Second Language Acquisition

Now in a fourth edition, this bestselling introductory textbook remains the cornerstone volume for the study of second language acquisition (SLA). Its chapters have been fully updated, and reorganized where appropriate, to provide a comprehensive yet accessible overview of the field and its related disciplines. To reflect current developments, new sections on using learner corpora, semantics and morphosyntax (within formal approaches to SLA), sociocultural approaches, gesture, priming research, and chaos theory have been added. Students will also find expanded discussions of heritage language learning, bilingualism, pragmatics, and much more.

The fourth edition retains the pedagogical features that students found useful in the current edition, and also incorporates new features. A new feature is the text boxes throughout the chapters that summarize key concepts and research literature. As with previous editions, discussion questions or problems at the end of each chapter help students apply their knowledge, and a glossary defines and reinforces must-know terminology. New supplemental material will be presented in a robust companion website with components for students and instructors.

By incorporating more coverage and interpretation of current theories, an emphasis on empirical findings, and a clearly written and illustrated presentation, *Second Language Acquisition* is an ideal textbook for the introductory SLA course in second language studies, applied linguistics, linguistics, TESOL, and language education programs.

Susan M. Gass is University Distinguished Professor, Dept of Linguistics and German, Slavic, Asian and African Languages, Michigan State University. She has served as president of the American Association of Applied Linguistics (AAAL) and the International Association of Applied Linguistics (AILA). Throughout her career, Sue has made groundbreaking contributions to advance the study of SLA, and remains one of the foremost leading figures in the field.

Jennifer Behney is Assistant Professor of Italian and Second Language Acquisition in the Department of Foreign Languages and Literatures at Youngstown State University. She completed her PhD in the Second Language Studies (SLS) program at Michigan State University in 2011 with a dissertation entitled *L2 Gender Facilitation and Inhibition in Spoken Word Recognition*. Her research interests include grammatical gender acquisition; facilitation and inhibition in spoken word recognition; eye-tracking and gender agreement marking; L2 syntactic priming; working memory, inhibition, and interaction; form-meaning connections in lexical access; and dialect/minority language preservation.

Luke Plonsky (PhD, Michigan State University) is Assistant Professor of Applied Linguistics at Northern Arizona University, where he teaches courses and conducts research on SLA, L2 pedagogy, and research methods. Luke's recent and forthcoming work in these areas can be found in journals such as *Annual Review of Applied Linguistics*, *Language Learning*, and *Studies in Second Language Acquisition* and in volumes published by CUP, Routledge, and Wiley-Blackwell.

Second Language Acquisition

An Introductory Course

Fourth Edition

Susan M. Gass

with
Jennifer Behney and
Luke Plonsky

Michigan State University
Youngstown State University and
Northern Arizona University

 Routledge
Taylor & Francis Group

NEW YORK AND LONDON

Please visit the companion website for this title at www.routledge.com/cw/gass

Fourth edition published 2013
by Routledge
711 Third Avenue, New York, NY 10017

Simultaneously published in the UK
by Routledge
2 Park Square, Milton Park, Abingdon, Oxon OX14 4RN

Routledge is an imprint of the Taylor & Francis Group, an informa business

First edition published by Lawrence Erlbaum Associates, Inc. 1994
Second edition published by Lawrence Erlbaum Associates, Inc. 2001
Third edition published by Routledge 2008

Library of Congress Cataloging in Publication Data
Gass, Susan M.
   Second language acquisition: an introductory course/Susan M.
   Gass with Jennifer Behney and Luke Plonsky.—4th ed.
   p. cm.
   Includes bibliographical references and index.
   1. Second language acquisition. I. Behney, Jennifer. II. Plonsky,
   Luke. III. Title.
   P118.2.S424 2013
   418—dc23   2012032782

ISBN: 978-0-415-89478-4 (hbk)
ISBN: 978-0-415-89495-1 (pbk)
ISBN: 978-0-203-13709-3 (ebk)

Typeset in Helvetica Neue and Optima
by Florence Production Ltd, Stoodleigh, Devon, UK

SFI Certified Sourcing
www.sfiprogram.org
SFI-00453

Printed and bound in the United States of America
by Edwards Brothers, Inc.

To the memory of my parents
Gertrude Zemon-Gass, PhD
H. Harvey Gass, MD
whose love, encouragement, and
support enabled me to do what I love doing.
Their memory is a blessing.
They live on in the generations of the future.
Samuel Zemon Ard
SMG

To Fabio
JB

To Mateo and Ruby, the two most fascinating
(and adorable) language learners in my life.
LDP

Contents

Figures

Tables

Preface

As I sit in Italy with my two-and-a-half-year-old grandson, I marvel, not only at his ability to learn English syntax (his native language), which progresses by leaps and bounds daily, but also at his ability to learn Italian, albeit not much. I am fascinated at how he knows that both a *gatto* and a *cat* go meow; that when one person gives something to him, he says *grazie*, and when another person gives something to him, he says *tank u*. A *horse* and a *cavallo* are the same thing. A *mucca* and a cow refer to the same animal, unless he is angry, then it's "that not *mucca*, that cow." After a few weeks in Italy, all dogs are now referred to as *cane*, regardless of language. This book takes these marvelous events and attempts to make sense of this highly complex phenomenon called language learning. I use these only as examples, because this book deals mostly with adults and brings in examples from children only as they relate to the main topic of this book, as a way of contextualizing the discipline of second language learning.

Learning a second language is something about which everyone seems to have an opinion. Even a casual airplane conversation with a seatmate, during which we are asked what we do, always elicits opinions about second language acquisition (SLA), some of which are accurate, some of which are not (I just patiently listen and smile). It is our intent to help set the record straight on this complex research area by bringing to the reader a bit of disciplinary history, accompanied by current directions.

The field of second language learning is old and new at the same time. It is old in the sense that scholars, for centuries, have been fascinated by the questions posed by the nature of foreign language learning and language teaching. It is new in the sense that the field, as it is now represented, only goes back about 40–50 years. In the earlier part of the modern phase, most scholarly articles emphasized language teaching and only had a secondary interest in language learning. In other words, the impetus for studying language learning originated in pedagogical concerns.

In the past 40 years or so, the field of SLA has developed into an independent and autonomous discipline, complete with its own research agenda. One only has to look at the increase in the number of conferences (of both a general and a topical nature) dealing exclusively with SLA, as well as special sessions on SLA as part of larger conferences. Furthermore, the field now has journals devoted exclusively to research in the field (*Studies in Second Language Acquisition, Language Learning, Second Language Research*), as well as others in which reports of second language studies comprise a major part (e.g., *Applied Linguistics, Applied Psycholinguistics, The Modern Language Journal*). There are also numerous edited volumes dealing with sub-areas of the field (e.g., language transfer, language input, language variation, Universal Grammar, Critical Period) and, in recent years, entire books concerned with sub-areas of the field, as well as numerous texts dealing with research methodologies. All of these attest to the vitality and vibrancy of the field. In this book, we present the old and the new as a way of helping the reader understand some of the history of the field and how we got to where we are today.

What is particularly noteworthy about the discipline of SLA is its interdisciplinary character. Second language research is concerned with the general question: How are second languages learned? With the belief that there are a number of perspectives one can take in answering this question, scholars have approached the field from a wide range of backgrounds: sociology, psychology, education, and linguistics, to name a few. This has both positive and negative effects on the field. The advantage is that, through the multiplicity of perspectives, we are able to see a richer picture of acquisition, a picture that appears to be more representative of the phenomenon of acquisition, in that learning a second language undoubtedly involves factors relating to sociology, psychology, education, and linguistics. On the other hand, multiple perspectives on what purports to be a single discipline bring confusion, because it is frequently the case that scholars approaching SLA from different (often opposing and seemingly incompatible) frameworks are not able to talk to one another. This is so because each perspective brings with it its own way of approaching data and its own research methodology. This book attempts to bring together these disparate threads, to place them within a coherent framework, and, importantly, to make the field accessible to large numbers of students with varying interests and varying goals for wanting to learn about second language learning. To that end, we take a multidisciplinary approach, in that what we have selected to present represents research with origins in other, well-established disciplines, but with implications for the central question: How are languages beyond one's primary language learned?

The book is designed to be used in an introductory course for advanced undergraduate or graduate students. The goal is to make the information contained herein available to students with a wide variety of background knowledge. The book can be used by those with a background in languages and/or linguistics and those with little or no background in these areas. The book developed out of the belief that the complexities of the field can, and should, be brought to the attention of many students, both those who are intending to delve further into the field and those who are only curious about the pervasive phenomenon of learning a second language.

This book has as its major focus second language learning. It is not a book that talks directly about language teaching, but we firmly believe that it is an important book for language teachers, in that it helps them understand the complex phenomenon that each and every student is struggling with. As teachers think about how to use this book, we encourage you to use some of the new pedagogical features in a way that best suits you and your students. We aimed the book at a broad audience, ranging from students who will use this as a stepping-stone as they pursue their advanced degrees in the field, to those in an advanced undergraduate program or MA program, whose main goal is to become teachers. For the former, some of the historical background may be more important as they begin their path to becoming professionals and eventually imparting this information to others. For the latter, a more cursory read can be given to those parts. Thus, more or less time can be given to any area by covering more than one chapter in a lesson or two or by extending chapters over a longer period of time. The "More to Do and More to Think About . . ." sections at the end of chapters can be used differently, depending on the students' goals. For example, more theoretical questions can be eliminated for those who are not planning PhD work; more pedagogical questions can be eliminated for those who are, and/or for students more interested in acquisition than pedagogy. It is our firm belief, however, that, regardless of ultimate goals, both groups (and those in between) can benefit from an understanding of how learning takes place.

This book is the fourth edition of one originally published in 1994, which I co-authored with Larry Selinker. The field has shown considerable growth since the first edition, and this edition reflects that growth, in part, by tracing the development of the field from its early stages to the present. This edition has been updated and rearranged, new sections have been added, and, in some cases, sections have been rewritten.

This edition has a number of new pedagogical features. For example, throughout each chapter there are "Time to Think . . ." and "Time to Do . . ." boxes, which are intended to encourage students to think about what they have just read and relate it to their own language learning experiences and, in some cases, to their own language teaching experiences (present or future). We have also put in boldface the first relevant mention of items in the glossary, so that students can find that item as they are reading. We have provided chapter summaries under the heading "Points to Remember," at the end of each chapter. Additionally, there is a companion website (www.routledge. com/cw/gass; for students and for teachers) that can be used for additional exercises. That website also includes PowerPoints that can be used for class presentations as well as other supplementary materials.

There are many people to whom we owe a debt of gratitude. First and foremost is Larry Selinker, who co-authored the first three editions with me. His influence on the field, on my thinking, and on this book has been enormous; without him, the field of SLA would not be where it is. A second individual to whom great thanks are due is Josh Ard, who has been instrumental in many areas of the book through all four editions. Josh provided detailed information on some of the original chapters. Through discussions with him, I have been better able to determine what is relevant and what is not. He painstakingly read through chapters, helped with references, and, in general, made extraordinarily perceptive comments throughout. He provided valuable clues as to what was involved in writing an introductory textbook, the goal of which was, in part, to "normalize" the field and make it informative and interesting to novices. His reading of the text many times over led to minor and major changes throughout. I am extraordinarily grateful.

Specific colleagues in the field provided detailed comments on earlier editions and completed surveys that helped us figure out where we could be clearer, where we needed to add parts, and where we needed to delete sections from earlier editions. We are grateful to all of them for their feedback. In particular, Bill VanPatten read through the manuscript of a previous edition and made perceptive comments about organization and ways to present research more clearly. Alison Mackey also read the entire manuscript of previous editions and many times made us rethink conclusions and suggested more research to look at. Her comments were detailed and insightful.

We have benefited from numerous individuals reading earlier versions of chapters of this edition. Some wished to remain anonymous, but you know who you are, and we thank you. Thanks also go to Jacqueline Aiello of New York University, Joyce Guat Ph Aw of Nanyang Technological University, National Institute of Education (Singapore), Jean-Marc Dewaele of Birkbeck, University of London, and Lucy Pickering of Texas A & M, for detailed comments on earlier versions of some of the chapters in this book. Debbie Pichler of Gallaudet University provided important comments on earlier versions of some chapters and also gave freely of her time to help us understand what is involved when sign language gets into the mix. We considered all of your comments (those from anonymous and non-anonymous sources) and, in many/most cases, were able to adjust the manuscript to align with your suggestions. In those cases where changes were not made, it is not because we did not think about doing so, but, in the end, we opted to leave chapters as we had originally planned, partly because, in many instances, we received suggestions such as "Change x" and "Don't change x."

Our colleagues and friends in the field deserve special mention. Although they have not all read the manuscript and may not all approve of the conclusions drawn from their writings, they have all been influential in our thinking and our development as researchers in the field. They are too numerous to mention, but they know who they are, and we thank them. Colleagues at Michigan State University have taught from this book and have helped us see where we could improve areas. A hearty thank you to all of you.

In expressing our gratitude to these individuals, we wish that we could also blame them for any errors (factual or interpretive) in this book. Alas, scholarly ethics do not allow us this luxury, and we accept all errors as our own.

In preparing for this fourth edition, Ivy Ip, our editor from Taylor & Francis, solicited opinions and feedback from prior users. In most cases, we do not know who these individuals are, but we hope that you will see your excellent suggestions reflected in these new pages. Thanks to Ivy for her patience and for soliciting comments, and thanks to those of you who are anonymous to us. Leah Babb-Rosenfeld and Rebecca Pearce worked with us through the preparation of this manuscript. I know that you had hoped for an earlier submission, and all I can do is express gratitude for your sticking with it. It goes without saying that your comments and patience throughout this process were always welcome.

A final group to be thanked consists of students over the years, many of whom provided welcome and helpful comments. Students have not hesitated to let us know when material was unclear and when some revision was necessary. There are too many to thank personally, but they are out there somewhere, possibly teaching courses in SLA. We hope that they have benefited from the material contained in those courses as much as we benefited from their feedback. In particular, LeAnne Spino volunteered to make comments on all aspects of the third edition. Her summary reflected comments that (1) came from her reading of the textbook and included suggestions for better wording and greater clarity; (2) were based on class discussion, where one concept or another could have been made clearer; and (3) included suggestions for additional, up-to-date references. A big thank you for volunteering to take on this task.

Others contributed in major and minor ways. Yeon Heo, my research assistant, went through all of the chapters to make them consistent. She saved us from many embarrassments, and we appreciate that. Others have read through individual sections and/or provided suggestions about their own research area that allowed us to be up to date or that helped us simplify the content (without destroying it), to make it more accessible to a nonspecialized audience. In particular, we recognize the significant contributions made by Rebecca Foote, Patti Spiner, and Nicole Tracy-Ventura. And, as usual, Russ Werner helped with technical support from beginning to end. Russ, you are one of a kind! I am grateful to Dean Karin Wurst of MSU's College of Arts and Letters for granting me time to complete this manuscript—I definitely needed to get out of town to do this. My leave from campus could not have taken place without the willingness of so many people to pick up the pieces that I left behind—Anna Davis, Pat Walters, Carol Wilson Duffy, and Larry Zwier of the ELC; David Prestel of CeLTA and our Iraq partnership; and Anne Baker and Joy Campbell of CLEAR/CeLTA. Thanks so much!

Special recognition to my partners in crime, Jennifer Behney, now of Youngstown State University, and Luke Plonsky, now of Northern Arizona University—it's a great partnership!

To you, the student, who will make use of the book, we have provided you with a summary of what is known today in the field of SLA. We hope that this book is but the beginning of a deeper quest into the nature of the learning process. We hope that your interest will be piqued by the text itself, but equally important is the emphasis we have placed on the follow-up activities for each chapter and moments within chapters to pause and reflect. It is our belief that these activities will give you the opportunity to think about the complexity and beauty of learning and using more than one language.

The subtitle of this book is *An Introductory Course*. It is well known in SLA circles that a truly introductory treatment of our field is difficult to achieve. We have tried hard and hope that we have been successful in our endeavor, and that we have succeeded in making the subject matter relevant and interesting to a wide range of students. Many of you will go on to be language teachers, and we hope to have given you an understanding of what your students are going through and how difficult and complex it is to learn a second or even third or fourth language.

Susan Gass
Collepino, Italy
July 4, 2012

CHAPTER ONE

Introduction

1.1 THE STUDY OF SECOND LANGUAGE ACQUISITION

How do people learn a second, or a third, or a fourth language? The simple answer is "with great difficulty." This book considers this basic question from a variety of perspectives.

What is the study of **second language acquisition**? It is the study of how second languages are learned. It is the study of how learners create a new language system with only limited exposure to a second language. It is the study of what is learned of a second language and, importantly, what is not learned; it is the study of why most second language learners do not achieve the same degree of proficiency in a second language as they do in their **native language**; it is also the study of why some individuals appear to achieve native-like proficiency in more than one language. Additionally, SLA is concerned with the nature of the hypotheses (whether conscious or unconscious) that learners come up with regarding the rules of the second language. Are the rules like those of the native language? Are they like the rules of the language being learned? Are there patterns that are common to all learners, regardless of the native language and regardless of the language being learned? Do the rules created by second language learners vary according to the context of use? Given these varied questions, the study of SLA impacts on, and draws from, many other areas of study, among them linguistics, psychology, psycholinguistics, sociology, sociolinguistics, discourse analysis, conversation analysis, and education, to name a few.

Given the close relationship between SLA and other areas of inquiry, there are numerous approaches from which to examine the questions raised above. Each area of inquiry examines second language data from a unique perspective, which includes goals, data-collection methods, and analytic tools. Thus, SLA is truly an interdisciplinary field. This introductory text attempts to shed light on the nature of SLA from multiple perspectives.

One way to define the field of SLA is to state what it is not. Over the years, the study of SLA has become inextricably intertwined with language pedagogy; in this

1

text, one goal is to disentangle the two fields. SLA is not about pedagogy, unless the pedagogy affects the course of acquisition (this topic will be explored in Chapter 13). Although it may be the case that those who are interested in learning about how second languages are learned are ultimately interested in doing so for the light this knowledge sheds on the field of language teaching, this is not the only reason SLA is of interest, nor is it the major reason scholars in the field of SLA conduct their research.

Let us briefly consider some of the reasons why it might be important for us to understand how second languages are learned.

• Linguistics

> When we study human language, we are approaching what some might call the human essence, the distinctive qualities of mind that are, so far as we know, unique to [humans].
>
> (Chomsky, 1968, p. 100)

The study of how second languages are learned is part of the broader study of language and language behavior. It is no more central or peripheral than any other part of linguistic study, which, in turn, has as its larger goal the study of the nature of the human mind. In fact, a major goal of SLA research is the determination of linguistic constraints on the formation of second language grammars. Because theories of language are concerned with human language knowledge, one can reasonably assume that this knowledge is not limited to first language knowledge, and that linguistic principles reflect the possibilities of human language creation and the limits of human language variation. This scope of inquiry includes second languages.

• Language pedagogy

Most graduate programs with the goal to train students in language teaching have required course work in SLA. Why should this be the case? If one is to develop language-teaching methodologies, there has to be a firm basis for those methodologies in language learning. It would be counterproductive to base language-teaching methodologies on something other than an understanding of how language learning does and does not take place. To give an example, some language-teaching methodologies are based exclusively on rule memorization and translation exercises. That is, a student in a language class is expected to memorize rules and then translate sentences from the native language to the language being learned, and vice versa. However, over the years, research in SLA has made language teachers and curriculum designers aware that language learning consists of more than rule memorization; it also involves learning to express communicative needs. The details of this conceptualization of what language learning is about have resulted in methodologies that emphasize communication. In other words, pedagogical decision-making must reflect what is known about the process of learning, which is the domain of SLA.

A second rationale related to language pedagogy has to do with the expectations that teachers have of their students. Let's assume that a teacher spends a class hour drilling students on a particular grammatical structure. Let's further assume that the students are all producing the structure correctly, and even in an appropriate context.

If, after the class is over and the drill is finished, a student comes up to the teacher and uses the incorrect form of what had just been drilled and drilled in spontaneous speech, what should the teacher think? Has the lesson been a waste of time? Or is this type of linguistic behavior to be expected? If a student produces a correct form, does that necessarily mean that the student has learned the correct rule? These sorts of issues are part of what teachers need to be aware of when assessing the success or failure of their teaching practices.

- **Cross-cultural communication**

We noted above some expectations that teachers have about students. Similarly, in interactions with speakers of another language/culture, we have certain expectations and we often produce stereotyped reactions. For example, we may find ourselves making judgments about individuals based on their language. It turns out that many stereotypes of people from other cultures (e.g., rudeness, unassertiveness) are based on patterns of nonnative speech. These judgments, in many instances, are not justified, because many of the speech patterns that nonnative speakers use reflect their nonnativeness, rather than being characteristics of their personality. As an example, consider the following exchange between a teacher and a former student (NNS = nonnative speaker; NS = native speaker):

(1-1)   From Goldschmidt (1996, p. 255)

> NNS: I have a favor to ask you.
> NS: Sure, what can I do for you?
> NNS: You need to write a recommendation for me.

Many teachers would, of course, react negatively to the seeming gall of this "request," perhaps initially thinking to themselves, "What do you mean I *need* to write a letter?", when most likely the only problem is this nonnative speaker's lack of understanding of the forceful meaning of *need*. It is our point of view that understanding how second languages are learned and how nonnative speakers use language allows us to separate issues of cross-cultural communication from issues of stereotyped behavior or personal idiosyncrasies.

- **Language policy and language planning**

Many issues of language policy are dependent on a knowledge of how second languages are learned. For example, issues surrounding **bilingualism**, such as the English Only Movement in the United States, or bilingual education (including immersion programs) can only be debated if one is properly informed about the realities and constraints of learning a second language. National language programs often involve decision-making that is dependent on (a) information about second language learning, (b) the kinds of instruction that can be brought to bear on issues of acquisition, and (c) the realities and expectations one can have of such programs. All too often, these issues are debated without a clear understanding of the object of debate, that is, the nature of how second languages are learned.

In sum, SLA is a complex field, the focus of which is the attempt to understand the processes underlying the learning and use of a second language. It is important to reemphasize that the study of SLA is separate from the study of language pedagogy, although this does not mean that there are not implications that can be drawn from SLA to the related discipline of language teaching, or that ideas that arise in classrooms cannot be useful in the understanding of SLA.

TIME TO THINK ...

What is your motivation for studying SLA? How do you think a knowledge of SLA will help you?

How would you describe the relationship between SLA and language pedagogy? Do you have to know something about SLA to teach well? Do you have to know something about teaching to understand SLA?

1.2 DEFINITIONS

The study of any new discipline involves familiarizing oneself with the specific terminology of that field. In this section, we present some basic terminology common to the field of SLA, accompanied by brief definitions. Other terms are introduced and defined as the text progresses. For an extensive list of definitions, see Loewen and Reinders' (2011) and VanPatten and Benati's (2010) books on key concepts.

- **Native language** (NL): This refers to the first language that a child learns. It is also known as the primary language, the mother tongue, or the **L1** (first language). In this book, we use the common abbreviation NL and/or L1.
- **Target language** (TL): This refers to the language being learned.
- **Second language acquisition**: This is the common term used for the name of the discipline and deals with the many areas covered in this book. In general, SLA refers to the process of learning another language after the native language has been learned. Sometimes, the term even refers to the learning of a third or fourth language. The important aspect is that SLA refers to the learning of a nonnative language *after* the learning of one's native or primary language. The second language is commonly referred to as the **L2**. As with the phrase "second language," L2 can refer to any language learned *after* the L1 has been learned, regardless of whether it is the second, third, fourth, or fifth language. By this term, we mean the acquisition of a second language both in a classroom situation, as well as in more "natural" exposure situations. In addition to referring to the discipline, as noted above, the term *second language acquisition* (not capitalized) can also refer to the process of learning another language.
- **Foreign language learning**: Foreign language is generally differentiated from second language in that the former refers to the learning of a nonnative language

in the environment of one's native language (e.g., French speakers learning English in France [EFL] or Spanish speakers learning French in Spain, Argentina, or Mexico [FFL]). This is most commonly done within the context of the classroom. Second language, on the other hand, generally refers to the learning of a nonnative language in the environment in which that language is spoken (e.g., German speakers learning Japanese in Japan [JSL] or Punjabi speakers learning English in the United Kingdom [ESL]). This may or may not take place in a classroom setting. The important point is that learning in a second language environment takes place with considerable access to speakers of the language being learned, whereas learning in a foreign language environment usually does not.[1] In this book, we use the generic term SLA to assume learning in a second language and a foreign language context.

- **Learners/L2ers**: Throughout this book, we often refer to those learning a second/foreign language as *learners*; one also finds the term L2ers to refer to the same group of individuals, although this term is not used in this book.
- **L2 acquisition**: This term, along with the more general term SLA, refers to the process of learning as well as to the field more generally.

TIME TO THINK ...

Consider your own language learning experience. Was it second language learning or foreign language learning, or both? Were they different experiences? In what ways? Consider differences and similarities in areas of pronunciation, grammar, and vocabulary. Is it easier to learn pronunciation in a second or a foreign language environment? What about grammar or vocabulary?

1.3 THE NATURE OF LANGUAGE

Fundamental to the understanding of the nature of SLA is an understanding of what it is that needs to be learned. A facile answer is that a second language learner needs to learn the "grammar" of the TL. But what is meant by this? What is language? How can we characterize the knowledge that humans have of language?

All humans with normal access to natural language acquire a language in the first few years of life. The knowledge acquired is largely of an unconscious sort. That is, very young children learn how to form particular grammatical structures, such as relative clauses. They also learn that relative clauses often have a modifying function, but in a conscious sense do not know that it is a relative clause, and could presumably not state what relative clauses are used for. Take as an example the following sentence:

(1-2)   I want the toy that the little boy is playing with.

A child could utter this fully formed sentence, which includes a relative clause ("that the little boy is playing with"), without being able to articulate the function of relative clauses (either this one, or relative clauses in general) and without being able to easily divide this sentence into its component parts. It is in this sense that the complex knowledge we have about our native language is largely unconscious.

There are a number of aspects of language that can be described systematically. In the next few sections, we deal with the **phonology**, **syntax**, **morphology**, **semantics**, and **pragmatics** of language.

1.3.1 Sound Systems

Knowledge of the sound system (phonology) of our native language is complex. Minimally, it entails knowing what are possible and what are not possible sounds in the language. For example, a native speaker of English knows that the first vowel sound in the German word Goethe is not a sound in English. This knowledge is reflected in recognition as well as in production, as generally a close English sound is substituted when one attempts to utter that word in English.

Phonological knowledge also involves knowing what happens to words in fast speech as opposed to more carefully articulated speech. For example, if a native speaker of American English wanted to express the following idea:

(1-3)   I am going to write a letter.

that person would undoubtedly say something like the following:

(1-4)   I'm gonna wriDa leDer.

We can see that speakers know when to combine sounds and when not to. We know that in "normal, fast" speech we combine words, but that in clearer, more articulated speech we do not.

A final point to make is that, as native speakers of a language, we know not only what are possible sounds and what are not possible sounds, but we also know what are possible combinations of sounds and what sounds are found in what parts of words. We know, for example, that in English, although [b] and [n] are both sounds of English, they cannot form a "blend" in the way that [b] and [r] can: *bnick[2] versus brain. Or, to take another example, consider the sound at the end of the word ping [ŋ], which is frequent in English. Native speakers of English know that it cannot appear at the beginning of words in English, although it can in other languages.

1.3.2 Syntax

In this section, we briefly describe what speakers know about the syntax of their language. This is what is frequently known as grammar, referring primarily to the knowledge we have of the order of elements in a sentence. We point out briefly that

PRESCRIPTIVE GRAMMAR - *rules* - How a language should be *used*.
DESCRIPTIVE GRAMMAR - language how it is *actually used*.
INTRODUCTION

there are two kinds of grammars that are generally referred to: (a) prescriptive grammar and (b) descriptive grammar. By prescriptive grammar, we mean such rules as are generally taught in school, often without regard to the way native speakers of a language actually *use* language. We have in mind such rules as "Don't end a sentence with a preposition," "Don't split infinitives," "Don't begin a sentence with a conjunction," "Don't use contractions in writing," and "Use *between* with two items and *among* with more than two" (Associated Press rule, as cited in Safire, 1999, p. 24). To illustrate that these so-called rules are something other than appropriate, McCawley (also cited in Safire), gives the following example: "He held four golf balls *between* his fingers." Even though there are more than two fingers involved, one cannot say: "He held four golf balls *among* his fingers." Additionally, many well-known versions exist of an anecdote involving Winston Churchill. One version refers to an editor who had rearranged something that Churchill had written so that the sentence in question would not end with a preposition. The story goes that Churchill responded with: "This is the sort of English up with which I will not put" (*The American Heritage Book of English Usage*, p. 27).

Linguists are concerned with descriptive grammars: They attempt to describe languages as they are actually used. Thus, when talking about knowledge of syntax, we are referring to descriptive grammars. The rules just stated are not always true of descriptive grammars, because native speakers of English may violate the prescriptive rules.

As with phonological knowledge, discussed in section 1.3.1, native speakers of a language know which are possible sentences of their language and which are not. For example, below, we know that sentences 1-5 and 1-6 are possible English sentences, whereas sentences 1-7 and 1-8 are not possible or are ungrammatical:

(1-5)   The big book is on the brown table.

(1-6)   The woman whom I met yesterday is reading the same book that I read last night.

(1-7)   *The book big brown table the on is.

(1-8)   *Canceling what's but general how then the two actually.

Thus, part of what we know about language is the order in which elements can and cannot occur. This is, of course, not as simple as the preceding examples suggest. Are sentences 1-9 and 1-10 possible English sentences?

(1-9)   Have him to call me back.

(1-10) That's the man that I am taller than.

For many speakers of English, these are strange-sounding; for others, they are perfectly acceptable.

Not only do we know which sentences are acceptable in our language, we also know which sentences are grossly equivalent in terms of meaning. For example, sentences 1-11 and 1-12 have the same general meaning, in the sense that they refer to the same event:

(1-11) Tom was hit by a car.

(1-12) A car hit Tom.

While we know that both sentences above can be assumed to be paraphrases of one another, we also know that they have slightly different functions in English. If someone asks, *What did that car hit?*, the most likely answer would be, *It hit Tom*, rather than *Tom was hit by it*. Thus, we as native speakers know, not only what is equivalent to what, but also when to use different grammatical patterns.

Another aspect of language that we know is how meaning is affected by moving elements within a sentence. For example, adverbs can generally be moved in a sentence without affecting the meaning, whereas nouns cannot. Sentences 1-13 and 1-14 are roughly equivalent in meaning:

(1-13) Yesterday Sally saw Jane.

(1-14) Sally saw Jane yesterday.

but (1-15) and (1-16) do not share a common meaning:

(1-15) Yesterday Sally saw Jane.

(1-16) Yesterday Jane saw Sally.

Thus, knowing a language entails knowing a set of rules with which we can produce an infinite set of sentences. As a demonstration of the rule-governed nature of language and our ability to comprehend novel sentences, consider 1-17:

(1-17) The woman wearing the green scarf ran across the street to see the gorilla that had just escaped from the zoo.

Even though this sentence is probably one you have never encountered before, you have little difficulty in understanding what it means.

1.3.3 Morphology and the Lexicon

The study of morphology is the study of word formation. In many cases, words are made up of more than one part. For example, the word *unforeseen* is made up of three parts: *un*, which has a negative function; *fore*, which means earlier in time; and *seen*, which means to visualize. Each part is referred to as a **morpheme**, which can be defined as the minimal unit of meaning.

There are two classes of morphemes that we can identify: bound and free. A bound morpheme is one that can never be a word by itself, such as the *un* of *unlikely*. A free morpheme is one that is a word in and of itself, such as *man*, *woman*, *book*, or *table*. Words can be created by adding morphemes, as in the following children's favorite:

establish
establish + ment
dis + establish + ment
dis + establish + ment + ari + an + ism
anti + dis + establish + ment + ari + an +ism

Not only do we know how to form words using affixes (prefixes, suffixes, infixes), but we also know what words can go with other words, as in *Mt. Everest is a high mountain*, but not **The Empire State Building is a high building*. *Tall* is more likely to describe a building than *high*.

1.3.4 Semantics

The study of semantics refers to the study of meaning. This, of course, does not necessarily correspond to grammaticality, because many ungrammatical sentences are meaningful, as can be seen in the following sentences:

(1-18) *That woman beautiful is my mother.

(1-19) *I'll happy if I can get your paper.

These and many other sentences, which may be uttered by nonnative speakers of a language, are perfectly comprehensible, despite the fact that they do not follow the "rules" of English. The reverse side of the picture is the sentence that is grammatically formed but that, because of the content, is meaningless (at least without additional contextualization), as in 1-20:

(1-20) That bachelor is married.

Knowledge of the semantics of a language entails knowledge of the reference of words. For example, in English, we know that a *table* refers to an object with a flat top and either three or four legs, or that a *leaf* most often refers to part of a tree. But, as native speakers, we also have to be able to distinguish between the meaning of the *leaf* of a tree and the *leaf* of a table. When we hear an advertisement on television for a table with extra leaves, it is this knowledge of homonyms that comes into play to help us interpret the advertisement in the manner intended. For a learner, of course, it is not so easy, as he or she might struggle to imagine a table with tree leaves.

Additionally, it is important to note that the limits of a word are not always clear. What is the difference between a *cup* and a *glass*? For many objects, the boundaries are obvious; for others, boundaries between objects are less so.

Referential meanings are clearly not the only way of expressing meaning. As native speakers of a language, we know that <u>the way we combine elements in sentences affects their meaning</u>. Sentences 1-21 and 1-22 are different in meaning. Thus, we know the extent to which syntax and meaning interrelate.

(1-21) The man bit the dog.

(1-22) The dog bit the man.

In some languages, the translation equivalents of those sentences (with possibly different intonation contours) can be interpreted as referring to the same event.

1.3.5 Pragmatics

Yet another area of language that we consider and that is part of what second language learners need to learn has to do with pragmatics, or <u>the way in which we use language in context</u>. For example, when we answer the telephone and someone says *Is Samuel there?*, we know that this is a request to speak with Samuel. It would be strange to respond *yes*, with the caller then saying *thank you* and hanging up, unless the caller did not want to carry on the conversation with Samuel present, or only wanted to know whether or not Samuel was present. <u>Clearly, the phrase *Is X there?* in the context of telephone usage is a request to speak with someone, and not an information question.</u> When the intent is the latter—as, for example, a parent checking on the whereabouts of a child—the conversation might be slightly modified.

(1-23) FATHER 1: This is Samuel's father. Is Samuel there?
　　　　　FATHER 2: Yes.
　　　　　FATHER 1: Thanks, I just wanted to know where he was.

Similarly, <u>word order, as discussed earlier, may have an effect on meaning</u> (see sentences 1-21 and 1-22) in some grammatical contexts, but in others, it does not.
　　　The following conversation exemplifies this:

(1-24) (Setting: Ice cream store; child, age 4)
　　　　　CHILD:　　　　I want a raspberry and vanilla cone.
　　　　　SHOPKEEPER: OK, one vanilla and raspberry cone coming up.
　　　　　CHILD:　　　　No, I want a raspberry and vanilla cone.
　　　　　SHOPKEEPER: That's what I'm getting you.

In this instance, the child was using word order to reflect the ordering of scoops of ice cream; the shopkeeper was not. Thus, what we have learned as adult native speakers of a language is what the real-life function of word order is in our language. In English, it does not necessarily refer to the ordering of physical objects.

TIME TO DO ...

Read the first few paragraphs of the article (see Link #1 in the Link section at the end of this chapter) and consider the following: As a native or very fluent speaker of English, is this passage (easily) comprehensible? Consider this question in light of what it means to know one's first language.

1.4 THE NATURE OF NONNATIVE SPEAKER KNOWLEDGE

We have briefly characterized some areas of language knowledge that a native speaker has of a language. Knowing a second language well means knowing information similar to that of a native speaker of a language. Given the complexity of the knowledge that must be learned, it should be clear that the study of the acquisition of that knowledge is a highly complex field.

The basic assumption in SLA research is that learners create a language system, known as an **interlanguage** (IL). This system is composed of numerous elements, not the least of which are elements from the NL and the TL. There are also elements in the IL that do not have their origin in either the NL or the TL. What is important is that the learners themselves impose structure on the available linguistic data and formulate an internalized system (IL).[3] Patterns in IL systems are both consistent and dynamic. What we eventually want to understand is: What is the nature of the IL system, how does it come to be, and why does it generally fail to be the same as a system underlying native speaker knowledge. With regard to the latter, an important question is: Why are learners exposed to something (often many times) but still remain unable to reproduce it in a way that matches that of native speakers?

Central to the concept of IL is the concept of **fossilization**, which generally refers to the cessation of learning. The *Random House Dictionary of the English Language* (Flexner & Hauck, 1988, p. 755) defines fossilization of a linguistic form, feature, rule, and so forth in the following way: "to become permanently established in the interlanguage of a second language learner in a form that is deviant from the target-language norm and that continues to appear in performance regardless of further exposure to the target language."

Because of the difficulty in determining when learning has ceased, one frequently refers to **stabilization** of linguistic forms, rather than fossilization or cessation of learning. In SLA, one often notes that IL plateaus are far from the TL norms. Furthermore, it appears to be the case that fossilized or stabilized ILs exist, no matter what learners do in terms of further exposure to the TL. Unfortunately, a solid explanation of permanent or temporary learning plateaus is lacking at present, owing, in part, to the paucity of **longitudinal** studies (see Chapter 3) that would be necessary to create the databases necessary to come to conclusions regarding "getting stuck" in another language.

TIME TO THINK ...

In what ways is your knowledge of a second language similar or different from your L1 knowledge?

The following sentences were produced by native speakers of Arabic:

1. I bought a couple of towel.
2. There is many kind of way you make baklawa.
3. There are about one and half-million inhabitant in Jeddah.

Which linguistic items (and arrangements of items) do you think come from the target language, which come from the native language, and which are autonomous? As a way to begin, think about whether learners of English of languages other than Arabic are likely to utter similar sentences.

1.5 CONCLUSION

In this chapter, we have presented a series of basic definitions to help the reader begin the journey of the study of SLA. As has been seen, inherent in an analysis of IL data is a focus on the learner and on the processes involved in learning. In the following chapters, we present additional information about ILs and variables found to be related to IL development, beginning with a discussion in Chapter 2 of ways of analyzing second language data.

POINTS TO REMEMBER

In this chapter, you have learned about:

●   SLA as an interdisciplinary discipline by nature, drawing on and contributing to a number of other social sciences that study human behavior, such as linguistics, education, psychology, and many others. The questions asked in these and other fields and the means or methods used to answer those questions have had a substantial influence on the interests of SLA researchers.

●   Many purposes exist for studying SLA and the numerous applications. Findings from SLA research are used to inform the practices and decisions made by language teachers and educational policymakers, among others.

●   Terminology:
    – NL
    – TL

- SLA
- Foreign language versus second language learning;

● Basic linguistic concepts:
  - sound systems/phonology
  - syntax
  - morphology
  - lexicon
  - semantics
  - pragmatics;

● Nonnative speaker knowledge and how it differs from native-speaker knowledge:
  - quantitatively (e.g., breadth of vocabulary);
  - qualitatively (e.g., conscious versus subconscious knowledge of structures and patterns).

SUGGESTIONS FOR ADDITIONAL READING

Language: Its structure and use (2012). Edward Finegan. Wadsworth.

Key concepts in second language acquisition (2011). Shawn Loewen and Hayo Reinders. Macmillan.

An introduction to language (2010). Victoria Fromkin, Robert Rodman, and Nina Hyams. Cengage Learning.

Key terms in second language acquisition (2010). Bill VanPatten and Alessandro Benati. Continuum Press.

Essential introductory linguistics (2000). Grover Hudson. Blackwell.

Linguistics: An introduction (1999). Andrew Radford, Martin Atkinson, David Britain, Harald Clahsen, and Andrew Spencer. Cambridge University Press.

Inside language (1997). Vivian Cook. Edward Arnold.

The language instinct: *How the mind creates language* (1994). Steven Pinker. Morrow.

MORE TO DO AND MORE TO THINK ABOUT ...

1. A teacher has drilled students in a structure called indirect questions:

   Do you know where my book is?
   Do you know what time it is?
   Did he tell you what time it is?

As a direct result of the drills, all students in the class were able to produce the structure correctly in class. After class, a student came up to the teacher and asked, "Do you know where is Mrs. Irving?" In other words, only minutes after the class, in spontaneous speech, the student used the structure practiced in class incorrectly. Describe what you think the reason is for this misuse. Had the lesson been a waste of time? How would you find out?

2. Consider the differences between child language acquisition and adult SLA. Specifically, consider the example provided in (1-2).

(1-2)   I want the toy that the little boy is playing with.

With regard to this sentence, we state in this chapter that,

> A child could utter this fully formed sentence, which includes a relative clause ("that the little boy is playing with"), without being able to articulate the function of relative clauses (either this one, or relative clauses in general) and without being able to easily divide this sentence into its component parts. It is in this sense that the complex knowledge we have about our native language is largely unconscious.

Do you think that this comment is also valid for adults learning a second language? Specifically, do you think that an adult needs to consciously learn the grammar of relative clauses *before* being able to use them spontaneously in IL? Take an example from your own language-learning or language-teaching experience and relate it to these child versus adult distinctions.

3. Create a list of some of the main reasons for the well-attested existence of fossilization in IL. Exchange your list with that of someone else and come up with a common list.

4. In section 1.3.2, we describe the types of knowledge that individuals have about sentences in their native language. We note that there is variation in native speakers' acceptance of sentences, as in sentences 1-9 and 1-10.

(1-9)   Have him to call me back.

(1-10)   That's the man that I am taller than.

Are these sentences acceptable to you? If not, what would you say instead? In what situations, if any, would you say these sentences? Consider how and when such variation might occur in terms of second language syntactic knowledge. If native speakers vary in what they think is or is not acceptable, how does that affect second language learning?

5. Following are English translations of compositions written by two school-children in their native language (Tatar) and compositions written by the same children in Russian, their L2. In all instances, the children were describing a picture.

Child 1 (written in Tatar):
The long awaited spring has come. The days are getting warmer and warmer. The blue sky is covered by white fluffy clouds. They skim like sailboats through the sky. The ice is breaking away on the river to the north. The birds have returned after having flown from us to a warm region. The apples have bloomed. Children are planting tomatoes, cucumbers, onions, and other vegetables. They are watering the trees. Azat is planting flowers. Rustam is watering the apples. The children are happily working in the garden. They are very happy.

Child 1 (written in Russian):
In the schoolyard there is a large garden. Children are digging in the earth. Children are working in the garden. In the garden there is a pine tree, an oak, and tomatoes. An apple tree is growing there. They are planting flower beds.

Child 2 (written in Tatar):
It was a beautiful spring day. The sun was shining. The birds who had returned from distant lands were singing. The trees were swallowed up by the greenery of the luxuriant spring foliage. The children have come into their garden. There the apple trees have already blossomed. Rustam is watering the flowers. The remaining children are planting vegetables. The teacher is watching the work of her pupils. She's pleased with their work, she smiles.

Child 2 (written in Russian):
In the schoolyard there is a large garden. Children are working there. The garden is big. In the garden there are trees. A child is planting a tree. A child is pouring water from a watering pot. In the garden a poplar is growing.

What kind of information (e.g., descriptive or evaluative) do these children include in their TL descriptions of these pictures? In their NL descriptions of the pictures? What similarities/differences are there between the NL and TL versions of these pictures?

6. In pairs, answer "True" or "False" to the following statements. Justify your responses. Once you come to a consensus, compare your answers with those of another pair. Note that, in some of the cases, arguments can be made for a "true" response as well as a "false" response.

(a) Any child without cognitive disabilities can learn any language with equal ease.

(b) Learning an L2 is a matter of learning a new set of habits.

(c) The only reason that some people cannot learn a second or foreign language is that they are insufficiently motivated.

(d) All children can learn a second language accent-free.

(e) All human beings have an innate capacity to learn language.

(f) Vocabulary is the most important part of learning an L2.

(g) Vocabulary is the most difficult part of learning an L2.

(h) Instruction is a waste of time.

(i) Learning an L2 takes no more time than learning an L1.

LINK

1.   http://goo.gl/5Km8W

Second and Foreign Language Data

2.1 DATA ANALYSIS

A central part of understanding the field of SLA is gained by hands-on experience in data analysis and data interpretation. This experience can be efficiently achieved with carefully organized data sets, that is, data gleaned from attested IL forms, but carefully organized to demonstrate particular structural points. It is the goal of this chapter to present several data sets and to provide a map through IL analysis in a step-by-step fashion. We hope that this will lead the reader to being able to understand and possibly challenge the logic and argumentation of each step.

A given about SLA data is that data may often be ambiguous with regard to their interpretation. Thus, it is frequently the case that there are no "correct" answers in analyzing IL data, as there might be in doing arithmetic or calculus problems. At best, there are better and worse answers, bolstered by better and worse argumentation. Importantly, the function of good argumentation is to lessen the ambiguity of analysis.

In the following sections, we present three sets of data accompanied by detailed explanations regarding the analyses of the data.[1] These sample analyses are not meant to represent the breadth of questions addressed in SLA. Rather, we include them to briefly introduce some of the issues inevitably encountered when working with second language production data.

TIME TO THINK ...

Think about interactions you have had with nonnative speakers of your L1 or of English. What are some of the common errors they make? Are these errors unique to speakers of one L1, or are they more or less common among different learners or in different modes (i.e., writing versus speaking)?

2.1.1 Data Set I: Plurals

The data presented here were collected from three adult native speakers of Cairene Arabic, intermediate to advanced speakers of English, shortly after they had arrived in the United States. The data source was compositions and conversations. In (2-1)–(2-19) are the utterances produced by these learners:

(2-1)   There are also **two deserts**.

(2-2)   I bought **a couple of towel**.

(2-3)   So, when I like to park my car, there is no place to put it, and **how many ticket** I took.

(2-4)   There is **many kind of way** you make baklawa.

(2-5)   **The streets** run from east to west, **the avenues** from north to south.

(2-6)   I go to university **four days** a week.

(2-7)   Just **a few month** he will finish from his studies.

(2-8)   Egypt shares **its boundaries** with the Mediterranean.

(2-9)   There is **a lot of mosquito**.

(2-10) **Many people** have **ideas** about Jeddah and other cities located in Saudi Arabia.

(2-11) When he complete **nine month** . . .

(2-12) He can spend **100 years** here in America.

(2-13) There are about **one and half-million inhabitant** in Jeddah.

(2-14) **How many month or years** have been in his mind?

(2-15) There are **many tents—and goats** running around.

(2-16) There are **two mountains**.

(2-17) **How many hour**?

(2-18) There are more than **200,000 telephone lines**.

(2-19) Every country had **three or four kind of bread**.

In order to describe the IL patterns of plural usage in these utterances, the first things to focus on are the phrases set in **boldface** type. Categorize them according to English-like and non-English-like patterns of plural usage, as in Table 2.1. Decide if the choice is clear or not, remembering that data are often ambiguous.

Thus, the first step is to make a list of the sentences according to the criteria of English-like or non-English-like.

TABLE 2.1 Sample Categorization of Plurals in Arabic–English IL

English-like	Non-English-like
(2-1) two deserts	(2-2) a couple of towel

In sentences 2-1, 2-5, 2-6, 2-8, 2-10, 2-12, 2-15, 2-16, and 2-18, the analysis of the phrase in boldface is clear; these sentences are English-like because they have an *s* plural marker on the noun, or, in the case of 2-10, also have a noun (*people*) that has a plural meaning.

In sentences 2-2–2-4, 2-7, 2-9, 2-11, 2-13, 2-17, and 2-19, the analysis is also clear, but, unlike the previous sentences, they are non-English-like because there is no plural marker on the noun.

The analysis of sentence 2-14 is not clear; the phrase in boldface is ambiguous, and there is a choice. What one notices is that the form *month*, as a plural, is non-English-like, whereas the form *years* is English-like. That is, there is IL variation within the same sentence. One analytical option is to say that, when any element of the plural phrase is non-English-like, then the whole phrase is non-English like. Another option is to create a third category, "Ambiguous." We prefer this latter solution, because placing TL categories on IL data is potentially misleading in terms of creating general IL rules for IL data (a point we return to later in this chapter). In this case, we see that there is IL variation in the same sentence; this presents a case that is fundamentally different from the others in this data set.

So, at this stage, the chart should look like the body of either Table 2.2 or Table 2.3.

TABLE 2.2 Possible Categorization of Plurals in Arabic–English IL

English-like	Non-English-like
(2-1) two deserts	(2-2) a couple of towel
(2-5) the streets, the avenues	(2-3) how many ticket
(2-6) four days	(2-4) many kind of way
(2-8) its boundaries	(2-7) a few month
(2-10) many people, ideas	(2-9) a lot of mosquito
(2-12) 100 years	(2-11) nine month
(2-15) many tents—and goats	(2-13) one and half-million inhabitant
(2-16) two mountains	(2-14) how many month or years
(2-18) 200,000 telephone lines	(2-17) how many hour
	(2-19) three or four kind of bread

TABLE 2.3 Possible Categorization of Plurals in Arabic–English IL

English-like	Non-English-like	Ambiguous
(2-1) two deserts	(2-2) a couple of towel	(2-14) how many month or years
(2-5) the streets, the avenues	(2-3) how many ticket	
(2-6) four days	(2-4) many kind of way	
(2-8) its boundaries	(2-7) a few month	
(2-10) many people, ideas	(2-9) a lot of mosquito	
(2-12) 100 years	(2-11) nine month	
(2-15) many tents—and goats	(2-13) one and half-million inhabitant	
(2-16) two mountains	(2-17) how many hour	
(2-18) 200,000 telephone lines	(2-19) three or four kind of bread	

The next step is an attempt to explain patterns. What are some possible IL generalizations that might account for this particular pattern of IL plural marking? First, we determine to what extent there is regularity in the data. We can easily see that there are frequent quantifying phrases (*kind of, how many*) in the non-English-like data. One initial hypothesis we might set up is:

Whenever there is a quantifying phrase or a nonnumerical quantifying word before the noun, there is no overt marking on the plural of that noun.

What we wish to do now is test the suggested generalization. In so doing, there are three possible answers one can get: The sentence in question *supports* the hypothesis, *does not support* it, or *is irrelevant* to the hypothesis. Our analysis is given in Table 2.4.

TABLE 2.4 Data Support for Arabic-English IL Pluralization Hypothesis

Support	Does Not Support	Irrelevant
(2-2) *a couple* of towel		
(2-3) *how many* ticket		
(2-4) *many kind* of way		
(2-7) *a few* month		
(2-9) *a lot of* mosquito		
(2-13) *one and half-million* inhabitant		(2-13) Is it a phrase?
(2-17) *how many* hour		
(2-19) three or four kind of bread		

Sentence 2-13 can be analyzed in one of two ways. Is it a numeral, or is it a phrase? In other words, does it represent an actual number or is it a phrase denoting "a large number"? Depending on the conclusion one comes to, it will either support this hypothesis or it is irrelevant to it. One also notes that it is written differently from the TL form (*one and a half-million*). One must ask if this will affect the analysis. We think not, but it does point to the ambiguity possibly generated by combining composition and conversation data. Sentence 2-14 is ambiguous, as pointed out earlier.

Therefore, the hypothesis stated earlier appears to be supported by these data. However, we have still not accounted for all of the data. We now have an IL hypothesis that is something like the following:

Mark all plural nouns with *s* except those that are preceded by a quantifying phrase or a nonnumerical quantifying word.

There are still possible exceptions to deal with:

1. **Sentence 2-11**: According to our rule, this should be *months*. However, one could account for this apparent exception by the pronunciation difficulty involved, notably the *nths* cluster at the end of the word. In fact, many native speakers of English simplify this cluster by pronouncing the end of the word *ns* rather than *nths*. Thus, simplification is common; the Arabic speakers simplified in one way; native speakers simplified in another.

2. **Sentence 2-14**: We noted that this was a problem in the initial categorization. Might it be the case that these learners have created an IL-particular rule that relates plural marking to type of conjunction? We do not know, of course, because one example of each cannot safely lead us to any general conclusion.

3. **Sentence 2-10**: This is possibly ambiguous. In one sense, it could be in our "Irrelevant" category in Table 2.4, in that we could view this as an unanalyzed **chunk**, that is, a group of words that the learner has learned as one big word, and has not broken down into its component words. For example, what is normally considered three words—*how are you*—might be understood by a learner as a greeting made up of one word *howru*. On the other hand, it could also be listed under "Supports," if we believe that the learner categorizes it as a nonplural form. Finally, it could be in our "Does Not Support" category, if we believe the learner conceptualizes it as a plural and has appropriately given the plural modifier *many*.

Knowing how to deal with apparent exceptions is just as important as knowing how to deal with the bulk of the data. Exceptions can be real, and, if in sufficient quantity, may suggest an incorrect initial hypothesis, or they may be reflections of another rule/constraint at play. In the examples presented here, we have attempted to explain away the apparent exceptions, and, in the case of one of them (*nine month*), have brought in additional data to show the reasonableness of using phonological simplification as an explanation.

Now we wish to go over what might be one of the most important questions of all: When you have reached the best possible analysis with the limited data at your disposal, and when there is still some uncertainty, what *further data* would you like from these learners to test your hypotheses? One type has already been mentioned with regard to sentence 2-13: More data that clearly differentiate oral from written production, because the IL rules generated might vary along this dimension. Another has also been hinted at: If one is trying to understand an individual's IL generalization, then one must only consider that individual's utterances. On the other hand, if one is using pooled data, as we have in this case, then it is to be expected that counter-examples will show up. Thus, for some purposes, we need to gather data where plural phrases are marked individual by individual, as SLA is characterized by sometimes rather large individual differences.

Additional data are needed to determine if the alternative explanations given for the apparent exceptions are correct or not. That is, there is a need to elicit (a) other words ending with difficult consonant clusters and (b) noun phrases with *or*. Yet another type of data we may wish to gather in relation to the data set under consideration might involve the various contexts in which these sentences were produced, which might bear on these IL performance data.

Thus far in this section, we have provided hands-on experience in data analysis and its interpretation. Our goal was to show that good argumentation can lessen the ambiguity inherent in most L2 data. We also noted that the analyses leave us with questions that can lead to further study, with new data being collected. The point here is that data should always be collected for a particular purpose, which usually arises from the unanswered questions of previous analyses. We illustrated this with a step-by-step discussion that could lead to further empirical work. In other words, research comes about by posing the question: "What else is there that we want to know?" In what follows, we consider some of the data from Data Set I, focusing on questions that cannot be answered from the data alone.

As noted, the data in this section represent a mixture of data sources. An initial problem is that the data source consists of compositions and conversations. Thus, for a thorough and meaningful analysis, one would want to know which sentences in that list are derived from compositions and which from conversations. Thus, if one is interested in finding out more about plurals in the L2 of Arabic speakers, it would be important to collect new data that separated these data sources from one another. This is particularly important when considering sentence 2-14, where the solution may be one of pronunciation. If that particular sentence came from a composition, we could essentially eliminate that explanation. Combining oral and written data in one data set is usually not based on sound principles other than the pedagogical purpose of the previous section.

Another difficulty with Data Set I is that the data are pooled across individuals, and thus the data of individual learners are not isolated. As learning is an individual task, one can question the reasonableness of not being able to identify individual learners. There are certainly good arguments for generalization beyond one individual, but, if a research goal includes being able to detail individual IL development (or nondevelopment), then one must either code for such individual differences or create a new study that focuses on such variation.

There are other factors of interest regarding particular sentences that one may wish to sort out through further data collection. As an example, consider sentence 2-14:

(2-14) **How many month or years** have been in his mind?

The IL phrase *month or years* is puzzling. How could it possibly be that after the quantifier *How many* one gets the plural without the *s* in *month* but with the *s* in *years* in the same phrase? The discussion in section 2.1 deals only with the fact that the analyst has the choice of analyzing that phrase as non-English-like or creating a third category called "ambiguous"; that is, where the phrase is both English-like and non-English-like.

We stated that we prefer the second solution because it does not place TL categories on L2 data. This has been called the "comparative fallacy" (Bley-Vroman, 1983). A goal of SLA research is to discover the system underlying a second language. Comparing L2 forms to TL standards may lead analysts down a path that precludes an understanding of the systematic nature of the learner system in question.[2] Sentence 2-14 presents a case that is indeed fundamentally different from the other sentences in the data set in question. Before one speculates further, one would like to see new data gathered concerning the specific question of whether, in *or* phrases in Arabic–English, plurality is expressed, as in this example, with a mixture of overtly marked plurals and non-marked plurals, or whether one is dealing with a one-time anomaly that can be safely ignored.

TIME TO DO ...

Look at the most recent issue of an SLA professional journal, such as *Studies in Second Language Acquisition, Language Learning,* or *Second Language Research.* Find an empirical study and look at the type of data that the researchers are considering. Do they present examples of target-like forms? Do they present examples of non-target-like forms? How are the researchers investigating the phenomenon?

We now turn to a data-analysis problem that deals with *-ing* marking on English verbs.

2.1.2 Data Set II: Verb + *-ing* Markers

The following utterances were produced by a native speaker of Arabic at the early stages of learning English. At the time of data collection, the learner had had no formal

English instruction. All of the sentences were gathered from spontaneous utterances.[3] In parentheses, we have provided the most likely intention (given the context) of these utterances, when the intention is not obvious from the forms produced.

(2-20) He's sleeping.

(2-21) She's sleeping.

(2-22) It's raining.

(2-23) He's eating.

(2-24) Hani's sleeping.

(2-25) The dog eating. (The dog is eating.)

(2-26) Hani watch TV. (Hani is watching TV.)

(2-27) Watch TV. (He is watching TV.)

(2-28) Read the paper. (He is reading the paper.)

(2-29) Drink the coffee. (He is drinking coffee.)

We have said that the learner is producing what in English would be represented by Verb + -ing structures. We have also noted that, in each case, her intention involves progressive meaning. Thus, an initial observation is that she has two forms she can use to express progressive meaning (*eating* versus *watch*).

One hypothesis we can make about these data is that the learner is using an IL rule that restricts the occurrence of Verb + -ing to sentence-final position. This is true 100 percent of the time, but such a purely structural hypothesis may ignore important semantic facts. A more complex hypothesis that takes into consideration semantic aspects could be the following:

Whenever there is an intended progressive, put the Verb + -ing form in final position.

This hypothesis can be easily rejected by sentences 2-26–2-29. We can attempt a second hypothesis about the use of the simple form of the verb:

Whenever there is no overt subject, the simple form of the verb is used.

This hypothesis is supported by sentences 2-27–2-29, but it, too, seems to tell us little about the use (or nonuse) of Verb + ing.

We now turn to the distinction between transitive versus intransitive sentences; that is, those sentences that have a verb and an overt object (*read the paper*) and those that do not (*sleep*). A third hypothesis can be formulated as follows:

The Verb + -ing form is used in sentences without overt objects. The simple form of the verb is used with transitive verbs with overt objects.

In this light, we notice that sentences 2-20–2-24 consist of a subject plus an intransitive verb; when this occurs, we see a form of the verb *to be* plus the Verb + *ing* form. In sentence 2-25, however, we see a subject that consists of a determiner (article) plus a noun (*the dog*); in this case, only the Verb + *-ing* element appears. This sentence is important for the ultimate explanation. In sentences 2-26–2-29, there is a transitive verb with an object, and the simple form of the verb is used. Here, we see the full force of the principle that the acquisition of a grammatical form is variable, with the Verb + *-ing* form occurring in intransitive sentences, and the simple form in transitive sentences.

How can we account for sentence 2-25? One explanation relates to processing limitations. This learner is able to deal with no more than two- and three-word utterances. It is for this reason that sentence 2-25 is central, as, if it were simply a matter of object presence/absence, we would have no way of explaining the lack of the verb *to be*. The presence of *the* and *dog* sufficiently complexifies the sentence to disallow any further elements.

There is yet another possible explanation having to do with this learner's analysis of the progressive. It is likely that the units *he's*, *she's*, *it's*, and *Hani's* (her husband) are stored as single lexical items. If these are stored as single words, then sentence 2-25 is not a problem, because, for this learner, the *s* is not part of the verb form (see section on chunking in Chapter 8).

TIME TO THINK ...

Beyond these explanations of nonnative-like learner production, can you think of any reasons why learners would have trouble acquiring the plural *-s* morpheme or other grammatical morphemes (e.g., *-s, -ed*)?

As in the previous section, we turn to a brief discussion of additional questions. We pointed out in this section that this Arabic–English speaker appears to express progressive meaning with and without *-ing*. This is one area where an anomaly exists. We can attempt to resolve the anomaly with further data collection, possibly involving types of verbs. Does transitive versus intransitive play a role in expressing progressive meaning? Does the existence of overt subjects play a role? Could it be that the *s* representing the verb *to be* is stored with the subject as one unit? Knowledge of the literature can be very helpful here, for there are attested cases (cf. Harley & Swain, 1984) where the first person singular of the verb *avoir* (to have) in learner French is *j'ai as* (I have), which is the combination of *j'ai* (*je* + *ai* [I + first person singular]) + *as* ([second-person singular form of *avoir*]). Each of these examples lends itself to further data collection with the goal of testing a particular hypothesis.

2.1.3 Data Set III: Prepositions

The last data analysis set we present concerns prepositions, which are known to be among the most difficult items to master in a second language. Examples of Arabic–English sentences with prepositions follow (intended meanings are in parentheses):

(2-30) You can find it **from Morocco til Saudi Arabia**. (from Morocco to Saudi Arabia)

(2-31) There is many kind **of way** you make baklawa. (there are many ways . . .)

(2-32) It's some kind **of different**. (It is quite different . . .)

(2-33) I don't like to buy a car **from Ann Arbor**. (in Ann Arbor)

(2-34) **Since long time**, I'm buying B. F. Goodrich. (for a long time)

(2-35) He finished his studies **before one month**. (a month ago)

(2-36) He will finish **from his studies**. (He will finish his studies.)

(2-37) They are many kinds of reptiles that live **at this planet**. (on this planet)

(2-38) I never help my mom **in the housework**. (with the housework)

(2-39) Egypt shares its boundaries with the Mediterranean Sea **on the north, the Red Sea from the east**. (on the north, the Red Sea on the east)

One noticeable factor in the use of prepositions by these learners is the different semantic areas involved: geographical versus temporal. We may wish to put forth the hypothesis that, in this IL, there is a rule that states:[4]

Use from for geographical locations.

This simple IL rule will work for most of the data, but not all. In sentence 2-39, we would predict *from the north*, and, in sentence 2-36, there is no explanation for *from his studies*. If this rule were borne out through the collection of further data, sentence 2-30 would provide a case of TL behavior by chance (Corder, 1981).

The next set of data from these learners involves phrases in which the TL requires a preposition.

(2-40) We used to pronounce everything **British English**.

(2-41) It doesn't give me problems **future**.

(2-42) He's working **his thesis** now.

(2-43) If I come early, I will register **fall**.

(2-44) The people are outside **this time**.

(2-45) About 20 kilometer out **Jeddah**.

(2-46) I'll wait **you**.

We might describe the behavior of these learners as involving a simplification strategy, although in this case that might be a dangerous generalization, for, as Corder (1983, 1992) pointed out, learners cannot *simplify* what they do not know. However, learners can clearly realize that they do not know how to use prepositions appropriately in English and adopt the following strategy:

Use no preposition except in specifically constrained instances.

A constrained instance was seen in the first set of sentences presented in this section, in which *from* was used in geographical phrases.

Now compare the third set of sentences gathered from the same learners with those of the first and second sets.

(2-47) Since I came **to the United States**.

(2-48) I have lived **in downtown Ann Arbor**.

(2-49) There are 25 counties **in Egypt**.

(2-50) You might think you are **in Dallas**.

(2-51) I have noticed there are many **of them**.

(2-52) They are genius **in this area**.

(2-53) I will go speak nice **to him**.

(2-54) Beginning **from 1:30 a.m. until 2:00 a.m.**

The third set of data presents correct TL forms, although, given what we know about covert errors,[5] some of them at least may only appear to be target-like.

The place expressions *in Egypt*, *in Dallas*, and *in this area* clearly negate the simple hypothesis stated earlier of using *from* for geographical locations. But we should be aware of the possibility that the learners may make a distinction between direction and location. Another possibility is that learners might produce more TL-like preposition usage when other than "obligatory" prepositions are required in the TL. In other words, when there are options, learners are more likely to get things right from sheer luck, even if they do not understand the full range of the language they hear (**input**). This possibility appears to hold for these data, despite the fact that the various options may result in a meaning change. One question that arises with all data collection is the appropriateness of ascribing meaning to learner utterances. This is best done through the NL, although clearly this is not always possible.

We turn now to questions that could not be answered with this data set and additional possible questions. What we observed was variation of a usual kind: "wrong" prepositions from the TL point of view varying with "correct" prepositions and, interestingly, with no prepositions where they are expected. We came up with an IL semantic rule ("Use *from* for geographical locations") that seemed to work some of the time, but again the data were pooled, and so it was hard to see how that rule might have varied according to individuals and according to oral versus written data. We saw that perhaps there is a variable IL rule that states: "Use no preposition except in specific instances." However, it is important to know what those instances might be. Another possibility we could not test with the data at hand, but which seems reasonable, is that there is a two-tier strategy, where the first decision is +/- preposition, and, if the decision is + preposition, then several possibilities might come into play— for example, always choose *X* for *Y* semantic function. Finally, one should never throw out the possibility of randomness playing a role in such an arbitrary area as TL preposition selection. Again, each of these hypotheses could lead to further data collection for a specific purpose.

TIME TO DO ...

In example (2-34), the learner produces the sentence "Since long time, I'm buying B. F. Goodrich." In some languages, *since* and *for* are translated with only one preposition (for example, in Italian with the preposition *da*). How would you explain to an L2 learner of English the difference between *since* and *for*?

A point mentioned in section 2.1 concerns the various contexts in which the IL sentences were produced and whether IL form may be coterminous with context or not (Selinker & Douglas, 1985; Tarone, 2000). In other words, can IL forms be shaped by the context in which they are produced?

Finally, from the preceding analyses, one could raise the question of how to formulate descriptive IL rules or principles and whether, with more relevant data, additional rules would be discovered. We have seen five types of interlanguage rules:

1. **Rule type A**: *Whenever X is present, do Y*. This type of rule appears twice, once with Arabic–English plurals, as in the following:

   Whenever there is a quantifying phrase or a nonnumerical quantifying word before the noun, there is no overt marking on the plural of that noun.

And again with Arabic–English marking (or not) for progressive meaning:

> Whenever there is an intended progressive put the Verb + -*ing* in final position.

Or, in a related form:

2. **Rule type B**: *Whenever there is no X, use Y.* This type of rule appears with progressives:

    > Whenever there is no overt subject, the simple form of the verb is used.

3. **Rule type C**: *Mark all Xs with Y except for those with feature Z.* This type of rule appears with plurals:

    > Mark all plural nouns with *s* except those that are preceded by a quantifying phrase or a nonnumeric quantifying word.

4. **Rule type D**: *The form X is used in sentences without Y. The alternative form Z is used in sentences with Y,* as in the following:

    > The Verb + -*ing* form is used in sentences without overt objects. The simple form of the verb is used with transitive verbs with overt objects.

5. **Rule type E**: *Use form X for function Y.* We see this with IL preposition use, as in:

    > Use *from* for geographical locations.

Thus, we may want to gather additional data to test whether or not these descriptive rules exhaust the potential for a given type of data set.

2.2 CONCLUSION

In general then, when we analyze data, either our own or data from the published literature, we want to always ask this question: What else do we want to find out that is not shown by the data presented? In other words, we always want to be sure that our data enable us to answer, with reasonable certainty, the questions we set out to answer. Additionally, in the case of data that are presented by other researchers, are the data presented thoroughly enough to support the conclusions drawn from them? Finally, it is important to note that the data presented here represent only a fraction of what the field of SLA is about, as will become clear in later chapters.

In the next chapter, we turn to ways in which data can be collected in SLA.

POINTS TO REMEMBER

- Data sets are made up of data taken from IL forms organized to demonstrate particular structural points.

- Exceptions to hypotheses that one makes when analyzing a data set could indicate that the hypothesis is wrong or that another rule or constraint is at play for those particular data. When data from different learners are pooled together, it is possible that differences in the data sets that do not support the hypothesis are due to individual differences among the ILs of individual learners.

- *Spontaneous utterance* refers to learner language that is produced spontaneously, as compared with *forced elicitation*, which is learner language that is experimentally obtained.

- Although pooled data are regularly presented in the literature, it is important to remember that individual differences in IL development may not be identifiable.

- The "comparative fallacy" (Bley-Vroman, 1983) refers to the tendency to place TL categories on IL data. This type of categorization can lead the researcher to miss important details about the systematic nature of the learner's IL.

- When looking at data, it is always important for a researcher to ask: What else do we want to find out that is not shown by the data presented?

SUGGESTIONS FOR ADDITIONAL READING

Exploring learner language (2009). Elaine Tarone and Bonnie Swierzbin. Oxford University Press.

Analysing learner language (2005). Rod Ellis and Gary Barkhuizen. Oxford University Press.

MORE TO DO AND MORE TO THINK ABOUT ...

1. In this chapter, we stated that data do not yield unique results. Is it always the case that data are ambiguous? Can you think of a case where unambiguous results are a possibility? Suppose you are told that, in Indian–English, extremely fluent speakers accurately produce sentences such as *I want to go there*, but do not produce sentences such as *I want her to go there*. Instead, they produce *I want that she go there*. What explanation is possible? Let's further suppose that the same can be said for speakers from a variety of unrelated native languages. Does this alter your view? Now suppose that you are further told that this is not true of all Indian–English speakers. Does this affect your answer? How can one determine the source of this IL system?

2. We noted in this chapter that, at times, it is not always possible to tell what targeted structure a learner has produced. The sentences that follow were produced by adult university students (data from J. Schachter, originally printed as Problem 8.1 in Selinker & Gass, 1984).

    (a) I am an accountant in Accounting Department of National Iranian Oil Company in Abadan which is one of the south cities of Iran.
    (b) There is a tire hanging down from the roof served as their playground.
    (c) Today you can find rural people that they don't have education.
    (d) My problem was to find a place has at least a yard for my children.
    (e) I wanted them to practice Chinese conversation what they learned every day.
    (f) When I return I plan to do accounting and supervising which is my interest and hope.
    (g) And it's a lovely view which you can see it from the plan.
    (h) Libya is quite a big country in which my home town is the biggest city.
    (i) Their philosophy depends on their education which they still working for it, as I am doing right now.
    (j) You can also go to the restaurant where you can have a good meal at a quiet table near the window.
    (k) I saw a group of people waiting for us.
    (l) Next week you give me a list of machine parts required in this contest.

    Identify the restrictive and nonrestrictive clauses in the L2 sentences. List the criteria you used for deciding whether a sentence contained a restrictive or a nonrestrictive relative clause. What difficulties did you have as you attempted to categorize these?

3. There is often a high level of inference in analysis of IL data. For example, when looking at learners' utterances during conversational interaction, it may be hard to determine what the speaker's intention was, and thus difficult to determine the target of the utterance. A consequence is that it may be difficult to classify the error in a sentence. As an example, consider the

following, in which a native speaker (NS) and a nonnative speaker (NNS) are attempting to determine the extent to which two similar pictures have differences.

NS: What about dogs?

NNS: I have a dogs, right.

NS: OK, I have dogs too. How about cats?

In this example, the speakers are engaged in a communicative task, working together to spot the differences between two similar pictures. They could not see each other's picture. At first sight, it is difficult to determine whether the learner's use of the indefinite article or the plural is non-target-like. In other words, in English, one could say either, "I have a dog" or "I have dogs."
In this case, an examination of the task allows us to see that the native speaker's picture has two dogs, and the learner's picture has only one. Thus, the article was correct, and the plural was incorrect. However, the native speaker interpreted it differently, assuming she meant that she also had more than one dog. Carry out a similar task in pairs, with one onlooker. Make a note of any potential ambiguities that could arise if you were carrying out the task with a learner. How would you go about resolving such difficulties in interpreting meaning?

4. There are numerous difficulties in assessing learner knowledge of reflexives. Consider the following sentence with the several options given as to who *himself* could refer to:

Larry said that Joseph hit *himself*.

(a) Larry

(b) Joseph

(c) Either Larry or Joseph

(d) Someone else

(e) Don't know

Native speakers of English know that *himself* can refer to Joseph and cannot refer to Larry. If you select (c) as the correct answer, do you know that (a) is not possible? In other words, does this format provide us with information about what is possible and what is not possible? If it does not, how might you design a task that would provide a researcher with this information?

5. The following utterances were produced by a native speaker of English learning Italian. They were part of a task (Behney, 2008) in which participants had to identify an object from a group of similar objects and colors. All nouns in Italian are either masculine or feminine. Italian has agreement between the definite article (*il* [masculine], *la* [feminine]), the noun, and adjectives, so that, if the noun is masculine, the article and the adjective will be as well; if the noun is feminine, the article and the adjective will also be feminine.

Utterance	Translation
il sole giallo	the sun(MASC) yellow(MASC)
la stella che e' nero	the star(FEM) that is black(MASC)
la luna che e' giallo	the moon(FEM) that is yellow(MASC)
la freccia bianca	the arrow(FEM) white(FEM)
la freccia che e' nero	the arrow(FEM) that is black(MASC)
il cerchio nero	the circle(MASC) black(MASC)
il cerchio grigio	the circle(MASC) gray(MASC)
la cuore che e' giallo	the heart(MASC) that is yellow(MASC)
il albero grigio*	the tree(MASC) gray(MASC)
la stella rossa	the star(FEM) red(FEM)
il sole grigio	the sun(MASC) gray(MASC)
il cerchio azzurro	the circle(MASC) blue(MASC)
il quadrato bianco	the square(MASC) white(MASC)
il triangolo azzurro	the triangle(MASC) blue(MASC)
la stella che e' giallo	the star(FEM) that is yellow(MASC)
la stella che e' bianco	the star(FEM) that is white(MASC)
il quadrato giallo	the square(MASC) yellow(MASC)
la stella che e' grigio	the star(FEM) that is gray(MASC)
la nuvola che e' bianco	the cloud(FEM) that is white(MASC)
il albero azzurro*	the tree(MASC) blue(MASC)
il triangolo rosso	the triangle(MASC) red(MASC)
il cuore grigio	the heart(MASC) gray(MASC)
il triangolo bianco	the triangle(MASC) white(MASC)
la luna che e' bianco	the moon(FEM) that is white(MASC)
il quadrato che e' grigio	the square(MASC) that is gray(MASC)
il cercolo che e' bianco	the circle(MASC) that is white(MASC)
la freccia gialla	the arrow(FEM) yellow(FEM)
il triangolo giallo	the triangle(MASC) yellow(MASC)
il cuore rosso	the heart(MASC) red(MASC)
il sole bianco	the sun(MASC) white(MASC)

*In Italian, this would be l'albero rather than il albero, because the definite article precedes a noun beginning with a vowel. We have left it in the original format, given that it does not affect the analysis.

Which of the utterances in the first column are correct, and which are incorrect?

Can you come up with an explanation for why the incorrect ones are incorrect? In other words, what IL "rule" has this learner come up with? What might be the reason for this learner's IL rule?

CHAPTER THREE

Where Do Data Come From?

3.1 DATA TYPES

Data are the essence of what second language researchers work with, but the question of where data come from is a complex one. In this chapter, we deal with some common issues in data collection. We point out that what we have selected here to discuss is only a very small number of data-collection methods. We further point out that many, although not all, second language research methods have their origins in research methods from other disciplines, notably linguistics, child language acquisition, sociology, and psychology. It is also important to be aware of the fact that particular research questions will often lead to a particular research methodology. In other words, data collection methodologies can only be understood in the context of the research questions being posed. We begin this discussion with a general issue, that of longitudinal versus **cross-sectional** data.

With regard to longitudinal studies, there are four characteristics to be discussed: (a) number of subjects and time frame of data collection, (b) amount of descriptive detail, (c) type of data, and (d) type of analysis.

Longitudinal studies are generally case studies (although not always, as we will see later), with data being collected from a single subject (or at least a small number of subjects) over a prolonged period of time. The frequency of data collection varies. However, samples of a learner's language are likely to be collected weekly, biweekly, or monthly.

Typical of longitudinal studies is the detail provided on a learner's speech, on the setting in which the speech event occurred, and on other details relevant to the analysis of the data (e.g., other conversational participants and their relationship with the subject). The following is a description of one longitudinal study, reported in Hakuta (1974a).

The data come from a longitudinal study of the untutored acquisition of English as a second language by a 5-year-old Japanese girl (Uguisu). Her family came to the

United States for a period of two years while her father was a visiting scholar at Harvard, and they took residence in North Cambridge, in a working-class neighborhood (Hakuta, 1974a, p. 287).

Hakuta went on to describe that the children Uguisu played with "were her primary source of language input." He also included a description of her school activity, saying that she went to "public kindergarten for two hours every day, and later elementary school, but with no tutoring in English syntax. Most of her neighborhood friends were in her same class at school" (Hakuta, 1974a, p. 287).

In most longitudinal studies (particularly those that are case studies), data come from spontaneous speech. This does not mean that the researcher does not set up a conversation to generate a particular type of data. It simply means that longitudinal studies do not fit into the experimental paradigm (to be discussed) of control group and experimental group. An important methodological question that arises in connection with spontaneous speech data collection is: How can a particular type of data be generated through spontaneous speech? Although there cannot be a 100 percent guarantee that certain designated IL forms will appear, the researcher can ask certain types of questions, in the course of data collection, that will likely lead to specific structures. For example, if someone were interested in the IL development of the past **tense**, learners could be asked during each recording session to talk about something that happened to them the previous day.

Analyses of data obtained through longitudinal studies (and particularly in case studies) are often in the form of descriptive, qualitative comments or narrative expositions. Although quantification of data may not be the goal of such studies, the researcher may report the frequency of occurrence of some form. In the reporting of results from longitudinally-collected data, there are likely to be specific examples of what a learner said and how their utterances are to be interpreted.

This type of data is highly useful in determining developmental trends, as well as in interpreting various social constraints and input influences on the learner's speech. On the other hand, a major drawback concerns the time involved. Conducting a longitudinal study requires time for collecting data at regular intervals, as well as for transcription of the speech, which is ideally accompanied by extensive detail on the social, personal, and physical setting in which the speech event took place. A second drawback is related to the lack of generalizability. Given that longitudinal studies are often limited in the number of subjects investigated, it is difficult to generalize the results. It is difficult to know, with any degree of certainty, whether the results obtained are applicable only to the one or two subjects studied, or whether they are indeed characteristic of a wide range of subjects, although for those working with longitudinal data, generalization is often not the goal. Rather, it is sufficient to know that a particular phenomenon has occurred. Another difficulty with spontaneously-produced longi- tudinal data, and perhaps the most serious one, is that, when learners produce a form, there is no way of probing their knowledge any further than what they have produced spontaneously (see data sets in Chapter 2). This is particularly the case if the researchers themselves have not collected the data, or if the researchers have not generated specific hypotheses and are not predisposed to gathering information about specific forms of speech. For example, if, in a particular set of spontaneously-elicited data, a learner only produces the present tense of verbs, does that mean that that is all the learner knows? We cannot interpret data only on the basis of what is actually present, because we do not know if absence of forms means lack of knowledge of forms.

A second type of data-collection method involves cross-sectional studies. Here, too, there are four identifiable characteristics that are generally associated with such studies: (a) number of subjects and time frame of data collection, (b) type of data, (c) descriptive detail, and (d) analysis of data.

A cross-sectional study generally consists of data gathered from a large number of participants at a single point in time, the idea being that we are able to see a slice of development, which is used to piece together actual development.

Unlike case studies, which are based primarily on spontaneous speech, cross-sectional data are often (but not always) based on controlled output. That is, the format is one in which a researcher is attempting to gather data based on a particular research hypothesis. The data, then, come from learners' performance on some pre-specified task.

The type of background information differs from what we have seen with longitudinal studies. Participants are not identified individually, nor is detailed descriptive information provided. A certain amount of background data is likely to be presented in tabular form, as in Table 3.1.

Because cross-sectional data involve large numbers of subjects, there is typically an experimental format to the research, both in design and in analysis. Results tend to be more quantitative and less descriptive than in longitudinal studies, with statistical analyses and their interpretation being integral parts of the research report.

One can use a cross-sectional design to create a **pseudolongitudinal** study. In such a study, the emphasis, like that of a longitudinal study, is on language change (i.e., acquisition), with data being collected at a single point in time, but with different proficiency levels represented. For example, if one were investigating the acquisition of the progressive, one would want to know not just what learners can do at a particular point in time (because the question involves acquisition and not static knowledge), but also what happens over a period of time. One way of gathering such data is through a longitudinal study, carefully noting every instance in which the progressive is, or is not, used. Another way of gathering information about linguistic development would be to take a large group of individuals, at three specified proficiency levels—let's

TABLE 3.1 Typical Data Presentation in a Cross-Sectional Design

Language Background	No. of Participants	Gender	Age	Proficiency
Arabic	24	13 F; 11 M	22–26	8 Beg/8 Int/8 Adv
Spanish	24	12 F; 12 M	23–28	12 Beg/12 Adv
Japanese	24	11 F; 13 M	21–23	20 Beg/4 Adv

say, beginner, intermediate, and advanced—and give each group the same test. The assumption underlying this method is that comparison of these three groups would yield results similar to what would be found if we looked at a single individual over time. The extent to which this assumption is warranted is controversial.

One advantage to a cross-sectional approach is the disadvantage of longitudinal data: Given that there are large numbers of subjects in the former, it is more likely that the results can be generalized to a wider group. The disadvantage is that there may be insufficient detailed information about the participants themselves and the linguistic environment in which production was elicited. Both types of information may be central to an appropriate interpretation of the data. This criticism, of course, is not so much a problem with the research approach, as it is with the way results are reported in the literature.

As noted earlier, longitudinal data are often associated with descriptive (or qualitative) data. Cross-sectional and pseudolongitudinal data, on the other hand, are often associated with quantitative or statistical measures. However, one can easily conduct statistical analyses on longitudinal data, and one can easily provide descriptive analyses of cross-sectional data. It is, furthermore, a mistake to assume that longitudinal data cannot be generalized. One may be able to put together a profile of learners based on many longitudinal studies.

Why would a researcher select one type of data-collection procedure over another? What is most important in understanding this choice is the understanding of the relationship between a research question and research methodology. There are certain kinds of questions and certain kinds of external pressures that would lead one to select one type of approach to research over another. If, for example, one wanted to gather information about how nonnative speakers learn to apologize in a second language, one could observe learners over a period of time, noting instances of apologizing (either in a controlled experiment or in a naturalistic setting). On the other hand, one could use a cross-sectional approach by setting up a situation and asking large groups of L2 speakers what they would say. The latter forces production, the former waits until it happens. Although many would argue that the former is "better," in that it more accurately reflects reality, it is also clear that one might have to wait for a considerable amount of time before getting any information that would be useful in answering the original research question. Thus, the exigencies of the situation often lead a researcher to a particular approach.

It would be a mistake to think of any of these paradigmatic boundaries as rigid; it would also be a mistake to associate longitudinal studies with naturalistic data collection. One can conduct a longitudinal study with large numbers of speakers; one can also collect data longitudinally using an experimental format. In a study on relative clauses, Gass (1979a, 1979b) gathered data from 17 L2 learners at six points in time (at monthly intervals). Thus, the study itself satisfied the typical definition of longitudinal. However, it did not satisfy the definition of a case study, as it did not involve detailed descriptions of the participants and did not include spontaneous speech. On the other hand, given the experimental nature of the study (which involved forced production of relative clauses), it more appropriately belongs in the category of cross-sectional.

In other words, the categories we have described are only intended to be suggestive. There is much flexibility in categorizing research as being of one type or another.

We next take a look at two studies to give an idea of the range of data that has been looked at in SLA.

First is a study by Kumpf (1984), who was interested in understanding how nonnative speakers expressed temporality in English. One way to gather such information is to present participants with sentences (perhaps with the verb form deleted) and ask them to fill in the blank with the right tense. This, however, would not give information about how that speaker uses tense in a naturalistic environment. Only a long narrative would give that information. Following is the text produced by the native speaker of Japanese in Kumpf's study. The participant is a woman who had lived in the United States for 28 years at the time of taping. For the purposes of data collection, she was asked to produce a narrative account.

> First time Tampa have a tornado come to.
> Was about seven forty-five
> Bob go to work, n I was inna bathroom.
> And . . . a . . . tornado come shake everything.
> Door was flyin open, I was scared.
> Hanna was sittin in window . . .
> Hanna is a little dog.
> French poodle.
> I call Baby.
> Anyway, she never wet bed, she never wet anywhere.
> But she was so scared and crying' run to the bathroom, come to me, and
>   she tinkle, tinkle, tinkle all over me.
> She was so scared.
> I see somebody throwin a brick onna trailer
> wind was blowin so hard
> ana light . . . outside street light was on
> oh I was really scared.
> An den second stop
> So I try to open door
> I could not open
> I say, "Oh, my God. What's happen?"
> I look window. Awning was gone.

(pp. 135–136)

With regard to temporality, there are a few conclusions that Kumpf draws from these data. One is that there is a difference between scene-setting information (i.e., that which provides background information to the story) and information about the action-line. These two functions are reflected in the use, or lack of use, of the verb *to be* with the progressive. In the scene-setting descriptions, descriptive phrases (*wind was blowin, door was flyin open, Hanna was sittin in window*), the past form of *to be* is apparent. However, when this speaker refers to specific events, no form of the verb *to be* was used (*somebody throwin brick onna trailer*).

A second finding from this study is the frequency with which certain types of verbs are marked with tense. The copula (*to be*) is tensed 100 percent of the time; verbs expressing the habitual past (*used to*) are tensed 63 percent of the time; and continuous action verbs (e.g., *try*) are tensed 60 percent of the time.

Could this information have been elicited through a controlled observation procedure? The first set of results (determining the differences between scene-setting and action-based information), probably not; the second set (frequency of verb tenses), probably could. In the first instance, it is difficult to imagine an experimental paradigm that would have elicited such information. In the second, one could more easily imagine setting up a situation (even using isolated sentences) in which the same results would have been obtained.

Because these data are limited to one speaker, one would like to know whether this is a general phenomenon or not. Results from studies such as this can be verified by attempting to force production from larger numbers of L2 learners. However, the fact that even one speaker made a distinction between the use of the verb *to be* and its nonuse suggests that this is a possible IL generalization. One question at the forefront of much SLA research is: Are the language systems that learners create consistent with what is found in natural language systems? This takes us back to the basic question: What are the boundaries of human languages? Given the primacy of questions such as these, the fact of a single individual creating a particular IL generalization (in this case, using or not using the verb *to be* to differentiate between two discourse functions) is enough to provide initial answers.

TIME TO THINK ...

It is said that, in quantitative research, the research questions guide the study, but that, in qualitative research, the research findings often emerge from the data. How might the first set of results from the Kumpf study (determining the differences between scene-setting and action-based information) be an example of a research finding emerging from the data without a prior research question?

Let's consider a study that gathers data within an experimental paradigm. Gass and Ard (1984) were concerned with the knowledge that learners have about various meanings of the progressive. Their database came from responses to four different tasks by 139 learners. In the first task, subjects were asked to judge the acceptability of sentences containing the various meanings of the progressive, as in 3-1 and 3-2:

(3-1)   John is traveling to New York tomorrow.

(3-2)   John travels to New York tomorrow.

In the second task, the sentences were embedded in short conversations:

(3-3) MARY: I need to send a package to my mother in a hurry.
       JANE: Where does she live?
       MARY: In New York.
       JANE: Oh, in that case John can take it. John is traveling to New York tomorrow.

In the third task, there were again isolated sentences, although these were in groups of five. Again, acceptability judgments were asked for.

(3-4) The ship sailed to Miami tomorrow.

(3-5) The ship is sailing to Miami tomorrow.

(3-6) The ship will sail to Miami tomorrow.

(3-7) The ship sails to Miami tomorrow.

(3-8) The ship has sailed to Miami tomorrow.

In the fourth task, they were given a verb form and asked to write as long a sentence as possible including that form.

What was found was that there was an order of preference of different meanings for the progressive. For example, most learners ordered the various meanings of the progressive so that the most common use was to express the present (*John is smoking American cigarettes now*); the next was the progressive to express futurity (*John is traveling to New York tomorrow*); the next to express present time with verbs of perception (*Dan is seeing better now*); the next with verbs such as *connect* (*The new bridge is connecting Detroit and Windsor*); and, finally, with the copula (*Mary is being in Chicago now*). The authors used this information to gain information about the development of meaning, including both prototypical meanings and more extended meanings. Through spontaneous speech alone (whether a case study or not), this would not have been possible. Only a forced-choice data task would elicit the relevant information. One should also note that controlled observations of spontaneous speech may underestimate the linguistic knowledge of a learner, particularly in those cases where the task is insensitive to the linguistic structure being elicited or is too demanding.

TIME TO THINK ...

What do you think are the difficulties of conducting a longitudinal study? What are the difficulties of conducting a cross-sectional study?

Have you participated in a research study? Was it longitudinal or cross-sectional?

3.2 LEARNER CORPORA

There may be times when a researcher does not want, or does not need, to collect original data. For example, if one wants to know about the emergence of certain forms, an existing corpus of L2 data might be the most useful. Additionally, many researchers are concerned with examining data from spontaneously produced contexts, rather than looking at experimentally produced data (see also section 3.3). **Corpora** allow this to happen.

The conceptual motivation behind the use of learner corpora is very similar to other empirical work in SLA in that it involves sampling learner language to be analyzed and then testing particular hypotheses or predictions regarding IL. A corpus-based approach, however, presents two major advantages that distinguish it from traditional techniques. First, learner corpora are manipulated and analyzed by computer, thus facilitating and automatizing much of the process. Of course, not all learner language is produced in an electronic format, and so a conversion from analog to digital is often necessary, a time-consuming and expensive task, particularly when the corpus consists of oral data. Second, learner corpora are generally much larger than non-corpus samples of learner data, often including over a million words. The International Corpus of Learner English (www.uclouvain.be/en-cecl-icle.html), for instance, has 3.7 million words. In addition to adding power to statistical analyses, large corpora enable researchers to more reliably assess the use of lexical items or structures that may be relatively infrequent in smaller samples of learner language. (See Figures 3.1 and 3.2

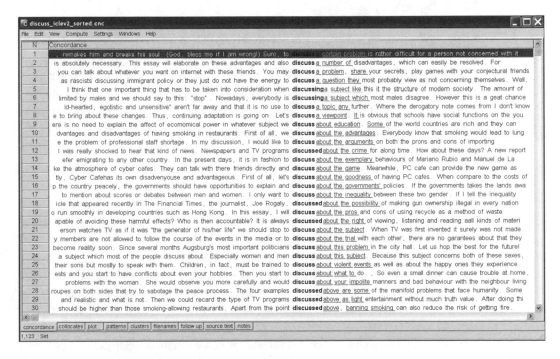

FIGURE 3.1 Right-Sorted Concordance of the Verb *Discuss* in ICLE (*Source*: From The International Corpus of Learner English. Reprinted by permission.)

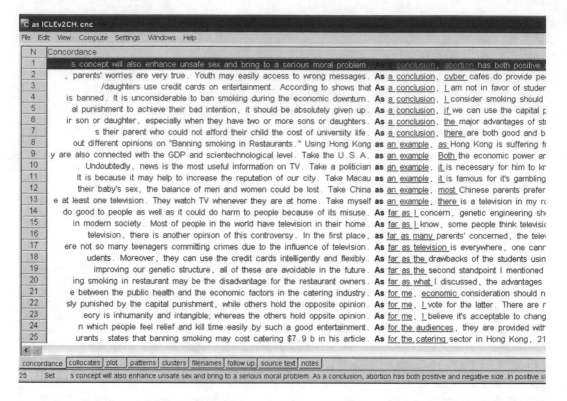

FIGURE 3.2 Left-Sorted Concordance of *As* in ICLE (*Source*: From The International Corpus of Learner English. Reprinted by permission.)

for examples of corpus data. Figure 3.1 shows uses of *discuss* by nonnative speakers, and Figure 3.2 shows uses of *as*.)

The benefits of using corpus methods to analyze learner production have prompted researchers interested in a wide range of variables in SLA to investigate features found in both oral and written data. Durrant and Schmitt (2009), for example, were able to compare **collocations** of L1 and L2 speakers, drawing from existing data in the International Corpus of Learner English (www.uclouvain.be/en-cecl-icle.html). Others develop their own corpora in order to address a particular question or measure a particular phenomenon not sufficiently present in an existing corpus. The Spanish Learner Language Oral Corpora 2 (SPLLOC 2: www.splloc.soton.ac.uk/splloc2/index. html; see Domínguez et al., in press) research team, for example, had a very specific interest—acquisition of tense and **aspect** morphology in L2 Spanish—and has collected learner production to answer a set of questions determined a priori. Still others cast a wider net in collecting learner-produced texts to enable a variety of questions related to learner language to be addressed. Collentine and Asención-Delaney's (2010) corpus is comprised of writing by first-, second-, and third-year learners of Spanish, totaling 432,511 words. Their 2010 study examined copula (the verb *to be*) choice in L2 Spanish in conjunction with a range of co-occurring features, both morphological and syntactic in nature. In addition to morphosyntax and lexis, corpus techniques have also been used to study L2 discourse beyond the sentence level (e.g., cohesion; Shea, 2011).

The main steps in carrying out a study using a learner corpus are as follows (see also Granger, 2012):

1. **Selecting and/or compiling learner production**: Does a suitable corpus already exist? How large does the corpus need to be, and how many unique learners and/or L1s are needed? (Although English is the best-represented language, L2 corpora have also been collected in Dutch, Finnish, French, German, Italian, Korean, Norwegian, Slovene, Spanish, and Swedish, among other L2s.) Would naturalistic/authentic production work, or are specific tasks required to elicit targeted linguistic features?

2. **Annotating the data** (optional): Does the corpus need to be tagged for parts of speech or other features? If so, is the grammatical or error tagger able to handle the irregularities of nonnative production?

3. **Extracting data**: What type of data is to be extracted (usually using a concordance program)? Collocations? Frequency counts? Relative error types (e.g., vocabulary, grammar, spelling) in a particular linguistic environment? This step often involves examining key words in context (KWICs) produced by the concordancing software. The following screen capture (Figure 3.3) displays KWICs resulting

TACTweb (1.0 (Beta A)) Results

Database Title:

Query: like

like (112)

```
A01 12        it's a boy and a girl who seems like they're talking to each other , it's on a
A01 31    , and on the last picture it seems like they have looking at the match football match
A01 57         (( yeah)) <57><A01> it looks like they're happy <58><T> (( yes actually they
B02 7      er no what country would you not like to live in  <8><A02> er I wouldn't like to
A02 8      to live in <8><A02> er I wouldn't like to live in . Germany <9><B02> why  <10><A02>
A02 10        why <10><A02> because I don't like the country <11><B02> <nv laugh</nv>
B02 27         being in <27><B02> ... well , I like to visit , countries so . I'm not quite sure
A02 28    okay . er a job you do at home and like <29><B02> pardon could you say it again
A02 30    <30><A02> a job you do at home and like <31><B02> well . I like sometimes to , clean
B02 31    at home and like <31><B02> well . I like sometimes to , clean my room , because it
A02 34    <34><A02> er . a country you would like to go to  <35><B02> I would like to go to
B02 35        like to go to <35><B02> I would like to go to Spain <36><A02> why  <37><B02>
A02 50      that er , and she really would like to go to Spain and er she = likes to clean
B02 54     ten minutes , and er she don't like to be in Germany , and she likes to be in
B02 54     like to be in Germany , and she like to be in Spain  <55><T> (( mm))  <56><B02>
B02 160   er , <hidden>)) <160><B02> well like these two they <161><T> (( yeah))  <162><B02>
B02 196     I felt joy because I <unclear> like them to win so I that was er that was what I
A03 20    their tickets and their = it looks like they're = <21><T> (( looks like they))
A05 18    <17><T> (( ah)) <18><A05> I don't like that <laughs>er and er no not more than that
B03 19    er . do you have some er heroes you like <laughs> <20><A05> heroes er like special
A05 20      like <laughs> <20><A05> heroes er like special person <21><B03> yeah [special
A05 22    [special person] <22><A05> [okay] I like er er er Johan = Olav Koss <laughs>the skater
```

FIGURE 3.3 Sample of KWICs of *Like* in the EVA Corpus of Norwegian School English

from a search for the word *like* in the EVA Corpus of Norwegian School English (http://kh.hd.uib.no/eva/eva.htm), with background information about the corpus at http://kh.hd.uib.no/eva/eva-sn1.htm.

4. **Analyzing and interpreting**: What is the focus of the analysis? What do the data say about L2 use and/or the predictions of theory that motivated the analysis?

The electronic format of corpus data and the culture of corpus-based research encourage scholars to make their data sets available online to be searched and analyzed by other researchers. SPLLOC2, for instance, can be freely accessed and downloaded on the project website (www.splloc.soton.ac.uk/splloc2/index.html) and searched using a number of criteria related to particular participants, tasks, and language forms of interest. Like many others, this particular corpus followed the CHILDES transcription format, so that the data are ready to be used with the CHILDES software (http://childes.psy.cmu.edu), CLAN, which is also free, to carry out a variety of analyses. Additional corpora that are freely available and searchable online include the International Corpus of Crosslinguistic Interlanguage (ICCI: http://cblle.tufs.ac.jp/llc/icci/search.php?menulang=en) and the *Corpus parlato di italiano* (http://elearning.unistrapg.it/osservatorio/corpus/frames-cqp.html), among many others. Other researchers, labs, and organizations make their corpora available upon request (e.g., the BUiD Arab Learner Corpus) or for purchase (e.g., The International Corpus of Learner English: www.i6doc.com/en/collections/cdicle/). Using existing data presents many obvious logistical advantages as opposed to designing and collecting a corpus from scratch. There are some significant drawbacks, however. Researchers who utilize existing corpus resources have no control over annotation on tasks or participant demographics, and, of course, they are limited to the tasks or instruments used by other researchers in collecting the corpus, which may or may not elicit features of interest.

TIME TO DO ...

Go to one of the learner corpora mentioned above (either of your L1 or your L2) and search for a particular word. Look at the results of how learners have used this word. Consider how you could use a learner corpus in an L2 study.

3.3 DATA ELICITATION

In addition to learner corpora, there are numerous ways of eliciting L2 data. As we mentioned earlier, many, but not all, have their origins in other disciplines. In the preceding section, we discussed corpus data. In this section, which is not intended to be inclusive, we present kinds of data and data-elicitation methods that have been used in L2 studies (see Gass & Mackey, 2007, for more detailed coverage).

3.3.1 Measuring General Proficiency

Thomas (1994), based on a survey of the literature, has identified four common ways of assessing proficiency: (a) impressionistic judgments, (b) institutional status (e.g., first semester of second-year French), (c) specific research-designed test, and (d) standardized tests. Because there are so many ways to measure proficiency, the field of SLA is left with considerable difficulty in comparing studies. This is unlike the field of child language acquisition (see Chapter 5), in which there is a well-accepted means of judging where a child is on the developmental scale.

As a precursor to a study, we often want to know where one might stand on a scale of overall proficiency. This is so in cases where one might want to conduct a pseudolongitudinal study in which development from beginning levels to more advanced levels is compared. Or, if one wants to compare two groups on some measure, one would probably want to ensure that the two groups are equal. There are a number of ways to do this. One way is through standardized language tests. These instruments can also (but not often) be used as a source of L2 data (cf. the work of Ard & Homburg (1983, 1992), discussed in Chapter 6).

Standardized language tests are often used as gauges for measuring proficiency levels. For example, one might categorize a group of advanced learners as those who have a TOEFL (Test of English as a Foreign Language) score above a certain level. Even with standardized tests, however, there is no absolute, accepted cutoff point for advanced, intermediate, beginner, and so forth. In fact, one difficulty in comparing SLA studies is that, because there is no accepted cutoff point, one researcher's advanced category may correspond to another's intermediate category. This is not the case with standardized measures, such as the Common European Framework of Reference, the American Council on the Teaching of Foreign Languages, or the Inter-agency Language Roundtable, where certain values are associated with descriptors of what it means to reach a particular level.

Another way of categorizing proficiency levels is through "seat time," that is, how much time one has spent studying a particular language (cf., Zyzik, 2006; Gass & Lee, 2011). It is obvious that just studying a language does not guarantee similar proficiency levels at the end. It is for this reason that researchers might opt for two degrees of separation, for example, first-year Spanish versus third-year Spanish, as did Gass and Lee (2011).

Self-proficiency ratings are sometimes used to gauge relative proficiency. Learners might be self-evaluated in terms of their abilities in various skills (reading, writing, and speaking). Much of the literature on self-assessment addresses concerns related to the value of self-reflection, **motivation**, and independence, thereby having an indirect impact on learning (De Saint Leger, 2009; Butler & Lee, 2010). However, there are instances when a self-assessment tool is used in the absence of other objective measures. Studies such as Ross (1998), LeBlanc and Painchaud (1985), and Malabonga et al. (2005) suggest that such measures can be valid, but also note that the instrument needs to be carefully designed (see Butler & Lee, 2006).

3.3.2 Measuring Nonlinguistic Information

Many studies do not involve actual language data, but rather deal with aspects of individuals, for example, aptitude, attitude, motivation, **learning styles**, and personality characteristics. There are many ways of gathering information about these attributes. Below, we discuss a few.

Questionnaires are commonly used to gain information about attitudes a learner may have toward language learning, either generally or toward the learning of a specific language (see Chapter 14). They are particularly useful when a large amount of data is desired. A standard questionnaire was developed by Gardner and Lambert (1972) and has been modified in numerous studies since. A sampling of the types of questions follows:

I am studying French because:

(a) I think it will someday be useful in getting a good job.
(b) I think it will help me to better understand French people and their way of life.
(c) It will allow me to meet and converse with more and varied people.
(d) A knowledge of two languages will make me a better educated person.
(e) Any other personal reason.

Another type of information is gained by asking participants to indicate their support (from *strongly in favor* to *strongly against*), on a six-point scale, for the following:

1. In the United States today, public officials aren't really very interested in the problems of the average person.

2. Having lived this long in this culture, I'd be happier moving to some other country now.

3. Compared to the people of France, Americans are more sincere and honest.

4. Family life is more important to Americans than it is to people in France.

Attitudinal ratings are also used in research on motivation and attitudes. Individuals are given polar opposites and asked to judge their impressions of a group of people (e.g., French people from France) on a seven-point evaluational scale:

(a) Interesting   ___:___:___:___:___:___:___   Boring
(b) Prejudiced   ___:___:___:___:___:___:___   Unprejudiced
(c) Happy   ___:___:___:___:___:___:___   Sad
(d) Hardworking   ___:___:___:___:___:___:___   Lazy

Most questionnaires are typically done by paper and pencil, although, with the advent of such websites as *Survey Monkey*, web-based questionnaires are becoming easier to construct and, hence, easier to administer (see Thompson et al., 2012, for an example of a web-based survey used to gain information about SLA graduate programs). Wilson and Dewaele (2010) discuss web-based questionnaires from the perspective of L2 research (see also Gosling et al., 2004, and Buchanan et al., 2005). They point to issues of participant selection, validity, reliability, and quality. Obviously, some of the same issues that pertain to all questionnaire designs are also relevant for web-based questionnaires. However, there are a few factors to consider when deciding whether to do a web-based or a paper–pencil questionnaire. For example, the following are advantages to using web-based surveys:

- cost;
- ability to reach a wider audience;
- data can be transferred directly onto a spreadsheet.

However, there are disadvantages as well:

- There is often little control over participants.
- It restricts the participants to those who are computer-literate and who have ready access to computers.
- With very large sample sizes, one might find significant associations just because of the large sample and not because of a meaningful association.

3.3.3 Verbal Report Data

There are times when researchers are interested in cognitive processes during language use. For this, they return to **verbal reports**, which can take a number of forms. Generally speaking, verbal reports are tools used to understand the cognitive processes involved when participants perform a task. To gather such data, individuals are asked to verbalize what they are thinking about as they are performing a specified

TIME TO DO ...

Are all language skills susceptible to think-alouds? Why or why not? If not, which ones are better suited for think-aloud protocols?

What is the role of the L1? Is it as easy to do a think-aloud in the L1 as in the L2? What are some of the issues?

How difficult do you think it would be to do a think-aloud?

Read the following passage (*The International*, August 6, 2012, produced by Headland Media) and verbalize your thoughts as you encounter words/phrases you don't know:

> But Prior took over the attacking role played by Pietersen on Saturday, cracking eight fours before he was ninth man out, top-edging a sweep against leg-spinner Imran Tahir to deep fineleg.
>
> Kemar Roach, voted player of the series, missed a half century as he was the only wicket to fall on the day, caught for 41 by Tim Southeee of the bowling of Kane Williamson, who induced an outside edge as the hosts claimed their first Test series against the tourists in 16 years.

EXAMPLE

Problem to be solved

A father, a mother, and their son are 80 years old together. The father is twice as old as the son. The mother has the same age as the father. How old is the son?

Student 1

1. a father, a mother and their son are together 80 years old
2. the father is twice as old as the son
3. the mother is as old as the father
4. how old is the son?
5. well, that sounds complicated
6. let's have a look

7. just call them F, M and S
8. F plus M plus S is 80
9. F is 2 times S
10. and M equals F
11. what do we have now?
12. three equations and three unknowns
13. so S . . .
14. 2 times F plus S is 80
15. so 4 times S plus S is 80
16. so 5 times S is 80
17. S is 16
18. yes, that is possible

19. so father and mother are 80 minus 16
20. 64

21. er . . . 32

Student 2

1. father, other and son are together 80 years old
2. how is that possible?
3. if such a father is 30 and mother too
4. then the son is 20
5. no, that is not possible
6. if you are 30, you cannot have a son of 20
7. so they should be older
8. about 35, more or less
9. let's have a look
10. the father is twice as old as the son
11. so if he is 35 and the son 17
12. no, that is not possible
13. 36 and 18
14. then the mother is
15. 36 plus 18 is 54
16. 26 . . .
17. well, it might be possible
18. no, then she should have had a child when she was 9
19. oh, no
20. no the father should, the mother should be older
21. for example 30
22. but then I will not have 80
23. 80 minus 30, 50
24. then the father should be nearly 35 and the son nearly 18
25. something like that
26. let's have a look, where am I?
27. the father is twice . . .
28. the mother is as old as the father
29. oh dear
30. my mother, well not my mother
31. but my mother was 30 and my father nearly 35
32. that is not possible
33. if I make them both 33
34. then I have together 66
35. then there is for the son . . . 24
36. no, that is impossible
37. I don't understand it anymore
38. 66, 80
39. no, wait, the son is 14
40. almost, the parents are too old
41. 32, 32, 64, 16, yes
42. the son is 16 and the parents 32, together 80

task. Verbal reports, which have been used in a wide range of fields, including psychology, business, math, to name just a few, can illustrate individual differences in approaching a problem. van Someren et al. (1994, pp. 5–6), through the example above, show that individuals think aloud as they carry out a task and reach the same conclusion by very different routes—in this case, one that is straightforward (and shorter) and uses algebra, and another one that appears somewhat circuitous, peppered with "guesses" and logic.

In this section, we deal with three general areas of verbal reports: **think-alouds**, **stimulated recalls**, and post-production interviews.

3.3.3.1 Think-Alouds

The example above represents a think-aloud protocol. During think-alouds in L2 research, learners may be presented with a task and asked to perform it. The examples below demonstrate the type of protocol obtained in a reading study (Cohen & Upton, 2007) and a writing study (Sachs & Polio, 2007).

The examples below (3-9, 3-10, and 3-11) from Cohen and Upton (2007, p. 16) demonstrate three types of reading behavior. The examples come from a reading subtest of the TOEFL exam, which consists of a reading passage followed by comprehension questions. (**Bold** indicates verbal reporting; underlined text refers to text from the test passage.)

(3-9) *Strategy*: jumping immediately to the word in the context of the passage before looking at the options to try to get a sense of the word's meaning

> **Well, this word** rate. [*Returns to passage.*] **Oh, when they report** positive feelings, **and** rate cartoons, **they become even happier**

(3-10) *Strategy*: reading a portion of the passage carefully.

> seep seep **I don't know this word. Let's go to the sentence in the text**.

(3-11) *Strategy*: using the understanding of the sentence and paragraph meaning to help select which option was the correct synonym or discard options that weren't.

> **I am sure that** "obviously" **doesn't make sense. It's either** "easily" **or** "intelligently." **For sure not** "frequently" . . . **I think it's** "easily" **because it's something about the effectiveness of the machine.** "Easily" **makes more sense in the passage.**

As these examples show, one is able to see a range of strategy use through the verbalizations of these learners.

The following example concerns writing, particularly reformulations (Sachs & Polio, 2007). Participants wrote a story based on a picture-story. Reformulations were given to the participants, and they compared their versions with the reformulated version, producing a verbal protocol as they were making their comparisons. The following day, participants revised their story. The think-alouds provided the researchers with information to allow them to detect places where there was **awareness** of original problems and consequent changes.

(3-12) *Original sentence*:

> One day, he noticed that his tammy is kind of terrible by looking at the mirror.

Reformulated sentence:

> One day, while looking in the mirror, a man noticed that his tummy looked pretty terrible.

Think-aloud:

> Ok, um, uh, I wrote, first of all, I wrote, he noticed that his tummy is kind of terrible, but native speaker's one is first of all, while looking in the mirror, a man noticed that his tummy looked pretty terrible, terrible. Mmm . . . I don't know why, I think . . . first of all, when I wrote this, I thought this is, I tried to write sentence . . . correctly, so I don't know why this is, why they, there is difference. Hm. By looking at the mirror, and while looking at the mirror, while looking. Ah, and I also didn't know that when I used, when somebody uses the word while, I thought a person has to put sub-subject while and looking. So . . . that's my, that's what I notice.

Revised sentence:

> One day, while looking in the mirror, a man noticed that his tummy looked pretty terrible.

On the day following the protocol, participants were given only their original story and were asked to write a revised story. As can be seen, the participant in the example above without a doubt noticed the changes that were made in the reformulation (particularly the word *while*) and incorporated them in the revision.

3.3.3.2 Stimulated Recall

Stimulated recall (see Gass & Mackey, 2000, for a detailed account of this methodology), a type of verbal report, differs from think-alouds in that the latter are performed during a task, and stimulated recalls, as the name implies, are performed after a task, and, importantly, there is a "stimulus" from the task to help the participant recall his/her thought processes during the preceding task.

Think-alouds are most often successful during reading or writing tasks and virtually impossible during oral tasks, because, quite obviously, one cannot perform an oral task and simultaneously talk about one's thoughts. It is for this reason that stimulated recalls have become common in studies of oral communication. In such instances, a task is performed (either audio- or video-recorded). As soon as possible after the task, a researcher reviews the audio or video (the stimulus) with the participant and asks the participant what he/she was thinking about during the task (not at the time of questioning, but at the time that the task was being performed). One needs to remember two important features of stimulated recalls: (1) There is a stimulus to jog the participant's memory; this is generally a video or an audio of the event, or, in writing research, something that the person has written or typed (a video of a screen could serve this purpose). (2) The learner must verbalize his/her thoughts that occurred during the original task. This latter is often difficult to ensure, but having a stimulus and having the recall close to the original event maximize the likelihood that thought processes are as accurate as possible. It is often the case that recalls can take place within minutes of the original event, with an interaction being recorded, and the participant viewing/listening to a video/audio immediately and responding to questions. Finally, the questions asked are important. A question such as "What were you thinking about when you said that?" is appropriate; a question such as "What are you thinking?" is not appropriate, because the time frame being asked about (during the event or at the moment of questioning) is not clear.

Below is an example taken from an experiment (Mackey et al., 2000) that used stimulated recall following an interactive task in which a NS and a NNS attempted to discover differences between two similar pictures. Examples (3-13) and (3-14) contain data from that study that show the kinds of thought processes that learners go through when they are receiving **corrective feedback**, in other words, feedback that lets them know that they have said something ungrammatical. In the first instance, the learner understood that *three?* indicated a problem. In the second example, taken from the same study, but with learners of Italian, the learner did not understand that a correction had been made.

(3-13) NNS: Three key
      INTERVIEWER: Three?
      NNS: Key er keys
      RECALL: After "key" again, I make a little effort to say "keys" because you have three. I was thinking try a little better English.

(3-14) NNS: C'è due tazzi
      "There is two cups (masc., plural)"
      INTERVIEWER: Due tazz—come?
      "two cup—what?"
      NNS: Tazzi, dove si puó mettere tè, come se [sic] dice questo?
      "Cups (masc. plural) where one can put tea, how do you say this?"
      INTERVIEWER: Tazze?
      "cups (fem. plural)?"
      NNS: Okay, tazze
      "Okay, cups (fem. plural)"
      RECALL: I wasn't sure if I learned the proper word at the beginning.

Thus, in the second example, the learner was focused on the actual word rather than the ending, whereas the interviewer was intending to correct the ending. It is through stimulated recall that this mismatch was revealed.

51

We now present examples of recall data from the Mackey et al. (2000) study that had to be discarded, because the validity of the data was questionable. As will be seen, it is very easy to confuse the time frame.

In example (3-15), the focus is on the time of the recall versus the time of the initial event (taken from Gass & Mackey, 2000).

(3-15) NNS: He also standing
       NS: He's standing
       NNS: Yeah
       RECALL PROMPT: Why did she repeat it after you?
       RECALL RESPONSE: Because I still speak lower . . . and maybe she don't
                          understand
       INTERVIEWER: She doesn't hear?
       RESPONSE (NNS):   Yeah
       INTERVIEWER: She doesn't hear or doesn't understand
       RESPONSE (NNS):   doesn't hear
       INTERVIEWER: Why does she say that?

In this instance, the interviewer only used the present tense and never mentioned the actual interactive event. This caused great difficulty, and the recall was not useable as a reflection of the learner's thoughts during the original interaction. In (3-16), the interviewer asked a clarification question, not a question related to the recall.

(3-16) NNS: Two people, three people is in the sea
       INTERVIEWER: All three people are in the sea
       NNS: The sea
       RECALL: I used I said people is three people is in the sea but I
                          have to say people are
       INTERVIEWER
       COMMENT: Did you understand that then?
       RECALL: Yeah?

The first recall comment is an explanation of what was wrong in the original interaction, but is not a recall comment. The interviewer tried to get back on track, but it was too late; the focus was already on the present. Finally, the question at the end, "Did you understand that then?", was leading. A more neutral question, such as "What were you thinking when she said 'all three people are in the sea'?", would have been more appropriate.

TIME TO THINK ...

Brainstorm some ways in which you could ask the question, "What were you thinking when you said . . .," if you were conducting a stimulated recall. How can you avoid leading questions?

The previous examples show how delicate and difficult data using stimulated recalls can be.

3.3.3.3 Post-Production Interviews

To illustrate this source of data collection, we turn to the study by Sachs and Polio (2007). Recall that they were concerned with how written feedback was used in revising. In addition to looking at actual data (feedback and revisions), they wanted to get additional information that could not be obtained with empirical data alone. For example, one of their questions was "Which activity was the easiest for you to do?" One response was:

> I think correction activity is more understand. Easier, more easier. Because more familiar, I think, more familiar, when I watched this paper, I feel it's more familiar. And . . . when I watched this paper, I felt, I recognized, this is wrong and this is right. I felt like that, so I think correction activity is more easy.

For those interested in teaching, it is of course important to know what type of revision is ultimately more useful for development, but it is also useful to know what learners' attitudes are toward various activities.

3.3.4 Language-Elicitation Measures

Earlier, we discussed data that address attitudes, motivation, and thought processes. In this section, we deal with data that, like corpus data, elicit samples of language. One common technique of data collection is known as elicited imitation. As the term implies, this is a technique whereby a subject hears a sentence (often tape-recorded) and then is asked to repeat it exactly. If the sentence is long enough, the learner will not be able to hold it in short-term memory long enough to repeat it. It is, therefore, stored as a semantic unit, and the learner imposes his or her own syntax on the sentence in attempting imitation. This then gives the researcher an indication of the structure of the learner's grammar. An example is given in (3-17) (Flynn, 1987):

(3-17) STIMULUS: The doctor called the professor when he prepared the breakfast.

RESPONSE: The doctor called the professor and the doctor prepared the breakfast.

These data are tightly controlled with regard to the type of structure one is attempting to gain information about. Like all elicitation measures, this one has its limitations and weaknesses. Some are not unlike those found in all experiments, namely the need to ensure an appropriate number of examples of each structure and the need to ensure comparable sentences (e.g., in terms of lexical difficulty, length, and phono-logical difficulty). Precisely what type of knowledge is reflected in an elicited imitation task is controversial. Do the results reflect a learner's underlying **competence**? Or are there task-performance issues, such as the learner's auditory and articulatory capabilities, that interfere (Chaudron & Russell, 1990)?

Many researchers are concerned, not with experimentally produced data, but with language that occurs in spontaneous situations. In an attempt to approximate naturally occurring, spontaneous data, researchers often ask a subject to tell a story, to provide an oral or written report on a movie, to write a composition, or to converse with a partner. Although there may be some controls exerted on the type of data obtained, it is largely unpredictable in terms of specific grammatical structures and, as mentioned earlier in this chapter, may underestimate the linguistic knowledge of the learner.

Perhaps one of the most controversial methods of doing L2 research is through the use of intuitional data. Broadly speaking, the term intuitional data refers to a type of metalinguistic performance. Participants in a study are asked about their intuitions (or judgments) as to whether or not a given sentence is acceptable (either linguistically or in a particular context). From this, one gains information about **metalinguistic knowledge**. For example, learners of English might be given sentences such as the following and asked whether they are good English sentences:

(3-18) He remembers the man who his brother is a doctor.

(3-19) We respect the man with whom you danced with him.

(3-20) He likes the girl who her uncle is a baseball player.

(3-21) He laughed at the boy whom he is taller than him.

(3-22) John admires the woman for whom you wrote the letter.

(3-23) He met the man whom you recommended.

Intuitional data have been widely used in SLA research, and yet, more than other research methods, they have been the subject of controversy. Historically, a considerable amount of SLA research has been (and continues to be) motivated by theoretical principles drawn from the field of linguistics. Along with this theoretical background have come methodologies typically used in linguistics. Primary among these methodologies for collecting linguistic data from native languages is that of grammaticality or acceptability judgment tasks.[1]

It is now commonplace for scholars, not only to think about language in terms of language use in everyday communicative situations, but also to examine language "as an object of analysis . . . in its own right" (Cazden, 1976, p. 603). Grammaticality judgments are one (but certainly not the only) form of metalinguistic performance, or language objectification.

In other words, one way of objectifying language is to state whether a given sentence is acceptable or not. What information can that give us? Native speakers' responses are used to infer the grammatical properties of a given language. That is, they are used to determine which sentences can be generated by the grammar of a language. Although this could conceivably be done by simple observation of spontaneous speech, judgment data can reveal more about a language than production data alone. For example, if a native speaker of Italian utters sentence 3-24, one can infer that that language has the word order of subject–verb–object (SVO):

(3-24) La bambina   guarda   il giocattolo.
　　　　the baby　　looks　　at the toy

However, with production data alone, one knows little more. One does not know what other kinds of word orders that language may or may not have. One does not know if the following sentence is also possible:

(3-25) Mangio io la pasta.
　　　　eat　　　I　　the pasta
　　　　"I eat the pasta."

In fact, VSO order is also possible in Italian,[2] a fact that may or may not be revealed by production data alone (at least not by spontaneous production data). A judgment task, on the other hand, will not miss this fact. In addition, it can provide information about what is not possible in the given language—something production data cannot do.

The use of grammaticality judgments, prevalent in work in linguistics, has been adopted by L2 researchers. However, the use of grammaticality judgments in L2 research has not been without difficulty or without controversy. Selinker (1972) argued that researchers should "focus . . . analytical attention upon the *only observable data to which we can relate theoretical predictions*: the utterances which are produced when the learner attempts to say sentences of a TL" (pp. 213–214). Although this view is still maintained by some, it has never been entirely accepted. Corder (1973), for example, argued that forced elicitation data were necessary.

Elicitation procedures are used to find out something specific about the learner's language, not just to get him or her to talk freely. To do this, constraints must be placed on the learner so that he is forced to make choices within a severely restricted area of his phonological, lexical, or syntactic competence (Corder, 1973, p. 41).

The question is: How valid are judgment data as measures of what a learner's grammar at a given point in time is capable of generating? There is clearly a difference between judgment data involving native speakers of a language and L2 judgment data. In the former, one is asking native speakers to judge sentences of their own language system in order to gain information about that same system. That is to say, the two systems are isomorphic. In the case of L2 learners, one is asking the learners to make judgments about the language being learned at a stage in which their knowledge of that system is incomplete. Here, however, inferences are made, not about the system they are being asked about, but about some internalized system of the learners (i.e., there may be a mismatch between the two systems in question).

An issue of importance here is that of **indeterminacy**, which refers to the incomplete (or lack of) knowledge a learner has of parts of the L2 grammar. As Schachter et al. (1976) pointed out, there are many sentences about which L2 learners have indeterminate knowledge. This is not to say that NSs of a language, either individually or collectively, do not have indeterminate knowledge, for surely they do, but the proportion of indeterminate knowledge in NS grammar is likely to be significantly different from that in learner grammars. For L2 learners, it is clear that indeterminacy exists, and it is conceivable that it embraces an even greater range of data than for native speakers of a language.

Obtaining information about nonindeterminate knowledge is less problematic when using production data, because, barring some sort of slip, the language produced is presumably generated by the learner's grammar. However, it is well accepted that production data are often inadequate for specific grammatical studies, as the examples of a given grammatical structure are often lacking. With grammaticality judgments, however, what we are asking learners to do is evaluate sentences of a language that they do not have total control over; many of the sentences being asked about are beyond the domain of their current knowledge base. Thus, responses to such sentences may represent little more than guesses. What is important to note is that grammaticality judgments are complex behavioral activities that must be used with caution and with full understanding of their limitations (Chaudron, 1983; R. Ellis, 1990a, 1991; Cowan & Hatasa, 1994; Gass, 1994; Goss et al., 1994; Mandell, 1999; Bader & Häussler, 2010).

Despite these difficulties, a significant amount of work has been done within the field of SLA using grammaticality judgments. Data, however, are collected in a variety of ways. In the simplest form, participants are asked to state whether a given sentence is acceptable in the TL or not. If, for example, a researcher wanted to know whether participants have learned that English does not allow **resumptive pronouns** in relative clauses (I saw the woman who *she* is your son's teacher), the researcher might give a list of sentences as was given in the beginning of this section and ask for judgments. However, it is difficult to confidently interpret these results, because one cannot be sure that a learner marked a sentence ungrammatical for the same reason that the researcher believes it to be ungrammatical. For this reason, the common technique is to ask learners to correct those sentences they have marked ungrammatical.

Another method is to ask, not for dichotomous judgments (correct/incorrect), but for judgments based on degree of certainty. Response sheets might look something like (3-26):

(3-26) He remembers the man who his brother is a doctor.

−3	−2	−1	0	+1	+2	+3
definitely incorrect			unsure			definitely correct

Intuitional data are not limited to judgments of grammaticality. Other means of obtaining judgments that reflect learners' intuitions are preference judgments, and rankings. In the former, participants are given sentences and are asked to judge whether the sentences (generally two) are equally grammatical, or whether one is more grammatical than the other. Example:

(3-27) That Mary had climbed a hill was orange.

(3-28) That Mary had climbed a hill was clear.

Or:

(3-29) Bill had built a boat.

(3-30) John had climbed a hill.

Ranking is a variation of the preference-type task just exemplified. The difference lies primarily in the number of sentences used and the lack of "same degree of grammaticality" as an option.

As mentioned earlier, the use of acceptability judgments in SLA research is not without controversy. However, what is not controversial is the need to get valid information about what individual learners know about the L2. That is, what is the nature of their grammatical system? Two additional methods have been used to determine this in recent years: truth-value judgments and sentence matching.

Truth-value judgments are frequently used for the investigation of learners' knowledge of reflexives. The issue with reflexives has to do with the interpretation of the reflexive pronoun, that is, to whom it refers. Given the following sentence (from Lakshmanan & Teranishi, 1994), what are the possibilities for interpretation?

(3-31) John said that Bill saw himself in the mirror.

In English, *himself* can refer to Bill, but not to John. However, in other languages, the equivalent of *himself* can refer to either John or Bill. The context is used to disambiguate these two possibilities. A research question might involve determining what knowledge learners have, if they are learning a language that allows both possibilities, even though their native language only allows one. The methodology involved in determining such knowledge has been the subject of numerous articles (e.g., Eckman, 1994a; Lakshmanan & Teranishi, 1994; Thomas, 1989, 1991, 1993, 1994, 1995; Wakabayashi, 1996; White, et al., 1997; see Glew, 1998 for a review). An example of a truth-value task can be seen in (3-32) (Glew, 1998).

(3-32) A boy and his father went on a bike ride together. The boy went down a hill very fast. "Don't go so fast!" shouted the father. It was too late, the boy fell off his bike and started crying. The father gave the boy a hug. Then the boy was happy again.

The boy was happy that the father hugged himself.
True   *False*

Truth-value judgment tasks are, of course, not without difficulties. For example, one could just ask a true/false question. Or, one could ask about all possibilities: (a) Can *himself* refer to *the boy*? (b) Can *himself* refer to *the father*? Or, one could make a statement: (a) *himself* cannot refer to *the boy* (T/F); (b) *himself* cannot refer to *the father*.

Another problem relates to the items themselves. Example (3-33) had to be thrown out of the database because of unexpected interpretations (Glew, 1998).

(3-33) Teresa and Madeleine went to a party one night. Teresa drank too much beer at the party. When it was time to go home, Teresa was worried because she didn't want to drive her car. "I'll drive you home," said Madeleine. "Oh, thank you Madeleine. I really appreciate it," said Teresa.

Teresa was happy that Madeleine drove herself home.
True   *False*

The expected answer was "False," but many participants wrote "True," because, technically, although we only know that Madeleine drove Teresa home, we may infer from the context that she also drove herself home. Thus, the item may be ambiguous, and the researcher may not know why a participant chose "True."

Another method that is claimed to provide information about grammatical and ungrammatical sentences is what is known as sentence matching. Sentence-matching tasks are performed with participants seated in front of a computer. They are presented with one sentence, which may be either grammatical or ungrammatical. After a short delay, a second sentence appears on the screen. Participants are asked to decide as quickly as possible if the sentences match or do not match, entering their decision by pressing specific keys on the computer. The time from the appearance of the second sentence to the participants pressing a key (i.e., the reaction time) is recorded and forms the database for analysis. Participants in a matching task are reported to respond faster to matched grammatical sentences than they do to matched ungrammatical ones (see Gass, 2001 for a discussion of this methodology).[3] The procedure is intended to provide some window on grammaticality, despite the fact that no specific judgments of grammaticality are being made.

TIME TO THINK ...

What are some of the advantages and disadvantages of the various intuitional data-elicitation methods? Can you think of others? Do you agree that the advantages are advantages and the disadvantages are disadvantages?

Another broad category of data-elicitation techniques is what can be called language games. Because there are many variations on this theme, we limit ourselves to some of the most common.

Participants can be paired, with one being told to teach the other how to use a particular computer program. Or, paired participants can be given two, almost identical, pictures and told to determine (without looking at each other's picture) what differences exist between the pictures. In a variation of the second one, participants can have two, almost identical, maps and have to describe to each other how to move an object (or an imaginary person) from one place to another. Other possibilities involve giving one participant a picture, with instructions to describe the picture so that another participant can draw it. Alternatively, one participant can describe an object so that another can guess what that object is. Finally, one participant can describe a picture to another, instructing his or her partner where to place stick-on objects on a board. What is common is that there is some sort of game involving two or more individuals, often with a single outcome.

What these methodologies have in common is the elicitation of speech, without an obvious focus on language or a particular language structure. Many of these studies have as their goal the investigation of conversational structure (see Chapter 12). Studies using these sorts of data can manipulate various social variables. For example, if one wanted to consider the role of age differences, pairs of different age levels could be involved; if one wanted to consider the role of gender differences, pairs would be constructed with this in mind; if one wanted to consider how the role of prior knowledge affects aspects of a conversation, participants would be paired in such a way as to incorporate that difference. This type of study is less appropriate when particular grammatical structures are the focus of a study, because, as mentioned earlier, there is no guarantee that the structures under consideration will appear in the data, or that they will occur with any frequency and in contexts appropriate for analysis.

TIME TO THINK ...

Think of your own L2 learning. If you learned your L2 in the classroom, did you play any language games? What were they? What grammatical structures or vocabulary were produced during the games? As a teacher, think of a particular grammar point that you intend to teach, or have taught. What language game could be used?

One final category of data collection to be discussed in this section is elicitation for the purposes of studying the acquisition of pragmatics. The most common measure is what is known as the discourse-completion questionnaire. This has been used in a number of studies to gather data from native and nonnative speakers concerning particular **speech acts** (apologies, compliments, refusals, requests, etc.).

Participants are given a (generally written) description of a situation in which the speech act under investigation is required. This is then followed by blank space in which the L2 learner is to write down what he or she would say in the given situation. An example of a situation in which the research focus was status differences in "giving embarrassing information" follows:

You are a corporate executive talking to your assistant. Your assistant, who will be greeting some important guests arriving soon, has some spinach in his/her teeth.

(Beebe & Takahashi, 1989, p. 109)

The learners are then to write down what they would say in response to this situation. To ensure that the correct speech act is given in their response, the printed page may have a mini-dialogue (Beebe et al., 1990, p. 69), as in (3-34), which is intended to elicit refusals:

(3-34) Worker: As you know, I've been here just a little over a year now, and I know you've been pleased with my work. I really enjoy working here, but to be quite honest, I really need an increase in pay.

YOU: _____

WORKER: Then I guess I'll have to look for another job.

Using a discourse-completion questionnaire is not the only means of gathering pragmatic data. Many techniques for data collection are not unlike those discussed earlier. For example, there are intuitional tasks, in which judgments of appropriateness are asked for, as in the following:

(3-35) You're a member of a research group. Many people are missing from a meeting and it is necessary for someone to notify them about the next meeting. Your boss turns to you and says:

(a) Notify those who are missing, OK?
(b) Perhaps you could notify those who didn't come?
(c) Could you please notify the others about our next meeting?
(d) How about getting in touch with the people who were absent?
(e) I'd appreciate it if you could notify the people who were absent.
(f) You will notify the people who were absent.

Respondents select the response that, given the constraints of the situation, they feel is the most appropriate.

Other research involving intuitional data requires participants to order utterances in terms ranging from most polite to least polite. The arguments for using intuitional data (or other means of forced data) as opposed to naturally occurring data are much the same as those presented earlier. One cannot obtain a sufficiently rich corpus of data unless one forces the issue. The disadvantages lie in the fact that one cannot automatically equate actual production data with data from questionnaires or other intuitional tasks. What we think we would say in a given situation is not necessarily the same as what we would actually say. Furthermore, it is unlikely that the contrived situations that researchers create would actually occur, or—if they do occur—that the given choices are the appropriate ones for the situation. For example, in the situation with spinach in someone's teeth, it is possible that the common response would be one in which a person refrains from comment, or even uses hand gestures.

3.4 PROCESSING DATA

There are times when researchers want to get deeper information about what learners are doing when they process language. We touched on this above when we talked about verbal reports and, in particular, with stimulated recall: there is a need to understand what learners are thinking about and how they process L2 speech or written texts. There are many ways of doing this (see Gass & Mackey, 2007; McDonough & Trofimovich, 2009; Jiang, 2012, for further elaboration). In this section, we select two such methods: reaction time and eye-tracking. We have selected these two because they reflect one tried and true method (reaction time) and one newer methodology (eye-tracking). Both are based on the assumption that certain responses to stimuli are reflective of how people process language.

3.4.1 Reaction Time

The underlying assumption of reaction-time research is that it takes time to respond to certain stimuli. We can infer cognitive processes by examining how long it takes to respond to a stimulus. In other words, the time it takes to react to something reveals something about how the mind works. Studies of this sort involve presentation of some stimuli and asking respondents to respond in some way, such as pressing a button or repeating a word. Time is measured from the beginning of the stimulus presentation to the time a button is pressed. To give an example, there may be times when one wants to gather information about learners' vocabulary knowledge. One could do this by asking them to identify words versus nonwords. This is known as a lexical-decision task. Responses are measured by having learners press a "yes" button on the computer (taped over a letter) or a "no" button, in response to the question "is this a word?" Reaction time or response time is measured from the onset of the appearance of the word on the computer screen to the time that it takes for the respondent to press the button. Within this paradigm, one could test the effects of frequency, word length, or familiarity, to name a few.

3.4.2 Eye-Tracking

Another method that has been used in recent years is eye-tracking. Eye-tracking uses a specialized piece of machinery (see below) that is able to track eye movements. In Figures 3.4 and 3.5, researchers (Winke et al., 2010) wanted to know when learners were using captions (in the boxed-in area below the video) and when they were looking at an actual video. Eye-tracking can give precise information about someone's gaze and, therefore, is frequently used in reading research. Figure 3.4 is a visual of an eye-tracker, and, in Figure 3.5, one can see by each dot precisely where one's gaze was directed while looking at the screen.

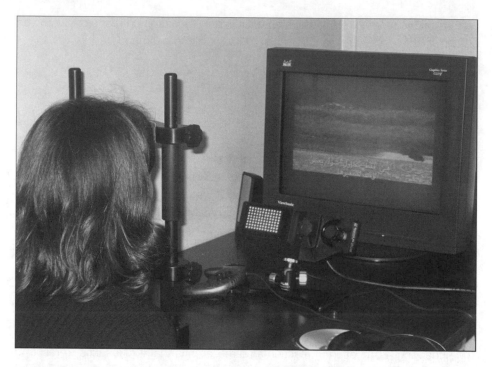

FIGURE 3.4 Picture of a Participant in an Eye-Tracking Experiment

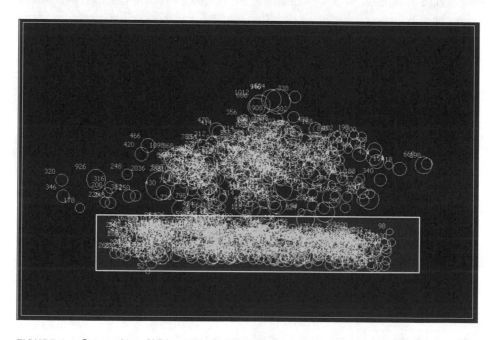

FIGURE 3.5 Screenshot of Video With Captions (in Area Outlined by Rectangle) at the Bottom and Video on the Top

Frenck-Mestre (2005) has noted that eye-movement recording provides a rich record of a person's linguistic behavior. As such, it gives empirical evidence of **attentional** processes (Duchowski, 2002) by providing a record of the duration of eye fixations, as well as other eye-movement information. Eye-tracking, in sum, provides underlying information about what learners are doing when they are watching something (e.g., reading a text, watching a video). For a review of eye-tracking research, see Godfroid et al. (in press), Dussias (2010), and the 2013 special issue of *Studies in Second Language Acquisition*.

3.5 REPLICATION

"The essence of the scientific method involves observations that can be repeated and verified by others" (American Psychological Association, 2010, p. 12). Much of SLA research is empirical, and such research is in need of replication. SLA research deals with human behavior and thus is often inconsistent. This is complicated by two additional factors: (a) the paucity of participants in many studies and (b) the nature of L2 knowledge. Many reported studies in the literature have a small number of participants. This makes it difficult to draw significant conclusions about acquisition (either the process or the product). The second point to consider is the nature of L2 knowledge. Learners are just that—*learners*. Often their knowledge is indeterminate (Schachter et al., 1976). As mentioned earlier, this refers to the fact that there are certain aspects of the L2 that learners are uncertain of. This may be because it is an aspect of language that they are "working on" and about which they do not yet have definite knowledge. Their linguistic behavior, then, will be inconsistent, with utterances such as the following virtually co-occurring:

(3-36) I am here since yesterday

(3-37) I have been here since yesterday

Polio and Gass (1997) have argued for the importance of replication, while at the same time acknowledging that "exact replication" is impossible, given that a replication study will deal with different individuals. Replication studies are an ideal way for those who are new to the field to get their hands dirty with actual data. Replication continues to be of significant concern in current research, with emphasis placed on increased robustness of results and generalizability (Porte, 2012).

3.6 META-ANALYSES

Replication is one way of verifying findings, but there are other ways to verify and compare results. When multiple studies have addressed a common question, it is often appropriate to summarize their results. This can be done through what is known as a **meta-analysis**, a systematic procedure for quantitatively synthesizing findings across studies. Like many of the data-elicitation types described earlier, whereby data from a sample of participants are combined or averaged, this technique also involves combining a sample of data points. However, in meta-analysis, samples do not come from individual people, but rather come from individual studies, and their data points are averages or effect sizes (e.g., Cohen's *d*, correlation coefficients [see Plonsky, 2012a, for an explanation of effect sizes]) to be precise. Thus, a meta-analysis is, in its most basic form, an average of averages.

As a tool for synthesizing previous research, meta-analysis enables L2 researchers to overcome several weaknesses inherent in traditional literature reviews (Oswald & Plonsky, 2010). For example, whereas reviews tend to rely heavily on the notion of probability and significance, a practice regarded by many quantitative methodologists from other social sciences, as well as our own (e.g., Brown, 2011; Nassaji, 2012; Norris & Ortega, 2000; Plonsky, 2009, 2011), as flawed and misleading, meta-analyses use effects sizes as the basis for all quantitative analyses. Another advantage of meta-analysis is the inclusive and quantitative approach it embodies, which eliminates the influence on fallible human reviewers that might result from studies presenting verbally compelling arguments or published in more visible or prestigious journals. We are not implying that the role of the expert reviewer is diminished in meta-analysis; rather, we emphasize that the quantitative and systematic nature of meta-analytic reviews contributes to increased objectivity, transparency, and replicability of outcomes.

Recognizing these and other benefits long-since enjoyed in fields such as education, psychology, and medicine, Norris and Ortega (2000) introduced much of SLA to meta-analysis in their oft-cited synthesis of research on the effectiveness of instruction. Since then, the use of meta-analysis in L2 research has increased exponentially (Norris & Ortega, 2010; Plonsky & Oswald, 2012). To date, approximately 40 SLA meta-analyses have been carried out, on topics such as feedback (e.g., Li, 2010a, 2010b), motivation (Masgoret & Gardner, 2003), strategy instruction (e.g., Plonsky, 2011), and interaction (e.g., Mackey & Goo, 2007). In addition, the field has also seen a number of papers discussing meta-analytic methods (e.g., In'nami & Koizumi, 2010; Oswald & Plonsky, 2010; Plonsky, 2012b), another indicator of growth and interest among SLA researchers.

Because meta-analysis is still relatively new to this field, it is hard to gauge the long-term impact it will have on the development of L2 theory, methods, and practice. However, we expect to see more and more areas of L2 research being synthesized using meta-analytic methods.

3.7 ISSUES IN DATA ANALYSIS

In this section, we focus on issues of analysis. The focus is not on statistical analyses, but rather on the type of information that is relevant to analyses of L2 data. The first issue we consider relates to the determination of development. The field of SLA has not yet come up with an index of development. That is, unlike in child language-acquisition research—which is heavily reliant on **mean length of utterance (MLU)**, a measure that averages the number of morphemes per utterance—there is no easy way of determining whether a given learner is more or less proficient than another. Thus, one cannot determine where on a developmental scale a given individual can be placed, as discussed earlier in this chapter. This is partly so because of the nature of L2 learning. Learners do not have a uniform starting point. From the beginning, their utterances vary in the degree of syntactic sophistication. Furthermore, ILs are unique creations. Although there may be similarities among speakers of a given NL learning the same TL, and although there may be similarities across TLs, each individual creates his or her own language system. Similarities may be found for a given grammatical structure (e.g., there are commonalities in relative-clause formation, regardless of language background). However, if we looked at an entire linguistic system, we would be less likely to find broad-sweeping similarities.

As mentioned in section 3.3, one way of determining a learner's place along a scale from lesser proficiency to greater proficiency is through the use of standardized tests. This is undoubtedly the most common way, as a quick perusal of research articles suggests. Another way of determining development is through categorization of individuals according to their placement scores for specific language programs (e.g., a beginning class, an advanced class, satisfaction of a university language requirement). However, these are only very rough measures, at best.

A more exact means for measuring syntactic development is what is known as the **T-unit**. A T-unit is an independent clause and any associated dependent clauses, that is, clauses that are attached to or embedded within it (Hunt, 1965). Thus, both (3-38) and (3-39) are T-units, but (3-40) is not:

(3-38) John woke up

(3-39) John woke up, although he was tired

(3-40) although he was tired

This was originally a measure used for determining syntactic development for native speakers, but it has been adapted for use with nonnative speakers by modification of the definition to incorporate error-free T-units rather than just T-units. Although this is a more precise measure than standardized tests, teacher evaluations, or class placement, it is most reliable with written data as opposed to oral data. Some researchers also use **C-units (communication-units)**, which are similar to T-units, but go beyond in that they incorporate short utterances (*yes, no, uh-huh*) that are important to a communicative event, but do not enter into an understanding of development or complexity.

In determining oral proficiency, the situation is even more complex, because there appear to be different measures, depending on whether one is considering monologue or dialogue data. Some of the measures that can be considered are pauses, speech rate, and self-corrections after a mistake has been made. For conversational data, additional factors come into play. For example, to what extent can a learner appropriately initiate topic changes? To what extent can nonnative speakers demonstrate appropriate conversational strategies (i.e., hold their own in a conversation)? This might include: (a) providing verbal cues to show that they are listening and/or following a conversation (e.g., *uh huh*, *yeah*) and (b) responding appropriately given the linguistic, social, and cultural context. To what extent do learners know when it is their turn to take the floor (a factor that may differ cross-culturally and individually)? Although all of these are clearly important measures in determining oral proficiency, we do not as yet know how each of these should be "weighted." Nor do we know what can be expected in terms of acquisition, a prerequisite to being able to place learners along a developmental continuum. A measure used for oral production is **AS-unit**—analysis of speech unit (cf. Foster, Tonkyn, & Wigglesworth, 2000). AS-units provide a means to include dysfluencies such as false starts and fillers, while also keeping track of clauses, which can provide information about development.

A second issue to be noted, and one that was dealt with in Chapter 2, is that data do not yield unique results. A researcher must interpret the results. In order to interpret the results, the analyst must first decide what data to include. That is, what are the relevant data for analysis? Another important consideration is the point of reference for comparison. Early research focused on comparisons between learner output and the NL on the one hand, and on learner output and the TL on the other. However, this type of comparison causes researchers to miss the generalizations that learners have constructed for themselves. This fact is often cited as a difference between longitudinal data (specifically, case studies) and cross-sectional experimental studies. The latter often do not provide the richness necessary to understand a learner's system; the former often do not provide specific information about what a learner's grammar includes and excludes.

To see the differences between these two types of studies with regard to the analysis of data, let's consider data presented by Huebner (1979, 1983). These data come from the spontaneous speech of a Hmong refugee from Laos, named Ge, who lived in Honolulu. In his home country, Ge had had no training in English, nor did he receive formal instruction while in Hawaii. Data collection began about one month after his arrival in Honolulu and continued every three weeks for approximately one year.

An initial analysis of the data from Ge's use of English articles was conducted using this particular methodology. The results are given in Figure 3.6.

What does Figure 3.6 tell us? First, it shows little development in terms of Ge's knowledge of the article system. Second, it does not show what it is about the article system Ge does and does not know. We have little information about the systematicity that underlies Ge's production and nonproduction of the English article. Further, comparing his data with the English article system suggests that Ge brings nothing more to the learning task than what he can figure out of that system. In other words, if one only compares what the learner is producing with the TL system, one misses the picture of what the learner's system is like. Making a one-to-one comparison between the IL and the TL may prevent the researcher from understanding the full system that the learner has created.

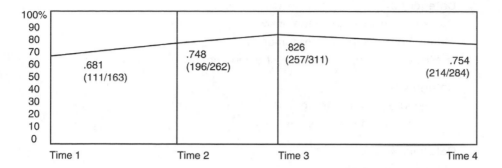

FIGURE 3.6 Percentages of Occurrences of Articles in Obligatory Standard English Environments (*Source*: From "Order-of-acquisition vs. dynamic paradigm: a comparison of method in interlanguage research" by T. Huebner, 1979, *TESOL Quarterly*, 13, 21–28. Reprinted by permission.)

Another way of analyzing the data is to bring into the analysis different possible meanings of articles. For our purposes, let's assume the correctness of Huebner's analysis. He claims two binary categories relevant to article use: (a) specific referent and (b) hearer's assumed knowledge. Noun phrase reference can thus be categorized into four types:

Category 1
+ specific reference
+ hearer's knowledge

Category 2
− specific reference
+ hearer's knowledge

Category 3
− specific reference
− hearer's knowledge

Category 4
+ specific reference
− hearer's knowledge

In English, Category 1 nouns use the definite article *the*; Category 2 is for generics and can use *the*, *a*, or *0*; Categories 3 and 4 function similarly, using either *a* or *0*. (In other languages, it is possible that only two forms exist, one used for Categories 1 and 2 and the other for 3 and 4; or another language still might have one form for Categories 1 and 2 and two separate forms for 3 and 4.)

Category 1
The President met with the Pope yesterday.
The teacher told me to do my homework.

Category 2

I am going to a movie tomorrow.

I am going to the movies tomorrow.

Movies are my favorite form of entertainment.

Category 3

A good person is hard to find.

It's hard to find good employees.

Category 4

I have a good idea.

I always have good ideas.

Table 3.2 shows the results based on this type of scheme. This table shows number of occurrences of each form (*the*, *a*, or *0*) according to the binary categories of specific referent and hearer's knowledge. The same four points in time are given.

As can be seen, these data differ from those in Figure 3.6, in that, in Table 3.2, clear differences exist between Time 1 and Time 4, whereas such differences were not apparent when only correct and incorrect examples were examined.

In Ge's native language, one of the most important concepts for a sentence is what is known as "topic–comment." The first part of the sentence is the topic, followed by a comment about that topic. Topics provide old information, thus, by definition, within the hearer's knowledge domain. Examples of topic–comment structures produced by Ge are given in 3-41 and 3-42 (Huebner, 1979, p. 27).

(3-41) en beibii, isa in da moder, en da owder broder.

"And the babies were placed between the adults."

(3-42) RESEARCHER: How did you cross the river?

GE: river, isa bowt

"As for the river, it was a boat."

TABLE 3.2 Number of Occurrences of Article Types Based on Four-Part Categorization Scheme (*Source*: From "Order-of-acquisition vs. dynamic paradigm: A comparison of method in interlanguage research" by T. Huebner, 1979, *TESOL Quarterly*, 13, pp. 21–28. Reprinted by permission.)

	Category 1			Category 2			Category 3			Category 4		
	da	a	0	da	a	0	da	a	0	da	a	0
Time 1	67	1	47	2	0	4	4	2	35	2	12	18
Time 2	133	0	40	1	0	4	3	5	56	33	0	2
Time 3	199	2	13	0	0	7	3	12	27	32	8	8
Time 4	154	2	22	1	0	10	3	9	40	13	8	23

At Time 1, there was less overt marking for Categories 1 and 2 than at any of the other time periods. At Time 2, there is a major increase in the marking of specific nouns (Categories 1 and 4), regardless of the status of the hearer's knowledge. By Time 4, *the* (da) is almost limited to Category 1 nouns, as it is in English. Huebner concluded that what this type of analysis provides is not a static indication of whether Ge is right or wrong when compared with Standard English. Rather, what we see is the dynamic movement toward English, guided by a movement from the underlying topic–comment structure of his NL to the underlying subject–verb structure of his TL. The first table of results shows minimal change; this latter analysis shows considerable change.

TIME TO THINK ...

Give an example of a generalization to an inappropriate context in English as would be measured by target-like use analysis.

In analysis of L2 data, there can be considerable difficulty in determining what the targeted structure is, and there can be differences in results depending on the methodology used for analysis, but there can also be differences in the results when using a similar methodology.

Pica (1984) demonstrated this discrepancy in an analysis of the acquisition of morphemes. She discussed two common methods for determining whether someone has acquired morphemes: **suppliance in obligatory context** and target-like use. She concentrated on the following question: What is the difference between these two methods? In the first method, suppliance in obligatory context, one determines whether or not Standard English requires a particular morpheme. For example, in sentence 3-43, it is obligatory to put an *-ing* on the word *dance*, because it is in the context in which a progressive is required.

(3-43) He is dancing.

One then looks at the L2 data and scores this in the following way: 2 points for correct form; 1 point for a morpheme misformation (e.g., *he's dances*), and 0 points for no morpheme (*he dance*). The following formula then applies:

$$\frac{\text{number of correct suppliance} \times 2 + \text{number of misformations}}{\text{total obligatory contexts} \times 2}$$

The second quantificational method, known as target-like use, incorporates the notion of distributional patterns. Although the suppliance-in-obligatory-contexts method provides detail on how accurate a learner is in those contexts where a form is required, it does not give information about possible generalizations to inappropriate contexts. In target-like-use analysis, the numerator consists of the number of instances of correct suppliance in obligatory contexts, and the denominator consists of not only the obligatory contexts, but also the nonobligatory contexts.

$$\frac{\text{number of correct suppliances in obligatory contexts}}{\text{number of obligatory contexts} + \text{number of suppliances in nonobligatory contexts}}$$

It is clear that these two formulae differ, but just how does this difference affect the interpretation of data? Pica compared three sets of data, one from a group of learners learning English in a classroom environment, one from a group of learners in a naturalistic environment (i.e., no instruction), and one from a third group of learners who learned both through informal means and through formal instruction. Table 3.3 gives the percentage scores for all three groups.

Depending on the analysis used, one comes up with different interpretations of the role of instruction versus noninstruction. For example, if we focus on the scores that come from the suppliance-in-obligatory-context method and examine the results for the progressive -*ing*, the conclusion we would come to is that the learning environment (instruction versus naturalistic) has little effect on the acquisition of the progressive. However, if we look at the results from the target-like-use method, we see an entirely different picture. Here, we would be forced to conclude that naturalistic acquisition is far superior to classroom instruction in learning the progressive.

Thus, the same database can yield different results about learners' knowledge of an L2 (in this case, about the knowledge they have about specific morphemes), depending on the way the data are quantified.

TABLE 3.3 Comparison of Suppliance in Obligatory Context (SOC) and Target Language Utterance (TLU) Percentage Scores for Each Group of Subjects According to Language Context (*Source*: From "Methods of morpheme quantification: Their effect on the interpretation of second language data" by T. Pica, 1984, *Studies in Second Language Acquisition*, 6, 69–78. Reprinted by permission.)

Morpheme	Instruction only			Naturalistic			Mixed		
	SOC	TLU	Diff.	SOC	TLU	Diff.	SOC	TLU	Diff.
Progressive -*ing*	97	69	−28	94	87	−7	98	74	−24
Plural -*s*	93	85	−8	74	72	−2	74	71	−3
Singular copular	95	89	−6	92	88	−4	97	94	−3
Progressive auxiliary	85	59	−26	76	71	−5	66	52	−14
Past irregular	75	66	−9	68	65	−3	73	64	−9
Past regular	51	47	−4	58	58	0	44	44	0
Third person singular	63	52	−11	25	22	−3	22	19	−3

Difficulties in determining what the targeted structure is that a learner has produced have been discussed in this chapter. There is an additional problem, particularly in attempting to deal with the role of the NL. How can we be sure about the facts of the NL? One concern is the role of dialects. For example, in many dialects in the United States, there is no difference between the vowel sounds in *cot* and *caught*. For many other American English speakers, the two words are kept distinct. If we were to conduct a study on the role of the NL in learning the phonology of a second language, how would we know whether a given speaker is of one dialect or another? The answer is relatively easy if we are aware that a difference exists (as in the case of English, owing to the fact that there are numerous descriptions that exist), but less easy if we are dealing with a language that has not been described as extensively. However, a more serious problem is the determination of the language variety to which a learner has been exposed.

As an example, consider two studies dealing with the acquisition of relative clauses, one published in 1974 by Schachter and the other by Gass (1979a, 1979b). The particular focus is what is known as **pronominal reflexes** (or pronoun retention/resumptive pronoun), a phenomenon—common in many languages (including informal English)—exemplified in (3-44).[4]

(3-44) There's two fellows that *their* dads are millionaires.

(Sinclair Lewis, *Babbitt*)

Table 3.4 was published in the 1974 study, and Table 3.5 was published in the 1979 studies.

What differences are there between Tables 3.4 and 3.5? In the 1974 study, Persian and Arabic are shown to have optional pronominal reflexes, whereas, in the 1979 study, Persian and Arabic are shown not to have pronominal reflexes. Similar differences appear in direct-object (DO) position. The discrepancy, it turns out, is one of dialect differences. Nonetheless, with different "facts" about the native language, it is easy to see how different results concerning the role of the native language can be obtained.

TABLE 3.4 Pronominal Reflexes in Five Languages (*Source*: From "An error in error analysis" by J. Schachter, 1974, *Language Learning*, 24, pp. 205–214, by Research Club in Language Learning. Reprinted by permission.)

	Subj.	DO	IO	OPrep	Poss.	OComp
Persian	(+)	+	+	+	+	+
Arabic	(+)	(+)	+	+	+	+
Chinese	–	–	+	+	+	+
Japanese	–	–	–	(+)	(+)	
English	–	–	–	–	–	–

	Subj	DO	IO	OPrep	Poss.	OComp
TABLE 3.5 Pronominal Reflexes in Five Languages (*Source*: From "Language transfer and universal grammatical relations" by S. Gass, 1979, *Language Learning*, 29, pp. 327–344, by Research Club in Language Learning. Reprinted by permission.)						
Persian	–	(+)	+	+	+	
Arabic	–	+	+	+	+	+
Chinese	–	–	+	+	+	
Japanese	–	–	–	–	(+)	
English	–	–	–	–	–	–

TIME TO THINK ...

Think about your own dialect in your L1. Are there certain phonological or syntactic differences between your dialect and the standard (or other dialects) of your language? Do you think that an analysis of language use by an L2 learner of your language would be compromised by this fact? Why, or why not?

One final, related point has to do with the entire notion of target from the learner's perspective. We have discussed the difficulty in assessing what the NL forms are that the learner brings to the L2 learning situation. There is an equally complex issue in that we do not always know what TL variety the learner is aiming at. When we spoke of pronominal reflexes, we assumed that English does not have these forms. However, it doesn't take more than a few minutes of listening to native speakers of English before we hear numerous instances of pronominal reflexes in spontaneously produced utterances. Thus, we cannot pretend to know precisely what knowledge base a learner brings to the learning situation, nor can we pretend to understand what TL model the learner has adopted.

3.8 WHAT IS ACQUISITION?

The question of what is acquired is not an easy one; it has been operationalized in different ways in the past. One can be misled into thinking that a correct utterance, or even two or three correct utterances, suggests that a particular structure has been acquired. However, as we will see in the remainder of this book, there are many factors that one must consider. For example, learners appear to **backslide**; that is, correct forms appear, but then seem to disappear. The reasons for this are often complex and will be covered at various points throughout the book. The fact of backsliding, however, underscores the need for, and difficulty of, pinpointing L2 knowledge.

Various definitions of acquisition of a form are possible: (a) the first appearance of a correct form, (b) a certain percentage of accurate forms (e.g., 90 percent), and (c) the "first of three consecutive two-week samples in which the morpheme is supplied in over 90 percent of obligatory contexts" (Hakuta, 1976a, p. 137). Considering language forms is limiting, however. For example, one needs to consider, not only the actual forms, but also the context in which the forms occur. In section 3.7, we mention the concept of obligatory contexts; that is, contexts in which a particular form is required in the TL. Consider the following hypothetical conversation:

RACHEL: I read three great books last week.
MIRIAM: Which one did you like best?
RACHEL: The book about Mr. Park's ex-wife who killed Nate Hosen.

Here, Rachel uses the definite article *the* before the noun *book*. English requires the use of *the* in this context, and, it is in this sense that we can talk about an obligatory context for the use of the definite article.

In sum, researchers use a variety of criteria to determine when acquisition has taken place, as is pointed out by Norris and Ortega (2012). However, one should not lose track of the important, and perhaps more interesting, factor of emergence. It is not just the point at which something is acquired that is of interest (unless one is comparing the point of acquisition of different forms), but it is also important to consider the stages that a learner goes through in acquiring a particular form, as was noted in the discussion of the definite article in section 3.7.

3.9 CONCLUSION

In this chapter, we have reviewed different methodologies for data elicitation and data analysis. Throughout the remainder of the book, the reader will be able to put this knowledge to use in doing additional problem sets and in determining what the strengths and/or shortcomings are of current research in SLA. We next move to a central factor in the study of SLA: **language transfer**. We approach this topic by first placing it in its historical context in Chapter 4. We then look at what we call a transition period (Chapter 5), and, finally, in Chapter 6, we move to alternative conceptualizations of the role of the NL.

POINTS TO REMEMBER

- Longitudinal studies take place over a longer period of time and involve a smaller number of participants (possibly only one). The data are often qualitative and narrative, with a focus on describing the context in which the data were collected and specific examples of what was said. Longitudinal SLA studies can follow the development of a language learner over time.

- Cross-sectional studies involve the collection of data from a large number of participants at one time and show a slice of development. Participants are not identified individually, and detailed description of the social context is not provided. The research is conducted in order to answer particular research questions.

- Learner corpora provide data from L2 learners. Corpora can provide a great deal of data to a researcher and can be easily manipulated and analyzed via computer.

- There are various ways in which data are elicited in the field of SLA. Some of these include: standardized language tests, questionnaires (psychology tests), verbal report data (think-alouds, stimulated recall, post-production interviews), and language-elicitation measures.

- Think-alouds are performed during the task, and stimulated recall is performed after the task. Both require the learner to reflect on his/her performance. In stimulated recall, there is a stimulus that stimulates the learner to recall his/her thought processes at the time.

- Intuitional data come from participants being asked about their intuitions about whether a given sentence is grammatical in a certain language. Grammaticality or acceptability judgments, preference judgments, rankings, truth-value judgments, and sentence matching are all used to elicit intuitional data. Such data-elicitation methods have come into SLA from the field of linguistics. The data can provide information that production data cannot, but such methods are controversial because of the indeterminacy of learner knowledge (i.e., learners are uncertain about particular aspects of the L2).

- Language games can elicit data while removing the focus from the language or particular language structures.

- Discourse-completion questionnaires are used to gather data about pragmatics, or how the language is used, including such speech acts as apologizing, refusing, or requesting. Discourse-completion questionnaires ask learners and native speakers about what they would say in certain situations.

- Research on how learners or native speakers process the language can involve reaction-time data and eye-tracking data. Reaction-time data refer to a measurement of how long it takes someone to respond to a particular stimulus.

- The need for replication studies in SLA is complicated by the fact that there are few participants in SLA studies, and the fact that learners have indeterminate knowledge about the L2.

- T-units and C-units are measures of syntactic development common in L2 research.

- An AS-unit is a measure of development commonly used for oral production.

- There are two types of quantificational methods of measuring morpheme acquisition. Suppliance in obligatory context refers to whether the language requires a morpheme in a particular context, and whether or not the learner has supplied the morpheme (number of correct suppliance × 2 + misformations, divided by total obligatory contexts × 2). Target-like use provides information about possible generalizations to inappropriate contexts (number of correct suppliances in obligatory contexts divided by number of obligatory contexts + number of suppliances in nonobligatory contexts).

- Backsliding refers to instances when correct forms appear but then seem to disappear in a learner's IL. There are various ways of determining acquisition of a form: first appearance, 90 percent correct use.

SUGGESTIONS FOR ADDITIONAL READING

Instruments for research into second language learning: Establishing a digital repository (IRIS). www.iris-database-org.

Conducting reaction time research in second language studies (2012). Nan Jiang. Routledge.

Replication research in applied linguistics (2012). Graeme Porte (Ed.). Cambridge University Press.

Ethnographic research in applied linguistics: Exploring language teaching, learning, and use in diverse communities (2012). Patricia Duff. Routledge.

The think-aloud controversy in second language research (2010). Melissa Bowles. Routledge.

A guide to doing statistics in second language research using SPSS (2010). Jenifer Larson-Hall. Routledge.

Questionnaires in second language research: Construction, administration, and processing (2nd ed.) (2009). Zoltán Dörnyei with Tatsuya Taguchi. Routledge.

The international corpus of learner English. Handbook and CD-ROM: Version 2 (2009). Sylviane Granger, Estelle Dagneaux, Fanny Meunier, and Magali Paquot. Presses Universitaires de Louvain.

Using priming methods in second language research (2009). Kim McDonough and Pavel Trofimovich. Routledge.

Case study research in applied linguistics (2008). Patricia Duff. Lawrence Erlbaum Associates.

Data elicitation for second and foreign language research (2007). Alison Mackey and Susan Gass. Lawrence Erlbaum Associates.

Collocations in a learner corpus (2005). Nadja Nesselhauf. John Benjamins.

Second language research: Methodology and design (2005). Susan Gass and Alison Mackey. Lawrence Erlbaum Associates.

Computer learner corpora, second language acquisition, and foreign language teaching (2002). Sylviane Granger, Joseph Hung, and Stephanie Petch-Tyson (Eds.). John Benjamins.

Conversation analysis (2000). Numa Markee. Lawrence Erlbaum Associates.

Stimulated recall methodology in second language research (2000). Susan Gass and Alison Mackey. Lawrence Erlbaum Associates.

Referential communication tasks (1997). George Yule. Lawrence Erlbaum Associates.

Evaluating research articles: From start to finish (1996). Ellen Girden. Sage Publications.

Second language classroom research (1996). Jacquelyn Schachter and Susan Gass (Eds.). Lawrence Erlbaum Associates.

The empirical base of linguistics: Grammaticality judgments and linguistic methodology (1996). Carson Schütze. University of Chicago Press.

Research methods in language learning (1992). David Nunan. Cambridge University Press.

Second language research methods (1989). Herbert Seliger and Elana Shohamy. Oxford University Press.

Understanding research in second language learning (1988). James Dean Brown. Cambridge University Press.

Developmental research methods (1987). Scott Miller. Prentice Hall.

Introspection in second language research (1987a). Claus Færch and Gabriele Kasper. Multilingual Matters.

Research design and statistics for applied linguistics (1982). Evelyn Hatch and Hossein Farhady. Newbury House.

MORE TO DO AND MORE TO THINK ABOUT ...

1. Consider the distinction between longitudinal and cross-sectional approaches to research methodology. Do you find this to be an important distinction? List several interlanguage structures you have observed (e.g., questions, articles). In pairs, come up with a rough design using one or the other of these approaches. Once you have done that, find another pair of students who has used the other approach (longitudinal or cross-sectional) and compare the advantages and disadvantages to each.

2. Find a journal article that deals with longitudinal data. How often were data collected? How much detail is provided about the participant(s)? About the environment in which learning took place? About data-collection procedures?

3. It is stated in this chapter that an advantage to a cross-sectional approach is "the disadvantage of longitudinal data." The discussion revolves around the generalizability of results. Is it necessary to set up these two approaches in this fashion? In other words, is there always a cross-sectional/longitudinal dichotomy? Does the concept of pseudolongitudinal approach resolve some of the difficulties suggested by a rigid dichotomy?

4. Explain the relationship between research questions and research methodology. What is meant by the strong claim that the two are always linked? Can the same research question be addressed using different methodologies? Devise a research question that focuses on the development of third person singular *s* for learners of English. Think of a situation where, owing to feasibility constraints, you have access to two adults learning English and you can see them several times a week. Devise a design based on this situation. Then, consider a situation where you teach English classes to adult migrants, but the class you teach changes every six weeks, at which point you have new students. What design might be appropriate for this situation? Can you answer your question with either design?

5. Reread the description of the Kumpf (1984) study (section 3.1). Evaluate the conclusion that her results could not have been obtained by a cross-sectional methodology.

6. In discussing Kumpf's (1984) work (section 3.1), we noted that some of the information that Kumpf dealt with (namely the determination of the frequency of verb tenses) could be obtained through an experimental design as opposed to a case study, which is what she utilized. How would you design an experiment to understand the acquisition of verb tenses?

7. Consider the various ways of collecting interlanguage data discussed here. Take each of the following and describe the advantages and disadvantages of each: (a) language tests, (b) psychological tests, (c) questionnaires, (d) attitudinal ratings, (e) elicited imitation, (f) spontaneous data, (g) language games, (h) intuitions. In your answer you will likely note that all of these are in some way controversial. What does that suggest about doing SLA research in general?

8. If you were to design an SLA study to investigate each of the following topics, what would an appropriate methodology be?

   (a) English articles;
   (b) text organizational structure;
   (c) a comparison of the effectiveness of native/nonnative teachers;
   (d) fluency.

9. The Pica (1984) study is discussed in some detail in this chapter. In light of her study, compare the research methods of "obligatory context" versus "target-like use." How are they fundamentally different? How do they supply different views of a particular learner's interlanguage at a particular point in time? Over time? Bley-Vroman (1983) called the former method "the comparative fallacy." One of Bley-Vroman's main points is that using the target language as a baseline for interlanguage description skews the interlanguage data away from looking at the interlanguage as an internal coherent system in its own right. Explain what you believe is meant by this. How do these two methods of analysis fare in this regard?

10. Analyze the following nonnative-speaker sentences using both the suppliance-in-obligatory-context method and the target-like-use method. Focus on the past irregular and the past regular verb forms and the plural -s.

    Yesterday morning, I seed two movies and writed three report. Then, in the afternoon, I seed one more movies. I enjoyed myself a lot.

11. Consider the following composition:

    Once upon a time there was a man who called "Taro Urashia" in small village in Japan. One day, when he take a walk near his home, he help one turtle on the seaside. Since he helped the turtle, he was able to get a chance to be invited from sea castle which is deep place in the sea.

    He had been entertained with music, good board, dance etc. every nights by beautiful girls of sea castle.

    Therefore, he forgot worldly presence and he did not notice how long did he stay there.

    Nevertheless he missed the new world, so he said that he wanted to go back to true world.

    Analyze this learner's use of articles, using the two methods of morpheme analysis discussed in section 3.7 (obligatory context versus target-like use). What differences did you find?

12. Let's assume you want to investigate how native speakers react to compliments by a second language speaker. Let's further assume that you believe that it is not so much the words people use that affect different native speaker reactions, but the stereotypes that native speakers have formed about particular groups of nonnative speakers. How would you go about investigating this?

13. Find two studies of SLA in which the categories beginning, intermediate, or advanced (or some similar attempt at determining proficiency or developmental level) are used. What are the criteria used for each of these? Are they the same for all categories used? Do you agree with the basis on which learners were categorized? What criteria would you use?

CHAPTER FOUR

The Role of the Native Language

An Historical Overview

4.1 INTRODUCTION

We turn now to one of the oldest and most continuously studied areas of SLA, that of the role of the NL, which has had a rocky history in the course of SLA research. This subfield of SLA has come to be known as language transfer. As we will see in this chapter, much of the history of this central concept has been related to varying theoretical perspectives of linguistics, psychology, and child language acquisition. The acceptance and/or rejection of language transfer as a viable concept has been related to the acceptance or rejection of the specific theory with which it has been associated. In this chapter, we include a discussion of some of the early work on second language learning; this is followed by issues related to this early period stemming from psychology and linguistics. Finally, a prevalent SLA means of dealing with **errors**, namely, **contrastive analysis**, is put into context and discussed, together with criticisms and shortcomings. These criticisms led to **error analysis**, which was the beginning of what might be called a transition period. This latter period is discussed in greater detail in Chapter 5.

It has always been assumed that, in an L2 learning situation, learners rely extensively on their native language. Lado, in his early and influential book *Linguistics Across Cultures* (1957), stated this clearly:

> individuals tend to transfer the forms and meanings, and the distribution of forms and meanings of their native language and culture to the foreign language and culture—both productively when attempting to speak the language and to act in the culture, and receptively when attempting to grasp and understand the language and the culture as practiced by natives.
>
> (Lado, 1957, p. 2)

Lado's work and much of the work of that time were based on the need to produce pedagogically relevant materials. To produce these NL-based materials, it was necessary to perform a contrastive analysis of the NL and the TL. This entailed making detailed comparisons between the two languages in order to determine similarities and differences (see section 4.3 for further elaboration).[1]

To understand why language transfer was accepted as the mainstream view of language learning, it is necessary to understand the psychological and linguistic thinking at the time Lado was writing. We review that literature briefly and then show how Lado's writings incorporated the theoretical positions of his time.

It is important at this juncture to clarify one important aspect of our understanding of the term *transfer*. Although the original term used in the classical literature on transfer did not imply a separation into two processes, **negative transfer** versus **positive transfer**, there has been some confusion in the use of the terms in the L2 literature. Implicit in the use of these terms is that there are two different underlying learning processes, one of positive transfer and another of negative transfer. However, the actual determination of whether or not a learner has positively or negatively transferred something is based on the output, as analyzed by the researcher, teacher, native speaker/hearer, when compared and contrasted with TL norms. In other words, these terms refer to the product, despite the fact that their use implies a process. In other words, there is a process of transfer; there is not a process of negative or positive transfer. Thus, one must be careful when using terminology of this sort, because the terminology often reveals a conflation between product and process. Further discussion of this concept appears in section 4.2.2.

4.2 BEHAVIORISM

Early research into language learning (both first and second) was heavily dependent on the dominant linguistic and psychological paradigms. In this chapter, we present some of the background as it relates more generally to language learning, in particular L1 learning.

TIME TO THINK ...

Think about your own L1 and L2(s). What aspects do you think you transfer from your L1 to your L2? Lexicon? Grammar? Pronunciation? Can you think of a specific example?

4.2.1 Linguistic Background

We turn now to a consideration of some of the common assumptions about language and language learning. Bloomfield's classic work, *Language* (1933), provides the most elaborate description of the behaviorist position with regard to language.

The typical behaviorist position is that language is speech rather than writing. Furthermore, speech is a precondition for writing. The justification for this position came from the facts that (a) children without cognitive impairment learn to speak before they learn to write; and (b) many societies have no written language, although all societies have oral language; there are no societies with only written, but no spoken, language systems.[2]

Within the behaviorist framework, speaking consists of mimicking and analogizing. We say or hear something and analogize from it. Basic to this view is the concept of habits. We establish a set of habits as children and continue our linguistic growth by analogizing from what we already know or by mimicking the speech of others. But what makes us talk and carry on conversation?

To understand the answer to this question within the behaviorist framework, consider the following information:

> Suppose that Jack and Jill are walking down a lane. Jill is hungry. She sees an apple in a tree. She makes a sound with her larynx, tongue and lips. Jack vaults the fence, climbs the tree, takes the apple, brings it to Jill and places it in her hand. Jill eats the apple.
>
> (Bloomfield, 1933, pp. 22–23)

Bloomfield divides a situation like this into three parts:

1. practical events before the act of speech (e.g., hungry feeling, sight of apple);
2. speech event (making sound with larynx, tongue, and lips);
3. hearer's response (Jack's leaping over the fence, fetching the apple, placing it in Jill's hand).

Thus, in this view, speech is the practical reaction (response) to some stimulus.

Although this describes the interrelationship between speech and action, it does not provide information about how children learn to behave in this way. Again, we turn to the Bloomfieldian description of how language acquisition takes place. "Every child that is born into a group acquires these habits of speech and response in the first years of his life" (Bloomfield, 1933, p. 29).

1. The first step is, interestingly, babbling generated by a child, although Bloomfield implies that it is somehow the imperfect repetition of something the child has heard. Assume the child produces something similar to *da*. "The sound vibrations strike the child's ear-drums while he keeps repeating the movements. This results in a habit: whenever a similar sound strikes his ear, he is likely to make these same mouth-movements, repeating the sound *da*. This babbling trains him to reproduce vocal sounds which strike his ear" (pp. 29–30).
2. The next step is a pairing of this stimulus with the response of a native speaker. The process depends on somebody, such as the mother, saying something that resembles the babbling. "For instance, she says *doll*. When these sounds strike the child's ear, his habit (1) comes into play and he

utters his nearest babbling syllable, *da*. We say that he is beginning to 'imitate.' Grown-ups seem to have observed this everywhere, for every language seems to contain certain nursery-words which resemble a child's babbling—words like *mama, dada*: doubtless these got their vogue because children easily learn to repeat them" (p. 30).

3. Bloomfield assumes that stimulus and response explain why the mother would say doll in the first place. "She says *doll* when she is actually showing or giving the infant his doll. The sight and handling of the doll and the hearing and saying of the word *doll* (that is, *da*) occur repeatedly together, until the child forms a new habit: the sight and feel of the doll suffice to make him say *da*. He has now the use of a word. To the adults it may not sound like any of their words, but this is due merely to its imperfection" (p. 30).

4. Bloomfield then has to argue that the absence of the stimulus somehow creates another stimulus that generates the same response. "Suppose, for instance, that day after day the child is given his doll (and says *da, da, da*) immediately after his bath. He has now a habit of saying *da, da* after his bath; that is, if one day the mother forgets to give him the doll, he may nevertheless cry *da, da* after his bath. 'He is asking for his doll,' says the mother, and she is right, since doubtless an adult's 'asking for' or 'wanting' things is only a more complicated type of the same situation" (p. 30).

5. In accordance with behaviorist theory, Bloomfield posits that correct performance yields better results: "If he says *da, da* imperfectly—that is, at great variance from the adults' conventional form *doll*—then his elders are not stimulated to give him the doll. In short, his more perfect attempts at speech are likely to be fortified by repetition, and his failures to be wiped out in confusion. This process never stops. At a much later stage, if he says *Daddy bringed it*, he merely gets a disappointing answer such as *No! You must say 'Daddy brought it'*; but if he says *Daddy brought it*, he is likely to hear the form over again: *Yes, Daddy brought it*, and to get a favorable practical response" (pp. 30–31).

TIME TO THINK ...

Think about Bloomfield's statement above that it is unlikely that children ever invent a word. Do you agree with that statement?

Think about the example of a child saying "bringed" that Bloomfield gives. What error has the child made here and why? Can you think of other similar examples of errors that children might make when learning their first language?

To sum up, from a theoretical perspective, the child learns to make the stimulus–response connection. One such connection is the uttering of the word *doll* (response) when the child sees the object (stimulus); another connection is the reverse: the child gets the doll (response) when he or she hears the word (stimulus). Thus, learning involves the establishment of a habit by means of which these stimulus–response sets become associated.

4.2.2 Psychological Background

The terminology used in a language-learning setting and the associated concepts (e.g., **interference/facilitation**) come from the literature on the psychology of learning. The leading psychological school of thought of the time was **behaviorism**. One of the key concepts in behaviorist theory was the notion of transfer just discussed. Transfer is a concept that was used extensively in the first half of the 20th century and refers to the psychological process whereby prior learning is carried over into a new learning situation. The main claim with regard to transfer is that the learning of task A will affect the subsequent learning of task B. What is of interest is how fast and how well you learn something after having learned something else. Some examples will help clarify this notion.

From a physical perspective, if someone knows how to play tennis and then picks up a table-tennis racquet for the first time, she or he will use the knowledge/skills that have been gained from playing tennis in this new, but related, situation. Thus, old knowledge/skills are transferred to a new situation.

In a transfer experiment related to verbal learning, a study by Sleight (1911) was concerned with the ability to memorize prose more easily if one has had "prior experience" in memorizing poetry. He compared four groups of 12-year-old children on their ability to memorize prose. Three groups had prior training on the memorization of (a) poetry, (b) tables of measures, or (c) content of prose passages. A fourth group had no prior training in any type of memorization. Following training, the groups were tested on their ability to memorize prose. The question was: "To what extent does poetry memorization, or more precisely, the skills used in poetry memorization, transfer to memorization of prose?" (The results were nonsignificant.)

Let's consider an example from the area of language learning. According to the initial view of language transfer, if speakers of a particular language (in this case, Italian) form questions by saying:

(4-1)   Mangia   bene   il bambino?
       eats   well   the baby
       "Does the baby eat well?"

then those same (Italian) speakers learning English would be expected to say,

(4-2)   Eats well the baby?

when asking a question in English.

A behaviorist notion underlying this expectation is that of habits and cumulative learning. According to behaviorist learning theory:

> Learning is a cumulative process. The more knowledge and skills an individual acquires, the more likely it becomes that his new learning will be shaped by his past experiences and activities. An adult rarely, if ever, learns anything completely new; however unfamiliar the task that confronts him, the information and habits he has built up in the past will be his point of departure. Thus transfer of training from old to new situations is part and parcel of most, if not all, learning. In this sense the study of transfer is coextensive with the investigation of learning.
>
> (Postman, 1971, p. 1019)

Although this statement is not specifically intended as a description of language learning, we can see how the concepts can be applied to L2 learning.

A distinction noted above that is commonly made in the literature is between positive transfer (also known as facilitation) and negative transfer (also known as interference). These terms refer, respectively, to whether transfer results in something correct or something incorrect, and not, as noted earlier, two distinct cognitive processes. As an example with relation to L2 learning, if a Spanish speaker is learning Italian, when asking a question that speaker might correctly produce

(4-3) Mangia bene   il bambino?
       eats   well   the baby

because, in Spanish, one uses the same word order to form questions.

(4-4) ¿Come bien   el niño?
       eats   well   the baby

This is known as positive transfer. However, if that same speaker is learning English and produces

(4-5) Eats well the baby?

the incorrect utterance is known as negative transfer. One can see, then, that the process is the same.

With regard to interference, there are two types noted in the literature: (a) *retroactive inhibition*—where learning acts backwards on previously learned material, causing someone to forget (language loss)—and (b) *proactive inhibition*—where a series of already learned responses tends to appear in situations where a new set is required. This is more akin to the phenomenon of L2 learning, because the first language in this framework influences/inhibits/modifies the learning of the L2.

Most of the literature on transfer of learning dealt with very specific laboratory experiments. The wholesale application of this framework to situations of L2 learning is questionable. There is little empirical evidence in support of the assumption that, for example, forgetting outside the laboratory is a function of the same variables and represents the same processes as those observed in formal laboratory situations. So, although it may be that learning task A affects the subsequent learning of task B in an experimental setting, one must question whether it is the case that this is so outside the lab. For example, when we go into a video-game arcade and play a particular kind of simulation game, such as driving, do we carry over what we do in that situation to driving on the road?

These views did not go unchallenged, and, in fact, the challenges were part of the early thinking of the field of SLA in the 1960s and 1970s. We return to this discussion in Chapters 5 and 6.

We turn now to the work on L2 learning that was based on these behaviorist positions. As noted earlier, Lado's work made these theoretical underpinnings explicit. Recall also that the major impetus for this work was pedagogical, as Fries makes clear in his foreword to Lado's book:

> Before any of the questions of how to teach a foreign language must come the much more important preliminary work of finding the special problems arising out of any effort to develop a new set of language habits against a background of different native language habits.
>
> Learning a second language, therefore, constitutes a very different task from learning the first language. The basic problems arise, not out of any essential difficulty in the features of the new language themselves, but primarily out of the special "set" created by the first language habits.
>
> (Fries, Foreword to Lado, 1957)

Thus, underlying much work in the 1950s and 1960s was the notion of language as habit. L2 learning was seen as the development of a new set of habits. The role of the NL, then, took on great significance, because, in this view of language learning, it was the major cause of lack of success in learning the L2. The habits established in childhood interfered with the establishment of a different set of habits.

From this framework emerged contrastive analysis, because, if one is to talk about replacing a set of habits (let's say, the habits of English) with another set of habits (let's say, those of Italian), valid descriptions are needed, comparing the "rules" of the two languages.[3]

4.3 CONTRASTIVE ANALYSIS HYPOTHESIS

What are the tenets of contrastive analysis? Contrastive analysis is a way of comparing languages in order to determine potential errors for the ultimate purpose of isolating what needs to be learned and what does not need to be learned in an L2 learning situation. As Lado detailed, one does a structure-by-structure comparison of the sound system, morphological system, syntactic system, and even the cultural system of two languages for the purpose of discovering similarities and differences. The ultimate goal is to predict areas that will be either easy or difficult for learners.

It is assumed that learners tend to transfer the habits of their native language structure to the foreign language and it is also assumed that this is the major source of difficulty or ease in learning the structure of a foreign language. Those structures that are similar will be easy to learn, because they will be transferred and may function satisfactorily in the foreign language. Those structures that are different will be difficult, because, when transferred, they will not function satisfactorily in the foreign language and will therefore have to be changed (Lado, 1957, p. 59).

The pedagogical materials that resulted from contrastive analyses were based on a number of assumptions, some of which have been discussed earlier in this chapter:

1. Contrastive analysis is based on a theory of language that claims that language is habit and that language learning involves the establishment of a new set of habits.
2. The major source of error in the production and/or reception of an L2 is the native language.
3. One can account for errors by considering differences between the L1 and the L2.
4. A corollary to item 3 is that, the greater the differences, the more errors will occur.
5. What one has to do in learning an L2 is learn the differences. Similarities can be safely ignored, as no new learning is involved. In other words, what is dissimilar between two languages is what must be learned.
6. Difficulty and ease in learning are determined, respectively, by differences and similarities between the two languages being contrasted.

There were two positions that developed with regard to the **Contrastive Analysis Hypothesis (CAH)** framework. These were variously known as the a priori versus the a posteriori view, the strong versus weak view, and the predictive versus explanatory view. In the strong view, it was maintained that one could make predictions about learning and, hence, about the success of language-teaching materials based on a comparison between two languages. The weak version starts with an analysis of learners' recurring errors. In other words, it begins with what learners do and then attempts to account for those errors on the basis of NL–TL differences. The weak version, which came to be part of error analysis, gained credence largely owing to the failure of predictive contrastive analysis. The important contribution of the former approach to learner data (i.e., error analysis) was the emphasis it placed on learners themselves, the forms they produced, and the strategies they used to arrive at their IL forms.

Those arguing against the strong version of contrastive analysis were quick to point out the many areas where the predictions made were not borne out in actual learner production (see examples 4-8–4-9).

However, there were other criticisms as well. Perhaps the most serious difficulty, and one that ultimately led to the demise of contrastive analysis, a hypothesis that assumed that the NL was the driving force of L2 learning, was its theoretical underpinnings. In the 1960s, the behaviorist theory of language and language learning was challenged. Language came to be seen in terms of structured rules instead of habits. Learning was viewed not as imitation but as active rule formation (see Chapter 5 for details).

The recognition of the inadequacies of a behaviorist theory of language had important implications for SLA, for, if children were not imitators and were not influenced in a significant way by reinforcement as they learned language, then perhaps L2 learners were not either. This became clear when researchers began to look at the errors that learners made. Similar to data from child language acquisition, L2 learner data reflected errors that went beyond those in the surrounding speech and, importantly, beyond those in the NL. For example, it is not uncommon for beginning L2 learners to produce an utterance such as (4-6), in which the learner attempts to impose regularity on an irregular verb:

(4-6)   He comed yesterday.

There was no way to account for this fact within a theory based primarily on a learner transferring forms from the NL to the TL.

Not only did errors occur that had not been predicted by the theory, but also there was evidence that predicted errors did not occur. That is, the theory did not accurately predict what was happening in nonnative speech.

Dušková (1984) presents data from Czech speakers learning English and Russian. She found that those learning English did not transfer bound morphemes, whereas the Czech learners of Russian did. Within a theory based on the transference of NL forms, this could not be explained, for why should transfer occur in one instance, but not in another?

Yet another example is given by Zobl (1980). In data from French speakers learning English and English speakers learning French, Zobl found inconsistencies in actual error production. In French, object pronouns precede the verb, as in (4-7).

(4-7)   Je les vois.
        I them see
        "I see them."

In English, object pronouns follow the verb. However, the following facts emerge in learner data:

(4-8)   By French learners of English:
        I see them. (produced)
        *I them see. (not produced)

(4-9) By English learners of French (Ervin-Tripp, 1974, p. 119; Selinker, Swain, & Dumas, 1975, p. 145) (none of these is possible in French):

 (a) Je vois elle.
   I see them.

 (b) Le chien a mangé les.
   The dog has eaten them.

 (c) Il veut les encore.
   He wants them still.

In other words, French learners of English never prepose the object pronoun. Rather, they correctly follow English word order, which in this case is in violation of French word order. With English speakers, the reverse occurs: They follow the NL word order. If the "habits" of one's native language are the driving force, then why should they be operative in one direction, but not the other?[4]

Yet another criticism of the role of contrastive analysis had to do with the concept of difficulty. Recall that a fundamental tenet of the CAH was that differences signified difficulty, and that similarity signified ease. Difficulty in this view was equated with errors. If a learner produced an error, or errors, this was a signal that the learner was having difficulty with a particular structure or sound.

But what actually constitutes a sign of difficulty? Consider the following example from Kellerman (1987, p. 82), in which a student wrote:

(4-10) But in that moment it was 6:00.

In a conversation with the student, the teacher wanted her to comment on her use of the preposition *in*. The student insisted that the correct form was *in*, but questioned whether it should be *it was 6:00* or *it had been 6:00*.

If we assume the dictionary definition of *difficulty*, which is "hard to do, make, or carry out," then it becomes difficult to apply this concept to the common equation of error with difficulty. Clearly, the learner was having difficulty in the sense of struggling with something that was hard for her to do, but in this case the struggle was with tense usage, even though there was no error reflecting that difficulty. On the other hand, there was no doubt in her mind about the correctness of the preposition. From her perspective, that was not an area of difficulty, despite the overt error. So, difficulty cannot be unilaterally equated with errors, although (within the CAH) errors are the predicted result of linguistic differences. Differences are based on formal descriptions of linguistic units—those selected by a linguist, a teacher, or a textbook writer. It is not a *real* measure of difficulty. To equate difference with difficulty attributes a psycholinguistic explanation to a linguistic description. It is a confusion of the product (a linguist's description) with the process (a learner's struggle with the second language).

We have mentioned some of the problems with assuming the validity of the CAH as Lado (1957) stated it. However, this discussion should not be interpreted as suggesting that there is no role for the NL in SLA, for this is clearly not the case.

What it does suggest is that there are other factors that affect L2 development, and that the role of the native language is far more complex than the simple one-to-one correspondence implied by the early version of the CAH.

Language learning is not just a matter of "linguistic hiccups" from NL to TL (as Sharwood Smith, 1978, noted [cited in Kellerman, 1979]). There are other factors that may influence the process of acquisition, such as innate principles of language, attitude, motivation, aptitude, age, other languages known; topics to be treated in subsequent chapters. For the present, suffice it to say that the acquisition of an L2 is far too complex a phenomenon to be reduced to a single explanation.

Two final points need to be made with regard to the significance of contrastive analysis and to Lado's pioneering work. First, it is an oversimplification to think that comparing two languages is a straightforward comparison of structures. Lado, in his detailed treatment, elaborated on ways in which languages might differ. After a discussion of ways in which different languages expressed similar meanings, Lado (1957, pp. 63–64) stated:

> In the above cases we assumed that the meanings signaled in the two languages were in some way equivalent even if not identical. We went so far as to call them "same." The difficulty in such cases depended on differences in the formal devices used in the two languages to signal the "same" meanings. We now turn to cases in which a grammatical meaning in one of the languages cannot be considered the same as any grammatical meaning in the other language.

Recognition of the complexity of comparing languages became apparent quite early, particularly in work such as that of Stockwell et al. (1965a, 1965b), who, rather than dichotomize the results of language comparison into easy and difficult and therefore dichotomize the needs of learning into a yes/no position, established a **Hierarchy of Difficulty** and, by implication, a hierarchy of learning. Included in this hierarchy are different ways in which languages can differ.

For example, in their framework, the most difficult category is that in which there is **differentiation**: The native language has one form, whereas the target language has two. According to this view, an English speaker learning Italian (or Spanish or French) would find the translation equivalent of the verb *to know* difficult, because, in Italian, there are two possibilities: *sapere*, meaning to know a fact, to have knowledge of something, or to know how to do something; and *conoscere*, meaning to be familiar or acquainted with someone. Second and third types of differences between languages occur when there is a category present in language *X* and absent in language *Y*. As an example, consider the English article system. Because Japanese does not have articles, a Japanese learner of English must learn a new category. An example of the third type is an English learner of Japanese where there is an absent category (i.e., no articles). A fourth difference is found in situations in which the opposite of differentiation occurs: that is, **coalescing** (e.g., an Italian speaker learning the English words *to know*). Finally, **correspondence** occurs when two forms are used in roughly

TABLE 4.1 Hierarchy of Difficulty (*Source*: Adapted from Stockwell, Bowen & Martin, 1965a, 1965b.)

Category	Example
Differentiation	English L1, Italian L2: *to know* versus s*apere/conoscere*
New category	Japanese L1, English L2: article system
Absent category	English L1, Japanese L2: article system
Coalescing	Italian L1, English L2: the verb *to know*
Correspondence	English L1, Italian L2: plurality

the same way (e.g., plurality in English and Italian). The hierarchy of these differences reveals the complexity of cross-linguistic comparisons (Table 4.1).

A second point concerning the significance of the CAH has to do with the importance of empirical validation and the limitations that Lado himself attributed to his work. As we discussed earlier, part of the criticism leveled against contrastive analysis was empirical: Not all actually occurring errors were predicted; not all predicted errors occurred. The lack of empirical basis was, in fact, noted by Lado (1957, p. 72):

Necessity of Validating the Results of the Theoretical Comparative Analysis
The list of problems resulting from the comparison of the foreign language with the native language will be a most significant list for teaching, testing, research, and understanding. Yet it must be considered a list of hypothetical problems until final validation is achieved by checking it against the actual speech of students. This final check will show in some instances that a problem was not adequately analyzed and may be more of a problem than predicted. In this kind of validation we must keep in mind of course that not all the speakers of a language will have exactly the same amount of difficulty with each problem. . . . The problem will nevertheless prove quite stable and predictable for each language background.

Historically, Lado's hypothesis inspired a generation of L2 researchers to conduct linguistic field work, that is, to check hypothetical contrastive analysis statements against the actual speech of language learners. This much-cited passage presages

TIME TO THINK ...

Think about your L1 and your L2. Can you come up with an example of each category of the Hierarchy of Difficulty for your L1 and L2? Would you agree with the hierarchy in terms of whether the example in the category of *differentiation* is more difficult than the example in the category of *new category*, etc.?

the current acceptance of the centrality of individual variation. One way of fulfilling Lado's injunction to check hypothetical problems against actual learner production was to refocus on learner errors, from which developed an approach called error analysis.

4.4 ERROR ANALYSIS

What is error analysis? As the name suggests, it is a type of linguistic analysis that focuses on the errors learners make. Unlike contrastive analysis (in either its weak or its strong form), the comparison made is between the errors a learner makes in producing the TL and the TL form itself. It is similar to the weak version of contrastive analysis, in that both start from learner production data; however, in contrastive analysis, the comparison is made with the NL, whereas, in error analysis, it is made with both the NL and the TL.

Even though the main emphasis in L2 studies during the 1950s and 1960s was on pedagogical issues, a shift in interests began to emerge. The conceptualization and significance of errors took on a different role with the publication of an article by Corder (1967) titled, "The significance of learners' errors." Unlike the typical view held at the time by teachers, errors, in Corder's view, are not just something to be eradicated, but rather can be important in and of themselves.

Errors can be taken as red flags; they provide windows into a system—that is, evidence of the state of a learner's knowledge of the L2. They are not to be viewed solely as a product of imperfect learning; hence, they are not something for teachers to throw their hands up in the air about. As with research on child language acquisition (see Chapter 5), it has been found that L2 errors are not a reflection of faulty imitation. Rather, they are to be viewed as indications of a learner's attempt to figure out some system—in other words, to impose regularity on the language the learner is exposed to. As such, they are evidence of an underlying rule-governed system. In some sense, the focus on errors was the beginning of the field of SLA, which at this point began to emerge as an area of interest, not only for the pedagogical implications that may result from knowing about L2 learning, but also because of the theoretical implications for fields such as psychology (in particular, learning theory) and linguistics.

Corder

In the same article, Corder was careful to distinguish between errors and **mistakes**. Mistakes are akin to slips of the tongue. That is, they are generally one-time-only events. The speaker who makes a mistake is able to recognize it as a mistake and correct it if necessary. An error, on the other hand, is systematic; it is likely to occur repeatedly and is also likely not to be recognized by the learner as an error. The learner, in this case, has incorporated a particular erroneous form (from the perspective of the TL) into his or her system. Viewed in this way, errors are only errors from a teacher's or researcher's perspective, not from the learner's. Taken from the perspective of a learner who has created a grammatical system (an IL), everything that forms part of that IL system by definition belongs there. Errors are only errors with reference to some external norm (in this case, the TL). For example, if a learner

ERROR x MISTAKE
systematic   1 time slip
not recognized   (auto-correction)

produces the following negative forms, and if we assume that these are consistent and form part of the learner's system, then it is only possible to think of them as errors with regard to English, but not with regard to the learner's system:

(4-11) No speak.

(4-12) No understand.

A great deal of the work on error analysis was carried out within the context of the classroom. The goal was clearly one of pedagogical remediation. There are a number of steps taken in conducting an error analysis.

1. **Collect data**: Although this is typically done with written data, oral data can also serve as a base.
2. **Identify errors**: What is the error (e.g., incorrect sequence of tenses, wrong verb form, singular verb form with plural subject)?
3. **Classify errors**: Is it an error of agreement? Is it an error in irregular verbs?
4. **Quantify errors**: How many errors of agreement occur? How many irregular verb form errors occur?
5. **Analyze source**: See later discussion.
6. **Remediate**: Based on the kind and frequency of an error type, pedagogical intervention is carried out.

Error analysis provides a broader range of possible explanations for researchers/ teachers to use to account for errors than contrastive analysis, as the latter only attributed errors to the NL. There are two main error types within an error-analysis framework: **interlingual** and **intralingual**. Interlingual errors are those that can be attributed to the NL (i.e., they involve cross-linguistic comparisons). Intralingual errors are those that are due to the language being learned, independent of the NL.[5] One would therefore expect similar intralingual errors to occur from speakers of a wide variety of L1s. Examples are given in Table 4.2.

Error analysis was not without its detractors. One of the major criticisms of error analysis was directed at its total reliance on errors, to the exclusion of other information. That is, critics argued, one needs to consider errors as well as non-errors to get the entire picture of a learner's linguistic behavior.

Perhaps the most serious attempt at showing the inadequacies of error analysis comes from a 1974 article by Schachter. She collected 50 compositions from each

TABLE 4.2 Categorization of Errors

Type	Source	NL	TL	Example
Interlingual	NL-based	French	English	*We just enjoyed to move and to play**
Intralingual	Regularization	All	English	*He comed yesterday*

*In French, verb complements are in the infinitival form. There is no *-ing* equivalent in French.

TABLE 4.3
RC Production (*Source*: From "An error in error analysis" by J. Schachter, 1974, *Language Learning*, 24, pp. 205–214, by Research Club in Language Learning. Reprinted by permission.)

NL group	Correct	Error	Total	% errors
Persian	131	43	174	25
Arabic	123	31	154	20
Chinese	67	9	76	12
Japanese	58	5	63	8
American	173	0	173	—

of four groups of learners of English: native speakers of Persian, Arabic, Chinese, and Japanese. Her research focused on the use of English restrictive relative clauses (RCs) by each of these four groups. The findings in terms of errors can be seen in column three of Table 4.3.

If we were to interpret these findings from an error-analysis perspective, we would have to conclude that the Japanese and Chinese speakers have control over the formation of English restrictive RCs and that the Persian and Arabic speakers do not. However, Schachter's analysis went beyond the errors to look at the total production of RCs, including error-free RCs. This analysis is presented in Table 4.3.

Including errors and non-errors is far more revealing with regard to the control speakers of various language groups have over restrictive RCs. Although it is true that the Persian and Arabic speakers had a greater percentage of errors than did the Chinese and Japanese learners, it is also the case that the Chinese and Japanese produced roughly half as many RCs as did the Persian and Arabic groups. What might account for this discrepancy, and why is it significant?

If one considers the ways in which the languages of Schachter's study form RCs, it becomes apparent why these results occur. Japanese and Chinese form RCs by placing the modifier (the RC) before the noun it modifies, as in the following examples:

(4-13) Japanese:

> Watashi-wa   Eigo-o   hanasu josei-o   mimashita.
> I subj.   English obj. talks woman obj. saw
> "I saw the woman who speaks English."

(4-14) Chinese:

> Wo   kandao   nei ge shuo   ying yu de   nuren.
> I   saw   the CL speaks   English language RM   woman
> "I saw the woman who speaks English."
> *CL = classifier; RM = relative marker*

Persian and Arabic RCs are similar to English, in that the RC is placed after the noun it modifies, as in the following examples:

(4-15) Arabic:

ana	raait	Al Emraah	allety	tatakalem	Al-Englizy.
I	saw	the woman	who	speaks	the English

"I saw the woman who speaks English."

(4-16) Persian:

an	zaenra	ke	inglisi	haerfmizaene	didaem.
that	woman	that	English	speaks	I saw

"I saw the woman who speaks English."

It thus seems reasonable to assume that, because of the great distance between the way in which the NL forms RCs (as in the case with Japanese and Chinese speakers) and the way in which the TL forms RCs, learners do not use the construction with great frequency. When they do use it, they use it cautiously and with a high degree of accuracy. The Persian and Arabic learners, on the other hand, use RCs more frequently (and are thus likely to produce more errors), because their NL structure is similar to the TL structure. Hence, the NL is a determining factor in accounting for the facts of RC production, and yet these facts would not be apparent through an error analysis alone.

A second difficulty with error analysis is the determination of what an error is an error of. Schachter and Celce-Murcia (1971) gave the following examples from Chinese learners of English:

(4-17) There are so many Taiwan people live around the lake.

(4-18) There were lots of events happen in my country.

(4-19) . . . and there is a mountain separate two lakes.

(4-20) . . . and there are so many tourist visit there.

At first glance, these look like RCs without the relative marker (*that, who, which*). However, another plausible explanation is one that accounts for these, not as failed attempts at RC productions, but rather as constructions parallel to topic–comment constructions in the NL of these speakers. That is, these learners are following an appropriate NL pattern of establishing a topic (*Taiwan people*, *lots of events*, *mountain*, *tourist*) and then making a comment about it (*they live around the lake*, *they happen in my country*, *it separates two lakes*, *they visit there*). This is not unlike the following construction in English: *You see that man? He just ran a red light*, as opposed to: *Did you see that man who just ran a red light?*

Schachter (1983, 1992) presented another example of an Arabic speaker learning English:

(4-21) But when oil discovered in 1948 and began export it in 1950 . . .

She interpreted this as a passive construction, the problem being the lack of the tensed form of the verb *to be*. However, it is not clear that this is the only interpretation. One could plausibly argue that this is not a passive, but that the verb *discover* could be interpreted in the TL by the learner as a verb that occurs in both transitive and intransitive variants (e.g., the verb *boil* in *I boiled the water* and *The water boiled*). Thus, there can be a discrepancy between what a researcher determines to be the targeted structure and what the learner was actually attempting to produce.

Yet another inadequacy of error analysis is the attempt to ascribe causes to errors. There is an assumption that, if a form is correct, then the underlying rule is also correct. However, consider a learner who produces the following two sentences:

(4-22) I wanted him to come.

(4-23) I persuaded him to come.

A reasonable assumption is that this learner has learned that these verbs require an infinitival complement. Let's further consider the following two hypothetical sentences, which occur at Stage 2:

(4-24) I enjoyed talking to my teacher.

(4-25) I stopped sending packages to my friend.

At this point, the conclusion would be that this learner has learned that there are verbs that require gerundive complements. However, at Stage 3, the learner produces:

(4-26) I saw him to come.

(4-27) I enjoyed talking to you.

One might assume, from looking at the first two stages, that the learner knows that there are two possibilities for forming verbal complements in English, and that, furthermore, the learner knows which verbs take which type of complement. However, when one realizes (in Stage 3) that the learner has not correctly sorted out the facts of English, then one is led to a different analysis: The learner applies infinitival complements at Stage 1, gerundive complements at Stage 2, and only later realizes (Stage 3) that some verbs take one type of complement, and other verbs take another type of complement. At this point, the learner has not yet learned which verb is of which type. The error in sentence 4-26 is significant in that it reveals that the learner does not have the correct rule worked out. However, the absence of error in the previous two stages does not necessarily mean correct rule formation; it only suggests a limited sampling bias. It is important to note that, despite the fact that the data from Stages 1 and 2 reflect correct English usage, they are further from the correct system than the data in Stage 3, which shows that the learner is aware of the fact that the two complement types depend on the main verb. In sum, error analysis alone cannot provide us with this information, because an assumption of error analysis is that correct usage is equivalent to correct rule formation.

Finally, we deal with another problematic area of error analysis, relating to the source of errors. Within the framework of error analysis, the assumption is that errors can be categorized as belonging to one source or another. Dulay and Burt (1974b) recognized the fact that sometimes one cannot determine whether an error is of one type or another. To reflect this, they established a category called *ambiguous goofs*, which is defined as "those that can be categorized as either Interference-like Goofs or L1 Developmental Goofs" (p. 115). An example of an interference-like goof is *hers pajamas*, produced by a Spanish-speaking child. This reflects Spanish noun–adjective number agreement and is not found among English-speaking children learning their first language. An L1 developmental goof, as in *He took her teeths off* (produced by a Spanish-speaking child), is not found in Spanish L1, but is a typical overgeneralization error of English L1 children. An ambiguous error, such as *Terina not can go* (produced by a Spanish speaker), can be interpreted either as an interference error, because it reflects a Spanish structure, or as a developmental error, because it is also found in English-speaking children learning their first language.

TIME TO THINK ...

Think of an error that you have heard an L2 learner of your NL make. Do you think the error could be defined as an interference-like goof or as a developmental goof? Is it immediately clear how to categorize that error?

However, is it reasonable to say that there must always be a single etiology for errors? That is, must errors be of type *X* or of type *Y*, but not both? A few examples will suffice to show that learner production may be influenced simultaneously by multiple sources (see Selinker & Lakshmanan, 1992, and Lardiere, 2007).

Dušková (1983) reports on the acquisition of the English article system by native speakers of Czech, a language that does not have definite or indefinite articles. She pointed out that the difficulty in ultimately getting the facts of the English article system correct is due to the lack of a comparable system in the NL. However, that alone does not account for all of the problems Czech speakers encounter. Compounding the problem for these Czech speakers is the English article system itself. Here are examples from her data:

(4-28) I should like to learn foreign language.

(4-29) It was very interesting journey.

(4-30) We shall use present solution.

(4-31) I visited Institute of Nuclear Energy in Ljublana.

(4-32) As in many other cases the precise rules do not exist.

(4-33) . . . working on the similar problem as I.

In the first four examples, there is a (possibly) straightforward explanation in terms of the native language, as no articles are present. However, in the last two examples, the definite article is used where either no article (4-32) or an indefinite article (4-33) would have been appropriate. Thus, whereas the major underlying source of the problem may indeed be the lack of a category in the NL, the TL also contributes, in that there are various functions of articles in English that the learner must sort out.

Error analysis yielded a number of studies in which patterns of acquisition were clearly attributable to knowledge of both the TL and the NL. Schumann (1979), in a study of the acquisition of negation, demonstrated the convergence of linguistic information from two systems. Schumann's study focused on the acquisition of English by Spanish speakers, but his data were also compared with similar acquisitional data from speakers of other languages. In general, he found similar patterns of development, but he also found important differences.

Schumann noted that, initially, negative utterances are formed by using the word *no*, which is placed before the verb, as in the following examples (Stage 1):

(4-34) no understand

(4-35) no you told me

(4-36) no swim

(4-37) no correct

A second stage of development is seen with the occurrence of *don't*, as in 4-38 and 4-39:

(4-38) don't like

(4-39) I don't saw him

Next, learners show an increased use of *not*, as opposed to *no*, as a negator (4-40):

(4-40) not today

They also use *not* following the verb *to be* and the auxiliary (4-41 and 4-42):

(4-41) I'm not old enough.

(4-42) I will don't see you tomorrow.

Still later, learners begin to use variants of *don't* (i.e., *doesn't*, *didn't*), as opposed to the previous stage, where *don't* was used in all cases (all persons, present/past).

(4-43) I didn't went to Costa Rica.

And finally, most learners sort out the facts of negation and learn that, in negation, *do* is the element that bears tense and person distinctions.

In looking at the source of errors, one notes that Spanish is a language with preverbal negation, the negative element being *no*.

(4-44) No voy.
     no I go
     "I don't go."

(4-45) El no puede ir.
     he no can go
     "He can't go."

What is most germane to this discussion of error analysis is the fact that, when these data are compared with the acquisition of English negation by NSs of languages other than Spanish (or languages similar to Spanish), slightly different facts emerge. For speakers of languages with preverbal negation (e.g., Spanish, Italian, Greek), Stage 1 is more persistent than it is with speakers of languages without preverbal negation (e.g., German, Norwegian, Japanese). In the speech of learners from this latter group, the *no* + verb stage is short, or even nonexistent.

Schumann concluded that, in the case of the Spanish speaker, two forces converge: the NL and the facts of development (children learning English also exhibit a preverbal *no* stage in the development of negation). However, in the case of speakers of languages such as Japanese, only one factor is at play: development. A single source will have less influence than converging sources and will lead the learner to move much more rapidly through the developmental sequence.

In sum, error analysis, although important in the recognition that learners were more than passive hiccupers of NL forms and functions, falls short in the analysis of L2 data in that it only sees a partial picture of what a learner produces of the L2. One cannot hope to appreciate the complexity of the learning situation by studying one limited part of it.

4.5 CONCLUSION

In this chapter, we presented an historical overview of the role of the NL, showing the transition from behaviorist contrastive analysis to a consideration of the actual speech of learners, through the prism of errors. In Chapter 5, we deal with the transition period in the understanding of the role of the NL, and, in Chapter 6, we discuss more recent conceptualizations of the role of the native language.

POINTS TO REMEMBER

- From behaviorism, the field of SLA took the idea that a child learns to mimic speech from adults. Language acquisition is a process of forming habits.

- Transfer is prior learning that is carried over into a new learning situation.

- The contrastive analysis hypothesis (CAH) is a method of comparing languages in order to predict what errors a learner will make and to isolate what needs to be learned in an L2 learning situation.

- Contrastive analysis was based on the idea that the more differences there are between the native language and the target language, the more difficult the task is for an L2 learner.

- A problem with the CAH was the fact that sometimes learners make errors that are not predicted by the hypothesis and other times do not make all the errors predicted.

- The Hierarchy of Difficulty according to the CAH: differentiation, new category, absent category, coalescing, correspondence.

- Error analysis is a type of linguistic analysis in which the errors that a learner makes are compared with the TL form itself.

- Interlingual errors are those that can be attributed to the NL.

- Intralingual errors are those that can be attributed to the TL and occur among learners of various L1s.

- Error analysis presented only a partial explanation of learner production.

SUGGESTIONS FOR ADDITIONAL READING

Rediscovering interlanguage (1992). Larry Selinker. Longman.

Language transfer in language learning (1992). Susan Gass and Larry Selinker (Eds.). John Benjamins.

Language transfer (1989). Terence Odlin. Cambridge University Press.

The role of the first language in foreign language learning (1987). Håkan Ringbom. Multilingual Matters.

Cross-linguistic influence in second language acquisition (1986). Eric Kellerman and Michael Sharwood Smith (Eds.). Pergamon.

An experimental study of phonological interference in the English of Hungarians (1971). William Nemser. Mouton.

A psycholinguistic study of phonological interference (1968). Eugene Brière. Mouton.

MORE TO DO AND MORE TO THINK ABOUT ...

1. The earliest known reference to NL influences can be found in the book of Judges, where, in Chapter 12, the famous story is told of "the men of Ephraim," who went out to battle and did not do so well. In order to detect who was a fleeing Ephraimite and who was not, the Gileadites set up a very practical language test for the Ephraimites, who tradition says could not pronounce the sound *sh*. The actual passage reads as follows:

> Jephthah then called together the men of Gilead and fought against Ephraim. The Gileadites struck them down because the Ephraimites had said, "You Gileadites are renegades from Ephraim and Manasseh." The Gileadites captured the fords of the Jordan leading to Ephraim, and whenever a survivor of Ephraim said, "Let me cross over," the men of Gilead asked him, "Are you an Ephraimite?" If he replied, "No," they said, "All right, say 'Shibboleth'." If he said, "Sibboleth," because he could not pronounce the word correctly, they seized him and killed him at the fords of the Jordan. Forty-two thousand Ephraimites were killed at that time.
>
> (Judges 12: 4–6. *The Holy Bible*, New International Version, Hodder and Stoughton, London, 1988)

Evaluate this story in light of the information on the effect of NL influence presented in this chapter. Can you think of other important cases where identification of a person by NL accent has played an important role?

2. As described in this chapter, beginning L2 learners produce sentences such as *He comed yesterday*, where regular rules are extended to irregular cases. What does this suggest about the formation of early IL? Can you think of cases in your own language learning where you have tried to impose such regularity improperly? Relate your characterization to the strengths and weaknesses of the contrastive analysis hypothesis.

3. Consider the two types of *interference* discussed in this chapter: retroactive and proactive. In terms of the former, under what circumstances might it be possible to lose some of your NL fluency? What parts of the NL might you predict would be most affected?

4. Consider the process of looking at structures across languages. Do you agree that one can easily note similarities of structures and differences of structures? Do you agree that these cannot equal ease and difficulty of learning? In what circumstances might similarities/differences be compatible with ease/difficulty of learning?

5. Describe the two major positions of contrastive analysis: a priori and a posteriori. In what ways is this a useful dichotomy? Suppose we were to say that, in reality, we are not dealing with a dichotomy, but with a continuum, where each of the named positions reflects one of the extremes. Does this

conceptualization alter your belief in the usefulness of these positions? Can one then say that the former is predictive, whereas the latter is explanatory?

6. As noted in this chapter, there is a lack of bidirectionality in cases such as the French–English word order of pronouns. In light of this, evaluate the following French sentences produced by NSs of English:

    (1)   *Il veut moi de dire français à il.*
           He wants me to say French to him.

               Correct form: *Il veut que je lui parle français*
               ("He wants that I to him speak French.")

    (2)   *Un chalet où on va aller à.*
           A cottage where one goes to go to.

           Correct form: *Un chalet où on va aller.*

    From context, we know that the intention of these sentences is:

    (1a)   He wants me to speak French to him.
    (2a)   A cottage that we're going to go to.

    Do you think these should be characterized as interference? Why or why not?

7. Compare the approaches to the analysis of L2 data discussed in this chapter—contrastive analysis and error analysis—with regard to the following:

    (a)   There may be covert errors. A classic example from Corder (1981) is the German speaker who says "You must not take off your hat," when the intent is "You don't have to take off your hat." In what sense is this an error? In what sense is it not?
    (b)   It might be more appropriate to talk about TL-like behavior. The fact that a learner has produced a correct form/sentence in a language does not necessarily mean that it is right.
    (c)   It is not always possible to provide a single explanation for IL data.

8. A number of problems arise with the incorporation of the concept of "transfer" from psychology into SLA. Primary among them is the emphasis on controlled experimentation in a laboratory setting, within the framework of the psychology of learning. To apply this to an L2 situation is difficult, because many other variables come into play in SLA that are difficult to control. For example, controlled material presented in a laboratory setting differs from an L2 learning situation in the complexity of what is being learned. What other differences can you think of between actual L2 learning and experimental learning?

9. In the discussion of errors, it was pointed out that errors are only errors from an external perspective (i.e., a teacher's or a researcher's). Is it possible that there are consistently incorrect forms (i.e., errors) that a learner recognizes

as errors, but that remain as errors because a learner does not know how to correct them? Do you think that these would be forms "ripe" for change? Or are they likely to fossilize?

10. Consider the Hierarchy of Difficulty discussed in section 4.3. Provide examples of each of these categories from your own learning experience. Do you agree that the proposed hierarchy represents degrees of difficulty, and that the ordering proposed is the correct one? Why, or why not?

11. Four compositions follow. First, do an error analysis of each. Describe the difficulties you encounter in doing this. Are there ambiguities? How could you resolve them? Do you know what the NLs are of these writers? What features determine your choice?

COMPOSITION 1

"THINGS ARE ROUGH ALL OVER" FOR SOCS AND GREASERS

There are many teenagers in *The Outsiders*, and each of them has several characteristics. There are many differences between the Socs and the Greasers, and each character who belongs to these groups has a different background. However, Cherry's saying, "Things are rough all over," applies to all characters in the story, so both the Socs and the Greasers have some "things" and "roughness." However, their "things" are not equally "rough."

Cherry says "Things are rough all over" as Soc. For Cherry and all the Socs, the part of rough is Rat race. Though they can get everything they want, it does not satisfy them. Because of it, the Socs take actions like Cherry said; we're always searching for something to satisfy us, and never finding it (p. 37). It might be suffering that the Greasers can not experience because they were not born in environment like the Socs. In addition, people who can not find something to satisfy them do antisocial behavior, and they are done to catch the hearts of their parents and people surrounded him. In the fact, Bob did so. His parents gave in to him, but he was not given loves from his parents. He came home drunker than anything to grab his parents' hearts, but he could not get his parents' love. In the other words, "things" are parents' love for Bob, and it was so "rough" for him, so "things are rough" to him. In addition, Cherry says to Ponyboy that the Socs also have sufferings, and it is not easy to solve them; that means Cherry's "things are rough all over."

Of course, not only the Socs but also the Greasers also have "things." For example, Johnny is not given love from his parents, Ponyboy's parents have been dead and he thinks his oldest brother hates him, and both his brothers, Sodapop and Darry, have worries about their brothers. Even Dallas, who seems so tough, suffers and wants to die. Thus, All of them have "things," but their "things" are not equally "rough." For example, Ponyboy's parents never return, and Dallas can't talk with anyone about his "things," but it is possible that Johnny's worry is able to be solved if Jonny talks with his parents. It means their things have two types; fist type is that they can not solve immediately, another type is that they can not solve any more. Moreover, each of their "things" has different difficulty to solve them. In the fact, Pony's brothers can resolve one of their "things" in the end of the story, but many characters still have their "things" by the end. Thus, each of the Greasers has different levels of "roughness."

Cherry wants Ponyboy to understand that both the Socs and the Greasers can not have it made. However, it is so difficult to Ponyboy to understand that because there is a big difference between the Socs and the Greasers. That is wealth. Ponyboy and all the Greasers have lived with preposition and poorness. In addition, the Socs also have their "things" and "roughness." However, the Greasers have problems of preposition and poorness besides their own "things," so "things" are also unequally "rough" between these two groups. When Ponyboy heard Cherry's words, he did not know about similarities and differences between the Socs and the Greasers. In the fact, he had some misunderstanding about the Socs; maybe it was money that separated us (p. 38), and I really couldn't see what Socs would have to sweat about. I thought if I had worries like them I'd consider I'm lucky (p. 36). In addition, he did not perceive "things" and "roughness" of the same team members. Therefore, it was so difficult to him to understand Cherry's words at that time. However, he came to understand Cherry's words gradually. He learned about his friends' and his brothers' suffering by talking with them, and he understood the Socs by hearing about Bob from Randy; he could find that all the Greasers have their "things" and "roughness," and even in the Socs who are rich kids also have worries same as the Greasers. Their worries are different, but it is the fact that all of them have some suffering. As Ponyboy noticed it, he was able to understand Cherry's words.

Cherry's words, "Things are rough all over," are true for all the Socs and the Greasers, but all characters in *The Outsiders* have different "things" and "roughness." The Socs have worries because of the wealth, and the Greasers also have worries because of their backgrounds. However, these differences are not important for Ponyboy. It is important for him that all people belonging to the Socs and the Greasers have suffering and worries, and it is significant that he know the other guys are also human.

COMPOSITION 2

FAMILY AND ITS POWER!

In society exists various groups and one of these is family. Family has an important meaning but sometime we misunderstand what really is! Surely, standard family consists of husband and wife and children but his sense is wider. Family are we, family are friends that share emotions, family is my grandfather, family is my class; it exists everywhere where people join together and form a group sharing everything. In this last month I have had a lot of opportunity to read and learn about it. For instance, I read the book *Nightjohn*, as well as seeing the movie, and I spent a lot of time in sharing thoughts with my classmates about this topic. The most cruel, but significant, example that I can use to explain family and its power is the why slave owners commonly broke up slave families. They had to maintain black people mentally weak to continue to live in their white status, and to reach such bad goal they separated its member to prevent rebellions. They had fear to lose power and money.

In fact, they had big cotton plantations and they owned black people; this gave them power in society and power on the slaves. They had this privileged life, for they hadn't to work but they had to scrutinize the slaves' works only. They were completely served and believed that their white status was superior of the black one. All this characteristics make them trust to be powerful, and to have the right to continue in such behavior. In the book there is a passage that I want to quote because it explains why white people had so fear of rebellion. "'Cause to know things, for us to know things, is bad for them. We get to wanting and when we get to wanting it's bad for them. They think we want what they got (39)." What they got was power, and they were so afraid to lose it that didn't hesitate in whipping slaves until death.

Another reason was money. Having a plantation and owning slaves meant to be rich because every slave has money value and all together formed the muster's wealthy. I want to narrate a passage in the *Nightjohn* that impressed me. The scenario developed in church among an argument between muster and slaves; he was furious and menaced to shot them with the gun, and, all of the sudden, *Sarny* stood up and cried out loud to didn't have fear to be shouted, because they were his wealth and he would never shot. Slaves worked in plantation that produced cotton; more over, they were money and could be traded if there was good opportunity. Indeed, *Sarny*'s mother was sold because she was a good breeder and muster did a good trade.

In the reason why master broke up slaves family lay hidden the family's power. Family is the place where the individual can find his own identity and to develop a sense of power. Identity is very important because everyone needs to know own root. This teaches us who we are and what are our values and our rights. In family we are socialized and we learn how to behave and what to aspect from our environment. Furthermore, everyday by sharing emotions, ideals, dream we grow and become stronger and capable to accept sufferance.

I'm positive with family. I met my wife seventeen years ago and we immediately engaged and after seven years we got married. Nine months ago Viola, my sweetie daughter, was born and I feel to have achieved what I had ever dreamed from my life. Power and money are nothing without love and family. Maybe this can seem a common sentence, but if you are in my condition, you know what I'm talking about. I can't imagine a life without my family, I get lost without it and I need to thank god for such luckiness.

I want to finish this essay remembered *Nightjohn* movie when *Delie* said him, "You have a new family now and everywhere you go you'll find a new one." This is a big truth! In life everyone have good and bad moments, but what is really important is to have someone to share with. Remember that family is everywhere! Family are friends, family are parents, strangers and family are my wife and my Viola.

---

adverbs -}
vocab. tint. NL
verb tenses -

COMPOSITION 3 highlight mistakes + errors - help students self - correct.

PEER PRESSURE INFLUENCES TEENAGERS

Peer pressure influences teenagers in many aspects. It may have positive or negative matters. Friends have the biggest influence on each other. Girls and boys in their teenage period like to stick with each other if they share the same interests, or even if they are in the same status. They also feel uncomfortable when they join new group that is different from the group they usually stick with. In the Outsider's novel, there are two groups; Greasers and Socs. Each group influences its members with different kinds of matters. ⟵

There are some usual influences among the members in each group. They do many things which might be in their culture, habits, or they follow each other by apery. For example, Greasers influence each other by letting their hair grow up and they do not like any body to tell them to cut it. Furthermore, most of Greasers wear blue jeans, T-shirts, and tennis shoes or boots. On the other hand, Socs wear nice, expensive clothes with leather shoes. I can see most of the Socs are rich and drive expensive cars while the Greasers who were poor, drive cheap cars and use simple things.

Moreover, there were some negative attitudes in both groups with their members. For example, there was a girl whose named was Cherry said to ponyboy, did not take it personally if I did not talk with you in school. She meaned by that she was from Socs and he was from Greasers and if she talked with him, she would lose her friends and they would give her bad treatment because of the race which they had against each other. Another thing, the guys influenced each other in many bad things: I could see most of them → badly smoked cigarettes and some drink alcohol even though others were young people. In addition for that, there was no body would stop them because there was no one telling them that the smoking and drinking caused many health problems in their life.

There were some bad attitudes from the friends who were surrounded ponyboy. I can see Dally was always trying to tell his friend ponyboy to be tough and strong against other people who faced him like Greasers. In addition, Dally most the time made fun of people, showed off and insulted children in front of his friends ponyboy and Johnny. People do not like get directions. For example, Derry the oldest brother of pony boy always gave him directions which ponyboy did not like while ponyboy liked his second oldest brother Soda more than Derry because he understood him more and considered him like adult and did not give him directions so I could see ponyboy influenced more form Soda.

There are also some positive effects to ponyboy from his friends who were around him. He had a good friend whose named was Johnny always helped him, did not like to fight with other people and one time he bought a book and gave it to him and told him keep reading the book, because book would be best friend and stay with you until you die. One time Johnny had telling ponyboy fight was not good and useless. In addition, there was also a good advice from him that he said to ponyboy several time "stay gold, stay gold and nothing good can stay." I can see also ponyboy learned to help people with his friends Dally and Johnny after the church had burned, even caused his life to death but he tried with them to take out people who were in church and to save their life with his brave and his friends encouragements.

In brief, peer pressure might be good and bad on adults and even more on teenagers. We need to get the positive things from good peer pressure and try to be away from people who have bad influence on us by the advice which Johnny said "stay good" and this would be a great full advice we can learn from life.

COMPOSITION 4

MY SIBLING'S RELATIONSHIP

Not everyone has luck to have brothers or sisters in the family, but I am the lucky one; I have one brother. He is one year old younger than me. He is not a lovely younger brother and I am also not a lovely elder brother. We always call each others full name, never call each other "brother"; however, we still respect and help each other. Of course, sometimes we do argue and fight, but we are still brothers. There are some similar and contracts relationships between the book, *The Outsiders*. I am going to compare with the book; however, let me tell you something about us first.

My brother and I both had learned music since when we were young. We both learned the same instruments: violin, piano and erhu (Chinese instrument) in the same music-elementary school. We both are studying in the U.S. right now. Music is important for both of us, because we had learned since we were young. It's pretty useful; the reason is we would have some common things to do for both of us. Sometimes we played in the same orchestra and sometimes we just played duet together. We always had good time when we play duet. Therefore, sometimes we would perform to some people. We used to study in the same high school for one year. We performed it at many places in that year. For instance, we played at the nursing house, many YMCA's and school's parties. We were happy about met lots of people and we hope they were enjoyed. As the book, brothers like to play each other. Darry, Sodapop, and Ponyboy enjoy the time they are together.

Every brother cares very much about their brothers. I can understand why Darry is very mad about Ponyboy being late to home after the movie, and after Darry and Sodapop very worry about Ponyboy when he and Johnny hide in the church. When my brother and I were in Taiwan, sometimes he went out with his friends until very late, and he did not call back home or my parents. I could not contact with him either. We were getting worried and angry about it. Therefore, I always kept telling him turn his cell phone on and let us know where he was going and when will he be back.

Every brother would protect their brothers. At begging of the book, Ponyboy got beaten by Socs. At that time, Darry and Sodapop saved Ponyboy. Later on in the story, even thought Dally is not Johnny and Ponyboy's brother, he still protects them as his younger brothers. He told them hide to the church, and tried to save them when they were in the fire. I would try to protect or help my brother when he gets troubles. I believe that he would do the same thing to me, too.

There is one thing I have in common with Darry; my brother and I don't really show love to each others just like Darry does not show love to Ponyboy. As I said before, my brother is not a lovely younger brother and I'm not a lovely older brother. We both think it's pretty nasty to be lovely. However, we still get alone pretty well. We still care each other very much.

As others brothers, sometimes we argue and fight. Like Darry argues with Ponyboy and hits him when Ponyboy was late back to the house. However, brothers are still brothers. There is one thing I think it's good to my brother and I. After we fight, we always get back to each other pretty soon. We don't really keep fighting and fighting. I think that's because we understand and we love each others.

CHAPTER FIVE

The Transition Period

5.1 INTRODUCTION

In Chapter 4, we saw the beginnings of more modern approaches to the discipline of SLA. We saw the field move from a behaviorist model of language learning to a broader view incorporating the notion of errors as providing information about how learners were organizing and processing their L2. In this chapter, we trace the development of what one might call a cognitive approach to learning. We first consider issues of child language acquisition, because it was this field that many of the earlier cognitive approaches to L2 learning drew from.

5.2 FIRST LANGUAGE ACQUISITION

The field of child language acquisition has been important in the development of SLA, particularly in the 1960s and 1970s, as SLA was beginning to establish itself as a viable research discipline. Over the years, much SLA research parallels developments in child language acquisition research and has drawn on concepts from that area of research to understand L2 phenomena. Many of the same questions have been, and continue to be, addressed, and some of the same theoretical explanations form the foundation of both fields.

In Chapter 4, we discussed a behaviorist theory of language when discussing the role of the native language. Primarily coming from research on child language acquisition (see Bloomfield's description of language learning in the previous chapter), during the 1950s and 1960s there were challenges to the behaviorist theory of language and language learning. Language came to be seen not as a set of automatic habits, but as a set of structured rules. These rules were claimed to be learned, not by imitation, but by actively formulating them on the basis of innate principles, as well as on the basis of exposure to the language being learned. Three examples from the child language literature provide evidence against the imitation view of language acquisition.

(5-1)   From Cazden (1972, p. 92; no age given)

> CHILD: My teacher holded the baby rabbits and we patted them.
> ADULT: Did you say your teacher held the baby rabbits?
> CHILD: Yes.
> ADULT: What did you say she did?
> CHILD: She holded the baby rabbits and we patted them.
> ADULT: Did you say she held them tightly?
> CHILD: No, she holded them loosely.

Despite the adult's modeling of the correct past tense form, the child continues to regularize the past tense by adding -ed rather than changing the vowel. Imitation clearly played no role at this point in this child's talk.

(5-2)   From McNeill (1966, p. 69; no age given)

> CHILD: Nobody don't like me.
> MOTHER: No, say "nobody likes me."
> CHILD: Nobody don't like me.
> (eight repetitions of this dialogue)
> MOTHER: No, now listen carefully; say "nobody likes me."
> CHILD: Oh! Nobody don't likes me.

(5-3)   Original data, age 3 years, 2 months

> CHILD: I don't see no trees.
> MOTHER: I don't see any trees. Not no trees, any trees.
> CHILD: No any trees. No any trees
> MOTHER: I don't see any trees.

In examples 5-2 and 5-3, the mother attempts unsuccessfully to model the correct form or even to overtly instruct the child. This type of example is often mocked in cartoons. One such cartoon shows a little boy saying, "Mommy, Dolly hitted me." The mother responds, "Dolly HIT me." The little boy's response was "You too?! Boy, she's in trouble!" (*Time Magazine*, November 1, 1999).

Recall Bloomfield's view of language learning in which he clearly stated that, when the child produces an incorrect form, the child receives a disappointing response with the admonition, "No, say it like this." The assumption is that the correct modeling (coupled with negative reinforcement) is sufficient to perfect the child's speech. However, as we have seen in the preceding examples, neither imitation nor reinforcement is a sufficient explanation of a child's linguistic behavior.

It became commonplace in the 1960s to see children as actively involved in creating grammars of their language, as opposed to being passive recipients imitating their surroundings. Children do not just soak in what goes on around them, but actively try to make sense of the language they are exposed to. They construct grammars. In so doing, they make generalizations; they test those generalizations or hypotheses;

and they alter or reformulate them when necessary—or abandon them in favor of some other generalization.

During the 1950s and 1960s, it became clear that the utterances of children displayed systematicity. Their language could be studied as a system, *not* just as deviations from the language they were exposed to. Thus, early utterances by children such as *no shoe* and *no book* are not best described as faulty imitation, but rather as representing the child's attempt to systematically express negation. It is these assumptions that have come to guide work in SLA as well. We turn next to some specifics of child language learning.

Learning a first language is an amazing accomplishment. It is a learning task perhaps like no other. At the onset of the language-learning odyssey, a child has much to determine about the language that she or he hears.[1] At the end of the journey, every child who is not cognitively impaired has an intact linguistic system that allows him or her to interact with others and to express his or her needs.

TIME TO THINK ...

Think about the complexity that children face when learning a language. Consider the concept of plurality and the language needed to express plurality and think about the input that children receive. A parent might have one potato chip in his/her hand and say, "Do you like potato chips?" Or, at another time, the parent might say, "Do you want a potato chip?" while holding more than one potato chip in his/her hand.

How do children figure out plurality? How does the child distinguish between the generic meaning expressed in the first one and the singular meaning of the second? Do you think that this is further complicated by the fact that, in response to the second question, when the child says "yes," he or she probably receives more than one potato chip?

Language is a form of communication, but children communicate long before they have language—at least in the way we normally think of language. Anyone who has lived in a household with an infant is aware of the various means that infants have at their disposal to communicate their needs. The most efficient of these is crying, but there are other, more pleasant means as well. Some of these include smiling[2] and cooing. Coos are not precisely like the regular speech sounds of language, but they do suggest that infants are aware of sounds and their potential significance. For example, from approximately four to seven months, infants use these cooing sounds to play with such language-related phenomena as loudness and pitch (Foster-Cohen, 1999).

5.2.1 Babbling

At approximately six months of age, infants turn to more language-like sounds in what is called **babbling**. Babbling most commonly consists of consonant–vowel sequences (e.g., bababa, dadada, and later bada). It is frequently the case that some of these early babbling sounds are taken to be "words" by parents or caregivers. For example, mamama is frequently, and perhaps wishfully, interpreted as referring to the child's mother, when in fact the sounds may be nothing more than sounds, with no meaning attached. The line between babbling and true words is often a fine one.

One device that children use fairly early to express meaning is intonation. Even before they have grammatical knowledge, they can use the appropriate stress and intonation contours of their language to distinguish among such things as statements, questions, and commands. A child can, for example, say *dada* with the stress on the second syllable. One can imagine the child doing so with her arms outstretched, with the intention of a command, something like, "Pick me up, daddy!" Or, one can imagine a child hearing what appears to be a door opening and saying dada with rising intonation. This might have the force of a question, such as, "Is that daddy?"

TIME TO DO ...

View the YouTube video (see Link #1 in the Links section at the end of this chapter) and consider the following:

1. Are these children having a real conversation? In what language?
2. How do you know?

How does babbling turn into word usage? Does this happen abruptly, or is the change a gradual one? Figures 5.1–5.3 show the relationship between babbling and actual word usage for three children between the ages of 11 months and 16 months.

There are a number of interesting points to be made about the data in Figures 5.1–5.3. First, for all three children, during the 5-month period there is a decrease in babbling and an increase in words, although the increase and decrease are not always linear. Second, there appears to be a point where each child "gets" the concept of words as referring to something. Once this occurs (month 14 for Child 1 and Child 2; month 15 for Child 3), there seems to be a drop-off in the amount of babbling that occurs.

5.2.2 Words

What function do words have for children? Words in early child language fulfill a number of functions: They can refer to objects, such as *ba* for bottle; they can indicate a wide range of grammatical functions, such as commands (*I want my bottle*); they can serve social functions, such as *bye* and *hi*. Children have to learn that words can serve each of these functions.

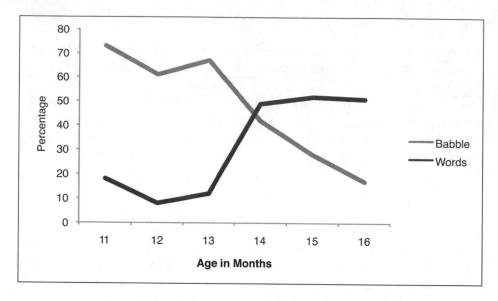

FIGURE 5.1 Relationship Between Babbling and Words: Child 1 (*Source*: Data from Vihman, 1996, cited in Foster-Cohen, 1999.)

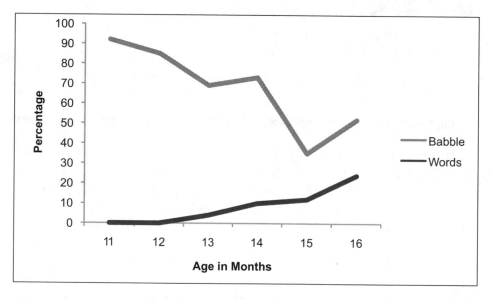

FIGURE 5.2 Relationship Between Babbling and Words: Child 2 (*Source*: Data from Vihman, 1996, cited in Foster-Cohen, 1999.)

Another point to bear in mind is that words in an adult's language do not always correspond to words in a child's language. What, in adult language, might be more than one word might be a single word for a child. For example, *allgone* is typically produced at the one-word stage in child language, even though it is comprised of two words in the adult language.

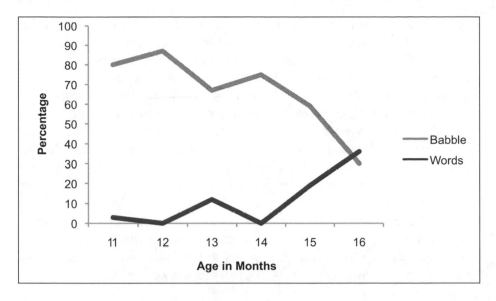

FIGURE 5.3 Relationship Between Babbling and Words: Child 3 (*Source*: Data from Vihman, 1996, cited in Foster-Cohen, 1999.)

There are other aspects of adult and child vocabulary that are not in a one-to-one correspondence. Children often **overextend** the meanings of words they know. For example, Hoek et al. (1986) noted one child's (19–20 months) use of the word *bunny* to refer to doll, hen, shoe, car, picture of people, giraffe, cow, bear, chair, lamp, puzzle, train, and so forth. At the same age, the child used *bear* to refer to a stuffed toy lion and a picture of a pig. At the same time, a physical object placed on a head (e.g., a book) might playfully be referred to as a hat, suggesting that the child can distinguish between objects and their functional uses.

In addition to overextension, children often underuse words. For example, one could imagine a child associating the word tree (in the dead of winter) with a leafless tree, but not using the word tree to refer to a tree with green leaves. In other words, children often use words with more restricted meanings than the word has in adult usage. This is known as **underextension**.

5.2.3 Sounds and Pronunciation

In these early stages, it is clear that the pronunciation of children's words is not exactly identical to that of adult speech. Among the earliest tasks that children face is figuring out the nature of the sounds they are hearing. Some sounds are distinguished quite early (e.g., the difference between the consonants in [ta] and [da]); others are, of course, learned later (wabbit for rabbit). Even when children start using words that more or less resemble adult words, at least in meaning, there are pronunciation differences. Common examples are substitutions, as in the rabbit example just given; deletion of syllables, as in *nana* for "banana"; deletion of sounds, such as *aypayn* for "airplane" and simplification, such as *fis* for "fish," or *baba* for "saba" (name of grandfather);

or sound rearrangements, such as *dadaf* for "safta" (name of grandmother). It is not always clear how to explain these phenomena. Are they a matter of motor control or of perception? The answer is—it depends. Foster-Cohen (1999) provided an interesting example from Smith (1973), whose child couldn't say the word *puddle*. He pronounced it as *puggle*. One could argue that this is a matter of pronunciation abilities, but a further look at this child's pronunciation showed that he used *puddle* for *puzzle*. Hence, this child was making a regular substitution (/g/ for /d/ and /d/ for /z/), but was perfectly capable of making the appropriate sounds, just not in the appropriate place. We also know that children often get angry when adults "imitate" them using their own (children's) pronunciation. For example, when an adult says, "oh, you want ice cweam [ice cream]," a child is likely to get angry and reply, "No, I want ice cweam, not ice cweam." Or, consider a child, 2 years, 4.5 months, who said, "dadaf sit front seat." The adult response: "dadaf sit front seat." Child: "no dadaf, dadaf." Adult: "Oh, safta sits in front seat?". Child: "Yes." This shows that children clearly can perceive a difference, although they do not make the difference in their own speech.

5.2.4 Syntax

Earlier, we talked about babbling and the move from babbling to words. This initial stage is often referred to as the one-word stage, because there is no word combination as of yet. The fact that children at this stage may use words such as *allgone* does not contradict this, for this word is likely to be only one word in the child's lexicon. After several months in the one-word stage, children start to combine words (usually at around 2 years of age). They might say something like "Mommy coming." What is typical of this phase is that the words that are used are content words (i.e., nouns and verbs). Function words, such as articles, prepositions, and grammatical endings, are notably lacking. As children move beyond the two-word stage, speech becomes **telegraphic**. The utterances used are much like the ones commonly used when sending a telegram—only the bare minimum, so as not to have to "pay" for any more than is necessary. For example, children's utterances might include "Aaron go home," "Seth play toy," "Ethan no go." As children's utterances become longer, it is appropriate for researchers to have a measure to determine complexity. MLU (mean length of utterance) is the standard measure used; it averages number of morphemes over 100 utterances and is a more realistic measure of development than is chronological age.

There are some typical stages that are found in further syntactic development. Lightbown and Spada (2006, pp. 6–7) provide the examples of the acquisition of question formation listed in Table 5.1. The important fact is that there is a predictable development for all children.

When we return to a discussion of SLA in later chapters, we will see that adults learning an L2 also have predictable sequences in terms of the acquisition of certain structures. However, the situation with L2 learners is more complex, because factors involving the NL may assume importance.

TABLE 5.1 Question Formation	
Stage 1.	Intonation: *Cookie? Mommy book?*
Stage 2.	Intonation with sentence complexity
	Yes/no questions. Children use declarative sentence order with rising intonation: *You like this? I have some?*
	Wh- questions. Question word with declarative order: *Why you catch it?*
Stage 3.	Beginning of inversion. *Wh-* questions maintain declarative order: *Can I go? Is that mine? Why you don't have one?*
Stage 4.	Inversion. *Do you like ice cream? Where I can draw them?* Use of *do* in *yes/no* questions (but not in *wh-* questions).
Stage 5.	Inversion with *wh-* questions. When negation needs to be included, the declarative form is maintained: *Why can he go out? Why he can't go out?*
Stage 6.	Overgeneralization of inversion *I don't know why can't he go out.*

5.2.5 Morphology

Much of the impetus for initial work in SLA stemmed from work by Brown (1973) and his astute observation that there was a predictable order of acquisition of certain inflectional morphemes in English. The three children he studied, Adam, Sarah, and Eve, learned English morphemes in roughly the same order, despite the fact that this did not always occur at precisely the same age. Brown's research revealed that the emergence of grammatical morphemes was consistent across these children, and that this emergence could be related to their overall development, measured in MLUs. The order of acquisition for these three children was: (1) present progressive, (2/3) prepositions *in*, *on*, (4) plural marker *-s*, (5) past irregular, (6) possessive (*-s*), (7) uncontractible copula (*is*, *am*, *are*), (8) articles (*a*, *the*), (9) past regular (*-ed*), (10), third person regular (*-s*), (11) third person irregular. What is interesting is that the order does not reflect the frequency of these morphemes in the speech of the children's parents.

There may be a number of reasons as to why this order rather than some other order exists. Among them are such notions as salience (e.g., the morpheme *-ing*, as in *walking*, can receive stress and is salient, whereas the morpheme *-ed*, as in *walked*, cannot), syllabicity (are they syllables?), and a lack of exception (the possessive ending *-'s* is used without exception, whereas the past tense *-ed* has exceptions in irregular verbs. We return to the order of morpheme acquisition later in this chapter in our discussion of SLA.

Another well-known study comes from Berko (1958), who devised a famous "wug" test to determine knowledge of grammatical morphemes. In this test, children were shown a picture of a novel animal and were told that this was a wug. Then they were shown a picture of two of the animals and were led into saying "there are two xxx." Even preschool children were able to correctly form plurals, which showed that they had understood the concept of plurality and the grammatical form to express plurality in English and were able to apply this knowledge to new contexts. At times, there is regularization of irregular forms (called overgeneralization), and children might say something like mices, not recognizing that the word mice is already plural. At a later stage, children learn that there are exceptions to regular patterns.

TIME TO DO ...

Go to Link #2 in the Links section of this chapter to see an example of Berko Gleason's wug test. What does the fact that even young children are able to correctly form the plural of *wug* tell us about language learning? Compare how this relates to what we learned about behaviorist views of language learning in Chapter 4.

One final point to make is that there are often prerequisites for learning certain forms, and there are often interrelationships between and among forms. An example can be seen in the acquisition of negatives and questions and the necessary prerequisite of knowledge of auxiliaries (e.g., forms of the verb *to be*, and forms of the verb *to do*). A very early stage involves only rising intonation, but once children are able to put words together, utterances with a *wh*- word (e.g., *where, what, who*) appear at the beginning of an utterance, such as "Where Ann pencil?", "Who that?", "What book name?" (examples from Foster-Cohen, 1999). As children become more sophisticated, other components begin to appear, such as modals, but there are examples without inversion, such as "What he can ride in?" (example from Klima and Bellugi, 1966). At a later stage, children begin to use auxiliaries and also correct order. As Foster-Cohen (1999) points out, as these question forms are developing for *wh*- questions, there is a similar development for *yes/no* questions. Akmajianet et al. (1995), referring to work by Foss and Hakes (1978) and Clark and Clark (1977), also note that negatives show a similar pattern, with single words such as *no* appearing first, followed by a negative word at the beginning of an utterance, such as "no eat," followed by negative modals or negative words in sentence internal position, such as, "He not big," "I can't do that." As with questions, this is followed by a wider range of auxiliaries, such as "I can't do it." Thus, the emergence of a number of different forms and structures is noted.

There are certain conclusions that we can draw about children learning their first language. Throughout this book, we will return to these, as most are applicable in an L2 context as well.

- Children go through the same developmental stages, although not necessarily at the same rate.
- Children create systematicity in their language and develop rules to govern their language knowledge and language use.

- The rules that are developed do not necessarily correspond to the rules of the adult language.
- There is overgeneralization of grammatical morphemes.
- There are processing constraints that govern acquisition and use.
- Correction does not always work.
- Language acquisition is not determined by intelligence.

TIME TO THINK ...

You have just read about some basics of child language acquisition. Which of these findings do you think are relevant for child SLA? Which are relevant for adult SLA? For example, children might use one word to refer to many objects—*dog* for any animal. Is that an area of interest if one is studying older children or adults?

Of additional concern to those interested in SLA is research on child SLA, to which we turn next.

5.3 CHILD L2 ACQUISITION

It has long been recognized that child SLA is a central and important part of the field of SLA. In fact, the so-called modern period of SLA received much of its impetus from studies on child SLA.

We begin by noting that the boundaries of child SLA are somewhat arbitrary. Child SLA refers to "acquisition by individuals young enough to be within the **critical period**, but yet with a first language already learned" (Foster-Cohen, 1999, pp. 7 8), or "successive acquisition of two languages in childhood" (McLaughlin, 1978, p. 99). What is eliminated from this definition is simultaneous acquisition of two (or more) languages in childhood; this generally falls under the cover term of bilingualism (see Chapter 15). The question of what constitutes simultaneous acquisition versus sequential acquisition is not an easy one to answer. Even though the precise beginning and end points of the period of child SLA are vague, we surely can take as core to the topic the ages between five and nine, when the primary language is mostly settled and before the effects from a critical or **sensitive period** (see Chapter 14) begin to manifest themselves.

That much research on adult SLA had its impetus in child L2 studies was noted by Selinker et al. (1975), where it was argued that the IL hypothesis originally formulated for adult SLA could be extended to nonsimultaneous child SLA. There, it was shown that strategies of language transfer, simplification, and overgeneralization of TL rules affected the L2 production of the 7–8-year-old children in the French immersion program studied. It was hypothesized that what made a crucial difference to the cognitive processes of the children involved were the settings in which the L2 was being learned. Learner systems did not develop (and possibly even fossilized) in settings where there was an absence of native-speaking peers of the TL. Thus, the quality of the input to the learner was seen as a central variable in L2 outcomes.

Within these two overall contexts of the presence and absence of native-speaking peers of the TL, McLaughlin (1978) claimed that there is no language transfer in child SLA unless the child is isolated from peers of the TL, the latter being the classic immersion setting. The idea is that, if the child has TL peers, there is a greater social context, where the child learns the L2 rules as if the L2 were an L1, with no language transfer occurring. There are several interesting hypotheses that McLaughlin (1978, p. 117) discusses, one being the regression hypothesis, according to which the child uses the language skills used in L1 acquisition with L2 data, but "at a very primitive and rudimentary level" (see Ervin-Tripp, 1974). A second hypothesis, the recapitulation hypothesis, involves the child recapitulating the learning process of a native speaker of the TL. In other words, when a child learns an L2, she or he uses the same processes available to children of the TL (Milon, 1974; Ravem, 1968, 1974).

However, McLaughlin also noted what could be considered counterevidence to this. Referring to work by Wode (1976), he pointed out that, "children *occasionally* use first-language structures to solve the riddle of second-language structures" (McLaughlin, 1978, p. 117, emphasis added). In other words, in child SLA, a child is more likely to use L1 structures when confronted with difficult L2 structures.

McLaughlin argued that the same processes are involved in all language acquisition; language learning is language learning. What is involved is a unitary process. He concluded that "there is a unity of process that characterizes all language acquisition, whether of a first or second language, at all ages" (McLaughlin, 1978, p. 202). His claim was that both L1 and child L2 learners use the same strategies in learning a language.

A general issue that is often a matter of discussion in the scholarly and lay literature is whether it is true that younger is better. McLaughlin concluded that it is not. In general, children have better phonology, but older learners often achieve better L2 syntax (see also Long, 1990). As is to be expected, more recent empirical work has shown that the picture is even more complex. Rocca (2007) presents evidence that, like L1 learners and unlike adult L2 learners, child language learners display morphological sensitivity. However, like adult L2 learners and unlike L1 learners, child L2 learners are influenced by language transfer, where language transfer can involve grammatical and lexical prototypical links. Thus, the view that the earlier the better cannot be taken as an absolute. The question of age differences is dealt with in Chapter 14.

We now briefly look at two earlier studies in child SLA that have proven influential: Hakuta (1974a, 1974b) and Ravem (1968, 1974). To compare them, we will focus on their study of the development of question formation in English.

Hakuta (1974b) studied a Japanese child learning English in the United States. Data were collected over an 11-month period, beginning when the child was age 5 years 4 months. The data were mixed, including TL-like and non-TL-like forms. A sample of the data is presented in (5-4).

(5-4)   From Hakuta (1974b, pp. 293–294):

> How do you do it?
> Do you have coffee?
> Do you want this one?
> What do you doing, this boy?
> What do you do it, this, froggie?
> What do you doing?
> Do you bought too?
> Do you put it?
> How do you put it?

With regard to question formation, the longitudinal data show gradual progression. As indicated by the first three examples, it appears that this child understands question formation in English. However, as the child progressed in English, she seemed to carry over the phrase *do you* as a chunk or, to use Hakuta's phrase, a **prefabricated routine**, producing both grammatical and ungrammatical questions. *Do you* appears to function as a chunk with both present and past tense (irregular) forms as late as eight months into data collection. In about the sixth to eighth month, *did* appeared in the data: *Did you call?* and *Did everybody saw . . .?* In general, this child seemed to follow a progression in which question forms (*why, where, when*) entered her system differentially. The data appear to represent idiosyncratic IL forms, but, on closer examination, can be argued to represent a gradual progression toward the acquisition of English forms.

Ravem (1968, 1974) studied a Norwegian child learning English in the United Kingdom. Data were collected every 3–4 weeks over a 4-month period, beginning when the child was 6 years 6 months old. As in Hakuta's study, the data included both TL-like and non-TL-like forms. Examples are given in (5-5).

(5-5)   From Ravem (1968, 1974)

> What dyou reading to-yesterday?
> What they doing?
> Like you ice cream?
> Like you me not, Reidun?
> What dyou do to-yesterday?
> What dyou did to-yesterday in the hayshed?
> When dyou went there?
> What you did in Rothbury?

Early on, this child seemed to be forming questions using mostly a declarative sentence word order: "you reading," "she (is) doing." Inversion, as would be predicted from both the NL (Norwegian) and TL (English) grammars, was not used except in *yes/no* questions. Eventually, the correct pattern of inversion was acquired for all question types.

Comparing the two studies in this area of question formation, we find that, even at the earliest stages, neither of the two children seemed to be using a direct language-transfer strategy with *wh-* questions; that is, we do not see in the Japanese–English IL questions such forms as, "That, what is . . .?", "You, how like . . .?", which would reflect the Japanese pattern, or, in Norwegian–English questions, such forms as "What reading you?", "What doing she now?", which would reflect the Norwegian pattern. However, in *yes/no* questions, inversion seems to happen early. In the case of the Japanese child, the correct use of the auxiliary appeared with some *wh-* words before others; with the Norwegian child, inversion occurred in some questions (*yes/no*) but not in others (*wh-* questions). Hence, there is no uniform pattern of the acquisition of question formation. Regarding the acquisition of the auxiliary *do*, we see changes, with the Japanese child moving from apparently correct forms to incorrect forms and then to correct forms again. We return to the concept of change from correct to incorrect to correct in Chapter 10 in our discussion of U-shaped learning.

5.4 CHILD L2 MORPHEME ORDER STUDIES

Earlier we discussed the **morpheme order studies** conducted by Brown (1973) within the context of child language acquisition. These studies, in some sense, became the cornerstone of early work in SLA.

As noted in Chapter 4, work in the area of language transfer traditionally focused on the behavioral aspects of SLA. However, in the early 1970s, a series of studies called the morpheme order studies was highly influential in the development of the field of SLA. These studies were strongly based on the idea developed by Dulay and Burt (1974a, 1974b, 1975) that child SLA was similar to child L1 acquisition. This came to be known as the **L1 = L2 Hypothesis**.

Chomsky (1959) attacked Skinner's work on behaviorism, bringing to light that a behaviorist position with regard to language learning was untenable. Viewing the learner as an active participant in the learning process and as a language creator was essential. For SLA, doing so entailed throwing off the shackles of language transfer. That is, because transfer was strongly associated with behaviorist thought, a way of arguing that L2 learning was not a behaviorist-based activity was to argue that transfer was not a major, or even an important, factor in attempts to account for L2 learning.

In order to challenge the concept of transfer, studies were conducted to show the percentage of errors attributable to the NL (although it should be noted that NL-based errors at this time were conceptualized as translation equivalents), as opposed to more subtle varieties of error source. For example, George (1972) claimed that one third of the errors in his corpus were attributable to the NL; Dulay and Burt (1975) claimed that fewer than 5 percent were so attributable in their data. However, these quantitative accounts of language transfer seem less interesting than the ones we examine later, which attempt to elucidate which aspects of language phenomena are transferable and which are not. As Richards and Sampson (1974, p. 5) recognize:

It would however be almost impossible to assess the precise contribution of systemic language interference at this time. . . . A number of factors interact in determining the learner's approximative system. Until the role of some of these other factors is more clearly understood, it is not possible to evaluate the amount of systemic interference due to language transfer alone.

In Chapter 4, we dealt with the criticisms of contrastive analysis. Many of these criticisms were empirical (i.e., predictions were not accurate). However, the most serious challenge to the CAH was theoretical. As stated earlier, the morpheme order studies were a reaction to earlier work that advocated a transfer (hence, behaviorist) approach to the study of how L2s are learned. Approaching the question from a mentalist perspective, Dulay and Burt (1974a, p. 37) proposed the **Creative Construction Hypothesis**:

> the process in which children gradually reconstruct rules for speech they hear, guided by universal innate mechanisms which cause them to formulate certain types of hypotheses about the language system being acquired, until the mismatch between what they are exposed to and what they produce is resolved.

In this view, there are L2 strategies that are common to all children, regardless of their NL. Importantly, emphasis is placed on the centrality of mental processes and the innate propensity for language that all humans have. Given that innateness is at the core of acquisition, it is further assumed that children reconstruct L2s in similar ways, regardless of their NL or the language being learned. In other words, processes involved in acquisition are assumed to be the same. Because the goal of research within the creative construction tradition was to substantiate these assumptions, research in child language acquisition assumed importance, because, in L1 acquisition, the nonbehaviorist position was unquestionable. What gave the behaviorist view any credence was the concept of transfer.

In order to empirically verify the hypotheses underlying creative constructionism, the morpheme order studies emerged, based on work initially done in child language acquisition by Brown (1973). Dulay and Burt's (1974a) study applied Brown's findings to child SLA. They hypothesized that similar patterns of development would be found in child L1 acquisition and child SLA. These results would suggest a similarity in processes between L1 and L2 learning. Furthermore, perhaps more importantly, if similar patterns of development were found to occur between two groups of children with different language backgrounds, one could conclude that developmental factors rather than NL factors were in play, and that universal mechanisms for SLA had to be considered primary.

Dulay and Burt's data come from the results achieved by 60 Spanish and 55 Chinese children on a standardized test of English L2 known as the **Bilingual Syntax Measure (BSM)**. The BSM consists of seven colored pictures about which children are asked questions designed to elicit responses on the English grammatical morphemes given in Table 5.2 (see Figure 5.4 for an example from the BSM).

TABLE 5.2 Areas of Investigation from the Bilingual Syntax Measure

Pronoun case	He doesn't like him.
Article	In the fat guy's house
Singular form of *to be* (copula)	He's fat.
-ing	He's mopping.
Plural	windows, houses
Singular auxiliary	She's dancing.
Past—regular	He closed it.
Past—irregular	He stole it.
Possessive	the king's
Third person singular	He eats too much.

FIGURE 5.4 Bilingual Syntax Measure (BSM) (*Source*: ©1973 by NCS Pearson, Inc. Reproduced by permission. All rights reserved.)

Using the picture in Figure 5.4, the experimenter is asked to "Point to BOTH houses using whole hand to point," while asking "WHAT ARE THESE?" The anticipated response *houses* would show correct usage of the plural /s/. Another question requires the experimenter to point to the doors of both houses at once and say "AND THESE?" with the anticipated response again involving the plural.

The researchers determined all of the instances in which each of these morphemes is required in English and then determined an accuracy score for each child based

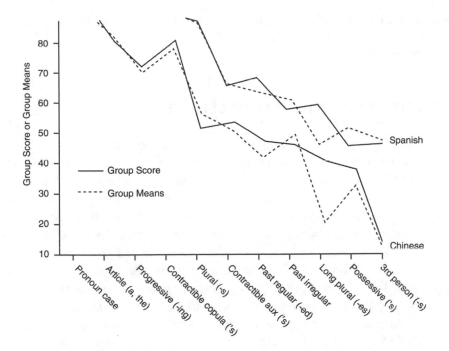

FIGURE 5.5 Comparison of L2 Sequences Obtained by the Group Score and the Group Means Methods (*Source*: From "Natural sequences in child second language acquisition" by H. Dulay & M. Burt, 1974a, *Language Learning*, 24, 37–53, by Research Club in Language Learning. Reprinted by permission.)

on a ratio of number correct/number required in English. In general, their results showed a similar pattern of development between the two groups of children (Spanish and Chinese), as can be seen in Figure 5.5, which includes two modes of scoring.

Had the results from the two groups differed, there would have been justification for attributing those differences to the NL. Because there were minimal differences, there was justification for attributing the similarity to universal developmental factors and for diminishing the significance of the role of the NL.

In Chapter 7 we deal with innatist approaches to SLA. In general terms, the main issue is the extent to which language acquisition (either first or second) is constrained by universal principles of language. Lakshmanan (1995) made the important point that, through research on child SLA (as opposed to adult SLA), we can obtain a better picture of the biological factors involved in SLA. For example, it would be interesting to find, as Lakshmanan claimed, that child SLA is constrained by universal principles, and that language transfer cannot be ruled out. If nothing else, this would suggest that such principles are available for at least some time after the acquisition of an L1. These issues will be revisited in later chapters. Despite the centrality of child SLA, there is a lack of detailed theory-driven work, as was noted by Foster-Cohen (1999), who pointed out that child SLA is a severely understudied area in relation to adult SLA, and an area wide open for research on many fronts. Recent work in SLA, however, does attempt to extend findings from adult L2 research to child language learners (e.g., Oliver, 1995, 1998, 2002; Mackey & Oliver, 2002; Oliver & Mackey, 2003; Philp & Duchesne, 2008).

5.5 ADULT L2 MORPHEME ORDER STUDIES

In the previous section, we discussed the work of Dulay and Burt (1973, 1974a, 1974b, 1975) on prepubescent children, which was important in its influence on moving the emphasis from a behaviorist view of language learning to a view of SLA that relied more on mental processes. It was not clear, however, whether the same findings would apply to the acquisition of an L2 by adults. Bailey et al. (1974) conducted an influential study to investigate precisely this issue. As with the Dulay and Burt study, there were two groups of learners, all learning English. The first group was comprised of 33 NSs of Spanish, and the second group, the non-Spanish group, was comprised of 40 NSs of a variety of languages (Greek, Persian, Italian, Turkish, Japanese, Chinese, Thai, Afghan, Hebrew, Arabic, and Vietnamese). The BSM was administered to these 73 adults. Results showed consistency with the results of the Dulay and Burt studies (Figure 5.6). Additionally, the two adult groups showed similar results, as is seen in Figure 5.7.

Thus, there appeared to be evidence for the lack of importance of NL influence. This being the case, the mentalist position embodied in Dulay and Burt's Creative Construction Hypothesis gained credence. On the basis of these studies, there was justification for positing a "natural order" of the acquisition of English morphemes.

Whereas the morpheme order studies did suggest a more or less invariant order, although far from rigid (see Krashen, 1977, for a review of such studies), there was

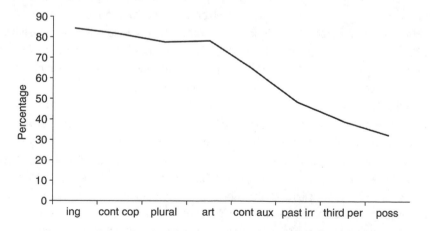

FIGURE 5.6 Relative Accuracy for Adult L2 Learners of English in Eight Functions (*Source*: Graph created from data appearing in "Is there 'a natural sequence' in adult second language learning?" by N. Bailey, C. Madden, & S. Krashen, 1974, *Language Learning*, 24, 235–243, by Research Club in Language Learning. Reprinted with permission.)

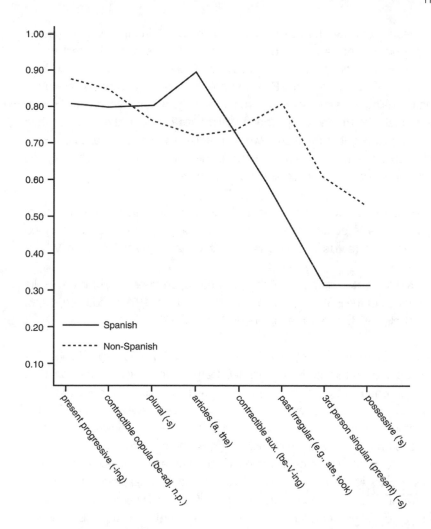

FIGURE 5.7 Comparison of Spanish and Non-Spanish Adults: Relative Accuracies for Eight Functions (*Source*: From "Is there a 'natural sequence' in adult second language learning?" by N. Bailey, C. Madden, & S. Krashen, 1974, *Language Learning*, 24, 235–243, by Research Club in Language Learning. Reprinted with permission.)

some evidence, even within these studies, of the role of the NL. For example, Larsen-Freeman (1975a, 1975b) found that NSs of Japanese (a language without an article system) learning English had lower accuracy scores on English articles than other groups. Additionally, Hakuta (1974a) found a different order of morpheme acquisition for a Japanese child learning English. In more recent years, Goldschneider and DeKeyser (2001) investigated the results from a range of studies, highlighting the role of saliency as a predictor of the order of English morphemes.

The morpheme order studies were not without problems, some of which are serious; others less so. Below, we list some of the common challenges to this body of research.

First, the results obtained may be an artifact of the BSM. In other words, the test itself may have biased the results, and any group of learners given this test would produce similar results. The most detailed study considering this problem came from Porter (1977). Porter administered the BSM to English-speaking children between the ages of 2 and 4, using the same scoring procedure as that found in one of Dulay and Burt's early studies (1973). The order of acquisition was closer to the L2 order than the L1 order, suggesting that the results were an artifact of the test measure, rather than a reflection of actual acquisition orders. However, this criticism may be unwarranted: two pieces of evidence are important here.

1. On closer inspection, we see that, depending on the accuracy of the method of "counting," there is actually little disagreement between the results obtained by Porter and the results of L1 studies (notably that of de Villiers & de Villiers, 1973).
2. Other L2 studies not using the BSM as a data-elicitation measure obtained results similar to those of the BSM (see Larsen-Freeman, 1975a, 1976; Andersen, 1976; Krashen et al., 1977; Krashen et al., 1978; Makino, 1979).

The second criticism concerns the Bailey et al. (1974) study specifically. The category *non-Spanish* in this study incorporated learners from such a wide variety of language backgrounds that whatever differences may have occurred owing to the L1 would be obliterated by such a large, disparate group (see review by Luk & Shirai, 2009). For example, some of the languages have article systems; some do not. Some of the languages have a rich system of morphology; others do not.

With regard to the morphemes themselves, morphemes with different meanings were categorized together. For example, from an acquisitional point of view, the English article system is more appropriately thought of as having separate morphemes (the indefinite article *a*, the definite article *the*, and nothing). This was discussed in Chapter 4 in connection with the data from Dušková (1983). Similarly, Andersen (1977) showed different behaviors of L2 learners with regard to the different English articles, suggesting that these morphemes should not have been grouped as a single grammatical structure.

A more serious criticism concerns the methodology itself. Do accuracy orders reflect developmental sequences? As we have pointed out in previous chapters, correct forms may not always signify acquisition of correct rule structures. Furthermore, considering whether or not a learner uses a form in its obligatory context in English misses those contexts in which it is not used in English, but in which the learner uses it. In other words, the total picture of a learner's use of a form is not taken into account. In particular, what is lacking are those instances in which learners have generalized a form to an inappropriate context. An example of this is given by Wagner-Gough and Hatch (1975) in their discussion of both the form and the function of linguistic elements in SLA. Their data came from a 5-year-old Iranian child. As with other children, he learned the *-ing* form earlier than other grammatical morphemes; in fact, his speech showed pervasive use of this form. However, the mere presence of *-ing* did not reflect acquisition. He used the progressive -*ing*, not only in appropriate contexts, but also in inappropriate ones. He used -*ing* when he intended to express:

(5-6) Immediate intentions:
I my coming. I my go my mother.
(= I'm going to come to you. I'm going to ask my mother.)

(5-7) Distant future:
I don't know Fred a my going, no go. I don't know coming, go.
(= I don't know if Fred is going or not. I don't know if he's coming or going.)

(5-8) Past events:
I'm find it.[3] Bobbie found one to me.
(= I found it. Bobbie found it for me.)

(5-9) Process-state:
Msty, Msty go in there. Hey Judy, Msty going in there.
(Msty is going in there. Hey Judy, Msty is going in there.)

(5-10) Imperative:
Okay, sit down over here! Sitting down like that!
(= Sit down over here! Sit down like that!)

Thus, given the method of counting correct use in obligatory contexts, the pervasive use of the progressive will yield correct forms in obligatory contexts. However, given the use in inappropriate contexts, it is difficult to maintain the argument that accuracy reflects acquisition.

Another criticism of the morpheme order studies is that there appears to be individual variation in learner data, and yet individual data are obscured with grouped data. The evidence for individual data was provided by Hakuta (1974a), whose study of one child suggested other than the natural order, and by Larsen-Freeman (1978), who, in analyzing her 1975 study, stated: "The results of this study showed individual variability and native language background to exert some influence on the way morphemes were ordered by language groups with a task" (p. 372).

The type of data elicited also appears to be problematic. Rosansky (1976) compared longitudinal and cross-sectional (grouped) data (see Chapter 3 for an elaboration of these terms) from six Spanish-speaking learners of English, finding that the two modes of analysis did not coincide (cf. Krashen, 1977, for a criticism of the Rosansky study).

Two final criticisms are noteworthy in that they reflect, not the studies themselves, but the conclusions that have been drawn from the studies.

First, the morpheme order studies investigated a limited number of grammatical morphemes (in general, 11 were considered). From these studies, researchers extended the implications to acquisition in general. Although it may be the case that there is a predicted order of the acquisition of English morphemes, it is not the case that all acquisition takes place in a predicted order, nor that there is justification to minimize the role of the NL.

Second, the major theoretical significance of the studies was to demonstrate that the NL was an insignificant influence and that behaviorism could not be maintained to account for the process of SLA. As a result of the diminishing importance of the NL, researchers believed that it could be argued that a cognitive view of the process of acquisition was the more appropriate theoretical stance to take. However, this line of argument attacks incorrect assumptions when it equates a behaviorist view of learning with the role of the NL. In other words, such an argument throws the proverbial baby out with the bathwater. It is more appropriate to question whether transfer is a habit-based phenomenon or not, because it is not inconceivable that one could adopt a cognitive view of SLA and maintain the significance of the NL. In fact, adopting a cognitive view and incorporating a strong role for the NL is the prevailing view in current SLA research.

In sum, the morpheme order studies have been, and continue to be, influential in our understanding of the nature of developmental sequences. However, it is not sufficient to posit an order without positing an explanation for that order. Although explanations have been forthcoming, they have, unfortunately, failed in their completeness. Part of the failure is due, once again, to the attempt to ascribe singular causality. Are morpheme orders due to perceptual saliency (e.g., -ing is easy to hear, -ed is not)? Are morpheme orders due to NL influences? Are they due to semantic factors, in that certain concepts may be semantically more complex than others? Are they due to syntactic complexity? Are they due to input frequency? The answer to all of these questions undoubtedly deserves a *yes* and a *no*. Long and Sato (1983) claimed that input frequency was the most likely explanatory factor, although they were quick to note that it was doubtful "that input frequency was the only factor likely to be involved" (p. 282). What is more realistic, yet subject to empirical verification, is that these factors all contribute to acquisition order. What is then left to be determined is the relative weighting each has. How do all of these factors converge to produce the particular orders obtained? (See Wei, 2000, for a theoretical perspective on the acquisition of morphemes within the context of SLA.) As mentioned earlier, clusters of determinants point to saliency as a major factor: perceptual salience, semantic complexity, morphophonological regularity, syntactic category, and frequency. Luk and Shirai (2009), however, in their investigation of English morphemes, find that Spanish NSs differ from NSs of Japanese, Chinese, and Korean in the order of acquisition, suggesting a role for the NL (see Chapter 6).

TIME TO THINK …

Think about what factors might explain morpheme acquisition order. What do you think are the most likely explanations? And why?

5.6 THE MONITOR MODEL

In the 1970s, an important theory of L2 learning was put forward on the basis of early morpheme order studies described above. It was known as the **Monitor Model** and consisted of five parts, described briefly below. It was developed in reaction to earlier behaviorist theories of SLA. Even though most of its parts have been discredited for lack of empirical evidence, it did represent an important change in thinking and, as such, represents an important milestone in the history of SLA.

5.6.1 The Acquisition-Learning Hypothesis

Krashen (1982) assumed that L2 learners have two independent means of developing knowledge of an L2: one way is through what he called *acquisition*, and the other is through *learning*:

> *acquisition* [is] a process similar, if not identical to the way children develop ability in their first language. Language acquisition is a subconscious process; language acquirers are not usually aware of the fact that they are acquiring language, but are only aware of the fact that they are using the language for communication. The result of language acquisition, acquired competence, is also subconscious. We are generally not consciously aware of the rules of the languages we have acquired. Instead, we have a "feel" for correctness. Grammatical sentences "sound" right, or "feel" right, and errors feel wrong, even if we do not consciously know what rule was violated. . . . In nontechnical terms, acquisition is "picking up" a language.
>
> The second way to develop competence in a second language is by language learning. We will use the term "learning" henceforth to refer to conscious knowledge of a second language, knowing the rules, being aware of them, and being able to talk about them. In nontechnical terms, learning is "knowing about" a language, known to most people as "grammar", or "rules". Some synonyms include formal knowledge of a language or explicit learning.
>
> (Krashen, 1982, p. 10)

In Krashen's view, not only does language development take place in two different ways, but learners also use the language developed through these two systems for different purposes. Thus, the knowledge acquired (in the nontechnical use of the term) through these means remains internalized differently. What is more, knowledge learned through one means (learning) cannot be internalized as knowledge of the other kind (namely, acquisition).[4]

How are these two knowledge types used differently? The acquired system is used to produce language. The acquisition system generates utterances because, in producing language, learners focus on meaning, *not* on form. The learned system serves as an "inspector" of the acquired system. It checks to ensure the correctness of the utterance against the knowledge in the learned system.

5.6.2 The Natural Order Hypothesis

According to this part of the Monitor Model, elements of language (or language rules) are acquired in a predictable order. The order is the same, regardless of whether or not instruction is involved. The "natural order" was determined by a synthesis of the results of the morpheme order studies and is a result of the acquired system, without interference from the learned system.

5.6.3 The Monitor Hypothesis

The Monitor is a construct central to Krashen's Monitor Model. The Monitor is related to the distinction discussed above between acquisition and learning. Recall that only the acquired system is responsible for initiating speech. The learned system has a special function—to serve as a monitor and, hence, to alter the output of the acquired system. Krashen presented a diagram of this event, as shown in Figure 5.8.

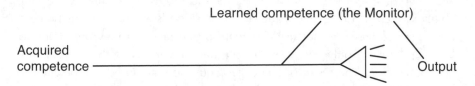

FIGURE 5.8 Acquisition and Learning in Second Language Production (*Source*: From *Principles and Practice in Second Language Acquisition* by S. Krashen, 1982, Pergamon. Reprinted by permission of the author.)

In Krashen's view, there are three conditions that must be met[5] for Monitor usage, although he claimed that, whereas these are *necessary* conditions, they are not necessarily *sufficient*, because the Monitor may not be activated, even when all three conditions have been satisfied. The three conditions for Monitor use are as follows:

1. **Time**: Learners need time to consciously think about and use the rules available to them in their learned system.
2. **Focus on form**: Although time may be basic, one must also be focused on form. Learners must be paying attention to how they are saying something, not just to what they are saying.
3. **Know the rule**: In order to apply a rule, one has to know it. In other words, one has to have an appropriate learned system in order to apply it.

The Monitor is intended to link the acquired and learned systems in a situation of language use. The Monitor consists of learned knowledge, and the only function of learned knowledge is to edit utterances. Following from this is the idea that the Monitor can only be used in production; it is useless in comprehension. How, then, do learners in a classroom setting ever comprehend the L2, as, for all intents and purposes, they have no acquired system? The following is an anecdote that describes how learned knowledge (if, by that, we mean conscious knowledge of rules) can be used in decoding:

> The other day while listening to the radio, I heard the announcer announce *wagunaa no kageki, kamigami no kasoware*. Knowing that *kageki* = "opera" and that *kami* = either "god" or "hair" or "paper," and knowing that there is a (fairly unproductive) rule in Japanese for pluralizing by reduplication, I concluded that *kamigami* must be the plural of *kami* "god," and that therefore *wagunaa* must be Wagner and *kasoware* must mean "twilight," and that I was in danger of hearing *Die Gotterdammerung*.
>
> (Gregg, 1984, pp. 82–83)

Gregg went on to report that he was using learned knowledge, not acquired knowledge, because he had never used the reduplication rule productively. As he explained, he used this rule consciously and quickly enough to turn off the radio in time not to have to listen to Wagner.

In addition to anecdotal evidence, which is clearly available to anyone who has used an L2, there are, once again, difficulties in terms of testability. As there are no absolute criteria for determining when the Monitor is in use and when it is not, any counterexample (such as non-Monitor use when there is a focus on form) can be countered with the argument that "there wasn't sufficient focus on form," or that mere focus on form is not a guarantee of Monitor use. In essence, with no way to determine whether it is in operation or not, there is no way to determine the validity of such strong claims. This is not to say that learners, or NSs, do not monitor their speech, for clearly this would not be accurate. (Self-correction is the result of monitoring.) The argument is against the theoretical notion of a monitor and its unique association with *learned* knowledge. We must thus distinguish between claiming anthropomorphic status for terms such as "the Monitor" and the psycholinguistic processes of monitoring.

5.6.4 The Input Hypothesis

In Krashen's view, the Input Hypothesis answers the basic question of how learning takes place. If there is a natural order, what mechanism exists to allow learners to move from one point to another? L2s are acquired "by understanding messages, or by receiving 'comprehensible input'" (Krashen, 1985, p. 2).

Krashen defined **comprehensible input** in a particular way. Essentially, comprehensible input is that bit of language that is heard/read and that is slightly ahead of a learner's current state of grammatical knowledge. Language containing structures a learner already knows essentially serves no purpose in acquisition. Similarly, language containing structures way ahead of a learner's current knowledge is not useful. A learner does not have the ability to "do" anything with those structures. Krashen defined a learner's current state of knowledge as i and the next stage as $i + 1$. Thus the input a learner is exposed to must be at the $i + 1$ level in order for it to be of use in terms of acquisition. "We move from *i*, our current level to *i* + 1, the next level along the natural order, by understanding input containing *i* + 1" (1985, p. 2).

Krashen assumed a **Language Acquisition Device (LAD)**, that is, an innate mental structure capable of handling both first and second language acquisition. The input activates this innate structure, but only input of a very specific kind (*i* + 1) will be useful in altering a learner's grammar.

In Krashen's view, the Input Hypothesis is central to all of acquisition and also has implications for the classroom:

1. Speaking is a result of acquisition and not its cause. Speech cannot be taught directly, but "emerges" on its own, as a result of building competence via comprehensible input.
2. If input is understood, and there is enough of it, the necessary grammar is automatically provided. The language teacher need not attempt deliberately to teach the next structure along the natural order—it will be provided in just the right quantities and automatically reviewed, if the student receives a sufficient amount of comprehensible input.

The teacher's main role, then, is to ensure that students receive comprehensible input. However, despite its attractiveness (and clearly no one would deny the importance and significance of input), there are numerous difficulties with the concept. First, the hypothesis itself is not specific as to how to define levels of knowledge. Thus, if we are to validate this hypothesis, we must know how to define a particular level (say level 1,340), so that we can know whether the input contains linguistic level 1,341, and, if so, whether the learner, as a result, moves to level 1,341. Krashen only stated that, "We acquire by understanding language that contains structure a bit beyond our current level of competence (*i* +1). This is done with the help of context or extralinguistic information" (1982, p. 21).

Second is the issue of quantity. Krashen states that there has to be sufficient quantity of the appropriate input. But what is sufficient quantity? How do we know whether the quantity is sufficient or not? One token, two tokens, 777 tokens? And, perhaps the quantity necessary for change depends on developmental level, or how ready the learner is to acquire a new form.

Third, how does extralinguistic information aid in actual acquisition, or internalization of a linguistic rule, if by *understanding* Krashen meant understanding at the level of meaning (see below and Chapter 16 for a different interpretation of understanding)? We may be able to understand something that is beyond our grammatical knowledge, but how does that translate into grammatical acquisition? As Gregg (1984, p. 88) stated: "I find it difficult to imagine extra-linguistic information that would enable one to 'acquire' the third person singular -*s*, or *yes/no* questions, or indirect object placement, or passivization."

As we will see in Chapter 12, input also figures prominently in emergentist accounts of SLA, where frequency of input is highly significant. Learners in this view are seen to extract regularities from the input, as opposed to regularities being imposed by **Universal Grammar (UG)**.

5.6.5 The Affective Filter Hypothesis

The phenomenon of affect and its relationship to L2 learning is well known and has been experienced by most language learners. One of the main concepts that appeared early in the L2 literature is what is known as the **Affective Filter**, which was intended to account in large part for why some people were able to learn L2s while others were not. As mentioned above, one way of accounting for nonlearning in Krashen's (1985) view was to claim that learners had not received comprehensible input in sufficient quantities; another would be to claim that an inappropriate affect was to blame. Affect, from Krashen's perspective, is intended to include factors such as motivation, attitude, self-confidence, and anxiety. Krashen proposed an Affective Filter. If the filter is up, input is prevented from passing through; if input is prevented from passing through, there can be no acquisition. If, on the other hand, the filter is down, or low, and if the input is comprehensible, the input will reach the acquisition device, and acquisition will take place. This is schematized in Figure 5.9.

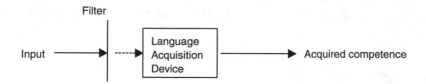

FIGURE 5.9 Operation of the Affective Filter (*Source*: From *Principles and Practice in Second Language Acquisition* by S. Krashen, 1982, Pergamon. Reprinted by permission of the author.)

According to Krashen, the Affective Filter is responsible for individual variation in SLA and differentiates child language acquisition from SLA, because the Affective Filter is not something children have/use.

The Affective Filter hypothesis captures the relationship between affective variables, on the one hand, and the process of SLA, on the other, by positing that learners vary with respect to the strength or level of their Affective Filters. Those whose attitudes are not optimal for SLA will not only tend to seek less input, but they will also have a high or strong Affective Filter—even if they understand the message, the input will not reach that part of the brain responsible for language acquisition, or the Language Acquisition Device. Those with attitudes more conducive to SLA will not only seek and obtain more input, they will also have a lower or weaker filter. They will be more open to the input, and it will strike "deeper" (Krashen, 1982, p. 31).

To summarize, according to Krashen, two conditions are necessary for acquisition: comprehensible input (in Krashen's technical sense) and a low or weak Affective Filter.

The Affective Filter, which shields the Language Acquisition Device from input necessary for acquisition, is what differentiates one individual from another; it is intended to explain why some learners learn and others do not. It is also intended to explain child–adult differences. The filter is not present (or, at least, not operative) in children, but is present in adults. But how does it work? Here, we are left without explanation. How is the input filtered out by an unmotivated learner? One of the functions of the filter noted by Dulay et al. (1982) is that it will determine what parts of the language will be attended to and in what order. However, a question to ask is: How can affect be selective in terms of grammatical structures?

Gregg (1984) gave the example of a Chinese NS with near-native-like knowledge of English. This speaker, however, had not acquired certain rules, such as third person singular -s. In Krashen's view, this incomplete knowledge of English would be due to the Affective Filter, but there is no explanation as to how the filter could let most of the input pass through and filter out third person singular.

The relationship between affect and SLA is not in doubt, but, in and of itself, it cannot explain how acquisition takes place or does not take place. The picture is, in actuality, far too complex.

Putting the parts of Krashen's model together, we can find difficulty in relating one part to another in a meaningful way. In general, the hypotheses are dependent on one another, and the arguments for one depend on the arguments for the others. For example, the Monitor is needed to account for discrepancies in the natural order; a Learning–Acquisition distinction is needed to justify the use of the Monitor. Thus, the argumentation is circular, rendering it vacuous.

TIME TO THINK ...

In what ways does the Monitor Model differ from earlier behaviorist explanations for L2 learning?

5.6.6 Limitations

Many of the limitations and criticisms have been dealt with above. A major limitation is the lack of emphasis on language production. Clearly, this is an important part of language learning, in that using language aids us in understanding what our own limitations are in terms of our knowledge of the L2. This will be taken up in greater detail in Chapter 12, when we deal explicitly with the role of output. In brief, Swain (1985) proposed the **Output Hypothesis**, which claimed that language use provides a forum for learning language other than mere practice of what has been learned.

5.7 CONCLUSION

In this chapter, we have dealt with the period in SLA history that formed a bridge between the early research in the field and what the field has become in the past three to four decades. In the following chapter, we return specifically to the role of the L1 in its more modern conceptualization.

POINTS TO REMEMBER

- The field of SLA has been closely tied to the field of child L1 acquisition since the beginning.

- Children all follow similar patterns in L1 acquisition, developing rule-based systems that are not necessarily affected by error correction.

- Child SLA refers to children who learn an L2 between the ages of five and nine, when the primary language is mostly settled, and before the effects from a critical or sensitive period.

- The L1 = L2 Hypothesis refers to the idea that child SLA is similar to child L1 acquisition.

- A mentalist approach to language acquisition posits that the processes of acquisition are the same, regardless of the NL or the language being learned.

- The Monitor Model marked a change in the field from behaviorist explanations for acquisition to a more innatist perspective. It consisted of five hypotheses: the Acquisition–Learning Hypothesis, the Natural Order Hypothesis, the Monitor Hypothesis, the Input Hypothesis, and the Affective Filter Hypothesis.

SUGGESTIONS FOR ADDITIONAL READING

Child language: Acquisition and development (2010). Matthew Saxton. Sage Publications Ltd.

Understanding child language acquisition (2010). David Singleton and Lisa Ryan. Hodder Arnold.

Childhood bilingualism: Research on infancy through school age (Child Language and Child Development) (2006). Peggy D. McCardle and Erika Hoff (Eds.). Multilingual Matters.

Child language: Acquisition and growth (2006). Barbara Lust. Cambridge University Press.

Understanding child language acquisition (2005). Paul Fletcher. Hodder Education Publishers. Hodder Arnold.

First language acquisition: The essential readings (Linguistics: The Essential Readings) (2004). Barbara Lust and Claire Foley (Eds.). Blackwell.

Language acquisition: The growth of grammar (2004). Maria Teresa Guasti. Bradford Books MIT Press.

The handbook of child language (2005). Paul Fletcher and Brian MacWhinney. Basil Blackwell.

The communicative competence of young children (1990). Susan Foster-Cohen. Longman.

MORE TO DO AND MORE TO THINK ABOUT ...

1. Watch the video in this YouTube excerpt (see Link #3 in the Links section at the end of the chapter).

   (a) Do you agree with your conclusion in the Time to Do . . . box in section 5.2.1?

   (b) Is "meaning" attached to what they are saying? Justify your response.

   (c) View the following video (see Link #4 in the Links section at the end of the chapter):
   — Do you think that this is a reasonable translation?
   — Create your own script of this exchange.

2. Give evidence that children's receptive skills precede their productive skills in L1 acquisition.

3. Which stages in the acquisition order of question formation from Table 5.1 do the following child question forms represent?

   (a) "Where we are going? Do you remember last time?"

   (b) "Daddy car?"

   (c) "I don't know where is the doggie."

   (d) "I have some?"

4. What can you hypothesize about a child's morphological acquisition based on the following statements?

   (a) "Grandma, I seed a lion at the zoo!"

   (b) "Gigi run fast!"

   (c) "Two cookie."

5. The following are parts of Krashen's various hypotheses. Respond to the following:

   Hypothesis 1: Do you agree that, because there may be a difference between learning in a classroom and acquisition outside a classroom, learners learn in two very distinct ways? A student once said: "If this is true and you have learned French in a classroom and go to France, then it won't help you." Is this a logical conclusion—that is, one that can be drawn from the distinction between acquisition and learning? Why or why not?

   Hypothesis 2: Do you agree that, if a learner tends to monitor his or her own form, doing so gets in the way of acquiring language? Integrate into your answer the concept of speed—that is, the idea that the monitor cannot be used at all times because of the speed of speech.

Hypothesis 3: Do you agree that one acquires all forms in a second language in a particular order, regardless of the input? Discuss this in terms of the three conditions of *time, focus on form,* and *know the rules.*

LINKS

1. http://tinyurl.com/4l8r4za

2. http://tinyurl.com/94pwrxg

3. http://tinyurl.com/4yquvpd

4. http://tinyurl.com/44eac2e

CHAPTER 6

Alternative Approaches to the Role of Previously Known Languages

6.1 REVISED PERSPECTIVES ON THE ROLE OF THE NATIVE LANGUAGE

As discussed earlier, the question of the NL was historically posed dichotomously. Is language transfer of major importance in forming ILs or is it not? This is evident in such statements as:

- "Language background did not have a significant effect on the way ESL learners order English morphemes" (Larsen-Freeman, 1978, p. 372).
- "Interference, or native to target language transfer, plays such a small role in language learning performance" (Whitman & Jackson, 1972, p. 40).
- "Direct interference from the mother tongue is not a useful assumption" (George, 1972, p. 45).

However, does the role of the NL have to be mechanical and uninteresting? Can there not be "selectivity" by learners in what is transferred and what is not transferred? If the latter question is answered in the affirmative, then transfer can be incorporated into a position consistent with a mentalist view of language. These topics are treated in this chapter.

During the mid to late 1970s those interested in SLA became less interested in a wholesale acceptance or rejection of the role of the NL. Rather, the emphasis was on the determination of *how* and *when* learners use their NL and on explanations for the phenomenon.

Most important in this discussion is the broadening and reconceptualization of language transfer and the concomitant examination of the terminology generally employed. Corder (1983, p. 86; 1992, p. 19) recognized the difficulty in continuing to use theory-laden terminology:

I have chosen the title of this paper deliberately, A Role for the Mother Tongue in Language Learning, because I do not wish to prejudice the nature of my discussion of that role by using the term "transfer" or even less by using the term "interference." I would like to hope that both these terms should be banned from use in our discussions unless carefully redefined. The fact is that they are both technical terms in a particular theory of learning, and unless one is adopting that particular theory in one's discussions, it is best to find other terms for any alternative theoretical position one may adopt. The danger of using such technical terms closely associated with particular theories is that they may perhaps quite unconsciously constrain one's freedom of thinking about the particular topic.

transfer/avoidance/ language loss (L1 or L2)/ rate of learning

It was for precisely these reasons that Kellerman and Sharwood Smith (1986) suggested the term **cross-linguistic influence**, which is sufficiently broad to include transfer, in the traditional sense, but also avoidance, language loss (whether of the L1 or of another L2), and rate of learning, all potentially conditioned by other languages that are known.

Beginning in the late 1970s, research on the role of the NL took on a different view, advocating a non-behaviorist position and questioning a close relationship between language transfer and behaviorism, instead taking on the position that transfer is part of a creative process.

That transfer was more appropriately viewed as something more than an involuntary hiccup that behaviorism implied could be seen in the work by Schachter (1974), in which she argued that there was avoidance of use based on facts of the native language, as discussed in Chapter 3. A second study, by Sjoholm (1976), further led to a rethinking and reconceptualization of the role of the NL. Sjoholm found that Finns (with Finnish as a dominant language) learning English made transfer-induced errors that could be traced to Swedish (their L2) rather than to Finnish. On the other hand, Swedish–Finnish bilinguals (with Swedish as their dominant language) made transfer-induced errors that were traceable to Swedish (their L1), not Finnish (their L2). Thus, it appeared that both groups relied more on Swedish than on Finnish. This is viable only if we take into account the learner's judgment, or perception, as to what is more likely to work in the L2.

A number of studies carried out in Finland, involving Finnish speakers learning English and Swedish speakers living in Finland also learning English, point to the advantage that the latter group has over the former group. This is attributed to the similarities that exist between Swedish and English and the lack of similarity between Finnish and English. As Ringbom (1987, p. 134) stated:

What emerges is a consistent difference in test results between groups which are very much the same culturally and educationally, but which have an entirely different linguistic starting point when they set out to learn English. One conclusion is that the importance of the L1 in L2-learning is absolutely fundamental.

TABLE 6.1 Participant Data from De Angelis (2005)

L1	L2 (n)
English	Spanish (37)
English	French (17)
Spanish	English (45)
Spanish	English and French (9)

As an explanation, he offered: "Similarities, both cross-linguistic and interlinguistic, function as pegs on which the learner can hang new information by making use of already existing knowledge, thereby facilitating learning."

This is further supported by more recent work, namely that by De Angelis (2005), who considered the acquisition of function and content words by first-year learners of Italian; the participant pool consisted of native speakers of Spanish and native speakers of English (see Table 6.1), who also knew other languages, as can be seen.

Each participant read a text (in either their Spanish L1 or English L1) and wrote a summary of that text in Italian. Typological similarity was an issue. The participants used function words from all languages they knew when there was typological similarity, as was the case with earlier studies, such as those by Ringbom. Particularly interesting are the results of native speakers of Spanish who also knew French. For them, both Spanish and French were perceived to be "useful" as they wrote in Italian, as evidenced by the fact that function words from both Spanish and French were used.

TIME TO THINK ...

Have you studied more than one L2? How did your knowledge of a previous L2 affect your acquisition of the L3? What things do you think transferred from your L2 into your L3, and what things from your L1 into your L3? Why do you think this might be?

6.1.1 Avoidance

It is clear that the NL may influence which structures a learner produces and which structures are not produced (i.e., avoidance). Evidence comes from work by Kleinmann (1977) in an investigation of Arabic speakers versus a group comprised of Spanish/Portuguese speakers (learning English) in the use of passives, present progressives, infinitive complements, and direct object pronouns. These four structures were predicted to be of differential difficulty for the learners, given the facts of their NLs. In addition to gathering production data, this study differed from Schachter's (1974) in that Kleinmann ascertained that the participants all "knew" the structures in question, at least from a comprehension perspective. Thus, the differential behavior between his groups could not be attributed to a lack of knowledge, but rather to some choice to use or not to use particular structures to express given concepts. The basis of the choice was related to the NL.

The source of avoidance is disputed. Whereas there is significant evidence that differences between the L1 and the L2 are the major source of avoidance, as was suggested in the preceding discussion, there is also evidence that the opposite occurs. That is, when great similarities exist between the L1 and the L2, the learner may doubt that these similarities are real. This is discussed below with particular reference to the work of Kellerman.

NL – TL differences (students avoids using new structures)

Still another view holds that avoidance has less to do with NL–TL differences, but rather is based on the complexity of the L2 structures in question. For example, in considering the acquisition of phrasal verbs (e.g., *come in*, *take away*, *lay aside*, *shut off*, *let down*, *mix up*), Dagut and Laufer (1985) found that Hebrew-speaking learners of English (Hebrew does not have phrasal verbs) in general preferred the one-word equivalent of the phrasal verbs (*enter*, *remove*, *save*, *stop*, *disappoint*, *confuse*). Within the category of phrasal verbs, they preferred those that are semantically more transparent (e.g., *come in*, *take away*) to those that are less transparent (*let down*, *mix up*). Thus, Dagut and Laufer concluded that the complexity of the TL structure had a greater impact on the issue of avoidance than did differences between the NL and the TL.

In a study of Dutch learners of English (Dutch, like English, has phrasal verbs), similar results were obtained by Hulstijn and Marchena (1989), who found differences between transparent and nontransparent phrasal verbs, but also found that learners did not accept phrasal verbs when there was close similarity between Dutch and English, most likely given their "disbelief" that another language could have a structure so similar to the "unusual" Dutch one.

Finally, in a study by Laufer and Eliasson (1993), there was an attempt to tease apart these variables. In their study of Swedish learners of English, attention was focused on the use or avoidance of English phrasal verbs (*pick up*, *put down*). Two tests (a multiple-choice test and a translation test) were given to advanced Swedish-speaking learners of English (Swedish is a language with phrasal verbs). The researchers considered whether the responses to (or translations of) Swedish phrasal verbs consisted of single-verb synonyms or English phrasal verbs. The results were compared with results from Hebrew-speaking learners of English (recall that Hebrew does not have phrasal verbs). Different types of phrasal verbs were considered,

TIME TO THINK ...

Are there certain structures that you avoid when using your L2? What are they? Do they exist in your L1? Is the avoidance due to differences between your L1 and your L2, or rather to the complexity of the L2 structure?

[handwritten margin note: Avoidance ? LI - L2 difference]

including figurative ones (e.g., *back up = support*, *turn up = arrive*) and literal ones (e.g., *come down = descend*, *put in = insert*). The researchers found that the best predictor of avoidance is the L1–L2 difference. Although L1–L2 similarity and inherent complexity (figurative versus literal phrasal verbs) have a role, the only factor that consistently predicts avoidance is the L1–L2 difference variable.

6.1.2 Differential Learning Rates

Ard and Homburg (1983, 1992) advocated a return to the original concepts embodied in the terminology of the psychology of learning. In particular, they viewed transfer as a facilitation of learning. They compared the responses of two groups of learners (Spanish and Arabic) to the vocabulary section of a standard test of English. Of major interest were the response patterns to different items. One would expect differences in response patterns to those items in which a Spanish word and an English word were cognates, as in the following example:

[handwritten margin note: Psychology viewed transfer as a facilitation of learning]

(6-1)   It was the first time I ever saw her *mute*.

    (a) shocked
    (b) crying
    (c) smiling
    (d) silent

but not to items in which all words were equally distant from the native languages of the learners, as in example (6-2):

(6-2)   The door swung slowly on its old _____.

    (a) fringes
    (b) braids
    (c) clips
    (d) hinges

[handwritten margin note: NL-TL similarities → help Language learners focus on other aspect of language (ex. vocab.)]

The Spanish learners did consistently better on this latter type of item than did the Arabic speakers. Ard and Homburg discussed this in light of learning time and, hence, accelerated learning rates. The Spanish speakers, because so many cognates exist between their NL and the TL, can focus more of their learning time on other aspects of language (in this case, other vocabulary items). It is the concentration on other vocabulary that results in a facilitation of learning. Thus, knowing a language that is related in some way to the TL can help in many ways, only some of which can be accounted for by the mechanical carryover of items and structures.

There is another perspective to be taken on the concept of differential learning rates. One such view was discussed in Chapter 4 with regard to Schumann's (1979) work on negation, where it was pointed out that a NL structure that corresponded to a TL developmental sequence was a factor in preventing learners from moving on to

[handwritten margin note: LEARNING RATE]

the next sequential stage. In other words, the internal system of the learner's L2 grammar exhibited delayed reorganization.

A similar view is adopted by Zobl (1982), who discussed the concepts of (a) delayed rule reorganization, or, in his words, "the pace with which a sequence is traversed" (p. 169), and (b) the number of structures in a given developmental sequence. With regard to pace of development, Zobl pointed to data from Henkes (1974) in which three children (French, Arabic, Spanish) were observed in their acquisition of English. A particular concern was the acquisition of the copula (the verb *to be*), a form present in French:

(6-3) Sa   maison   est   vieille.
      his   house   is   old

[handwritten note: don't have the copula "to be" → French take more time to learn.]

and in Spanish:

(6-4) Su   casa   es   vieja.
      his   house   is   old

but absent in Arabic:

(6-5) baytuhu   qadimun.
      house his   old
      "His house is old."

Consistent with the work of the time, and notably a diminution of the importance of the NL, Henkes attempted to show that, for the Arabic child, the lack of use of the English copula is not NL-related, as both of the other two children also failed to use the copula consistently. However, as Zobl pointed out, what is particularly interesting is the fact that, whereas the Arabic child continued to use the copula variably, even at a fairly advanced state of syntactic acquisition, the other two children regularly employed the copula at this stage. Thus, although the same pattern of copula use was observed in all three children, it took the Arabic child longer to get the facts of English sorted out, owing to the absence of the category in the NL.

6.1.3 Different Paths

The previous section dealt with rate of acquisition across a similar path. In many instances, however, paths of acquisition are not identical for speakers of all languages. Zobl (1982) compared the acquisition of the English definite article by a Chinese-speaking child and a Spanish-speaking child. With the Chinese-speaking child, early evidence of a form that appears to serve the function of a definitizer is the use of *this*. What is further noteworthy is that, when there is NS modeling of *this*, it tends to be retained in the child's speech, whereas, when there is a model of the definite article *the*, it is deleted or changed to *this* (see Table 6.2).

TABLE 6.2 Data from Chinese-speaking Learner of English (*Source*: From "A direction for contrastive analysis: The comparative study of developmental sequences" by H. Zobl, 1982, *TESOL Quarterly*, 16, pp. 169–183. Reprinted by permission.)

	NS	NNS
1.	Is this airplane your brother's?	*This airplane . . . Brent*
2.	Show me the airplane.	*Show me airplane?*
3.	Put it on the chair.	*Chair? This one?*
4.	Ask Jim "Where's the turtle?"	*Jim, where's turtle?*
5.	You want to push the pen.	*I want to push pen.* *Push, pencil*
6.	Is the table dirty?	*Yes, this is dirty.* *Table is dirty.*
7.	Whose bike is this?	*This . . . Edmond's.* *Mark, I want this bike.*
8.	What are you going to do with the paper?	*I want this paper school.*
9.	Ask Jim if he can play with the ball.	*Jim, can you play the ball?*
10.	Ask Jim if you can have the pencil.	*Jim, you want this pencil?*
11.	Is he washing the car? What is he doing?	*Washing car.*

On the other hand, from the beginning of data collection with the Spanish-speaking child, both *this* and *the* were frequent, as can be seen in Table 6.3.

Furthermore, when modeling of *the* occurred, there was not the same change to *this* as was seen with the Chinese-speaking child. Additional examples from the native Spanish-speaking child are given in Table 6.4.

The differences between these two children suggest that facts of their NLs led them down two different paths—the Chinese child through a stage in which *this* occurs before the definite article, and the Spanish child to a starting point in which the definite article and the demonstrative *this* co-occur.

A similar perspective comes from Wode (1977), who argued that there is a predictable order of structures and that certain developmental structures must be used by learners before the NL can be expected to have an influence on L2 production. He discussed the acquisition of English negation by German L1 children.

The first stage of negation, as we have already seen, is preverbal *no*, in which there is no evidence of NL influence.

(6-6) No cold.

(6-7) No play baseball.

TABLE 6.3 Data from Spanish-speaking Learner of English (*Source*: From "A direction for contrastive analysis: The comparative study of developmental sequences" by H. Zobl, 1982, *TESOL Quarterly*, 16, pp. 169–183. Reprinted by permission.)

1.	Hey hey this. Here the toy.
2.	The car.
3.	Lookit this. Lookit this cowboy. Here. This cowboy. Indians D'Indians. That d'Indians.
4.	This one . . . that truck. I gonna open that door. Get the car. Shut the door.
5.	The car. Same thing this car.

TABLE 6.4 Data From Spanish-speaking Learner of English (*Source*: From "A direction for contrastive analysis: The comparative study of developmental sequences" by H. Zobl, 1982, *TESOL Quarterly*, 16, pp. 169–183. Reprinted by permission.)

	NS	NNS
1.	Look.	*Lookit the little house.*
2.	You gonna draw the man?	*The man.*
3.	Guero, she wanna know what are you making.	*I make. I make it the blue.*
4.	Are you going to get me a cup?	*Where's the cup? Get the cup.*

Only at a later stage do the following sentences appear:

(6-8)   That's no right.

(6-9)   It's no Francisco.

At this stage of development, the child is able to see a similarity between German and English negation, because, in German, the negative morpheme appears after the verb *to be*.

(6-10) Es ist nicht wahr.
        it is not true

It is at this stage that these German-speaking children produce the sentences in 6-11 and 6-12, sentences that are clearly influenced by German, which forms negatives by placing the negative marker after the verb in main clauses:

(6-11) I'm steal not the base.

(6-12) Marylin like no sleepy.

Thus, learners must see some resemblance between the language they are learning and their native language before they are able to recognize that the NL might be "useful" to them. This can also be stated as the **Transfer to Somewhere Principle**, which we deal with in section 6.1.5.

6.1.4 Overproduction

Not only are there different paths of development, but we also find quantitatively different uses of forms, depending on the native language. For example, Schachter and Rutherford (1979) examined compositions written in English by Chinese and Japanese speakers. Both of these languages are of the type that relies heavily on the concept of topic. Sentences are organized around a topic–comment structure, as in 6-13:

(6-13) As for meat [topic], we don't eat it anymore [comment].

What Schachter and Rutherford found was an overproduction of sentences like the following:

(6-14) It is very unfortunate that . . .

and sentences with *there is* or *there are*:

(6-15) There is a small restaurant near my house in my country. Many things of the restaurant are like those . . .

They claimed that these structures were being used to carry the weight of a particular NL discourse function, even though the TL makes use of other forms for that same function. They hypothesized that the NL is at play here: There is an influence of NL function (the need to express topic–comment-type structures) to L2 form. Han (2000) further investigated this structure supporting earlier research, claiming that this structure, which she refers to as a *pseudo-passive*, becomes more like a target-like passive as learners become more syntactically sophisticated. She examined spontaneous writing of two Chinese learners of English (advanced proficiency), finding both a true passive and a structure that looks more like a topic–comment structure in the same writing, as is shown below.

(6-16) From Han (2000, p. 88):

They told me that the attractive offer will be sent to me a bit later since **what I sent to them have not received**.

1970 - Role of NL was put on
"when" and "under what
conditions" perspective
THE ROLE OF PREVIOUSLY KNOWN LANGUAGES

The first part of this sentence includes a target-like passive, whereas the second part, *what I sent to them* (topic) and *have not received* (comment) are more L1-like. What is noteworthy, however, is that the first part of the sentence may be somewhat formulaic and may have been used as a formulaic chunk from a letter the writer had received. Clearly, this example shows that the L1 exerts a subtle influence, even at later stages of proficiency.

6.1.5 Predictability/Selectivity

In the late 1970s, interest in the role of the NL shed its earlier dichotomous perspective and took on a *when* and *under what conditions* perspective. That is, the question was: Under what conditions does transfer take place?

Andersen (1983) developed the Transfer to Somewhere Principle, which stated that:

> A grammatical form or structure will occur consistently and to a significant extent in interlanguage as a result of transfer *if and only if* there already exists within the L2 input the potential for (mis-)generalization from the input to produce the same form or structure.
>
> (p. 178)

This proposal has limitations (for example, this is limited to syntax, and there is little possibility of disproving it, because the potential must be in the mind of the learner, and it is difficult to show that there was no potential), but it does contribute to the discussion in which the learner and his/her perceptions, rather than merely language, are at the center.

The notion underlying contrastive analysis—that similarities implied learning ease and that differences implied learning difficulty—proved to be invalid. Kleinmann (1977) suggested the opposite: When something in the L2 is very different from the L1, there is a novelty effect. In his study, this was the case with the progressive, which is absent in Arabic, and yet Arabic speakers learned this English structure early and well. It may be that the frequency of the progressive in English, along with its perceptual saliency, leads learners to notice that structure more easily than other structures.

TIME TO THINK ...

Kleinmann considered the novelty effect of the English progressive among native Arabic-speaking learners. What other structures can you think of in your NL that are not present in other languages you know. Did you notice a novelty effect? Was it important? Do you think it made it easier or more difficult to learn because of that?

Supporting evidence comes from Bardovi-Harlig (1987) who examined differences in the order of acquisition between sentences such as (6-17) and (6-18).

(6-17) Who did John give the book to?

(6-18) To whom did John give the book?

Theoretical considerations based on what is termed **markedness** (forms more common among the languages of the world are unmarked, whereas those less common are marked; see Chapter 7 for a detailed discussion of the concept) predict the acquisition of 6-18 before 6-17. However, the data show the reverse pattern: 6-17 is acquired before 6-18. Bardovi-Harlig identified salience as the main contributing factor to the unexpected outcome. In her terms, salience is defined as the availability of input. It is because there is a greater quantity of input for sentences such as 6-17, as opposed to 6-18, to which learners are exposed that the acquisition patterns are what they are.

The role of salience in SLA received greater support from Doughty (1991) in a study of relativization. She compared three groups of learners engaged in a computer-assisted language-learning project. The groups differed in the format of presentation of the language material. In addition to a control group, there were two experimental groups: a meaning-oriented treatment group and a rule-oriented treatment group. As the names suggest, in the latter group there were explicit metalinguistic statements about RCs, whereas, in the meaning-oriented treatment group, there were no such explicit statements. If it is correct that salience can come about through focusing a learner's attention on particular grammatical features, then one would expect that the rule-oriented treatment group would do better on a posttest than the other two groups. This was not the case: The two experimental groups improved more or less equally. However, a closer examination of the experimental materials brings us back to the question of salience and what it is that makes something salient. There are many ways in which increased salience can be brought about. Among these is frequency of input (possibly at both ends—that is, highly frequent and highly infrequent items/structures). Form-focused instruction is yet another (see Chapter 13 on instructed SLA). However, there is a caveat—studies cannot in absolute terms determine how externally manipulating salience impacts what happens in a learner's head.

Returning to Doughty's study, we see that both saliency and redundancy (i.e., frequency) were built into the tasks of the meaning-oriented treatment group. In the experimental material, this group saw reading passages with certain features, namely head nouns and RC markers, highlighted on the screen. Additionally, there was typographical capitalization of the juxtaposed head noun and RC marker, thereby visually making this part of the reading passage salient to the learner. Thus, if salience has an important role in SLA, Doughty's results (given her particular methodology) are what would be predicted, as both forms of pedagogical intervention focused on drawing learners' attention to RC formation. (We return to the concept of attention in Chapter 10.)

salience x Redundancy
⤷ frequency of use in L2
⤷ availability
of input of L2
THE ROLE OF PREVIOUSLY KNOWN LANGUAGES

Thus, as Kleinmann (1977) suggested, some L1–L2 differences may prove to be relatively "easy" to learn, owing to their saliency in the L2 input. In a similar vein, Ringbom (1987) pointed out that similarities may obscure for the learner the fact that there is something to learn. Oller and Ziahosseiny (1970) suggested that learning is "the most difficult where the most subtle distinctions are required either between the target and native language, or within the target language" (p. 186).

Both the Ringbom and the Oller and Ziahosseiny views are consistent with placing the learner (rather than just the learner's language) at the center. How the learner relates the first to the second language is of primary importance in understanding how L2 learning is affected by knowledge of the L1.

One of the most interesting proposals in the area of cross-linguistic influences was that made by Kellerman (1979). Fundamental to his view of the role of the NL is the learner's perception of the distance between the L1 and L2. The significance of this work, and other work of the time, is the attempt to place the study of transfer, or cross-linguistic influences, within a cognitive domain, thereby discrediting the implicit assumption of the necessary relationship between transfer and behaviorism. In this view, the learner is seen to be making decisions (albeit clearly not conscious decisions) about which forms and functions of the NL are appropriate candidates for use in the L2. The constraints on language transfer transcend the linguistic boundaries of similarity/dissimilarity between the NL and TL and encompass as a major variable the learner's decision-making processes relating to the potential transferability of linguistic elements. This is not to say that similarity/dissimilarity dimensions are irrelevant, for clearly this is not the case. Considerations of similarity/dissimilarity are central to a learner's decision-making processes.

If learners use the NL to make predictions about the TL, what is the basis on which these decisions are made? In Kellerman's framework, linguistic information is categorized along a continuum, ranging from language-neutral information to language-specific information. What is meant by this?

Language-neutral items are those items a learner believes are common across all languages (or at least the NL and TL). The accuracy of this belief is irrelevant, because what is of concern is how the learner views the situation. Language-neutral parts of language might include writing conventions, certain aspects of semantics, stylistics, and/or certain grammatical structures. It is reasonable to assume that, without prior knowledge, a prototypical speaker of English brings to a language-learning situation the belief that all languages use commas, periods, quotation marks, question marks, and so forth, in the same ways as they are used in English. Similarly, our same speaker of English is likely to believe that all languages are able to express the semantic concept embodied in (6-19):

(6-19) The ball rolled down the hill.

Our learner would probably begin with the assumption that learning to express this concept in an L2 only involves learning the specific lexical items and appropriate word order of the language being learned.

From the domain of syntax, there are also structures in an L2 to which learners most likely expect to find translation equivalents. Simple structures such as 6-20 are not likely to be considered structures that other languages do not have.

(6-20) The sky is blue.

At the other extreme of the continuum are language-specific items. These are elements that a learner views as unique to his or her language. Included in this category are a great deal of the syntactic structure of a language, much of the phonology of language, idioms, inflectional morphology, slang expressions, and collocations.

None of these categories is absolute. For example, idioms and collocations can be of different types, with some being more transparent than others. An idiom such as *kick the bucket* would most likely be considered language-specific by most people, given that the meaning of the composite cannot be easily determined from the meanings of the different words. Learners would not be expected to do a word-for-word translation of the idiom when using a second language. Thus, an English speaker learning Italian would be unlikely to say something like this:

(6-21) *Quel vecchio   ha dato   un calcio   al   secchio.
        that   old [man]   has given a kick   to the   bucket
        "That old man kicked the bucket."

On the other hand, a collocation such as *make a difference* appears to be more transparent in meaning; hence, our speaker might indeed be expected to say this:

(6-22) Quel libro   ha   fatto   una   differenza.
        that book   has   made   a   difference
        "That book made a difference."

The knowledge reflected in this continuum, representing how one views one's own NL in terms of **language-specific** versus **language-neutral** items, is known as a learner's **psychotypology**.

However, the language-specific/language-neutral continuum is not intended to be absolute. An additional, important variable is perceived language distance (presumably closely related to actual language distance). Languages that are closely related may influence learners in their beliefs about what is language-neutral and what is language-specific. For example, whereas we suggested earlier that phonology may be considered language-specific, this may only be the case for learners learning very dissimilar languages (e.g., Japanese speakers learning Polish). Spanish speakers learning Italian may consider all of their NL phonology as being the same as, or at least quite similar to, that of the TL phonology. Hence, in this learning situation, we would expect to find much more transfer. This is schematized in Figure 6.1.

	Close									Distant
Neutral	X	X	X	X	X	X	X	X	X	X
	X	X	X	X	X	X	X			
	X	X	X	X	X					
	X	X	X							
	X	X								
Specific	X									

FIGURE 6.1 Schematized Version of Kellerman's Model of Language Transfer

[handwritten margin notes: learner's perception of differences between L1 & L2 + learner's perception of organization of language-specific and neutral (language-specific and neutral)]

The *X*s in Figure 6.1 indicate the extent to which the NL is expected to influence the L2. What is crucial is that the degree of language closeness is based both on a learner's *perception* of the distance (not necessarily the actual language distance) between the languages and on the learner's perception of the organization of his/her NL (i.e., the extent to which parts of one's language are considered language neutral/language specific, and the extent to which the determination of language specificity is rigid or is susceptible to change, based on the perception of language distance).

TIME TO THINK ...

What types of problems could arise for learners of an L2 that they perceive to be very similar to the L1? In the example above of Spanish learners of Italian, what problems might such learners have with Italian phonology?

In an empirical study, Kellerman (1979) attempted to show how intuitions about NL semantic space are used to predict translatability of items (in this case, various meanings of a single lexical item), from which one can infer transferability.

To determine NL influences, he gave Dutch learners of English a list of Dutch sentences with various meanings of the word *breken* (to break; see Problem 1 in "More to Do and More to Think About . . ." at the end of the chapter), and asked them which of the translation equivalents they thought could be used in English.

What Kellerman found was that the concept of *coreness* was important. Coreness is determined by a combination of such factors as frequency, literalness, concreteness, and listing in a dictionary. In considering lexical items with multiple meanings, we can differentiate between core meanings and noncore meanings. Core meanings are those that are most frequently used (*He broke his leg, She broke his heart*), have literal meaning (*He broke his leg*), are concrete rather than abstract (*The cup broke*), and are listed first in a dictionary or are the first to come to mind. It is unlikely that any dictionary would give the meaning in *His voice broke when he was 13* as one of the first meanings of the verb *to break*. Similarly, a teacher, when asked to explain the meaning of *break* in class, is unlikely to use the sentence *The news story broke at six o'clock* as the first (or even any) attempt at definition.

[handwritten margin notes: coreness — most frequently used meaning, concrete and comes 1st in the dictionary]

	Close								Distant
Core	X	X	X	X	X	X	X	X	X
	X	X	X	X	X	X	X		
	X	X	X	X	X				
	X	X	X						
	X	X							
Non-core	X								

FIGURE 6.2 Revised Model of Language Transfer

Core meanings are likely to be equivalent to language-neutral items, whereas the noncore meanings are likely to be equivalent to language-specific items. What does this say for a theory of transfer? To answer this question, consider Figure 6.2, which is a revised version of Figure 6.1.

In probabilistic terms, we can predict where transfer will and will not occur. The greatest likelihood of transfer is in core elements, regardless of perceived distance. The second area of probable transfer is between languages perceived as close (e.g., Spanish/Italian, Dutch/German), regardless of the status of core versus noncore elements.

Placing the learner in the center of the determination of transfer also implies that these predictions are not absolute across time. It may be that a learner begins learning a language with the expectation of great similarity, only to find that there are more differences than originally anticipated. This would necessitate a revision in what was considered transferable. Conversely, a learner might begin the study of an L2 with the expectations of great differences, only to find that there are more similarities than originally anticipated. Hence, the categories of language-neutral (coreness) and language-specific (noncoreness) are variable, along with the perceived NL–TL distance.

In summary, there are three interacting factors in the determination of language transfer: (a) a learner's psychotypology, that is, how a learner organizes his or her NL; (b) perception of NL–TL distance; and (c) actual knowledge of the TL.

Transfer, then, is only predictable in a probabilistic sense. One can never predict, in any given situation, whether a learner will be influenced by the facts of the NL or not. In terms of falsifying this view, one must also think in probabilistic terms. What would count as counterevidence? Large numbers of learners going against the predictions of this learner-centered model of transfer would call into question its predictive value. A single occurrence would not. A single instance of a learner transferring a nonpredicted element—let's say, the idiom *kick the bucket*—would not serve to counter the validity of this model.

Recent work on language transfer has added new dimensions to our understanding of the concept, with notions such as "conceptual transfer" being introduced. This refers to the transfer of semantic concepts. Odlin, who in 1989 provided the first general summation of language-transfer studies, later (2005, 2008) considered research on linguistic relativity, as well as investigations of the transfer of concepts and meaning. In a study by Odlin and Alonso-Vázquez (2006), the evidence indicates that what is seemingly a present or past perfect verb phrase can have distinct meanings in the IL that vary considerably according to the learner's L1. French-speaking learners of English tend to overuse the English perfect in referring to past events (e.g., *I have gone to Rome last year*). In contrast, Turkish speakers often use the past perfect to refer to events that they have no direct knowledge of, as in *My friend had gone to Rome last year*, while the same learners use the simple past for events that they do have direct knowledge of, as in *I went to Rome last year*. The differences between the use of the perfect by French speakers and that by Turkish speakers reflect grammatical and conceptual meanings in their native language. Turkish systematically contrasts past events that a speaker knows of first hand from past events known only from inference or hearsay. This obligatory contrast in Turkish often finds its way into IL English verb phrases, as the French *passé composé* influences Francophones' choices of perfect forms. These studies show that the language-specific semantic and conceptual character of the L1 has important implications for our concept of language transfer that are only beginning to be understood.

Importantly, however, language transfer cannot be understood at all if concern is limited to two languages, the native and one target; one must also consider at least a third language to determine whether another language group without the feature in question also behaves similarly (this would eliminate transfer as an explanation) or differently (this would suggest transfer as an explanation).

6.1.6 L1 Influences in L2 Processing

As the field of SLA continues to develop, a greater emphasis has been placed on how learners process language. This area is discussed in greater detail in Chapter 10, but we include a brief discussion here as it relates to the role of the L1. Frenck-Mestre (2005) reviews studies that suggest different processing strategies between learners and NSs where the learners resemble NSs of the L1 rather than NSs of the L2. She analyzes the results of learners of French (NSs of Spanish and of English) processing sentences such as *Jean saw the daughter of the woman who was leaving the shop*. Each group of learners (English and Spanish) was divided into two levels of proficiency, depending on their length of residence in France. Spanish and French NSs each have a tendency to interpret *who was leaving the shop* as referring to the first noun phrase (*the daughter*), whereas English interprets the RC as referring to the second noun phrase, *the woman*. Beginning learners rely on their L1 processing strategies as they comprehend these sentences, whereas more advanced learners (the English learners of French) move to an L2 processing strategy and interpret the RC as referring to the first noun phrase. This suggests an important role for L1 processing when learners are confronted with the L2[1] (see also Clahsen & Felser, 2006a; Dussias & Sagarra, 2007; Witzel et al., 2009; and a review by Dussias, 2010).

In a series of three experiments, VanPatten and Keating (2007) investigated the acquisition of tense processing by L2 learners (English speakers learning Spanish). They found that learners begin with a universal processing principle that, in this case, was based on words that indicate time, such as *yesterday*, *last week*, and not on

TIME TO DO ...

Think about the sentence: *Jean saw the daughter of the woman who was leaving the shop.* Who was leaving the shop, the daughter or the woman? (Don't overthink it. Use your first intuition.) Now translate the sentence into another language that you know (either an L2 or, if you are not an NS of English, your L1). Who was leaving the shop, the daughter or the woman? Has your answer changed?

tense markings such as the *-ed* ending on verbs. Because NSs of English rely on time adverbs, whereas NSs of Spanish rely on tense markings, it appeared as if they were relying on L1 processing strategies. However, the situation is actually more complex because Spanish-speaking learners of English also rely on time adverbs. Hence, one can conclude that there is a strong preference for a strategy of time-adverb reliance. It is only in later stages of proficiency that appropriate L2 strategies are consistently used. It may be that, with more complex syntax, as in the case of the Frenck-Mestre studies, a greater reliance on the L1 may be found.

6.1.7 Morpheme Order

As was discussed earlier, the morpheme order studies were instrumental in attempts to minimize the role of the L1 by showing a more or less universal order of acquisition of English morphemes; this was known as the natural order and was supported by many (e.g., R. Ellis, 1994; Mitchell & Myles, 2004), years after the original formulation. It will be recalled that one of the criticisms of the morpheme studies is that there was not a careful examination of individual languages. Luk and Shirai (2009), however, rectified this in their analysis of English learning by speakers of Spanish, Japanese, Korean, and Chinese. What was found was that Spanish speakers followed what was predicted by the natural order, but the others did not. They generally acquired the plural *-s*, articles, and possessive *'s* later or earlier than would be predicted. This was attributed to the fact that the grammatical categories examined in their overview were absent in the NLs of those learners who did not follow the natural order. This strongly suggests a role for the NL, even in those areas (grammatical morphemes) hitherto believed to be impervious to NL influence.

6.2 CONCLUSION

In this chapter, we have dealt specifically with more recent views of the role of the NL. Throughout this book, we return to the issue of the NL and its role in L2 learning. Clearly, the NL is pervasive in all areas of learning, as has been shown in this chapter and as is seen in all domains of L2 study. For this reason, the issues surrounding this construct were introduced in this and preceding chapters and will be discussed throughout the chapters in this book (see, for example, Chapters 7 and 8).

POINTS TO REMEMBER

- The idea of transfer or interference became less associated with behaviorism in the late 1970s. Researchers began to realize that learners could have cross-linguistic influences from the L1 (or other L2s) when learning a new language, but still be actively creating their language, not simply imitating.

- L1–L2 difference can predict the amount of avoidance that learners show in using particular structures.

- L1–L2 similarities can result in differential learning rates, different learning paths, overproduction of L1-influenced forms, and predictability/selectivity.

- Saliency of a form in the L2 may lead to it being learned more quickly, regardless of whether it is present in the L1 or not. There are various ways in which saliency can be defined.

- Similarities between the L1 and L2, rather than being the easiest things to learn, may prove the most difficult, in particular when there are subtle distinctions between the two languages.

- Semantic and conceptual facts about the L1 can affect a learner's choice of forms in the L2; for example, French learners of English tend to overuse the present perfect in English for past events, because of the existence of the *passé composé* in French.

- Recent research into learners' processing of language has shown that the L1 can affect how learners process the L2.

- More recent research into the morpheme order studies has shown that not all learners follow the order, as previously thought. The L1 of the learner appears to make a difference in the order of morpheme acquisition that the learners follow.

SUGGESTIONS FOR ADDITIONAL READING

Cross-linguistic influences in the second language lexicon (2006). Janusz Arabski. Multilingual Matters.

Effects of the second language on the first (2003). Vivian Cook (Ed.). Multilingual Matters.

Cross-linguistic influence in third language acquisition: Psycholinguistic perspectives (2001). Jasone Cenoz, Britta Hufeisen, and Ulrike Jessner (Eds.). Multilingual Matters.

Foreign language and mother tongue (2000). Istvan Kecskés and Tunde Papp. Lawrence Erlbaum Associates.

Language transfer in language learning (1992). Susan Gass and Larry Selinker (Eds.). John Benjamins.

Language transfer (1989). Terence Odlin. Cambridge University Press.

The role of the first language in foreign language learning (1987). Håkan Ringbom. Multilingual Matters.

Cross-linguistic influence in second language acquisition (1986). Eric Kellerman and Michael Sharwood Smith (Eds.). Pergamon Press.

MORE TO DO AND MORE TO THINK ABOUT ...

1. The data that follow are from responses of 81 native speakers of Dutch who were learning English (data from Kellerman, 1979). Students were given each of the grammatical Dutch sentences in the first column (all with the word *breken*—"to break") and were asked to indicate if they believed that the English translation equivalents (in the second column) were grammatical in English. The degree to which they thought each sentence would be possible in English is given in the third column as a percentage of the 81 respondents who said it was grammatical.

Dutch Sentence (all are grammatical)	English Equivalent	% Responses Translatable
1. Welk land heeft de wapenstilstand . **gebroken**	Which country has broken the ceasefire?	28
2. Zij **brak** 't wereldrecord.	She broke the world record.	51
3. Zij **brak** zijn hart.	She broke his heart.	79
4. De golven **braken** op de rotsen.	The waves broke on the rock.	35
5. Hij **brak** zijn woord.	He broke his word.	60
6. Hij **brak** zijn been.	He broke his leg.	81
7. Het ondergrondse verzet werd **gebroken**.	The underground resistance was broken.	22
8. Dankzij 'n paar grapjes was 't ijs eindelijk **gebroken**.	Thanks to a few jokes, the ice was finally broken.	33
9. 'n Spelletje zou de middag enigszins **breken**.	A game would break up the afternoon a bit.	11
10. Zijn val werd door 'n boom **gebroken**.	His fall was broken by a tree.	17
11. 't Kopje **brak**.	The cup broke.	64
12. Nood **breekt** wet.	Necessity breaks law (a saying).	34
13. Sommige arbeiders hebben de staking **gebroken**.	Some workers have broken the strike.	9

Dutch Sentence (all are grammatical)	English Equivalent	% Responses Translatable
14. Na 't ongeluk is hij 'n **gebroken** man geworden.	After the accident, he was a broken man.	61
15. Zijn stem **brak** toen hij 13 was.	His voice broke when he was 13.	17
16. De man **brak** zijn eed.	The man broke his oath.	47
17. De lichtstralen **breken** in het water.	The light rays break (refract) in the water.	25

(a) Consider the percentage of sentences judged translatable in column 3. Order these sentences in terms of greater to lesser translatability of the Dutch word *breken*.

(b) Consider the English translation equivalents in column 2. Given the meanings of the Dutch sentences, what differences are there that might account for the varying degrees of translatability ascribed to them? For example, how do you account for 81 percent acceptance for item 6, 79 percent acceptance for item 3, but only 64 percent acceptance for item 11?

(c) How might your analysis predict the translatability of the equivalent of *break* in your native language or in another language you know?

2. Compare the Contrastive Analysis Hypothesis prediction of transfer with Kellerman's predictions. In what ways do they differ? In what ways are they similar?

3. The following data are from NSs of Czech learning English and Czech speakers learning Russian (Dušková, 1984). Column 1 (L2 English) represents unattested forms (indicated by *). In other words, Czech learners never produce plurals or past tense forms, as given in column 1.

As can be noted, there is widespread transfer of endings from Czech to Russian, but not from Czech to English. Why do you think this is so? Why should these facts be troublesome for an NL-based theory of SLA?

	L2 English	NS Czech	L2 Russian	NS Russian
Plural forms	*teacherele	ucitelé ucitelé	ucitele	ucitelja
	*workwomanici	delnice delnice	rabotnice	rabotnicy
Past tense	*arisenul	vznikl vzniknul	vozniknul	voznik
	*he dieel	umrel umrel	on umrel	on umer

4. Tape-record three different L2 speakers (with different NLs). Ask NSs of English to identify the NL of the speakers on the basis of the accent. Is it relatively easy? What made it easy or difficult for them to make the appropriate identification? Now take the compositions given in Problem 11 of Chapter 4. Can you make the appropriate identification? What made it easy or difficult for them to make the appropriate identification in this instance?

5. Consider the phenomenon of avoidance discussed in this chapter. It has been primarily investigated in the domain of syntax. Why do you think this emphasis has occurred? Can avoidance be as easily studied in phonology? In vocabulary? Why, or why not? How valid is it to attribute avoidance to lack of use? Could one conceptualize lack of use as not necessarily avoidance, but as *deliberate* choice of another structure? How could one empirically investigate this possibility?

CHAPTER SEVEN

Formal Approaches to SLA

[handwritten annotations:]
Independent Discipline with strong ties to other disciplines ⟶ sociocultural orientations

linguistic
focus: product of acquisition

psychology
focus: process by which learning system is created

sociolinguistics
focus: social factors that influence language system to be created and used.

7.1 INTRODUCTION

Linguistics has impacted research in SLA since the early days of the development of the field, with many linguistic theories having had some relevance. In this chapter, we deal with what are known as formal approaches. By this is meant an approach that takes language form as its subject matter. Specifically, the focus is on the learner's linguistic system (or competence). A formal linguistic theory is used to describe that system. There are a number of such theories that have attempted to do this, but L2 research has focused primarily on generative linguistic theory and, more specifically, on Universal Grammar, the most well-known of generative theories. Within formal approaches, areas such as pragmatics and other social constraints are not the focus of study. This does not mean that those working within this paradigm deny the importance of these areas; they are just not areas of focus. The main focus of attention in this chapter is on generative approaches to morphosyntax and on phonology; **typological universals** are discussed in Chapter 9.

As we stated in Chapter 1, the field of SLA, a relatively young discipline, has been influenced in its formation by other disciplines. In turn, SLA has also exerted influence on these source disciplines. At present, some would conceptualize SLA as an independent field, with its own research agenda and with a multidisciplinary focus, whereas others would conceptualize it as a subdiscipline of one source discipline or another. It is our view that, because SLA has a substantial body of research and a strong research tradition, it is best thought of as an independent discipline, with strong ties to other disciplines.

In this and Chapters 9–11, we focus on three areas in which the SLA relationship with other academic disciplines has been most heavily felt: linguistics (this chapter and Chapter 9), psychology (Chapter 10), and sociolinguistics, broadly construed to include sociocultural orientations (Chapter 11). This is not to say that these are the only areas with which SLA has strong ties. Rather, they are selected as representative. We focus generally on the influence on SLA from these disciplines, but in a few places we discuss what influence SLA has, or can have, in the other direction. With regard to the influence each of these fields has on SLA, the difference can be found in the general emphasis: linguistics focuses on the products of acquisition (i.e., a description of the linguistic systems of L2 learners), psychology focuses on the process by which those systems are created (e.g., a description of the way in which learners create learner systems), and sociolinguistics focuses on social factors that influence the acquisition of the linguistic system and the use of that system. However, one feature all areas share when considering SLA is a concern with the essential learning problem: how is it that learners acquire, when they do, the complexities of an L2?

This chapter deals with nativist approaches to language, which claim that at least some aspects of language learning involve innateness. Within this general category, two main positions are noted: **general nativism** and **special nativism.** The general-nativist position (see Eckman, 1996; Hamilton, 1996; O'Grady, 1996, 2005; Wolfe-Quintero, 1996) maintains that there is no specific mechanism designed for language learning. Rather, "there are general principles of learning that are not particular to language learning but may be employed in other types of learning" (Eckman, 1996, p. 398). Special nativism includes theories of language (learning) that posit special principles for language learning, principles that are unique to language (learning) and that are not used in other cognitive endeavors. Both the general-nativist and special-nativist positions agree that there is something innate involved in language learning, but it is the nature of the innate system that is in question: Is it available only for the task of language learning, or is it also available for more general learning tasks? This chapter treats only the special-nativist approach, known as UG, given its pervasiveness over the years.

7.2 UNIVERSAL GRAMMAR

The UG approach to SLA begins from the perspective of learnability. The assumption of innate universal language properties is motivated by the need to explain the uniformly successful and speedy acquisition of language by children, in spite of insufficient input. This is known as the Logical Problem of acquisition.

In UG theory, universal principles form part of the mental representation of language, and it is this mental grammar that mediates between the sound and meaning of language. Properties of the human mind are what make language universals the way they are. As Chomsky (1995, p. 167) noted: "The theory of a particular language is its *grammar*. The theory of languages and the expressions they generate is *Universal Grammar* (UG); UG is a theory of the **initial state** S_o of the relevant component of the language faculty." The assumption that UG is the guiding force of child language acquisition has long been maintained by many; it is now commonplace to apply it to SLA. After all, if properties of human language are part of the mental representation of language, one can safely assume that they do not cease being properties in just those instances in which a nonnative language system is being employed.

160

universal
requirement
(e.g. everyone drives on
↑ the same
side)

specific variations
(e.g. some countries chose
right and some chose
left)

FORMAL APPROACHES TO SLA

The theory underlying UG assumes that language consists of a set of abstract principles that characterize core grammars of all natural languages. In addition to principles that are invariable (i.e., all languages have them) are parameters that vary across languages. Cook (1997, pp. 250–251) made an interesting analogy between driving a car and principles and parameters:

> Overall there is a principle that drivers have to keep consistently to one side of the road, which is taken for granted by all drivers in all countries.[1] Exceptions to this principle, such as people driving down motorways on the wrong side, rate stories in the media or car chases in action movies. The principle does not, however, say, *which* side of the road people should drive on. A parameter of driving allows the side to be the left in England and Japan, and the right in the USA and France. The parameter has two values or "settings"—left and right. Once a country has opted for one side or the other, it sticks to its choice: a change of setting is a massively complex operation, whether it happens for a whole country, as in Sweden, or for the individual travelling from England to France. So, a universal principle and a variable parameter together sum up the essence of driving. The principle states the universal requirement on driving; the parameter specifies the variation between countries.

TIME TO THINK ... UG → *innate language facility that limits the extent to which languages can vary.*
→ why? → kids "know" things that were never taught.

Using the analogy of driving on one side of the road or another, brainstorm some possible principles that all languages follow and give examples of the way parameters for different languages vary for these particular principles.

How does UG relate to language acquisition? If children have to learn a complex set of abstractions, there must be something other than the language input to which they are exposed that enables them to learn language with relative ease and speed. UG is postulated as an innate language facility that limits the extent to which languages can vary. That is, it specifies the limits of a possible language. The task for learning is greatly reduced if one is equipped with an innate mechanism that constrains possible grammar formation. Before relating the question of UG to SLA, we turn briefly to issues from child language acquisition to explain the basic argumentation of this theory.

The theoretical need for an innate language faculty is based on a negative argument. The claim is that, on the basis of language input alone, children cannot attain the complexities of adult grammars. Innate linguistic properties fill in where the input fails. What does it mean to say that the input is insufficient? It is not merely an antibehaviorist notion that argues against an input/output scheme. Rather, it is based on the fact that children come to know certain properties of grammar that are not obviously learnable from input, as illustrated by the following examples from English discussed by White (1989):

(7-1)   I want to go.

(7-2)   I wanna go.

(7-3)   John wants to go but we don't want to.

(7-4)   John wants to go but we don't wanna.

(7-5)   Do you want to look at the chickens?

(7-6)   Do you wanna look at the chickens?

(7-7)   Who do you want to see?

(7-8)   Who do you wanna see?

Examples 7-1–7-8 show the range of possibilities for changing *want to* to *wanna*. However, there are many times in English where the sequence *want to* cannot be replaced by the informal *wanna*, as in 7-9–7-12:

(7-9)   Who do you want to feed the dog?

(7-10) *Who do you wanna feed the dog?

(7-11) Who do you want to win the race?

(7-12) *Who do you wanna win the race?

Without prior information to guide learners, it would be difficult to determine the correct distribution of *want to* versus *wanna* in informal English. The input does not provide sufficiently specific information about where to use *wanna* and where not to use it. White explained that there are principles of UG involving question formation to account for the distribution of these English forms. Briefly, sentence 7-7 can be represented by something like *You want to see X*, and 7-9 by something like *You want X to feed the dog*. Note the location of *X*, the element about which a question is being asked. In 7-9, but not in 7-7, the question is about an element (*X*) that is placed between *want* and *to*. This is what effectively blocks contraction. In 7-7, *want* and *to* are adjacent, thereby allowing contraction; that is, no intervening element blocks it. Importantly, the input alone does not provide this information. This argument is called the **Poverty of the Stimulus**.

One could, of course, argue that direct or indirect intervention is indeed forthcoming, and that one does not need innateness to explain language acquisition. However, in most instances, the language-learning environment does not provide information to the child concerning the well-formedness of an utterance (Chomsky, 1981, 1986); even when it does, it provides information only about the ungrammatical (or inappropriate) utterance, and not about what needs to be done to modify a current hypothesis. Furthermore, as we saw in Chapter 5 (section 5.2), even with explicit correction, children's grammars are often impervious to change.

[handwritten margin notes: "informs learner that his/her utterance is deviant with regard to the norms of the language learned." — "e.g. 'that's not right' or 'what did you say?'" — "sentences in a language that provide input for learner"]

Theoretically, there are two kinds of evidence available to learners as they make hypotheses about correct and incorrect language forms: **positive evidence** and **negative evidence**.[2] Positive evidence comes from the speech learners hear/read and thus is composed of a limited set of well-formed utterances of the language being learned. When a particular sentence type is not heard, one does not know whether it is not heard because of its impossibility in the language or because of mere coincidence. It is in this sense that the sentences of a language that provide the input to the learner are known as positive evidence. It is on the basis of positive evidence that linguistic hypotheses can be made. Negative evidence, on the other hand, is composed of information to a learner that his or her utterance is deviant with regard to the norms of the language being learned. We provide more detail on this in Chapter 12. For now, suffice it to say that negative evidence can take many forms, including direct correction, such as *That's not right*, or more subtle corrections, such as *What did you say?*

The child language literature suggests that negative evidence is not frequent (see Brown & Hanlon, 1970, and the theoretical arguments by Baker, 1979), is often ignored, and can therefore not be a necessary condition for acquisition. Because positive evidence alone cannot delineate the range of possible and impossible sentences, and because negative evidence is not frequently forthcoming, there must be innate principles that constrain a priori the possibilities of grammar formation.

TIME TO THINK ...

If we think about young children, we recognize that negative evidence is, in fact, available in some form, namely, when adults rephrase children's ill-formed utterances. Does the availability of such feedback in fact solve the logical problem of language acquisition? Why, or why not?

In sum, UG is "the system of principles, conditions, and rules that are elements or properties of all human languages" (Chomsky, 1975, p. 29). It "is taken to be a characterization of the child's prelinguistic state" (Chomsky, 1981, p. 7). Thus, the necessity of positing an innate language faculty is due to the inadequate input, in terms of quantity and quality, to which a learner is exposed. Learning is mediated by UG and by the L1, as we will see below. *[handwritten margin notes: "Universal Grammar" and "Language Learning is mediated by UG + L1."]*

How does this relate to SLA? The question is generally posed as an access-to-UG problem. Does the innate language faculty that children use in constructing their NL grammars remain operative in SLA? More recently, this question has been formulated as an issue of initial state: What do L2 learners start with?

7.2.1 Initial State

The question posed in this section is: What is the nature of the linguistic knowledge with which learners begin the SLA process? That is, what is the unconscious linguistic

[margin notes, handwritten:]
child language acquisition ≠ adult language learning

innate language faculty (constrains grammars of L2 learners and L1 learners)

knowledge that learners have before receiving L2 input, or, to take a variant of the question, what are early L2 grammars like? The two variables influencing this debate are transfer (i.e., the availability of the L1 grammar) and access to UG (i.e., the extent to which UG is available).

Two broad views are discussed here: the **Fundamental Difference Hypothesis (FDH)** (Schachter 1988; Bley-Vroman, 1989, 2009), which argues that what happens in child language acquisition is not the same as what happens in adult SLA, and the **Access to UG Hypothesis**, which argues that the innate language faculty is alive and well in SLA and constrains the grammars of L2 learners as it does the grammars of child L1 learners. We take a look at each of these positions, the latter in actuality being made up of several branches.

[margin notes, handwritten:]
– L2 learners don't have access to UG / construct grammar based on NL
– what they know about UG is influenced by NL
– L2 have a language system formed

7.2.1.1 Fundamental Difference Hypothesis

As was seen in Chapters 4 and 5, much of the work in SLA was driven by the notion that L1 and L2 acquisition involve the same processes. This is not to say that differences were not noted; rather, proposals to account for these differences were made, with an attempt to salvage the major theoretical claim of L1 and L2 similarities.

The FDH, as originally formulated (Bley-Vroman, 1989), starts from the belief that, with regard to language learning, children and adults are different in many important ways. For example, the ultimate attainment reached by children and adults differs. In normal situations, children always reach a state of "complete" knowledge of their native language. In SLA (at least, adult SLA), not only is "complete" knowledge not always attained, it is rarely, if ever, attained. Fossilization, representing a non-TL stage, is frequently observed (Han, 2004; Long, 2007).

Another difference concerns the nature of the knowledge that these two groups of learners have at the outset of language learning. L2 learners have at their command knowledge of a full linguistic system. They do not have to learn what language is all about, at the same time that they are learning a specific language. For example, at the level of performance, adults know that there are social reasons for using different language varieties.[3] What they have to learn in acquiring an L2 system is the specific language forms that may be used in a given social setting. Children, on the other hand, have to learn, not only the appropriate language forms, but also that there are different forms to be used in different contexts.

Related to the idea that adults have complete knowledge of a language system is the notion of equipotentiality, expressed by Schachter (1988). She pointed out that children are capable of learning *any* language. Given exposure to the data of a language (i.e., the input), a child will learn that language. No language is easier to learn than another; all languages are equally learnable by all children. This is not the case with L2 learners. Spanish speakers have less difficulty learning Italian than they do Japanese. If language relatedness (perceived or actual) were not a determining factor in ultimate success, we would expect all learners to be equally able to learn any L2. This is not borne out by the facts.

One final difference to mention is that of motivation and attitude toward the TL and TL community (see Chapter 14 for a fuller discussion). It is clear that, as in any learning situation, not all humans are equally motivated to learn languages, nor are they equally motivated to learn a specific language. Differential motivation does not appear to impact a child's success or lack of success in learning language. All human beings without cognitive impairment learn an L1.

In sum, the basic claim of the original FDH was that adult L2 learners do not have access to UG (see section 7.4 for a discussion of the revised version of this hypothesis). Rather, what they know of language universals is constructed through their NL. In addition to the NL, which mediates access to UG, L2 learners make use of their general problem-solving abilities. L2 learners come to the language-learning situation knowing that a language contains an infinite number of sentences; that they are capable of understanding sentences they have never heard before; and that a language has rules of syntax, rules of combining morphemes, limits on possible sounds, and so forth. With specific regard to syntax, learners know that languages can form questions, and that the syntax of questions is syntactically related to the syntax of statements. They know that languages have a way of modifying nouns, either through adjectives or RCs.

This information is gleaned by means of knowing that the NL is this way and by assuming that these facts are a part of the general character of language, rather than a part of the specific nature of the native language. Thus, the learner constructs a pseudo-UG, based on what is known of the NL. It is in this sense that the NL mediates knowledge of UG for L2 learners. The FDH has been significantly revised; these revisions are dealt with in section 7.4.

[handwritten margin note: L2 learning: 1. full transfer/full access 2. minimal trees 3. Initial hypothesis of syntax 4. full access (no transfer)]

7.2.1.2 Access to UG Hypothesis

The opposing view to the FDH is the Access to UG Hypothesis. The common perspective is that, "UG is constant (that is, unchanged as a result of L1 acquisition); UG is distinct from the learner's L1 grammar; UG constrains the L2 learner's interlanguage grammars" (White, 2003, p. 60). White (2003) outlines five positions (only four of which are dealt with here) with regard to the initial state of L2 learning: the first two take the L1 as the basis of the initial state, and the second two take UG as the initial state: (1) **Full Transfer/Full Access**, (2) **Minimal Trees**, (3) **Initial Hypothesis of Syntax**, and (4) **Full Access (without transfer)**.

Before beginning the discussion of access to UG, it is important to make one further distinction and that is between lexical and **functional categories**. In addition to principles, part of the innate language component consists of lexical and functional categories. Lexical categories are the categories that we learn about in school: nouns, adjectives, verbs, adverbs, and so forth. These are referred to as content words. Functional categories, on the other hand, are words that serve particular functions (e.g., articles, possessives), or they may be categories consisting of grammatical morphemes (e.g., plurals, tense markers). Functional categories can be thought of as grammatical elements that, in a sense, form the glue of a sentence. Examples of functional categories are determiners (e.g., *a, the, our, my, this*), complementizers

Functional
Category:
↳ fixed set
of words in
a language.

Lexical
Category:
↳ can be
added/mo-
dify words
as needed
(can create
new words:
e.g. dotcom).

(e.g., *if*, *whether*, *that*), and grammatical markers (past tense endings, case markings, plural endings, and gender marking). These differ from lexical categories in a number of ways. In general, functional categories represent a fixed set of words in a language, whereas lexical categories can be added to as the need arises (consider the recent addition to the English lexicon of the word *dotcom*, as in *dotcom industry* or in the recent *Time* magazine headline, "Doom Stalks the Dotcoms").[4]

TIME TO THINK ...

What other examples of recent lexical-category additions to English can you think of besides dotcom? And in another language that you know?

However, the most important distinction has to do with whether or not a class of words is associated with lexical properties. Prepositions, for example, though typically having the functional category characteristic of a fixed set of words in a language, are best thought of as a part of the lexical category. This is so because prepositions are often associated with such roles as agent (who does what to whom), patient (who is the recipient of the action), and location. For example, in English, the preposition *by* can be associated with an agent in passive sentences (*John was kissed by Mary*), and the preposition *in* can take on the role of location (*John was kissed in the park*).

Prepositions can often provide important cultural information, as well. An example is the Italian preposition *in*, which behaves like a functional category at times: for example, *in* occurs before countries—*in Italia*—versus the preposition *a*, which occurs before cities—*a Roma*. However, when Italians get married, they have to register their marriage at the local city hall, and the woman, while keeping her original name, is officially listed as *XY in Z*, where *Z* is the husband's family name. So, when Maria Caruso marries Carlo Pavarotti, her official name becomes: *Maria Caruso in Pavarotti*, with the preposition *in*, in this case, taking on great cultural meaning.[5] Maybe this mixed character is why prepositions are so difficult to learn, as we noted in the IL data set of section 2.1.3, and why they are a problem for any characterization of UG.[6]

Much research that addresses the question of SLA from a formal approach has changed the focus from parameter-resetting to acquisition of formal features of the L2. This is a reflection of the field, in that more recent configurations of UG consider parameters to be housed in specific formal features. The learner is seen to map features from the L1 in a new way in the L2. There is currently debate over whether features that are not represented in the L1 can ever be truly acquired in the L2. For example, if a learner of a language with grammatical gender comes from an L1 in which there is no grammatical gender, will that learner be able to acquire grammatical gender in the L2 in a native-like way? The question is complicated by the fact that learners are likely to produce different kinds of errors in their marking of grammatical gender, including errors with lexical, syntactic, morphological, and/or processing sources (Spinner & Juffs, 2008).

learners
map features
from L1 to L2

A question for acquisition is: are functional categories available at early stages? Or, is most learning at that stage purely lexical? A second issue is whether functional features are available at all in L2 learning. In some views, the only features and categories available to L2 learners are those that are present in their L1. Those features not in the L1 are not acquirable, leaving L2 learners with non-target-like syntactic representations. This is known as the **Representational Deficit Hypothesis** (see Hawkins, 2003), although there are different names given to this particular approach, namely, the **Failed Functional Features Hypothesis** (Hawkins & Chan, 1997).[7] A different position is what is known as the **Missing Surface Inflectional Hypothesis** (Prévost & White, 2000).[8] The claim is that there is no representational (i.e., syntactic) deficit, but the issue is one of difficulty of mapping intact representations (not representations with deficits) onto the surface morphology of the L2. In other words, there are no underlying representational deficits. This latter position is often accompanied by what is known as the **Prosodic Transfer Hypothesis** (Goad et al., 2003). In this view, one of the reasons that learners do not acquire L2 morphology is because of the transfer of L1 phonological representations. (For an overview, see Lardiere, 2012.) Although more related to processing than to representation, another approach to representation comes from Clahsen and Felser (2006a, 2006b, 2006c), who proposed the **Shallow Structure Hypothesis**. This position maintains that processing by L2 learners, when compared with that of NSs, involves less detail in their syntactic

TIME TO DO ...

Grammatical gender acquisition in the L2 by learners who do not have gender in the L1 is one area in which research in support of the Representational Deficit Hypothesis and the Missing Surface Inflection Hypothesis has been conducted. These studies often use tasks such as a picture-identification task, where learners receive a stimulus in the L2 such as this Spanish sentence from White, Valenzuela, Kozlowska-Macgregor, and Leung (2004):

> María contesta: "Sí, claro, va a hacer mucho sol. Ponlas ahí cerca de la roja."
> (Maria answers: "Yes, of course, it is going to be very sunny. Put them over there by the red$_{FemSing}$ [one]").

Learners are then given three pictures, from which they must choose the correct item that is being referred to by *la roja*. In this case, they see a suitcase (*la maleta$_{FemSing}$*), a book (*el libro$_{MascSing}$*), and socks (*los calcetines$_{MascPl}$*).

Which picture must the learners choose in this example? What does it tell us if they choose the wrong picture? Do you think we can draw conclusions about their acquisition of gender from such a task?

representations during sentence comprehension. In other words, there is a fundamental difference between NSs and L2 learners in the way they process sentences. If learners do not come up with complete syntactic representations, how do they comprehend? The proposal is that other areas of language (lexical, pragmatic, semantic) come into play. Processing of sentences can be native-like only when representation involves "closely adjacent constituents" (Clahsen & Felser, 2006a, p. 111 et passim).

We now turn to different conceptualizations of the roles of the L1 and UG as possible starting points for L2 acquisition.

L1 as the base

1. **Full Transfer/Full Access**: This position assumes that the starting point is the L1 grammar, but that there is full access to UG during the process of acquisition (Schwartz & Sprouse, 1994, 1996, 2000; Schwartz, 1998; Whong-Barr, 2005). The learner is assumed to use the L1 grammar as a basis but to have full access to UG when the L1 is deemed insufficient for the learning task at hand. L1 and L2 learning differ, and there is no prediction that learners will eventually attain complete knowledge of the L2. This is the case because starting with an L1 grammar makes it impossible to reach the L2 grammar, assuming that only positive evidence is useful for grammar formation.

2. **Minimal Trees Hypothesis**: In the previous position, Full Transfer/Full Access, learners draw on both the L1 and UG. The first option was to draw on the L1 and, where that was insufficient, to draw on UG. This position also maintains that both the L1 and UG are available concurrently (Vainikka & Young-Scholten, 1994, 1996a, 1996b). However, the L1 grammar that is available contains no functional categories, and these categories, initially, are not available from any source. The emergence of functional categories is not dependent on the L1, and, hence, there is no transfer in this area; rather, they emerge in response to L2 input. The development of functional categories of learners from different languages will be the same. In this view, learners may or may not reach the final state of an L2 grammar, depending on what is available through the L1 and what is available through UG. They should be able to reach the final state of an L2 grammar with regard to functional categories.

UG-based

1. **The Initial Hypothesis of Syntax** (Platzack, 1996): This position maintains that, as in child language acquisition, the starting point for acquisition is UG.

2. **Full Access/No transfer**: This position maintains that, as in child language acquisition, the starting point for acquisition is UG (Epstein et al., 1996, 1998; Flynn, 1996; Flynn & Martohardjono, 1994). There is a disconnection between the L1 and the developing L2 grammar. A prediction based on this position is that L1 and L2 acquisition will proceed in a similar fashion, will end up at the same point, and that all L2 acquisition (regardless of L1) would proceed along the same

path. Learners should be able to reach the same level of competence as native speakers. If there are differences, they are **performance**-related rather than competence-related.

In the following sections, we examine data that bear on these issues of access to UG. There are two types of relevant data: data relating to **UG principles** that are invariant, and data relating to **UG parameters** that vary across languages.

{ – structure dependence (language is not a string of unstructured segments).

7.2.2 UG Principles → Invariant

White (1989) reported on a study by Otsu and Naoi (1986) dealing with the principle of structure dependence. The basic concept behind this principle is that linguistic principles operate on syntactic (or structural) units. That is, most importantly, according to this view, what makes language knowledge different from other types of knowledge is the notion of structure dependency; language is not just a string of unstructured segments. White pointed out that this accounts for the grammatical question in 7-14 and the ungrammaticality of 7-15, both stemming from the question in 7-13.

(7-13) The boy who is standing over there is happy.

(7-14) Is the boy who is standing over there _____ happy?

(7-15) *Is the boy who _____ standing over there is happy?

The rule for question formation makes reference to the subject, which, in the case of 7-13 is a complex subject consisting of a determiner phrase (*the boy*) and a RC (*who is standing over there*). The rule does not make reference to a nonstructural unit, such as "the first verb." Thus, *yes/no* questions are formed by moving the main verb to the front of the sentence, not by moving the first verb in the sentence to the front (as in 7-15).

Otsu and Naoi tested knowledge of structure-dependency among Japanese learners of English. In Japanese, questions are formed by adding a question particle to the end of a sentence. No word-order changes are made. The learners tested knew how to form simple questions and passed a test showing knowledge of RCs, but they had no knowledge of question formation involving complex subjects. It was hypothesized that, if a UG principle, structure dependence, were operative, it could not have come into the learner-language system through the L1, as the L1 does not have a principle of structure dependence relevant to question formation. Thus, the only way the principle of structure dependence could have come into the learners' L2 grammar was through direct access to UG. In general, the results of this study support the notion that learners' grammars are constrained by principles of UG, in this case the principle of structure dependence.

Another study relevant to the issue of UG principles is one by Schachter (1989). She tested the principle known as subjacency, which limits the amount of movement that can take place within sentences. Consider the following contrived conversation:

} subjacency principle

SPEAKER 1:   I agree with the idea that David loves Mary Jo.
SPEAKER 2:   I didn't hear you. *Who do you agree with the idea that
David loves?

The ungrammaticality of *Who do you agree with the idea that David loves?* is due to the fact that, in English, movement of the question word from the position of the original noun phrase (*Mary Jo*) to its new sentence-initial position is constrained by the distance and intervening syntactic structures between the two positions.[9] In Speaker 2's sentence, the necessary syntactic relationships cannot hold; that is, the movement rule is violated, and, hence, the sentence is ungrammatical.

Schachter (1989) tested knowledge of this principle by eliciting grammaticality judgments from NSs of Indonesian, Chinese, and Korean learning English. In a separate article, Schachter (1990) added a group of Dutch speakers to her database. The languages in question have different requirements on subjacency. In Korean, there is no evidence of subjacency; in Chinese and Indonesian, there is some evidence of subjacency, although, in both of these languages, *wh-* movement is more limited than in English; and, in Dutch, subjacency restrictions are much the same as in English. The results of Schachter's study suggest that the Dutch speakers recognize that English is constrained by the principle of subjacency; the results for the other groups are not as clear. The Korean-speaking learners, in keeping with the no-access position, were not constrained by subjacency. The Chinese and Indonesian speakers behaved more English-like than the Korean speakers, but their IL grammars could not be said to be constrained by the principle of subjacency.[10]

Empty category Principle

A third example comes from White's (2003) discussion of the results of studies based on the Empty Category Principle (ECP) (Chomsky, 1981). In essence, the ECP is a way of accounting for asymmetry found in the use or nonuse of case particles. Examples can be seen from Japanese in 7-16–7-18.

(7-16) John   ga   sono   hon   o   yonda.
       John   NOM   that   book   ACC   read-PAST
       "John read that book."

(7-17) John   ga   sono   hon   yonda.
       John   NOM   that   book   read-PAST

(7-18) *John   sono   hon   o   yonda.
       John   that   book   ACC   read-PAST

Here, 7-16 is grammatical, with both a nominative and an accusative case marker; 7-17 is possible, with a nominative case marker and no accusative case marker, but 7-18 is ungrammatical, because it has only an accusative case marker, but no nominative case marker. Kanno (1996) investigated whether beginning learners of Japanese were able to recognize this discrepancy, arguing that, if they recognized the asymmetry in the early stages of learning, one could assume that the ECP functions in early L2 learning.[11] Both L2 learners and NSs of Japanese accepted accusative case-drop sentences more than nominative case-drop ones. This suggests that ECP does in fact function in the early grammars of L2 learners.

Thus, with regard to UG principles, there is conflicting evidence as to whether learners have direct access to UG, have access through the NL, or have no access at all.

- range of options to choose from
- if UG is available, it's difficult to reset parameters
- once a parameter is set, all related properties are affected (there are consequences for grammar)
- UG constrains grammar development

7.2.3 UG Parameters

There are certain linguistic features that vary across languages. These are expressed through the concept of linguistic parameters. Parameters have limited values. In learning an L1, the data a child is exposed to will determine which setting of a parameter that child will select. Although parameters are not invariable, as we saw with principles, they are limited, thereby easing the burden on the child. In other words, if parameters exist, the child's task is eased, because there is a limited range of options to choose from.

The issue for SLA is the determination of whether and how a given linguistic parameter can be reset. Let's assume a parameter with two values. Let's further assume a NS with an NL setting in one way, who is learning an L2 with a setting in another way. If UG is available to that learner, there should be little difficulty in resetting the parameter, because the speaker has access to both settings through UG. If UG is operative only through the L1 (as the FDH suggests), then we would expect only those features that are available through the L1 to manifest themselves in the L2. Finally, if UG is not operative at all, we would expect none of the UG features to be available.

One of the most interesting aspects related to the concept of parameters is that they involve the clustering of properties. Once a parameter is set in a particular way, all related properties are affected. In other words, there are consequences for other parts of the grammar. We examine one such parameter, known as the pro-drop parameter. This parameter encompasses a number of properties, namely (a) the omission of subject pronouns, (b) the inversion of subjects and verbs in declarative sentences, and (c) *that*-trace effects—that is, the extraction of a subject (leaving a trace) out of a clause that contains a complementizer. A language will either have all of these properties or none of them. Languages such as Italian and Spanish are [+pro-drop] and have all of the associated properties, whereas English and French are [-pro-drop], having none of them. Examples from English and Italian that illustrate the differences follow:

Italian	*English*
Omit subject pronouns	*Obligatory use of subject pronouns*
Va al cinema stasera.	She is going to the movies this evening.
goes to the movies this evening	*is going to the movies this evening

Subject verb inversion

| È arrivata Laura. | Laura has arrived. |
| is arrived Laura | *has arrived Laura |

That-trace

| Chi hai detto che è venuto? | Who did you say came? |
| who you said that is come | *Who did you say that came? |

White (1985) and Lakshmanan (1986) presented data from Spanish and French learners of English (White) and Spanish, Japanese, and Arabic learners of English (Lakshmanan) on precisely these three structures.[12] White found that the learners did not recognize these three structures as related. Although there was a difference in judgments of acceptability between the Spanish and the French speakers on the first type of sentence (i.e., those with and without overt subject pronouns), there was no difference between the two groups on the other two types of sentences. Thus, these learners did not see these three properties as a unified parameter. Lakshmanan's results were similar. Her groups of learners responded similarly to the first two sentence types, but differently with regard to the third, again suggesting that these properties were not seen by these learners as unified under the umbrella of a single parameter.

There is evidence, however, that is more compelling with regard to the clustering of properties. Hilles (1986) assumed different properties of the pro-drop parameter in her investigation of the acquisition of English by a native speaker of Spanish named Jorge: (a) obligatory pronoun use; (b) use of nonreferential *it*, as in weather terms (*it's raining*, *it's pouring*), and use of nonreferential *there*, as in *There is rain in the forecast*; and (c) use of uninflected modals (e.g., *must*, *could*). Hilles showed that these three features were related in the speech of her learner. Specifically, there was an inverse relationship between Jorge's lack of referential subject use and the appearance of modal verbs. As Jorge began to use subject pronouns in English (i.e., as his null-subject use went down), he also began to use modals as noninflected forms. Hilles hypothesized that the triggering factor for the switch from [+pro-drop] to [-pro-drop] was the use of nonreferential subjects. This was an indication that this learner had truly understood the mandatory nature of subjects in English.

With specific regard to pro-drop, Park (2004) analyzed pronominal subjects and objects, observing that Spanish speakers learning English frequently drop subject pronouns, whereas Korean speakers learning English frequently drop object pronouns. She attempts to account for this discrepancy through the interpretability of agreement features in the native languages. One also observes that parameter-resetting did not occur.

The results of research on L2 parameters, like those of the research on principles discussed in 7.2.2, are mixed. There are data supporting the view that UG constrains the grammars that learners can come up with; there are data arguing against this position. Thus, the answer to the question of whether L2 acquisition is fundamentally the same as L1 acquisition is *no*; the answer to the question of whether L2 acquisition is fundamentally different from L1 acquisition is also *no*. Although it may be the case that universal principles (either typological or formal) guide L2 acquisition, it is also the case that there are areas of conflict between NL and TL grammars, yielding grammars that fall beyond the domain of what would be predicted if the only constraining factors were universals. White (2003, p. 149), following her discussion of parameters, concludes that, "despite conflicting evidence and conflicting theories, results from several studies suggest that interlanguage grammars conform to parameters of UG."

[margin note: conflict between NL grammar and TL grammar]

Within the Minimalist framework (Chomsky, 1995, 2000, 2002), the lexicon (discussed in the next chapter) assumes great importance (see section 7.2.4 for additional discussion of Minimalism). Parameterization within the Minimalist Program is no longer in the syntax, but in the lexicon. Most of the constraints on language, described earlier in terms of complex principles and parameters, are now the result of a handful of general constraints on movement and the specific information stored in the lexicon of individual languages. Furthermore, most of the parametric variation relates to grammatical features such as tense and agreement. When we think of learning vocabulary, what we typically think of is learning the meanings of words (e.g., what the word *chair* refers to or what *subterfuge* means). However, knowing that, for example, *break* is defined as "to disjoin or reduce to pieces with sudden or violent force" (*American Heritage Dictionary*) is only part of what we know about the word *break*. Knowing a word entails much more than that, and the additional knowledge is as important as any other piece of knowledge we have of language. For example, we also know that the verb *break* is irregular in its past tense formation, whereas *love* is not. We know that a sentence such as 7-19 is a good English sentence, but 7-20 is not, unless one thinks of the meaning "to break under interrogation" (thanks to Ildikó Svetics for pointing this interpretation out to us).

[margin note: LANGUAGE CONSTRAINTS: result of general constraints on movement and specific information in lexicon.]

(7-19) Harvey broke the glass jar.

(7-20) Harvey broke.

We know that some verbs require objects (*hit*), other verbs allow objects but do not require them (*eat*), and still other verbs generally disallow objects (*sleep*). This is part of what we know about a language. Within Minimalism, parameters are part of the lexicon, and language learning is largely lexical learning.

An example of how parametric variation is attached to the lexicon comes from the use of reflexives. Given an English sentence such as 7-21, speakers of English recognize that the word *herself* must refer to *the girl*:

(7-21) The mother told the girl to wash herself.

However, the same is not true in sentence 7-22, where *her* can refer to the mother or to someone else.

(7-22) The mother told the girl to wash her.

Thus, the word *herself* in English contains information about possible antecedents. Other languages choose different options. For example, in Japanese, one reflexive form, *zibun*, can be ambiguous, as in 7-23 (from Lakshmanan & Teranishi, 1994):

(7-23) John-wa   Bill-ga   kagami-no n aka-de   zibun-o mita to   itta
       John-TOP   Bill-NOM   mirror-GEN inside-LOC self ACC saw that said
       "John said that Bill saw self in the mirror."
       (Either John or Bill can have seen himself.)

In 7-24, the reflexive *zibun-zisin* removes the ambiguity.

(7-24) John-wa Bill-ga kagami-no naka-de zibun-zisin mita to itta.
       "John said that Bill saw himself in the mirror."
       (John cannot have seen himself.)

Languages thus contain information in the lexicon that signals grammatical relationships. The central role of the lexicon is dealt with in the following chapter.

7.2.4 Minimalist Program

[handwritten margin note: MERGE: how lexical items are put in right order.]

[handwritten margin note: AGREE: agreement with structure]

[handwritten margin note: MOVE: how elements can be displayed]

[handwritten annotation: BASIC OPERATION OF MERGE, AGREE AND MOVE.]

In the Minimalist Program, the underlying assumption is that, in all languages (and therefore in UG), there are basic operations of *merge*, *agree*, and *move*. The first of these determines how the lexical items in a given language are put in the correct order; *agree* stipulates that certain features of a given language must show agreement within a structure; and *move* determines how the elements in a structure can be displaced. Features "are the primitive, elemental units that make up the lexical items of every language, and the differences between languages are due to differences among these features" (Lardiere, 2009, p. 173). Gender, for example, is a feature that is instantiated in some languages but not in others. Features may be interpretable, which means that they have some type of semantic value. For example, the number feature on the English word *cats* in the sentence *The cats eat.*, or, more precisely, on the plural *-s* morpheme, has semantic value; it tells us that there is more than one cat. However, the number feature on the verb *eat* (as compared with the singular *The cat eats.*) has

---

TIME TO DO ...

Watch the video of an interview with Noam Chomsky (see Link #1 in the Link section at the end of this chapter) and discuss the following questions: What are the two factors that determine the "mature state of knowledge" (final state) according to Chomsky? Where do we get evidence about this final state, or mature grammar? How can we determine whether particular properties of the final state are attributable to the initial state (UG)? What, according to Chomsky, are human beings preprogrammed for?

no semantic value. It Is only there for syntactic agreement purposes and therefore is an uninterpretable feature. What is important is the fact that these three operations are universal.

There is an important question that is in need of resolution: Are universals the major organizing factor of learner-language grammars?

7.2.5 Falsification

In trying to come up with a parsimonious account of how L2s are acquired, it is necessary to have a theory that will explain (and predict) the facts of learner grammars. In order to determine the accuracy of our theories, an important consideration is the issue of falsification. Our theory must predict what will occur and what will not occur. It is only in this way that we can test the accuracy of our hypotheses. In other words, our theories need to be falsifiable, based on the data.

Learner languages are highly complex systems and, to some extent, are unique and constantly changing, making it difficult to make absolute predictions. Thus, it is more appropriate to think about probabilistic predictions. Unlike L1 grammars, no two individuals have the same L2 grammar, and, hence, there is no way of predicting what will happen to a grammar when new information is added, causing changes in the existing system. One might think of this as the kaleidoscope factor. Each kaleidoscope pattern differs. Any change in the system (a shake or twist to the kaleidoscope) will result in a different, unpredictable pattern.[13] One can make certain predictions, but, given the many factors involved in a kaleidoscope (does one twist the box or shake it, how hard, etc.?), one cannot make absolute predictions. One can only establish guidelines within which all of the images are likely to fall.

[handwritten note: NO 2 language learners have the same L2 pattern.]

The advantage of research within a UG framework is that, because it is based on a well-defined linguistic theory, more accurate predictions can be made, although the arguments made earlier regarding absolute versus probabilistic predictions still hold (see also Pinker, 1987).

When there are counterexamples—that is, when the predictions are not borne out—there are various approaches one can take: (a) assume a no-access to UG position, as we have seen with regard to the FDH; (b) attribute the results to methodological problems; (c) attribute the results to an undefined performance component; (d) attribute the results to mapping factors; or (e) assume the theory is false.

Because the predictions are based on theoretical constructs that are abstractions which have to be argued rather than empirically verified, and because the theory is in a state of development, there is little concrete evidence that one can bring to bear to show that the linguistic analysis of a principle or parameter is indeed the correct one. Thus, if one maintains the assumption that L2 grammars are natural grammars, then SLA data can be brought into the arguments in the field of linguistics in the determination of linguistic principles and parameters.

Because of the changing nature of the linguistic constructs on which it is based, UG-based research is difficult to falsify. Upon being confronted with data apparently contradicting the predictions of UG access, it is equally possible to argue that the underlying linguistic formulation was the incorrect one.

To illustrate this point, reconsider the discussion of the pro-drop parameter. We noted that there were differing views as to what constituted the appropriate clusters in this parameter. In White's study, the predicted clusterings were not evidenced in the data. A possible conclusion she comes to is as follows:

> It is of interest that some recent proposals suggest that the possibility of VS word order [i.e., subject inversion] is not, in fact, part of the pro-drop parameter, but derives from other principles of grammar (Chao 1981; Safir 1982; Hyams 1983), a position that these results would be consistent with.

> (White, 1985, p. 59)

Thus, rather than assuming a no-access position, White suggests the possibility that the parameter has been inaccurately described.

Yet another way of viewing the falsification problem is to allow for violations of universals, as these violations are temporary, given the ever-changing nature of learner languages. UG then serves as a "corrective mechanism" (see Sharwood Smith, 1988). A violation is only to be taken as a serious violation if it can also be shown that the person's interim system (i.e., his or her learner language) has stabilized. This would mean that most cross-sectional studies would have to be eliminated, because it is only with longitudinal data that we can determine whether a grammar has stabilized/ fossilized or not. There is an added difficulty here. As we have no independent means of determining whether stabilization/fossilization has taken place, we can never know when we are confronted with a stabilized grammar and when we are not. Thus, if we are to take this view, we cannot determine whether or not universal principles are violated. However, if the principles are followed, then we can conclude that L2 grammars are constrained by the particular principles. If the principles are not followed, there is little that can be concluded. We have no way of determining with certainty that the principles are permanently not followed.

If we consider the initial-state discussion earlier in this chapter, it is clear that there are difficulties defining what is meant by *initial state*. For example, how early must data be to be relevant? First day of exposure, first utterance? What about a period of non-production before production begins? Is this relevant? Does it exist? If these data are relevant, then is there any way of falsifying certain claims (for example, whether functional categories are in place or not)?

To take a similar example, recall that one of the questions in UG-based research is the extent to which functional categories are available in early stages of learning. For example, it is frequently the case that there is little morphological marking in early L2 production, suggesting the absence of functional categories. However, plural marking is often absent at very late stages of SLA, making it difficult to maintain that omission is solely due to an absence of functional categories. Therefore, on the surface, one might consider a certain type of data as evidence of falsification, whereas different explanations might be plausible for the same phenomenon in different contexts.

7.3 TRANSFER: THE GENERATIVE/UG PERSPECTIVE

In Chapters 4–6, we discussed historical and current views of transfer. Conducting SLA research within a paradigm such as the one discussed in this chapter necessitates a reconsideration of the concept of transfer. The question arises: What new insights do recent linguistic approaches and, in particular, theoretical paradigms provide regarding the old concept of transfer?

White (1992) provided detail on this issue. She notes four areas that make current views of the phenomenon of transfer truly different from earlier conceptualizations, particularly those embodied in the framework of contrastive analysis. We deal with three of these areas here: levels of representation, clustering, and learnability.

7.3.1 Levels of Representation

Within a theory of UG, our knowledge of syntax is best represented by positing different levels of grammatical structure. To simplify matters, assume that there is an underlying structure and a surface structure. To understand the difference, consider 7-25:

(7-25) Visiting relatives can be boring.

This sentence can be parsed in one of two ways, each with a different meaning:

(7-26) When I visit relatives, I am bored.

(7-27) Relatives who visit me can be boring.

The two different meanings are a result of two different underlying syntactic structures that can be computed for sentence 7-25. The surface structure is 7-25, but there are two different possible deep structures for this sentence, namely 7-26 and 7-27. The deep structure then provides the semantic contents, or the meaning of the sentence, and the surface structure provides the phonological form of the sentence.

If sentences have multiple levels of representation, one can imagine that transfer could occur, not just on the basis of surface facts, but also on the basis of underlying structures (see Tarone et al., 1976).

7.3.2 Clustering

With regard to clustering, recall that, within a UG theory claiming that learning involves setting/resetting of parameters, there are properties that cluster together within a parameter. Within this framework (as with typological universals, discussed in Chapter 9), one is concerned with how multiple properties of language do or do not behave in a like fashion. Further, there is evidence that mixed values are adopted for multivalued parameters and continuous linguistic features (for examples, see Broselow & Finer, 1991; and Gass, 1984).

[Handwritten annotation at top: SUBSET PRINCIPLE } language learning can proceed on the basis of INPUT alone.]

Within earlier approaches to transfer (particularly a contrastive analysis approach), there was no way to show how related structures were linked in the minds of L2 learners. Nonetheless, a model that involves structural relatedness clearly represents an innovative approach to language transfer.

7.3.3 Learnability

A UG perspective on SLA is heavily dependent on arguments of learnability. In particular, the issue of positive evidence is central, because learners construct grammars on the basis of the input (the positive evidence to which the learner is exposed), together with principles of UG. However, there are some language structures that may be in a superset/subset relationship, which accounts for the fact that, even if there is full transfer and full access, learning may not always be successful. In fact, a learning principle, the Subset Principle, has been proposed that ensures that language learning can proceed on the basis of input alone. When there are multiple possibilities in a language, child learners adopt the most restrictive grammar possible, so that she or he can proceed to learn the appropriate forms on the basis of input alone. If she or he were to assume a superset grammar, there would be no way to retreat from that grammar. Consider adverb placement in French and English. In French, adverbs can be positioned in a greater number of places than in English. In English, sentence 7-28 is ungrammatical, whereas the French counterpart is not.

(7-28) *The man is drinking slowly his coffee.

If an English-speaking child were to start with a grammar that allowed all possibilities for adverb placement, it would be difficult to learn, on the basis of positive evidence (input) alone, that the grammar (English) was actually more restrictive.

Looking at this across languages, we can see that the input necessary for the learner may be different depending on the superset/subset relationship of the two languages in question on a particular feature. For a French learner learning English, she or he has to learn that 7-28 is ungrammatical (and, in fact, this is learned late and is characteristic of a French person speaking English), whereas, an English learner learning French only has to hear the broader range of possibilities to know that French has more possibilities for adverb placement.

Where positive evidence is readily available, allowing a learner to reset a parameter, little transfer (and, when present, of short duration) is predicted (as in the case of the L2 being a superset of the L1). On the other hand, when positive evidence will not suffice to provide learners with adequate information about the L2, possibly necessitating negative evidence, transfer is predicted (as when the L2 is a subset of the L1).

7.4 THE FUNDAMENTAL DIFFERENCE HYPOTHESIS REVISED

In 2009, Bley-Vroman substantially revised the FDH, as it had been conceived 20 years previously. While maintaining the notions of reliability and convergence in NL learning—

[handwritten top annotations:] NL learning – reliability notion: a child reliably learns his/her language completely
CONVERGENCE → all children converge on the same end product of learning (same grammar)

reliability, meaning that a child reliably learns his/her language completely, and convergence, meaning that all children of a particular society converge on the same end product of learning, that is, the same grammar—and the notion that foreign-language learning is marked by neither reliability nor convergence, Bley-Vroman noted that important advances in linguistic theory had made it necessary to revisit the FDH, incorporating notions from Minimalism. As all languages make use of all of the operations of *move*, *agree*, and *merge*, there is no need for an L2 learner to have access to UG in order to set the parameters in the L2. He/she has access to everything in UG through his/her L1.

Previous UG theory held that the learner's task in learning a new language was to pick up on what parameters were set for that language. As certain parameters within a language tend to co-occur or cluster together (e.g., languages such as Spanish or Italian that are pro-drop tend to also have free subject–verb inversion and *that*-trace effects), the learner would only need to realize some of the individual structures in order to set the metaparameter for that language and to trigger the acquisition of all the other structures that cluster together with it. However, as we saw earlier, SLA research—as well as some L1 research—has found that learners do not, in fact, get these other structures for free when they realize one of the structures; individual structures are acquired individually.

Other findings include the fact that not all factors that were believed to be strong evidence for the existence of UG in SLA are due to UG, but rather are due to nongrammatical factors, such as semantics-discourse structure and processing. The original FDH gave great importance to the difference between domain-specific processes, such as L1 learning, and domain-general processes involved in other types of learning. However, the revised FDH concedes that the processes used in the language faculty may be used in other faculties as well, and therefore the distinction between native- and foreign-language learning as calling on different learning mechanisms must be revised.

Another construct is that of patches. We all have areas in our NL that we are unsure of or which we take time to think about. For example, the distinction between *lie/lay* is often problematic for NSs of English, or, in the area of agreement, which do NSs say: *Either you or she know/knows the answer*? Native speakers often aren't sure which one to use. Learners may have many patches, and NSs have only a few, small patches. This may be a quantitative difference, but not a fundamentally different one.

TIME TO THINK …

Consider the examples given above of structures for which native speakers of English have patches. When does one use *lie* and when does one use *lay*? Which do you prefer: *Either you or she know the answer.* or *Either you or she knows the answer.*? What other examples of patches that native speakers of English have can you think of?

[handwritten right-margin annotations:] L2 LEARNING → can't rely on Reliability nor on convergence

All languages make use of move, agree, and merge, so there's no need for a L2 learner to have access to UG in order to set parameters in the L2. The learner can access UG through L1.

7.5 SEMANTICS AND THE SYNTAX–SEMANTICS INTERFACE HYPOTHESIS

7.5.1 Semantics

[handwritten: why learners are able to learn some parts of language, but not others.]

In the SLA literature, semantics is the area that has been paid the least attention. In this section, we highlight one recent proposal that deals with semantics and that addresses some of the same issues discussed in this chapter, namely, why is it that learners are able to learn some parts of language, but not others. For a recent review of semantics in L2 learning, see Slabakova (2012).

[handwritten margin note: learners learn syntax and semantics but have problems with inflectional morphemes.]

Slabakova proposed the **Bottleneck Hypothesis** (2006, 2008) as a means of explaining the difficulty that learners have in acquiring an L2. As in other approaches to L2 acquisition, the Bottleneck Hypothesis states that learners are able to acquire syntax and semantics, but the main challenge is inflectional morphemes, and formal features are what cause problems. In other words, there is a bottleneck in the acquisition of the correct mapping of inflectional morphemes in the L2. Slabakova (2012) points out that,

> inflectional morphemes carry the features that are responsible for syntactic and semantic differences among languages of the world, so it is logical that once these morphemes and their features are acquired, the other linguistic properties (word order, interpretation, etc.) would follow smoothly.
>
> (p. 140)

7.5.2 Syntax and Semantics: The Interface Hypothesis

[handwritten margin note: Structures that involve interface are harder to be learned.]

The Interface Hypothesis (Sorace, 2000, 2003, 2005, 2011) contends that structures that involve an interface between syntax and another cognitive domain (syntax–semantics, syntax–pragmatics, and syntax–lexical-semantics interfaces) are more difficult to acquire than structures that don't involve such an interface. The Interface Hypothesis was proposed to account for the nonconvergence (i.e., not all learners converge on the same end grammar) and residual optionality of L2 learning, in particular among near-native or very advanced L2 learners. Recent research has indicated that certain interfaces are more problematic than others; the syntax–pragmatics interface results in more nonconvergence than the syntax–semantics interface.

7.6 PHONOLOGY

[handwritten: pronunciation and perception patterns / Accent]

Another area where SLA and linguistics intersect is phonology. The study of L2 phonology is not unlike other areas of L2 acquisition, in that it attempts to account for the patterns of knowledge and use of L2 learners, in this case of pronunciation and perception. It is commonly accepted that the NL origin of an L2 speaker is often identifiable by his or her accent. In fact, NNS pronunciation is often the source of humor, as in the case of comedians mimicking particular accent types, or in cartoon characters adopting nonnative accents.

The acquisition of an L2 phonology is a complex process. An understanding of how learners learn a new phonological system must take into account linguistic differences between the NL and the TL systems, as well as universal facts of phonology. Phonology is both similar to, and different from, other linguistic domains. It is similar to what we have seen in other parts of language, in that some of a learner's pronunciation of the L2 is clearly attributable to the NL, whereas some is not. It is different in that not all of the concepts relevant to syntax are applicable to phonology. For example, avoidance is a common L2 strategy used when a syntactic construction is recognizably beyond one's reach. Thus, if a learner wants to avoid passives, it is relatively easy to find an alternative structure to express the same concept. However, if a learner wants to avoid the sound [ð], as in *the* in English, it would be virtually impossible. Phonology differs from syntax in that, in the former, but not the latter, most people can detect the linguistic origin of a speaker (although see arguments in Ioup, 1984, relating to what she calls a syntactic accent).

As discussed in Chapter 4, in its simplest form, the CAH did not make accurate predictions. It did not predict why speakers of language *X* learning language *Y* would have difficulty with a given structure, whereas speakers of language *Y* learning language *X* did not have difficulty with that same structure. These discrepancies were also evident in phonology. As an example, consider Stockwell and Bowen's (1965) proposed Hierarchy of Difficulty (Table 7.1). The hierarchy (ordered from most difficult to least difficult) attempts to make predictions of difficulty based on whether or not phonological categories are absent or present and, if present, whether they are obligatory or optional.

Thus, if a learner has an NL that has no **phonemic** contrast between two sounds (e.g., /l/ and /r/) and is learning a language where that contrast is obligatory, she or he will have difficulty. However, if the L1 and the TL both have the same contrast, there will be little difficulty in learning.

TABLE 7.1 Hierarchy of Phonological Difficulty (*Source*: Adapted from R. Stockwell and J. Bowen. *The Sounds of English and Spanish* (p. 16). Chicago: University of Chicago Press, 1965. Reprinted with permission.)

NL	TL	
0	Obligatory	difficult
0	Optional	
Optional	Obligatory	
Obligatory	Optional	
Obligatory	0	
Optional	0	
Optional	Optional	
Obligatory	Obligatory	easy

TIME TO THINK ...

Do you have an accent when you speak in your L2? If so, what specifically marks you as an NNS of your L2? Are there specific sounds or phonemic contrasts in the L2 that are difficult for you?

[handwritten margin note top-left:] MOST COMMON ↑

[handwritten margin note top-right:] sounds that are most commonly/more used in a certain language

7.6.1 Markedness Differential Hypothesis

Hierarchies of this type are also proposed within other phonological frameworks. In particular, Eckman (1977) proposed what he called the **Markedness Differential Hypothesis**, which was based on a phonological theory of markedness. One way to think of markedness is that an unmarked form, whether phonological or syntactic, is one that is more common, more usual, in the world's languages than a marked one. It is perhaps easier to understand this concept in an area other than phonology. If we consider words denoting professions, avocations, or societal roles, we see that male terms are the basic ones (e.g., *actor*, *poet*, *host*, *hero*), whereas the female counterparts have suffixes added on to the male term (*actress*, *poetess*, *hostess*, *heroine*). The male term is taken to be the basic one (unmarked), and the female term is the marked derivative.

[handwritten margin note left:] unmarked e.g. male forms (actor, poet, host, hero).

[handwritten margin note left:] marked e.g. female forms (actress, poetess, hostess, heroine)

If we apply the same concept to phonology, we can describe cross-linguistically which sounds are common to many languages (the unmarked ones) and which are not (the marked ones). Dinnsen and Eckman (1975) proposed that voicing contrasts[14] in languages are not uniform in all positions in a word. Table 7.2 gives linguistic facts on which the proposed Markedness Differential Hierarchy was based. The linguistic information shows a progression from least-marked (most frequent, and possibly easiest) language type to most marked.

[handwritten margin note left:] least-marked = most frequent ↕ most-marked = least frequent

The hierarchy reflecting this is known as the **Voice Contrast Hierarchy**, which states that a contrast in initial position is the least marked, and a contrast in final position is the most marked. The interpretation of this is such that we can predict that a language that maintains a marked contrast (i.e., a contrast in word-final position) also maintains a contrast in all positions that are less marked.

How does this apply to an L2 learning situation? What is predicted is that a speaker of a language with a more marked NL structure (or, in this case, a more marked contrast) than that which occurs in the TL will have an easier time learning the TL structure/contrast than a speaker whose NL is less marked than the TL. This correctly predicts, for example, that a speaker of English (with a voicing contrast in final position [*tab* vs. *tap*]) will have no difficulty in producing German words where there is no contrast in final position. On the other hand, a German speaker learning English has to learn to make a contrast in final position (a more marked structure than the German NL) and will be expected to produce errors.

Thus, within the Markedness Hypothesis Framework, the interest is not in denying the importance of transfer (although most work in which transfer was minimized

TABLE 7.2 Markedness Differential Hierarchy (*Source*: From "A functional explanation of some phonological typologies" by D.Dinnsen and F. Eckman. In R. E. Grossman, L. J. San, & T. J. Vance (Eds.), *Functionalism* (pp. 126–134). Chicago: Chicago Linguistic Society, 1975. Reprinted by permission.)

Description	Languages	
Languages that maintain a superficial voice contrast in initial, medial, and final positions	English, Arabic, Swedish, Hungarian	More frequent
Languages that maintain a superficial voice contrast in initial and medial positions, but fail to maintain this contrast in final position	German, Polish, Greek, Japanese, Catalan, Russian	
Languages that maintain a superficial voice contrast in initial position, but fail to maintain this contrast in medial and final positions	Corsican, Sardinian	
Languages that maintain no voice contrast in initial, medial, or final positions	Korean	Less frequent

recognized the inevitability of using the NL in the area of phonology), but in determining the principles that underlie its use. It is for this reason that the CAH was not abandoned in phonology with the same vigor as in syntax. Rather, the attempt was made to reconfigure it and incorporate additional principles.

What work in phonology shows, not unlike work in syntax, is that one must consider both the facts of the NL and developmental or universal facts in attempting to understand why learners produce the language they produce, and why they create the kinds of IL rules that underlie their production.

However, there is more to the picture than purely linguistic information. Sociolinguistic information is also relevant to an understanding of L2 phonology. Beebe (1980) showed that the social values of sounds in the NL affect transfer. Her study dealt with the acquisition of English pronunciation by native speakers of Thai. In Thai, the phoneme /r/ is pronounced in many different ways, depending on the linguistic and social context. In her English data from Thai NSs, she found that the formal variety of a Thai /r/ (a trilled r) was used in formal English contexts, but not in informal ones. Svetics (personal communication) similarly reported that two Greeks, when speaking English, pronounced [dʒ] and [tʃ], as in *bridge* or *lunch*, as [dz] and [ts], respectively, because the former two sounds are only used in Greek by uneducated individuals.

Most of the studies reported on thus far considered individual sound segments, but recent work has looked at units larger than individual segments; for example, syllables (Broselow et al., 1998; Carlisle, 1998). Young-Scholten and Archibald (2000), in their review of L2 syllable structure, asked a number of important questions, including: To what extent are L2 syllables constrained by allowable L1 syllable structures, and to what extent do universal principles apply or even prevail? As in other areas of SLA, it appears that both forces are operational.

Not only are sounds of a language transferred, but there is also evidence that learners attempt to maintain their NL syllable structure. When the TL permits syllable structures that are not permitted in the NL, learners will make errors that involve altering these structures to those that would be permitted in the NL (Broselow, 1987). For example, in Spanish, the initial English sequence in *snob* is not a permissible sequence in word-initial position. Spanish speakers are known to insert an epenthetic (addition of an additional sound) vowel, producing *esnob.* Similarly, Arabic speakers pronounce the English word *plastic* as [bilastik]. (In Arabic there is no contrast between [p] and [b] in word-initial position, which results in [bilastik] rather than [pilastik].)

As with other areas of phonology, one can order syllable types in terms of markedness, so that learners moving from a language with a less marked syllable structure (e.g., consonant/vowel [CV]) to one that has a more marked syllable structure [consonant–vowel–consonant (CVC)] tend to produce language closely approximating the NL syllable structure. On the other hand, evidence of conformity to the NL syllable structure by a speaker of a language with a more marked syllable structure is not apparent.

Thus, L2 syllable structure is in part shaped by the NL. It is, however, also affected by universal tendencies. Tarone (1980) showed that L2 learners of English simplified L2 syllables (e.g., through deletion or through epenthesis), even though the syllable type was allowed in the L1. An example is the addition of a final sound to the English word *sack* by Korean learners, resulting in [sæke], even though the sequence of CVC is allowable in Korean. Tarone suggested that learners revert to the basic (universal) CV syllable structure, regardless of L1.

It is well known that certain consonant clusters are difficult for L2 learners (e.g., fi*fth*, fis*ts*). Another universal tendency that has been proposed is that clusters of consonants tend to sort themselves out earlier at the beginning of words than at ends of words. This is borne out by L2 data. Anderson (1987) looked at English L2 data from Egyptian-Arabic and Chinese speakers. Egyptian-Arabic has no initial clusters, but does have final clusters. Chinese has neither. Yet both groups were found to have more difficulty with final clusters than with initial clusters.

Young-Scholten and Archibald (2000), in their review of L2 syllable structure, pointed to type of exposure as a possible factor involved in acquisition. They noted that L2 learners use epenthesis more than L1 learners as a simplification strategy.

Young-Scholten (1995, 1997) and Young-Scholten et al. (1999) argued that, when exposure comes from a classroom context where there is a reliance on written texts, epenthesis is frequent, regardless of the L1. If exposure does not come through written texts, epenthesis as a simplification strategy is less frequent. Young-Scholten's argument is that written information makes it more likely that learners will retain phonological information. This, however, does not obviate the need for simplification when learners' L1 constrains their phonology. Another possible means for simplification is through deletion (e.g., of unstressed syllables—a strategy used in child language acquisition). Young-Scholten and Archibald pointed out that this is rare in adult L2 learners, precisely because of their familiarity with the written text. Hence, they are left with the other common simplification strategy of epenthesis.

7.6.2 Similarity/Dissimilarity: Speech Learning Model

In addition to considering notions of markedness, there has also been an emphasis on similarity between the L1 and the L2. Flege (1992, 1995) claims that L2 sounds that are similar/equivalent to L1 sounds are difficult to acquire, because the learner does not perceive them or classify them as different and, hence, does not set up a new category of contrast. Flege's **Speech Learning Model** (1992, 1995) makes the following claims:

> A new phonetic category can be established for an L2 sound that differs phonetically from the closest L1 sound if bilinguals discern at least some of the phonetic differences between the L1 and L2 sounds. . . . Category formation for an L2 sound may be blocked by the mechanism of equivalence classification. When this happens, a single phonetic category will be used to process perceptually like L1 and L2 sounds (diaphones). Eventually, the diaphones will resemble one another in production.
>
> (Flege, 1995, p. 239)

More recently, he elaborates on this:

> The Speech Learning Model also hypothesizes that the perceived phonetic dissimilarity of an L2 sound from the closest L1 sound is a determinant of whether a new phonetic category will or will not be established for the L2 sound. The more distant from the closest L1 speech sound an L2 speech sound is judged to be, the more likely it is that L2 learners—regardless of age—will establish a new category for the L2 sound.
>
> (Flege, 2007, p.15)

Flege's claims have been substantiated reasonably well (Flege, 1987a, 1987b, 1990, 1993; Aoyama et al., 2004), although, as has been discussed elsewhere in this book, constructs are not always clear cut in SLA research. For example, how does one define *similar?* Does the theory need to be supported in total, or is probabilistic approximation sufficient?

Additional work by Flege et al. (2006) relates L2 pronunciation, not to similarity necessarily, but to length of residence as opposed to age. This conclusion was based on pronunciation judgments of the English speech of Korean children and adults. The researchers found that the greatest predictor of pronunciation was length of residence, which corresponds to amount of input.

Major and Kim (1999) modified the work of Flege by proposing the Similarity Differential Rate Hypothesis, which makes a slightly different claim, that is, that there is a rate difference between the acquisition of similar versus dissimilar sounds, with dissimilar sounds being acquired faster than similar sounds.

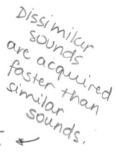
Dissimilar sounds are acquired faster than similar sounds.

In the next sections, we deal with two approaches to L2 phonology: Optimality Theory and the **Ontogeny Phylogeny Model**.

7.6.3 Optimality Theory

Optimality Theory is a relative newcomer to the theoretical scene in linguistics (see Prince & Smolensky, 1997) and an even later arrival in SLA. It had its beginnings in phonology, but has more recently extended its domain to syntax and semantics. Optimality Theory does not avail itself of the concept of rules per se, but rather, the basic concept is one of universal constraints and the rankings of those constraints. Constraints are innate and apply across all languages. There are two constraint types: faithfulness constraints and markedness constraints. The former match the input with the output, and the latter ensure the well-formedness of the output. There are, at times, conflicts among constraints, but these conflicts are resolved by a language-specific ordering of constraints. Variation across languages is a result of the differential ordering of constraints, and L2 learning involves the reranking of NL constraints. Tesar and Smolensky (1996, 1998) claim that "reranking of constraints will stop when learners no longer detect differences between their own output and the language surrounding them" (as cited in Levelt et al., 1999, p. 294).

Hancin-Bhatt and Bhatt (1997) investigated the acquisition of English beginnings and ends of words by Spanish and Japanese learners. The main task in question was to listen to two sentences (one grammatical and one ungrammatical) and repeat the sentence that was grammatically correct. Embedded in these sentences was the target (a pseudo-word) item (in italics). Below are examples of two sentences:

(7-29) Mary hopes they are ready to *frulm* today.

(7-30) Mary hopes them are ready to *frulm* today.

They analyzed the results within the framework of Optimality Theory: Some of the errors were due to language-specific rankings, while others were due to rankings that are universally dominant.

Hancin-Bhatt (2000) investigated the acquisition of syllable codas by Thai learners of English. Thai is more restrictive than English as to what can occur in syllable-final position. Hancin-Bhatt found that there is an interaction between NL constraint rankings and TL constraint rankings. She makes the argument that the rerankings that occur in the course of acquisition occur in an ordered fashion.

Broselow et al. (1998) investigated simplification of English words by Mandarin speakers. They argued that simplification was the result of constraint rankings, bringing in the concept of markedness to talk about constraint rankings. They refer to the emergence of the unmarked, by which they mean that the IL will have constraints that are ranked low in both the L1 and the L2 and, hence, masked by the effect of higher ranking constraints. This is the source of novel L2 pronunciations.

Substitutions are a widespread and recognized phenomenon in the pronunciation of an L2. Lombardi (2003, citing Edwards, 1994) illustrates the effect of this in the following anecdote: "One of my favourite errors occurred in an American war film, subtitled in French. One of the soldiers peers into the distance, and another says, 'Tanks?' The subtitle reads 'Merci'" (Lombardi, 2003, p. 225).

Lombardi (2003) considered the substitutions that Russian and Japanese speakers make when trying to produce English interdental sounds. Russian speakers have a [θ] to [t] pattern, and Japanese speakers a [θ] to [s] pattern. Using data from a range of languages, she argues that constraint rankings better account for this phenomenon than do rule-based approaches, given that the latter often require the addition of new rules. Learners begin with a universal substitution (that of using stops). She argues that this is the initial state that comes from UG, but that there are ranking constraints that also influence the phonological output of L2 learners, namely an L1-based reranking.

Eckman et al. (2003) continue work on contrasts that have been common in the phonology literature. They consider three types of contrasts: (a) the TL has two contrasting sounds, neither of which is present in the NL; (b) the TL has two contrasting sounds, one of which is present in the NL; and (c) the TL has two contrasting sounds, both of which are present in the NL, but which do not contrast. Their general hypothesis was that L2 phonological rules conform to the general principles of phonological theory available in L1 learning. As an example, they considered predicted stages of development for a Korean learner learning English. For example, they predict the following stages for the acquisition of [s] and [š], which in Korean are in allophonic variation (sounds that vary only in pronunciation based on surrounding sounds, but which do not yield a meaning difference), an example of contrast (c) above.

[handwritten margin note: TYPES OF CONTRASTS]

Stage 1: No contrast: *sea* and *she* are pronounced [ši].
Stage 2: Partial contrast: distinction between derived words and non-derived words (*messing* and *meshing* versus *sea* and *she*). The former are distinct, but the latter pair are homophones.
Stage 3: Full contrast: native rules are not applied in any context, derived or basic.

Their investigation of L2 learners in a cross-sectional and instructional setting suggested that, indeed, the acquisition of phonological contrasts adheres to universal principles of phonology. Their work relies on the concept of rules, whereas Optimality Theory relies on constraints. Eckman and his colleagues argue that their data on contrasts cannot be captured within an approach, such as Optimality Theory, that only allows constraints.

[handwritten margin note: Acquisition of phonological contrast adheres to Universal Principles of Phonology]

In sum, research in this area shows both NL influences as well as universal influences, a finding common to syntax as well.

7.6.4 Ontogeny Phylogeny Model

[handwritten note: captures similarities between L1 and L2 and universals.]

This model is intended to capture the basic patterns of ILs. In particular, it captures phonological relationships between L1 and L2, as well as universals. Major (2001) states these relationships as follows: "L2 increases, L1 decreases, and U [universals] increases and then decreases" (p. 82). At the early stage, the learner only has a first language and a "dormant" U (except those parts of U that are operational in the L1). It is important to note that U refers to the "universals of language that are not already part of the L1 or L2 system" (p. 83). This relationship is illustrated by Figures 7.1–7.6.

- L1
- L2 Similar
- U

FIGURE 7.1
Stage 1 (*Source*: © 2001 from *Foreign Accent* by R. Major. Reproduced by permission of Lawrence Erlbaum Associates, a division of Taylor & Francis Group.)

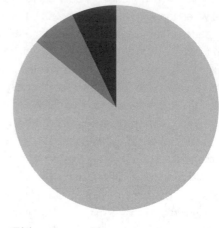

- L1
- L2 Similar
- U

FIGURE 7.2
Stage 2 (*Source*: © 2001 from *Foreign Accent* by R. Major. Reproduced by permission of Lawrence Erlbaum Associates, a division of Taylor & Francis Group.)

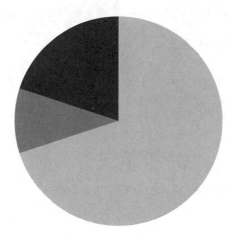

- L1
- L2 Similar
- U

FIGURE 7.3
Stage 3 (*Source*: © 2001 from *Foreign Accent* by R. Major. Reproduced by permission of Lawrence Erlbaum Associates, a division of Taylor & Francis Group.)

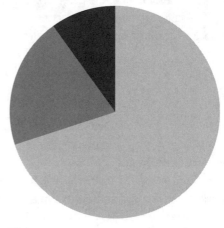

- L1
- L2 Similar
- U

FIGURE 7.4
Stage 4 (*Source*: © 2001 from *Foreign Accent* by R. Major. Reproduced by permission of Lawrence Erlbaum Associates, a division of Taylor & Francis Group.)

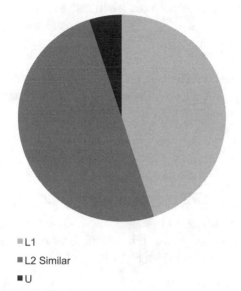

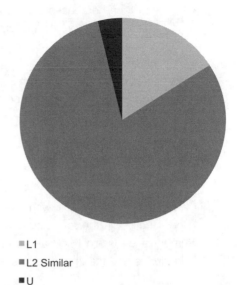

■ L1
■ L2 Similar
■ U

■ L1
■ L2 Similar
■ U

FIGURE 7.5
Stage 5 (*Source*: © 2001 from *Foreign Accent* by R. Major. Reproduced by permission of Lawrence Erlbaum Associates, a division of Taylor & Francis Group.)

FIGURE 7.6
Stage 6 (*Source*: © 2001 from *Foreign Accent* by R. Major. Reproduced by permission of Lawrence Erlbaum Associates, a division of Taylor & Francis Group.)

There are four corollaries to the Ontogeny Phylogeny Model, namely, the chronological, stylistic, similarity, and markedness corollaries. The first is intended to capture L2 development; the second, contextual variation (e.g., formal, casual speech); the third, similarity/dissimilarity in language; and the fourth, issues of markedness in language. As can be seen below, each corollary specifies the relationship between the three constructs: L1, L2, and Universal (U).

- **Chronological Corollary:** IL develops chronologically in the following manner: (a) L2 increases, (b) L1 decreases, and (c) U increases and then decreases (p. 85). This is demonstrated in Figures 7.1–7.6.

- **Stylistic Corollary**: IL varies stylistically in the following manner: As style becomes more formal, (a) L2 increases, (b) L1 decreases, and (c) U increases and then decreases (p. 93).

- **Similarity Corollary**: In similar phenomena, IL develops chronologically in the following manner: (a) L2 increases slowly, (b) L1 decreases slowly, and (c) U increases slowly and then decreases slowly. Thus, the role of L1 is much greater than U, compared with less-similar phenomena. By implication, the less similar the phenomena (i.e., the more dissimilar), the more important the role of U is compared with L1 (p. 100).

- **Markedness Corollary**: In marked phenomena, IL develops chronologically in the following manner: (a) L2 increases slowly, (b) L1 decreases (at a normal rate) and then decreases slowly, and (c) U increases rapidly and decreases slowly. Thus, except for the earliest stages, the role of U is much greater than L1, compared with less-marked phenomena (p. 107).

As can be seen, Major incorporates IL development (chronological), a well as variation captured through the stylistic corollary, and linguistic relationships, such as similarity and markedness.

7.7 CONCLUSION

This chapter has dealt with the acquisition of linguistic phenomena from a formal perspective. In the following chapter, we deal with the lexicon, which has assumed importance within Minimalism, and, in Chapter 9, we turn to functional models of language and the impact of these approaches on the study of SLA.

POINTS TO REMEMBER

- The field of linguistics has had an important influence on SLA. Linguistic approaches to SLA focus on a description of the linguistic systems of L2 learners. These approaches claim that at least some aspects of language learning is innate and are referred to as nativist.

- Universal Grammar (UG) is the set of abstract principles that underlie all natural languages. Languages vary in terms of the parameters that they have, but they all follow the underlying principles of UG. UG is the innate language faculty that limits the extent to which languages can vary.

- The Poverty of the Stimulus argument in favor of an innate language faculty refers to the fact that learners of a language know more about what can and cannot be done in a language than they could have possibly learned from the input alone.

- Positive evidence of what is possible in a language refers to the well-formed utterances that learners are exposed to in the input. Negative evidence refers to information provided to the learner that his/her utterance is deviant with regard to TL norms (i.e., wrong). Because of the infrequency of negative evidence and the fact that positive evidence does not make it clear to the learner whether he/she has not heard a particular form because it is not possible in the language or because of coincidence, nativists argue that there must be innate principles that the learner is born with that constrain grammar formation.

Positive evidence x Negative evidence ↳

- Some L2 research has considered what the initial state is that an L2 learner begins with. Do learners have access to this innate language faculty when learning an L2?

- The original Fundamental Difference Hypothesis stated that there is a fundamental difference in how L1 learners and L2 learners learn the TL in terms of ultimate attainment, and the fact that all L1 learners fully acquire the L1, whereas there is a lot of variability among L2 learners. Thus, the original FDH claimed that adult L2 learners do not have access to UG.

- There are various theories about whether or not L2 learners have access to UG when learning the L2.

- More recent research from nativist perspectives has focused on whether L2 learners can acquire features of the L2 that are not present in their L1. These theories include the Representational Deficit Hypothesis, the Missing Surface Inflection Hypothesis, the Prosodic Transfer Hypothesis, and the Shallow Structure Hypothesis.

- The Fundamental Difference Hypothesis was revised. Learners have access through their L1 to the operations of merge, agree, and move (i.e., UG), as described in the Minimalist Program. Language learning may not draw on a different learning mechanism than other types of learning, and the difference between L1 and L2 learning may not be as different as previously stated.

- The Bottleneck Hypothesis states that learners are able to acquire syntax and semantics, but that there is a bottleneck in the acquisition of inflectional morphemes.

- The Hierarchy of Phonological Difficulty predicts that learners will have the most problems with obligatory phonemic contrasts in the L2 that are not obligatory phonemic contrasts in the L1, whereas the contrasts that exist in both the L1 and the L2 will not be problematic.

- The Markedness Differential Hypothesis is based on a phonological theory of markedness, with a progression from least marked (easiest) language types to most marked (most difficult).

- L2 syllable structure is shaped by the NL but also by universal tendencies, such as simplifying to CV (through deletion or epenthesis).

- Flege's Speech Learning Model states that a new phonetic category will be formed for the L2 if the learner perceives it as significantly different from an L1 phonetic category.

- Optimality Theory deals with faithfulness constraints that match the input with the output and markedness constraints that ensure the well-formedness of the output. L2 learning involves the reranking of NL constraints.

- The Ontogeny Phylogeny Model captures phonological relationships between L1 and L2, as well as universals.

SUGGESTIONS FOR ADDITIONAL READING

First and second language acquisition (2011). Jürgen Meisel. Cambridge University Press.

Meaning in the second language (2008). Roumyana Slabakova. Mouton de Gruyter.

Investigations of the syntax–semantic–pragmatics interface (2008). Robert Van Valin Jr. (Ed.). Benjamins.

Ultimate attainment in second language acquisition: A case study (2007). Donna Lardiere. Lawrence Erlbaum Associates.

Fossilized second language grammars: The acquisition of grammatical gender (2005). Florencia Franceschina. John Benjamins Publishing Company.

Inquiries in linguistic development: In honor of Lydia White (2006). Roumyana Slabakova, Silvina A. Montrul, and Philippe Prévost (Eds.). John Benjamins.

Exploring the syntax–semantics interface (2005). R. Van Valin. Cambridge University Press.

Second language acquisition and universal grammar (2003). Lydia White. Cambridge University Press.

Tense and aspect morphology in L2 acquisition (2002). Rafael Salaberry and Yasuhiro Shirai (Eds.). John Benjamins.

Foreign accent (2001). Roy Major. Lawrence Erlbaum Associates.

Second language syntax: A generative introduction (2001). Roger Hawkins. Blackwell.

The development of past tense morphology in L2 Spanish (2001). Rafael Salaberry. John Benjamins.

Tense and aspect in second language acquisition: Form, meaning, and use (2000). *Language Learning Supplement*. Kathleen Bardovi-Harlig. Blackwell.

Syntactic theory and the structure of English: A minimalist approach (1997). Andrew Radford. Cambridge University Press.

The minimalist program (1995). Noam Chomsky. The MIT Press.

Language acquisition studies in generative grammar (1994). Teun Hoekstra and Bonnie D. Schwartz (Eds.). John Benjamins.

Linguistic perspectives on second language acquisition (1989). Susan Gass and Jacquelyn Schachter (Eds.). Cambridge University Press.

Chomsky's universal grammar (1988). Vivian Cook. Basil Blackwell.

MORE TO DO AND MORE TO THINK ABOUT ...

1. This chapter has dealt with the concept of language universals and their relationship to SLA. Consider the notion of IL universals. What might these be? How would these relate to the concept of language universals?

2. In what ways can universals affect the development of IL grammars in terms of the nature of how grammatical knowledge relates to input? Recall that, within the UG framework, learnability takes on a central role. How does this concept relate to Kellerman's (1979) notion of transfer, discussed in Chapter 5? Focus particularly on his notion of a learner's psychotypology and of transfer being related to the learner's perception of language distance and language specificity/neutrality.

3. In this chapter, we considered clustering and its effect on L2 grammars, particularly in regards to the pro-drop parameter. What might the function of the use or nonuse of pronouns be? That is, why are pronouns obligatory in English and not so in other languages? How can our knowledge of parameter clusterings help language teachers?

4. Suppose that linguistic research finds that the clusterings are incorrect—that, in fact, the clusterings involve other linguistic properties. What sort of dilemma would this finding pose to L2 researchers? How might the dilemma be turned around to put L2 researchers in a position of making valuable contributions to arguments about the nature of language? How would language teachers fit in to this debate, and what would their contributions to it be?

LINK

1. http://tinyurl.com/9a9x4hw

spelling/ Meaning/ Pronunciation

CHAPTER EIGHT

The Lexicon → vocabulary

→ lack of vocabulary or wrong word choices can make communication fail

→ Lexicon is essential for comprehension

→ Lexical errors are disruptive to communication

→ Learners need Lexical skills to produce and understand sentences.

FORM   MEANING   USE

8.1 THE SIGNIFICANCE OF THE LEXICON

In SLA research to date, there has been much less attention paid to the lexicon than to other parts of language, although this picture is quickly changing (see Singleton, 1999a, 1999b; Nation, 2001; Bogaards & Laufer, 2004; Laufer & Nation, 2012). Furthermore, there are numerous reasons for believing that lexis is important in SLA. In fact, the lexicon may be the most important language component for learners, a notion that has developed in SLA owing, in part, to influences from outside the field. For example, even Chomskyan scholars and those who work within the Minimalist framework (see Chapter 7), who had at one point dismissed the importance of vocabulary, now claim that language learning is largely lexical learning (e.g., Chomsky, 1989). Tomasello (2003) goes even further, arguing that, "learning words and learning grammatical constructions are both part of the same overall process" (p. 93). Moreover, the importance of understanding vocabulary knowledge and development has been highlighted—and, at the same time, perhaps also made more complex—as researchers and theoreticians have begun to move away from discrete classification of language forms as either lexical or grammatical and toward a more encompassing and accurate view of lexicogrammar (e.g., Liu & Jiang, 2009).

Another take on the importance of the L2 lexicon is that, of all error types, learners consider vocabulary errors the most serious (Politzer, 1978, as cited in Levenston, 1979, p. 147). Additionally, large corpora of errors consistently indicate that lexical errors are the most common among L2 learners. Meara (1984, p. 229) cited Blaas (1982) as indicating that lexical errors outnumbered grammatical errors by a 3:1 ratio in one corpus. Corpus-based findings such as these have been confirmed in classroom-based studies as well, where both teachers and learners have been found to draw attention frequently to lexical issues. For example, Lyster (1998) found that 80 percent of learners' lexical errors received corrective feedback, in comparison with 70 percent for phonological, and 56 percent for grammatical, errors. Likewise, Ellis et al. (2001a) found that, of the errors corrected by the teacher, almost 40 percent targeted vocabulary. Students, as well, have been found to explicitly draw attention to lexical forms (e.g., J. N. Williams, 1999; R. Ellis et al., 2001b; Zhao & Bitchener, 2007; Alcón Soler & Garcia Mayo, 2008). In J. N. Williams (1999), for example, 80 percent of learners' language-related questions pertained to vocabulary. Moreover, NSs find lexical errors to be more disruptive than grammatical errors (Johansson, 1978, as cited in Meara, 1984, p. 229). Gass (1988b) seconded this argument, noting that grammatical errors generally result in structures that are understood, whereas lexical errors may interfere with communication. As an example, consider 8-1. The listener may notice an error in 8-1 and may infer that the speaker is nonnative, but still would probably understand what was intended.

(8-1)   Can you tell me where is the train station?

On the other hand, consider an error cited by Gairns and Redman (1986, p. 3):

(8-2)   I feel sorry for people who live in the suburbs.

Presumably, the typical NS of English who heard this would wonder what the speaker felt was wrong with suburbs—perhaps they are too stilted and boring. Gairns and Redman argued that this utterance, made by a NS of Spanish, was presumably motivated by the Spanish "false friend" *suburbio*, meaning "slum quarter, shantytown." The average English NS would misunderstand the sentence and never consider that the speaker had chosen the incorrect lexical item.

Many linguistic theories place the lexicon in a central place, which also suggests its importance in language learning. Levelt (1989, p. 181) maintained that the lexicon is the driving force in sentence production (i.e., in encoding or sentence generation), which he described as a formulation process:

> Formulation processes are lexically driven. This means that grammatical and phonological encodings are mediated by lexical entries. The preverbal message triggers lexical items into activity. The syntactic, morphological, and phonological properties of an activated lexical item trigger, in turn, the grammatical, morphological and phonological encoding procedures underlying the generation of an utterance. The assumption that the lexicon is an essential mediator between conceptualization and grammatical and phonological encoding will be called the *lexical hypothesis*. The lexical hypothesis entails, in particular, that nothing in the speaker's message will *by itself* trigger a syntactic form, such as a passive or a dative construction. There must be mediating lexical items, triggered by the message, which by their grammatical properties and their order of activation cause the Grammatical Encoder to generate a particular syntactic structure.

The lexical hypothesis ←

Levelt was referring to production by competent, adult NSs, but it is also the case that the lexicon is an important factor, if not the most important factor, in accounting for the bulk of L2 data.

The lexicon is also important in comprehension, especially oral comprehension, as Altman (1990) showed in her overview of sentence comprehension. Lexical information is clearly used in helping to determine syntactic relationships, and comprehension is of great importance to SLA. If words cannot be isolated from the speech stream, and if lexical information cannot be used to interpret the utterances, the input will not be comprehended. Thus, comprehension of the input depends to a large extent on lexical skills (see section 8.4). The lexicon is also important in reading, but, in the vast bulk of the world's orthographies, the writing system itself, by virtue of having spaces between words, guides readers in the isolation of individual words.

In summary, there are various reasons for saying that the lexicon is important for L2 learners. Both learners and NSs recognize the importance of getting the words right, and lexical errors are numerous and disruptive. In general, learners need good lexical skills to produce sentences and to understand them.

8.2 LEXICAL KNOWLEDGE: WHAT DOES IT MEAN TO KNOW A WORD?

A major task of L2 lexical research is to discover what L2 learners know about the lexicon of the L2. In order to achieve this through empirical investigation, however, theory must first provide a robust and thorough model of the types of knowledge an L2 learner can have about a particular word and words in general. Much of the research in this domain has sought to address this issue and the related one of how to best measure lexical knowledge. As should become clear in reading this section, vocabulary knowledge is surely a multifaceted construct (see Laufer & Nation, 2012).

8.2.1 Production and Reception

An initial consideration is that learners appear to have differing degrees of knowledge of their L2 lexicon. Nation (2001, p. 27) lists the following as word knowledge types necessary if one is to be considered to have complete knowledge of a word:

- **form**:
    - spoken (what does it sound like? *eight* sounds like [eit]);
    - written (spelling);
- **meaning**:
    - form and meaning (what is the meaning of a particular form?);
    - concept and referents (what concepts are included?);
    - associations (what words do we think of when we hear this form?);
- **use**:
    - grammatical functions (the patterns the word occurs in);
    - collocations (what words can occur with the word, for example, with *vacation*, one says *take*);
    - constraints on use (e.g., registers—in what contexts do we expect to hear this word?).

The above examples reflect receptive knowledge, but there is also productive knowledge to consider, which deals with aspects of pronunciation (knowing how to pronounce a word, as opposed to recognizing it), spelling, nuances of meaning (as opposed to getting the general meaning), grammatical constraints (e.g., *impact* as a verb takes a direct object, but *impact* as a noun occurs in the phrase *has an impact on*).

As an example, consider the word *overextended*. There are many things we have to know, some of which are listed below.

Receptive knowledge includes:

- recognizing the word in writing or orally;
- knowing the general meaning;
- knowing the specific meaning in a specific context of use;
- knowing that it is made up of the component parts—*over*, *extend*, *-ed*;
- knowing that it has a possible negative connotation (as opposed to *overqualify*, which may or may not have a negative connotation);
- knowing that it generally occurs with *himself*, *herself*, *oneself*, *themselves*, *ourselves*, *yourself*;
- knowing that the opposite is *underextended*.

On the other hand, productive knowledge involves greater specificity and includes, among others:

- knowing how to accurately pronounce a word or correctly spell it;
- knowing the precise meaning in a variety of contexts;
- knowing that *She overextended herself* is OK, but that *She overextended her chair* is probably not OK, in the absence of a highly specific context;
- knowing the precise context of use.

TIME TO THINK ...

Think of a low-frequency word in your L2. Think of all the aspects of receptive and productive knowledge that you know about this word, using the example of *overextended* above as a guide. Do you think that this would be easy or difficult to teach? Why, or why not?

Learners generally have a wider range of receptive[1] vocabulary than productive vocabulary. However, as discussed in Teichroew (1982), the picture is really more complicated. Lexical knowledge cannot be captured by means of a simple dichotomy. Teichroew proposed that vocabulary knowledge can best be represented as a continuum, with the initial stage being recognition, and the final being production

[handwritten margin note: productive knowledge]

(see also Stewart et al., 2012). In Teichroew's view, production should not be viewed in a monolithic fashion, for productive knowledge includes producing both a range of meanings as well as appropriate collocations (i.e., what words go together), as has been described above. For example, in our discussion of the word *break* with regard to the work of Kellerman (Chapter 6), we noted the many meanings of that word. Initially, learners may know the meaning of *break* as in *break a leg* or *break a pencil*, and only with time do they learn the full range of meanings and such collocations as *His voice broke at age 13*. (We return to a discussion of production and reception in sections 8.5.1 and 8.5.2 below.)

[handwritten margin note: POTENTIAL VOCABULARY / REAL VOCABULARY]

Another distinction to be made is one between *potential* and *real* vocabulary (Berman et al., 1968, as cited in Palmberg, 1987, p. 21). Potential vocabulary consists of words a learner will recognize, even though she or he has not yet seen them in the L2. Examples would be common scientific and technological terms. Much of this vocabulary spreads from language to language, with little indication of whether the term was first coined by a Russian, English, German, or Danish speaker. Real vocabulary consists of words the learner is familiar with after (and because of) exposure.

[handwritten margin note: 3 TYPES OF VOCABULARY KNOWLEDGE: passive, controlled-active and free active / different developmental rates: / passive - fasten / free-active - slowest]

Laufer and Paribakht (1998), using research by Laufer (1998), investigated three types of vocabulary knowledge: passive, controlled active, and free active. Passive knowledge involves understanding the most frequent meaning of a word, controlled-active knowledge involves cued recall (e.g., a test item might include *The railway con_____ the city with its suburbs*, where the first few letters of a word are included to eliminate other possibilities), and free-active knowledge involves spontaneous use of the word. Laufer and Paribakht found that these three knowledge types developed at different rates. Passive vocabulary knowledge was the fastest, whereas active (particularly free active) was the slowest. Furthermore, passive vocabulary was always larger than active vocabulary, although there was a difference between learners in a foreign-language setting and those in an L2 setting. The gap between knowledge types was smaller in the foreign-language setting, suggesting a strong role for the environment in learning.

[handwritten note: → the way how language system is represented in the mind of the learner]

8.2.2 Knowledge and Control

[handwritten note: → processing system fo control actual performance]

A different distinction was drawn by Bialystok and Sharwood Smith (1985), namely, between *knowledge* and *control* (see Chapter 10). Knowledge was defined as "the way in which the language system is represented in the mind of the learner (the categories and relationships in long-term memory)," whereas control was defined as "the processing system for controlling that system during actual performance" (p. 104). The authors made an analogy to a library. The knowledge is in the books and in the way they are organized, and control is in the way the books are accessed. With regard to the latter, the library/language user needs to know how to determine which books are in the library and how to locate the books. The first time one uses a library, it is difficult to find one's way around, but, with repeated use, access gets easier and more efficient.

The distinction made between knowledge and control is particularly useful with regard to vocabulary, because it is not bound to just reception or production. Rather, both production and reception include information regarding knowledge and control.

However, the analogy has its drawbacks. In considering the library analogy as it is applied to the lexicon, there are a number of questions to be addressed, among them: What is a representation? How exhaustive are the representations? In other words, do the representations capture everything we know about words?

The library analogy, although useful, does not capture the dynamic, changing nature of the L2 lexicon. Books in a library are static and unchanging. A book purchased 10 years ago does not change in any significant way on the owner's shelf. Unchanging, static, formalized, symbolic descriptions cannot account for all of lexical learning.

The library metaphor may work reasonably well for phonological knowledge of the lexicon. There is a need for some sorts of phonological idealization, or what may be called *representations*, if only as targets for pronunciation (see Linell, 1982; Ard, 1989). However, representations do not capture everything important about lexical pronunciations. For example, they do not capture special effects (including unusual patterns of stress or emphasis) a speaker may choose to place on a word. In certain situations, a speaker may address an interlocutor as *darling*, while imitating the pronunciation of a Gabor sister to show affectation.

Tyler (1989, p. 444) noted that, "the representation of a word cannot contain all the various and subtle interpretations that the word could have in different real-world contexts." She noted that pragmatic inferencing is required, along with real-world knowledge. The point of this for SLA is that learners have to know more than just the representation to be able to use a word and understand it in a way approximating NSs.

In sum, finding meaning is not simply a matter of finding stored, fixed information. Rather, constructive processes are involved in finding meanings for words. Because processes are involved, we cannot rule out the possibility that there can be varying degrees of control over these processes. Similarly, we demonstrate later that processes in using words, such as in production and in comprehension, have to be learned. Thus, we can talk of varying degrees of knowledge of the processes. Knowledge and control are both important, but their relationship is more intertwined than sequential. One does not just have knowledge and then try to control it.

8.2.3 Breadth and Depth

This, in general, is tantamount to a distinction between quantity and quality. Breadth of knowledge refers to the number of words learners know (Nation, 2001; Nassaji, 2004). On the other hand, depth of vocabulary knowledge is a quality measure (Read, 1993, 2000; Meara, 1996; Nassaji, 2004). Earlier, we discussed what knowing a word entails, and it is this complexity that is referred to as vocabulary knowledge depth. This might include, not only the meaning of the word, but also semantic relationships with other words, syntactic patterning, collocations, pronunciation, and so forth.

Research has shown that both breadth and depth of knowledge play a role in comprehension, although most studies have investigated reading comprehension. For example, numerous studies (e.g., Koda, 1989; Coady et al., 1993; Haynes & Baker, 1993; Laufer, 1997a, 1997b; Qian, 1999; Schmitt et al., 2011) have shown that there is a relationship between breadth of knowledge and reading comprehension. (See Stæhr, 2009, for an example of a rare study of the relationship between vocabulary knowledge and listening comprehension.) Jeon and Yamashita (2011) recently meta-analyzed research on the correlation between learners' reading comprehension and real-word decoding (i.e., a measure of breadth of vocabulary knowledge). Synthesizing across 14 studies, the findings portray a fairly strong relationship between the two. In addition to breadth of knowledge, depth of knowledge has been found to be a better predictor of L2 reading comprehension than just breadth of knowledge. For instance, Nassaji (2004) found that depth of knowledge could be tied to particular strategy use (e.g., identifying, evaluating, and monitoring), to more effective lexical inferencing strategies, and to the success of inferencing. The following excerpts illustrate the difference in lexically skilled and lexically less skilled participants in his study.

Lexically skilled:
"Sewage in their nose . . ." "smell of their sewage in their nose . . ." "have dust between their toes and the smell of sewage in their nose . . ."

I think, there a lot of dirty things around the city and that those things are making smells, and the smell goes to their noses, so sewage are things like dirty things, garbage, like, according to this . . . "and the smell of the sewage in their nose." Yes.

Lexically less skilled:
". . . and the smell of sewage in their nose . . . in their nose . . . their toes . . ." "the toes and the smell of sewage in their nose," "their toes . . ." umm . . . because it is in their nose, I think . . . "between their toes . . ." I am not sure . . . because something in their nose their . . . mmm . . . is . . . mmm . . . maybe it's their . . . it's their . . . I'm not sure. "the smell of sewage . . ." it's the smell . . . the sewage it is something . . . there is some smell . . . may be sew . . . I'm not sure.

The differences between these two excerpts are striking. The first major difference is that the lexically less skilled participant is primarily repeating what is in the text, peppered with *umms* and other hesitation phenomena. She or he never focuses on the actual meaning of the text. The first participant repeats a large chunk of relevant speech that includes *dust between their toes*. And, *dust* provides an important clue in unraveling the meaning of *sewage*.

Pulido (2003) looked at a range of issues (proficiency and topic familiarity) with regard to reading comprehension, but germane to this discussion is the finding that sight vocabulary knowledge (which measured breadth of knowledge of a limited set of vocabulary items, namely, the nontargeted words in the experimental reading passages) had an impact on incidental vocabulary gain. Laufer (1997b) went a step further claiming that, at least for L2 readers, the "threshold for reading comprehension is, to a large extent, lexical" (p. 21; see also Stæhr, 2009; Horst, 2010; Schmitt et al., 2011; Schmitt & Schmitt, in press).

Read (2004) discussed various ways of conceptualizing depth of knowledge, including precision of meaning, comprehensive word knowledge, and network knowledge. He noted that different researchers mean different things by depth of knowledge, with some using meaning, others using comprehensiveness, and others using network associations. He further notes that any of these terms is problematic, because the lexicon is "something that is inherently ill-defined, multidimensional, variable and thus resistant to neat classification" (p. 224).

[handwritten margin note: DEPTH OF KNOWLEDGE]

As can be seen, knowing an L2 word involves different ways of knowing, including receptive and productive knowledge. In the next section, we consider more specific details of what learners have to know about a word, including its meaning, subcategorization restrictions, associations, and collocations.

[handwritten note: place of each word in a sentence (place can change meaning)]

[handwritten margin note: student tend to transfer from L1 to L2]

8.2.4 Subcategorization

As NSs of our language, we know that some verbs require objects, some verbs require indirect and direct objects, some verbs require animate subjects, and so forth. Additionally, NSs of English, for example, know how to interpret the role certain noun phrases play in the action described by the verb. For example, a native English speaker knows the relationships between 8-3 and 8-4:

(8-3) *X* rents *Y* to *Z*.

(8-4) *Z* rents *Y* from *X*

Or, a native speaker of Italian knows that, in 8-5, even though the subject is "the dogs," the meaning is "I like dogs" (the dogs are pleasing to me).

(8-5) mi   piacciono   i cani
       to me   please (pl)   the dogs
       "I like dogs."

This is an area of difficulty, as we will see in Chapter 10 (section 10.2.3) in the discussion of input processing. Thus, it is not enough to know the meanings of individual words. In 8-3 and 8-4, a speaker must know that, when *rent* is accompanied by *to*, the subject is the owner. On the other hand, when *rent* is accompanied by *from*, the subject is the person who takes possession of the property for a short time.

This type of information can differ from language to language. Adjemian (1983) found that L2 learners tended to transfer lexical patterns from their L1 to their L2. The scope of his research was the lexical acquisition of French by native English speakers and of English by native French speakers. The following sentences were produced by the native French speakers learning English:

(8-6)   At sixty-five years old they must *retire themselves* because this is a rule of society.

(8-7)   They want to *fight themselves* against this (tuition increase).

Note that the reflexives in these sentences are not intended to indicate emphasis. In the translation equivalents of these sentences in French, the verbs require the reflexive morpheme *se* (*se retirer* and *se battre*).

English learners of French produced ungrammatical sentences such as 8-8:

(8-8)   Elle marche les chats.
        She walks the cats.

Sentence 8-8 is ungrammatical in French because the verb *marcher*—"to walk"—cannot take a direct object. Another verb (*se promener*) must be used. Learners in both cases assume that verbs in their L2 take the same kinds of subjects and objects as they do in their native language.

TIME TO THINK ...

Consider the vocabulary errors that the L2 learners made in 8-6, 8-7, and 8-8. When learning your L2, did you make similar errors? Have you heard learners of your L1 make similar errors in vocabulary? How could you deal with these in a pedagogical context? Do you consider these to be vocabulary errors? Why or why not? If not, what type of error is it?

8.2.5 Word Associations and Networks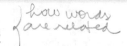

Part of what is involved in knowing a word and, in particular, in knowing a word in a manner similar to NSs is the association that is made to other words. Meara (1978) investigated the lexical associations made by learners of French. Modern theories of lexical semantics are concerned with the relationships between words. Word associations are a reasonable means of determining how individuals relate words. Meara found that learners tended to produce rather different associations from those made by NSs of French. NSs primarily gave paradigmatic (semantically-related and the same part of speech) or syntagmatic (word combinations) associations, based on semantic factors:

Paradigmatic

Stimulus	*Response*
man	woman
	dog
	boy
	child

Syntagmatic

Stimulus	*Response*
brush	teeth
hold	hands
black	mark
bank	robber

Learners tended to give responses based on phonological similarity, such as *plafond*—"ceiling"—or *professeur*—"professor"—to the stimulus *profond* "deep." A possible interpretation is that the learners had not constructed the network of relationships necessary for fluent word associations in their L2. A later study by Schmitt and Meara (1997) investigated word associations by Japanese learners of English, specifically word associations and their relationship with verbal suffixes. The authors found that the ability to produce native-like word associations, not surprisingly, is related to suffix knowledge as well as to vocabulary size and general proficiency.

In both our L1 and our L2, we establish networks that may be semantic networks, syntactic networks (words behave in similar/same ways syntactically), phonological networks, and so forth. Essentially, a lexical network involves the linking of words in some way. Henriksen (1999) uses exactly this approach in her discussion of depth of vocabulary knowledge. Various forms of word-association measures have been used in L2 research (e.g., Söderman, 1993; Schmitt, 1998a; Singleton, 1999a, 1999b; Meara & Fitzpatrick, 2000), with considerable discussion on development in terms of a movement from phonological to semantic associations.

8.2.6 Word Formation

Knowledge of the lexicon also involves knowing how to combine elements to create novel lexical items. The importance of word formation varies from language to language. Word formation is much less important in English than in many other languages. Hankamer (1989) noted that Turkish contains much more productive derivational morphology than does English, allowing it to form more words through morphology. The situation is even more extreme in a language such as Eskimo or in a language with both verbal and nominal incorporation, such as Chukchee. For example, in Chukchee, verbs meaning "to whale hunt," "to walrus hunt," and "to reindeer hunt" are formed from the words meaning "hunt," "whale," "walrus," and "reindeer."

Another factor that should be pointed out for English word formation is that many of the complicated words in English are taken from Latin and Greek. The average English speaker is not aware of how these words are formed. The situation is different in German. The German word *Wasserstoff* means "hydrogen" and is a part-by-part translation (*hydro* means "water," which is *Wasser* in German, and *gen* means "substance" or *Stoff* in German). A German speaker is thus more likely to recognize the word-formation process in *Wasserstoff* than is an English speaker in *hydrogen*. We might expect German speakers to be more sensitive to word-formation processes in general in learning an L2 as well.

Olshtain (1987) investigated the development of word-formation processes by learners of Hebrew. She considered the use of new words from the perspective of production and interpretation. In the case of production tasks, learners showed a progression toward TL patterns. For example, NSs tended to provide innovative words in tasks 74 percent of the time, advanced learners 67 percent, and intermediate learners only 19 percent. Additionally, when intermediate learners did innovate, the mechanisms they used differed from those of both advanced learners and native speakers. Only the intermediate students relied predominately on suffixes, emphasized in their language classes as the major means of forming new words. Both the advanced learners and NSs used a greater variety of means of forming new words. They were much more likely to use compounding, blending, and root changing than were the intermediate learners. However, on an interpretation task, a task that required learners to assign meaning to new words, neither group of learners performed like NSs. On this task, learners were asked to interpret words out of context. The inability to interpret words in a native-like fashion, even by those who *produced* words like NSs, suggests that even advanced speakers are highly context bound in their use of the L2.

8.2.7 Formulaic Language, Collocations, and Chunking

Individual words often appear together on a regular basis. For example, NSs of English, when confronted with an economics article and seeing the word *underdeveloped*, might predict that the next word will be *nation* or *country*. In other words, the choice of the next word is quite narrow. Other collocations, such as *broad daylight*, *green with envy*, and *deep sigh* are common in language and are often processed as single units. These are different from idioms such as *kick the bucket* and multiword structures that signify a particular meaning and are represented by single words in many languages, such as *yellow jacket*. Unfortunately, in English, orthography is not always a good indicator of the status of words. *Matchbox*, *match-box*, and *match box* are all attested spellings. Learners have to learn these multiword units as wholes. Of course, in a perceptual situation, a learner may err and interpret bound phrases like these word by word. The interpretation gained in this manner will generally not make any sense in its context.

An important factor about these combinations is that they are not totally free. In fact, there are strong statistical or frequency-based constraints on possible co-occurrences, as is shown in gap-filling tests. Consider what words could be chosen in the following frames:

I'm afraid I have some _____ news.

She looked out the window and breathed a _____ sigh.

I wonder what's wrong. She's been in there a _____ time.

He's very stubborn. He's had a _____ will ever since he was a baby.

I know that's true as a _____ rule, but this may be an exception.

Akhmatova (1974, p. 24) suggested that:

> It follows that word-combination becomes "free" in the sense of not having any constraints imposed upon it only when words are combined by *creative* or "imaginative" speakers who are not content with merely reproducing the already existing complexes. Words are combined "freely" only by people who strive for novelty and originality. It is mainly in fiction or other types of imaginative speaking and writing that we find word-combinations that are really "free."

Until recently, relatively little attention had been paid to these problems in L2 learning. Meara (1983, 1987) gave only four sources for collocations in his bibliographies for vocabulary in an L2: Alexander (1982), Binon and Cornu (1985), Brown (1974), and Cowie (1978). All of these studies dealt only with the pedagogical problem. None discussed how learners acquire competence in word combinations and collocations.

In recent years, research has looked at collocations as one form of language chunk. We discussed chunking[2] and prefabricated patterns in Chapter 5. Essentially, we can think of chunks as prefabricated patterns where the learner may not know how to "unpackage" the component parts, as was seen with the Japanese child Uguisu's use of *doyou* as a single, unanalyzed unit. Or, one can think of chunks as a form of collocation where, with repeated exposure, we learn that *take a bath* or *take a shower* go together, as opposed to *do a bath* or *do a shower*. One can further see that this reduces the learning burden, in that storage is often limited to a small number of items, and, if some of them are multiword, less processing time is presumably involved.

As an example, one might think of learning a language with a different script. At first, we have difficulty in determining the different parts of letters. Let us consider the following examples from Hebrew, Arabic, and Korean.

Hebrew: ז ל ו

Arabic: ک ش ق

Korean: 언 어

When learning a language with a different script it is often difficult to recognize individual letters (and even more difficult to produce the letter) or to determine one letter from another. With repeated exposure, learners can see each letter as a unified whole, much as those familiar with a Latin script can see the letters *a, b, c* as unified wholes, without seeing the individual strokes, and can identify the letter quickly and effortlessly. At a later stage, we chunk larger items together, such as individual words, and can understand them without seeing the component parts. For example, very frequent words, such as *the* or *and* are recognized without being decomposed into each letter.

Learners are often forced to be innovative in their word combinations. The result is that misunderstandings abound. Consider the following example. Normal synonyms for *local* include *parochial* and *provincial*. Consider the differences between the following statements:

(8-9)   The *Detroit Free Press* is a local paper.

(8-10) The *Detroit Free Press* is a parochial paper.

(8-11) The *Detroit Free Press* is a provincial paper.

The first of these descriptions is just a matter-of-fact account. The second two ascribe pejorative evaluations about the quality of the newspaper. A learner who said one of the latter two might be surprised to hear an interlocutor object that she thinks the paper is pretty good. When we hear something unusual, we assume that the speaker had a good reason to say things in this unusual manner. The problem for the learner is to learn how not to be innovative and to stick to the standard combinations.

From a more strictly theoretical perspective, Nation (2001) characterizes N. Ellis's position on chunking (2001) as follows:

> Language knowledge and language use can be accounted for by the storage of chunks of language in long-term memory and by experience of how likely particular chunks are to occur with other particular chunks, without the need to refer to underlying rules. Language knowledge and use is based on associations between sequentially observed language items. This viewpoint sees collocational knowledge as the essence of language knowledge.
>
> (p. 318)

This view, though popular, is not supported unanimously. Others (e.g., Wray, 2002) have proposed that learners approach and process words that they are exposed to as individual units, without retaining probabilistic or collocational information.

In order to test and further refine these and other proposals, chunks, collocations, idioms, and other types of **formulaic language** have been the object of much attention recently, in both the theoretical and empirical literature. Within this domain, one strand of research has examined the nature of L2 learners' knowledge and the means by which formulaic language is processed. Siyanova and Schmitt (2008), for example, compared native and nonnative speakers on two types of collocational knowledge: perceived frequency and processing. Despite learners' ability to produce a large number of collocations, the results point to a marked advantage for NSs for both, even when compared with advanced learners. Similarly, using eye-tracking, Siyanova-Chanturia et al. (2011) found that NNSs read idioms and figurative language more slowly than completely literal equivalents, a difference not found for NSs (see also Conklin & Schmitt, 2008). Taken together, these studies support the notion that, despite processing more slowly than NSs, NNSs are sensitive to the frequency with which the individual words in formulaic language or chunks co-occur.

A second and less developed strand of research within this domain has been concerned with the process by which formulaic language can be learned. Many of the experiments in this area build on the research described in the previous paragraph, which has found NSs to be able to process collocational patterns. This line of research is also somewhat more practically oriented in nature. For example, an interesting experiment regarding idiom learning was conducted by Bogaards (2001), in which Dutch learners of French were presented with French idioms. He presented new words and idioms with similar meanings to the learners and found that multiword expressions that contained known words (e.g., *homme à femmes* versus *dragueur* — both meaning "womanizer") were easier to learn than words that are completely new. He suggests that initial knowledge of form helps learners as they learn new meanings attached to those forms. In another study, Durrant and Schmitt (2009) found that adult learners, like NSs, are sensitive to collocational patterns and that they do process and learn lexical input formulaically, as opposed to individually or as a series of discrete lexical items. Consequently, the authors conclude, learners' gaps in collocational knowledge can, in theory, be remedied, given sufficient input.

TIME TO DO ...

Visit the *Oxford Collocation Dictionary Online* for Advanced English Learners at the following website : www.ozdic.com/. Search for a few English words. Are the collocations listed frequent ones in your opinion?

8.3 INFLUENCES ON L2 VOCABULARY AND DEVELOPMENT

8.3.1 The Role of the L1

In all aspects of language learning, the L1 (or other languages known) undoubtedly plays an important role. The lexicon is no exception. Singleton (1999a, 1999b) reviews a number of studies and comes to the conclusion that there is connectivity between the L1 and the L2 lexicon. Note that he uses the term connectivity to rule out a disconnect between the two lexica, as well as to rule out total integration. "L1 and L2 lexis are separately stored, but that the two systems are in communication with each other — whether via direct connections between individual L1 and L2 lexical nodes, or via a common conceptual store (or both)" (pp. 189–190). He also raises the question of individual differences and notes, "that the relationship between a given L2 word and a given L1 word in the mental lexicon will vary from individual to individual" (p. 190). What is particularly interesting is that he attributes this to factors of acquisition and the extent to which formal and/or semantic connections are made by the learner of the L1 and L2 word.

There is evidence to suggest that the lexica of both languages remain activated, even with advanced proficiency in an L2 (Kroll & Stewart, 1994; Jared & Kroll, 2001; Marian & Spivey, 2003). This, they claim, is the case, even though automaticity increases with proficiency (see Segalowitz & Hulstijn, 2005). Sunderman and Kroll

(2006) report that, in words that have close forms (neighbors) in the L1 and L2, there is influence from both languages, even when performing a task in only one of the languages. They cite the example in English of the word *gate*, which has neighbors in English (*game*) and in Spanish (*gato*—cat). Regardless of what language a task is being conducted in, both languages show influence of neighbors in both languages. Sunderman and Kroll (2006) investigated English-speaking learners of Spanish at two levels of proficiency and found that there was L1 activation for both groups, but that the sensitivity to the L1 translation decreased with increasing proficiency. Titone et al. (2011) found that the strength of a cognate effect depended on the age of learning the L2; it is an important variable only when the L2 is learned early.

In general, one finds a facilitation effect for cognates, with cognates being recognized faster than noncognates when presented with words out of context (e.g., Dijkstra et al., 1999; Costa et al., 2000; Lemhöfer & Dijkstra, 2004; Schwartz et al., 2007). With words in context, the results have been mixed. Most research has been conducted with nouns, but verbs also show a cognate effect (see Van Assche et al., in press). The general explanation has to do with the notion that, when one encounters a cognate, there is activation of multiple aspects of a word, including orthographic, phonological, and semantic (see Dijkstra et al., 2010).

Qasem and Foote (2010) examined the ability of Arabic-speaking, low- and high-proficiency learners of English to identify translation equivalents, with three types of critical conditions: distractors that were orthographically related, morphologically but not semantically related, or semantically related. The findings of the study showed that NL interference occurred in all three conditions and for both groups, thus indicating that L1 form and meaning may influence the perception of L2 vocabulary items.

Jiang (2000, 2002, 2004) proposed and presents evidence to support a three-stage model of adult L2 vocabulary learning. The first stage is a lexical association stage, in which learners recognize some form as a word. They understand the meaning of the word because they associate it with their L1—hence, the association phase of learning. This phase of lexical representation only contains the form of the word (phonology, orthography) and something that points it to a comparable word in the L1. All processing is done through the L1 translations. With continued exposure and use, the semantic/syntactic information from the L1 is transferred to the L2 word. At this point, the lexical representation contains L2 form information and the transferred syntactic and semantic information that has been transferred from the L1, and there is a direct link between the L2 word (weak or strong) and the conceptual representation. He calls this the L1 lemma mediation stage, as processing still involves L1 information. The third stage is one in which L1 information is discarded, but Jiang (2000) suggests that, for many words, the second stage remains the steady-state stage. His various empirical studies verify these claims with Korean learners of English (Jiang, 2004) and Chinese learners of English (Jiang, 2002).

Lee (2007) argues against Jiang's semantic transfer hypothesis, pointing out that L2 proficiency, but not L1 influence, is a key factor in explaining semantic over-generalization, at least within the conceptual domains that Jiang explored. Specifically,

Lee added a NNS comparison group, pointing out that, in any L1 transfer research, there have to be at least two groups of NNSs. Otherwise, one is left not knowing whether transfer or developmental factors are involved. In Lee's study, highly advanced Korean ESL learners were compared with advanced Korean ESL learners, highly advanced Chinese ESL learners, and NSs of English, with respect to semantic over-generalization in contextualized environments. The findings revealed the comparable overgeneralization behaviors of highly advanced Korean ESL and highly advanced Chinese ESL groups, indicating that the semantic overgeneralization may be an indicator of L2 development, but not of cross-linguistic influence.

In the next sections, we focus on incidental and incremental learning.

8.3.2 Incidental Vocabulary Learning

happens when learners are focused on comprehending meaning. (reading or listening).

A great deal of attention has been paid to what is known as **incidental vocabulary learning** (see Gass, 1999, for a discussion of the controversial nature of this term). Wesche and Paribakht (1999a, p. 176) defined incidental learning as what takes place when "learners are focused on comprehending meaning rather than on the explicit goal of learning new words." In other words, learning is a by-product of something else (e.g., reading a passage).

A number of studies have shown that incidental learning can indeed occur through reading or listening (e.g., Brown et al., 2008; Vidal, 2011). Rott (1999) examined exposure through reading and its effect on acquisition and retention of vocabulary. Her study of the acquisition of German by NSs of English investigated the effects of differential exposure to lexical items: exposure two, four, or six times. The results showed that only two exposures were sufficient to affect vocabulary growth, and that six exposures resulted in the greatest amount of knowledge growth. Retention, following exposure, was greater for receptive knowledge than for productive knowledge.

Paribakht and Wesche (1997) divided learners of English into two instructional conditions. In one group, learners read passages and answered comprehension questions. In the other group, learners read passages and then did vocabulary activities. The same words were targeted for both groups. Although both groups made gains in vocabulary knowledge, the first group's knowledge was limited to recognition, whereas the second group acquired productive knowledge as well.

In a follow-up study, Paribakht and Wesche (1999), using think-aloud and retrospective methodology, focused on the strategies that learners used in the process of learning a new word. Inferencing was one of the most common strategies that learners appealed to. Surprisingly, dictionary use did not predominate (see also Fraser, 1999). Learners used morphological and grammatical information as aids in the inferencing process.

Gu and Johnson (1996) investigated lexical strategy use by Chinese university students learning English. Strategies such as guessing from context, dictionary use (for learning purposes, as opposed to comprehension only), and relying on word formation were noted. Oral repetition correlated with general proficiency, but visual repetition (writing words over and over, memorizing the spelling letter by letter, writing new words and translation equivalents repeatedly) negatively predicted vocabulary size and general proficiency. In general, there was more than one way to achieve vocabulary growth: through extensive reading, as well as by employing a wide range of strategies.

TIME TO THINK ...

What vocabulary learning strategies do you use in your L2? What do you think is the best way to learn new words? What strategies are not useful to you?

Hulstijn et al. (1996), in their study of advanced learners of French (Dutch NSs), found that the availability of a bilingual dictionary or marginal glosses fostered acquisition of word meanings. They claimed that, when there is access to external information (e.g., dictionaries or glosses), the formation of a form–meaning relationship is fostered by repeated exposure. In other words, if a learner looks up the meaning of an unknown word the first time that word is encountered, each subsequent encounter reinforces the meaning of the word. On the other hand, when no such external information is available, learners often ignore an unknown word (see also Paribakht & Wesche, 1999), or infer incorrect meanings. Thus, repeated exposure alone, without some connection to the word's meaning or use, has little effect.

R. Ellis and He (1999), in an investigation of the role of negotiation in incidental vocabulary learning, found that, when learners have the opportunity to use new lexical items in a communicative context (including negotiation), those words are retained (in the short and long term) to a greater extent than when they are only exposed to input. However, Newton (1995) found that negotiation was not always a precursor to learning a new vocabulary word. Other factors, such as task type, played a role in whether or not a word was learned. Gass (1999) proposed that incidental learning is most likely to occur when the words in the two languages are cognates, when there is significant exposure, and when related L2 words are known.

In other cases, greater intentionality (e.g., through attention) is required (see Elgort, 2011), as found by several recent studies looking at the role of feedback and inter-action in vocabulary development (e.g., de la Fuente, 2006; Alcón Soler, 2007; Jeon, 2007; Strapp et al., 2011). Plonsky and Loewen (in press), for example, integrate the interactionist approach to language development with Schmitt's (2008) notion of engagement to study the individual and combined effects of several variables on vocabulary development. To this end, the authors recorded and transcribed an entire semester of an intermediate Spanish L2 class, in order to track the frequency of use and form-focused episodes of 12 words. Using these data, along with additional information about each word, such as whether or not it was targeted by the textbook, the researchers then assessed each variable as a possible predictor of vocabulary learning, as measured by pre-post gains. The results suggest that no single variable, such as frequency, can predict lexical development. For example, some high-frequency words showed low gains, whereas others that occurred with low frequency resulted in high gains. In the latter cases, one of two scenarios were observed: Either the word received significant attention to form, or it had some kind of personal or social relevance to the learners, similar to Jeon's (2007) argument for the role of communicative value (see also Laufer & Rozovski-Roitblat, 2011).

Hulstijn and Laufer (2001) and Laufer and Hulstijn (2001) relate retention of vocabulary learning to the concept of *depth of processing* (Craik & Lockhart, 1972), which, in its simple form, predicts that memory retention is dependent on whether something is shallowly or deeply processed. We have discussed earlier that knowing a word involves many possibilities, including understanding the phonological form, the meaning, collocations, etc. It is predicted that processing a vocabulary word at the level of meaning is more deeply processed than processing at the level of phonological form, and, presumably, knowing meaning and collocations suggests even deeper processing (see also Craik & Tulving's [1975] richness of encoding). Hulstijn and Laufer and Laufer and Hulstijn take these concepts a step further by introducing the involvement load hypothesis. Involvement, in their model, consists of need, search, and evaluation. Need refers to motivation, and the need can be either moderate or strong; it is strong when it is motivated by the internal needs of the learner, and it is moderate when it is motivated by an external source (e.g., a teacher). Search and evaluation are both cognitive constructs. The former refers to the attempt to determine the meaning of a word (e.g., looking it up in a dictionary). Evaluation represents an attempt to determine whether the word is the correct one, given the context. Evaluation involves a decision, for example, following a comparison of one meaning of a word with other meanings. This would be moderate involvement, but, if a decision involves combination of the new word with other words, this is strong involvement.

Laufer and Hulstijn (2001) analyzed a number of studies and their effect on vocabulary retention, showing that, in general, the tasks that were effective were those that had high involvement. Hulstijn and Laufer (2001) conducted an experiment to determine if greater involvement would lead to greater retention of receptive knowledge. They constructed three tasks with different levels of involvement (reading comprehension with glosses in the margins, reading comprehension plus fill in the blank, and writing a composition using the target words). It was predicted that writing a composition would entail the greatest involvement, and reading with glosses, the least. Their participants were learners of English from the Netherlands and Israel. The Israeli participants fully support the order, but the Dutch students performed better on the reading with glosses in the margins than on the reading with filling in the blank. In general, the greater use that learners make of vocabulary items, the greater the likelihood that they will retain these items, both in form and in meaning.

Kim (2008) built on the work of Laufer and Hulstijn in two carefully designed studies that sought to test the involvement load hypothesis. Study 1 looked at immediate and

high involvement

↓

high gains

delayed vocabulary gains resulting from three tasks, one at each level of involvement. Study 2 also looked at immediate and delayed vocabulary gains, but using two different tasks designed to induce the same level of involvement. Both studies found support for the involvement load hypothesis. Study 1 showed higher gains, both immediate and delayed, resulting from the higher-involvement tasks, and study 2 found similar gains, again both immediate and delayed, for the two tasks.

These studies are not unlike what we we will see in the discussion of the Output Hypothesis in Chapter 12, namely, using language promotes acquisition. They also suggest that breadth of vocabulary knowledge is only relevant when accompanied by depth of knowledge.

8.3.3 Incremental Vocabulary Learning

Learning vocabulary is not a one-time affair. In other words, it is unrealistic to believe that a learner hears a word or, in the case of some pedagogical methods, memorizes a word, with the outcome being full knowledge of the word. It is, perhaps, sufficient to think about what happens when we encounter words, even in our native language, that we don't know. One interesting fact is that, once that happens, we seem to encounter that word quite frequently, making us wonder how we could have missed it for so long. Learning the meaning and use of the word requires us to listen to how it is used in different contexts and, perhaps, even to consult a dictionary before being brave enough to attempt to use it ourselves. Thus, a first encounter with a word may draw a learner's attention to that item. Subsequent encounters provide learners with opportunities to determine relevant semantic and syntactic information. The important point is that learning words is a recursive process and does not occur instantaneously (see also Schmitt, 1998b). In fact, Paribakht and Wesche (1993) developed a Vocabulary Knowledge Scale with five stages: (a) the word is unfamiliar; (b) the word is familiar, but the meaning is not known; (c) a translation into the NL can be given; (d) the word can be used appropriately in a sentence; and (e) the word is used accurately, both semantically and grammatically. (See Stewart et al., 2012, for a recent study of the extent to which learner knowledge of the different levels within the Vocabulary Knowledge Scale is unique.)

VOCABULARY KNOWLEDGE SCALE

↓

5 stages

Schmitt (1998b) conducted a longitudinal study investigating the acquisition of 11 words by three adult advanced learners of English during a one-year period of time.

TIME TO DO ...

Consider the five stages of the Vocabulary Knowledge Scale listed above. Find five words in your L2 (in a dictionary or on a website), one for each of the five categories (i.e., one word that is unfamiliar to you, one word that is familiar but the meaning is unknown to you, etc.). Do you think you went through the preceding stages to get to your current stage for each word?

His focus was on four kinds of knowledge: spelling, associations, grammatical information, and meaning. The results were not conclusive. Spelling was not a problem for any of the learners. For association knowledge, two of the learners developed, but one did not. With regard to meaning knowledge, none of the learners had anything more than partial mastery of all the meaning senses. Two of the learners made progress in meaning knowledge; one did not. The one who did not was not the same as the one who did not make progress in association knowledge. For grammatical knowledge, only one student made steady progress; the other two were somewhat erratic across the time period. What was not found, however, was any sort of developmental hierarchy of knowledge types.

8.4 USING LEXICAL SKILLS

Thus far in this chapter, we have primarily dealt with lexical knowledge. We now turn our attention toward things learners do, or try to do, with words. We look at lexical skills involved in using language. A particular goal of this discussion is to relate L2 research findings to psycholinguistic research. We compare certain findings about how learners use words with descriptions of psycholinguistic processes, to determine what relationships, if any, exist.

8.4.1 Production

The primary evidence about L2 lexical use comes from production. Production processes and strategies may have a strong effect on what learners produce. In ordinary conversation, learners generally rely on sentence-production processes, except in unusual situations where they repeat something that has been memorized as a whole, such as a chunk. Even many experimental and/or standardized tests, such as gap-filling exercises or tests in which learners select from a list of words to fit in a context, may encourage learners to run through an analogue of sentence production to complete the task. For example, individuals might be asked to fill in the blank:

Credit card payment is _____ to lock-in any instant purchase fares.

They (learners or NSs) may use skills normally used in sentence production to fulfill the task, by generating a word that would be meaningful and would make sense in the syntactic environment.

As mentioned earlier, there is good reason to believe that lexical information is crucial in the sentence-production strategies of competent NSs. Hence, it at first seems paradoxical that little evidence of this is found in the early stages of SLA. Klein and Perdue (1989) provided a thorough discussion of principles that might determine word-order arrangements by L2 learners in naturalistic (untutored) settings. In their conclusion, they wrote:

The objective ... was to analyze whether there are any principles according to which learners with a limited repertoire put their words together. It was shown—with some exceptions and some degree of uncertainty—that there are basically three rules which determine the arrangement of words in early learner varieties (plus one rule for the type of NP [noun phrase] which may occur in a specific position): a phrasal, a semantic, and a pragmatic rule.

(p. 326)

In this article, there was no specific discussion of the role of particular words, even though the particular words in a sentence are major factors in determining the semantics and/or pragmatics. Yet, there is no indication from the data in that study that learners are yet attending to particularities of lexical items that go beyond general semantic and pragmatic factors. It may be that the stage described by Klein and Perdue is one in which this degree of analysis is not yet available for the learners. Until they control the vocabulary better, specific lexical factors are ignored in sentence production in favor of more global factors.

Ard and Gass (1987) presented further evidence of the fact that lexical information plays little role in early stages. They found that, in earlier stages of SLA, grammaticality judgments were relatively uniform, with particular lexical items making little difference. As acquisition progressed, there was much more difference among responses to the same structure with different words. They looked at learner judgments about such sentences as the following:

1. The teacher demonstrated the new machine to the students.
2. The teacher showed the new machine to the students.
3. The teacher demonstrated the students the new machine.
4. The teacher showed the students the new machine.
5. The judge told the lawyer his decision.
6. The judge informed the lawyer his decision.
7. The judge told his decision to the lawyer.
8. The judge informed his decision to the lawyer.
9. The judge told the lawyer of his decision.
10. The judge informed the lawyer of his decision.

Ard and Gass found that learners at relatively low levels of acquisition were more likely to judge sentences with *demonstrate* and *show* (and with *tell* and *inform*) uniformly (i.e., all correct or all incorrect) than were learners at higher stages of acquisition. They interpreted this to mean that the learners, as they progress, learn important additional lexical information, namely which structures are possible for particular words.

The studies by Klein and Perdue and by Ard and Gass suggested that, in early stages, learners tend to ignore specific lexical information and rely on other information, namely syntax, semantics, or pragmatics.

In summary, learners have to, and do, learn the lexical constraints on sentence production. However, we still do not know much about the details of how this sort of learning takes place. The evidence indicates that learners initially make little use of lexical information (Ard & Gass, 1987; Klein & Perdue, 1989), or that learners use lexical information appropriate for the L1 (Adjemian, 1983).

Sentence-production strategies may also play a part in explaining some of the findings of Blum-Kulka and Levenston (1987) for the acquisition of what they call lexical–grammatical pragmatic indicators. For example, the Hebrew construction *efšar* + infinitive ("possible" + infinitive) is limited to situations that express a speaker's perspective. Thus, 8-12 is acceptable; 8-13 is not:

(8-12) Efšar leqabel et hamaxberet selax leqama yamim?
"Is it possible to have/receive your notebook for a few days?"

(8-13) Efšar latet li et hamaxberet?
"Is it possible to give me the notebook?"

Blum-Kulka and Levenston found that learners of Hebrew fail to make this distinction and, from the perspective of standard Hebrew, often overgeneralize *efšar* to all requests. They did not present any additional evidence about the knowledge these learners have of *efšar*, but it is certainly possible that this word, with a following infinitive, has been learned with the meaning "possible," and, thus, these learners have no awareness of additional connotations. On the other hand, these learners may know this additional information and be unable to use it in free speech. There are many situations in L2 learning when learners are unable to do everything in real-time production that they may show knowledge of. For example, Russian learners of English will generally learn about the use of articles before they can use them well in production. It can be concluded that the nature of sentence-production processes contributes to learner difficulties in lexical use.

Levelt (1989) presented a detailed model of sentence production. A blueprint of the basics is given in Figure 8.1.

Levelt argued that formulation processes are primarily lexically driven, although he did not discuss SLA data but did provide information on child L1 acquisition and cross-linguistic differences in language production.

First of all, we should note that Levelt divided the production process into two stages. The speaker initially conceives of a preverbal message. This, in itself, is a complex activity. Levelt mentioned that, as a part of conceiving of a preverbal message, a speaker must establish a purpose. A speaker must "order information for expression, keep track of what was said before . . . attend to his own productions, monitoring what he is saying and how" (1989, p. 9). The cover term that Levelt used for all of this is conceptualizing, and the name for the processing system that does this is the **Conceptualizer**. The Conceptualizer determines the notions that will be expressed in the actual verbal message. The preverbal plan, the output of the Conceptualizer, must be converted into actual words (and ultimately speech). The processing system that does this is called the **Formulator**.

Levelt noted that languages differ in their requirements about what must be specified by the Conceptualizer. Spanish has a three-way distinction for spatial deixis

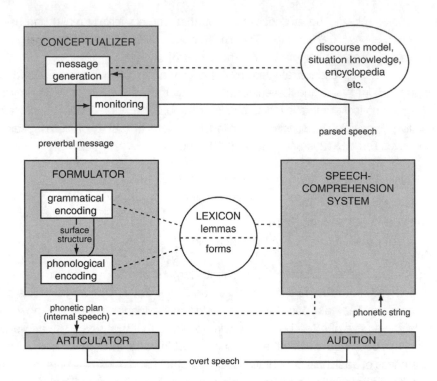

FIGURE 8.1 A Blueprint for the Speaker. Boxes Represent Processing Components; Circle and Ellipse Represent Knowledge Stores (*Source*: From *Speaking: From intention to articulation* by W. J. M. Levelt. Reprinted by permission. © 1989 Massachusetts Institute of Technology Press.)

(*este* "this (here)," *ese* "that (there)," *aquel* "that (way over there)").[3] Levelt gave the additional example of classifiers, based on concepts such as shape. For example, in several languages, including some in Australia, Africa, and the Americas, adjectives must agree with nouns in *class*. Class is partially determined by such things as whether the noun is long and thin, or a liquid, or round. In some instances, English codes information that other languages do not. For example, as Levelt noted, tense is an obligatory category in English, but is not in many other languages, the example he gave being Malay.

Levelt argued that there is no reason to believe that speakers of different languages think differently or view the world differently. Rather, the Conceptualizers must present different information to be coded in different languages. He suggested that, in language acquisition, there needs to be feedback between the Formulator and the Conceptualizer.[4] As we learn our NL, we learn what information is needed. Once this state is reached, "it is no longer necessary for the Conceptualizer to ask the Formulator at each occasion what it likes as input. In short, the systems have become autonomous" (Levelt, 1989, p. 105).

Let us now consider SLA. In Levelt's terms, learners have to acquire a new Conceptualizer. The Formulator is a different matter. Whether or not they are consciously aware that they have to plan differently in producing sentences in an L2, the natural tendency would seem to be to rely on the Formulator developed in acquiring the L1.

Let us now reconsider the examples of *efšar* in Hebrew and articles for Russian learners of English. It is not enough for learners to know the complexities of these elements. They must also modify their Conceptualizer to add the relevant information to the plans for production and learn how to formulate the correct structures. If English speakers learning Hebrew ignore the issue of speaker's perspective in generating the conceptual plan for the sentence, then the Formulator will not have access to the distinction, and the overgeneralization found by Blum-Kulka and Levenston would be expected. Similarly, if Russian learners of English do not consider specificity in constructing conceptual plans, there is little reason to believe that correct article use would be formulated.

The distinction between the Conceptualizer and Formulator may also play a role in explaining the common use of what one might call lexical decompositions by learners. Learners frequently use circumlocutions such as *go up* for monomorphemic words such as *climb*. If the Conceptualizer produces a plan that provides semantic notions, as Levelt suggested, then it may be easier for learners to produce the utterance by using higher-frequency words that are less specific. We would expect learners to have more difficulty finding lower-frequency words than do NSs. The model developed by Levelt may be useful in explaining facts of L2 production (see also de Bot et al., 1997), but this awaits additional research.

[margin note: common use of lexical decompositions by learners.]

8.4.2 Perception

Different languages utilize different distinctions in their phonological systems. For example, many of the world's languages utilize tone as a distinctive feature in separating words. English, of course, does not. On the other hand, English utilizes distinctions between tense and lax vowels (as in *sheep* vs. *ship*) that are not used to distinguish words in other languages. Given these differences in phonological inventories, it is not surprising to find that speakers of different languages tend to use different strategies in word perception, as has been noted in a series of studies by Cutler (e.g., 1990).

Cutler (1990) found that English speakers use a strategy of focusing on strong syllables (i.e., those containing an unreduced vowel) in word recognition. There are various sorts of data for this proposal. One type comes from studies in which participants are asked to respond whenever they hear a particular target word. They were more likely to erroneously respond to *trombone* when the target was *bone* than to trumpet when the target was *pet*. The second syllable in *trombone* is strong, whereas it is weak in *trumpet*. A second type of evidence comes from tasks in which participants are asked to determine which word is a part of a nonsense word. They were able to find *mint* with greater speed and accuracy in the nonsense word *MINTef* than in the nonsense word *mintEEF* (the capital letters indicate the stressed syllable).

Cutler (1990) suggested that this strategy of focusing on strong syllables is not found in French, where there is no phonological motivation for it. French speakers tend to pay equal attention to all syllables. Spanish phonology and Chinese phonology are similar to French in their treatment of syllables. In other words, they pay equal attention to stressed and unstressed syllables. This makes the following finding by Meara (1984, pp. 234–235) particularly intriguing:

> We have also carried out studies on Spanish speakers, and these suggest that there may be some *unexpected* [italics added] and interesting differences between the way native speakers of English and Spanish handle words. At the moment we are working on the idea that syllables play a much more important role in the representation of words for Spanish speakers than is the case for English.

Meara also claims that Chinese speakers "pay more attention to the ends of words than English speakers do" (p. 234). This does not mean that Chinese speakers pay less attention to other syllables than they do to final syllables. If English speakers are focusing on the strong syllables, which tend not to be final in polysyllabic words, and if Chinese and Spanish speakers tend to attend to all syllables equally, then these patterns are just what we would expect. It seems likely that a major reason that Spanish and Chinese learners perform differently with English words is that they are utilizing the processing strategies they learned in their NLs.

Word perception is generally the primary problem in understanding ongoing speech, as mentioned earlier. If the words are not perceived correctly, then the listener is unlikely to be able to determine the meaning of the discourse. Being able to understand enough words in real time to follow a conversation is a difficult task in an L2, one that usually requires considerable work with the language.

Even among competent speakers of a language, lexical considerations are often paramount in explaining the flow of a conversation. Typically, investigators looking at a conversation analyze transcripts of the conversation. However, as Linell (1985) noted, this often gives an unrealistic picture of what the participants in the conversation have to do. We can read a transcript in any order, in particular, referring back when it is helpful. This gives much more of an impression of semantic wholeness than is usual in actual, ongoing speech. Participants in a conversation cannot retain everything in memory. Instead, they often attend only to limited features in the conversation. For example, responses are often based on a particular word or group of words that a conversational partner said. Especially because speech is planned before another interlocutor finishes, words early in the interlocutor's utterance are likely to be very important. Consider the following segment of an interview. This example was taken from a textbook designed for ESL learners (Cornelius, 1981, p. 124).

INTERVIEWER: On the matter of careers, a lot of the jobs that people go into are sort of lifetime careers. What about baseball? Is it a full lifetime career?

CORNUTT: It's been—uh . . . I mean, it's been . . . Baseball's been my life so far . . . you know. I mean, I know someday—could be tomorrow—that I'm going to be out of it.

INTERVIEWER: But how long can you expect to . . . to play, let's say actively?

CORNUTT: Well, I think that—of course, me—I've set goals, and I made my first goal, which was to make it to the big leagues. And now, my next goal is to make it through four years . . . and get my pension. And after that, everything is.

INTERVIEWER: But how many years can you expect to play professional ball . . .?

CORNUTT: It's . . . it's diff—I'm a pitcher, and it's difficult, as a pitcher, to really say how many years . . . because you never know whether you're going to have a sore arm, whether it's going to go on you or wh . . . what the problem may be. But uh . . . as a pitcher, I guess the prime—I'm 24 years old now, and this is my sixth year—and the prime time for a pitcher is 27 to 30.

In classes, both NSs and NNSs felt that Cornutt was either rude and uncooperative or misunderstood the questions. The fact that the interviewer was more fluent and kept asking questions that, in retrospect, appear to be different phrasing of the same question reinforces the belief that the canonical interpretation of each question was something like *How long will your baseball career last?*

Cornutt and the interviewer are both NSs of English. The conversation can be even more divergent if a nonnative listener misinterprets a word and uses that misinterpreted word as the key word on which to base a response. Unfortunately, not enough is known about how lexical perceptions affect discourse by NNSs.

8.5 CONCLUSION

In this chapter, we have shown the complexities and importance of the lexicon. Unfortunately, less research on the L2 lexicon has taken place than its importance might warrant. It is one of the most difficult areas for learners to acquire with any large degree of success.

POINTS TO REMEMBER

- The lexicon has started to receive more attention in SLA as the driver of language production and reception.

- Complete knowledge of a word includes knowledge of its form, meaning, and use, as well as its pronunciation, spelling, nuances of meaning, and grammatical constraints.

- Distinctions have been made between receptive and productive knowledge of vocabulary; potential and real vocabulary; passive, controlled-active, and free-active vocabulary knowledge; vocabulary knowledge and vocabulary control; and breadth and depth of knowledge.

● Learners must know, not only the meaning of a word, but also its subcategorization restrictions, associations, and collocations.

● Chunks, collocations, idioms, and other types of formulaic language have become the object of much SLA research. Chunks are prefabricated patterns where the learner may not know how to "unpackage" the component parts.

● The L1 plays an important role in the L2. Recent research suggests that both the L1 and L2 are activated when using the L2.

● Incidental vocabulary learning refers to learning of words that is a by-product of something else (e.g., reading a passage).

● The involvement load hypothesis is based on the idea of need, search, and evaluation. Need refers to motivation. Search refers to the attempt to determine the meaning of a word. Evaluation represents an attempt to determine whether the word is the correct one, given the context.

● Vocabulary learning is incremental, in that it doesn't happen instantaneously, but is a recursive process.

SUGGESTIONS FOR ADDITIONAL READING

Topics in formulaic language (2012). Charlene Polio (Ed.). Special issue of *Annual Review of Applied Linguistics*. Cambridge University Press.

Current perspectives in second language vocabulary research (2012). David Hirsh. Peter Lang.

Researching vocabulary: A vocabulary research manual (2010). Norbert Schmitt. Palgrave.

Connected words: Word associations and second language vocabulary acquisition (2009). Paul Meara. John Benjamins.

Modelling and assessing vocabulary knowledge (2007). Helmut Daller, James Milton, and Jeanine Treffers-Daller (Eds.). Cambridge University Press.

Formulaic sequences: Acquisition, processing, and use (2004). Norbert Schmitt (Ed.). John Benjamins.

Vocabulary in a second language: Selection, acquisition and testing (2004). Paul Bogaards and Batia Laufer (Eds.). John Benjamins.

Learning vocabulary in another language (2001). I. S. P. Nation. Cambridge University Press.

Vocabulary in language teaching (2000). Norbert Schmitt. Cambridge University Press.

Exploring the second language mental lexicon (1999). David Singleton. Cambridge University Press.

Incidental L2 vocabulary acquisition: Theory, current research, and instructional implications (1999). Special issue of *Studies in Second Language Acquisition*, *21*, Marjorie Wesche and Sima Paribakht (Eds.).

Vocabulary and language teaching (1988). Ronald Carter and Michael McCarthy (Eds.). Longman.

Second language vocabulary acquisition (1997). James Coady and Thomas Huckin (Eds.) Cambridge University Press.

Vocabulary: Description acquisition and pedagogy (1997). Norbert Schmitt and Michael McCarthy. Cambridge University Press.

MORE TO DO AND MORE TO THINK ABOUT ...

1. In this chapter, we noted that Levelt's model of speech production in Figure 8.1 was intended for L1 cross-linguistic data. What implications might the model have for L2 speech production? What aspects of L2 use might the model not be able to account for? For example, can it accommodate NL transfer?

2. Provide examples of lexical complexities from English or from another language you know and speculate what sort of learning difficulties might arise.

3. The following data are from intermediate level ESL students in an intensive course program. The students are from a variety of NLs. Part I is from oral data, and Parts II and III are from written compositions:

    Part I:
    (1) I had one *discuss* with my brother.
    (2) You have a business *relation* (relationship).
    (3) You get happy very *easy*.
    (4) There will be two *child*.
    (5) You say he's a *science*.
    (6) We have to think about Franklin, the *science*.
    (7) She has a good chance to *life*.
    (8) Maybe they don't finish their *educated*.

    (a) How do the forms in italics differ from Standard English usage?
    (b) Is there a predictable relationship between these learner forms and standard usage?

Part II:

  (1)   Actually such *behaves* lead mostly to misunderstanding.
  (2)   The people give presents to *they* friend and their family.
  (3)   Some people didn't *belief* this was a better way.
  (4)   No matter how *differ* in age between us.
  (5)   *Differ* from other parents in my country, they never told us what we must study.
  (6)   Taught me how to choose the more *advantages* values.
  (7)   This is a strange but *interest* continent.
  (8)   The most *advantage* way.

(c) Focus on the words in italics in each sentence. Work out a generalization and explanation for the patterns you find.

(d) Is the generalization you have come up with consistent with the generalization you found in Part I?

Part III:

  (1)   Soccer is the most common *sporting*.
  (2)   America refused continual *supported our military request*.
  (3)   When he was 7 years old, he went *schooling*.
  (4)   About two hours driving *eastern* from Chicago.
  (5)   After finished my college *studied*, I went to my country.
  (6)   Doctors have the right to *removed* it from him.
  (7)   There is a night for *asleep*.
  (8)   Moreover it may lead to *conflicting*.
  (9)   I am not going to get married when I will *graduation* the school.

(e) Work out an IL generalization that might account for the forms in italics. How can you explain it?

(f) Does this generalization change the one(s) you came up with for Parts I and II? If so, how?

(g) Given the data presented in all three parts of this problem, what strategy/strategies have these learners come up with regarding lexical use?

4. The data in this problem are from both written and oral sources. The native language is Arabic.

Part I:

  (1)   You eat a cabbage roll *one time*.
  (2)   I need my hair to be *tall*.
  (3)   I hope to become *bigger* than this age.
  (4)   *Close* the television.
  (5)   And imagine that kind of people *graduate* every night from the bars.
  (6)   You have hard time *to collecting* your money.

(7)   So, when I like to park my car, there is no place to *put it,* and *how many ticket I took.*

(8)   I did not *find my money in the street.*

(9)   This "sambousa" is not sweet or *pastry.* It's main course.

(10) If I will not follow from *first,* I will not understand.

(11) If you *appreciate* your money, you won't buy American car.

(12) If you appreciate your money, you won't buy American car. You'll pay *expensive.*

(a)   Describe (sentence by sentence) what these students are doing in terms of word meaning.

(b)   Provide sentence-by-sentence interpretations of these utterances.

(c)   What IL generalizations might account for these data? Provide a justification for your conclusions. What general strategy has been adopted in the acquisition of English word meaning by these learners?

Part II:

The following are the intended meanings of the sentences from Part I. These are the meanings that were discerned from playback sessions in the NL.

(1)   You ate a cabbage roll once.

(2)   I want my hair to be long.

(3)   I am looking forward to the day when my children will be older.

(4)   Turn off the television.

(5)   And imagine the kind of people who will leave the bar every night.

(6)   You have a hard time earning your money.

(7)   Because there are not enough parking spaces, I get a lot of tickets.

(8)   Money doesn't grow on trees.

(9)   The "sambousa" is not a dessert. It's a main course.

(10) If I don't follow the lectures from the beginning, I won't understand.

(11–12) If you value your money, you won't buy an American car. You will pay a lot of money if you do.

(d)   Compare your interpretations from Part I with those given in Part II. What differences do you find? What do these differences suggest about NS biases in interpretation?

(e)   Do the results of your comparison affect or change your previous IL generalizations? If so, how and why?

5.   After learning a new word that we believe we have never heard before, it seems to appear frequently in both written and oral contexts. How would you explain this phenomenon? Is it just that the word has become more frequently used, or is it a learner's perception? Is it unique to an L2 context, or does this happen in one's native language as well?

CHAPTER NINE

Typological and Functional Approaches

9.1 INTRODUCTION

This chapter has as its main focus two different approaches to SLA: typological and functional. Typological approaches stem from the study of the patterns exhibited in languages worldwide, and functional approaches have as their main interest the study of how language functions. Functional approaches generally entail a consideration of multiple areas of language, such as tense–aspect, which combines verb meanings, morphological form, and phonology.

9.2 TYPOLOGICAL UNIVERSALS

The study of typological universals stems from work in linguistics by Greenberg (1963). In this approach to the study of universals, linguists attempt to discover similarities/ differences in languages throughout the world. That is, the attempt is to determine linguistic typologies, or what types of languages are possible. One of the most import- ant discoveries of this approach is that one can generalize across unrelated and geographically nonadjacent languages regarding the occurrence and co-occurrence of structures. Many of the typological universals are expressed in terms of implications, such that, if a language has feature *X*, it will also have feature *Y*. In Greenberg's original work, many universals (or universal tendencies) were based on word order, as in the following: "In languages with prepositions, the genitive almost always follows the governing noun, while in languages with postpositions it almost always precedes the noun" (Greenberg, 1963, p. 78).

For example, in languages with prepositions, such as French, Russian, and Italian, we expect to find the noun representing what is being possessed preceding the possessor. In fact, this is the case. All three languages form genitives in the same way:

French:

(9-1) le   chien   de mon   ami
       the   dog   of my   friend

Russian:

(9-2) Sobaka   moego   druga
       dog   my GEN   friend GEN

Italian:

(9-3) il   cane   di mia   madre
       the   dog   of my   mother

In languages with postpositions, such as Turkish, what in English and many languages are called prepositions follow the noun, as can be seen in 9-4 and 9-5, where the morphological markers follow the noun:
Turkish:

(9-4) From *Language Files* (Jannedy et al., 1994, p. 153)

    (a) deniz = an ocean

    (b) denize = to an ocean

    (c) denizin = of an ocean

(9-5) Example of genitive (from Comrie, 1981)

    ev-   in   pencere- s-   i
    house   possessor   window   separates vowels possessed
    "the window of the house"

English is somewhat exceptional in that it allows, not only the predicted order (*the leg of the table*), but also the unpredicted word order (*my friend's dog*).

Other language universals can be stated in rigid (or absolute) terms; for example:

Languages with dominant verb–subject–object (VSO) order are always prepositional.

This universal can be exemplified by a language such as Welsh, which has verb-first word order and prepositions (example from Comrie, 1981, p. 81):

(9-6) Lladdwyd   y dyn   gan y   ddraig.
       Killed-passive the man   by the   dragon
       "The man was killed by the dragon."

Why is an understanding of language universals important to the study of SLA? One of the early questions regarding the nature of L2 systems was the extent to which they could be considered a natural language:

> Underlying the IL hypothesis is the unwritten assumption that ILs are linguistic systems in the same way that Natural Languages are. (By "natural language" I mean any human language shared by a community of speakers and developed over time by a general process of evolution.) That is, ILs are natural languages.
>
> (Adjemian, 1976, p. 298)

What does it mean to say that ILs are natural systems? It does not mean that all ILs are as complex as all natural languages, for clearly they are not. The majority of complex syntax does not develop until late in the process of learning. What it does mean is that, if a given linguistic phenomenon appears to be impossible in any of the world's languages, then it will also be an impossible form in an L2 system.

As an example, we consider word-order phenomena from a selection of languages of the world. In Hindi, French, and Japanese, the following sentences are possible:

Hindi (*Language Files*, Jannedy et al. 1994):

(9-7) Ram-ne   seb   kʰaya
       Ram   apple   ate
       "Ram ate an apple."

(9-8) Ram Angrezi bol   səkta   hɛ
       Ram English speak   able   is
       "Ram can speak English."

(9-9) larke-ne čari-se   kutte-ko mara
       Boy   stick with dog   hit
       "The boy hit the dog with a stick."

(9-10) jis   lark-ne kutte-ko mara   vo   mera   bhai   he
       which   boy   dog   hit   he   my   brother is
       "The boy who hit the dog is my brother."

(9-11) Ram-ki   bahin
       Ram's   sister
       "Ram's sister"

(9-12) safed   pʰul
       white   flower

French:

(9-13) Jean   a mangé   une pomme.
       Jean   has eaten an apple
       "Jean ate an apple."

(9-14) Jean   peut parler   anglais
       Jean   an   speak   English
       "Jean can speak English."

(9-15) Le garçon   a frappé   le chien   avec   un baton.
       The boy   has hit   the dog   with   a stick
       "The boy hit the dog with a stick."

(9-16) Le garçon qui   a frappé   le chien   est   mon frère.
       The boy   who   has hit   the dog   is   my brother
       "The boy who hit the dog is my brother."

(9-17) La soeur   de   Jean
       The sister   of   Jean
       "Jean's sister"

(9-18) une fleur   blanche
       a flower   white
       "a white flower"

Japanese (*Language Files,* Jannedy et al. 1994):

(9-19) Taroo-ga   ringo-o   tabeta
       Taroo   apple   ate
       "Taroo ate an apple."

(9-20) Taroo-wa   Eigo-ga   hanaseru
       Taroo   English speak   can
       "Taroo can speak English."

(9-21) sono   otokonoko-wa   boo-de   inu-o   butta
       that   boy   stick with   dog   hit
       "That boy hit the dog with a stick."

(9-22) inu-o   butta   otokonoko-wa   watashi-no   otooto-da
       dog   hit   boy   my   brother is
       "The boy who hit the dog is my brother."

(9-23) Taroo-no   imooto
       Taroo's   sister
       "Taroo's sister"

(9-24) shiroi   hana
       white   flower
       "white flower"

If we consider the categories of object, verb, auxiliaries, prepositions/postpositions, nouns and RCs, possessives, and adjective noun order, we can see the possible generalizations based on these data and from English (Table 9.1).

We can think of languages as being head-initial or head-final, where the head is a verb, or a noun, or a preposition in relation to other units within its constituent. Thus, in a head-initial language, the verb will precede the noun, and, in a head-final language, the verb will follow the object. If we consider one of the basic differences in languages, the order of verbs and objects, the patterns in Table 9.2 occur.

TABLE 9.1 Word Orders

	Hindi	French	Japanese	English
Basic order (V + O)	OV	VO	OV	VO
Aux + verb	V Aux	Aux V	V Aux	Aux V
Preposition + noun (Postposition)	N Post	Prep N	N Post	Prep N
N + RC	N + RC	N + RC	RC + N	N + RC
Possessive	Poss + N	N + Poss	Poss + N	Both
Adjective + N	Adj + N	N + Adj	Adj + N	Both (Adj + N dominant)

TIME TO THINK ...

Think about a language that you know that is not listed in Table 9.1. How would you complete the table for that language? Is it more similar to Hindi and Japanese or to French and English?

There are some oddities, that is, languages or parts of languages where the predicted patterns do not obtain, as in the following examples:

- **Hindi and Japanese RCs**:
  - From these data, Hindi and Japanese appear to be OV languages; that is, the object precedes the verb.
  - The RC precedes the noun in Japanese but follows it in Hindi.

- **English adjective–noun order**:
  - From these data, English appears to be a VO language; that is, the verb precedes the object.
  - The adjective precedes the noun, rather than following it, as in other VO languages.
  - There are instances where the adjective follows the noun:
    - ○ She likes all things Japanese/She likes all Japanese things.

The question, then, for SLA is: To what extent do the constraints that govern natural languages also govern learner language systems? Put differently, to what extent is the variability of learner languages limited? Would we be likely to find evidence of ILs that violate these generalizations? More specifically, would a Japanese speaker learning English be likely to postpose a preposition (i.e., use postpositions rather than prepositions)? One answer to this question has been formulated as the **Structural Conformity Hypothesis**: "All universals that are true for primary languages are also true for interlanguages" (Eckman et al., 1989, p. 195).

TABLE 9.2 OV and VO Word Orders

OV (head-final)	VO (head-initial)
V Aux	Aux V
N Postposition	Preposition N
?	N + RC
Poss N	N + Poss?
Adj + N	?

There are many ways in which universals can be expected to affect the development of L2 grammars: (a) They could absolutely affect the shape of a learner's grammar at any point in time. If this is correct, there would *never* be any instance of a violation of a given universal evident in L2 grammars. (b) They could affect acquisition order, whereby more marked forms would be the last to be acquired, or, in the case of **implicational universals**, one could expect fewer errors in the less marked forms. Or, (c) They could be one of many interacting forces in determining the shape of learners' grammars.

Some universals may be thought of as having greater influence than others. For example, if we return to the word-order examples given earlier, we saw that English word order with regard to noun–adjective order is not consistent with the prediction made by knowing that English is a verb–object language. What might we expect the implication of this universal to be with regard to learner language? Gass and Ard (1980) reported on data from Spanish learners learning English and English learners learning Spanish. They predicted that, for universals based on historical factors, the effect on ILs is not as strong as universals based on other motivating factors (e.g., physical factors, as in the case of some aspects of phonetics). They argue that the English adjective–noun order is an artifact of historical factors and will not significantly affect IL development. This prediction was borne out in their examination of 29 compositions of Spanish learners of English, ranging from novice to high-intermediate. Of the 141 examples of nouns and adjectives, there was only one instance of a noun–adjective sequence. Additionally, as noted by Dvorak and reported in that article, English learners of Spanish initially make errors in the adjective/noun sequence, although the problem is straightened out early. Thus, it appears that the issue is more one of NL influence than of universal influence.

9.2.1 Test Case I: The Accessibility Hierarchy

We turn to a few test cases in which typological/implicational universals are investigated from an SLA perspective. Perhaps the most widely discussed implicational universal is one dealing with RC formation. The universal itself, known as the **Accessibility Hierarchy (AH)**, was discussed at length by Keenan and Comrie (1977). The basic principle is that one can predict the types of relative clauses that a given language will have, based on the following hierarchy:

Accessibility hierarchy:

SU > DO > IO > OPREP > GEN > OCOMP[1]

Two claims are important here. First, all languages have subject RCs; and, second, predictions can be made such that, if a language has a RC of the type *X*, then it will also have any RC type higher on the hierarchy, or to the left of type *X*. Thus, if we know that a language has object-of-preposition relatives (*That's the woman about whom I told you*), we know that it also has subject, direct-object, and indirect-object relatives. There is no a priori way to predict the lowest RC type, but, when the lowest type is known, we are able to make claims about all other RC types in that language.[2]

There have been further claims that the hierarchy reflects the ease of relativization and/or certain discourse constraints.[3] If this is the case, ease or difficulty should not differentially affect languages that an individual uses. That is, if it is truly a matter of difficulty that makes OComp RCs less frequent (and more difficult) in languages of the world, then OComp relatives should not be more difficult than other RC types in only one of the language systems that a learner has available (i.e., the NL versus the TL).

To substantiate this claim, Gass (1979a, 1979b) presented data from learners of English with a wide range of native languages (Italian, Arabic, Portuguese, Persian, French, Thai, Chinese, Korean, and Japanese). In that study, based on data from (a) free compositions, (b) sentence combining, and (c) grammaticality judgments, it was argued that the production of RCs by L2 learners could be predicted on the basis of the AH. Figure 9.1 is an illustration of the results from the sentence-combining task of that study. With the exception of the genitive,[4] the predictions of the AH are borne out.

A second important aspect of the hierarchy is the implication regarding the use of resumptive pronouns (pronominal reflexes) in RCs. Examples of sentences with resumptive pronouns are given in 9-25 and 9-26:

(9-25) She danced with the man who [*he] flew to Paris yesterday.

(9-26) The woman whom he danced with [*her*] flew to Paris yesterday.

There is an inverse relationship between the hierarchy and resumptive pronouns, such that it is more likely that resumptive pronouns will be used in the lower hierarchical positions than in the higher ones.

Resumptive Pronoun Hierarchy:

OCOMP > GEN > OPREP > IO > DO > SU

Hyltenstam (1984) investigated resumptive pronouns in some detail. His data come from the acquisition of Swedish as an L2 by speakers of Spanish, Finnish, Greek, and

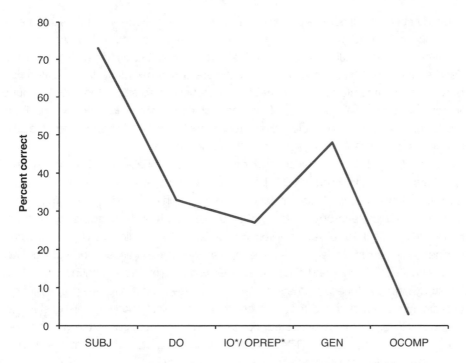

FIGURE 9.1 Percentages of Sentences Correct on Combining Task (All Groups) (*N* = 188).
*These two positions have been combined owing to their analogous behavior in English relative clauses (*Source*: From "Language transfer and universal grammatical relations" by S. Gass, 1979b, *Language Learning*, *29*, 327–344, by Research Club in Language Learning. Reprinted by permission.)

Persian. These languages vary in the positions that can be relativized, as well as in the optional and obligatory use of resumptive pronouns. Swedish has the full range of RCs (SUBJ to OComp), but has no resumptive pronouns in any of the RC positions. Hyltenstam used a picture-identification one in which participants were asked a question such as, "Who is in picture number 5?", with the target response being a relative clause, "the man who is running." The results from Hyltenstam's study conform to the predictions of the hierarchy, with more pronominal reflexes occurring in positions lower on the hierarchy than in those positions higher on the hierarchy.[5]

In sum, the results from studies on the universal predictions of the Accessibility Hierarchy support the notion that learner grammars are constrained in a similar way to natural-language grammars. There is general support for the universality of the Accessibility Hierarchy, although, in recent years, work in this area has expanded to cover a wider range of languages. Hamilton (1994) takes this research a step further and questions the extent to which this universal truly is universal. In general, however, the evidence does support this universal principle.

In more recent years, it has become clear that the range of studies on relative clauses has been limited, and that a broader consideration of languages is needed. In fact, Comrie (2003) proposes a different typology for some East Asian languages.

O'Grady et al. (2003) noted a preference for subject over direct-object RCs in Korean. Additionally, Cho (1999) presented data from Korean that supported the Accessibility Hierarchy. However, Jeon and Kim (2007) considered two kinds of Korean RCs: head-external and head-internal RCs. There are a number of syntactic differences between these two RC types. In a study of 40 learners of Korean, Jeon and Kim found limited support for the predictions of the Accessibility Hierarchy. In head-external RCs, there was a preference for subject over direct-object RCs, but, in head-internal relative structures, evidence for that preference did not exist.

In a study of the acquisition of Japanese by Cantonese, English, and Korean speakers, Ozeki and Shirai (2007) introduced another level of complexity—that of animacy. They considered oral data and found that even low-proficiency learners used more direct-object and oblique (other than subject and direct-object, e.g., object of preposition) RCs than subject relatives, contradicting the predictions of the hierarchy. Further, a subset of the learners (Chinese and English NSs) associated subject RCs with animate head nouns and direct-object RCs with inanimate head nouns. In a follow-up study with Cantonese learners of Japanese, Ozeki and Shirai used a sentence-combining task. They found that subject and direct-object relatives were easier than oblique RCs, as would be predicted, but that, when learners converted direct-object and oblique RCs into subject RCs, it was nearly always done with animates as heads. Thus, the selection of RC types is sensitive to animacy.

Kanno (2007), in a study of Chinese-, Sinhalese-, Vietnamese-, Thai-, and Indonesian-speaking learners of Japanese, found that having a semantic cue available aids in the processing of RCs. Interestingly, when processing becomes difficult (e.g., when a semantic cue is not available), properties of the L1 affect interpretation.

All in all, research on RCs suggests that the hierarchy is adhered to, but that the situation shows greater complexity (e.g., semantics, language specifics) than thought in the early years of research. As Eckman (2007, p. 327) states,

> If the [Noun Phrase Accessibility Hierarchy] is not as strongly supported when other language types are brought into the data pool, then we need to make hypotheses about what kinds of principles could be postulated that would subsume both the SLA data from RC acquisition in European languages as well as the SLA data from typologically distinct languages.

TIME TO THINK ...

Which of the RC types exist in your L1 and L2 (SU > DO > IO > OPREP > GEN > OCOMP)? Are resumptive pronouns used in your L1 and your L2? If they are, are they more common with RCs lower on the hierarchy? Does animacy play a role in RC construction in your L1 or L2?

9.2.2 Test Case II: The Acquisition of Questions

A second test case of the relationship between universals and SLA comes from data on the acquisition of questions. Eckman et al. (1989) return to some of the early Greenbergian universals (Greenberg, 1963) to determine whether these universals, developed on the basis of natural-language data, could also be said to be valid for L2 learner data. Eckman et al. stated the two universals and their SLA interpretation as follows (1989, pp. 175, 188):

1. *Wh-* inversion implies *wh-* fronting: "Inversion of statement order (in *wh-* questions) so that verb precedes subject occurs only in language where the question word or phrase is normally initial."

    1(a)   Reinterpreted for learner languages as:
    "The relative frequency of occurrence of subject–verb inversion in *wh-* questions is never larger than the relative frequency of occurrence of the fronting of the *wh-* word."

2. *Yes/No* inversion implies *wh-* inversion: "This same inversion (i.e., inversion of statement order so that verb precedes subject) occurs in *yes/no* questions only if it also occurs in interrogative word questions."

    (2)a   Reinterpreted for learner languages as:
    "The relative frequency of occurrence of subject–verb inversion in *yes/no* questions is never larger than the relative frequency of occurrence of subject–verb inversion in *wh-* questions."

These universals are interpreted to suggest that the presence of subject–verb inversion in *yes/no* questions (a question that requires a *yes/no* answer) in a language, as in 9-27, implies the presence of a verb (auxiliary in English) before the subject in *wh-* questions, as in 9-28:

(9-27) Will you see my friend?

(9-28) Whom will you see?

This, in turn, implies the presence of *wh-* fronting (where the *wh-* word is at the beginning of the sentence), as in 9-29:

(9-29) Whom will you see? (vs. You will see whom?)

Thus, if a language has *yes/no* inversion, it will also have verbs before subjects in *wh-* questions and it will also have *wh-* words at the beginning of sentences. In markedness terms, *yes/no* inversion is the most marked, and *wh-* fronting the least.

To evaluate these claims as they relate to SLA, Eckman et al. (1989) gathered data on question formation by 14 learners of English, who were NSs of Japanese,

Korean, or Turkish. The data show that, in fact, learners are constrained by the implicational universal. Those learners who had acquired the most marked question type (*yes/no* inversion) had also acquired the other two. Interestingly, and herein lies one of the main difficulties of SLA research, of the 14 participants, data from one did not follow the predictions of the universal. How is this to be interpreted, a question we addressed in Chapter 2? Does it suggest that the universal is not valid for L2 data? If so, the result would be the invalidation of the claim that the range of the domain of language universals is all human languages, including learner languages.

An alternative interpretation lies in the explanation of the one exception. Are there extenuating circumstances that might mitigate against the strength of this universal? Because there are so many factors that compete in SLA (including NL, TL, pragmatics, processing limitations, attitude, motivation, attentiveness), it is unlikely that predictions can be made in an absolute fashion. It is only when the exceptions seem to outweigh the predictions of universals that we can begin to invalidate claims. In other words, the most we can hope for with L2 predictions are tendencies or probabilistic predictions. In fact, with the one exception in the study by Eckman et al. (1989), the researchers provided an explanation related to processing constraints. Thus, for 13 of the participants, the linguistic universal wins out, but, for one, a processing principle relating to less complex versus more complex structures wins out. Why processing principles provide the major constraints for one individual, while linguistic universals provide the major constraints for the majority, remains an unanswered question. This result highlights the importance of individual variation.

9.2.3 Test Case III: Voiced/Voiceless Consonants

A third study that we discuss in the context of language universals comes from the domain of phonology. The data presented in Eckman (1981a, 1981b) are from speakers of Spanish and Mandarin Chinese learning English. The area of investigation is word-final voiced and voiceless consonants. Table 9.3 presents data from the Spanish speakers, and Table 9.4 presents data from the Mandarin Chinese speakers.

From the data in Table 9.3 (the Spanish-speaker data), one can observe the following: Word-final obstruents (sounds in which the airstream is obstructed) are voiceless.[6] The data from the Mandarin speakers are somewhat different in that we do not see devoicing. Rather, what we see is the following: Add a *schwa* (ə) following a word-final voiced obstruent (*schwa*s represent reduced sounds, as in [dəpartrmənt] —department). Thus, both groups of speakers begin with the same problem—how to resolve the difficulty of producing words with word-final voiced obstruents, which is a marked structure. The Spanish speakers solve the problem by devoicing the obstruents; the Mandarin speakers resolve the problem by adding a *schwa* to the end of words. There are two questions that need to be addressed: Why should both groups have the same problem? Why should each group attempt to resolve it in a different manner?

The answer to the first question involves a consideration of two facts, one relating to the NL and the other to language universals. With regard to the NL, neither language

TABLE 9.3 IL Data from Spanish Speakers (*Source*: From "On the naturalness of interlanguage phonological rules" by F. Eckman, 1981b, *Language Learning*, 31, pp. 195–216, by Research Club in Language Learning. Reprinted by permission.)

Learner 1		Learner 2	
IL phonetic form	Gloss	IL phonetic form	Gloss
[bɔp]	Bob	[rav]	rob
[bɔbi]	Bobby	[ravər]	robber
[rɛt]	red	[bɔp]	Bob
[rɛðər]	redder	[bɔbi]	Bobby
[bik]	big	[smuθ]	smooth
[bigər/biɣər]	bigger	[smuðər]	smoother
[bref]	brave	[rɛθ/rɛð]	red
[brevər]	braver	[rɛðər]	redder
[prawt]	proud	[du]	do
[prawdəst]	proudest	[riðu]	redo
[wɛt]	wet	[bek]	bake
[wɛtər]	wetter	[priβek]	prebake
[sik]	sick	[wɛt]	wet
[sikəst]	sickest	[wɛtər]	wetter
[ðə]	the	[sef]	safe
[son]	zone	[sefəst]	safest
[fʌsi]	fuzzy	[ðə]	the
[faðər]	father	[ðis]	this
[fris]	freeze	[pig]	pig
[tæg]	tag	[bæd]	bad
[bɛd]	bed	[bɛt]	bed
[pɪg]	pig	[bik/big/biɣ]	big

has a voice contrast in final position. With regard to universal markedness principles, it has been argued (see Chapter 7) that a voicing contrast in final position is the most marked (and, hence, presumably the last voicing contrast to be learned). Both of these facts combine to predict the learner language facts that we have seen, namely a difficulty with voicing contrast in final position.

The second question, regarding the differential resolution to the problem, is more difficult to deal with. The Spanish speakers' solution of devoicing final obstruents is one found in many languages of the world; for example, German, Catalan, Polish, and Russian. The Mandarin speakers' solution, however, is unlike patterns found in other

TABLE 9.4 IL Data from Mandarin Speakers (*Source*: From "On the naturalness of interlanguage phonological rules" by F. Eckman, 1981b, *Language Learning*, 31, pp. 195–216, by Research Club in Language Learning. Reprinted by permission.)

Learner 1		Learner 2	
IL phonetic form	Gloss	IL phonetic form	Gloss
[tæg/tægə]	tag	[ænd/ændə]	and
[rab/rabə]	rob	[hæd/hædə]	had
[hæd/hæsə]	had	[tɔb/tɔbə]	tub
[hiz/hizə]	he's	[stadɪd/stadɪdə]	started
[smuðə]	smoother	[fɪʊd/fɪʊdə]	filled
[rayt]	right	[bɪg/bɪgə]	big
[dɛk]	deck	[rɛkənayzdə]	recognized
[zɪp]	zip	[ɪz/ɪzə]	is
[mɪs]	miss	[sɛz/sɛzə]	says
[wɛt]	wet	[wɛtə]	water
[dɪfər]	differ	[afə]	offer
[ovər]	over	[lidə]	leader
[bigər]	bigger		
[kɪkɪn]	kicking		
[tægɪn]	tapping		
[lebər]	label		
[lɛtər]	letter		
[blidɪn]	bleeding		
[lidə]	leader		

languages of the world. At first glance, this could be taken as evidence that learner languages do not fit within the domain of natural languages, for here we have a learner language rule unlike a rule in any natural language. However, the creation of a nonnatural-language rule, like the one presented here, can be explained on the basis of the language contact system. In natural languages, one does not have the conflict between two language systems, as we have with the formation of L2 grammars.

In Mandarin Chinese there are no obstruents (voiced or voiceless) in word-final position. Thus, to devoice the obstruents, as the Spanish speakers do, does not solve the initial problem of violating NL constraints, as another constraint would be violated as a result. Hence, the Chinese speakers opt for a solution that combines the NL phonetic constraints of absence of word-final obstruents with the frequent use in the TL of the vowel *schwa*.

TIME TO DO ...

As stated above, German is one language where final obstruents are devoiced. Listen to the examples of voiced consonants that are devoiced in German on the webpage (see Link #1 in the Link section at the end of this chapter).

Can you hear the devoiced consonants? Do you think it would be easy or difficult for you to do this (assuming that you are not a NS of German!)?

9.2.4 Falsifiability

In the history of SLA research, what has the mechanism been for dealing with linguistic counterexamples? Within the domain of typological universals, researchers have weakened their strong claims to probabilistic ones or frequency claims, as we saw with regard to question formation in the case of the Structural Conformity Hypothesis, in particular. A second related way is to claim that the IL itself is shown in the variation, compared with what native speakers do (Selinker, 1966). A third common means has been the attempt to explain the exceptions, generally with recourse to the NL or the TL, or to the methodology used in data collection. For example, when the addition of *schwa* in word-final position by the Mandarin Chinese learners of English was discussed (section 9.2.3), the fact that the Chinese learners created a system unlike any system known in the domain of L1s (and, hence, supposedly outside of the domain of language universals), the attempt was made to explain the pattern in terms of the facts of the NL and the TL. Similarly, in the work on RCs (section 9.2.1), the predictions made by the AH were not borne out in all cases. Attempts have been made to account for the discrepancies in terms of the data-collection method.

There has been little attempt to claim that the universal is inaccurately described —a logical possibility, as we will see later. Because the linguistic facts of typological universals, being based on surface facts of languages, are reasonably well established, it is unlikely that this latter possibility would carry much weight. Nevertheless, were there widespread evidence that typological universals did not hold for learner languages, and there were no compelling arguments as to why this should be so, there would be two possible conclusions: (a) The domain of language universals is that of natural languages and not L2s, or (b) the domain of language universals is that of all linguistic systems—any failure to comply with a putative language universal would then be taken as evidence that the description of that universal is incorrect.

9.2.5 Typological Universals: Conclusions

For implicational universals to have any importance in the study of SLA, two factors must be taken into consideration. First, one must understand why a universal is a universal. It is not sufficient to state that L2s obey natural-language constraints because that is the way languages are. This only pushes the problem of explanation back one step. SLA can contribute to the general study of language by showing whether universal constraints are operative in newly created languages. However, it can only contribute to a general understanding of language if it can also explain if, and why, a particular universal is a universal. Second, there must be an arguable relationship between the features in question. In other words, there must be a connection between the feature that is implied and the feature that does the implying, which essentially boils down to a relationship between more-marked and less-marked forms.

The first of these factors relates to the underlying explanation for the implication; the second relates to the plausibility of joining what might appear to be two unrelated grammatical forms. Explanations have generally taken the form of processing constraints, functional considerations, or pragmatics. These explanations have in common the fact that they deal with the way language functions and the ways humans use language. However, the picture may be more complex; current research attempts to determine whether learners relate structures that are said to be related by the theoretical model on which the descriptions are based. In fact, Gass and Ard (1984) and Eckman (1992) argued that not all language universals will equally affect the formation of L2 grammars. Gass and Ard argued that one must look at the underlying source of the universal and understand why structures are related to determine whether they will, or will not, affect SLA, whereas Eckman claimed that universals must involve the same structure (e.g., RCs, question formation) before they will have an effect on the development of L2 grammars.

In Chapter 7, we discussed the kind of evidence necessary for language learning to proceed (see Chapter 7). Typological approaches have had little to say about the type of evidence necessary for learning and, hence, have had little to say about learnability issues.

Finally, we turn to the role of the L1. We can schematize three approaches to transfer in Table 9.5. Universal Grammar, as can be seen, deals with underlying structures, whereas typological approaches and contrastive analysis only deal with surface forms of language. With regard to the second category, the issue of clustering of properties is part of typological approaches and UG, but has no role to play in contrastive analysis. Third is the issue of learnability, which is at the heart of UG, but not of typological approaches (where the concern is patterns across languages) or contrastive analysis.

TABLE 9.5 Differences in Three Approaches to the Study of Transfer

	Universal Grammar	Typological	Contrastive analysis
Levels of analysis (deep)	+	-	-
Property clusters	+	+	-
Learnability	+	-	-

9.3 FUNCTIONAL APPROACHES

In Chapter 7 and the early sections of this chapter, we considered ILs from the perspective of linguistic structures. The second part of this chapter looks at SLA from the perspective of how language functions, that is, how language is used for communication purposes. The major concern in this section is how different forms are used to express different functions, in other words, how form and function relate to one another. Whereas, in the preceding chapters, we considered isolated parts of language (e.g., syntax, morphology, lexicon), because functional approaches consider meaning as central, they simultaneously take into account many aspects of language, including pragmatics, semantics, syntax, morphology, and the lexicon, with multiple levels of language being considered simultaneously. We first turn to tense and aspect and then to issues of discourse.

9.3.1 Tense and Aspect: The Aspect Hypothesis

A major question asked by researchers studying tense and aspect is: How do learners recognize what morphological markers (e.g., past tense, progressive) go with what verbs?

As we showed earlier, the issue of the acquisition of morphological items has long been a feature of L2 research. Earlier work looked at the actual morphemes and tried to determine the order in which they are acquired. In the 1980s, a more sophisticated approach was taken to the L2 acquisition of tense–aspect morphology. The **Aspect Hypothesis** claims that, "first and second language learners will initially be influenced by the inherent semantic aspect of verbs or predicates in the acquisition of tense and aspect markers associated with or affixed to these verbs" (Andersen & Shirai, 1994, p. 133). This approach is semantic in nature and focuses on the influence of lexical aspect in the SLA of tense–aspect morphology. The original impetus for the hypothesis came from L1 acquisition studies, specifically Antinucci and Miller (1976), who carried out a study of L1 acquisition of Italian and English (see critique by Weist et al., 1984). Andersen (1986, 1991) formulated the hypothesis in its present form, with a specific focus on SLA (see also Andersen & Shirai, 1994; Bardovi-Harlig, 1994).

Andersen (1986, 1991) presented a study of two NSs of English, one child and one adolescent, learning L2 Spanish. He noticed an interesting distinction in their development of tense–aspect marking: the past tense (preterit) markers emerged with punctual and achievement verbs, whereas the imperfect markers emerged with verbs that indicate states. These verb types are illustrated in the following examples:

(9-30) se partió (punctual)
        it broke

(9-31) enseñó (achievement)
        s/he taught

(9-32) tenía (state)
        s/he had (imperfect form)

Punctual verbs, according to Andersen (1986, p. 311), are "momentary in duration. They may be thought of as being reduced to a point." Bardovi-Harlig (1999a) characterizes aspectual classes as follows:

> States persist over time without change (e.g., *seem, know, need, want,* and *be,* as in *be tall, big, green*). Activities have inherent duration in that they involve a span of time, like *sleep* and *snow*. They have no specific endpoint as in *I studied all week* and, thus, are atelic (e.g., *rain, play, walk,* and *talk*). Achievements capture the beginning or the end of an action (Mourelatos, 1981) as in *the race began* or *the game ended* and can be thought of as reduced to a point (Andersen, 1991). Examples of achievement verbs include *arrive, leave, notice, recognize,* and *fall asleep*. Accomplishments (e.g., *build a house* or *paint a painting*) are durative like activities and have an endpoint like achievements.
>
> (p. 358)

Based on his empirical results, Andersen postulated a sequence of developmental stages. The development of the past tense seemed to spread from achievement verbs to accomplishment verbs to activities and finally to states. The situation is different for the imperfect, which appears later than the perfect. It spreads in the reverse order—from states to activities to accomplishments, and then to achievements. Thus, Andersen argued that, when tense–aspect morphology emerged in the IL of these two participants, it was constrained by lexical aspect in terms of the types of verbs described above.

A similar phenomenon has been reported in a variety of L2 naturalistic and classroom settings (e.g., Kumpf, 1984; Kaplan, 1987; Flashner, 1989; Robison, 1990, 1995; Bardovi-Harlig, 1992a, 1992b; Bardovi-Harlig & Reynolds, 1995; Hasbún, 1995; Shirai, 1995; Bardovi-Harlig & Bergström, 1996; Shirai & Kurono, 1998; Rocca, 2002; see also reviews by Andersen & Shirai, 1994, 1996 and Bardovi-Harlig, 1999a, 2000). Findings from research in a number of TLs generally show the following:

1. **Past/perfective morphology** emerges with punctual verbs and verbs indicating achievements and accomplishments. The morphology then gradually extends to verbs expressing activities and states.
2. **Imperfective morphology** emerges with durative and/or stative verbs (i.e., activities and states), then gradually spreads to achievement/accomplishment and punctual verbs.
3. **Progressive morphology** is strongly associated with durative and dynamic verbs (i.e., activities).

Other studies are revealing in this regard. First, in a classroom setting, Housen (1995) observed, over a 3-year period of time, six learners of L2 English, whose native languages were French and Dutch. Data from the children, 8 years old at the beginning of the study, were longitudinally collected at 6-month intervals. Housen's results were mixed; the influence of telicity on perfective morphology was not as strong as predicted.

The strongest support for the Aspect Hypothesis came from the progressive marker, which was initially restricted to activities and then gradually covered all aspectual classes. It even overextended to states. Examples follow in 9-33–9-36:

(9-33) She dancing. (activity)

(9-34) And then a man coming . . . (accomplishment)

(9-35) Well, I was knowing that. (state)

(9-36) Other boys were shouting "watch out!" (achievement)

The French learners were overall less proficient than the Dutch learners and never reached the stage where they could use the regular-past morphology productively. Transfer factors were also involved in that learners appeared to be predisposed by the basic distinctions in their L1 tense–aspect system to look for similar distinctions in the L2 input, specifically in the case of the past/nonpast distinction, where Dutch is closer to English. However, in the progressive/nonprogressive distinction, where neither of the NLs obligatorily encodes progressive aspect, the learners seemed to resort to universal conceptual prototypes and appeared to interpret the progressive as a marker of inherent durativity.

In another study, Rohde (1996, 2002) analyzed naturalistic L2 data of four L1 German children learning English during a 6-month stay in California. An analysis of uninflected and other nontarget-like verb forms showed the following:

- use of progressive with infinitive or first/third person plural function:

    (9-37) I can fishing.
    (9-38) They going all, all the fishes going round my eggs and they bite.

- use of progressive in past contexts:

    (9-39) I think Birgit was kissing.
    (9-40) We was going up there.

- omission of past inflections on irregular and unfamiliar verbs:

    (9-41) Tiff, I sleep yesterday outside.
    (9-42) I just kick him.

- marking of future events with the construction *I'm* + verb:

    (9-43) I'm go home.
    (9-44) I'm get it for Tiff.

- unsystematic use and nonuse of inflections:

    (9-45) What do your foot? [German: Was macht dein Fuss? = What does your foot do?]
    (9-46) Hey Johnny is loving me.

As a result of these findings, Rohde maintains that the Aspect Hypothesis applies, with an important caveat: The influence of lexical aspect is gradient and wanes according to the learner's age, the particular L1/L2s involved, and the length of TL exposure.

The Aspect Hypothesis is a rich hypothesis drawing upon many forms of linguistics. It is important to note that very early forms of temporal expression appear without any overt linguistic marking. How then do learners express temporality? Bardovi-Harlig (1999a) suggested four ways: (a) build on conversational partner's discourse, (b) infer from context, (c) contrast events, and (d) follow chronological order in narration. These are essentially pragmatic means for accomplishing what learners are unable to accomplish within their linguistic means.

The next stage is the beginning of the learner's use of language to express temporality. Predominant in this phase is the use of adverbials (e.g., *yesterday*, *then*, *after*, *often*, *twice*). It is interesting that the ready availability and sufficiency of adverbials may delay acquisition of temporality (Giacalone Ramat & Banfi, 1990). In fact, Dietrich et al. (1995) suggest that some untutored learners may not progress past this stage (see discussion of Kumpf's work in Chapter 3).

TIME TO THINK ...

Brainstorm a list of adverbials in English or another language that learners might use to express temporality. Think about whether the adverbials can express past, present, future, progressive, and perfective meanings. Do you think that reliance on these adverbials might delay acquisition of temporality? In what ways have you used temporal adverbs to express time in your L2?

In a study by Wulff et al. (2009), the authors considered different possibilities to explain emergence of form. They did this through a triangulation of data, including corpus data (L1 and L2) and judgments by native speakers as to prototypicality of form. As with many aspects of L2 learning, they found no single factor responsible for the emergence of form; rather, numerous factors together (including frequency and prototypicality) drive learning. Added to this, one needs to consider L1 influence. Izquierdo and Collins (2008) considered two groups of learners of French (Spanish L1 and English L1), finding that those with Spanish as an L1 (whose L1 is similar to the L2 in the domain tested, namely the distinction between perfective and imperfective, which exists in both) take advantage of the similarity, whereas English learners (whose L1 differs from the L2 in that no distinction is made) rely more on verb semantics and "partially understood pedagogical rules" (p. 351). However, the role of the L1 is not quite so straightforward. Gabriele (2009) investigated aspects of learners of Japanese as an L2 (English L1) and English as an L2 (Japanese L1). The specific area of study was the present progressive in English and an imperfective marker in Japanese.

She found that the learners of Japanese were better able to acquire the Japanese imperfective marker than the learners of English were to acquire the present progressive. In particular, they were able to understand the semantics of the imperfective in the L2 and, importantly, were able to rule out interpretations that would have been based on their L1. She proposed two possibilities to explain this: grammatical complexity and features of the input.

Finally, Ayoun and Salaberry (2008) considered French learners of English with up to 7 years of study. They point to the fact that there is a task effect that comes into play, suggesting a representation of language that is still fragile, even after numerous years of study. They also point to the possibility of different stages of development, with some learners in their study relying on the L1 and others showing only a limited effect of the L1.

In sum, the area of research that deals with tense–aspect suggests a multiplicity of factors at play in explaining variability in acquiring this central feature of language.

9.3.2 The Discourse Hypothesis

Another way of looking at the acquisition of tense–aspect is not to consider lexical meaning, as with the Aspect Hypothesis, but to look at the structure of the discourse in which utterances appear. In general, there are two parts to discourse structure: background and foreground. Foreground information is generally new information that moves time forward. Background information is supporting information. Unlike foregrounded material, it does not provide new information, but might serve the purpose of elaborating on the information revealed through the foregrounded material. Within the context of the **Discourse Hypothesis**, it is claimed that "learners use emerging verbal morphology to distinguish foreground from background in narratives" (Bardovi-Harlig, 1994, p. 43). An example of how this might come about was seen in Chapter 3 in the discussion of data from Kumpf (1984).

Jarvis (2002) investigated article use in English by L2 learners from the perspective of discourse universals. His data from Finnish-speaking and Swedish-speaking learners of English were gathered from written narratives (in two parts) of a silent film. The narratives were analyzed by isolating all referents to the film's female protagonists and categorizing these references as to the contextual category: (a) new topic, (b) new comment, (c) current topic, (d) current comment, (e) known topic, and (f) known comment. These were defined in the following way (p. 395):

New topic
A previously unmentioned NP[7] referent that serves as the subject . . . of the main clause of a T-unit where no other NP referent has been mentioned previously.

New comment
A previously unmentioned NP referent that does not meet the criteria for a new topic.

Current topic

A NP referent that was mentioned in the preceding T-unit or earlier in the current T-unit and is the subject of the main clause of the current T-unit or as the only NP referent in the main clause that was mentioned previously.

A NP referent in a subordinate clause—though not in reported speech—if it is coreferential with the topic . . . of the main clause.

Current comment

A NP referent that was mentioned in the preceding T-unit or earlier in the current T-unit but does not meet the criteria for current topic.

Known topic

A NP referent that was mentioned earlier in the text, but not in the preceding T-unit or earlier in the current T-unit, and is the subject of the main clause or the only NP referent in the main clause mentioned previously.

Known comment

A NP referent that was mentioned earlier in the text, but not in the preceding T-unit or earlier in the current T-unit, and does not meet the criteria for known topic.

The results show a complex interplay between the NL and discourse constraints, suggesting that learners distinguish between new, current, and known NP referents, although the NL does influence these choices. The distinction between topic and comment is less straightforward, and Jarvis suggests that this may cast doubt on the universality of this distinction, although he acknowledges that his learners were not at the very early stages of acquisition. One interesting suggestion made is that learners may simultaneously entertain multiple hypotheses regarding article use.

Bardovi-Harlig (2004a, 2004b, 2005) investigated learners of English, showing that *will* emerges prior to *going to* as an expression of futurity. Bardovi-Harlig (2004a) considers three explanations: (a) formal complexity, (b) *will* as a lexical marker, and (c) the **one-to-one principle**. The one-to-one principle "is a principle of one *form* to one meaning" (Andersen, 1984, p.79, emphasis in original). With regard to formal complexity (*going to* is more complex than *will*), she argues that this might explain why *will* emerges first, but not why *going to* is infrequently used.[8] The second explanation that she explores is the possibility that learners perceive *will* as a lexical rather than a grammatical marker. This fits in with the general observation that lexical marking often precedes grammatical or morphological marking in SLA. In other words, learners use lexical items (e.g., *tomorrow*) before using grammatical means to express future. This is made easier by the fact that it is a single word, and, further, her data show only few instances of the reduced form (*'ll*). The third explanation relies on the one-to-one principle first articulated by Andersen (1984): "an IL should be constructed in such a way that an intended underlying meaning is expressed with one clear invariant surface form (or construction)" (p. 79). This principle, he claims, is a "first-step" in constructing an L2 grammar and guides learners as they construct "a minimal but functional IL system"

(p. 79). Bardovi-Harlig argues that *will* is the general future marker at the early stages. If the one-to-one principle is valid, in order for *going to* to enter the system, learners have to assign a new meaning, separate from the meaning of *will*. Following Dahl (1985, 2000), Bardovi-Harlig (2004a) makes the argument that *going to* has the meaning of "'in preparation' or impending use. The concept of 'immediacy' may be built in to the meaning associated with the form" (p. 133).

Bardovi-Harlig (1998), through data from L2 learners of English, finds support for both the tense–aspect and discourse hypotheses. She comes to the following conclusions (p. 498):

1. Achievements are the predicates most likely to be inflected for simple past, regardless of grounding.
2. Accomplishments are the next most likely type of predicate to carry the simple past. Foreground accomplishments show higher rates of use than background accomplishments.
3. Activities are the least likely of all the dynamic verbs to carry simple past, but foreground activities show higher rates of simple past inflection than background activities. Activities also show use of progressive, but this is limited to the background.

These findings clearly show that lexical meaning (as seen by the distinction among verb types) is one determinant of verbal morphology; discourse structure (as seen by the differential use of morphology for foreground vs. background material) is another. Thus, both the Aspect Hypothesis and discourse structure work together to account for the way tense–aspect morphology and meaning are acquired.

9.3.3 Concept-Oriented Approach

The **concept-oriented approach** starts with the assumption that learners begin with the need to express a given concept, for example, an event in the past. Thus, basic to this approach is the need to map certain functions that the learner wants to express to the form that she or he needs to express them. With adult learners, the function (i.e., concept) is already known, as the relevant concepts are available through their L1. Earlier in this chapter, we discussed Andersen's one-to-one principle, which is essentially an expression of one form/one meaning. Andersen (1990) discusses the possibility of multifunctionality, recognizing that there are times when a learner needs to "search" the input to understand additional meanings expressed in the input. An example might be the present progressive, which can mean an act in the present (*I am writing these words now*) or an act in the future (*I am flying to Shanghai tomorrow*). A great deal of research within this analytical framework has been conducted by Bardovi-Harlig, who has considered the acquisition of tense in numerous places (e.g., 2004a, 2004b, 2006, 2007), as well as in work by the European Science Foundation (e.g., Dietrich et al., 1995).

9.4 CONCLUSION

In sum, what has emerged from research in the domain of linguistics discussed in this and Chapter 7 is that universals (both typological and UG-based) clearly have an important impact on the formation of L2 grammars. What is in need of further examination is the extent to which universals operate alone or in consort with NL and TL facts, and the discovery of whether or not all universals equally affect L2 grammars.

POINTS TO REMEMBER

- Typological approaches to SLA deal with similarities between the languages of the world. Functional approaches deal with how language functions.

- The Interlanguage Structural Conformity Hypothesis holds that universals that are true for natural languages are true for ILs as well.

- An example of a typological universal is the Accessibility Hierarchy, which claims that there is a hierarchy of RCs, where one can predict the types of RCs that a given language will have. Learners have generally been found to follow this hierarchy in their order of acquisition.

- Another example of a typological universal that has been investigated in SLA is the acquisition of questions. If a language has subject–verb inversion in yes/no questions, then it will also have a verb before the subject in *wh-* questions, which in turn means that it will also have *wh-* fronting.

- The typological universal of word-final voiced obstruents (most marked) is handled in different ways by Spanish- and Mandarin-speaking learners of English. L1 Spanish learners of English pronounce final voiced obstruents as voiceless (e.g., Bob → [bɔp]), whereas Mandarin-speaking learners of English add a *schwa* after the final voiced obstruent (e.g., rob → [rabə]).

- The Aspect Hypothesis claims that learners initially use the semantics of a verb to know which tense and aspect markers to use with that verb. Achievement and accomplishment verbs are associated with past-tense morphology, activities and states are associated with imperfective morphology, and activities are associated with progressive morphology.

- Discourse structure, in terms of foreground and background, is another means by which learners acquire verbal morphology.

SUGGESTIONS FOR ADDITIONAL READING

Research design and methodology in studies on L2 tense and aspect (2012). Rafael Salaberry and Lloren Comajoan (Eds.). Mouton de Gruyter.

The Oxford handbook of tense and aspect (2012). Robert I. Binnick. Oxford University Press.

A dynamic approach to second language development: Methods and techniques (2011). Marjolijn Verspoor, Kees de Bot, and Wander Lowie (Eds.). John Benjamins.

Functional categories in learner language (2009). Peter Jordens and Christine Dimroth. Mouton de Gruyter.

Beyond the aspect hypothesis: Tense–aspect development in advanced L2 French (2005). Emmanuelle Labeau. Peter Lang.

The L2 acquisition of tense–aspect morphology (2002). Rafael Salaberry and Yasuhiro Shirai (Eds.). John Benjamins.

Foreign accent: The ontogeny and phylogeny of second language phonology. (2001). Roy Major. Lawrence Erlbaum Associates.

Tense and aspect in second language acquisition: Form, meaning, and use (2000). Kathleen Bardovi-Harlig. Blackwell.

Crosscurrents in second language acquisition (1991). Thom Huebner and Charles A. Ferguson (Eds.). John Benjamins.

MORE TO DO AND MORE TO THINK ABOUT ...

1. Take the example of RC formation, as discussed in this chapter. It was claimed that there is a universal such that every language that has indirect-object relativization also has direct-object relativization. What sort of data would you want to gather to substantiate this claim for SLA? This universal is a static claim; that is, it makes a claim about a given language/IL at a given point in time. Consider it from an acquisitional point of view. What would the language learning prediction be? Does this universal predict acquisition order? What sort of experimental design would you use to test this?

2. Consider the notion of resumptive pronouns in relative clauses discussed in this chapter. In ILs it is common to find sentences like the following:

   That's the man whom I told you about [*him*].

   Let's assume that sentences like this are produced by speakers who have pronominal reflexes in their NL. To what would you attribute this IL form?

   Assume that the sentence below is produced by speakers of a language with no pronominal reflexes. To what would you attribute this IL form? Are these analyses in contradiction? How would you reconcile these differences?

That's the woman that I'm taller than her.

These IL sentences are common in some dialects of English, particularly in colloquial speech. How does this affect your analysis?

3. Consider the case where you have a language in which genitive phrases follow nouns, as in the following French example:

Le chien   de mon ami
the dog   of my friend

In English, two structures are possible, one in which the possessor follows the noun and one in which it precedes it.

The dog of my friend
My friend's dog

Whereas both of these English sentences are possible, the first one sounds strange. On the other hand, of the following two groups of sentences in English, it is the second group that is less likely to be said:

The leg of the table
A leg of lamb

The table's leg
A lamb's leg

How would you explain this? What would you predict regarding a learner's IL production? Considering both transfer and input, how would a learner figure out the facts of English? As a teacher, how might you explain this?

A French/Italian/Spanish speaker learning English has to go from one form to two, whereas the other direction requires a learner to go from two forms to one. Which do you think would be more difficult, and why?

4. Considering the previous problem, let's assume that a hypothetical learner has sorted out the correct English facts about possession. Then she encounters *the book of Job* and has also become aware of the ungrammaticality of *Job's book* in this context. Do you think that this might then alter her original analysis? Do you think she might begin to produce phrases like *the table's leg* or might go into a restaurant and order *a lamb's leg*? Why, or why not?

5. Consider the following definitions for the basic meanings of the progressive/present/future tenses in English:

(a) Progressive (*to be* + verb + *-ing*): ongoing witnessed activity that persists for an extended period of time.
(b) Simple present (base verb): lawlike regular state or expected events characteristic of their subject at the present time.
(c) Future (*will* + verb): states or events expected in foreseeable future.

The data presented here are from Spanish and Japanese learners of English (data from Gass & Ard, 1984). These learners had been asked to judge the acceptability of the following sentences in English.

	Spanish n = 52	Japanese n = 37
	% acceptable responses	
1. Dan sees better.	65	43
2. Dan is seeing better now.	81	19
3. Mary is being in Chicago now.	8	5
4. John is travelling to New York tomorrow.	8	32
5. The new bridge connects Detroit and Windsor.	79	73
6. The new bridge is connecting Detroit and Windsor.	46	24
7. John travels to New York tomorrow.	8	19
8. John will travel to New York tomorrow.	86	81
9. John is smoking American cigarettes now.	88	76
10. The new bridge will connect Detroit and Windsor.	67	87
11. Fred smokes American cigarettes now.	56	51
12. Mary will be in Chicago now.	10	14
13. John will smoke American cigarettes now.	10	3
14. Mary is in Chicago now.	88	92

Focus on the progressive, simple present, and future tenses. For each, order the sentences from those most frequently judged acceptable to those least frequently judged acceptable. Do this separately for each of the two language groups. Are the two language groups comparable? What explanation can you give for the different percentages of each of the two language groups? What explanation can you give for the differential acceptability of the various uses of each tense by both groups? In your answer you might want to consider the different semantic concepts embodied in each of the verb tenses: completed action, incomplete action, and action in progress.

What do these data suggest about the interaction between syntax and semantics in SLA?

Consider sentences 4 and 7, the translation equivalents of which are possible in Spanish. However, the acceptability of these sentences in English is low in the Spanish speakers' judgments. How can you account for this? What does this suggest about the interaction of the NL and language universals?

What do these data suggest about the acquisition of tense–aspect systems in an L2? Is acquisition gradual or is it an all or nothing phenomenon?

6. The data below are from a native speaker of Arabic enrolled in an intermediate level of an intensive English program. He had seen a movie titled *Little Man, Big City*. The following is his oral account of that movie.

> I saw today a movie about a man in a big city. I want to tell you about a movie, my friend. The movie began with a man about forty years old or forty-five in his apartment in the city and he was disturbed by alarm clock, TV, and noisy outside the house or outside the apartment and he woke up in a bad temper and he wanted a fresh air, he went when he opened the window to get this fresh air, he found a smoke, smoke air, dirty air. The movie also showed that the man not only disturbed in his special apartment or special house, but in everything, in work, in street, in transportation, even in the gardens and seashores. Man in the city has to wake up very early to go to the work and he has to, as the movie shows, he has to use any means of transportation, car, bus, bicycle and all the streets are crowded, and he has no no choice or alternatively to use and he is busy day and night. At day, he has to work hard among the machines, the typewriters and among papers, pencils and offices in the city. And when he wanted to take a rest in his house or outside his house in the garden or the seashore . . . He can't because the seats are crowded with people. When he wanted to take a meal in restaurant, the restaurant is crowded, everything is crowded in the city and very, very— it's not good place or good atmosphere to to live in. The movie showed that. And the man began to feel sick and thus he wanted to consult the doctors to describe a medicine or anything for for health, but the doctors also disagreed about his illness or they couldn't diagnose his illness correctly. This they show at first. Want to make us know about the life in the city. The man began to think about to find a solution or answer for this dilemma. OK dilemma? Dilemma. He thought that why not to go to the open lands and to build houses and gardens and and to live in this new fresh land with fresh air and fresh atmosphere and why don't we stop smoking in the factories by using filters, filters and stop smoking from the cars and all industrial bad survivals or like smoking like dirty airs and so on. The man also wanted to make kids or childrens in the houses not to play or to use sports inside houses, but to go outside the houses in the garden and to play with balls, basket anything. They like to play. And also he wanted to live in a quiet and calm apartment. People inside houses must not use TV in a bad way or a noisy way. Must use it in a calm way or in a quiet way and that, I think, that is a good solution or a good answer for this city dilemma.

Categorize the data by separating this speaker's use of the present tense from his use of the past tense. Focusing on tense shifts, from past to present and vice versa, work out an IL generalization that might account for this shift.

7. Below is a written version of the same movie by the same speaker:

> I saw a movie about a man in a city (big city). I want to tell you what I saw and what is my opinion. The movie began with a man about forty years old, in his apartment in a big city. He was disturbed by many things like Alarm O'Clock, T.V., Radio and noisy outside. He want a fresh air, but he could not because the city is not a good place for fresh air. There are many factories which fill the air with smoke. The movie showed the daily life of a man in the city. He is very busy day and night. He had to go to his work early by any means of transportation, car, bus, bicycle. The streets are crowded, everything in the city is crowded with people, the houses, streets, factories, institutions and even the seashores. Man in a big city lives a hard and unhealthy life, noisy, dirt air, crowded houses and smoke are good factors for sickness. The man in the big city tried to find answer to this dilemma. Instead of living in crowded, unhealthy places, he wanted places that must be used for living. People must live in good atmosphere climate and land. Gardens, which are god places for sports, must surround houses. My opinion is that man's solution for the problem is good and acceptable especially for health.

Categorize the data by separating the speaker's use of the present tense from his use of the past tense. Focusing on tense shifts, from past to present and vice versa, work out an IL generalization that might account for this shift.

LINK

1. http://tinyurl.com/cdayu5a

CHAPTER TEN

Looking at Interlanguage Processing

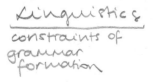

Linguistics × Psychology
constraints of   Mechanisms
grammar   involved in
formation   SLA

10.1 INTRODUCTION

As with the field of linguistics, the field of psychology has significantly influenced the study of SLA. In this chapter, we outline approaches to SLA with a basis in psycholinguistic processing rather than in linguistic structures. In linguistics, the emphasis is on constraints on grammar formation, whereas, in psychology, the emphasis is on the actual mechanisms involved in SLA, as well as on issues (e.g., working memory capacity) that affect those mechanisms. This is not to say that there is no overlap, only that each approach has its own particular emphasis.

We begin the chapter by discussing processing approaches, in particular, **Processability Theory**, information processing, and **input processing**. In the following section, we deal with concepts that are prevalent in the psycholinguistic literature and that relate to L2 learning, namely, attention, **working memory**, and **syntactic priming**. We then turn to a discussion of **emergentism** in L2 learning. This is followed by a section on a **dynamic systems** approach. We then finally consider knowledge types (acquisition/learning, **declarative/procedural**, **implicit/explicit**) and the interface between knowledge types.

10.2 PROCESSING APPROACHES

Processing approaches are characterized by a concern with the processing mechanisms and capacities of the human brain and how those mechanisms and capacities operate within the context of L2 learning. The first approach we deal with is known as Processability Theory.

10.2.1 Processability Theory

Processability Theory relies on the concept of a linguistic processor. In its simplest form, Processability Theory (cf. Pienemann, 1999, 2007, and the review by Pienemann & Keßler, 2012) proposes that production and comprehension of L2 forms can take place only if they can be handled by the linguistic processor. Understanding how the processor works allows predictions to be made about the developmental paths that learners take. As an example of how this works, consider the sequence that learners of English follow when learning questions. In Table 10.1 (based on Pienemann & Johnston, 1987) is the proposed developmental sequence for the acquisition of English questions.

This model makes a strong prediction of word-order development such that, in Stage 1, a learner will start off (apart from single words and/or chunks) with canonical order, such as SVO. Stage 2 involves some movement, but movement that does not interrupt the canonical order. This is followed by Stage 3, in which canonical order is interrupted. In Stage 4, grammatical categories are recognized. And, finally, in Stages 5 and 6, learners recognize substrings.

The question arises as to why question formation should be subject to the kind of constraints seen in this model. One explanation, which has been put forward by Clahsen (1984), includes three processing mechanisms that constrain movement from one stage to the next:

1. **Canonical order strategy**: This predicts that strategies that separate linguistic units require greater processing capacity than strategies that involve a direct mapping onto surface strings. For example, early learners generally use a single, basic word order (e.g., in English, SVO). Elements do not interrupt this sequence.

2. **Initialization/finalization strategy**: When movement takes place, elements will be moved into initial and/or final position, rather than somewhere in the middle of a sentence. This aids in both processing and memorization, given research findings of the salience of first and last positions.

3. **Subordinate-clause strategy**: Movement in subordinate clauses is avoided. In general, subordinate clauses are processed differently, because one has to hold material in memory without a complete semantic analysis. When movement is learned, it happens in main clauses before it does in subordinate clauses.

These processing strategies, which deal with movement, are claimed to account for the acquisition order of English questions, which, of course, require movement.

Within this approach, there is a Processability Hierarchy, which, in short, states that the processor checks on the match between the grammatical information within a sentence. What this means is that, within a sentence such as *The girl walks to school*, the processor checks to see if parts of a sentence match; in this case, the match involves singularity—singular subject *the girl* and singular verb *walks*. However, in order for this matching to work, learners need to develop a number of procedures, for example, procedures for putting together parts of the sentence (e.g., *the* and *girl*) and procedures for comparing relevant grammatical information (for example, in a language in which there is no subject–verb agreement, such a matching procedure is not

TABLE 10.1 Developmental Stages of English Question Formation (*Source*: From *Stepping up the pace—Input, interaction and interlanguage development: An empirical study of questions in ESL*. Unpublished Doctoral Dissertation, University of Sydney, Australia by A. Mackey, 1995. Reprinted by permission.)

Developmental stage	Example
Stage 1: Single units:	
Single words	What?
Single units	What is your name?
Stage 2: SVO:	
Canonical (basic) word order with question intonation	It's a monster?
	Your cat is black?
	You have a cat?
	I draw a house here?
Stage 3: Fronting (*wh-* word/*do*):	
Direct questions with main verbs and some form of fronting	Where the cats are?
	What the cat doing in your picture?
	Do you have an animal?
	Does in this picture there is a cat?
Stage 4: Pseudo inversion: yes/no questions, verb *to be*:	
In yes/no questions, an auxiliary or modal (e.g., *can/could*) is in sentence-initial position	Have you got a dog?
	Have you drawn the cat?
In *wh-* questions, the verb *to be* and the subject change positions	Where is the cat in your picture?
Stage 5: *Do*/auxiliary second:	
Q-word → auxiliary/modal → subject (main verb, etc.)	Why (Q-word) have (auxiliary) you (subject) left home?
Auxiliary verbs and modals are placed in second position after *wh-* question words and before subjects (applies only in main clauses/direct questions)	What do you have?
	Where does your cat sit?
	What have you got in your picture?
Stage 6: *Can* inversion, negative question, tag question:	
Can inversion: *wh-* question inversions are not present in embedded clauses	Can you see what the time is?
	Can you tell me where the cat is?
Negative question: A negated form of *do*/auxiliary is placed before the subject	Doesn't your cat look black?
	Haven't you seen a dog?
Tag question: An auxiliary verb and a pronoun are attached to the end of a main clause	It's on the wall, isn't it?

relevant). Lack of agreement would suggest that the learner has not yet developed appropriate procedures for matching grammatical information. Pienemann (1999) established a hierarchy relevant to the ordering of procedures, as follows:

1. no procedure (e.g., single-word utterances);
2. category procedure (e.g., adding a plural morpheme to a noun);
3. noun-phrase procedure (e.g., matching gender as in *la casa* [the house], where both determiner and noun are feminine);
4. verb-phrase procedure (e.g., movement of elements within a verb phrase);
5. sentence procedure (e.g., subject–verb agreement);
6. subordinate-clause procedure (e.g., use of a particular tense based on something in the main clause).

hierarchy of ordering procedures (one procedure is a prerequisite for the next.

This hierarchy is implicational in that one procedure is a prerequisite for the next. Even though these are universal procedures, there is some leeway for learners to create individual solutions to processing limitations. For example, in Table 10.1 above, we saw the following examples for Stage 3 questions:

(10-1) Where the cats are?

(10-2) What the cat doing in your picture?

(10-3) Do you have an animal?

(10-4) Does in this picture there is a cat?

Learners produced a range of forms to avoid the complexity of movement. As noted, the principles are invariant. What is less understood are the language-specific facts representing a range of languages (for an example of how one determines relevant procedures for a language, see Kawaguchi, 2005).

We turn our attention next to another psycholinguistic approach to SLA, information processing.

10.2.2 Information Processing: Automaticity, Restructuring, and U-Shaped Learning

McLaughlin (1990a) noted two concepts that are fundamental in L2 learning and use: **automaticity** and **restructuring**. Automaticity refers to control over one's linguistic knowledge. In language performance, one must bring together a number of skills from perceptual, cognitive, and social domains. The more each of these skills is routinized, the greater the ease with which they can be put to use.

Restructuring refers to the changes made to internalized representations as a result of new learning. Changes that reflect restructuring are discontinuous or qualitatively different from a previous stage. Learning means the inclusion of additional information that must be organized and structured. Integrating new information into one's developing L2 system necessitates changes to parts of the existing system, thereby

[handwritten margin note top: therefore, the more information can be automatically handled, the more attentional resources are available for new information]

restructuring, or reorganizing, the current system and creating a (slightly) new L2 system. Mere addition of new elements does not constitute restructuring.

An underlying assumption in looking at SLA from the perspective of these two concepts is that human beings have a limited capacity for processing. Central to the ability to process information is the ability to attend to, deal with, and organize new information. Because of the limited capacity that humans have available for processing, the more that can be handled routinely—that is, automatically—the more attentional resources are available for new information. Processing resources are limited and must be distributed economically, if communication is to be efficient. Put differently, trying to read a difficult scholarly article is done less efficiently if one is watching TV simultaneously. Too much attention is drawn away from the article, to the TV. When there are no other demands on our attention (e.g., reading the article in the quiet of the library), it takes less time to read and understand the article (see section 10.3.1. for a more detailed discussion of the role of attention in SLA.).

[handwritten margin note left: Assumption: humans have a limited capacity for processing. BUT — have ability to process info. - attend to, deal with and organize new information.]

10.2.2.1 Automaticity and Restructuring

[handwritten note: fast, unconscious, effortless processing]

One way of viewing SLA is to see it as the acquisition of complex skills, much like learning other skills, such as playing tennis or playing the violin. From this perspective, the role of automaticity assumes great importance. When learning to play tennis, for example, one cannot deliberate about every movement of the racquet or movement of one's feet. Rather, when skilled players approach the net, they automatically move their feet in a particular way and get the racquet set, without thinking deliberately about each step or position of the racquet.

There are a number of ways that automaticity can be conceptualized, but the most central of these is that there is fast, unconscious, and effortless processing.

[handwritten margin: AUTOMATIZATION IN SLA.]

TIME TO THINK …

Think about the tennis metaphor above. When speaking your L2, do you feel like you are focusing on each step (swing of the racquet) or do you speak (and understand) your L2 without thinking about each detail? What factors affect how automatized your use of the L2 is?

When there has been a consistent and regular association between a certain kind of input and some output pattern, automatization may result. That is, an associative connection is activated. This can be seen in the relative automaticity of the following exchange between two people walking down the hall toward each other:

[handwritten margin: (Association between input and output) → An associative connection is activated. Iv. Japanese Prime Minister and Clinton]

SPEAKER 1: Hi.
SPEAKER 2: Hi, how are you?
SPEAKER 1: Fine, and you?
SPEAKER 2: Fine.

[Handwritten margin note top: PROCESSING RESOURCES ARE LIMITED AND MUST BE DISTRIBUTED ECONOMICALLY IF COMMUNICATION IS TO BE EFFICIENT.]

The conversational routine is so automatic in a language one knows well that most people have had the experience of responding "fine" before the question is even asked, and of responding "fine" when it turns out that a different question is being asked, as in the following conversation:

JULIE: Hi, Sue.
SUE: Good morning, Julie.
JULIE: Fine, and you?

A comparable example took place at a G8 summit in Okinawa, Japan. Prior to the summit, Prime Minister Mori of Japan spent time brushing up on his English. Upon meeting President Clinton, he apparently became flustered and, instead of saying *How are you?*, said instead: *Who are you?* President Clinton responded: *I'm Hillary Clinton's husband*. However, Prime Minister Mori, unaware that he had asked the wrong question, was anticipating a response something like *I'm fine, and you?* and responded *I am too.*[1]

Crookes (1991) discussed the significance of planning and monitoring one's speech. It is at the level of planning (e.g., preplanning an utterance) that a learner makes a decision about what to say and what structures to use. That is, a learner has some choice over which structures will be used and, hence, practiced. Assuming that practice is a way toward ultimate automatization, then it is clear that decisions of what to practice are crucial in the determination of future language use. Thus, as Crookes pointed out, preplanning (see Chapter 13 for an additional discussion of planning) is important in determining what will and what will not become automatized and, as a result, what parts of one's IL will become more automatic.

Similar arguments have been made by Bialystok (1978), who argued that explicit knowledge can become implicit through the use of practice. Practice can, of course, take place in the classroom and can be determined by the learner through the preplanning of utterances.

There is empirical evidence to support the benefits of planning in affecting the complexity of the discourse (Crookes, 1989; R. Ellis, 1987a; J. Williams, 1990). In general, planning an utterance leads to the ability to utilize more complex language, which, in turn, can lead to the automatization of complex language and the ability to plan language with even greater complexity.

The role of monitoring is also important. Here, it is important to differentiate between monitoring as part of a theoretical construct developed by Krashen and *monitoring* that refers to the activity of paying attention to one's speech. In the latter use of the term, one can imagine a situation in which learners, in monitoring their speech, note the successful use of a form and are then able to use it in a subsequent conversation. That is, through careful monitoring of one's own speech, one can pick out successful utterances and use them as a basis for future practice (see Crookes, 1991). Controlled processing is yet another mechanism of language use. With controlled processing, the associations have not been built up by repeated use. Rather, attentional control is necessary. Thus, one would expect a slower response. Consider the same

257

greeting situation as given earlier, but this time in a language unfamiliar to you. If you were learning Japanese and someone said to you:

SPEAKER 1: Genkideska ("How are you?")

the response, *anatawa*, would not come so easily or automatically. It might take some attention for you to dig up the appropriate response to that question. The distinction between controlled and automatic processing is one of routinization and the creation of associations in long-term memory, not one of conscious awareness, as Krashen's acquisition-learning distinction suggests. The distinction is also not one of separateness, because automatic processing presupposes the existence of controlled processing.

SLA, in this view, takes place by the initial use of control processes. With time and with experience in specific linguistic situations, learners begin to use language more automatically, thus leaving more attentional resources for new information that requires more control. Segalowitz (2003) points out that the picture in reality is not so clear cut. Grammatical learning is not simply a matter of moving from the knowledge of examples to automatic use based on rules; nor does it move from the effortful use of rules to automatic retrieval of chunks stored in memory. DeKeyser (2001) and Segalowitz suggest a need to investigate these two modes together (rule-based learning and exemplar-based learning) in order to understand how learners put information together to produce language in a way that NSs do, that is, fast, effortlessly, and unconsciously.

The construct of attention (see section 10.3.1) is intimately connected to automaticity, in that, when information use (e.g., in production or in reading, or in going to the net in tennis) is automatic, there is less attention paid to each action along the way. Consider Table 10.2 from McLaughlin et al. (1983). Here we have a sketch of different types of processing information depending on two variables: degree of control and degree of attention.

TABLE 10.2 Possible L2 Performance as a Function of Information-Processing Procedures and Attention to Formal Properties of Language (*Source*: From "Second language learning: An information-processing perspective" by B. McLaughlin, T. Rossman, & B. McLeod, 1983, *Language Learning*, *33*, pp. 135–158, by Research Club in Language Learning. Reprinted by permission.)

Attention to formal properties of language	Information processing	
	Controlled	Automatic
Focal	(Cell A) Performance based on formal rule learning	(Cell B) Performance in a test situation
Peripheral	(Cell C) Performance based on implicit learning or analogic learning	(Cell D) Performance in communication situations

There are various ways in which learners can approach the process of learning an L2, depending in large part on where they focus attention. Cell A reflects a learner who focuses attention on formal properties of learning in a controlled way. This would most likely be the type of learner who would come out of a formal, classroom-learning experience. Cell C reflects a learner in a situation in which the use of the language is not automatic, but in which the use of the language does not necessitate explicit attention. Cells B and D reflect automatic, routinized language use. In Cell B, however, task demands, such as a formal test, might necessitate a learner's attention, whereas Cell D reflects the normal situation of language use by NSs and by fluent NNSs. Segalowitz (2003) describes the interaction as follows:

Practiced Mental components speed up with use

> As various component mental activities become practiced, their time of operation will speed up, and less of the total time of performance will be devoted to those particular mental operations. Mechanisms that were formerly rate-determining because they were quite slow may, after training, no longer be so because they operate so quickly that other, slower mechanisms become the rate-determining components by default. The now fast mechanisms may operate so rapidly that the remaining slower processes may not be able to interfere with their operation. The products of these now fast mental operations may no longer be available for verbal report and hence not experienced as being consciously executed, etc. In this sense, they have become automatic.
>
> (pp. 386–387)

The second concept of import within the framework of information processing is that of restructuring, which takes place when *qualitative* changes occur in a learner's internal representation of the L2 or in the use of procedures—generally from inefficient to efficient. In terms of child language acquisition, McLaughlin described restructuring in the following way: "Restructuring is characterized by discontinuous, or qualitative change as the child moves from stage to stage in development. Each new stage constitutes a new internal organization and not merely the addition of new structural elements" (1990a, p. 117).

RECONSTRUCTING ↓ qualitative changes ↓ every new stage constitutes a new internal organization, and not only adding.

To return to the kaleidoscope analogy mentioned in Chapter 7, if a new colored element were inserted into the system, with no other changes, restructuring would not have taken place. If, on the other hand, a new element were added, disturbing the existing system and thereby necessitating reorganization, restructuring would have taken place. Table 10.3 presents data from R. Ellis (1985a) to illustrate this.

At Time 1, only one form, *no*, is used. At Time 2, a new form, *don't*, has entered this learner's system. Now *no* and *don't* are being used in apparent **free variation** in both indicative and imperative forms. By Time 3, this learner has created a system in which there are the beginnings of a one-to-one correspondence between form and function. *Don't* is now the only form used for imperatives, whereas, for indicatives, both forms remain. Thus, restructuring takes place at Time 3, when the learner has begun to sort out the form-function relationship. The learner in this case is reorganizing and reshuffling her L2 knowledge until she has appropriately sorted out form–function relations (if that stage is ever reached).

TABLE 10.3 Evidence of Restructuring (*Source*: From *Understanding second language acquisition* by R. Ellis. Oxford, England: Oxford University Press, 1985a. Reprinted by permission.)

Time 1	Time 2	Time 3	Time 4
I am no go.	I am no go.	I am no go.	I am no go.
No look.	No look.	Don't look.	Don't go.
I am no run.	I am don't run.	I am don't run.	I am no run.
No run.	Don't run.	Don't run.	Don't run.

Lightbown (1985, p. 177) provides the following rationale for restructuring:

> [Restructuring] occurs because language is a complex hierarchical system whose components interact in nonlinear ways. Seen in these terms, an increase in error rate in one area may reflect an increase in complexity or accuracy in another, followed by overgeneralization of a newly acquired structure, or simply by a sort of overload of complexity which forces a restructuring, or at least a simplification, in another part of the system.

A final example of restructuring comes from the work of Ard and Gass (1987), who examined the interaction of syntax and the lexicon. They gave two groups, of high- and low-proficiency learners, a grammaticality-judgment task containing four sentence types. Results showed that there was less differentiation among lexical items in the lower-proficiency group than in the higher-proficiency group. Different lexical items in the same syntactic frame did not have a great effect on the less-proficient learners' judgments of English sentences. Thus, sentences such as 10-5 and 10-6 were more likely to be responded to in a like manner by the lower-level learners than by the more proficient learners.

(10-5) The judge told the lawyer his decision.

(10-6) *The judge informed the lawyer his decision.

One can interpret these findings to mean that low-proficiency learners interpret sentences syntactically, ignoring semantic and lexical aspects of sentences. At higher levels, greater lexical and semantic differentiation was noted. What this research suggests is that learners may begin with a given rule that covers all cases of what they perceive to be a particular structural type. A second step occurs when an additional rule becomes available to them. They now have two choices available. Either they can alternate the rules (as in the early stages of the negative forms *no* and *don't*, discussed earlier) or they can alter the first and possibly the second of these rules until the correct distribution and patterning are established. Thus, when, as a function of proficiency, additional syntactic patterns become available to learners, destabilization occurs, and it is destabilization that is at the base of language change.

McLaughlin and Heredia (1996) relate restructuring, or representational changes, to a novice–expert continuum, whereby researchers study changes that take place when a beginner at some skill gains greater expertise. In their summary, they note that "experts restructure the elements of a learning task into abstract schemata that are not available to novices, who focus principally on surface elements of a task. Thus, experts replace complex subelements with schemata that allow more abstract processing" (p. 217).

In relating this to language learning, one can think of chunk learning (see Chapter 8), whereby learners have fixed phrases, but may not have unpackaged these phrases into anything meaningful. Rather, the string of sounds is a chunk with a holistic meaning. As a learner becomes more proficient, the component parts become clear. In these situations, when this occurs, a learner's speech may, on the surface, appear simpler, but may, in reality, represent greater syntactic sophistication. Thus, the learner has moved from formulaic speech to speech that entails an understanding of structure. To put this somewhat differently, the learner is moving from exemplar-based learning to a stage in which representations are more rule-based.

10.2.2.2 U-Shaped Learning

Destabilization, as discussed above, is a consequence of restructuring and often results in what are known as **U-shaped patterns**.[2] U-shaped patterns reflect three stages of linguistic use. In the earliest stage, a learner produces some linguistic form that conforms to target-like norms (i.e., is error-free). At Stage 2, a learner appears to lose what s/he knew at Stage 1. The linguistic behavior at Stage 2 deviates from TL norms. Stage 3 looks just like Stage 1, in that there is again correct TL usage. This is illustrated in Figure 10.1.

Lightbown (1983) presented data from French learners of English in a classroom context. She examined the use of the -ing form in English among sixth-, seventh-, and eighth-grade learners. Sentence 10-7 was a typical Grade 6 utterance when describing a picture.

(10-7) He is taking a cake.

By Grade 7, 10-8 was a typical response to the same picture.

(10-8) He take a cake.

How can we account for an apparent decrease in knowledge? Lightbown hypothesized that, initially, these students were presented only with the progressive form. With nothing else in English to compare it to, they equated it with the simple present of French. That is, in the absence of any other verb form, there was no way of determining what the limits were of the present progressive. In fact, with no other comparable verb form in their system, learners overextended the use of the progressive into contexts in which the simple present would have been appropriate. When the

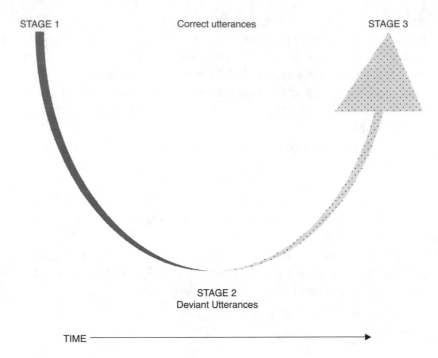

FIGURE 10.1 Schema of U-Shaped Behavior

simple present was introduced, learners not only had to learn this new form, but they also had to readjust their knowledge about the present progressive, redefining its limits. Evidence of the confusion and subsequent readjustment and restructuring of the progressive was seen in the decline in both use and accuracy. It will take some time before these learners eventually restructure their L2 knowledge appropriately and are able to use both the progressive and the simple present in target-like ways. Thus, given these data, a U-shaped curve results (assuming eventual target-like knowledge), as in Figure 10.2.

TIME TO THINK ...

Can you think of any learners of an L2 who have experienced a U-shaped learning pattern? What was the structure that the learner showed a U-shaped pattern with? What factors do you think might have led to the change from target-like use to nontarget-like use and back to target-like use?

[extreme limitation of input or compromised input]

10.2.3 Input Processing

This area of research deals with how learners comprehend utterances and, particularly, how they assign form-meaning relationships and is attributed largely to the work of VanPatten and his colleagues (see 2012 for a review). Different researchers have looked at various aspects of this issue.

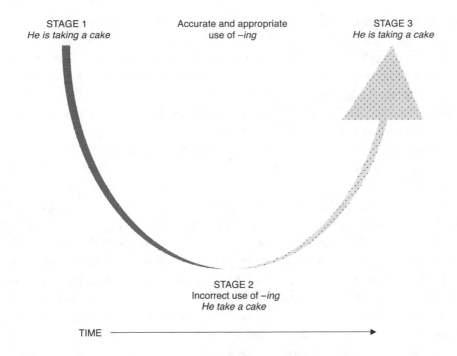

STAGE 1
He is taking a cake

Accurate and appropriate
use of *–ing*

STAGE 3
He is taking a cake

STAGE 2
Incorrect use of *–ing*
He take a cake

TIME

FIGURE 10.2 Schema of U-Shaped Behavior: Use of *-ing*

Because this approach has been largely addressed in the context of language teaching, we defer a more thorough discussion to Chapter 13. For the purposes of this chapter, we point out simply that the proposed principles and their corollaries attempt to account for how processing takes place—from meaning to form. Within each principle are corollaries that attempt to account for why certain parts of an utterance/sentence take center stage rather than others (content words, lexical items before forms, nonredundant information, etc.), and why meaning might override form (e.g., lexical semantics, real-world knowledge/events, and context).

There are other approaches to the processing of input as well. For example, O'Grady (2003) suggests that,

> the computational system may be too underpowered to reliably execute the more demanding tasks involved in natural language processing. . . . Whereas children routinely overcome this deficit, its effects in the case of adults may be longer lasting, contributing to the pattern of partial attainment that is typical of second language learning.
>
> (p. 53)

He also suggests (p. 58) that L2 learning is a venue for observing "the acquisition device functioning under conditions of duress—either because of extreme limitations on the available input (as in the case of classroom learning) or because one or more of its component modules have been compromised, or both." He suggests that structural complexity is a source of processing difficulty. Research to support this view is seen in work by O'Grady et al. (2003), who found that, in comprehension of RCs, subject RCs were easier than direct-object RCs (73.2 percent versus 22.7 percent) for their group of learners of Korean, suggesting structural complexity as a source of the difficulty. Jeon and Kim (2007) find support for the difference in RC types, although their study raises additional questions regarding RC structures in Korean, as well as issues of animacy. The issue of computational complexity is supported by these data, as it is in other data based on RC production.

Carroll (2001) proposed the **Autonomous Induction Theory**, which attributes difficulties in learning an L2 to parsing problems. Acquisition moves forward when there is a failure in the parsing of utterances. Learning is an inductive process in this view (learning takes place by the learner being presented with examples (input) and making generalizations from those examples) and is triggered by a failure to process incoming stimuli. Parsing involves a categorization of the stream of sounds that one hears into some meaningful units (e.g., lexical, functional, syntactic). When one hears an L2 utterance, one has to assign appropriate relationships, that is, one has to parse the elements into something that makes sense. Thus, let's assume a complex sentence such as *That's the cat whom the dog bit*. Let's further assume that a learner hears this and parses it as if it were *That's the cat who bit the dog*, given that the latter is an easier RC structure, when considering the Accessibility Hierarchy. Finally, let's assume that the learner knows from prior events that it was the dog who had done the biting. It is at this juncture that there is a signal to the parser that there needs to be an adjustment. This is not to say that there will always be a positive result, and that the parsing mechanism will be adjusted; it is to say that this is the mechanism by which such adjustments may take place. As Carroll (2007, p. 161) puts it, the language acquisition device "is triggered when the parsing system fails."

Clahsen and Felser (2006a, 2006b), based on processing mechanisms of child L1 learners and adult L2 learners (as well as adult NSs), found different emphases in terms of parsing. For children learning their L1 and adult NSs, syntax-based principles dominate. Children do not make use of lexical–semantic or referential information to the same degree as adults. This, they suggest, may be owing to different abilities at lexical retrieval and different working-memory capacities. Adult L2 learners were found to rely less on syntactic information and more on lexical–semantic and pragmatic information (see discussion in section 10.4.1 regarding the **Competition Model**). They proposed the Shallow Structure Hypothesis, "according to which the sentential representations adult L2 learners compute for comprehension contain less syntactic detail than those of native speakers" (p. 35)[3] (see also discusion in Chapter 7).

In sum, these approaches deal with the important role that the processing of language input plays, although the emphases are slightly different, with VanPatten's main concern being establishing form-meaning connections, O'Grady's emphasis on computational complexity, Carroll's on the parser, and Clahsen and Felser on the different parts of grammar used in comprehension/processing.

10.3 PSYCHOLINGUISTIC CONSTRUCTS

In this section, we deal with some psycholinguistic constructs that have, in recent years, figured prominently in helping us understand the nature of L2 learning.

10.3.1 Attention

According to *The American Heritage Dictionary*, attention refers to "the concentration of the mental powers upon an object." It has come to be one of the most important constructs in L2 research. In fact, Schmidt (2001) claims that it "appears necessary for understanding nearly every aspect of second and foreign language learning" (p. 6). There are a number of approaches to attention and particularly to its relationship with awareness. One of the early treatments of attention in the SLA literature came from Tomlin and Villa (1994). They proposed three components of attention: alertness (readiness to receive incoming stimuli), orientation (direction of resources to stimulus), and detection (registration of stimulus). Detection is the major component and is what drives learning. The other two are, in a sense, support, as they contribute to the likelihood that detection will occur. In this model, detection does not entail awareness, and, consequently learning can take place without awareness.

Schmidt (1990, 1993a, 1994, 1995, 2001) proposed the *noticing hypothesis*. Awareness (through attention) is necessary for noticing, which in turn is essential for learning. Underlying this hypothesis is the idea of noticing a gap. Schmidt and Frota (1986) suggested that, "a second language learner will begin to acquire the target-like form if and only if it is present in **comprehended input** and 'noticed' in the normal sense of the word, that is consciously" (p. 311). The idea presented here is that learning requires a learner to be actively involved or attending to L2 forms in order for learning to take place (see Robinson et al., 2012, for an overview). In Chapter 12, we return to some of these concepts, in particular, the concept of output, or using the language as a way of recognizing difficulty and of consequently noticing L2 forms. The importance of the role of noticing has been debated (cf. Robinson, 1995, 2003a; Schachter, 1998; Truscott, 1998; J. N. Williams, 2005; Carroll, 2006, 2007; Truscott & Sharwood Smith, 2011). The major debate centers around the question of how much and what kind of attention is necessary for learning (Godfroid et al., in press) and what the developmental stage of learning has to be to make attention effective (Mackey & Philp, 1998; Philp, 2003). Robinson (1995, 1996) utilizes both the Tomlin and Villa and Schmidt models in his account of attention. He claims that noticing is just a later stage in the model, and that detection is prior to it, thereby combining both approaches into an expanded model.

Yet another approach to the role of attention is detailed in Chapter 16 and is based on Gass's (1988a) integrated model of SLA. She adds **apperceived input** into the mix, which is a stage before noticing, more akin to Tomlin and Villa's stage of detection, but there is not a level of awareness at this point.

There have been a number of studies considering the role of attention and awareness in language learning, with most showing a connection between awareness and learning. For example, in a series of studies, Leow and his colleagues (Leow 1997, 2000,

2001; Rosa & O'Neill, 1999; Rosa & Leow, 2004) showed, through verbal report data during a task, that there was an association between awareness of a form and the learning of that form. They were also able to show that levels of awareness were an important part in understanding when learning took place. They found that awareness at the level of noticing was less important than awareness at the level of understanding. J. N. Williams (2004), on the other hand, found that there could be learning without awareness. In a carefully designed study of an artificial microlanguage, participants first learned the meanings of nouns and determiners in this language. They then listened to a series of words and had to repeat each one out loud, state if the referent of the noun was animate or inanimate, and translate the word into English. There were determiners that designated whether the nouns were animate or inanimate. There was a test phase following this treatment phase, in which participants were given an English phrase and had to choose between two translations. One phrase had the correct determiner (animate or inanimate) plus noun, and the other had the incorrect determiner and noun. The next phase was to determine if the learners were aware of the animacy relationship; if they were, they did not continue with the study. Only those who were not aware of the determiner–noun animacy relationship continued. These learners performed better than chance on a later test, suggesting that they were able to learn even though there had not been an indication of awareness.

In another study, Gass et al. (2003) considered attention from the perspective of its differential role on different parts of the grammar (lexicon, morphosyntax, syntax). Learners were placed into a focused attention group or a non-focused attention group. They found that learning occurred in both conditions, suggesting that learning without attention might indeed be possible (although, clearly, learners in the non-focused attention group might have figured out the scope of the study and were able to attend to the object of inquiry). Focused attention was most beneficial for syntax and least for the lexicon. In addition, there was a diminished effect for proficiency, with focused attention having a greater effect in early stages of learning.

One area of recent research has considered the role of output in promoting noticing. Izumi and Bigelow (2000) found that output did not draw learners' attention to the grammatical structure in question (English past hypothetical conditional). Uggen (2012), in a conceptual replication of Izumi and Bigelow and using qualitative data, did find that output influenced subsequent noticing of vocabulary and it also affected awareness of what the linguistic gaps were in an individual's knowledge of the L2. Importantly, as with the Gass et al. (2003) study, learning was differentiated, in this case by the complexity of the structure investigated (present versus past hypothetical conditional).

Other, more sophisticated measures have been used in recent years to investigate the construct of noticing. For example, Godfroid et al. (in press) and Spinner et al. (in press) used eye-tracking methodology, to determine noticing for vocabulary acquisition in the former and gender agreement in the latter. Unfortunately, over the years, the terms *noticing*, *attention*, and *awareness* have lacked in precision (see review of these terms and concepts by Godfroid et al., in press). As Godfroid et al. point out, some studies have focused on noticing as attention, some on noticing as awareness, and some on noticing as both. One of the reasons for this difficulty centers on the empirical evidence for noticing: How do we know if something has been noticed? As research techniques become more sophisticated, as with the ability to track eye movements (which presumably reflect ongoing processing), the greater the likelihood that we will come to a more thorough understanding of these concepts and their role in L2 learning.

Attention and memory are closely aligned in many accounts of L2 learning. We turn next to this latter area of research.

storage

previously called SHORT-TERM MEMORY

structures and processes used by humans to store and manipulate information.

10.3.2 Working Memory

manipulation of information.

Over the past decade, there has been significant interest in the psychological construct of working memory in SLA research (see J. N. Williams, 2012, for an overview). In brief, working memory refers to the structures and processes that humans use to store and manipulate information. The term that preceded working memory was most often short-term memory. The major difference is that working memory focuses on the manipulation of information, rather than just the storage of information, as was the case with short-term memory. Miyake and Shah (1999) provide a useful definition: working memory consists of "those mechanisms or processes that are involved in the control, regulation, and active maintenance of task-relevant information in the service of complex cognition, including novel as well as familiar, skilled tasks" (p. 450).

There are a number of models of working memory in the psychology literature. For example, a common one is the Baddeley and Hitch model (1974), which proposes two slave systems that are responsible for system maintenance (see also Baddeley, 2003a, 2003b). One system is known as the articulatory loop, and the other as the visuospatial sketch pad. The articulatory loop contains phonological information that is maintained by articulating the phonological information. For example, when you want to remember a phone number and you do not have pen and paper to write it down, you will repeat it over and over until you can get to a phone to dial the number, or can find pen and paper to write it down. The second slave system is the visuospatial sketch pad, which, as its name implies, stores visual and spatial information.

Additional to the two slave systems is the central executive, which is the overall supervisor and coordinator of information. The central executive focuses attention on some things, inhibits others, and is the overall coordinator when more than one task needs to be done at a time. Baddeley (2000) extended this model to include a fourth component, an episodic buffer, which is the holder of information that includes and integrates other information (e.g., visual, semantic, phonological). For example, consider

Overall supervisor and coordinator - focuses attention on some things, inhibits others.

central executive

2 slaves system

Episodic Buffer

holds info and integrates info

the situation in which someone says something to you, but you are only half paying attention. If the speaker prods you to respond, you can probably recall the words uttered, but this capability will only last for a short period of time.

A slightly different conceptualization of working memory comes from Conway et al. (2005). They see working memory as "a multicomponent system responsible for active maintenance of information in the face of ongoing processing and/or distraction" (p. 770). One's ability to maintain information is the result of domain-specific storage (with processes of rehearsal) and "domain-general executive attention" (p. 770). They provide the following exemplification of how this might work in novice and experienced chess players:

> [A] novice chess player will rely more on domain-general executive attention to maintain game information (e.g., recent moves or future positions) than on domain-specific skills (e.g., learned strategies and position patterns). In contrast, an expert chess player typically will rely more on domain-specific processes and skills to maintain information. However, even the expert might need to call upon executive attention under some circumstances, such as playing the game in particularly demanding situations or under some sort of cognitive or emotional load.
>
> (pp. 770–771)

L2 requires emotional and cognitive effort

One can readily imagine how this might apply to learning an L2, where there are numerous competing demands, some of which are emotional (speaking an L2 in front of others), and some of which involve great cognitive effort.

Working-memory capacity varies from individual to individual. So, the ability to juggle numerous language tasks also varies from individual to individual. This is generally referred to as working-memory capacity. There are numerous techniques that researchers have used to determine working-memory capacity, and, like all elicitation measures, there is difficulty in perfectly aligning the elicitation task with the underlying construct. It is important to note that defining the construct and measuring it are not the same. Most measures use a dual-task format, combining some memory measure with a processing task. Common among these is the reading span task (cf. Daneman & Carpenter, 1980). In these tasks, participants may read a number of sentences and are told to remember the last word of each sentence. At the end of a set of sentences (usually two to six), they are asked to write down (in order) the last word of each sentence. So that rehearsal will not take place, often they are asked to respond to the plausibility of each sentence.

TIME TO DO …

Go to Link #1 in the Link section at the end of this chapter and try a reading span working-memory task for yourself. Note the dual-task format: typing the sentence and remembering the last word.

In recent years, there have been a number of studies relating working-memory capacity to language learning. The results are not always straightforward. Many of these use some sort of span task (listening or reading), and the question arises as to the language of the working-memory task. An interesting study by Miyake and Friedman (1998) found links between L1 and L2 working memory scores, but most important for language learning is the finding that there is a relationship between L2 working memory and comprehension of syntax. Similarly Harrington and Sawyer (1992) and Osaka and Osaka (1992) found correlations between L1 and L2 working-memory scores. Mackey et al. (2002), finding a relationship between working memory and noticing, also found a correlation between L1 and L2 working-memory scores.

Service et al. (2002) and Gass and Lee (2011) found that the correlations between L1 and L2 working memory depended on proficiency. In the Gass and Lee study, there was a significantly weaker correlation with lower-proficiency learners than with more advanced speakers.

Two other considerations enter into an understanding of the role of working memory: (1) the language of the working memory task and (2) the closeness of the languages in question. In the case of the former, most working-memory tests are done in one's NL, assuming that working memory is an individual trait and not dependent on language. Unfortunately, with L2 research, it is not always possible to conduct working-memory tests in the NL of the participants. In the case of the second, van den Noort et al. (2006) suggest that the interaction between working-memory capacity and language proficiency may be language-specific.

Some studies have used simple, verbal working-memory measures (such as a digit span task, which measures capacity for number storage by presenting participants with a series of numbers that they repeat back; the number of digits presented increases in length, depending on performance) and, therefore, only tap the storage component, whereas other studies use more complex measures that tap both storage and processing, such as a reading or listening span task. Here again, there is not uniformity as to differences in L1 and L2 capacities. For example Ardila et al. (2000) used a digit span task with bilingual Spanish–English speakers. There were differences between the languages that they were tested in, namely between early and late bilinguals (Ardila, 2003).

Other studies have considered phonological short-term memory and the relationship of this construct to L2 learning. These measures relate to the articulatory/phonological loop subsystem of Baddeley's model. Generally, this refers to the ability to hear phonological input and to repeat it. The most common means of eliciting data to reflect this capacity is the nonword pairs recall test, although known words have also been used. In this test, participants hear a stimulus of nonword (phonologically possible in the language of administration) and, after a pause, are asked to repeat the string of sounds.

Phonological short-term-memory capacity has been linked to a number of areas of L2 learning, most specifically vocabulary and syntax. For example, Papagno and Vallar (1992) compared phonological short-term-memory capacity with the ability to

269

repeat known and novel words and found a relationship between short-term-memory capacity and novel words, but not known words, probably owing to the fact that semantic representations were presumably already in place for the known words. Service and Craik (1993) showed a relationship between phonological short-term memory and the ease or efficiency with which new vocabulary was learned. It has also been linked to general oral fluency (O'Brien et al., 2007) and to general language performance (Kormos & Sáfár, 2008).

Service and Kohnonen (1995) conducted a longitudinal study of L2 English (L1 Finnish), also noting a relationship between phonological short-term-memory capacity and the acquisition of L2 vocabulary.

Not only is there an apparent relationship between the learning of vocabulary and an individual's phonological short-term-memory capacity, but there is also a relationship with the learning of grammar.

An important part of learning a new language is the ability to retain relevant information long enough to figure out what it means or to analyze it syntactically. It therefore stands to reason that those who have the capacity to do this to a greater extent would also be those who are more successful at learning all aspects of language.

Other studies have supported the relationship between phonological short-term memory and the learning of grammar. For example, N. Ellis and Schmidt (1997), in a laboratory study using an artificial language, found a relationship between the phonological memory task and the learning of the grammar of this new language. (The language had SOV word order and had noun–adjective agreement, singular–plural agreement, and transitive/intransitive marking.)

In yet another study using an artificial language, Williams and Lovatt (2003) used L1 English speakers with Italian words as an L2 (none of the participants knew Italian) and a semi-artificial language (using Italian as the base). The results showed that phonological short-term memory was related to rule learning and even to abstract aspects of grammar.

Working-memory research in SLA is in its infancy. As with other constructs in SLA, it is not always clear how best to measure it. Many of the differences in L2 working-memory research need to be understood in the context of data collection (see Conway et al., 2005, for an excellent overview of the methodology involved in reading span tasks).

10.3.3 Syntactic Priming

Syntactic priming is said to occur when a previously uttered or comprehended syntactic structure (the prime) is repeated, when an alternate structure is available (Bock, 1989). An example is given in 10-9 below, from McDonough (2006, p. 182).

(10-9) A: The man shows his wife the boot.

B: A teacher is teaching some kids a game.

Learners A and B were involved in a picture description/matching activity. Speaker A used a double-object dative to describe a picture. Immediately following this, speaker B used the same construction to describe another picture, even though speaker B could have used a prepositional dative ("A teacher is teaching a game to some kids"). Priming has been argued to be a fluency-enhancing vehicle, as it improves communication by reducing speech onsets, requires less processing effort, and leads to more fluent formulations (Ferreira & Bock, 2006). Smith and Wheeldon (2001) found that speakers started sentences with primed noun phrases more quickly than other sentences, and Bock and Loebell (1990) found that primed passive sentences were produced more fluently than active sentences. Bock and Griffin (2000) showed that syntactic priming persists, with as many as 10 sentences intervening between the prime and the target, unlike semantic priming for individual words, which decreases by 30–100 percent with just one intervening word. Boyland and Anderson (1998) likewise found syntactic priming after 20-minute delays. It is also argued that syntactic priming is implicit learning (see below), because it does not require the intention to remember or replicate the form (priming is actually greater when remembering is not encouraged [Bock, 1986]), that it is inaccessible to consciousness, it is complex and abstract, and is an incidental consequence of the performance of a task. Furthermore, syntactic priming, like learning, has been shown to have an inverse preference effect; that is, lesser known material is learned more, or the less common structure shows more priming than the preferred structure (Bock, 1986; Hartsuiker & Kolk, 1998; Hartsuiker, Kolk, & Huiskamp, 1999; Bock & Griffin, 2000; Scheepers, 2003). For example, in Hartsuiker and Westenberg (2000), participants preferred the participle-final Dutch structures at the start, but, after priming of auxiliary-final structures, that became the preferred structure.

The phenomenon of syntactic priming has been well documented in various contexts, with various populations, and using various tasks. The phenomenon has recently been taken up in the L2 literature (see McDonough (2006) and McDonough & Trofimovich (2009), who focused on the acquisition of English double-object datives; McDonough & Mackey (2008), where the focus was on English question forms by native speakers of Thai; and Kim & McDonough (2008), who investigated the L2 acquisition of English passive sentences by native speakers of Korean).

The question remains as to which syntactic structures are susceptible to priming and which are less likely to benefit from priming. McDonough (2006) suggested that more complex target structures are susceptible to priming in the L2, and that priming might be partially responsible for the facilitating effect of interaction in L2 acquisition. This is supported by Behney (2008), who found syntactic priming of a more complex target structure of subject RCs as opposed to the alternate structure of noun–adjective noun phrases in native English-speaking learners of Italian. Behney and Gass (in press), in a study involving RCs and structural difficulty, found that natural learning paths and structural difficulty can be at odds with the effects of priming and extensive use of structures.

TIME TO DO ...

Complete the following sentence prompts so that they make grammatical sentences. Complete each in order as quickly as possible, with the first thing that comes to mind.

1. The yachtsman loaned the spare lifejacket _____ .
2. The happy child gave the present _____ .
3. The generous girl lent _____ .
4. The sturdy shelf held _____ .
5. The ad hoc committee decided _____ .
6. The unscrupulous salesman sold the gullible tourist _____ .
7. The champion cyclist showed the team manager _____ .
8. The tennis fan handed _____ .
9. The rambunctious child broke _____ .
10. The pub offered a free beer _____ .
11. The Swedish pen pal mailed a scenic postcard _____ .
12. The injured climber showed _____ .
13. The sound of the choir _____ .
14. The train from Montreal arrived _____ .
15. The messenger handed the countess _____ .
16. The senior lecturer loaned the visiting professor _____ .
17. The head waiter gave _____ .
18. We lingered in the restaurant _____ .
19. The Impressionist painting was hung _____ .

Now go back and identify 1–3, 6–8, 11–13, and 16–18 as double-object datives (e.g., *The man shows his wife the boot.*) or prepositional datives (e.g., *The man shows the boot to his wife.*). Note that the first two sentence prompts of each trio constrained you to produce one type of dative. The third sentence prompt of each trio could be completed with either type of dative. Was it more likely for you to complete numbers 3, 8, 13, and 18 with the same type of dative as in the two preceding sentences?

(These sentence prompts were used in Pickering and Branigan (1998) to show that syntactic priming occurs in written discourse as well as spoken discourse.)

) emphasis: language usage / +input

10.4 EMERGENTIST MODELS

In emergentist approaches to language learning, also referred to as constructivist approaches, emphasis is on usage. Learning does not rely on an innate module, but rather it takes place based on the extraction of regularities from the input. As these regularities or patterns are used over and over again, they are strengthened. Frequency accounts (N. Ellis, 2002) are an example. Frequency accounts of SLA rely on the assumption that "humans are sensitive to the frequencies of events in their experience" (p. 145). The approach is exemplar-based, in that it is the examples that are present in the input that form the basis of learning and from which regularities emerge. According to N. Ellis (2002, p. 144), "comprehension is determined by the listeners' vast amount of statistical information about the behavior of lexical items in their language." In other words, language is not driven by an innate faculty; rather, the complex linguistic environment provides the information from which learners abstract regularities. Assuming that aspects of language are sensitive to frequency of usage, there are implications for how one conceives of grammar. The representation of language, in this view, relies on the notion of variable strengths that reflect the frequency of the input and the connections between parts of language. Learning is seen as simple instance learning (rather than explicit/implicit induction of rules), which proceeds based on input alone; the resultant knowledge is seen as a network of interconnected exemplars and patterns, rather than abstract rules.

Even though connectionist approaches have been around for a number of years, it is only recently that research within an L2 context has begun to take place. **Connectionism** is a cover term that includes a number of network architectures. One such approach is parallel distributed processing (PDP). At the heart of PDP is a neural network that is generally biologically inspired in nature. The network consists of nodes that are connected by pathways. Within connectionism, pathways are strengthened or weakened through activation/use.

Learning takes place as the network (i.e., the learner) is able to make associations, and associations come through exposure to repeated patterns. The more often an association is made, the stronger that association becomes. New associations are formed and new links are made between larger and larger units, until complexes of networks are formed. Recall the discussion of the morpheme order studies in Chapter 5. One of the explanations for the order of acquisition of morphemes comes from Larsen-Freeman (1976), who proposed that frequency of occurrence is a major determinant. To place this explanation within the framework of connectionism, we would want to say that learners are able to extract regular patterns from the input to create and strengthen associations, although they may not be aware that this is what they are doing. N. Ellis and Schmidt (1997), in an experiment based on a connectionist model, supported Larsen-Freeman's suggestion, finding frequency effects for the acquisition of L2 morphology.

Not many L2 studies have been conducted within the framework of connectionism.[4] As noted earlier, connectionist systems rely, not on rule systems, but on pattern associations. Thus, if such a model is to work, we will need to have a clear understanding of how to determine strength of associations. It stands to reason that the strength of associations will change as a function of interaction with the environment, or, put differently, with the input. It is to be noted that, in the case of SLA, the strength of association may already (right or wrong) be present; that is, a pattern of connectivity may already have been established, even though it may be an incorrect one vis à vis

L1 associations are already strenghten and fixed, making L2 harder.

↓

the older the learner the less able s/he is to establish new connection patterns.

the TL. In other words, the L1 is already in place, and, therefore, there is a set of associations with their strengths fixed. These associations can possibly interfere with the establishment of an L2 network.

Sokolik and Smith (1992) devised a computer-based experiment on the learning of French noun gender. The program was designed to be trained on and tested on French nouns, without any discourse context (e.g., article or adjective agreement). Regular nouns were used (including words ending in -*tion* or -*esse*, which are feminine, and words ending in -*eur* or -*ment*, which are masculine), as well as irregular nouns (e.g., *peur* "fear," which is feminine). The program was able to correctly identify noun gender and to identify the gender of words never before encountered. When a set of unrelated, preexisting weights was added to the model, learning was slowed. Sokolik (1990) suggested that, as a function of age, learners are less able to establish connectionist patterns. We turn next to the Competition Model, which also relies on the establishment of cues and the strength of cues.

10.4.1 Competition Model

FORM AND FUNCTION CANNOT BE SEPARATED.
→ concerns about how language is used

The basis for the Competition Model comes from work by Bates and MacWhinney (1982), although more recent research (e.g., MacWhinney, 2002, 2005) expands on the underlying concepts. The Competition Model was developed to account for the ways monolingual speakers interpret sentences. A fundamental difference between this model and what we have seen with a UG model (Chapter 7) is that, whereas the latter separates the form of language from its function, the Competition Model is based on the assumption that form and function cannot be separated. According to MacWhinney et al. (1984, p. 128), "the forms of natural languages are created, governed, constrained, acquired and used in the service of communicative functions."

It is important to understand that the Competition Model, similar to other psycho-linguistic approaches to SLA, is concerned with how language is used, as opposed to being concerned with a determination of the underlying structure of language.

We provide a brief description of the main tenets of the Competition Model before considering its application to an L2 context. A major concept inherent in the model is that speakers must have a way to determine relationships among elements in a sentence. Language processing involves competition among various cues, each of which contributes to a different resolution in sentence interpretation. Although the range of cues is universal (i.e., the limits on the kinds of cues one uses are universally imposed), there is language-specific instantiation of cues and language-specific strength assigned to cues.

Let's consider two languages with different word-order possibilities: English and Italian. English word order is rigidly of the form subject–verb–object (SVO). Consider the English sentence in 10-10:

(10-10)   The cows eat the grass.

NSs of English use various cues to determine that *the cows* is the subject of the sentence and that *the grass* is the object. First, a major determining cue in understanding this relationship is word order. NNSs of English know that, in active declarative sentences, the first noun or noun phrase is typically the subject of the sentence. Second, knowledge of the meaning of lexical items contributes to correct interpretation (cows eat grass, rather than grass eats cows). Third, English speakers use animacy criteria (i.e., whether the noun is animate or inanimate) to establish grammatical relationships. Finally, morphology (in this case, subject–verb agreement) contributes to interpretation, because the plurality of *the cows* requires a plural verb (*eat*). In sum, all elements converge in coming up with the interpretation of *the cows* as the subject and *the grass* as the object.

There are examples in language where interpretation is not so straightforward. In other words, there are examples where convergence is not the result. In these instances, the various cues are in competition. Let's assume a sentence such as 10-11.

(10-11)   The grass eats the cows.

Here, English speakers are surprised; there is competition as to which element will fill the subject slot. Using word order as a cue, *the grass* should be the subject; using meaning and animacy as cues, *the cows* is the most likely subject; using morphology as a cue, it is *the grass*, because it is the only singular noun in the sentence. Thus, in this unusual sentence, there is a breakdown in our normal use of cues; as a result, there is competition as to which noun phrase will fill the slot of subject. Different languages resolve the conflict in different ways. English uses word order and agreement as primary determinants. Other languages, such as Italian, resolve the problem of interpretation in a different way.

The following are examples from Italian that illustrate some of the word-order possibilities (which vary in intonation as well as syntax) in that language:

							Word order
(10-12)	Giovanna	ha	comprato	il	pane.		SVO
	Joan	has	bought	the	bread		
(10-13)	Allora,	compro	io	il	vino.		SVO
	then	buy	I	the	wine		
	"Then, I'll buy the wine."						
(10-14)	Ha	comprato	il	vino	Aldo.		VOS
	has	bought	the	wine	Aldo		
	"Aldo bought the wine."						
(10-15)	No,	il	vino	l'	ha	comprato	Antonella.	OVS
	no	the	wine	it (obj.)	has	bought	Antonella	
	"No, it's Antonella who bought the wine."						

Given the large number of word-order possibilities, how is interpretation possible in a language such as Italian? How does an Italian speaker know which noun is the

NL influence in L2 learning in sentence structure (word order)

↓

Meaning based comprehension takes precedence over grammar-based one.

⊕

students follow cues that are dominant in their NL first, and then, if it fails, they use meaning comprehension strategy.

subject of the sentence? Or, in this conversation, how does an Italian know who is going to do what, or who is responsible for what? In Italian, word order assumes a lesser role in interpretation than it does in English, and morphological agreement, semantics, and pragmatics assume greater importance.

For SLA, the question is: how does one adjust one's internal speech-processing mechanisms from those appropriate for the NL to those appropriate for the TL? Does one use the same cues as are used in the NL, and are those cues weighted in the same way as they are in the NL? Or, do these mechanisms from the NL constrain interpretation as one is trying to understand a rapidly fired message in the TL.

One possibility is that, in L2 sentence interpretation, the learner's initial hypothesis is consistent with sentence interpretation in the NL. However, there may be universal tendencies toward the heavy use of particular cues. What methodology is used to gather information of this sort? In general, the methodology in the L2 studies based on the Competition Model is the same. Learners whose NL uses cues and cue strengths that differ from those of the TL are presented with sentences designed to present conflicting cues and are asked to determine what the subjects of those sentences are. Thus, NSs of English learning Italian would be given a sentence such as 10-16:

(10-16) La   matita   guarda   il   cane.
　　　　the   pencil   looks at   the   dog

and would be asked to determine whether the subject is *la matita* "the pencil" or *il cane* "the dog." Using English cues, it would be *the pencil*, because word order takes precedence over all other cues. Using Italian cues, it would be *the dog*, because semantic and pragmatic cues are the strongest (in the absence of a biasing agreement cue).

A number of studies have been conducted using this paradigm. One of the findings is that, under certain circumstances, a meaning-based comprehension strategy takes precedence over a grammar-based one. For example, English speakers learning Italian (Gass, 1987) and English speakers learning Japanese (a language that relies on the pragmatics of the situation for sentence interpretation, as well as on case-marking and lexico-semantic information; Harrington, 1987; Kilborn & Ito, 1989; Sasaki, 1991, 1994) readily drop their strong use of word-order cues and adopt meaning-based cues as a major cue in interpreting Italian and Japanese sentences. On the other hand, Italian speakers learning English and Japanese speakers learning English maintain their NL meaning-based cues as primary, not readily adopting word order as a major interpretation cue.

Although the tendency of learners to adopt a meaning-based strategy as opposed to a grammar-based one is strong, there is also ample evidence that learners first look for those cues that are dominant in their NL as their initial hypothesis. Only when that appears to fail (i.e., when learners become aware of the apparent incongruity between L1 and L2 strategies) do they adopt what might be viewed as a universal prepotency: that of using meaning to interpret sentences.[5]

Particularly relevant to this area of research is the finding (Sasaki, 1994) that English learners of Japanese make use of rigid word order as a cue (in this case, the SOV word order of Japanese), even before they figure out how rigid Japanese word order is. In other words, English NSs assume rigid word order as the first hypothesis, just like in their NL. Their first task is to figure out what that word order is. Once they figure out that Japanese has SOV order, they rigidly apply the new word order. This is supported by data from Japanese learners of English, who were asked to differentiate between sentences such as 10-17 and 10-18 in terms of identifying the appropriate subject of the second verb (Gass, 1986).

(10-17) The man told the boy to go.

(10-18) The man promised the boy to go.

The data showed that learners first learned that English is a rigid word-order language, before learning what the appropriate word order is.

One cannot, however, lose sight of the important role of context. For example, Sasaki (1997a, 1997b) showed that individual variation in responses is a significant factor, and that the context of presentation of sentences affects the way sentences are interpreted. His 1994 study of Japanese learners of English and English learners of Japanese showed effects of proficiency: There is greater or lesser dependence on case-marking clues depending on proficiency level.

Rounds and Kanagy (1998) investigated English-speaking children in Japanese immersion programs. Their results conflict with some of the previous results, in particular those suggesting an overreliance on semantic strategies. The children in the Rounds and Kanagy study selected a word-order strategy, relying on the basic SOV order of Japanese. According to Sasaki's (1991) prediction, they should have soon learned that the word-order strategy would fail, because Japanese has OSV as well as SOV order; in other words, the learners should have soon realized that word order is not a sufficient cue to sentence interpretation in Japanese. In the Rounds and Kanagy study, however, the children continued to use word order as their primary strategy. The researchers attributed this result to the environment in which the study took place; that is, the input children received was limited, in that it came primarily from their teacher and limited reading materials that contained mostly SOV sentences. Thus, in trying to understand how learners interpret sentences, there are numerous complex conditions that need to be taken into account.

In sum, research conducted within the Competition Model suggests that learners are indeed faced with conflicts between NL and TL cues and cue strengths. The resolution of these conflicts is such that learners first resort to their NL interpretation strategies and, upon recognition of the incongruity between TL and NL systems, resort to a universal selection of meaning-based cues, as opposed to syntax-based cues, before gradually adopting the appropriate TL biases as their L2 proficiency increases. What then is involved in L2 processing, at least with regard to comprehension, is a readjustment of which cues will be relevant to interpretation and a determination of

context plays an important role.

the relative strengths of those cues. What is not known is how learners recognize which NL cues lead to the wrong interpretation and which cues lead to the correct interpretation. In fact, Bates and MacWhinney (1981) noted that one L2 user, even after 25 years of living in the TL country, still did not respond to sentence interpretation tasks in the same way as NSs of the TL.

As with the linguistic approaches we have considered, there are certain difficulties inherent in looking at and interpreting data in this way. One such difficulty is what we might call processing uniqueness. Is there only one way of arriving at a particular interpretation? Assume that learners are presented with the following sentence and are asked to respond to that sentence in terms of the grammatical subject:

(10-19)   The pencil sees the boys.

Assume also that the learners select *the boys* as the subject. Are they doing this because they have a preference for animate objects as subjects—that is, their strategy is "select the animate noun"—or do they make this selection because they are rejecting inanimate nouns as possible subjects? In this latter case, their strategy is "choose anything but the inanimate noun." It is often difficult to differentiate between these two different strategies.

A second difficulty in the interpretation of the results concerns fundamental differences between syntax-based languages and meaning/pragmatics-based languages. One of these differences is mathematical. In a word-order language, such as English, there is one basic word-order possibility in declarative sentences (although, clearly, English can move words around, as in *That movie, I want to see it* [OSVO]). In Italian, there are many possibilities, as we have seen. Thus, the difference may not be one of syntax and semantics, but one of the kind of evidence one needs to confirm or disconfirm hypotheses. If one starts from an English L1 position, with one basic word order, all that one has to do is hear/read the many Italian possibilities. On the other hand, if one begins with an Italian L1 position, in the absence of negative evidence (see Chapter 7), or correction, there is no way of knowing that the many Italian possibilities are not possible in English. In this latter case, learners hear one possibility (SVO order); the absence of other possibilities in the input may mean that they do not exist or that, coincidentally, they have not been heard. Thus, in the case of the English speaker learning Italian, learning (and adjustment of cue strengths) can take place on the basis of positive evidence alone. In the case of the Italian speaker learning English, negative evidence may be necessary for the learner to realize that word order is a reliable cue in English. This alone would predict that the learning of English in this area would be a more difficult task than the learning of Italian. Which interpretation is the appropriate one is a matter as yet undetermined.

A recent extension of the Competition Model is the Unified Competition Model (MacWhinney 2008, 2012), which, without changing the basic ideas, includes neurocognitive, developmental, and social elements that "control the core competition" (MacWhinney, 2012, p. 215). These controlling factors happen at the moment of speaking and may be "risk" or "support" factors.

[handwritten margin note, top left: process of neurodevelopment / as a child grows, patterns become more and more entrenched]

[handwritten margin note, top right: establishment of new encoding dimensions e.g. vocabulary learning (hearing a word 1 time is not enough for real learning to happen) → the stronger the consolidation the less frequently one needs to encounter a word.]

As an example, consider the concepts of **entrenchment** and **resonance**. MacWhinney points out that entrenchment is a process of neurodevelopment having its origin in the functioning of the brain. As an infant matures, his/her brain becomes more committed to L1 patterns: patterns become entrenched. One can imagine that language closeness facilitates learning owing to the commitment made to certain patterns, whereas, with languages where the differences are great, "entrenchment . . . can lead to problems" (MacWhinney, 2012, p. 216). Entrenchment is considered a risk factor, but can be counteracted by resonance. L2 patterns can be encoded, as it is through resonance that new encoding dimensions are established. MacWhinney illustrates this through vocabulary learning. We know that it is rarely the case that just encountering a word in an L2 is sufficient for learning. This is not dissimilar from other parts of L2 learning where, as Gass (1988b) pointed out, encountering anything for the first time may only set the stage for learning rather than result in learning. MacWhinney claims that "robustness accumulates with practice" (p. 216), and that practice needs to be incrementally spaced further and further apart. He finds evidence of this practice in work by Pimsleur as far back as 1967, in which Pimsleur relates memory to vocabulary (although he includes structures as well), explicitly laying out a schedule for presentation of vocabulary. Clearly, this is an example of a successful and common pedagogical practice awaiting a theoretical explanation. MacWhinney provides that explanation, attributing it to the use of "resonant neural connections" in the brain. When one accesses a memory trace over and over again, a consolidation of that trace results. Once this happens, one needs only to reactivate this consolidation on an occasional basis. The stronger the consolidation, the less frequently one needs to encounter a word.

TIME TO THINK ...

Think about learning an L2 and not encountering a word for a long period of time. What happens? Do you immediately remember the meaning? Do you often recognize the word as something you have encountered, even though you may not know the meaning?

In sum, learners are seen as sorting out the complexities of language through repeated exposure, through the extraction of regularities, and through the demands of use. Form–function mappings are dependent on the reliability of the input. That is, the more reliable a cue (e.g., word order in English), the easier (and faster) it is to learn.

10.4.2 Frequency-Based Accounts

Frequency-based accounts of L2 learning (see N. Ellis, 2012, for a review) claim that learning arises from the input, without positing an innate linguistic system to interact with the input data. Underlying this claim is the assumption that,

[margin note: LEARNING MEMORY + PERCEPTION ↓ are affected by frequency of usage.]

learning, memory and perception are all affected by frequency of usage: the more times we experience something, the stronger our memory for it, and the more fluently it is accessed. The more recently we have experienced something, the stronger our memory for it, and the more fluently it is accessed.

(N. Ellis, 2012, p. 195)

Thus, the more frequent something is in the input, the more likely we are to learn that item (lexical item/structure) and remember it. The regularities that we finally internalize emerge from the data rather than from an innate structure. It is while we engage in conversations or some communicative activity that we are able to learn constructions/patterns/structures. We return to the idea of the importance and significance of conversation in Chapter 12. Learning in this view involves extracting regularities from the input, but, clearly, it is not as straightforward as what we see with child language acquisition. What they can induce is not without blinders, some of which have been discussed elsewhere in this book, such as the role of the NL and attention. As discussed above, the more language is entrenched, the greater it becomes a blinder, thereby blocking appropriate induction of TL patterns. That frequency is significant in L2 learning (ranging from pronunciation to spelling) has been discussed by N. Ellis (2002); learners are sensitive to effects of frequency, as would be expected by the simple realization that common words in a language are learned early—*cane* ("dog" in Italian) is undoubtedly learned earlier than a word rarely encountered, such as *pachino* (a small tomato), or, at least, encountered only in specific/narrow contexts.

[margin note: The more language is entrenched the more it blocks NL. ↓ common words are learned earlier than rarely used/encountered words.]

10.5 DYNAMIC SYSTEMS

There are many terms that are used in the literature, almost interchangeably, to refer to similar notions: **complexity**, **chaos theory**, **complex adaptive systems**, **non-linear systems**, and dynamic systems. They are better thought of as a class of systems that refers to ways in which complex systems change and develop over time.

De Bot (2008) defines chaos as "referring to the fact that the outcomes of interactions of variables over time cannot be predicted using conventional mathematics. Thus, chaos is unpredictability rather than lack of order" (p. 167). He delineates two main characteristics: (1) "chaos can emerge out of the interaction of variables, and differences in initial conditions," (p. 167) and (2) "that there is universal order in seemingly chaotic patterns" (p. 167). Complexity is "a chaos of behaviors in which the components of the system never quite lock into place, yet never quite dissolve into turbulence either" (Waldrop, 1992, p. 293, cited in De Bot, 2008).

Complexity theory, chaos theory, and dynamic-systems theory offer a view of how learning takes place consistent with emergentist views. In fact, an emergentist conceptualization takes into account that language is a complex system and that properties of that system are determined as they interact with the environment (cultural, social, discoursal). As Larsen-Freeman et al. (2011, p. 5) note, "complexity theorists question and offer an alternative to the notion that objects and events can best be understood

[margin note: EMERGENTIST CONCEPT]

by reducing them to static entities (Sumara 2000: 268)." What separates these theories from previous approaches to SLA is the fact that the focus is not on isolated parts of language and cause–effect relationships; rather, they study SLA from a holistic perspective, considering how changes in one subsystem impact and relate to other subsystems. We have all heard of the butterfly movement in one part of the world and the effect that that movement has, thousands of miles away. This interrelationship of many systems is complex and is at the heart of complexity theory. Language is a dynamic system, and each instance of language use contributes to change. If we think about feedback that learners receive in many contexts (e.g., from a teacher), we understand that feedback contributes to the learner's developing system and results in a different sort of complexity (recall the kaleidoscope analogy).

Language is dynamic

As Larsen-Freeman (2012, p. 75) points out, "language has the shape that it does because of the way that it is used, not because of innate bio-program or internal mental organ . . . there may be domain-general evolutionary prerequisites to language that support its use and acquisition." Among those evolutionary prerequisites are, "the ability to imitate, to detect patterns, to notice novelty, to form categories, or the social drive to interact, to establish joint attention with another, to understand the communicative intention of others" (p. 75). What stands out in this approach is the dynamic and changing nature of the system, a system that evolves as a result of learners determining regularities from the input that they encounter.

Language is shaped by how it is used

Larsen-Freeman (1997) was one of the early researchers to recognize the potentiality of a dynamic-systems approach to L2 learning, pointing out, in particular, that language (and, by extension, L2s) has the characteristics of dynamic and complex systems. As she notes, those interested in chaos/complexity "are interested in how disorder gives way to order, of how complexity arises in nature" (p. 141). For example, the process is known to be dynamic, complex, and nonlinear; they are self-organizing and open (increased input effects changes in the system). She expands upon a number of issues that can be illuminated by thinking of them within a dynamic-systems approach, among them being definitions of learning, assessment, instability/systematicity, individual differences, and instructional impact. To this, N. Ellis and Larsen-Freeman (2006) add numerous other characteristics of an emergent system, including such concepts as discussed in this chapter (e.g., noticing, interface—see below), as well as topics (e.g., motivation) discussed in other chapters of this book. A dynamic-systems approach shows promise in that it appreciates, and even demands, not a cause–effect relationship in language development, but rather a multiplicity of factors that interact within an individual to effect change.

language complexity → chaos complexity ↓ HOW DISORDER GIVES WAY TO ORDER.

EMERGENT SYSTEM } noticing, interface, motivation ...

↳ DYNAMIC SYSTEMS — Demands a multiplicity of factors than interact within an individual to effect change.

10.6 KNOWLEDGE TYPES

In this section, we approach the topic of knowledge types by assuming that SLA is like other types of cognitive learning, and the emphasis is on describing, in terms of general cognition, how linguistic knowledge is acquired and organized in the brain.

There are a number of ways in which one can represent L2 knowledge. Some have already been mentioned in previous sections but will be dealt with in greater detail here. We first deal with the acquisition–learning distinction.

[handwritten: focus meaning and production]

10.6.1 Acquisition/Learning → *[handwritten: focus: produce accurate forms of the language.]*

As noted in Chapter 5, Krashen (1982) proposed, for L2 learning, two parallel and independent systems: acquisition and learning. The former is used in language production, when learners are focused on meaning. The latter then checks what is generated by that acquired system to ensure that the forms are accurate. In other words, the two systems have two different functions: production and checking of meaning and form.

[handwritten: → knowledge about something | conscious awareness]

10.6.2 Declarative/Procedural → *[handwritten: Learning and storage of facts | motor and cognitive skills]*

Another distinction is between declarative and procedural knowledge, or sometimes declarative and procedural memory. Declarative knowledge is concerned with knowledge *about* something, and declarative memory underlies learning and storage of facts (e.g., Newfoundland dogs are generally black). With regard to language, declarative knowledge relates to such aspects of language as word knowledge (collocation, pronunciation, meaning). In general, this information is relatively accessible to conscious awareness; that is, we can retrieve that information when called upon to do so. Procedural knowledge or procedural memory relates to motor and cognitive skills that involve sequencing information (e.g., playing tennis, producing language). Using language (e.g., stringing words together to form and interpret sentences) is thought to involve procedural knowledge and, unlike declarative knowledge, is relatively inaccessible. The distinction between these two has important consequences for learning, because it is thought that, with age, the ability to use procedural knowledge to learn new operations decreases, and older L2 learners need to rely more on declarative information in learning. O'Grady (2006) uses this to account for the difficulty in learning past tense in English by L2 learners. Using data from Goldschneider and DeKeyser (2005, p. 72) that show the difficulty involved in the English past tense, O'Grady suggests that the difficulty has to do, not with the relatively transparent phenomenon of adding -ed to a verb that refers to a past event, but with the difficulty in computing aspect (see Chapter 9), because tense depends on the prior determination of aspect.[6] It is this computation that makes past-tense acquisition difficult for learners.

[handwritten: procedural knowledge]

10.6.3 Implicit/Explicit → *[handwritten: Declarative memory (conscious awareness)]*

A distinction that has its roots in psychology is that of implicit and explicit know-ledge, not unrelated to the distinction discussed in the previous section. Declarative memory can be seen as forming the basis of explicit knowledge, and procedural knowledge underlies implicit knowledge. Where there is a difference, however, is that, in the case of explicit versus implicit knowledge, awareness is a key issue

[handwritten margin notes: Focus; Acquisition → meaning; Learning → form; AWARENESS]

EXPLICIT LEARNING × IMPLICIT LEARNING

input processing with conscious
intention

LOOKING AT INTERLANGUAGE PROCESSING

input process without
intention / natural
process

(see DeKeyser, 2003; Doughty, 2003; N. Ellis, 2005; R. Ellis, 2005; R. Ellis & Loewen, 2007; Isemonger, 2007). Even though there may be a general relationship between declarative/procedural and explicit/implicit, the relationship cannot be considered rigid, as there may be instances when declarative memory contains information that is not explicit.

A related distinction is between **implicit** and **explicit learning**. The latter, as Hulstijn (2005) notes, "is input processing with the conscious intention to find out whether the input information contains regularities and, if so, to work out the concepts and rules with which these regularities can be captured" (p. 131). On the other hand, implicit learning "is input processing without such an intention" (p. 131). N. Ellis defines the concept of implicit learning without reference to input processing. In his words, implicit learning is "acquisition of knowledge about the underlying structure of a complex stimulus environment by a process which takes place naturally, simply and without conscious operations" (N. Ellis, 1994, p. 1). Explicit learning "is a more conscious operation where the individual makes and tests hypotheses in a search for structure" (N. Ellis, 1994, p. 1). Both types of knowledge can be used in generating utterances by NSs and NNSs, although NSs presumably rely much less on explicit knowledge than on implicit knowledge. The use of explicit knowledge may be relegated to particular difficulties, such as the *lie–lay* distinction in English. Viewing knowledge as a continuum, it is easier to conceptualize explicit knowledge becoming implicit (through practice, exposure, drills, etc.) and vice versa.

Explicit knowledge can become implicit and vice versa.

With regard to L2 learning, there are a number of issues to consider. First, what can be learned implicitly and what cannot be? Second, and a corollary, is implicit knowledge convertible to explicit knowledge?

TIME TO THINK ...

Can most NSs of English use *the* versus *a* correctly? Can they explicitly state the appropriate context of use of these forms? Why do you think this is the case? Consider the reverse. When learning an L2, is it possible to have explicit knowledge about something (i.e., state what the rule is) but not be able to consistently use it correctly?

There is evidence that some associated forms can be learned implicitly, even, for example, much of syntax, which can be learned through the regularities in the input. However, the question of implicit learning of form-meaning connections is not determined. DeKeyser (1995), in a study focusing on, inter alia, gender and number and using an artificial language did not find evidence of implicit learning of form-meaning connections. J. N. Williams (2004, 2005), adding animacy to the mix, did find evidence of form-meaning connection learning, even when the learners stated that they were not aware of the connection, but, to complicate the picture, Hama and Leow (2010), in a similar study, did not find such evidence. In a follow-up study, Leung and Williams (2012) took a more refined approach, considering, not whether or whether not, but when. They found that some can learn some form-meaning connections implicitly (in their case, animacy), whereas others are not so amenable to this kind of learning (in their case, relating the size of objects).

[handwritten annotation: → level out analysis and mental organization of linguistic info. →] *[handwritten annotation: speed + efficiency of access to info.]*

10.6.4 Representation/Control

Bialystok and Sharwood Smith (1985) noted that there are two aspects of importance in describing knowledge of a language: knowledge representation (the level of analysis and mental organization of linguistic information) and control over that knowledge (the speed and efficiency with which that information can be accessed; see also section 8.2.2). They made four points about the nature of learners' grammatical knowledge and how that knowledge differs from NS knowledge in a number of ways:

1. extent of analysis in the grammar;
2. greater analytic sophistication does not necessarily entail greater approximation to the TL;
3. reanalysis does not necessarily entail greater complexity (depth of analysis);
4. greater analysis does not necessarily entail greater conscious awareness.

We elaborate on Points 2–4 below.

With regard to Point 2, increasing ability to analyze TL structures does not necessarily entail correctness. What is meant by increased analysis? In many instances, learners use what are referred to as prefabricated patterns or language chunks, concepts introduced in Chapter 5, and discussed in Chapter 8. Prefabricated patterns are those bits of language for which there has been no internal analysis:

> [Prefabricated patterns] enable learners to express functions which they are yet unable to construct from their linguistic system, simply storing them in a sense like larger lexical items ... It might be important that the learner be able to express a wide range of functions from the beginning, and this need is met by prefabricated patterns. As the learner's system of linguistic rules develops over time, the externally consistent prefabricated patterns become assimilated into the internal structure.
>
> (Hakuta, 1976b, p. 333)

For example, consider the data in 10-20–10-23 from a child L2 speaker (Wong-Fillmore, 1976):

(10-20)   Lookit, like that.

(10-21)   Looky, chicken.

(10-22)   Lookit gas.

(10-23)   Lookit four.

Presumably, this child uses the phrase *lookit* or *looky* to get the attention of another individual and has not understood that *lookit* is made up of the two words *look at*.[7] At a later point in time, however, this child produces the following:

(10-24)   Get it, Carlos.

(10-25)   Get it!

(10-26)   Stop it!

One might speculate that the child, at this point, reanalyzed *lookit* as being comprised of *look* and *it*, thus allowing him to extend his L2 use to novel environments, such as those seen in 10-24–10-26. There is no evidence from these data that the correct target analysis of *look* and *at* was ever reached by this child, although there were different stages of analysis that the child went through.

Point 3, above, addresses the issue of reanalysis. Reanalysis does not necessarily mean that the learner is moving in a TL direction, nor that the analysis has become any more complex. Recall the examples given in Chapter 4, in which a learner first produces sentences such as the following:

(10-27)   I wanted him to come.

(10-28)   I persuaded him to come.

Later, the learner produces:

(10-29)   I enjoyed talking to my teacher.

(10-30)   I stopped sending packages to my friend.

In Stage 1, the learner only produces infinitival complements; in Stage 2, the learner only produces gerundive complements. There has been a reanalysis of the English complement system, although the second stage is no closer to the English system than the first stage, nor can it be considered any more complex than the first stage. In fact, in terms of sophistication, Stage 2 could be considered less complex than Stage 1, because, in Stage 1, the learner has used an object and, in the case of pronouns, has to assign case to it.

Point 4 addresses conscious awareness. The use of a system (correct or incorrect vis-à-vis TL norms) is not dependent on a learner's conscious awareness of the system, nor on his or her ability to articulate what the system is. What increased analysis does is allow the learner to make greater use of the system. Thus, determining the component parts of a chunked phrase allows the learner to use those component parts in other linguistic contexts. Increased awareness may or may not come as a result.

10.7 INTERFACE OF KNOWLEDGE TYPES

We have discussed various ways of representing knowledge. In this section, we outline three ways in which there is an interface between knowledge types.

10.7.1 No Interface

[handwritten: Nothing learned can be used fluently through unconscious speech.]

This position is best represented by Krashen's acquisition-learning distinction. It is clear that learners have different ways of internalizing information. The question, however, is whether or not learners develop two independent systems. Krashen stated explicitly that what has been learned cannot become part of the acquired system. However, if evidence of an acquired system is fluent, unconscious speech, then it is counterintuitive to hypothesize that nothing learned in a formal situation can ever be a candidate for this kind of use. The counterargument would consist of saying that information about a particular grammatical structure, for example, is housed in two separate linguistic systems; if nothing else, this is clearly an inefficient way for the brain to cope with different kinds of information.

A second objection to the distinction between acquisition and learning comes from consideration of those learners who learn language only in a formal setting. Let's further specify those learners whose instruction is in the NL, as opposed to the TL. By Krashen's definition, we would expect that they only have a learned system, as there is no way of "picking up" information for their acquired system. Recall that speaking is initiated through the acquired system. In such instances, how would learners ever generate utterances? Without an acquired system, there would be no initiation of L2 production.

A third objection to the distinction drawn within this framework has to do with falsifiability. Krashen provided no evidence that learning and acquisition are indeed two separate systems, a proposal that, at best, is counterintuitive; nor has he provided a means for determining whether they are or are not separate. Lack of specific criteria leaves one with no means of evaluating the claims. The hypothesis remains an interesting one, but nothing more than that.

10.7.2 Weak Interface

[handwritten: explicit knowledge and implicit knowledge are related and are dissociable but cooperative.]

N. Ellis (2005, 2007) argues for a relationship between explicit knowledge and implicit knowledge. Essentially, he argues that they are "dissociable but cooperative" (2005, p. 305). His argument is more subtle than a view which states that explicit knowledge gets turned into, or is converted into, implicit knowledge. Both can work cooperatively in any given instance. He provides the example of walking—we only think about walking when something goes awry, as when we stumble (or when speaking and we can't find the right word). At that point, we can call in a system of explicit knowledge, at those moments when implicit knowledge fails us. This is also the case in normal communication. As fluent NSs, we rarely think about our speaking except when we stumble. In his view, conscious and unconscious processes are involved at all steps of the way in any cognitive task, language being no exception.

1. Knowledge (that) → observation/analysis/verbal inst.
2. skill → move from declarative knowledge to procedural knowledge
2. Knowledge (how) LOOKING AT INTERLANGUAGE PROCESSING
3. Automatization of procedural knowledge.

10.7.3 Strong Interface

DeKeyser (1997) argues that L2 learning is like other forms of learning, both cognitive and psychomotor. The basic argument is that, regardless of what one is learning (e.g., language or tennis), learning progresses from knowledge *that* (declarative), relating to some skill or behavior, to knowledge *how* (procedural), and finally to automatization of procedural knowledge. The first type of knowledge can be obtained through observation and analysis, or through verbal instruction (or both). The next step is to move from the stage of conceptualization (declarative knowledge) to using that knowledge (procedural knowledge)—in other words, to some sort of performance (producing language, understanding language, swinging a tennis racquet). However, this is only the beginning, for procedural knowledge needs to become fast and without deliberation. Practice (whether time spent in training, such as Roger Federer playing tennis, or time spent using an L2 in a foreign country, such as is the case for language learners) is necessary to ensure that particular behaviors are quick, and there is diminished attention paid to the particular task (in the case of language learners, producing and/or understanding language).

DeKeyser (1997) presented data from learners of an artificial language who had been presented with four rules. One group received comprehension practice for two rules and production practice for the other two. A second group received production practice for the two rules that the first group had received comprehension practice on, and comprehension practice for the two rules that the first group had received production practice on. A third group had an equal amount of production and comprehension practice for all rules. Through reduced error rates and faster reaction times for those rules that they had practiced, participants showed movement from declarative knowledge to proceduralization to automaticity (a slower process than proceduralization). This suggests that declarative knowledge (rule presentation in this case) followed by practice led to greater proceduraliazation and automaticity, that is, more robust knowledge. What was interesting was that there was a lack of evidence of skill transfer (from production to comprehension, and vice versa), suggesting the skill-specificity of L2 knowledge. This is further supported in work by de Jong (2005), whose work with learners of Spanish showed that practice in aural comprehension yielded greater speed in comprehension, but not a reduced number of production errors.

10.8 CONCLUSION

In this chapter, we have reviewed psycholinguistic approaches to the study of SLA. We have illustrated the major concerns of such approaches, focusing on the ways in which L2 learners organize their L2 knowledge, on how learners use L2 knowledge, and on how subsequent learning affects the restructured organization of L2 knowledge. Nevertheless, how this processing is integrated in a detailed way into the formation of IL structure is far from clear. There has been little emphasis on contextual factors, which add to our understanding of this puzzle. We next move to a consideration of social and contextual variables as they affect the learning and production of an L2.

POINTS TO REMEMBER

- Like the field of linguistics, the field of psychology has influenced SLA. Psycholinguistic approaches to SLA focus on the mechanisms involved in SLA, not on grammatical formation.

- Processability Theory claims that learners can only comprehend and produce forms if they can be handled by the linguistic processor. Developmental sequences can be predicted based on how the processor works. One such developmental sequence is the acquisition of English questions.

- Automaticity refers to control over linguistic knowledge that becomes routinized. Restructuring refers to changes made to learning that has already been internalized because of new learning.

- People have a limited capacity for processing information. The more automatized information is, the more attentional resources that one has available to learn new information.

- U-shaped learning refers to a pattern of learning new forms where learners begin using the target-like form, then revert to nontarget-like forms, and then finally return to the target-like form.

- Input processing refers to approaches such as VanPatten's, which focuses on form-meaning connections, O'Grady's, which focuses on computational complexity, Carroll's, which focuses on the parser, and Clahsen and Felser's, which focuses on parts of grammar used in processing.

- There are different views of how attention is related to SLA and learning. In Tomlin and Villa's three-part model (alertness, orientation, and detection), awareness is not necessary for detection, or learning, to take place. Schmidt's noticing hypothesis claims that awareness is necessary for noticing, which is necessary for learning.

- Working memory refers to the processes that the brain uses to store and manipulate information. As the ability to carry out language tasks varies from individual to individual, working-memory tests are becoming common in SLA research. Many working-memory tests have a dual-task format, in that it is necessary to store some information while processing some other information.

- Syntactic priming is said to occur when someone uses the same syntactic structure that he/she has previously used/heard or compre-hended (rather than use an alternate structure). It has been suggested that syntactic priming might play a role in SLA, and that more developmentally advanced or more target-like structures may be primed in learners.

- Emergentist or constructivist models claim that language learning does not result from an innate language faculty, but rather it is the result of the linguistic environment, from which learners abstract regularities and recognize patterns.

- The Competition Model deals with how speakers determine relationships between parts of a sentence. It is based on the idea that language processing involves competition between various cues that lead to different interpretations of the sentence.

- There are different ways in which L2 knowledge can be described: acquisition vs. learning, procedural vs. declarative, implicit vs. explicit. There are different theories as to whether there is any interface between the knowledge types: no interface, weak interface, or strong interface.

SUGGESTIONS FOR ADDITIONAL READING

A dynamic approach to second language development (2011). Marjolin Verspoor, Kees de Bot, and Wander Lowie. John Benjamins.

Using priming methods in second language research (2009). Kim McDonough and Pavel Trofimovich. Routledge.

Complex systems and applied linguistics (2008). Diane Larsen-Freeman and Lynne Cameron. Oxford University Press.

Handbook of cognitive linguistics and second language acquisition (2008). Peter Robinson and Nick Ellis (Eds). Routledge.

Special issue of The Modern Language Journal: Dynamic systems (2008, *92*:2).

Special issue of Applied Linguistics: Language emergence (2006, *27*: 4).

Rethinking innateness: A connectionist perspective on development (1996). Jeffrey Elman, Elizabeth Bates, Mark Johnson, Annette Karmiloff-Smith, Domenico Parisi, and Kim Plunkett. MIT Press.

Attention and awareness in foreign language learning (1995). Richard Schmidt (Ed.). Second Language Teaching and Curriculum Center, University of Hawai'i at Manoa.

Implicit and explicit learning of languages (1994). Nick Ellis (Ed.). Academic Press.

MORE TO DO AND MORE TO THINK ABOUT ...

1. Consider the difference between linguistic products (i.e., the IL form) and psycholinguistic processes (the internal mechanisms used to arrive at those forms). The Competition Model claims that learners use particular cues to arrive at appropriate interpretation. How can learners come to know that the NL interpretation strategy may be an inappropriate one for the L2? Do you think that it would be easier to go from a language such as Italian, which allows for a wider range of sentence types, to one such as English, which allows for a smaller set of sentence types? Or would the opposite be true?

2. Fries (1945) discussed the sentences *The man killed the bear* and *The bear killed the man*. In that discussion, he said that there is essential meaning, not only in the form of words (*man/men* and *bear/bears*), but also in their arrangements. Therefore, the words *kill*, *bear*, and *man* alone do not provide all essential information for understanding the meaning of the sentence *The bear killed the man*. "There must be some method or device for pointing out the performer of the act and distinguishing him from the one upon whom the act is performed" (Fries, 1945, p. 28). How does this view differ from the one expressed by the Competition Model? Relate Fries's discussion to what you would expect Italian learners of English and English-speaking learners of Italian to *produce* in terms of word order in an L2. When would you expect communication breakdowns? What sorts of breakdown would you expect? Would you expect production to be as much of a problem as perception? Would you expect Italian learners to use free word order in English? Why, or why not? Are there other aspects of language that might help disambiguate free-word-order sentences in Italian?

3. Consider the following data, from a beginning learner of English with Arabic as an L1 (Hanania, 1974). Data are given from four points in time.

    Time 1:
    No (imperative)
    No English ("I can't speak English")

    Time 2:
    No (answer to question)
    I can't speak English
    My husband not here
    Not raining

    Time 3:
    No (answer to question)
    I can't speak English
    My husband not here

My husband not home
Don't touch
Don't touch it

Time 4:
My husband not here
Hani not sleeping
I can't speak English
No, I can't understand
I don't know
Don't eat
No, this is . . . (answer to question)

What is the progression from the first time period to the fourth, in terms of this learner's development of English negation? Give specifics about her knowledge at each time period.

There is some evidence that *can't* and *don't* are being used as unanalyzed units. What evidence can you bring to bear to support this conclusion?

Focus on Time 4. Do *can't* and *don't* still seem to be unanalyzed units? Why, or why not? Has restructuring taken place?

4. The following sentences were produced by an 11-year-old Spanish-speaking child who had lived in the United States since age 7 (data provided by B. Wald, originally printed as problem 1.5 in Selinker & Gass, 1984). The intended meanings of the child's utterances (gleaned from context) are given in parentheses.

    When I do something they don't hit me. (When I do something wrong they don't hit me).

    The mother doesn't want to take him away. (His mother didn't want to take him away.)

    He doesn't hear 'cause he was already dead. (He didn't hear because he had already died.)

    He don't buy us nothing. (He never buys us anything.)

    She don't help her nothing, *muy floja*. (She never helps her; she's real lazy.)

    They still doesn't know 'cause they work in another country. (They hadn't found out yet because they were working in another country.)

What systematic distinction does this learner make between her use of *don't* and *doesn't*? What does this suggest about imposing TL interpretation on L2 utterances?

LINK

1. http://cognitivefun.net/test/21

CHAPTER ELEVEN

Interlanguage in Context

[handwritten annotations, connected by arrows from the title:]
Social context
L2 is not a static phenomenon
social status of interlocutor
gender differences
tasks required from learner
relationship between learner and interlocutor

11.1 INTRODUCTION

This chapter focuses on social and contextual variables as they affect the learning and production of an L2. The emphasis is on how a developing IL system is dependent on the social context in which learning takes place. The basic premise is that L2 data do not represent a static phenomenon, even at a single point in time. Many external variables (such as the specific task required of a learner, social status of the **interlocutor**, the relationship of the interlocutors to one another, gender differences, and so forth) affect learner production and the developing IL system.

11.2 SOCIOCULTURAL APPROACHES

Sociocultural theory stems from work by Vygotsky that deals with general issues of human mental development (see Vygotsky, 1978, 1987 and works by Frawley & Lantolf, 1985; Aljaafreh & Lantolf, 1994; Lantolf & Thorne, 2006; 2007; Lantolf, 2012). Sociocultural theory attempts to account for learning by bringing together factors internal to the learner, as well as those external to the learner.

[handwritten annotation:] Vygotsky Sociocultural Theory → social contexts and internal processes

Over the years, there has been an increased emphasis on language use. One consequence of this emphasis is that the field has begun to incorporate approaches that go beyond the purely linguistic and psycholinguistic orientations that had been prevalent and that had focused on "in the head" phenomena of acquisition. Sociocultural theory is grounded in the ontology of the social individual and represents a fundamentally different way of looking at language and learning than what has been discussed in other parts of this book. In general, a sociocultural approach considers language and, by extension, SLA as contextually situated; it is concerned with situated language as it relates to internal processes.

11.2.1 Mediation

There are a number of concepts that are different from more traditional approaches to SLA, namely, **mediation** and **regulation**, **internalization**, and the **Zone of Proximal Development (ZPD)**. Mediation is the most important of these, because sociocultural theory rests on the assumption that human activity (including cognitive activity) is mediated by what are known as symbolic artifacts (higher-level cultural tools), such as language and literacy, and by material artifacts. These artifacts mediate the relationship between humans and the social and material world around us. To think of this in more concrete terms, one can consider how humans have developed tools to ease what might otherwise be an arduous process. If one wanted to put strands of wool together to create material, one could hold the strands taut and interweave other pieces of wool. However, over time, humans have developed tools to mediate the weaving process, namely, a loom with all of its component parts (e.g., the reed, the heddles, and a shuttle). Within sociocultural theory, humans use symbols as tools to mediate psychological activity and to control our psychological processes. This control is voluntary and allows us to attend to certain things, to plan, and to think rationally. The primary tool that humans have available is language, and it is a tool that allows us to connect to our environment (both physical and social). Language gives humans the power to go beyond the immediate environment and to think about and talk about events and objects that are far removed, both physically and temporally.

Regulation is a form of mediation. As children learn language, they also learn to regulate their activities linguistically. There are three stages of development on the way to self-regulation. The first stage involves the use of objects as a way of thinking (object-regulation). One can think of parents using objects (e.g., pieces of candy) to help children learn the abstract concept of counting. A second stage is known as other-regulation, whereby learning is regulated by others rather than objects. Finally, self-regulation, the final stage, occurs when activities can be performed with little or no external support. This occurs through internalization of information (e.g., addition without the use of pieces of candy, although some external support is required in the case of more complex mathematical manipulations).

11.2.2 Internalization

Another concept central to sociocultural theory is internalization. This is the process that allows us to move the relationship between an individual and his/her environment to later performance. One way that internalization occurs is through imitation, which can be both immediate and intentional and delayed, as seen, for example, in early-child-language research by Weir (1962), in which imitation/practice was observed by children when they were alone in bed. This is also known as **private speech** and has been observed in L2 classrooms by Ohta (2001; see discussion in Chapter 13) and by Lantolf and Yáñez (2003). The items focused on by learners in these imitation/private-speech situations are controlled by the learner and not necessarily by the teacher's agenda.

294

learning results from interpersonal activity that creates basis for individual functioning. (distance between actual development and the potential level of development)

INTERLANGUAGE IN CONTEXT

11.2.3 Zone of Proximal Development *- VYGOTSKY*

Another concept that is associated with sociocultural theory is known as the Zone of Proximal Development (ZPD), defined by Vygotsky (1978, p. 86) as: "the distance between the actual developmental level as determined by independent problem solving and the level of potential development as determined through problem solving under adult guidance or in collaboration with more capable peers." What this means is that learning results from interpersonal activity, and it is interpersonal activity that forms the basis for individual functioning. This clearly embodies the social nature of learning and underscores the importance of collaborative learning as it shapes what is learned (see Chapter 13).

11.2.4 Private Speech *→ it's the way learners regulate task performance*

Lantolf and Thorne (2006, 2007) show the applications to SLA. For example, the concept of private speech as a means of regulating a task by imposing order on that task (through meta-comments about the task itself), has been noted throughout the literature. In a study by McCafferty (1994), when describing a picture sequence, learners used regulatory language (e.g., *I see a man . . .* or *What do I see?*), a phenomenon absent in NS descriptions of the same picture. This was argued to be an example of how learners use private speech to regulate task performance. In other words, private speech is proposed to be a way to regulate complex tasks, and it is through self-regulation that researchers come to understand the processes used by learners.

TIME TO THINK ...

Look at a picture and try to describe it in your L2. Are you using private speech as you do the task? What meta-comments do you make to yourself? How do you think this would differ if you were more or less proficient in your L2?

11.2.5 Learning in a Sociocultural Framework *⟨ imitation ⟨ ZPD*

Learning within a sociocultural framework relies on two mechanisms: imitation and the ZPD. As Lantolf (2012) points out, imitation is very different from the earlier views discussed in this book, which involved little cognitive energy. A cognitive approach to imitation, as taken in the sociocultural framework, sees imitation as a mechanism by which learners build up their resources, to be used at a later time. This is not unlike the imitation that occurs when thinking about chunked learning (see Chapter 8) or prefabricated patterns (see discussion of Hakuta's work in Chapter 5), in which learners may imitate a sequence from the input without necessarily unpacking the component parts. In this case, one can think of imitation as a stepping-stone whereby learners

[handwritten top:] RECAST – form of mediation

[handwritten margin note left:] imitation interfaces with ZPD

may store exemplars for later use. Lantolf (2012) provides the following example from a learner of German:

(11-1) LEARNER: Ich   rufe   meine   Mutter   jeden   Tag
                 I   call   my   mother   every   day
       TEACHER: jeden Tag an
                 every day (prefix from verb *anrufen* [to call]
       LEARNER: Ich rufe meine Mutter jeden Tag an

In this instance, the teacher provided a partial **recast**, for which there was uptake/imitation by the learner. However, it was unlikely that this was just repetition or mindless imitation; at a later point in time, the same student uttered the following incorrect utterance: *Ich empfehle das neus Buch an* (I recommend the new book). In this example, the learner used the incorrect separable prefix *an*, presumably by analogy to/imitation of the correction made earlier by the teacher. Thus, imitation was a mechanism used, not just for the sake of imitation, but to create something new, albeit incorrect in this case. What is important to keep in mind is that imitation interfaces with the ZPD. In other words, recasts, a form of mediation, are effective when they are sensitive to a learner's ZPD.

[handwritten note across text:] Gesturing enhances comprehensibility and helps learners overcome their lexical difficulties, elicit vocabulary from interlocutor, deal with difficulty in coreference.

[handwritten margin left:] Thinking for speaking :) when learners speak thinking takes an unique function

11.2.6 Gesture and SLA

[handwritten:] to solve interpersonal problems

The study of gesture in SLA is of recent interest (see McCafferty, 2004a, and Gullberg & McCafferty, 2008) to researchers. Gullberg and McCafferty list a number of studies that suggest the benefits of gesturing and other forms of nonverbal communication for L2 learners, both in and out of a classroom context. It is interesting to note that there are studies that investigate gesturing during descriptions of verbs expressing motion. The framework for such studies comes from Slobin's (1996, 2003) **thinking-for-speaking**. According to this view, when one speaks, thinking takes on a unique function, with the verbalization of events being influenced by the linguistic categories of our language. Slobin (1996, p. 76) refers to this as, "the expression of experience in linguistic terms." He goes on to say, "Whatever effects grammar may or may not have outside of the act of speaking, the sort of mental activity that goes on while formulating utterances is not trivial or obvious" (p. 76). According to McNeill (2000a, 2000b, 2005), speaking and gesture form a single unit, what he refers to as a *growth point*. In other words, they form a single unit of meaning, even though the media are different.

[handwritten margin left:] GROWTH POINT: speaking and gesture form a single unit of meaning (even though media are different)

There are many ways in which an understanding of gesture can enhance an understanding of L2 learning. Gullberg and McCafferty (2008) point to a number of such areas. Gesturing may enhance the comprehensibility of utterances, given that there is additional input available to accompany verbal input. From a learning perspective, research also focuses on how learners use gestures, at times to overcome their own lexical difficulties, but also to elicit vocabulary from interlocutors, or even to deal with difficulties with coreference (Gullberg, 1998). Within a sociocultural framework, McCafferty (2004b) argues that L2 learners use gesture to solve interpersonal problems, a type of *gesturing for thinking*. In his study of a Taiwanese student studying English in the US, he shows that an NS interlocutor used gesture to aid comprehension, but, importantly, for the purposes of understanding how gestures are used by learners, the L2 learner used abstract deictic gestures, a type of virtual organizer—in other words, gesturing for thinking.

One area that is of interest in the study of gesture is space and motion events, a topic dealt with by Slobin (1996). From a typological point of view, languages can be categorized as being satellite-framed (English) or verb-framed (Spanish, Korean) (see Talmy, 2000). What this means is that the former express the path of a motion in adverbs or particles (see example 11-2 from Negueruela et al., 2004), and the manner of the motion is expressed in the verb.

Satellite - framed language & Verb - framed language

(11-2) Satellite-framed language:

The little bird hops out of the cage.

In this example, the manner of the bird's movement is seen in the verb *hop*, whereas the trajectory of that movement is seen in *out of*. Spanish and Korean differ in this regard, as can be seen in 11-3 and 11-4 (Spanish) and 11-5 (Korean, from Choi & Lantolf, 2008).

(11-3) El   pajarito   sale   de   la   jaula   dando   saltitos
        the   little bird   leaves   from   the   cage   giving   hops

(11-4) El   pajarito   da   saltitos   y   sale   de   la   jaula
        the   little bird   gives   hops   and   leaves   from   the   cage

(11-5) Entek   mith-ulo   kwulle-e   nayly-e   ka
        Hill   below toward   roll-INF   descend-INF   go
        goes rolling down a hill

In the Spanish examples, the verb (*sale*) includes both the motion and the path, with the phrase *dando saltitos* providing information about the manner (*giving hops*). In Korean, the path of the motion is expressed through the two verbs (roll and descend), one showing the path (*roll*) and the other the trajectory (*descend*). Manner is expressed separately from the verb (*below-toward*). In the case of English speakers learning Spanish, they rely on their L1 patterns. However, for Spanish speakers learning English, this is not the case. As Negueruela et al. (2004) note,

> from the perspective of inner speech . . . their [the participants'] perception of the motion depicted in the story was oriented by their internalized conceptual meanings that had been inculcated during the early years of their ontogenetic formation as they were drawn into the cultural practices of their respective speech communities.
>
> (pp. 141–142)

[handwritten margin note: Human cognition results from the full context (historical, social, material, cultural) in which experiences take place.]

Choi and Lantolf (2008) considered L2 speakers of English and Korean (L1s were Korean and English, respectively) and found that they were able to shift their orientation for path of motion, but were less able for manner of motion. The suggestion, then, is that there may be a hierarchy of difficulty, in that path is easier than motion from the perspective of L2 acquisition.

In sum, in this view, human cognition results from the full context (historical, social, material, cultural) in which experiences take place. Thus, the experiences we have and the interactions we engage in are crucial in the development of cognition. Language is a tool (a symbolic artifact) that mediates between individuals and their environment. For L2 situations, learning moves from a social process to a psychological process. In other words, the need for negotiated mediation changes over time. What might require a teacher or other individual can, over time, shift to a solely internal process.

[handwritten margin note: language is a toll that mediates between individuals and their environment]

[handwritten margin note: in L2 learning moves from a social process to a psychological process.]

[handwritten note: learners alternate forms (eg. no/don't)]

11.3 VARIATION

ILs seem to exhibit more variability than do NLs (see Bayley & Tarone, 2012, for an overview). For example, a learner might alternate between forms to express the same language function. Examples are given in 11-6 and 11-7, in which the learner alternates between *no* and *not*.

(11-6) My husband not here.

(11-7) No English.

What is the source of this variability? Earlier, we discussed one source of variability with regard to the variable use of the two forms of negation, *no* and *don't*. Initially, the variation in the use of these two forms was nonsystematic. That is, the forms were used interchangeably, with no apparent difference in meaning. With increased proficiency, the nonsystematic use of these forms became a source for learners' hypotheses about their use. There was a gradual establishment of a one-to-one form–function relationship. Thus, variation was the initial step in the eventual emergence of target-like usage. A similar example comes from R. Ellis (1984) in his description of an 11-year-old boy, a native speaker of Portuguese learning English. He produced the following two utterances:

(11-8) No look my card.

(11-9) Don't look my card.

During this child's first month in the United Kingdom, he produced 18 negative utterances, 17 using *no*, and 1 using *don't* (11-9). In the following month, there was an increase in the number of *don't*s, although *no*s were still more frequent. In the sixth month, negatives with *not* were most frequent. Thus, the number of *no*s decreased, and the number of *don't*s increased. In the middle of the transition period, there was considerable variation between the two forms.

Similar data are seen in the domain of phonology. Gatbonton (1978), in a cross-sectional study involving three sounds—[θ], as in *thing*; [ð], as in *soothe* or *the*; and [h], as in *behind*—found that learners begin with a single sound that is used in all linguistic environments. At a later point in time, a second sound enters the system. The second sound is then in free variation with the first. Later stages involve sorting the forms out into their appropriate environments.

Variationist perspectives on SLA (e.g., Adamson, 1988; Tarone, 1988; Preston, 1989; Bayley & Preston, 1996) focus "on the correlations of social facts and linguistic forms, the influence of linguistic forms on one another, and the place of variation within the study of language change" (Preston, 2002, p. 141). Preston (2000, 2002) makes the important connection between variationist approaches to SLA and their psycholinguistic underpinnings. In particular, he outlines three areas (levels, in his words) of interest and argues for a psycholinguistic account for each one.

In the first instance, there is a linking between sociocultural information and linguistic forms. This is illustrated in Figure 11.1.

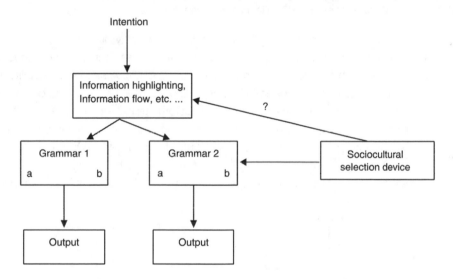

FIGURE 11.1 A Level I Psycholinguistic Model of Interlanguage Variation (*Source*: Preston, 2000. Reprinted by permission.)

Preston (2002) argues that, "speakers have two (or more) forms available in their linguistic . . . competences . . . and another device (some sort of sociocultural one) tells them which to choose" (p. 144). This model incorporates those individuals with more than one grammar (bilinguals) to choose from, as illustrated in Figure 11.1. A choice of one form or another may be based on a set of probabilistic weights that are part of each occurrence.

There is a second area to Preston's model, and that is the variation due to linguistic, as opposed to social, factors. In fact, Preston points out that linguistic variation is generally stronger than choices made on the basis of sociocultural factors. Figure 11.2 illustrates the inclusion of linguistic information into his model.

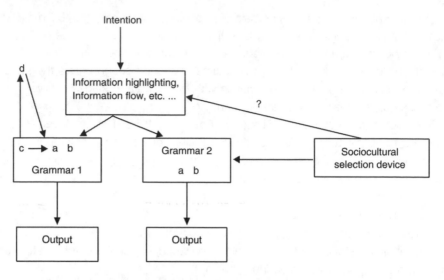

FIGURE 11.2 A Level II Psycholinguistic Model of Interlanguage Variation
(*Source*: Preston, 2000. Reprinted by permission.)

This model incorporates linguistic influence (looking at only one of the grammars of a bilingual speaker). In this instance, there are two modes of influence. One is a "linguistic fact" (c), which influences the selection of (a) or (b). A second possibility is that this "linguistic fact" (c) is influenced by something outside the grammar (d), which could be nonlinguistic (such as information status). Both are presumed to be possible.

A third area of variationist research concerns language change, which, in some sense, is what learning another language is about, albeit, in L2 learning, it happens much more rapidly than in language change in the more traditional sense. In Figure 11.3, Preston incorporates shading that represents areas of weakness in a grammar.

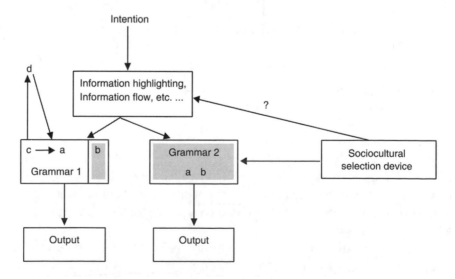

FIGURE 11.3 A Level III Psycholinguistic Model of Interlanguage Variation
(*Source*: Preston, 2000. Reprinted by permission.)

One might think about this in terms of areas of language that are more susceptible to change (cf. Gass, 1988a).

If we consider Grammar 1 as the NL, one can see that there is less possibility for change than in Grammar 2 (the L2). Preston (2002) makes the interesting claim that, the later structures are learned, "the weaker the grammar at those points and the less reliable respondent judgments about that territory will be (exactly as we have discovered in SLA 'incompleteness' or 'fossilization' studies, e.g., Coppieters, 1987; Johnson & Newport, 1989)" (p. 150). In other words, one expects more variability in judgments (which Preston claims to reflect performance) in learner languages than in NLs. In the next sections, we refer to studies that deal with these areas of influence on form.

11.4 SYSTEMATIC VARIATION

[handwritten margin notes: two or more sounds/grammatical vary contextually — variations that are linguistically based — variations that are sociolinguistically determined.]

There is another type of variation that may occur from the early stages—systematic variation. Systematic variation is evidenced when two or more sounds/grammatical forms vary contextually. Some variation is linguistically based, other is sociolinguistically determined. We deal first with linguistically based variation.

11.4.1 Linguistic Context

In a study investigating phonological variation by NSs of Japanese learning English, Dickerson (1975) found that the target sound [r] was more frequently used before a low vowel (e.g., [a]) than before a mid vowel (e.g., [I], [ɛ], or [ɔ]), and more frequently before a mid vowel than before a high vowel ([i] or [u]). Figure 11.4 is taken from

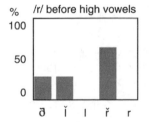 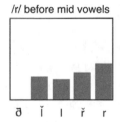 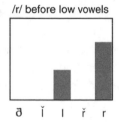

Variants of /r/ by Japanese learners of English

[ɖ]	voiced nonretroflexed flap
[ǐ]	voiced lateral flap
[l]	voiced lateral
[řˇ]	voiced retroflexed flap
[r]	voiced retroflexed semiconsonant

FIGURE 11.4 Pronunciation of English /r/ in Three Different Linguistic Environments (*Source*: From "Interlanguage phonology: current research and future directions" by L. Dickerson and W. Dickerson, 1977. In S. Corder and E. Roulet (Eds.), *The notions of simplification, interlanguages and pidgins and their relation to second language learning*, Actes du 5ème Colloque de Linguistique Appliquée de Neuchâtel (pp. 18–29). AIMAV/Didier. Reprinted by permission.)

/R/ →

Linguistic
context
affects
morphology
(e.g. plural)
and
syntax
(e.g. negation)

Dickerson and Dickerson (1977). Five pronunciations for English /r/ are exemplified as a function of the phonetic environment in which they occur. As can be seen, not only are different variants used, but also the patternings differ, depending on the following vowel.

Similarly, Sato (1984) considered the reduction of consonant clusters in English by two Vietnamese children. Examples of reductions are given in Table 11.1.

Sato noted a difference in the TL production of consonant clusters, depending on whether the cluster was at the beginning of the syllable or at the end. Syllable-initial clusters were more accurately produced than syllable-final clusters (see also Chapter 7).

Linguistic context has been found to affect morphology and syntax as well. In morphology, Young (1991) investigated the use of plural markings by L2 learners. In a study of Chinese NSs learning English, Young collected interview data from 12 learners on two separate occasions, using two different interviewers. The 12 individuals were divided into two proficiency levels (high and low), on the basis of their results on standardized test scores. Young provided evidence for variation in the use and nonuse of the plural /s/, even on the same lexical item. Examples from his data are given in 11-10 and 11-11.

(11-10) MARY: The store is . . . a . . . just sells all the *books*
   MARY: all the *book* is have to ship from Taiwan

(11-11) JENNIFER: I think because my brother . . . a . . . hate girls when he was a
   INTERVIEWER: Really?
   JENNIFER: Mm.was terrib- . . . he she . . . he's very strange I mean he . . . you know even he was in the high school he wouldn't talk to *girl* you know

Young established a number of hypotheses, only some of which are relevant to a discussion of the linguistic context in which plural nouns occur. He found that there was variation conditioned by the phonological environment (by both the preceding and following segment). A summary of these results showing the precise conditioning factors is given in Table 11.2.

TABLE 11.1 Reduction of English Consonant Clusters by Vietnamese Children (*Source*: Adapted from "Phonological processes in second language acquisition: Another look at interlanguage syllable structure" by C. Sato, 1984, *Language Learning, 34*, 43–57.)

Standard English		Learner production
[groʷ]	"grow"	[goʷ]
[pleis]	"place"	[pəleis]
[læst]	"last"	[læ]

TABLE 11.2 Phonological Environment as a Constraint on /s/ Plural Marking (*Source*: Adapted from *Variation in interlanguage morphology* by R. Young, 1991, New York: Peter Lang. The probability weights are based on VARBRUL, a statistical package (Pintzuk, 1988; Rand & Sankoff, 1990) designed for analyzing variation data. Probability weights allow researchers to determine what the possible influence might be that would predict when something will occur.)

Factor	% of plural usage	Probability weights
Preceding segment		
Nonsibilant fricative (/f/, /v/)	78	.67
Vowel	71	.53
Stop (/p/, /t/, /k/, /b/, /d/, /g/)	66	.53
Nasal (/m/, /n/)	58	.46
Sibilant (/s/, /z/, /ð/, /ʃ/)	54	.41
Lateral (/l/)	42	.30
Following segment		
Vowel or glide (/w/, /y/)	70	.56
Pause	64	.49
Consonant or liquid (/l/, /r/)	60	.44

Interestingly, these results hold only for low-proficiency learners. For higher-proficiency learners, the most important factor in determining whether or not plural nouns are marked with /s/ is the presence or absence of plural markings elsewhere in the noun phrase. Contrary to what would be expected from data of natural languages (and from pidgins), there is a greater likelihood for plural nouns to be marked in a phrase such as *two boys* than in phrases such as *the boys*. This is so in what Young referred to as measure nouns (years, days, minutes, kilometers, dollars, etc.). Examples from Young's (1991) study are given in 11-12–11-16.

(11-12) I stay Boston only only five da-five days

(11-13) It's a drive it's twenty minutes

(11-14) I come Philadelphia its a . . . mm . . . forty years

(11-15) The second day the stock of RCA the market can drop by two dollars. dram- you know drastically

(11-16) So in fact the distance is very long . . . about . . . twelve to thirteen kilometers.

In phrases where plurality is not indicated redundantly, there is less likelihood of *-s* marking on the noun.

In addition to the phonological environment, there are other factors that relate to plural marking. For example, Young found that syntactic determinants, as well as determinants based on the position of the noun within the NP, also affect plural marking. In fact, the greatest influence was the position of the noun within the NP (whether a pronominal modifier or head).

In syntax, there is, similarly, variation based on linguistic context. Hyltenstam's (1977) study of the acquisition of Swedish negation by NSs of 35 different languages serves as an illustration. In Swedish, the placement of the negative word *inte* is dependent on whether the negated verb is in a main clause or a subordinate clause, as seen in 11-17 and 11-18.

(11-17) Kalle   kommer   inte   idag.
        Charlie   comes   not   today
        "Charlie isn't coming today."

(11-18) Det är   skönt   att   Kalle   inte   kommer   idag.
        it's   fine   that   Charlie not   comes   today
        "It's fine for Charlie not to come today."

Learners begin with a simple undifferentiated hypothesis: one-to-one correspondence between form and function

The first stage learners follow in the acquisition of Swedish negation is to uniformly put the negator before the verb, not differentiating between main and subordinate clauses. This is consistent with what we have seen earlier, in that learners begin with a simple, undifferentiated hypothesis: There is a one-to-one correspondence between form and function. When learners, as a function of greater proficiency, begin to recognize that their own systems do not correspond to the language they are exposed to, there is a need to revise the current hypothesis, in many cases resulting in greater complexity. In the case of Swedish, the change to the TL system has, as an intermediate stage, the placement of the negative marker after some finite auxiliary verbs. This then spreads to more and more verbs. At this stage, there is then variability between placement before and after verbs. The same pattern is repeated with nonauxiliary finite verbs. At this point, learners are still not in conformity with the target system; they must now begin the process of differentiating between main and subordinate clauses. This takes place in the same gradual way as before, with the learners first placing the negator before main verbs, and only later before both main and auxiliary verbs. What is important to note is that, all through this process, there is considerable variability, depending in large part on whether the context is a main verb or an auxiliary verb.

Thus, systematic variation is found in phonology, morphology, and syntax. It is evidence of learners' need to impose regularity on their own IL system.

11.4.2 Social Context Relating to the Native Language → *Phonology*

There are sources other than the linguistic environment that govern variation, such as social factors relating to the NL.

One of the earliest studies to consider the role of social factors in SLA was that of Schmidt (1977), in which he investigated the pronunciation of the sounds /θ/ as in *thing* and /ð/ as in *this* by two groups of Cairene Arabic speakers. One group was comprised of university students, and the other of working-class men. In colloquial Egyptian Arabic, there are lexical triplets with the sound /θ/ alternating with /s/ and with /t/, as in the three possible pronunciations of the word *third*: θaːli θ, saːlis, and taːlit. The main difference in Schmidt's two groups of NSs occurred in the use of the /θ/ variant in Arabic. All of the university students produced the /θ/ variant some of the time, whereas the majority of the working-class group never pronounced words using the /θ/ variant. Thus, the /θ/ variant appears to be a prestige variant, associated with the educated class. What is important to note is that, in terms of Classical Arabic, the /θ/ variety is the correct one.

Schmidt's study was additionally concerned with the pronunciation of /θ/ in English. Because /θ/ is a prestige form in Egyptian Arabic, it could be assumed that the more formal the situation is for elicitation of English, the greater the occurrence of /θ/. Schmidt's database consisted of 34 NSs of Arabic, from whom three types of data were elicited, ranging in formality from reading a passage (the least formal), to reading a word list, to reading pairs of contrasting words (the most formal). The percentage of /θ/ variants for each of these elicitation tasks is given in Table 11.3.

TABLE 11.3 Percentage of /θ/ Variants from Cairene Arabic Speakers on Three English Tasks (*Source*: Adapted from Schmidt, 1977.)

Reading a passage	Reading a word list	Reading pairs of contrasting words
54	73	73

A closer look at a subset of the participants revealed that they could be divided into two groups—those who terminated their studies after secondary school and those who did not. Here, the results parallel those we saw earlier with the data from Arabic: The more educated group used a higher percentage of /θ/s in English than the less educated group, although, for both groups, there was variation along the formality–informality scale. These results are given in Table 11.4.

Thus, social factors in the native culture—in this case, a formality/informality distinction as well as NL prestige forms—influence the forms learners use in an L2.

Most studies of social context have focused on phonology (Major, 2001). One such study was that of Beebe (1980), who investigated the use of /r/ by Thai learners of English. Beebe's participants were given two tasks: in one, learners were engaged in conversation, and, in the other, learners read from a word list. Thus, one was an informal situation (although it was taped), in which language was not the focus, and the other was a formal one, in which there was a greater focus on language. In Beebe's analysis, she considered instances of initial /r/ and instances of final /r/. In final position, the correct TL variant was used 41.1 percent[1] of the time in the informal situation, whereas, in the formal situation (i.e., reading a word list), the correct TL variant was used 72.2 percent

TABLE 11.4 Mean Scores for the /θ/ Variable in English and Arabic for Two Groups of Secondary Students (*Source*: Adapted from Schmidt, 1977.)

		6 learners (less educated)	16 learners (more educated)
Arabic:	Reading passage	8.66	45.63
	Word list	43.33	70.62
	Minimal pairs	68.33	78.75
English:	Reading passage	111.66	60.25
	Word list	40.00	86.25
	Minimal pairs	53.33	79.38

TABLE 11.5 Percentage of TL Variants of /r/ (*Source*: Adapted from Beebe, 1980.)

	Informal conversation situation	Formal situation (reading a word list)
/r/ in final position	41.1	72.2
/r/ in initial position	38.5	8.9

of the time (although it is to be noted that there were far fewer tokens in the formal situation than in the informal one). In looking at the data from the pronunciation of initial /r/, the pattern is reversed. In the informal situation, the accuracy rate was 38.5 percent. In the formal situation, the accuracy rate was 8.9 percent (see Table 11.5).

The situation that we find relating to final /r/ is what would be predicted on the basis of task type, as is discussed later in this chapter. However, the initial /r/ data are puzzling in this regard. Beebe proposed an explanation that relates to the role of the NL. The NL variants used in the formal situation are, in fact, prestige variants of initial /r/ used in Thai. Thus, in the word list, the socially prestigious form is being transferred to a TL context, as we saw with Schmidt's Arabic data.[2]

Thus, variation in L2 use may have a basis in the social norms of the NL. However, there are other sources of variation. We consider conversational partner (or interlocutor), task type, and conversational topics in the next section.

TIME TO THINK ...

Think about the two pronunciations of -*ing* in English (i.e., [ɪŋ] or [ɪn]). Under what circumstances would you use each of the variants? When would you not use one of the variants? Do you think that one variant might be more common in conversation and another when reading a word list? Can you think of other examples of phonological variation in English?

11.4.3 Social Context Relating to Interlocutor, Task Type, and Conversational Topic

We often adjust our speech style according to the situation and the speaker with whom we are talking. It is well known that the way we speak in a family situation is different from the way we speak in a formal job interview. We turn to similar issues in the understanding of NNS speech.

One way of accounting for speech effects attributed to interlocutor differences is through Speech Accommodation Theory (Giles & St. Clair, 1979; Giles & Smith, 1979; Thakerar et al., 1982), which begins from the observation that speech patterns tend to converge/diverge in social interaction. Thakerar et al. (1982, p. 207) defined convergence and divergence as follows:

> Convergence . . . a linguistic strategy whereby individuals adapt to each other's speech by means of a wide range of linguistic features including speech rates, pause and utterance lengths, pronunciations, etc. . . . whereas divergence refers to the manner by which speakers accentuate vocal differences between themselves and others.

Why should speakers accommodate their speech to that of others? The reasons are social in origin. Speaking like others (not unlike dressing in a manner similar to others) is intended to have the benefit of gaining the approval of others. It also identifies one as a member of the same social group, class, or ethnic background. The studies designed to consider IL variation from this perspective in general find convergence among speakers. For example, in a study by Beebe and Zuengler (1983), data were collected in Thai from Chinese–Thai children in two separate interviews, one with an ethnic Chinese speaker and one with an ethnic Thai speaker. (Chinese was the L1 and Thai was the L2 of these children.) Beebe and Zuengler focused on six Thai vowels and two Chinese consonants, given in Tables 11.6 and 11.7.

As can be seen, the interlocutor had an effect on the speech of these NNSs for both vowels (Table 11.6) and consonants (Table 11.7). They accommodated to the speech of their interlocutors by making speech adjustments that made them sound more Thai-like or more Chinese-like, depending on the ethnic background of the interlocutor.

Perhaps one of the most frequently investigated topics within the sociolinguistic–SLA literature concerns the differential results obtained as a function of data-elicitation tasks. The basis of this work is that of Labov (e.g., 1969, 1970), who noted that different forms are likely to occur, depending on the speech situation.

Tarone (1979, 1983) extended Labov's work, which had been based on observations of NSs, to the L2 learning context. She argued that missing from the original IL formulation is the idea that an L2 learner's system is a variable one, changing when the linguistic environment changes. (In fact, the title of one of her early articles (1979) was "Interlanguage as Chameleon.") According to Tarone, the learner's grammatical system exhibits more systematicity or consistency in the vernacular style,

[handwritten left margin: VERNACULAR STYLE X SUPERORDINATE STYLE]

TABLE 11.6 Percentage of Thai Variants (Standard Bangkok Thai) Used by 61 Bilingual Chinese–Thai Subjects with Thai and Chinese Interviewers (all interviews were conducted in Thai) (*Source*: From "Accommodation theory: An explanation for style shifting in second language dialects" by L. Beebe & J. Zuengler. In N. Wolfson & E. Judd (Eds.), *Sociolinguistics and second language acquisition* (pp. 195–213). Newbury House, 1983. Reprinted by permission.)

Interviewer Variant	Thai	Chinese
[uu]	47	35
[ɛɛ]	42	31
[əə]	30	23
[o]	61	48
[aa]	65	61
[a]	92	91

[handwritten left margin: least attention is paid to the form of one's speech (more systematic, but least accurate). most internally consistent]

[handwritten below table: least likely to be influenced by the TL system = ⊃ ACCURATE / LEAST ⊃ ACCURATE]

[handwritten left margin: most attention is paid to the form of one's speech (Focus: speech) ↓ more influence from TL ↓ Most accurate, but least systematic system]

TABLE 11.7 Percentage of Chinese Variants Used by 61 Bilingual Chinese–Thai Subjects with Thai and Chinese Interviewers (*Source*: From "Accommodation theory: An explanation for style shifting in second language dialects" by L. Beebe & J. Zuengler. In N. Wolfson & E. Judd (Eds.), *Sociolinguistics and second language acquisition* (pp. 195–213). Newbury House, 1983. Reprinted by permission.)

Interviewer Variant	Thai	Chinese
[ŋ]	11.5	16.1
[k]	5.8	10.7

and less in what she calls the *superordinate* style. These two systems are defined in terms of the amount of attention paid to speech. The vernacular system is that system in which the least attention is paid to the form of one's speech, and the superordinate style is that system in which the most attention is paid to speech form. These two, then, reflect the outer boundaries of a continuum of styles, the use of which is partially determined by attention to form, which in turn is at least partially determined by the social setting of a speech event.

An early study in this area is by Dickerson and Dickerson (1977). Earlier, we discussed these data in terms of linguistic context. Here, we focus on this research as a function of task type (see Figure 11.5).

The data from Japanese speakers of English relate to the production of /r/ in two contexts: following a consonant and preceding either a mid vowel or a high vowel. As can be seen from the data, there are differences in accuracy as a function of the type of task (free speech, dialogue reading, word-list reading) the learner is engaged in.

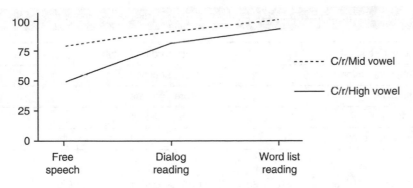

FIGURE 11.5 Pronunciation of /r/ as a Function of Task (*Source*: From "Interlanguage phonology: current research and future directions" by L. Dickerson and W. Dickerson (1977). In S. Corder and E. Roulet (Eds.), *The notions of simplification, interlanguages and pidgins and their relation to second language learning*, Actes du 5ème Colloque de Linguistique Appliquée de Neuchâtel (pp. 18–29). AIMAV/Didier. Reprinted by permission.)

It is hypothesized that these three tasks can be ordered along a continuum of attention to speech: There is less specific focus on form in the free-speech situation and more with the word list. Accuracy is observed to the greatest extent in those tasks in which there is the greatest focus on form. However, there is difficulty with this conceptualization of the relationship between task type and accuracy, because there is no independent evidence that these tasks should be ordered in this way. Perhaps, most attention is found in the dialogue reading. Or, perhaps the amount of attention is not uniform among all individuals across task types. If this latter possibility is the case, one would expect individuals to vary as to which task demands the most or least attention.

An important consideration is the relationship between accuracy and systematicity. Recall that the vernacular is believed to be the most systematic, but, in the data from Dickerson and Dickerson, we saw that it was also the least accurate. Systematicity is intended to mean only that there is the least invasion from other systems. Thus, one could expect that the vernacular, because it is the most internally consistent, is least likely to be influenced by the TL system. Hence, it will also be the least accurate. On the other hand, the superordinate style is one in which the most attention is paid to speech and in which there appears to be the most influence from the TL, and, hence, it is representative of the most accurate, but possibly the least systematic, system. This can be schematized in the following way (Table 11.8).[3] This table is intended to be illustrative only, because, in fact, one can think of these styles as a continuum.

Attention to speech as the only variable involved in accounting for different forms may be too simplistic an explanation for variation. Gass (1980), in an investigation of the acquisition of relative clauses, compared two task types. She used a grammaticality-judgment task and a sentence-combining task. In the former, learners were asked to judge the grammaticality of sentences in their L2. In the latter task, learners were given

309

[Handwritten annotations at top: "EACH TASK PERFORMED BY A LEARNER PLACES DIFFERENT DEMANDS"]

TABLE 11.8 Vernacular and Superordinate Styles

Vernacular style	Superordinate style
Less attention to form	More attention to form
Less accurate	More accurate
Systematic	Less systematic
Less likely to be influenced by TL	More likely to be influenced by TL

sentences, such as 11-19, and were told to combine them into a single sentence, with the targeted sentence being something like 11-20:

(11-19) The boy ran home. The boy was crying.

(11-20) The boy who was crying ran home.

The main focus was on the use of the NL by L2 learners. In comparing the results of the two tasks (acceptability judgment and sentence combining), Gass found that the results between the tasks were not identical, leading her to emphasize that different data-elicitation techniques may yield different conclusions. In particular, with a sentence-combining task, there is a possibility of avoiding the target structure. The point is that the concept of attention to speech may be less important than understanding the processes involved in doing various tasks. For example, the grammaticality-judgment task is primarily a decoding task in which two steps are involved in deciding to reject or accept a given sentence. First, learners must interpret the sentence in some way. Second, they must determine if it fits the patterns of English as represented by their IL. In other words, a learner must attempt to match the sentence with an internalized linguistic system. On the other hand, a sentence-combining task is a production task in which a learner must focus on the form of the sentence, while simultaneously maintaining the original meaning. Thus, each task that a learner performs will place different demands on the learner, attention to speech being but one.

[Handwritten annotations in margin: "First: sentence interpretation", "Second: determine if patterns of English are represented by IL.", "Attempt to match the sentence with an internalized linguistic system"]

Even in data that do reflect more clearly a difference in attention to form, the results do not bear out the hypothesized relationship between accuracy and attention to speech, as exemplified by the Dickerson and Dickerson data. In particular, Sato (1985) found the opposite relationship to hold. In her study of word-final consonant production and consonant clusters of a Vietnamese child learning English, the trend observed by Dickerson and Dickerson did not hold. Data were collected from three tasks at four points in time: (a) free conversation, (b) oral reading of continuous text, and (c) elicited imitation of words and short phrases. (At Time 4, Task 2 was replaced by the recitation of a rehearsed text.) Tables 11.9 and 11.10 give the results from the tasks used.

As can be seen, in neither the production of consonants nor in the production of consonant clusters does the predicted relationship hold, although, once again, it is not clear which task would be the one with the most attention paid to speech. Sato clearly pointed out that defining speech styles only in terms of attention to speech is an overly simplistic view of how learner production varies.

310

TABLE 11.9 Target-like Production of Word-final Consonants by Task (% Correct) (*Source*: From "Task variation in interlanguage phonology" by C. Sato. In S. Gass & C. Madden (Eds.), *Input in second language acquisition*. Newbury House, 1985. Reprinted by permission.)

Task	Time 1	Time 2	Time 3	Time 4
Conversation	52.00	72.41	73.55	68.96
Oral reading	61.54	61.65	63.70	70.81
Imitation	78.57	64.52	79.45	72.73

TABLE 11.10 Target-like Production of Word-final Clusters by Task (% Correct) (*Source*: From "Task variation in interlanguage phonology" by C. Sato. In S. Gass & C. Madden (Eds.), *Input in second language acquisition*. Newbury House, 1985. Reprinted by permission.)

Task	Time 1	Time 2	Time 3	Time 4
Conversation	5.88	5.41	21.69	14.63
Oral reading	19.78	28.89	30.69	6.15
Imitation	12.50	26.92	49.17	31.82

Tarone, too, recognized the limitations of a linear, monolithic perspective on variation. In a 1985 study, she looked at morphemes that informal observation had indicated were often omitted even by advanced learners. She found that it was not the case that the vernacular was the least accurate. In this study, there were three tasks: (a) grammaticality judgment (most attention to form), (b) oral interview about the learner's major field of interest, and (c) oral narration (least attention to form).

Tarone's analysis and explanation of these findings incorporated the notion of discourse function. That is, one cannot simply say that the type of task will dictate what forms will be used. One also needs to look at the function of those forms within a discourse context. For example, plural /s/ did not shift along the predicted continuum; other morphemes—such as third person singular—conformed to the hypothesized attention-to-form–accuracy relationship; still others—such as English articles and direct-object pronouns—exhibited a trend opposite to what was predicted. Tarone's explanation resides in the contextual roles of these different forms. In context, the third person singular is redundant. That is, there are other cues in the sentence or the preceding context that specify the person and number of the verb. On the other hand, in a narrative context and, perhaps to a lesser extent, in discussing one's field, articles and pronouns are important in maintaining and establishing appropriate relationships. Thus, the demands of the narrative and interview tasks were such that there was greater pressure for accuracy of certain forms but not of others. The morphemes that were needed to convey meaning and that provided a cohesive narration were increasingly provided as the tasks required more focus on meaning. At the same time, the morphemes that were empty in terms of meaning were increasingly deleted as the task required more focus on meaning. That is, attention was a factor as tasks increased or decreased in their focus on form, but not all morphemes were equal in the amount of attention they attracted. Morphemes that carried meaning were attended to and supplied more as tasks required more focus on meaning, while morphemes that carried no meaning were attended to and supplied less.

Whereas attention to form and discourse function may contribute to the internal consistency of learner systems, discourse topic is important as well. Eisenstein and Starbuck (1989) gathered oral data from 10 learners of English as an L2 on two topics: one that an individual had specified as being a topic of great interest, and the other that the individual had specified as being of little or neutral interest. They included accuracy measures on a number of grammatical categories, including tense usage, verb formation, verb meaning, and tense meaning. In general, accuracy was lower on those topics in which there was emotional investment; in other words, on those topics that had been designated as having great interest for the subject. One could argue that this is related to the notion of attention to speech, because it is precisely in instances of high investment that one would expect great attention to the meaning and, as a result, less attention to form.

There is additional evidence for the effect of topic on L2 production (Woken & Swales, 1989; Zuengler, 1989), although, in both of these studies, it was not linguistic accuracy that was considered, but linguistic behaviors. In Zuengler's study, she paired an NS and an NNS who were majoring in the same field (statistics, dairy science, or electrical engineering). Each pair had two conversations, one on a neutral topic about which each was presumed to have equal knowledge (food), and the other on a topic relating to their major. In some pairs, the NS was further along in his/her studies, and in others it was the NNS who had more advanced topic knowledge. The measures that were considered were interruptions, amount of talk, and the number of questions asked. All of this contributed to a determination of conversational dominance. The results suggest that conversational dominance is not conditioned by linguistic knowledge alone, because NSs did not uniformly dominate the conversations. Rather, dominance was better understood in terms of content knowledge.

A similar study was conducted by Woken and Swales (1989), who also varied topic knowledge. Their participants (native and nonnative pairs) differed in terms of their knowledge of computers. Each NNS had expertise in a particular computer program, whereas none of the NSs were familiar with the program. The task involved the NNS instructing the NS on the use of the program. Woken and Swales' measures consisted of linguistic measures (such as number and length of clauses and number of questions asked) and nonlinguistic measures (such as number of vocabulary explanations and direction-giving). Their results are similar to those of Zuengler, showing that dominance and control in a conversation must be considered to be complex phenomena. The common view is that NSs control the conversation by virtue of the fact that they have more linguistic resources available to them. However, the effect of topic knowledge (as well as other social variables, such as status and familiarity) must be taken into account. Thus, there is a complex interaction of many factors that shape the nature of conversational and linguistic behaviors involving NNSs.

Selinker and Douglas (1985) argued that L2 research must take into account the notion of context as an internal construct. One aspect of context is variation as a function of elicitation task, which we dealt with earlier in this chapter. Another has to do with the concept of *discourse domain,* which the authors define as "internally-created contexts, within which . . . Il structures are created differentially" (p. 190). That is, learners create discourse domains that relate to various parts of their lives and are important to them. IL forms are created within particular contexts or particular discourse domains. The evidence adduced comes from a learner who produces different IL structures within different discourse domains. Selinker and Douglas's argument rested on their belief that various aspects of SLA (e.g., transfer, fossilization, avoidance) occur differentially within discourse domains. To illustrate this, consider 11-21 and 11-22. In the former, the interviewer is discussing with Luis the contents of a technical article on engineering. In 11-22, the topic of discussion is food. In both episodes, Luis forgets a crucial word.

[Margin handwritten notes: CONTEXT AS AN INTERNAL CONSTRUCT ↓ learners create discourse domains that relate to various parts of their lives and are important to them. ↓ transfer fossilization avoidance play a role.]

(11-21) L = Luis (NNS); I = interviewer (NS)

L: . . . and then this is eff-eh-referring that the contractor maybe didn't adjust the equipment to the co-site conditions—maybe this you know the equipment can be effected by the—what is that the—I lost the word—I mean—because no—for—you have one equipment here in for example one estate and you want to move that equipment to for example you are working Michigan and you want to move that equipment to Arizona or a higher estate—you have to adjust your equipment because the productivity of the equipment eh gets down—eh because of the different eh height of the (project) place

I: oh   I   see the a the ah altitude

L: yeah the altitude—that is [the word =

I: [that's the word

L: = I was looking for

I: yea the altitude—the altitude makes a difference

L: makes a difference in the productivity of the equipment

(11-22) L: I don't know if you know what machaca is

I: tell me—I think I've had it once before

L: No—you you get some meat and you put that meat eh to the sun an after that you—I don't know what is I—I learned that name because I went to the sss—farmer jack I saw that—you make like a little then— oh my god—then you = you = forget it (laugh)

I: (laugh) make it into strips?

L: OK like a—you you have a steak no?   you first

I: uh huh

L: in the sun—you have

I: then it gets rotten and you throw it away

313

L: ummm—no no no no no only one day or two days

I: hmmm

L: after that with a stone you like escramble that like ah—

I: you grind it up?

L: Yes that psss you you start to what is that word oh my god

I: mash?

L: exactly you have to you start making mash that meat

In the nontechnical domain, he appears willing to use a strategy of abandonment (note his *forget it* in his second turn). In the technical domain, the same communication breakdown does not occur, because Luis is able to continue without the necessary word. This he does by describing the process, presumably in the hopes of either getting his idea across or of eliciting the word from the native-speaking interviewer. In the conversation about food, Luis enters into a negotiated interaction with the interviewer, resulting in a mutual word search. That is, both conversational participants have as their goal the search for the appropriate lexical item. Thus, in these two examples, the NNS uses two distinct **communication strategies** in his attempt to explain a concept to an NS.

TIME TO THINK ...

Think about the episodes in 11-21 and 11-22 where Luis is describing a technical and a nontechnical topic. What role do you think gesture might have played in the interactions? How might gesture have facilitated the communication?

We have seen that there is considerable variation in L2 learner data. The variation can be of two sorts, free and systematic, although systematic variation is far more prevalent. When forms vary systematically, there are a number of determining factors, some of which are linguistic, others of which are sociolinguistic or situational. R. Ellis (1987b, p. 183) proposed a role for both free and systematic variation in L2 development. Free variation occurs as an initial stage when two (or more) forms are involved. The next stage (systematic variation) involves consistency of form–meaning relationships, with overlapping forms and meanings. The final stage, the categorical-use stage (assuming that a learner reaches that point), is the correct form–meaning assignment. This is shown in the diagram in Figure 11.6.

To take the data presented in Chapter 10 (Table 10.3) regarding the use of *no* and *don't*, we can match the data up with the model presented in Table 11.11. What is interesting to note is that the categorical-use stage for this learner is not the correct TL one.

That learners vary in their production of TL forms is not in dispute. What is a matter of dispute, however, is the appropriate way of representing linguistic knowledge. Those whose major interest is in Chomskyan linguistics (see arguments in Gregg, 1990, and Jordan, 2005) take as the domain of SLA research the determination of linguistic

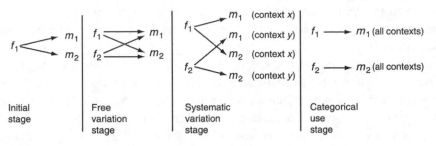

f = form
m = meaning
'context' refers to both situational and linguistic contexts

FIGURE 11.6 The Role of Free and Systematic Variation (*Source*: From *Second language acquisition in context*, by R. Ellis, 1987a, Prentice Hall. Reprinted by permission.)

TABLE 11.11 Stages of IL Variation

Initial stage	*no* for all forms
Free-variation stage	*no/don't* interchangeably
Systematic-variation stage	*don't*/imperatives *no* and *don't*/indicatives
Categorical-use stage	*don't*/imperatives *no*/indicatives

competence. Competence, being a representation of abstractions, is not variable. Variability in this view is part of performance, that is, part of putting language knowledge to use at a given point in time. On the other hand, SLA researchers such as R. Ellis (1990b) and Tarone (1990) view L2 knowledge itself as variable. That is, it is not a matter of performance, but variability is part of what learners know about their L2. Eckman (1994b) argued that the resolution of this issue lies, not in theoretical argumentation over what is and what is not in the domain of a theory of SLA, as Gregg (1990) argued, but rather in empirical argumentation. On the side of those who argue that the appropriate domain for the study of SLA is linguistic competence, one would want to see evidence that such a theory could indeed account for the well-established phenomenon of variation. On the other hand, those who argue that variation data are crucial to a theory of SLA would want to show that those data cannot be accounted for in a competence model of SLA.

There is evidence to suggest that context is essential to understanding how acquisition takes place. Kormos (1999), in a review of studies dealing with monitoring and self-repair, showed that error detection is dependent on social context. For example, some contexts will necessitate a much greater level of accuracy than others. In other words, learners will self-correct according to the interlocutor and social context. It follows, then, that, if we assume that learners' self-correction contributes to learning, context is important in understanding what is and is not learned.

Another study relevant to the issue of context is that of Tarone and Liu (1995). They argued, on the basis of interactional data in three settings, that a learner's involvement "in different kinds of interactions can differentially affect the rate and route of the acquisition process" (p. 108). The data come from a Chinese NS learning English in Australia. At the onset of data collection, the child was almost 5 and, at the end, he was almost 7 years old. Data were collected in three situations: (a) in interactions with teachers, (b) in interactions with peers, and (c) in interactions with the researcher (in English, although the researcher was an NS of Chinese). Tarone and Liu considered the rate and route of the acquisition of interrogatives. With regard to rate, they argued that new forms nearly always emerge in one context (interaction with the researcher), then spread to the context with peers, and then to interactions with teachers. What is important, however, is the fact that new forms emerge from interactions themselves, and the differential demands of each interaction differentially allow for the emergence of new forms. In other words, different contexts push the learner to produce new forms to a greater extent than other contexts (see Tarone, 2000; R. Young, 1999).

[margin note: Different contexts push learners to produce new forms]

The issue has come to the fore in articles by Firth and Wagner (1997, 1998), Kasper (1997), Long (1997), Poulisse (1997), and Gass (1998). The arguments revert back to earlier arguments of what the domain of a theory of SLA is. The difference in opposing views can be reduced in simple terms to a difference in acquisition and use, a distinction that is often blurred. Acquisition is fundamentally a psycholinguistic process (see Tarone, 2000), and the question is: To what extent is that psycholinguistic process affected by social context?

[margin note: Acquisition is a psycholinguistic process]

Figure 11.7 refers to the general field of research as L2 studies, eliminating the misleading term *acquisition*. Acquisition is used: (1) in the true sense of acquisition (the process of obtaining new knowledge), (2) as a product, and (3) as language use. The left part of Figure 11.7 refers to areas of acquisition studies, where there is little dispute about the contribution of those areas to knowledge. The solid lines connecting SLA and contributing areas of research (transfer and universals) represent an unquestionable connection. Similarly, the solid lines between L2 use and its sub-areas represent unquestionable connections.[4] The dotted lines represent areas for which

[margin note: Meanings of acquisition]

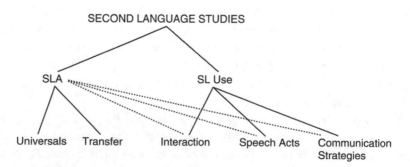

FIGURE 11.7 A Characterization of Research in SLA (*Source*: From "Apples and oranges: Or, why apples are not orange and don't need to be: A response to Firth and Wagner" by S. Gass (1998), *The Modern Language Journal*, *82*, 83–90. Reprinted by permission.)

argumentation and empirical evidence must be brought to bear. In Chapter 12, we make the argument that interaction is a central part of learning. In the current chapter, we have seen areas in which variation may also be considered to be important to an understanding of SLA.

Færch and Kasper (1987) similarly avoided the term *acquisition*. As they noted, "we have chosen to refer to the field of study as second language (SL) research, thus avoiding the bias towards developmental issues implicit in the more common term 'second language acquisition research'" (p. 5). Seliger (1983, p. 190) made a similar point about the importance of distinguishing between two major areas of concern. The first type of study is those

(a) which are concerned with describing how the learner uses what he has acquired either by describing the external sociolinguistic or ecological conditions for such use or by describing the internalized system which he maintains which enable him to produce interlanguage performance. Such research, while obviously important and legitimate begins with the assumption that the learner's output is the product of *a system in place*.

(b) The second type of study is that concerned with explaining how interlanguage sources of knowledge are learned or acquired in the first place. That is, the second area of study is concerned with describing the process of the *acquisition of interlanguage systems*.

Seliger (1983) suggested the term *Second Language Studies* rather than *Second Language Acquisition* to cover the broad range of topics currently embraced by this disciplinary area. This exchange of articles has had an impact on the field of SLA, as argued in Gass, Lee, and Roots (2007), by opening up the door to a wide range of studies examining language in context, in particular within a social–interactional framework. We have already discussed sociocultural theory; in the next section, our attention shifts to conversation analysis.

11.5 CONVERSATION ANALYSIS

Common to the approaches to SLA discussed in this chapter is an understanding of language quite different to that in other approaches discussed elsewhere in this book. Language is not an isolated phenomenon that can be understood out of its social context. Consequently, learning is not situated in an individual's cognition; that is, it is not an intrapsychological process. Rather, it is linked to social and local ecology; it is adaptive to an emergent set of resources that are embodied in social interaction, and learning is anchored in the social practices that a learner engages in. In this view, linguistic utterances are sensitive to, and reliant upon, their interactional context. Unlike other approaches discussed in previous chapters, with a social-interactive perspective on language, the linguistic code cannot be understood as an

social ecology

TABLE 11.12 Analysis from a CA Perspective (Mori, 2004)

Lines 39–49	Conversation analysis
David: °nan da?° 　　[°(wata-) .ss::° 　*What is it?[°(I–)* 　　.ss::°(39)	Line 40—asks question about what David wants to say. Focus is on the lack of indication of appropriate ownership Lines 39→ use of Japanese suggests the importance of Japanese in classroom
Alan: [ANO: 　　watashi 　　no uchi O::,　　　aa:: abunaiku:: 　　naritai 　　toKI::, (0.4) 　　d[onna:: *Uhm when I want my hou::se to be:: ah: dangerous ((incorrect)),* *(0.4) what ki::nd(40–41)*	Lines 40–41—Alan formulates question that turns out to be basically a translation of English, but has the opposite meaning in Japanese
Teacher: [abunaku 　　naritai? *want to be dangerous?* (42) 　　(0.4)　　　(43)	
Alan:　　　aa[::: *aa::: (44)* David:　　　[uheheh *uheheh(45)* Alan:　　　abu- aa[:::::: *dan- aa::::: (46)*	Lines 44–46—Alan reacts to repair and reflects on what he said Line 45—David points out that what Alan has said is not correct
David: [>°ie ie ie [a　　　ie°< *No nono oh no (47)*	Line 47—David points out that what Alan has said is not correct
Alan: [a! <u>yeah</u> abunaku 　　naritai toki:: *oh! yeah when we want to be dangerous (48)*	
	<u>Summary</u>: Focus is on the language used, who initiates the question, and whose "original" language problem it was. Uses body language and gaze to support idea of ownership of language problem. Motivations are attributed to different participants a propos each one's desire to show the teacher how he is engaged in the task and engaged in learning.

isolated phenomenon, ~~outside~~ of its social context. Nor can one understand how learning takes place without the support of the social context. Isolated grammaticality judgments or experiments of psycholinguistic processing make little sense within this paradigm.

Conversation analysis (CA) is one manifestation of a social-interactionist perspective. Evidence for learning is embedded in the changes in accomplishment of social activities, not necessarily in the linguistic code used to express those activities. In other words, because language learning is a social activity, it is important that the focus be on a speaker's orientation toward language. One can view language in this framework as linked to social and local ecology, and the linguistic encoding of utterances is sensitive to their interactional contexts.

language learning is a social activity

What evidence is there that learning has taken place within this framework? One piece of evidence is the kinds of activities in which learners engage (e.g., social interactions) and are successful. Thus, activities are the starting point for the study of human functioning, and one can view the changes in activities as evidence that learning has taken place. Only language in its natural environment serves as data in this framework, and only the interactional configuration of a speaker's orientation toward language serves as useful data. This is not to say that certain learning conditions (e.g., attentional focus) are not relevant. Rather, they are investigated through the course of activities.

Mori (2004) presents data from a Japanese classroom. Table 11.12 is an excerpt from that study, along with the type of analysis that was given to the data.

Kasper (2004) also presents data from learners of German (two excerpts) to show the contextual moorings necessary for interpretation (see Table 11.13).

A conversational analysis considers only what is observable, although this excerpt suggests that this is not always easy to avoid. We turn next to another area of language in context, that of communication strategies, or how language is used when the communication tool is not that of one's NL.

TABLE 11.13 Analysis from a CA Perspective (*Source*: Kasper, 2004.)

Interaction	Conversation analysis
NS: okay:,wie geht es dir? *how are you?*	The initial exchange is a routine adjacency pair. The NS questions the response by saying *warum* (why).
NNS: es geht gut, *I'm okay,*	This question shows the NS's "orientation to the event as a learning activity whose main purpose it is to
NS: ja?　　(.) warum? *are you?* (.) *why?*	'get the learner to talk,' and to her interactional charge as provider of environments for learner talk."
NNS: u::mm (.) ts uh i- °er° am wochendende? It was lange? (　)= *at the weekend? it was long?*	The NS responds as if this were a normal conversation. Therefore, the participants co-construct this "hybrid interactional form" that reflects "normal" conversation, as well as an event for language practice.
	Comment: This is clearly an emic perspective that attempts to get inside the head of the participants.

TIME TO THINK ...

Notice the detailed transcriptions used in CA? What differences do you see between the transcripts above and other transcriptions of interactions in this and earlier chapters in the book?

[handwritten margin note: 3 components: 1) problematicity 2) consciousness 3) intentionality]

11.6 COMMUNICATION STRATEGIES

[handwritten note: Attempt to express meaning when facing difficulty in L2.]

Learners are frequently faced with a need to express a concept or an idea in the L2 but find themselves without the linguistic resources to do so. A communication strategy must be employed. A communication strategy (to be differentiated from learning strategies, to be discussed in Chapter 14) is a deliberate attempt to express meaning when faced with difficulty in the L2.[5] Bialystok (1990, p. 1) reports the following incident:

> While living in Colombia, a friend of mine wanted to buy some silk. The Spanish word for silk, *seda*, however, is apparently used for a variety of synthetic substitutes. Eager to have the genuine product, my friend went into the local shop and, roughly translated from Spanish, said something like the following to the shopkeeper: "It's made by little animals, for their house, and then turned into material."

The person described in this episode did not know an unambiguous word for *silk*, nor the words for *silkworm* or *cocoon*, and thus had to resort to various descriptive devices to get the meaning across. The use of circumlocutions such as these is known as a communication strategy. Other examples of communication strategies include: approximation, literal translation, language switch, and avoidance. Examples are given in 11-23–11-26 (from Tarone, 1977).

(11-23) Approximation
       IL form = pipe
       TL form = waterpipe

(11-24) Literal translation
       IL form = He invite other person to drink
       TL form = They toasted each other

(11-25) Language switch
       IL form = balon
       TL form = balloon

(11-26) Avoidance
       IL form = the water (mumble)
       TL form = The water spills

In dealing with the notion of communication strategies, most researchers have *(handwritten: COMPONENTS OF COMMUNICATION STRATEGIES)* included three components in a definition of communication strategies: problematicity, consciousness, and intentionality (see Dörnyei & Scott, 1997, for an overview). Problematicity means that the learner, in using a communication strategy, must have first recognized that there is a problem of communication that must be overcome. *(handwritten: 1) PROBLEMACITY (recognize that there's a communication problem that must be overcome).)* Inherent in the notion of consciousness is the idea that learners must be aware that they have encountered a problem and be aware of the fact that they are, in fact, doing something to overcome that problem. Including intentionality as part of a definition of communication strategies implies that learners have control over various options and make choices about which option will have a particular effect (Bialystok, 1990). *(handwritten: 2) CONSCIOUSNESS do something to overcome the problem)*

There are difficulties with all of these components of a definition of communication strategies. First, much of the language used when there is a problem is the same type of language used when there is no problem. If this is the case, it is difficult to include problematicity as part of the definition. For instance, suppose that someone finds a *(handwritten: 3) INTENTIONALITY control over options to make choices.)* calculator (never having seen one before) and attempts to describe it to another person with the statement in 11-27 (Bialystok, 1990):

(11-27) C'est une petite machine avec des nombres.
"It's a small machine with numbers."

It is difficult to claim that, in this case, the speaker has recognized a problem, because the speaker is faced only with the task of describing an unknown object and has no idea that there is a name for the object. There are many instances of language use in which we are forced to describe objects; in these instances, there may be no sense of problematicity in the sense of being faced with a communication breakdown of any sort. If it is the case that nonproblematic language use makes use of the same type of strategy that is used in so-called problematic language use, it is difficult to use problematicity as a defining characteristic.

It is equally difficult to equate consciousness with communication strategies. As Bialystok noted, communication difficulties are solved with a small set of strategies, even in varied circumstances. Given the consistency of strategy use, it is not easy to make an argument about consciousness. That is, learners do not confront each new problematic situation with conscious choices, but rather pull from a small set of regularly used strategies. This is closely tied with the idea of intentionality. If choices are routinized, it is unlikely that there are conscious choices available.

In a review of the literature on communication strategies, Bialystok concluded that communication strategies do not have a privileged status. Rather, they are part of the *(handwritten: communication strategies)* same processes involved in nonstrategic language use:

They are the adjustments to the ongoing processes responsible for language acquisition and use that allow processing to be maintained. They are the means by which a system can perform beyond its formal limitations and communication can proceed from a limited linguistic system.

(1990, p. 147)

[handwritten margin: — Acquisition of L2 / — use of L2]

11.7 INTERLANGUAGE PRAGMATICS

[handwritten margin: Appropriate way to use words and sentences in L2. ↓ Go beyond the literal meaning]

Interlanguage pragmatics deals with both the acquisition and use of L2 pragmatic knowledge. We noted in Chapter 1 that, in learning an L2, one must learn more than just the pronunciation, the lexical items, and the appropriate word order; one must also learn the appropriate way to use those words and sentences in the L2. For example, we pointed out that one must learn that, within the context of a telephone conversation, *Is Josh there?* is not only a request for information but is also a request to speak with that person. In fact, children are known to respond to this question only on the basis of an information request, such that a typical response from a child is *yes*, with no further indication that he or she will call the person to the phone. Thus, a child in learning an L1 must learn to go beyond the literal meaning of utterances to understand the pragmatic force. The same can be said for L2 learning and use. Consider 11-28, an example of a conversation between a British tourist and an NS of Finnish, provided by Maisa Martin (personal communication):

(11-28) TOURIST: We're trying to find the railway station. Could you help us?

      NS OF FINNISH: Yes. (full stop)

In Finnish, the pragmatic force of a request for directions does not coincide with the pragmatic force in English. Thus, despite a Finnish NS's perfectly grammatical English, one often finds what might be interpreted as abrupt responses.

[handwritten margin: speech acts → functions of language: complaining, thanking, apologizing, refusing...!]

Much of the work in IL pragmatics has been conducted within the framework of *speech acts*. Speech acts can be thought of as functions of language, such as complaining, thanking, apologizing, refusing, requesting, and inviting. Within this view, the minimal unit of communication is the performance of a linguistic act. All languages have a means of performing speech acts, and presumably speech acts themselves are universal, and yet the *form* used in specific speech acts varies from culture to culture. Thus, the study of L2 speech acts is concerned with the linguistic possibilities available in languages for speech-act realization and the effect of cross-cultural differences on both L2 performance and the interpretation by NSs of L2 speech acts.

It is easy to imagine how miscommunication and misunderstandings occur if the form of a speech act differs from culture to culture. In 11-28, a native speaker of British English and a native speaker of Finnish were seen to differ in the ways they ask for directions and interpret requests for directions. When breakdowns occur, they are frequently disruptive, because NSs attribute, not linguistic causes to the breakdown, but personality (individual or cultural) causes. Thus, in 11-28, the British tourist is likely to have interpreted the Finnish speaker's response as rude and/or uncooperative. Or, similarly, consider the response to the situation in 11-29, produced in English by an NS of Hebrew (Cohen & Olshtain, 1993, p. 54):

(11-29) *Context*: You promised to return a textbook to your classmate within a day or two, after xeroxing a chapter. You held onto it for almost two weeks.

CLASSMATE: I'm really upset about the book because I needed it to prepare for last week's class.

RESPONSE: I have nothing to say.

It is clear that this response sounds rude to an NS of English and suggests a lack of willingness to apologize. However, what was meant was the translation of something equivalent to *I have no excuse*.

In terms of language learning, the area of pragmatics is perhaps one of the most difficult areas for learners, because they are generally unaware of this aspect of language and may be equally unaware of the negative perceptions that NSs may have of them as a result of their pragmatic infelicities. Miscommunication resulting from NS perceptions of relatively proficient NNSs (as opposed to learners with low-level comprehension and productive skills) is often serious in terms of interpersonal relations, because the source of the difficulty is more likely to be attributed to a defect in a person (or a culture; e.g., Americans are insincere, Israelis are rude, Japanese are indirect), than to an NNS's inability to map the correct linguistic form onto pragmatic intentions. As Gumperz and Tannen (1979, p. 315) point out, because the interlocutors "assume that they understand each other, they are less likely to question interpretations." This is precisely the communicative situation that Varonis and Gass (1985a, 1985b) labeled the most dangerous: Without a shared background, linguistic system, and specific beliefs, "when one interlocutor confidently [but inaccurately] interprets another's utterance, it is likely that participants will run into immediate problems because they do not share a common discourse space" (1985a, p. 341).

We take the speech act of refusal as a way of illustrating the speech-act research paradigm. Refusals occur in all languages. However, not all languages/cultures refuse in the same way, nor do they feel comfortable refusing the same invitation or suggestion. That is, not all cultures view the same event as allowing a refusal. How does this affect L2 use?

Refusals are a highly complex speech act, primarily because they often involve lengthy negotiations, as well as face-saving maneuvers to accommodate the noncompliant nature of the speech act. Because oral refusals are the result of an initial request (*Would you like to come to my house for dinner tonight?*), they preclude extensive planning on the part of the refuser.

A study by Beebe et al. (1990), in which the major concern was the existence of pragmatic transfer, deals specifically with L2 refusals. Four groups of NSs of Japanese and English (two NS controls and two L2 groups) filled out a **Discourse Completion Test** involving 12 situations, including refusals of requests, refusals of invitations, refusals of suggestions, and refusals of offers. In describing the setting, it was made clear that the refuser was to take the role of either a higher- or lower-status person. Each situation involved an initial segment of written speech, followed by a blank, and then followed by a rejoinder that forced the participants to write a refusal in the preceding blank. In analyzing the results, the authors considered the order of semantic formulae. Semantic formulae consist of such factors as expressions of regret, excuses, offer of alternatives, and promises. For example, a refusal to a dinner invitation at a friend's house might elicit the following response: *I'm sorry, I have theater tickets that night. Maybe I could come by later for a drink.* The order of formulae in this refusal is (a) expression of regret, *I'm sorry*; (b) excuse, *I have theater tickets that night*; and (c) offer of alternative, *Maybe I could come by later for a drink.*

The data from this research suggest evidence of pragmatic transfer. The range of formulae used is similar from language to language, but the *order* in which the formulae are used differs from language to language. For example, Table 11.14 shows Beebe et al.'s data from refusals of requests:

[handwritten margin note: pragmatic transfer]

TABLE 11.14 Order of Semantic Formulas in Refusals of Requests When Refuser is of a Higher Status (*Source*: Adapted from Beebe, Takahashi, and Uliss-Weltz, 1990.)

Japanese NSs	English by NSs of Japanese	NSs of American English
Positive opinion/empathy	Positive opinion/empathy	Positive opinion
Excuse	Excuse	Regret
		Excuse
		Can't

Other work involving refusals, but using a different methodology for data elicitation, suggests that a complex and negotiated interaction takes place in L2 refusal situations. Research by Houck and Gass (1996) and Gass and Houck (1999) on refusals, using role play as a means of data collection, showed that the refusals in these role plays were often lengthy interactions in which the participants negotiated their way to a resolution. An example is given in 11-30:

(11-30) *Setting*: The NNS is a guest in a family's home. The family members have gone to a neighbor's home for a few minutes. The NNS has been instructed not to let anyone in. The NS in this role play is playing the part of a cousin passing through town who would like to come in and wait for her cousin.

NS: Oh hi how are you doing?
NNS: oh fine thank you
NS: is uh is uh Quentin in
NNS: no uh no sh I'm not
NS: no he's not in
NNS: uh no no he's not in
NS: ahh where'd he go
NNS: ahh he goes to neighbor house
NS: ah well do you mind if—I'm I'm his cousin and I'm just passing through Lansing tonight and I'm I'm on my way to Detroit. I'm on a on a business trip and and uh I'd like to see him. I've got about half

an hour or so. Would you mind if I come in and wait for a minute or so until he comes back

NNS: ah no wait wait I'm a guest to uh this home the—I can't uh I don't uh uh um I can't I don't know what uh I do this situation then eh

NS: I'm sorry?

NNS: uh he he don't tell me uh

NS: ahh

NNS: if another person come in his home

NS: yeah yeah but I I I'm his cousin I'm sure it's going to be ok

NNS: but I don't know

NS: I I know it'll be all right

NNS: my first time to meet you I don't know you

NS: y'know actually this is the first time I've met you too how do you do

NNS: wait wait I think uh I think uh he came back uh not so late

NS: nice to meet you uh huh

NNS: yeh—uh please wait uh your car

In this example, the two speakers hemmed and hawed, cut each other off, self-corrected, modified and elaborated their positions, and generally became involved in negotiating semantic, pragmatic, and social meaning. The episodic nature of this example, with multiple refusals, requests, and rerequests, has not been documented in NS speech.

Acceptances are also difficult. Considering the following situation: A professor invites a number of students to lunch on the occasion of their graduation. An NNS replies to the invitation as follows:

(11-31) Thank you for the invitation. I would be willing to come.

To an NS of English, this response is strange, if not rude. Willingness suggests a possible reluctance, and one wonders who is doing whom a favor.

In coming to an understanding of L2 pragmatics, one must ultimately deal with the wide range of social variables that might determine how language is used. For example, what is the relationship between the two people involved in a particular speech event? Are they of equal status? Are they of equal age? Are they of the same sex? Are there other people witnessing the speech event? What is their relationship to those speaking?

IL pragmatics, in dealing with how people use language within a social context, must take into consideration, not only how language is used (i.e., how grammatical forms are used to express semantic concepts), but also what it is being used for, and who it is being used with.

The bulk of research on IL pragmatics has focused on pragmatic use rather than on acquisition (see Bardovi-Harlig, 2012, for a review). In pointing this out, Bardovi-Harlig (1999b) and Kasper and Schmidt (1996) made the important point that there is a dearth of studies dealing with changes in, or influences on, pragmatic knowledge.

325

Kasper and Schmidt also outlined a number of research questions that need to be addressed regarding the acquisition of L2 pragmatic knowledge. We list some of those questions here. As can be seen, they share themes with many of the issues related to other parts of language discussed in this book.

1. Are there universals of pragmatics, and how do these universals affect the acquisition of L2 pragmatic knowledge?
2. What are the issues relating to methodology and measurement?
3. What is the role of the NL?
4. Is development of L2 pragmatic knowledge similar to the development of L1 pragmatic knowledge?
5. Is there a natural route of development?
6. What is the role of input? Instruction? Motivation? Attitude?
7. What are the mechanisms that drive development?

To this, Bardovi-Harlig (2004c) adds the question of native-like attainment: "the question of whether (or to what extent) adults can acquire the pragmatics of a second language is at the heart of interlanguage pragmatics research" (p. 6).

Bardovi-Harlig (1999b) emphasized the need to consider the development of pragmatic knowledge together with grammatical knowledge. Hence, for learners who do not have a variety of verbal forms as part of their linguistic repertoire, their use of verbal forms to express pragmatic functions will be limited. Scarcella (1979), for instance, found that low-level learners relied on imperatives when making requests in every situation. As proficiency increased, imperatives were appropriately restricted to subordinates and intimates. Bardovi-Harlig (1999b, p. 694) gives the following example:

(11-32) *Context*: Graduate students addressing a faculty advisor.

> ADVISOR: OK, let's talk about next semester.
> NS: I *was thinking of* taking syntax.
> NNS: I *will* take syntax.

According to Bardovi-Harlig, this example suggests that the NNS shows an understanding of the core meaning of *will* as an indicator of the future, but does not understand the subtlety of use of the progressive as a marker of the future. Thus, the pragmatic extension of progressives to refer to the future is a later developmental stage (see also Bardovi-Harlig, 2012, for a review).

Bardovi-Harlig and Dörnyei (1998) conducted a study in which participants were shown video clips of events and were asked if they noticed pragmatic and/or grammatical infelicities, and how serious these were. Interestingly, the learning environment played a role in interpretation of severity of error. Second language learners were more sensitive to pragmatic errors than foreign-language learners, both in terms of noticing them and in terms of judging them as serious.

The range of issues in IL pragmatics is broad. Bardovi-Harlig (2004c) conducted a thorough review of a range of studies, including comprehension/judgment and production studies. She reports studies that show that learners can achieve native-like performance, and others that show the opposite. Many issues remain, including the evaluation of success (e.g., does t appear rude because they don't know the appropriate L2 pragmatic norms, or because he or she is a rude person?), as well as detailed descriptions of interactions with a range of learners and in a range of contexts.

TIME TO THINK ...

When learning your L2, what areas were difficult for you pragmatically? Did you make any gaffes based on an incomplete understanding of the L2 pragmatics? What were they? At what point did you realize that there was a problem?

11.8 LANGUAGE LEARNING IN A STUDY-ABROAD CONTEXT

In recent years, the role of context has spread to an understanding of the significance of living abroad for language learning. As one might imagine, the range of variables is extensive: how long, what living arrangements, what level of proficiency, to name a few. All of these questions are significant, as the question about language learning in a study-abroad setting cannot be answered as yes/no, but must be considered in light of numerous variables. As Collentine and Freed (2004) state, with relation to articles in a special issue of *Studies in Second Language Acquisition* (2004), they "provide no evidence that one context of learning is uniformly superior to another for all students, at all levels of learning, and for all language skills " (p. 164).

Some studies have attempted to understand broad issues, whereas others have focused narrowly on an understanding of what happens in a study-abroad setting. Included In these latter studies are issues of attitude and even culture shock. An example comes from Kinginger (2004), in her study of Alice, an American student from a low socioeconomic background, who had a driving passion to study French. When she arrived in France, her emotional reactions entered into the picture and became a source of frustration, interfering with her ability to learn.

Linguistic improvement in a study-abroad context depends on numerous factors, some of which are dependent on the length of the program, the social networks that students build, the living arrangements, and, of course, the language instruction provided (Churchill & DuFon, 2006). Magnan and Lafford (2012), in their review of learning in a study-abroad setting, report that longer stays yield more gains, and also yield a greater commitment to the study of language. A second issue relates to the language-learning backgrounds of the participants. There is a threshold to learning (see Lafford, 2006) such that lower-level students tend to learn more, particularly in the areas of oral interaction. However, they may not be as well prepared to deal with aural and written input (cf. Freed, 1990) as are more advanced learners. Without a doubt, living with a host family is beneficial for language and cultural learning. However,

Linguistic improvement in study-abroad contexts

327

this is not without problems, as interpersonal variables can enter into the picture, making language learning and cross-cultural understanding problematic. All of these issues must be understood against the backdrop of an individual's needs, orientations, personalities, learning styles, attitudes, goals, and motivation.

TIME TO DO ...

Interview a student who has studied abroad. Question him/her about changes in his/her language proficiency, about culture shock, and about his/her commitment to studying the target language and target culture. Would he/she recommend study abroad to other learners of the same L2?

11.9 CONCLUSION: SLA AND OTHER DISCIPLINES

In this chapter and preceding chapters, we have concerned ourselves with the relationship between SLA and other disciplines, notably linguistics, psychology, and sociolinguistics. Of course, these are not the only areas that relate to SLA. Others—such as neurolinguistics, sociology, anthropology, communication, artificial intelligence/natural-language processing, cognitive science, and philosophy—are also potential contributors to an understanding of the nature of SLA.

We have presented data to show how a linguist, a psycholinguist, and a sociolinguist would look at L2 data. But what about the opposite direction? What is the significance of SLA data to an understanding of these source disciplines? There are different perspectives one can take on this issue. Gass (1989) and Gass and Schachter (1989) argued, with regard to the fields of linguistics and SLA, that there are important, bidirectional implications to the relationship. We extend that argument to other fields as well. In other words, it is our belief that, not only is SLA dependent on other disciplines for models, theories, and ways of asking and answering questions, but it also gives back to those fields a broader perspective on the nature of human language and the human mind.

The argument made in Gass and Schachter (1989) focused on the bidirectionality of SLA and linguistics. With regard to the disciplines discussed in this and previous chapters, it is clear that the disciplines form the starting point of SLA research. However, there is another side to this story. If linguistics, psychology, and socio-linguistics (or whatever other disciplines might be involved) attempt to understand broader issues of the human mind, then any theory emanating from these disciplines must incorporate findings from L2s, for they too are systems produced by humans. Any theory that fails to account for L2 data, in this view, would be lacking.

A weaker view is one that attributes an enhancing position to SLA. That is, L2 data would not falsify linguistic theories, theories of psychology, or models of sociolinguistics, but would enhance those theories or models. What is meant by enhancement? In Chapter 5, we presented data from Kellerman on language transfer.

One of the important notions he developed was what he referred to as *psychotypology*. By understanding what a learner transfers and does not transfer from the NL, we gain insight into the organizational structure that humans impose on their NL. Thus, knowledge of that structure is gained through the window of L2 data. Using L2 data provides researchers with the means of viewing humans in an active, dynamic situation of language use.

POINTS TO REMEMBER

- Sociolinguistic approaches to SLA are focused on the context in which a language learner learns the L2.

- Sociocultural theory takes into consideration the mediation (language is a tool that mediates between us and our environment), regulation (of objects, others, and self), internalization (moving the relationship between an individual and his/her environment to later performance), and the Zone of Proximal Development (learning results from interpersonal activity).

- Gestures may make input more comprehensible to learners or may help learners to overcome lexical difficulties or solve interpersonal problems.

- Interlanguages show more variation, both syntactic and phonological, than native languages do. Some variation is linguistic in nature, and some is sociolinguistic. The native language, the task type, the conversational topic, and the interlocutor can all play a role in sociolinguistic variation.

- Second language studies refers to research on both the acquisition of a second language and the use of a second language.

- Social-interactional approaches consider language learning, not as an intrapsychological process, but rather as a process that occurs within a social context. Social interactional approaches include Conversation Analysis and Sociocultural Theory.

- Communication strategies are deliberate attempts to express meaning in the second language when faced with difficulty, such as not knowing a particular word.

- Interlanguage pragmatics refers to how learners must learn, not only the vocabulary and grammar of an L2, but also the appropriate ways to use those words and structures in the L2. Speech acts are functions of the language and include complaining, thanking, apologizing, refusing, requesting, and inviting.

- The effects of study abroad on language learning depend on many factors, including proficiency level, living arrangements, and time spent in the target language environment.

SUGGESTIONS FOR ADDITIONAL READING

Context, individual differences and pragmatic competence (2012). Naoko Taguchi. Multilingual Matters.

Alternative approaches to second language acquisition (2011). Dwight Atkinson (Ed.). Routledge.

Sociocultural theory in second language education: An introduction through narratives (2011). Merrill Swain, Penny Kinnear, and Linda Steinman. Multilingual Matters.

Sociocultural research on second language teacher education: Exploring the complexities of professional development (2011). Karen Johnson and Paula Golombek (Eds.). Routledge.

Sociocognitive perspectives on language use and language learning (2010). Robert Batestone (Ed.). Oxford University Press.

Second language teacher education: A sociocultural perspective (2009). Karen Johnson. Routledge.

Sociocultural theory and the teaching of second languages (2008). James Lantolf and Matthew Poehner. Equinox.

Gesture: Second language acquisition and classroom research (2008). Steven McCafferty and Gale Stam. Routledge.

Advanced language learning: The contribution of Halliday and Vygotsky (2006). Heidi Byrnes (Ed.). Continuum.

Language learners in study abroad contexts (2006). Margaret DuFon and Eton Churchill (Eds.). Multilingual Matters.

Living and studying abroad (2006). Michael Byram and Anwei Feng (Eds.). Multilingual Matters.

Sociocultural theory and the genesis of second language development (2006). James P. Lantolf and Steve Thorne. Oxford University Press.

Interlanguage pragmatics (2005). Kathleen Bardovi-Harlig and Beverly Hartford (Eds.). Lawrence Erlbaum Associates.

The ecology and semiotics of language learning: A sociocultural perspective (2004). Leo Van Lier. Kluwer Academic Publisher.

Pragmatic development in a second language (2003). Gabriel and Kenneth R. Rose. Blackwell.

Sociocultural theory and second language learning (2000). James P. Lantolf (Ed.). Oxford University Press.

Second language acquisition in a study abroad context (1998). Barbara Freed (Ed.), John Benjamins.

Communication strategies: Psycholinguistic and sociolinguistic perspectives (1997). Gabriele Kasper and Eric Kellerman. Longman.

Pragmatics (1996). George Yule. Oxford University Press.

Second language acquisition and linguistic variation (1996). Richard Bayley and Dennis Preston (Eds.). John Benjamins.

Variation in interlanguage morphology (1991). Richard Young. Peter Lang.

Communication strategies (1990). Ellen Bialystok. Basil Blackwell.

MORE TO DO AND MORE TO THINK ABOUT ...

1. In sentence 11-31, we saw an example of an NNS's lack of pragmatic competence when responding to a professor's invitation to lunch to celebrate graduation ("Thank you for the invitation. I would be willing to come."). Why is this response inappropriate in this situation? What would you respond to your professor in this situation? Think about your L2 if you have one. Would you respond in the same way as in your L1? If possible, try to find an NS of your L2 and ask them if they think your response is appropriate in the situation.

2. In a study by Maier (1992), written apologies were collected in a business context. The task that was given to both NNSs and NSs of English follows:

   > Yesterday was not your lucky day. On your way to a job interview in another city, your car broke down on the highway. By the time you reached a telephone it was after 5:00 and no one answered your call at the office. When you called this morning, the secretary in the personnel department told you that you were no longer being considered for the position because you had not only missed your interview, but you had also failed to call. You explained your situation and were told that the only possible way to get another interview would be to write a letter to the personnel manager. If your letter was convincing enough, you might get another chance. Write a letter to the personnel manager to explain why you missed your appointment yesterday. Persuade her to give you another interview.
   >
   > (Maier, 1992)

   Below are excerpts from the responses from the NSs and NNSs (the grammatical errors from the NNSs' responses have been edited out). Identify these responses according to whether you believe they were written by an NS or an NNS. What are the characteristics that led to your choice? Consider not only the style of what is said, but also the content of the responses. What do you think is the effect of the different responses on a reader?

   (a) Please accept this letter of apology for not being able to meet with you yesterday for our scheduled interview.

   (b) First, I want to say sorry for not attending the job interview.

(c) I apologize for missing the interview.

(d) I would like to take this opportunity to apologize for missing the scheduled meeting.

(e) Due to circumstances beyond my control, I was unable to participate in the scheduled interview on Wednesday.

(f) Last Thursday I missed your interview by accident.

(g) I would like you to give me another chance.

(h) I would very much appreciate your consideration once again and also be grateful to you to be able to reschedule our meeting.

(i) Please consider me once again for the interview.

(j) I would be very grateful if, under the circumstances, you would grant me another interview.

(k) I hope you will give me a chance to interview again.

(l) Would you please give me one more chance . . . Please, please give me one more interview.

(m) I would like to be a part of your organization.

(n) I am very interested in your company. Working in the ABC Corporation is my dream. I cannot give up my dream.

(o) I really, really want to work in your company. It is for this reason that I graduated from my school. I really want to make good use of my studies.

(p) I remain very interested in this position.

(q) I'm sure I'll never let you down.

(r) I believe that I can handle this job well enough. You already know what my background is.

(s) I'll call again at 10 on Wednesday morning, February 20, hoping to hear your positive response.

(t) I look forward to your reply.

(u) I hope you give a good prompt response.

3. What do the bar graphs in Figure 11.4 in this chapter suggest about the role of the phonetic environment in phonetic learning?

4. There are many speech acts that could be studied as part of L2 use. Take one of the following and gather data from L2 speakers in their use of the particular speech act: complaining, insulting, thanking, apologizing, requesting, refusing, complimenting, suggesting. In gathering data, consider such factors as gender, status, and familiarity. How do they affect your results?

5. As a follow-up to Problem 4, gather baseline NS data (from the L1 and the L2 of the speaker) and determine, if possible, the source of the NNS speech-act behavior.

6. In this chapter, we discussed the significance of the interlocutor in determining NNS speech patterns. Consider the data given in Figures 11A.1 and 11A.2. In this study, Young (1986) tape-recorded data from six

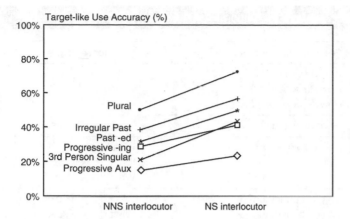

FIGURE 11A.1 Effect of Interlocutor on TLU Accuracy of Bound Morphemes and Progressive Auxiliary (*Source*: From *Variation in interlanguage morphology*, by R. Young, 1991, published by Peter Lang. Reprinted by permission.)

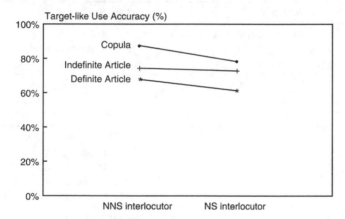

FIGURE 11A.2 Effect of Interloctuor on TLU Accuracy of Free Morphemes (*Source*: From *Variation in interlanguage morphology*, by R. Young, 1991, published by Peter Lang. Reprinted by permission.)

intermediate ESL learners. Each NNS was recorded in two separate interview situations, one with an English interviewer and one with an NNS interviewer.

How would you interpret these data? What conclusions can you draw regarding the effect of the interviewer on the speech patterns of these learners?

7. The data in Table 11A.1 are from a Japanese child learning English (Hakuta, 1974b). The data show her acquisition of questions in English. What can you determine from these data about this child's acquisition of past-tense questions? Is the acquisition of the past auxiliary (*did*) in questions a case of all or nothing, or does acquisition appear to be gradual?

TABLE 11A.1 Contexts Requiring Past Auxiliary *Did* in Question Form

Month	Present-tense forms	Past-tense forms
3	Why do you do? How do you make? How do you draw that?	
4	What do you do?	Where did you get that?
5	How do you break it?	What did she say? What did you say? What did you say?
6	Do you bought too? Do you bought this too? Do you put it? Do you put it? How do you put it? How do you put it?	What did you do? What did you say?
7	How do you do it?	How did you get it?
8	Do you saw these peppermint? Do you saw some star eye? Do you saw some star eye?	Did you call? Did everybody saw some blue hairs?
9		Did you see the ghost? Did you know we locked the door when we come to here?
10		Did you use some blue? Why did you do that? Why did you get this? Why did you go to a hospital? Why did you draw?
11		What did you say? What did camel say? Did I made that? Did I make that? Did you see that? Did you see me? Why did you put this? I didn't correct this one, did I?
12		Did you what?

8. The graphs in Figure 11A.3 are the results for four IL forms from Japanese and Arabic learners of English. All learners were tested using three elicitation measures: (a) a grammaticality-judgment test; (b) an oral interview, focusing on the learner's field of study; and (c) an oral narrative of events (video).

    Which of these three elicitation measures do you think requires the most attention to form? The least? Why?

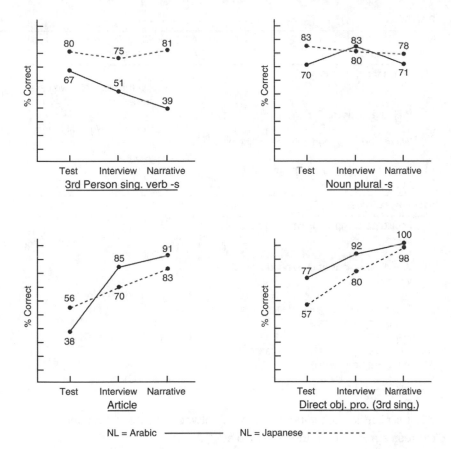

FIGURE 11A.3 Style Shifting on Four IL Forms by Two NL Groups on Three Tasks (TL—English). (*Source*: From "Variability in interlanguage use: A study of style-shifting in morphology and sytnax" by E. Tarone, 1985, *Language Learning*, *35*, 373–404, by Research Club in Language Learning. Reprinted by permission.)

Given your assessment of a progression from most attention to least attention to speech and the hypothesis that ILs would be most influenced by the TL on those tasks that required the most attention to form, how do these data bear on this issue? Are the results similar for all four IL forms? If not, what differences are there and how do you account for those differences?

9. The data in this problem reflect ways in which NSs and NNSs express agreement and disagreement (data from Porter, 1983). Part I deals with agreement and Part II with disagreement. The NSs and NNSs were discussing three stories, all of which included the need to rank characters in the story in terms of which character is the most reprehensible, which character should be saved, and which is the most useful for surviving at sea.

PART I

NSs Initial responses	NNSs Initial responses
1. That's the same as mine.	
	1. Well, in the first, third we have the same.
2. Well, that's close.	
	2. It's agree, no? We're agree.
3. We're kind of agreed on some of them.	
	3. We are agree.
4. Well, I thought she was pretty bad too, but . . .	

After some discussion	After some discussion
5. I could go along with switching a little bit.	
	4. All right.
6. Well, I'm somewhat convinced by what you say.	
	5. I changed my mind.
7. That is somewhat good idea, I guess, in the extreme case.	
	6. It's OK. I think is OK.
8. I think basically you have a somewhat legitimate argument.	
	7. Yeah, I change to seven.

What similarities/differences are there between the ways NSs and NNSs express agreement in these examples?

PART II

NSs	NNSs
1. (I ranked them—those two the worst.) Really, I ranked Abigail and Slug the worst.	
	1. No!
2. At this point, I was very arbitrary.	
	2. Well, I disagree with you.
3. But I don't know how it works.	
	3. I'm no agree with that.
4. I thought . . . but who would know for sure.	
	4. But that is not important.
5. Oh! It didn't even enter my head.	
	5. Is wrong.
6. I wouldn't necessarily agree with that.	
	6. No, no, forget it!
7. So I had him kind of towards the end of my list.	
	7. I'm not sure about
	8. I didn't really pay attention of that part.
	9. Is very difficult

What similarities/differences are there between NSs and NNSs in expressing disagreement? Considering both parts of this problem, do you think that the NNSs appear rude? If so, why? If not, why not? Do the NSs appear rude? Why or why not?

10. The following is a proposed taxonomy of communication strategies (modified from Tarone, 1977):

> Avoidance (message abandonment)
> Paraphrase
>> Approximation
>> Circumlocution
> Conscious transfer
> Literal translation
> Language switch.

Classify the following utterances (from Bialystok, 1990, pp. 63–69) into one of the above categories. All are produced by English-speaking children learning French. What problems, if any, do you encounter in the classification? Evaluate the strategy used here in terms of the notions of problematicity, consciousness, and intentionality described in this chapter.

swing:	C'est une sorte de, tu peux dire, chaise que quand tu "move." Des fois, c'est sur des arbres. [It's a kind of, you could say, chair for when you move. Sometimes it is in the trees.]
playpen:	On peut mettre un bébé dedans. Il y a comme un trou. [You put a baby in it. It is like a hole.]
wooden spoon:	On l'utilise pour prendre . . . si on mange . . . [You use it to make . . . if you eat]
garden hose:	Quelque chose qui est sur le mur et il y a un fausset avec un . . . [Something that is on the wall and there is a tap with a . . .]
spatula:	Quelque chose que tu utilises souvent pour enlever quelque chose. [Something that you use often for picking up something.]
garden chair:	De fois on le met dehors quand le soleil brille, ou sur la plage. [Sometimes you put it outside when the sun shines, or on the beach.]
can opener:	C'est un object que tu . . . tu ouvres des "tins," des bôites en métal. [It's something that you . . . you open the, tins, the metal boxes.]

can opener: C'est quand tu as une petite bouteille et il y a une machine et tu veux ouvrir la. [It's when you have a little bottle and there is a machine and you can [sic] open it.]

screwdriver: On utilise pour faire . . . il y a des gris, des rouges. Le rouge c'est comme on met tes mains au-dessus. L'autre part ça peut faire tu mettre les . . . [You use it to make . . . there are some grey and some red. The red is like you put your hands under it. The other part is so you can make the . . .]

wagon: Tu peux mettre des animaux ou des personnes dans et tu le tire. [You can put animals or people in it and you pull it.]

beater: C'est pour si on veut "mixer" [It's for if you want to mix.]

wrench: Quand tu as quelque chose qui est "stuck." Quand on a une bouteille du jus ou quelque chose et puis on veut ouvrir la petite chose que est sur la bouteille. [When you have something that is stuck. When you have a bottle of juice or something and then you want to open the little thing that is on the bottle.]

garden hose: Quand tu as un jardin et tu veux que le jardin a de l'eau. [When you have a garden and you want the garden to have water.]

child's car seat: C'est une chaise pour bébé que tu mets dans la voiture pour tu sois "safe," sauf. [It's a chair for a baby that you put in a car to keep you safe.]

rubber stamp: Le part brun regarde comme c'est une tête. [The brown part looks like a head.]

CHAPTER TWELVE

Input, Interaction, and Output

12.1 INTRODUCTION

It is commonly believed that learning an L2 involves learning the rules of grammar of the L2 (often in the form of memorization), along with vocabulary items and correct rules of pronunciation. Putting those rules to use in the context of conversation is then construed as a natural extension of grammar acquisition. This view implicitly assumes that language use does not vary from L1 situations to L2 situations, in that all that would be needed to successfully converse in an L2 would be to plug in the correct forms to say the same thing as one does in one's NL. In this chapter, we show how this view is an overly simplistic one. In so doing, we deal with the nature of the input to L2 learners, feedback to learners, and language production (output). We focus on the interrelationship of L2 use (especially conversation) and language learning.

12.2 INPUT

As we discussed in Chapter 4, earlier conceptualizations of L2 learning were based on a behaviorist view in which the major driving force of language learning (at least for children) was the language to which learners were exposed (the input). Because, in that view, learning a language involved imitation as its primary mechanism, the language that surrounded learners was of crucial importance. However, as behaviorist theories fell into disfavor, so did research interest in the input to the learner.

Interest shifted to the internal mechanisms that a learner (child or adult) brings to the language-learning situation, with research focusing on innateness and the nature of the innate system. As has been discussed elsewhere in this book, learners were viewed as creators of language systems, and, at least in the case of children, the input they received was of minor importance. If children only need to discover which of a limited number of possibilities are represented in their language, then it is possible that only a few instances of exposure are sufficient to trigger the appropriate language forms. As a consequence of this view, the significance of the input was minimized.

Corder, in 1967, made an important distinction between what he called input and **intake**. Input refers to what is available to the learner, whereas intake refers to what is actually internalized (or, in Corder's terms, "taken in") by the learner. Anyone who has been in a situation of learning a second/foreign language is familiar with the situation in which the language one hears is totally incomprehensible, to the extent that it may not even be possible to separate the stream of speech into words. This is input, because it is available to the learner; it is not intake, because it "goes in one ear and out the other," and it is not integrated into the current learner-language system. This sort of input appears to serve no greater purpose for the learner than does language that is never heard. Conceptually, one can think of the input as that language (in both spoken and written forms) to which the learner is exposed.

What is the nature of the input to a language learner? Ferguson (1971) noted that, in language directed toward linguistically deficient individuals (young children, NNSs of a language), NSs make adjustments to their speech in the areas of pronunciation, grammar, and lexicon. Speech directed toward young children he called **baby talk** (now known variably as **motherese**, **caretaker speech**, or **child-directed speech**); speech directed toward linguistically deficient NNSs he called **foreigner talk**.

Table 12.1, adapted from Hatch (1983), presents a partial listing of characteristics of foreigner-talk speech. In general, foreigner-talk adjustments reveal speech patterns that would not ordinarily be used in conversations with NSs. Some features are the same or similar to caretaker speech, the language spoken to young children. Some of the most salient features of foreigner talk include: slow speech rate, loud speech, long pauses, simple vocabulary (e.g., few idioms, high-frequency words), repetitions and elaborations, and paucity of slang.

Additional examples are given in Table 12.2. In these examples, which come from a single kindergarten teacher's instructions to her students, there is a gradation from talk to NSs to nonproficient L2 speakers. The teacher adjusts her speech as a function of the proficiency of her students.

TIME TO DO ...

Can you think of the ways in which you modify your speech to those who are less proficient than you? How does this compare with what you saw in Tables 12.1 and 12.2? If you have taught a foreign language, do you think that you have adjusted your speech? How?

Characteristics of foreigner talk are not always so obvious. Consider 12-1 and 12-2, which come from a survey on food and nutrition that NNSs conducted over the telephone (Gass & Varonis, 1985, p. 48):

TABLE 12.1 Summary of Foreigner-Talk Features (*Source*: Adapted from Hatch, 1983.)

Slow rate = clearer articulation

Final stops are released
Fewer reduced vowels
Fewer contractions
Longer pauses

Vocabulary

High-frequency vocabulary
    Less slang
    Fewer idioms
Fewer pronoun forms
Definitions:
    Overtly marked (e.g., *This means X*)
        Semantic feature information (e.g., *a cathedral usually means a church, that's a very high ceiling*)
        Contextual information (e.g., *if you go for a job in a factory, they talk about a wage scale*)
Gestures and pictures

Syntax

Short and simple sentences
Movement of topics to front of sentence
Repetition and restatement
New information at the end of the sentence
NS grammatically repeats/modifies learners' incorrect utterances
NS fills in the blank for learners' incomplete utterances

Discourse

NS gives reply within a question
NS uses tag questions
NS offers correction

TABLE 12.2 A Progression of Foreigner Talk (*Source*: Kleifgen, 1985.)

To an NS kindergarten class:	These are babysitters taking care of babies. Draw a line from *Q* to *q*. From *S* to *s* and then trace.
To a single NS:	Now, Johnny, you have to make a great big pointed hat.
To an intermediate-level NS of Urdu:	Now her hat is big. Pointed.
To a low-intermediate-level NS of Arabic:	See hat? Hat is big. Big and tall.
To a beginning-level NS of Japanese:	Big, big, big hat.
To a beginning-level NS of Korean:	Baby sitter. Baby.

(12-1) NNS: How have increasing food costs changed your eating habits?
NS: Well, we don't eat as much beef as we used to. We eat more chicken, and uh, pork, and uh, fish, things like that.
NNS: Pardon me?
NS: We don't eat as much beef as we used to. We eat more chicken and uh, uh pork and fish. . . . We don't eat beef very often. We don't have steak like we used to.

(12-2) NNS: There has been a lot of talk lately about additives and preservatives in food. In what ways has this changed your eating habits?
NS: I try to stay away from nitrites.
NNS: Pardon me?
NS: Uh, from nitrites in uh like lunch meats and that sort of thing. I don't eat those.

In these two examples, there was little indication of modified speech in the initial responses to the NNSs' questions. This is, perhaps, because the questions were scripted and rehearsed, and, despite the obvious nonnativeness of the caller (Spanish in the first example and Arabic in the second), there was an appearance of fluency. However, once the NNS said *Pardon me*, the NS in all likelihood realized the difficulty involved in the conversation and made modifications. In this case, the modification was not syntactic or phonological, as one typically expects with foreigner talk. Rather, the NS restated, repeated, and elaborated on the responses, the implication being that, given more information, the NNS would have an easier time understanding.

There are still other ways of modifying speech. From the same database come the following two examples:

(12-3) NNS: How have increasing food costs changed your eating habits?
NS: Well, I don't know that it's changed THEM. I try to adjust.
NNS: Pardon me?
NS: I don't think it's changed MY EATING HABITS.

In 12-3 (emphasis added), the NS specified the noun object more fully once the NNS indicated a lack of understanding. In 12-4 (emphasis added), implicit grammatical information is made more explicit by adding the subject and the auxiliary verb:

(12-4) NNS: How have increasing food costs changed your eating habits?
NS: Oh, rising costs we've cut back on the more expensive things. GONE to cheaper foods.
NNS: Pardon me?
NS: WE'VE GONE to cheaper foods.

In looking at a composite picture of these data, one finds that modification of one's speech when addressing NNSs is a variable matter, with NSs reassessing an

NNS's linguistic ability during the course of a conversational interaction. That is, one might engage in a conversation assuming either fluency on the one hand or lack of fluency on the other hand. However, as a result of a continuing conversation, one's assessment of the language ability, or language proficiency, of an NNS is likely to change. This will often result in a change in the speech patterns during the conversation. *[without language comprehension learning does not take place]*

What are the functions of foreigner talk in terms of language learning? Generally, one can claim that, by hearing speech that has been simplified in the ways just described, the L2 learner will be better able to understand. It is a given that, without understanding the language, no learning can take place. Although understanding alone does not guarantee that learning will occur, it does set the scene for learning. However, not all types of foreigner talk are created equal. In a review of the literature, Parker and Chaudron (1987) showed that simplifications resulting from discourse elaboration or modification of the conversational structure are more likely to aid comprehension than those simplifications that result from simplification at the linguistic level (i.e., foreigner talk). *[PARKER & CHAUDRON ↓ simplification and modification in foreign speech aid comprehension]*

Input, whether or not in the form of foreigner talk, is crucial in any account of L2 learning, but there is more to consider, as we will see throughout this chapter.

*[What factors determine COMPREHENSIBILITY?
1. pronunciation
2. ability to produce gramatically correct sentences
3. familiarity with a specific NNS
4. familiarity with non native speakers in general
5. familiarity with discourse topic]*

12.3 COMPREHENSION

Crucial to the success of any conversation is the ability to understand and to be understood. Lack of comprehension is a characteristic of many conversations involving NNSs. What factors determine comprehensibility?

The first area of concern in a discussion of comprehension is the NS's ability to understand the NNS's pronunciation. However, this is clearly not the only factor; the NNS's ability to use the L2 grammatically is yet another. In fact, in a study using a matched-guise format,[1] NS listeners were asked to judge sentences read by the same NNS (each of 14 NNSs read one pair of sentences, all of which were then randomized). The sentences varied according to whether or not they were grammatical. One version was grammatical, and the other was not. Given that one speaker read both versions, pronunciation remained constant. Examples of grammatical and ungrammatical pairs are given in 12-5 (from Varonis & Gass, 1982, p. 135):

(12-5) Grammatical: It is unusual for him to have a new car.
      Ungrammatical: He is unusual to have a new car.

      Grammatical: He always spends his holidays at home.
      Ungrammatical: He does spend his holidays always at home.

When asked to judge the NNSs' pronunciation on a two-pronged scale (*good* and *not good*), NSs for the most part judged the grammatical sentences as being spoken by a speaker with good pronunciation, and the ungrammatical sentences as spoken by a speaker with bad pronunciation. Although grammaticality had an influence on the majority of the responses, there were some speakers for whom grammaticality had little effect on NS judgments. These were the speakers who were judged, on an independent rating, to have very good or very bad pronunciation; that is, the two extremes. Thus, understanding an NNS's speech is dependent on at least the grammaticality of the NNS's speech, as well as the pronunciation. From these studies, we can conclude that, in interpreting NNS utterances, grammar is less important than pronunciation and vocabulary. Why should this be the case? The main explanation has to do with range of choices. There is a more limited number of grammatical possibilities (or grammar rules) in language than there are vocabulary items or possible pronunciations. That is, if a learner fails to mark agreement or puts items in the wrong order, there is a greater likelihood that an NS can fall back on his or her grammatical knowledge to make sense of what a learner is saying. However, if a learner uses an inappropriate or nonexistent vocabulary item, the NS may be sent down a comprehension path from which there is little possibility of return.

[margin note: in L2 output: Grammar is less important than pronunciation and vocabulary.]

TIME TO THINK ...

If grammar is less important than pronunciation and vocabulary, what are the implications for those language-teaching practices where the emphasis falls on grammar instruction as a way toward intelligibility?

The second area of concern in a discussion of comprehension is the NNS's ability to understand. In conversation, indications of understanding are given in a number of ways. Most common are what are called **backchannel cues**. These are generally verbal messages, such as *uh huh* or *yeah*, which are said during the time another person is talking.[2] When a conversation is face to face, as opposed to over the telephone, head nods can also serve the same function. To understand how important these backchannel cues are in conversation, consider a telephone conversation in which you are talking to someone who is not giving frequent indication that he or she is listening. In other words, consider a conversation in which there is complete silence on the other end. It does not take long before you begin to wonder if anyone is there. NNSs of a language quickly learn how to give appropriate backchanneling cues, without the concomitant ability to actually understand the conversation.

[margin note: Backchannel cues: messages, words, hints, gestures that show that the other person is understanding the conversation]

In the following conversation (from Varonis & Gass, 1985a, pp. 332–333), we see how the major NNS contribution to this conversation is the provision of backchannel cues. During the course of the conversation, the NNS has little understanding of what the NS is saying but uses backchannel cues as a way of keeping the conversation going. The setting: A native speaker of Spanish, studying English in the United States, called a store to inquire about the price of a TV set. However, he did not realize that, when he looked up the telephone number in the telephone book, he had looked up numbers for TV repair shops. The following is a transcription of that telephone conversation:

(12-6) *NNS*

2. Hello could you tell me about the price and size of Sylvania color TV?

4. Could you tell me about price and size of Sylvania TV color?

6. Uh 17 inch huh?

8. Yeah TV color

10. OK.

12. Uh huh.

14. Ah Sony please.

16. Or Sylvania.

18. Uh huh.

20. OK.

22. Hm hm.

24. Hm hm.

26. OK.

28. Hm hm.

NS

1. Hello

3. Pardon?

[Pause]
5. What did you want? A service call?

7. What did you want a service call? Or how much to repair a TV?

9. 17 inch.

[Silence]
11. Is it a portable?

13. What width is it? What is the brand name of the TV?

15. We don't work on Sonys.

17. Sylvania?

19. Oh, Sylvania OK. That's American made.

21. All right. Portables have to be brought in.

23. And there's no way I can tell you how much it'll cost until *he* looks at it.

25. And it's a $12.50 deposit.

27. And if he can fix it that applies to labor and if he can't he keeps the $12.50 for his time and effort.

29. How old of a TV is it? Do you know off hand?

30. 19 inch.

31. How old of a TV is it? Is it a very old one or only a couple years old?

32. Oh, so so.

33. The only thing you can do is bring it in and let him look at it and go from there.

34. New television please.

35. Oh you want to know [Silence] how much a new television is?

36. Yeah I want buy one television.

37. Do we want to buy one?

38. Yeah.

39. Is it a Sylvania?

40. Sylvania TV color.

41. Well, you know even, even if we buy 'em, we don't give much more than $25 for 'em. By the time we fix 'em up and sell 'em, we can't get more than

42. Hm hm.

43. $100 out of 'em time we put our time and parts in it.

44. Is it 17 inch?

45. Well, I don't . . . the only thing I can tell you to do is you'd have to come to the shop. I'm on the extension at home. The shop's closed. [Silence]

46. 19 inch? You don't have?

47. Do we have a 19 inch?

48. Yeah.

49. No, I've got a 17 inch new RCA.

50. OK. Thank you. Bye.

51. Bye

If we look only at the NNS's speech (the left column), it is clear that it is dominated by *yeah*s, *uh huh*s, *hm hm*s, and *OK*s. Yet, it is clear from the transcript that the NNS never realized that the NS was talking about repairing TVs. It is likely that this NNS's use of a large number of appropriately placed backchannel cues is what led the NS to continue the conversation (see Hawkins, 1985, for a lengthier discussion of the role of signals of apparent understanding and actual understanding).

The more familiar NSs are with NNS speech, either through individual contact or through language background, the easier it is for NS comprehension to take place. In a study in which familiarity with NNS speech was the object of investigation (Gass & Varonis, 1984), it was found that the more experience NSs had in listening to NNS speech, the more they understood. In particular, comprehension appears to be facilitated by three factors: (a) familiarity with a particular NNS, (b) familiarity with nonnative speech in general, and (c) familiarity with the discourse topic. Experience with a particular NNS will result in ease of comprehension. This is not unlike what happens with child speech, as it is frequently the case that young children are only understood by their caregivers. General experience in conversations with NNSs also facilitates comprehension. A teacher of English to NNSs, for example, is more likely to understand other NNSs than someone who has had little or no interaction with NNSs. Finally, if the topic of the discourse is familiar, it is more likely that understanding is aided by an NS's ability to fill in with prior knowledge when individual words may not be understood. As Labov and Fanshel (1977, p. 82) stated (based on NS conversations), "most of the information needed to interpret actions is already to be found in the structure of shared knowledge and not in the utterances themselves," where shared knowledge can refer, not only to actual real-world knowledge, but also to linguistic knowledge, such as pronunciation, grammar, and vocabulary.

We have seen that problems between an NS and an NNS can occur for a variety of reasons; when there is a lack of comprehension between speakers, they will often stop the flow of conversation to question what is not understood. In other words, they will negotiate the meaning of an utterance. To better understand this and how it differs from what happens in NS speech, we next look at the nature of NS conversation.

It is commonly acknowledged that, in most conversations, the discourse progresses in a linear fashion. When participants in a conversation share a common background (social/cultural/language), the turn-taking sequence proceeds smoothly, with each speaker responding to what the previous speaker has said, while maintaining his or her own sense of direction in the discourse. In other words, barring loud noises, inattentiveness, and so forth, participants in a conversation have an understanding of what has been said, of what was intended, and of how their contribution to the conversation fits in with previous contributions (by them or by others).

In discourse where there is not shared background, or in which there is some acknowledged *incompetence* (e.g., incomplete knowledge of the language being spoken, or lack of knowledge of the topic), the conversational flow is marred by numerous interruptions, as in the following example from Gass and Varonis (1985, p. 41):

(12-7) NNS: There has been a lot of talk lately about additives and preservatives in food. How—

NS: —a a a lot, a lot of talk about what?

NNS: Uh. There has been a lot of talk lately about additives and preservatives in food.

NS: Now just a minute. I can hear you—everything except the important words. You say there's been a lot of talk lately about what [inaudible]

347

NNS: —additive, additive, and preservative, in food—
NS: Could you spell one of those words for me, please?
NNS: A D D I T I V E.
NS: Just a minute. This is strange to me.
NNS: H h.
NS: Uh—
NNS: 'n other word is P R E S E R V A
NS: —oh, preserves
NNS: Preservative and additive.
NS: —preservatives, yes, okay. And what was that—what was that first word I didn't understand?
NNS: OKAY in—
NS: —Additives?
NNS: OKAY.
NS: —Additives and preservatives
NNS: Yes.
NS: Ooh right . . .

In this example, the entire exchange is one in which the NS seeks clarification about a word in the first question from the interviewer. She asks twice for clarification and then follows that up with a request for the spelling of the word she does not understand. This is followed by an incorrect repetition (*preserves*) and a further **clarification request** about another word (*additives*). Finally, there seems to be comprehension, and the interview moves forward.

[handwritten margin note: CLARIFICATION REQUEST]

[handwritten note: - language is learned via Input, output and feedback. - involves: negotiation, recasts, feedback. - learning is stimulated by communicative pressure]

12.4 INTERACTION

Interaction has been dealt with in SLA from a variety of perspectives, for example, psycholinguistically (see N. Ellis, 2009) and from a variationist perspective (see Tarone, 2009). Philp (2009, p. 255) describes current interaction research as seeking

to explain the cognitive processes involved in L2 learners' comprehension, processing, and use of language, including how learners make sense of input, recognize novelty or anomaly of form, and manipulate language to express meaning. It explores how the learners' noticing of form connects with and alters existing explicit and implicit knowledge, leading to reformulation of a developing system of L2 grammar and use.

The **interaction approach** accounts for learning through input (exposure to language), production of language (output), and **feedback** that comes as a result of interaction (see summaries by Gass and Mackey [2006, 2007] and Mackey, Abbuhl, and Gass [2012]). In the view of Gass (2003), interaction research "takes as its starting point the assumption that language learning is stimulated by communicative pressure and examines the relationship between communication and acquisition and the mechanisms (e.g., noticing, attention) that mediate between them" (p. 224). Interaction involves a number of components, including negotiation, recasts, and feedback. Similarly, Mackey et al. (2012, p. 8) state: "The interactionist approach posits that the interactional 'work' that occurs when a learner and his/her interlocutor (whether a native speaker or more proficient learner) encounter some kind of communication breakdown is beneficial for L2 development." In what follows, we discuss the concept of **negotiation of meaning**. This is followed by a section on output, within which we further discuss negotiation and focus on recasts, as parts of a broader concept of feedback.

When the flow of conversation is interrupted, as in 12-7, participants often compensate by questioning particular utterances (*You say there's been a lot of talk about what?*) and/or requesting conversational help (*could you spell one of those words for me?*). In other words, they negotiate what was not understood. Negotiation of this sort allows participants to maintain, as well as possible, equal footing in the conversation, providing the means for participants to respond appropriately to one another's utterance and to regain their places in a conversation after one or both have slipped.

Thus, negotiation of meaning refers to those instances in conversation when participants need to interrupt the flow of the conversation in order for both parties to understand what the conversation is about, as in example 12-8 (see also 12-7). In conversations involving NNSs, negotiations are frequent, at times occupying a major portion of the conversation. An example is given in 12-8 (Varonis & Gass, 1985b, pp. 78–79):

(12-8)   J = NS of Japanese; S = NS of Spanish

    J: And your what is your mm father's job?

    S: My father now is retire.

    J: Retire?

    S: Yes.

    J: Oh yeah.

    S: But he work with uh uh institution.

    J: Institution.

    S: Do you know that? The name is . . . some thin like eh control of the state.

    J: Aaaaaaaah.

    S: Do you understand more or less?

    J: State is uh . . . what what kind of state?

    S: It is uhm.

    J: Michigan State?

    S: No, the all nation.

    J: No, government?

    S: All the nation, all the nation. Do you know for example is a the the institution mmm of the state mm of Venezuela.

[handwritten margin note: Meaning Negotiation: → negotiation of comprehension.]

349

J: Ah ah.

S: Had to declare declare? her ingress.

J: English?

S: No. English no (laugh) . . . ingress, her ingress.

J: Ingress?

S: Ingress. Yes. I N G R E S S more or less.

J: Ingless.

S: Yes. If for example, if you, when you work you had an ingress, you know?

J: Uh huh an ingless?

S: Yes.

J: Uh huh OK.

S: Yes, if for example, your homna, husband works, when finish, when end the month his job, his boss pay—mm—him something

J: Aaaah.

S: And your family have some ingress.

J: Yes ah, OK OK.

S: More or less OK? And in this in this institution take care of all ingress of the company and review the accounts.

J: OK I got, I see.

S: OK my father work there, but now he is old.

In the preceding conversation, the speakers spend the majority of their time involved in straightening out the meaning of words, specifically, *retire*, *institution*, *state*, and *ingress* ("income"). In conversations involving nonproficient NNSs, exchanges of the sort exemplified in 12-8 are frequent, with considerable effort going into resolving nonunderstandings as opposed to exchanging ideas or opinions (the typical material of conversation).

As we have seen, not only is the form of the speech produced by NSs modified in conversations with NNSs, but also the structure of the conversation itself. Long (1980) was the first to point out that conversations involving NNSs exhibited forms that did not appear to any significant degree when only NSs were involved. For example, **confirmation checks** (*Is this what you mean?*), **comprehension checks** (*Do you understand? Do you follow me?*), and clarification requests (*What? Huh?*) are peppered throughout conversations in which there is a nonproficient NNS participant. Examples of each are given in 12-9–12-12.

(12-9)   Comprehension check
NNS: I was born in Nagasaki. Do you know Nagasaki?

(12-10)   Comprehension check
NNS1:   And your family have some ingress.
NNS2:   Yes ah, OK OK.
NNS1:   More or less OK?

350

(12-11) Confirmation check

NNS1: When can you go to visit me?

→   NNS2: Visit?

(12-12) Clarification request

NNS1: . . . research.

NNS2: Research, I don't know the meaning.

TIME TO DO ...

Find another speaker of your L2 in your class. Ask that person to draw a picture as you describe a picture from a magazine in your L2. Don't let him/her see the picture as you describe it. Note any confirmation checks, comprehension checks, or clarification requests that occur during your interaction.

Furthermore, different kinds of questions are asked, often with the answer being suggested by the NS immediately after the question is asked (example 12-13):

(12-13) From Long (1983, p. 180)

NS: Do you like California?

NNS: Huh?

NS: Do you like Los Angeles?

NNS: Uhm . . .

NS: Do you like California?

NNS: Yeah, I like it.

In 12-13, there is an indication of nonunderstanding (*Huh?*), with the result being a narrowing down of the topic (*California* → *Los Angeles*), followed by a final repetition of the original question. These conversational tactics provide the NNS with as much information as possible as she attempts to ascribe meaning to the NS's stream of sounds.

In 12-14, the NS asks an "or-choice" question. That is, the NS not only asks a question, but also provides the NNS with a range of possible answers. The example is from a personal observation made in an ESL classroom, during the first class back after a long holiday break. The teacher had asked a student what he did over the break. He responded that he had just relaxed.

(12-14) NS: Where did you relax?

[Silence]

NS: Did you relax out of town or in East Lansing?

NNS: East Lansing.

Recognition of this mode of NNS discourse is exploited in the play *Fully Committed* by Becky Mode (1995), in which the NS gives multiple choices when the NNS does not understand. The setting is a restaurant reservations office (telephone).

(12-15) Sam: How can I help you?
  Watanabe: My name is Watanabe. "W" as in Wisconsin, "A" as—
  S: Okay. How can I help you?
  W: I want to take a table.
  S: Okay, when would you like to come in?
  W: We are four people.
  S: All right. When would you like to come in?
  W: Four people.
  S: Okay . . . What day of the week would you like to come in?
  W: Four
  S: I'll be right with you ma'am. [*Puts her on hold, takes a deep breath, then returns*] Sorry about that.
  W: No have four?
  S: No, no. [*Trying a new tactic*] Four people on Monday? Tuesday? Wednesday?
  W: Ohhh! Tuesday.
  S: Okay, Tuesday. Would you like to come in for lunch or dinner?
  W: Lunch!
  S: Okay! Lunch on Tuesday. What time?
  W: Seven p.m.
  S: Ma'am. That's dinner
  W: Dinner?
  S: Yes seven p.m. is dinner and we are fully committed for dinner on Tuesday.
  W: Ful-ly?
  S: We don't have any tables.
  W: Oh, I call you back.

In this excerpt, Sam, the NS, clearly understands that this is a difficult conversation and offers choices (*Monday? Tuesday?*) and rephrases fully committed (*We don't have any tables*), when it is apparent that the NNS does not know that word.

There are other, perhaps more subtle, differences between conversations involving only NSs and those involving at least one nonproficient NNS. For example, in conversations with NNSs, there is frequently a willingness on the part of everyone to change topics, often abruptly.

(12-16) Topic shift
  NNS1: Are you going to attend today's party?
  NNS2: I don't know yet, but probably I'll attend. [long pause, with intermittent "hm"s] So when will you go back to Japan?

Topic shifts may also result from prolonged attempts to negotiate the meaning, as in 12-17 (from Hatch, 1978, pp. 420–421).

(12-17) NS: Who is the best player in Colombia?
NNS: Colombia?
NS: Does uh . . . who is *the* Colombian player?
NNS: Me?
NS: No, in Colombia, who is *the* player?
NNS: In Colombia plays. Yah.
NS: No, on your team. On the Millionarios.
NNS: Ah yah, Millionarios.
NS: No, on the Millionarios team.
NNS: Millionarios play in Colombia. In Sud America. In Europa.
NS: Do, do they have someone like Pele in Colombia?
NNS: Pele? In Colombia? Pele?
NS: In Colombia? Who is, who is "Pele" in Colombia? Do you have someone?
NNS: In Bogota?
NS: Yeah, who is the best player?
NNS: In Santo de Brazil?
NS: OK [gives up] and are you center forward?

In all of the examples provided in this section, the effect of NS and NNS modifications (whether intentional or not) is to aid the NNS in understanding. This reduces the burden for the NNS, in that he or she is assisted by others in understanding and in producing language appropriate to the situation. However, one could also argue that outward signs of negotiation and resolution of that negotiation are only strategies to show solidarity, rather than true indications of meaning negotiation (Hawkins, 1985; Aston, 1986).

One should not be misled, however, into thinking that comprehension is the same as acquisition. Comprehension, in the usual sense of the word, refers to a single event, whereas acquisition refers to a permanent state. (Other ways of viewing the notion of comprehension will be discussed in Chapter 16.)

In Chapter 11, we discussed conversation analysis (section 11.5). We presented data from Mori (2004), with her CA interpretation, and data from Kasper (2004), with her CA interpretation. Below we present the same snippets of conversation with an interpretation that would be given by someone within an interactionist framework. We include the CA interpretation for purposes of comparison. See Table 12.3.

Data from Kasper (2004) presented in Table 12.4 below, come from a German classroom. We present the excerpts and the analyses from an interactionist perspective and from a CA perspective, to make it easier to see how the difference in orientation leads to different foci of the analysis.

TABLE 12.3 Data from Mori (2004) with a CA and Interactionist Perspective

Lines 39–49	Conversational analysis	Input–interaction

David: °nan   da?°
    [((wata-)
.ss::°
What is it? [((I–) .ss::((39)
Alan: [ANO:
    watashi
    no   uchi   O::,
    aa:: abunaiku::
    naritai
    toKI::, (0.4)
    d[onna::
Uhm when I want my hou::se
to be:: ah: dangerous
((incorrect)), (0.4)
what ki::nd (40–41)
	Line 40—asks question about
	what David wants to say.
	Focus is on the lack of indication
	of appropriate ownership
	
	Lines 39→ use of Japanese
	suggests the importance of
	Japanese in classroom
	
	Lines 40–41—Alan formulates
	question that turns out to be
	basically a translation of English,
	but has the opposite meaning
	in Japanese
		Line 39—request for assistance
		—probably for a word
		Line 40—serves as a trigger for
		feedback for teacher

Teacher: [abunaku naritai? *want to be dangerous? (42)* (0.4) (43)		Line 42—teacher provides Line 43—pause possibly indicates "thinking" where Alan is attempting to process the feedback
Alan: aa[::: *aa::: (44)* David: [uhe heh *uhe heh (45)* Alan: abu- aa[::::::: *dan- aa::::: (46)*	Lines 44–46—Alan reacts to repair and reflects on what he said Line 45—David points out that what Alan has said is not correct	Line 44—Alan indicates an understanding of feedback Line 45—David also indicates an understanding of what was wrong with Alan's utterance (see Pica, 1992; Mackey, 1999; Ohta, 2001, about learning that can take place by nonparticipants)
David: [>(ie ie ie [a ie(< *No no no oh no (47)*	Line 47—David points out that what Alan has said is not correct	Line 47—David indicates an understanding of what was wrong with Alan's utterance
Alan: [a! yeah abunaku naritai toki:: *oh! yeah when we want to* *be dangerous (48)*		Line 48—Alan accepts feedback recognizing a problem with his utterance
	Summary: Focus is on the language used, who initiates the question and whose "original" language problem it was. Uses body language and gaze to support idea of ownership of language problem. Motivations are attributed to different participants a propos each one's desire to show the teacher how he is engaged in the task and engaged in learning	**Summary**: Focus is on feedback that student receives and the perception of that feedback by both participants, resulting in an apparent recognition of the correct form. Uses pauses as an indication of "thinking" time that precedes verbal recognition. No social motivations are attributed. Researchers search for evidence of learning (e.g., pauses, repetitions, verbal recognition of learning)

Data from Kasper (2004) with a CA and Interactionist Perspective

Interaction	Conversational analysis	Input–interaction
NS: okay:, wie geht es dir? *how are you?* NNS: es geht gut, *I'm okay,* NS: ja? (.) warum? *are you? (.) why?* NNS: u::mm (.) ts uh i- °er° am wochendende? It was lange? ( )= *at the weekend? it was long?*	The initial exchange is a routine adjacency pair. The NS questions the response by saying *warum* (why). This question (?) shows the NS's "orientation to the event as a learning activity whose main purpose it is to 'get the learner to talk,' and to her interactional charge as provider of environments for learner talk." The NS responds as if this were a normal conversation. Therefore, the participants co-construct this "hybrid interactional form" that reflects "normal" conversation" as well as an event for language practice	An input–interaction analysis of this exchange would focus, if comments were made on this exchange, on the learner and her reaction to the strange NS response, with emphasis on the hesitation phenomena of the NNS and would "suggest" that this might be an indication of the fact that she was possibly thrown off by the unexpected response to a seemingly formulaic response. The input–interaction analysis would only look at surface facts and would not ascribe motivation to the NS as to why she responded in the way she did. Or, if such an interpretation were made, it would be bolstered by additional evidence, such as stimulated recall
	Comment: This is clearly an emic perspective that attempts to get inside the head of the participants.	**Comment**: The need to bolster arguments from the participants is, of course, antithetical to a CA analysis, given the distance that the researcher keeps from the investigated parties and the need to interpret from "afar"

As can be seen from these two examples, a transcription within the interactionist perspective does not include the same level of detail or elaboration, as these aspects of conversation do not enter into what might count as learning. Activities are not central to an interactionist framework, and thus learning as increased accomplishment within an activity is not relevant (see also Gass, 2004).

TIME TO THINK ...

Think about your own experiences learning an L2. Have you had experiences negotiating meaning with an NS of the L2 or with a more proficient NNS of the L2? How were the breakdowns in communication repaired?

12.5 OUTPUT

Up to this point, we have dealt with the concept of input. We have also focused on conversational or interactional modifications that come as a result of an exchange in which a non-proficient NNS is involved. There is one final concept that needs to be mentioned, and that is **comprehensible output** (see Swain, 1985, 1995, 2005).

Input alone is not sufficient for acquisition, because, when one hears language, one can often interpret the meaning without the use of syntax. For example, if one hears only the words *dog*, *bit*, *girl*, regardless of the order in which those words occur, it is likely that the meaning *The dog bit the girl* is the one that will be assumed, rather than the more unusual *The girl bit the dog*. Similarly, if one hears a sentence such as *This is bad story*, one can easily fill in the missing article. Little knowledge, other than knowing the meanings of the words and knowing something about real-world events, is needed.

This is not the case with language production or output, because one is forced to put the words into some order. Production, then, "may force the learner to move from semantic processing to syntactic processing" (Swain, 1985, p. 249). In fact, the impetus for Swain's original study was the lack of L2 development by immersion children, even after years of academic study in that L2. Swain studied children learning French in an immersion context, suggesting that what was lacking in their development as native-like speakers of French was the opportunity to use language productively, as opposed to using language merely for comprehension. She compared results on a number of different grammatical, discourse, and sociolinguistic measures for sixth-grade children in a French immersion setting and sixth-grade native-French-speaking children. The lack of proficiency on the part of the immersion children, coupled with their apparent lack of productive use of French, led Swain to suggest the crucial role for output in the development of an L2.

It is trivial to state that there is no better way to test the extent of one's knowledge (linguistic or otherwise) than to have to use that knowledge in some productive way—whether it be explaining a concept to someone (i.e., teaching) or writing a computer program, or, in the case of language learning, getting even a simple idea across. However, output has generally been seen, not as a way of creating knowledge, but as a way of practicing already existing knowledge. This was certainly the thrust behind early methods of language teaching in which the presentation–practice (i.e., drill and repetition) mode was in vogue. A second traditional role assigned to output was that it was the way in which additional (and perhaps richer) input could be elicited. The idea that output could be part of learning was not seriously contemplated prior to Swain's important paper in 1985, in which she introduced the notion of comprehensible output, or pushed output. What is meant by this concept is that learners are pushed or stretched in their production as a necessary part of making themselves understood. In so doing, they might modify a previous utterance, or they might try out forms that they had not used before.

Comprehensible output refers to the need for a learner to be "pushed toward the delivery of a message that is not only conveyed, but that is conveyed precisely, coherently, and appropriately" (Swain, 1985, p. 249). In a later explication of the concept, Swain claimed that,

> output may stimulate learners to move from the semantic, open-ended, non-deterministic, strategic processing prevalent in comprehension to the complete grammatical processing needed for accurate production. Output, thus, would seem to have a potentially significant role in the development of syntax and morphology.
>
> (Swain, 1995, p. 128)

Mackey (2002) demonstrates this notion through the following example and the comments that followed this learner's struggle with the appropriate word.

(12-18) Example of pushed output

> NNS: And in hand in hand have a bigger glass to see.
> NS: It's err. You mean, something in his hand?
> NNS: Like spectacle. For older person.
> NS: Mmmm, sorry I don't follow, it's what?
> NNS: In hand have he have has a glass for looking through for make the print bigger to see, to see the print, for magnify.
> NS: He has some glasses?
> NNS: Magnify glasses he has magnifying glass.
> NS: Oh aha I see a magnifying glass, right that's a good one, ok.

Recall comments following this episode:

> In this example I see I have to manage my err err expression because he does not understand me and I cannot think of exact word right then. I am thinking thinking it is nearly in my mind, thinking bigger and magnificate and eventually magnify. I know I see this word before but so I am sort of talking around around this word but he is forcing me to think harder, think harder for the correct word to give him so he can understand and so I was trying. I carry on talking until finally I get it, and when I say it, then he understand it, me.

As is clear from these comments (made immediately following the original exchange), this learner struggled to come up with the appropriate expression. She was pushed through the negotiation sequences to make her language clearer.

In what ways can output play a central role in the learning process?[3] We consider four possible ways that output may provide learners with a forum for important language-learning functions: (a) receiving crucial feedback for the verification of these hypotheses; (b) testing hypotheses about the structures and meanings of the target language; (c) developing automaticity in IL production; and (d) forcing a shift from more meaning-based processing of the L2 to a more syntactic mode.

Izumi et al. (1999) specifically investigated the noticing function of output, finding partial support for this hypothesis and pointing out the need to balance cognitive and linguistic demands. In particular, participants were exposed to written input and had to underline words that they felt would be essential to their subsequent reproduction of the same passage. The experimental group was then given a production task, whereas the control group was not. This was followed by a second exposure (again with underlining) and a second reproduction by the experimental group. Participants noticed the targeted feature (past hypothetical conditional, such as, *If Kevin got up early in the morning, he would eat breakfast*) and incorporated the feature into their output, but this did not carry over into a posttest. In a second phase, both groups produced a written essay on a topic that called for the use of the target form. Despite the fact that the results after the first phase did not show retention on the posttest, there was greater improvement on this written essay by those who had produced output than by those in the control group, who had not been involved in a production task in phase 1, thereby suggesting that output may indeed be important for acquisition.

Izumi and Izumi (2004), in a study on the acquisition of RCs, had an experimental treatment that allowed for an output group and a non-output group, finding that the output group did not outperform the non-output group. Their output task was a production task that may not have allowed for the focus on form that they had intended. As discussed in Chapter 10, Uggen (2012), in her study of the role of production, found that subsequent noticing of vocabulary was influenced by prior production. She also found evidence that production impacted a learner's awareness of his/her L2 knowledge gap. This was not the case, however, for all structures examined; structural complexity played a role.

In another study, McDonough (2005) found evidence for language use (output), but her participants were engaged in an interactive task that forced attention to form, unlike the type of task in Izumi and Izumi's study. She tested the output hypothesis directly in her study of Thai learners of English questions in which four groups carried out communicative tasks. The four groups focused on salience (enhancement) and opportunity to modify following feedback. Examples from each of the four groups are provided below:

(12-19) Enhanced opportunity to modify

> NNS: What angel doing in this situation?
> NS: What angel doing? Huh?
> NNS: What is angel doing?

In this example, the response directs attention to the inaccurate form, followed by a clarification request that gives the learner an opportunity to modify his/her output.

(12-20) Opportunity to modify

> NNS: What happen for the boat?
> NS: What?
> NNS: What's wrong with the boat?

Here, there is a request for clarification, but no enhancement or drawing attention to the problematic part of the utterance.

(12-21) Feedback without opportunity to modify

> NNS: What we do with it?
> NS: What we do? Uh, let's see well we could talk about the purpose if you want.

The NS in this example points to the problem through the response by making the error salient, but continues without giving the learner an opportunity to modify her language.

(12-22) No feedback

> NNS: Where you going the last holiday?
> NS: To Laos

Despite the error, there is no feedback, only a response. This detailed study provides evidence that the best predictor of acquisition, in this case operationalized by the acquisition of more advanced questions, is the opportunity to modify one's speech.

12.5.1 Feedback

Feedback is an important source of information for learners. Most generally, it provides them with information about the success (or, more likely, lack of success) of their utterances and gives additional opportunities to focus on production or comprehension. There are numerous ways of providing feedback to learners, from the explicit (stating that there is a problem) to the implicit (feedback during the course of an interaction). R. Ellis (2008) refers to input-providing feedback (e.g., recasts—see section 12.5.1.2) and output-promoting feedback (e.g., *What did you say?*). In this and the subsequent sections, we address the role of feedback and suggest ways that different types of feedback may impact learning. Figure 12.1 illustrates this concept with the mediating factor of attention.

Through interaction, learners' attention is drawn to some element(s) of language, with the possible consequence that that element/those elements will be incorporated into a learner's developing system.

TIME TO THINK ...

Think about language teaching (you as a teacher, or you as a student): how do you feel when you are given feedback? Some argue that it is humiliating for students and don't provide feedback. Do you agree? Why or why not? Is there a difference between feedback on oral production and on written production? Is one more acceptable than the other? Why or why not?

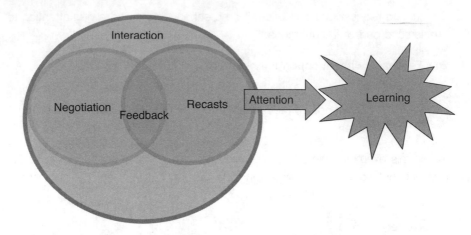

FIGURE 12.1 A Model of Interaction (*Source*: From "Input, interaction, and output: an overview" by S. Gass and A. Mackey, 2006. In K. Bardovi-Harlig and Z. Dörnyei (Eds.), *Themes in SLA Research, AILA Review*, 3–17. With permission by John Benjamins Publishing Company, Amsterdam/ Philadelphia, www.benjamins.com.)

In Chapter 7, where we discussed the role of negative evidence (information that a particular utterance is deviant vis-à-vis TL norms), it was pointed out that, at least with regard to children, it cannot be a necessary condition for acquisition. What, then, about L2 learning? It is undoubtedly the case that adults (at least those in formal learning situations) do receive more correction than children, and it may further be the case that adults must have negative evidence (i.e., that it is a necessary condition) in order to accomplish the goal of learning an L2 (Gass, 1988a; Schachter, 1988; Birdsong, 1989; Bley-Vroman, 1989). Although this research has been based primarily on theoretical arguments, there is some empirical evidence that negative evidence is, in some instances, necessary for SLA.

White (1991) investigated the question of how learners learn not to do something in the L2 that is present in the NL, in this case adverb placement by French children learning English. French learners of English have to learn that English allows subject–adverb–verb (SAV) order (*He always runs*) and that it does not allow subject–verb–adverb–object (SVAO) order (**He drinks always coffee*). White's study consisted of five classes of French NSs learning English as an L2 (two classes at Grade 5 and three classes at Grade 6) and one control group of monolingual NSs of English. One of the Grade 5 groups and two of the Grade 6 groups were given explicit instruction on adverb placement, as well as exercises and correction on adverb placement; the other groups were given instruction on questions using the same types of exercises, but no explicit instruction on adverbs. The classroom treatment lasted two weeks. All children were given pretests, posttests immediately following the treatment sessions, a second posttest five weeks later, and a follow-up test a year later. The tests consisted of grammaticality-judgment tasks (with correction), preference tasks, and a sentence-manipulation task. By comparing the groups' performance, White was able to show that negative evidence did indeed promote the learning of adverb placement. However, the effects of the treatment were not as long lived as anticipated, as the two groups did not differ on their performance one year following the treatment.

Feedback occurs naturally and in classrooms. One might think that feedback is frequent in language classrooms, but this is not always the case. For example, Zyzik and Polio (2008) found that, in Spanish literature courses, there was virtually no feedback, despite the fact that one of the goals of these classes is language learning. Loewen (2003) found variation in feedback even within the same language school and from student to student. Thus, the benefits of feedback are not consistently available to everyone.

[handwritten margin note: feedback is not consistently available to everyone.]

12.5.1.1 Negotiation

[handwritten note: focus on incorrect forms enables learners to search for additional confirmatory or nonconfirmatory evidence. is a type of negative evidence. feedback through negotiation serves as corrective function]

Negotiation serves as a catalyst for change, because of its focus on incorrect forms. By providing learners with information about incorrect forms, negotiation enables learners to search for additional confirmatory or nonconfirmatory evidence. If we accept that negotiation as a form of negative evidence and as a way of providing feedback serves the function of initiating change, we need to ask what factors determine whether the initiated change results in permanent restructuring of linguistic knowledge. As with any type of learning, there needs to be reinforcement of what is being learned. This is schematized in Figure 12.2. If additional input is not available, learners do not have the opportunity to obtain confirmatory/nonconfirmatory evidence. This, in fact, may explain the results of White's study. Without additional focused evidence, it is not surprising that the learners did not retain knowledge of English adverb placement. In other words, acquisition appears to be gradual and, to state the matter simplistically, takes time and often requires numerous "doses" of evidence. That is, there is an incubation period extending from the time of the initial input (negative or positive) to the final stage of restructuring and output.

[handwritten margin note: Acquisition is gradual and takes time and requires numerous "doses" of evidence.]

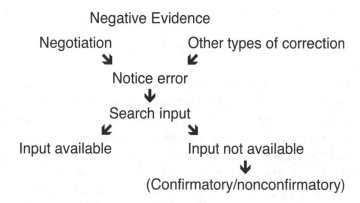

Negative Evidence

Negotiation   Other types of correction

Notice error

Search input

Input available   Input not available

(Confirmatory/nonconfirmatory)

FIGURE 12.2 Function of Negative Evidence (*Source*: © 1997 from *Input, interaction and the second language learner* by S. Gass. Reproduced by permission of Lawrence Erlbaum Associates, a division of Taylor & Francis Group)

Negative evidence ——> shows what's not possible in the L2 when it is possible in the NL.

Although White's study is important in showing that negative evidence may be necessary to trigger a permanent change in a learner's grammar, it does not show that positive evidence (i.e., input) alone is insufficient. (In fact, the question group of White's study received little information about adverbs from the naturalistic classroom data to which they were exposed.)

↓ triggers permanent changes in grammar

positive evidence ↓ alone is not sufficient ↓ shows to learners that there's info in L2 that might be different in NL.

Trahey and White (1993) conducted a follow-up study to determine the effect of positive evidence. Their study consisted of two Grade 5 classes of French students learning English. Both classes were given an input flood of English adverbs (positive evidence only) over a two-week period. The same timetable as that used in the earlier White studies was used, with the exception of three-week rather than five-week follow-up testing and no testing one year later. What they found was that input was sufficient for learners to notice that SAV order is possible in English, but that it was not sufficient to detect the ungrammaticality of SVAO sentences. Thus, these two experiments showed that positive evidence can reveal to learners the presence of information in the L2 that is different from their NL, but that negative evidence is necessary to show what is not possible in the L2 when it is possible in the NL. Trahey (1996) showed that an abundance of positive evidence a year after exposure yielded knowledge of grammatical sentences, but did not succeed in eradicating the ungrammatical sentences. Thus, positive evidence alone is not sufficient.

LEARNERS RESPOND DIFFERENTLY TO DIFFERENT TYPES OF FEEDBACK.

Other studies of feedback have also suggested that feedback obtained through negotiation serves a corrective function (Gass & Varonis, 1989; Pica et al., 1989). Pica et al. provided evidence that learners respond differentially to different types of feedback. In their study, one important focus was on different types of NS signals to NNS errors. They found that the greatest amount of modification comes in response to clarification requests, as in the following example, taken from Nobuyoshi and R. Ellis (1993, p. 204), as opposed to seeking confirmation through modeling:

Greatest amount of modification ↕ comes from clarification requests

(12-23) NNS: He pass his house.
NS: Sorry?
NNS: He passed, he passed, ah, his sign.

CORRECTION ↓ facilitator of acquisition

What this suggests is that the fact that the NNS is *forced* to make the actual correction, as opposed to hearing and perhaps thinking about the correct form, is in itself a facilitator to acquisition. However, again, we are left with the unknown factor of longer-term retention.

This same study that suggested longer-term retention after focused attention is that of Nobuyoshi and R. Ellis (1993). Learners had to describe a series of pictures that depicted events that had happened the previous weekend and the previous day. The experimental group received feedback through clarification requests that focused on past-tense forms. The control group did not receive such focused feedback. The results can only be considered suggestive, given the very small sample size. However, in the experimental group, two of the three participants were able to reformulate the correct forms after feedback and were able to maintain the correct forms at a subsequent administration one week later. In the control group, none of the participants showed an accuracy gain.

Similarly, Lightbown (1992) compared corrective feedback provided by teachers immediately after the occurrence of an error in a communicative activity with feedback on audiolingual drills or pure practice activities. She found that, in both cases, learners were able to self-correct, but only in the first case was the self-correction incorporated into their L2 systems, as evidenced by use of the targeted form outside of the classroom.

An early study on the effect of corrective feedback on grammatical reorganization was carried out by Carroll et al. (1992). The comparison was between groups with corrective feedback and groups with no corrective feedback. The linguistic focus was on regular noun formation in French. After receiving training on the relationship between verbs and nouns (e.g., attelé–attelage, "harnessed"/"harnessing"), learners were given new words to manipulate. Some participants were corrected, and others were not. The results showed that corrective feedback was important in the learning of individual items, but that it had little effect on a learner's ability to generalize this information to new items.

Takashima (1995), in a study of Japanese learners of English, investigated the effects of feedback that was focused on two morphological forms (past tense and plural)[4] versus feedback that was communication-oriented. The focused feedback was in the form of clarification requests (Sorry?, What did you say?). Groups of students had to work together to make up a story based on a sequence of pictures, of which each student in the group had only one. One student was then nominated to tell the story to the class. This was the actual feedback session, as the teacher provided either focused morphological feedback or content feedback. The accuracy rate for past tense increased at a faster rate during the time of the study (11 weeks) in the focused morphological-correction group as opposed to the content-correction group. Further, the magnitude of the difference increased as a function of time. Improved accuracy was noted for the particular student who was corrected (in front of the class), as well as for those students who were in the class observing the interaction. Interestingly, when considering the actual reformulations by individual students, there was no correlation between the reformulated utterances and improvement on the use of the structure on tests. This further suggests that the actual interaction does not constitute change itself, but is only a catalyst for later change. Illustrative of this is the following excerpt from Takashima (1995, p. 77), in which the first clarification request appears to fall short of the mark, in that the student makes no change, but, as the storytelling continues, the student seems to be more sensitive to the past-tense forms, even self-correcting in the last turn.

(12-24) S = student; T = teacher

> S: One day, the fairy, sting the magic wand to Cinderalla.
> T: Sorry?
> S: One day, the fairy sting the magic wand to Cinderalla.
> T: OK.
> S: Cinde, ah, Cinderaella changed into, the beautiful girl. [Laugh] Ah, and, the, Cin, Cinderella wen Cinderella went to the palace by coach. The, the prince fall in love at a first glance.

T: Sorry?

S: Ah, the prince fall in, falled falled in love Cinderella at a first glance. And they dance, they danced . . . Ah, Cin, Cinderella have, Cinderella have to go home.

Input enhancement

Here, the input has been enhanced through clarification requests, and the output has similarly been enhanced (Takashima's term), apparently as a function of the **input enhancement**.

TIME TO THINK ...

If you learned your L2 in a classroom, did you find teacher feedback helpful? Was the intention of the feedback always clear? Was it more useful for some areas than others (e.g., syntax, vocabulary, pronunciation)?

12.5.1.2 Recasts

less direct form of feedback
is a reformulation of an incorrect utterance

Recasts are another form of feedback, although they are less direct and more subtle than other forms of feedback. A recast is a reformulation of an incorrect utterance that maintains the original meaning of the utterance, as in 12-25, where the NS reformulates the NNS's incorrect question (Philp, 1999).

(12-25) NNS: Why he want this house?

→   NS: Why does he want this house?

Recasts are complex. For example, one must consider: Is it a partial recast? A full recast? A response to a single error or to multiple errors (how many changes are made)? We present two examples that illustrate forms that recasts can take. In 12-26, a recast with rising intonation, the auxiliary is added, and the verbal morphology is corrected (Philp, 1999, p. 92). In 12-27, the verb form is corrected (from future to subjunctive, required after *avant que*) without rising intonation (Lyster, 1998, p. 58).

(12-26) NNS: What doctor say?

         NS: What is the doctor saying?

(12-27) S = student; T = teacher

S: Avant que   quelqu'un   le   prendra.
     before   someone   it   will take
     "Before someone will take it."

T: Avant que   quelqu'un   le   prenne.
     before   someone   it   takes
     "Before someone takes it."

There have been a number of recent reviews of recasts in the L2 literature, focusing on experimental as well as theoretical concerns (Nicholas et al., 2001; R. Ellis & Sheen, 2006; Long, 2007; Mackey & Goo, 2007; Loewen, 2009). Because recasts are an indirect form of correction, it is important to question to what extent they are relevant to acquisition. To this end, there have been a number of empirical studies focused specifically on the effectiveness of recasts. The results from these studies are mixed. However, as Goo and Mackey state (2013), many of the studies that argue against the effectiveness of recasts are methodologically problematic. For a more general review of quantitative methods including designs, analyses and reporting practices in interaction research, see Plonsky & Gass, 2011.

Lyster and Ranta (1997) collected data from children in Grades 4–6 enrolled in French immersion programs. Their research considered recasts by teachers following errors and, importantly, the reaction by the student ("uptake," in their terminology) in the subsequent turn. They argued that uptake "reveals what the student attempts to do with the teacher's feedback" (p. 49). Even though there were numerous instances of recasts found in the data, they did not appear to be particularly effective. Rather, students were more prone to repair utterances following other types of feedback.

Unfortunately, an immediate response may not be revealing, in that learners may be "mimicking or repeating without true understanding" (Gass, 2003, p. 236). This makes recasts a somewhat elusive concept to deal with, and research often produces mixed results. For example, Mackey and Philp (1998) found that an immediate response by a learner was not necessarily related to development, whereas Nabei and Swain (2002) and Lyster (2004) found the reverse. As noted elsewhere in this chapter, it is not always possible to judge what the effects of learning are by considering only immediate reactions.

Lyster (1998), using the same database as reported on in the Lyster and Ranta (1997) study, divided recasts into four types, depending on two features: (a) declarative versus interrogative and (b) confirmation of the original utterance or additional information. Lyster found that there was some confusion between the corrective and approval functions of recasts. He argued that recasts may not be particularly useful in terms of corrective feedback, but they allow teachers to move a lesson forward by focusing attention on lesson content rather than on language form.

Lyster (2004) compared the benefits of recasts and prompts in a study that took place in immersion classrooms. He includes the following four types of prompts:

(12-28) Clarification requests
     STUDENT: Et le coccinelle. . . "And the (M) ladybug."
     TEACHER: Pardon? "Sorry?"
     STUDENT: La coccinelle . . . "The (F) ladybug."

(12-29) Repetitions
     STUDENT: La chocolat. "(F) Chocolate."
     TEACHER: La chocolat? "(F) Chocolate."
     STUDENT: Le chocolat. "(M) Chocolate."

365

(12-30) Metalinguistic clues

STUDENT: Parce qu'elle cherche, euh, son, son carte
"Because she's looking for, um, her, her (M) card."

TEACHER: Pas son carte. "Not her (M) card."

STUDENT: Euh, sa carte? "Um, her (F) card?"

(12-31) Elicitation

TEACHER: Il vit où un animal domestique? Où es-ce que ça vit?
"Where does a pet live? Where does it live?"

STUDENT: Dans un maison. "In a (M) house."

TEACHER: Dans . . .? Attention. "In . . .? Careful."

STUDENT: Dans une maison. "In a (F) house."

Data were collected within the context of a fifth-grade-content French immersion classroom. Teachers either provided no feedback, recasts, or prompts. The focus was on grammatical gender in French. Determination of learning was made through both oral and written tasks following the five-week treatment sessions. He found that form-focused instruction with prompts was more successful than with recasts, based on the written measures. There was not a significant difference on the oral assessment measures. This study was conducted in a content-based classroom where there are numerous nonlinguistic demands made on the learner, possibly making it difficult to focus on the subtle corrective function of recasts.

The results of a study by Ammar and Spada (2006) are similar to those of Lyster (2004). Their study took place in intensive English classes (L1 French) in Montreal, with Grade 6 pupils. The target grammatical area was possessive determiners (*his/her*), a structure notably difficult for French learners of English. Prompts turned out to be more effective than recasts. The effectiveness of recasts depended, in part, on proficiency level, with more advanced learners receiving more benefit than learners of lower proficiency. Ellis et al. (2006) looked at metalinguistic explanation (explicit feedback) and recasts (implicit feedback), finding that, on tests of both explicit and implicit knowledge, the metalinguistic explanation group outperformed the recast group, most likely due to recognition of the overtly corrective nature of metalinguistic feedback. Explicit feedback benefited both implicit and explicit knowledge.

In general, a number of studies have suggested that there is a positive effect for recasts on later learning (see Nicholas et al. 2001, and Mackey & Goo, 2007, for reviews). Leeman (2003) looked at noun–adjective agreement in Spanish in attempting to determine the benefits of recasts, particularly because they serve to provide positive evidence in a salient way. She had three experimental groups: (1) recasts, which she proposed provided both negative evidence as well as enhanced salience of positive evidence; (2) negative evidence; and (3) enhanced salience of positive evidence. She found that the first and third groups (recast group and enhanced-salience-of-positive-evidence group) showed posttreatment benefits. In this way, she was able to separate out the various parts of recasts (positive and negative evidence). Thus, it appears that recasts are useful owing to the enhanced salience provided in recasts rather than negative evidence. Han (2002) investigated consistency of use of past-tense morphology.

[handwritten annotations at top: "4 conditions for usefulness of recasts. ① individualized attention ③ developmental readiness ② consistent focus ④ intensity."]

She found that recasts were beneficial, but proposed four conditions for their usefulness: individualized attention, consistent focus, developmental readiness, and intensity.

In a study of the acquisition of past tense in an interactive context, McDonough (2007) compared clarification requests and recasts, finding that both positively influenced the acquisition of past tense. However, in a study on the acquisition of the comparative and past tense, R. Ellis (2007) considered the effect of recasts and metalinguistic feedback, not finding a positive effect for recasts. However, the treatment time in his study was much shorter than in other studies investigating the impact of recasts on the development of English past-tense morphology.

Ishida (2004) considered Japanese morphology in her study of recasts. In general, her results show a positive and lasting effect for recasts. Like Han (2002), she points to the need to consider developmental readiness in a full understanding of the utility of recasts. Iwashita (2003) also considered the acquisition of Japanese word order and locative-initial constructions. She investigated more than just recasts, but, in general, found different effects for interaction moves (recasts, negotiation, models). Recasts were beneficial only for one of the verb forms. This further suggests the need to determine developmental readiness in order to fully understand the effect of recasts or any other interactional move. Mackey and Philp (1998) also found positive learning effects following recasts for the development of question formation.

McDonough and Mackey (2006) provide a detailed study on recasts, looking at the relationship between: (1) recasts and learning and (2) learning and immediate responses to recasts. In an interaction-based study with Thai learners of English, they considered the acquisition of English questions. There were two experimental groups (recast and no feedback). Within the recast group, there were two recast types, as in 12-32 where there was an opportunity to respond and 12-33 where there was no response opportunity.

[handwritten margin annotation: "RECASTS STUDIES"]

(12-32) Recast with opportunity to respond—from McDonough and Mackey (2006)

> LEARNER: Why he must say it like that?
> NS: Why did he say that?
> LEARNER: Yeah

(12-33) Recast with no opportunity to respond—from McDonough and Mackey (2006)

> LEARNER: How many sister you have?
> NS: How many sisters do I have? I have one sister.

They characterized responses to recasts in one of two ways: as a pure repetition, or as what they termed a primed production, where there was some novel production. Examples of each are given in 12-34 and 12-35 below.

(12-34) Repetition—from McDonough and Mackey (2006)

> LEARNER: When it happen?

NS: When did it happen?

LEARNER: When did it happen?

(12-35) Primed production—from McDonough and Mackey (2006)

LEARNER: Why he hit the deer?

NS: Why did he hit the deer? He was driving home and the deer ran out in front of his car

LEARNER: What did he do after that?

Their study included three posttests, and development was operationalized as two questions, with unique lexical items in different tasks. Both recasts and primed production were predictive of ESL question development. What was particularly interesting is that mere repetition of the recasted form (uptake, in Lyster and Ranta's framework) did not correlate with development.

mere repetition doesn't foster development

Other studies that show a positive effect for recasts point to two main problems with recast studies: the concept of uptake and the data to be included in analysis. Mackey and Philp (1998) pointed out that uptake (as defined by Lyster & Ranta, 1997) may be the wrong measure to use in determining effectiveness. Their data represented an attempt to go beyond the turn immediately following a recast. They make the point (cf. Gass & Varonis, 1994; Gass, 1997; Lightbown, 1998) that, if one is to consider effectiveness (i.e., development/acquisition), then one should more appropriately measure delayed effects. In particular, Mackey and Philp considered the effects of interaction, with and without recasts, on learners' knowledge of English questions. Their results showed that, for more advanced learners, recasts plus negotiation were more beneficial than negotiation alone. This was the case even though there was not always evidence for a reaction by the learner in the subsequent turn.

A study by Long et al. (1998) also attempted to determine the role of recasts (in this case, as opposed to models). They investigated (a) the acquisition of ordering of adjectives and a locative construction by English learners of Japanese, and (b) the acquisition of topicalization and adverb placement by English learners of Spanish. Their results were mixed, inasmuch as only one of the learner groups (Spanish) showed greater learning following recasts as opposed to models. Furthermore, these findings were true for adverb placement only.

A problem having to do with the data used for analysis was noted by Oliver (1995). Frequently, after a recast, there is no opportunity for the original speaker to make a comment. This may be owing to a topic shift, as in 12-36 (Oliver, 1995, p. 472), or the inappropriateness of making a comment because the recast had been in the form of a *yes/no* question, and the appropriate response would not be a repetition, but a *yes/no* response.

(12-36) From Oliver (1995, p. 472)

NNS: A [c]lower tree.

NS: A flower tree. How tall is the trunk?

When the lack of opportunity/appropriacy is included, the percentage of incorporated recasts greatly increases. Lyster (1998) argued that the context of language use in these studies (child–child dyadic interactions in Oliver's research, and teacher–student interactions in his own research) is different, and that, in fact, in classrooms, the teacher often keeps the floor, thereby (as mentioned earlier) drawing attention to content and not to language form. In his 2004 study, Lyster compares recasts with prompts (see examples 12-28–12-31 above), finding the superiority of prompts over recasts given the opportunity for some form of uptake.

An important literature review by Goo and Mackey (2013) seeks to shed light on the effectiveness of recasts, pointing out that some of the research that downplays a role for recasts in learning is actually comparative—recasts versus prompts/metalinguistic feedback. As they point out, these studies are less useful than ones that attempt to delve deeply into what function recasts are serving, in that different feedback types have different roles in learning. They also point to certain methodological issues, some of which have been dealt with in this section, such as opportunities for output modification and complexity of the recast.

There is one final issue to address before concluding this section on feedback. What do learners perceive? In a study by Mackey et al. (2000), data were collected from 10 learners of English as an L2 and 7 learners of Italian as a foreign language. The study explored learners' perceptions of feedback provided to them through task-based dyadic interaction. In the interactions, learners received feedback focused on a range of morphosyntactic, lexical, and phonological forms. After completing the tasks, learners watched videotapes of their previous interactions and were asked to introspect about their thoughts at the time the original interactions were in progress. Examples of the interactions and the recall comments of the learners follow:

(12-37) Morphosyntactic feedback (perceived as lexical feedback)

>NNS: C'è due tazzi.
>"There is two cups (m. pl.)."
>INT: Due tazz-come?
>"Two cup—what?"
>NNS: Tazzi, dove si puó mettere té, come se dice questo?
>"Cups (m. pl.), where one can put tea, how do you say this?"
>INT: tazze?
>"Cups (f. pl.)?"
>NNS: ok, tazze.
>"Ok, cups (f. pl)."
>*Recall*: I wasn't sure if I learned the proper word at the beginning.

(12-38) Phonological feedback correctly perceived

>NNS: Vincino la tavolo è.
>"Near the table is (the correct form is *vicino*)."
>INT: Vicino?
>"Near?"

NNS: La, lu tavolo.
"The ? table."

Recall: I was thinking . . . when she said *vicino* I was thinking, OK, did I pronounce that right there?

(12-39) Lexical feedback correctly perceived

NNS: There is a library.
NS: A what?
NNS: A place where you put books.
NS: A bookshelf?
NNS: Bok?
NS: Shelf.
NNS: Bookshelf.

Recall: That's not a good word she was thinking about library like we have here on campus, yeah.

The results showed that learners were relatively accurate in their perceptions about lexical, semantic, and phonological feedback, and less so with morphosyntactic feedback (see also Hawkins, 1985). Thus, there may be a differential role for feedback in different linguistic areas, as also suggested by Pica (1994). Perhaps morphosyntactic feedback is not noticed because, as is typical in a conversational context, individuals are focused on meaning, not on language form. Phonological and lexical errors can interfere with basic meaning and, hence, need to be attended to on the spot, if shared meaning is to result.

TIME TO THINK ...

How do you feel when someone recasts you in your L2? Does it ever interrupt the flow of communication? Do you always pick up on the correction? Why do you think you do in some cases, but not in others?

output is a way of testing hypo...
producing language help create
analyticity that allows learners
think about language).
evidence: self-correction

12.5.2 Hypothesis Testing

The notion of hypothesis testing has been central to research in SLA for a number of years (see Schachter, 1983, 1992). Output, particularly when it occurs as part of a negotiation sequence, is a way of testing a hypothesis. This is not to say that hypotheses are being consciously tested every time an L2 speaker produces an utterance. It is to say, however, that, through negotiation and through feedback, learners can be made aware of the hypotheses that they are entertaining as they produce language. That is, the activity of using language helps create a degree of analyticity that allows learners to think about language (see section 12.5.3).

Swain (1995, pp. 133–134) suggested that learners are, in fact, involved in testing hypotheses, and that they use the forum of interaction to work through those hypotheses. In support of this position, Swain presented the following example from two L2 learners (age 13) in attendance at an immersion program in Canada. The teacher had just read aloud a text, and the students, having taken notes on the reading, worked in pairs to reconstruct the text as closely as possible, in terms of both content and form. The sentence they were working on in this example is: *En ce qui concerne l'environment, il y a beaucoup de problèmes qui nous tracassent* ("As far as the environment is concerned, there are many problems that face us") (Swain, 1995, pp. 133–134; translation, pp. 143–144).

(12-40) K = student; G = student; T = teacher

K: Wait a minute! No, I need a Bescherelle [verb reference book]. Please open the Bescherelle at the page with, OK, at the last page [i.e., the index]. OK look for *tracasse*, one page two pages.

G: *Tra, tra, tracer.*

K: *Tracasser* page six. Look for it please.

G: No problem.

K: It's on page . . .

G: Verb [on page] six. OK, it's the same as *aimer*. [i.e., it is conjugated in the same way, and *aimer* is given as the standard example for all verbs with this pattern of conjugation.]

K: Let me see it please [reading from the page]. The *passé simple*. [K is trying to find a first person plural version of the verb which sounds like *tracasse*, the word he has written in his notes, but is unable to find one].

G: Perhaps it's here.

K: No, it's just *nous aime* [pause] ah, the present. *Tracasse*. Isn't it *aimons, tracasse* [to teacher who has just arrived]? You don't say *nous tracasse* [what he has written down in his notes]. Shouldn't it be *nous tracassons*?

T: It's the *problems* that are worrying us [deliberately not directly giving the answer].

K: *Nous tracassons.*

G: Oh [beginning to realize what is happening].

K: Yeh? [So what?]

G: The problems which are worrying us. Like the [pause]. It's the problems [pause] like, that concern us.

K: Yes, but *tracasse* shouldn't it be <o–n–s>?

G: *Tracasse.* It's not a, it's not a [pause], yeh, I dunno [unable to articulate what he has discovered].

K: OK, it says problems which worry us. Therefore, is *tracasse* a verb that you have to conjugate?

> T: Uh huh.
>
> K: So is it *tracassons?*
>
> T: It's the **problems** which are worrying us.
>
> G: Us, it's it's not, yeh, it's the problems, it's not, it's not us.
>
> K: Ah! E–n–t [third person plural ending] OK. OK.

As Swain explains, the question here relates to the morphology of the French verb and the use of an RC. The difficulty lies in the fact that Student K had taken the French phrase *nous tracasse* without taking into consideration that the entire constituent was *qui nous tracasse* ("that we are faced with"). In the first instance, it appears that *nous*—"we"—is the subject, and that the verb should therefore be *tracassons* to agree with the first person plural subject. In actuality, *nous tracasse* is part of the relative clause *qui nous tracasse*, with *qui*—"that"—as the third person subject. The entire dialogue is one in which Student K is at first puzzled, then verbalizes the problem, and then works to understand the syntax and, hence, the morphology. In sum, it is through this interaction that this child is able to come to a correct conclusion after an initial, faulty hypothesis.

Another piece of evidence supporting the fact that learners test hypotheses through production is self-correction. Negotiation sequences produce many instances of corrective feedback to learners, from NSs and NNSs alike. And, importantly, these instances appear to have long-lasting effects on language development in some cases. In the following examples (Gass & Varonis, 1989, pp. 80–81), it appears that Hiroko is in some sense ready to accept a correction (12-41). Her quick and easy acceptance of Izumi's *at* suggests a tentativeness that bespeaks hypothesis testing, rather than a conviction of the correctness of her own utterance.

(12-41) HIROKO: Ah, the dog is barking to—

        IZUMI: At

       HIROKO: At the woman.

(12-42) HIROKO: A man is uh drinking c-coffee or tea uh with uh the saucer of the uh uh coffee set is uh in his uh knee.

        IZUMI: In him knee.

       HIROKO: Uh on his knee.

        IZUMI: Yeah.

       HIROKO: On his knee.

        IZUMI: So sorry. On his knee.

In 12-42, it appears that both Hiroko and Izumi are tentative and are in a sense fishing for the right form. This is supported by the frequent hesitation on the part of Hiroko in her initial utterance and by the apology on Izumi's part at the end. Other examples (also discussed in section 12.5) suggest the longer-term retention that results from these negotiations. This can be seen in 12-43 (Gass & Varonis, 1989, p. 78):

(12-43) ATSUKO: Uh holding the [kʌp].
       TOSHI: Holding the cup?
      ATSUKO: Hmm hmmm . . .
                [seventeen turns]
       TOSHI: Holding a cup.
      ATSUKO: Yes.
       TOSHI: Coffee cup?
      ATSUKO: Coffee? Oh yeah, tea, coffee cup tea cup.
       TOSHI: Hm hm.

The initial clarification request by Toshi suggests to Atsuko that something is wrong with her pronunciation of the word *cup* [kʌp]. This indication caused her to notice something in her pronunciation that did not match the expectation of her partner. The remainder of the dialogue was one of hypothesis testing, in which she matched her phonetic formulation to her partner's.

Pica et al. (1989) showed that clarification requests yielded modifications in learner output. The authors suggested that learners "test hypotheses about the second language, experiment with new structures and forms, and expand and exploit their interlanguage resources in creative ways" (1989, p. 64). This was in contrast to an earlier study by Pica (1988) in which there were not a large number of self-corrections following feedback. However, in the latter study, Pica only considered immediate responses to feedback, showing only that the interaction did not result in immediate change, not that it did not *stimulate* change. There may be other variables in operation when we determine whether or not there is an effect for feedback. Lin and Hedgcock (1996) analyzed data from classroom learners of Spanish (NSs of Chinese) versus well-educated (but not schooled) learners of Spanish (also NSs of Chinese). They found differences between these two populations in their ability to detect ungrammaticality and to incorporate negative feedback provided to them.

More direct evidence of hypothesis testing, however, comes from Mackey et al. (2000) in which they used a stimulated research procedure (see Gass & Mackey, 2000). They video-taped interactive tasks and, immediately following, replayed the video, asking learners what they were thinking about at the time of the interaction. Example 12-44 (from their study, but not published therein) below illustrates the notion of hypothesis testing.

(12-44) Hypothesis testing (INT = interviewer)

      NNS: *poi un bicchiere*
            then a glass
      INT: *un che, come?*
            a what, what?
      NNS: *bicchiere*
            glass

Recall by NNS: I was drawing a blank. Then I thought of a vase but then I thought that since there was no flowers, maybe it was just a big glass. So, then I thought I'll say it and see. Then, when she said "*come*" (what?), I knew that it was completely wrong.

"I'll say it and see" suggests that she was using the conversation as a way to see if a hypothesis was correct or incorrect.

12.5.3 Automaticity

[handwritten margin note: consistent and successful mapping (practice) of grammar to output results in automatic processing]

A third function of output is the development of fluency and automaticity of processing (see Chapter 10). As discussed earlier, the human mind can be viewed as a limited processing system. Certain processes are deliberate, requiring a significant amount of time and working-memory capacity. Others are routine and automatic, involving less time and capacity. McLaughlin (1987, p. 134) claimed that automatization involves "a learned response that has been built up through the consistent mapping of the same input to the same pattern of activation over many trials." Here, we extend this notion to output: the consistent and successful mapping (practice) of grammar to output results in automatic processing (see also Loschky & Bley-Vroman, 1993).

12.5.4 Meaning-Based to Grammar-Based Processing

[handwritten margin note: output forces learners to move from semantic processing to syntactic processing]

In some sense, the study of output began with an understanding of the difference between meaning-based and grammar-based use of language. Swain's initial hypothesis stated that output "may force the learner to move from semantic processing to syntactic processing" (1985, p. 249). This notion has been dealt with throughout the book and is not elaborated on here. Suffice it to say that processing language only at the level of meaning will not, and cannot, serve the purpose of understanding the syntax of the language, a level of knowledge that is essential to the accurate production of language.[5]

In sum, output provides learners the opportunity to produce language and gain feedback, which, through focusing learners' attention on certain local aspects of their speech, may lead them to notice either (a) a mismatch between their speech and that of an interlocutor (particularly if, as part of the feedback, a linguistic model is provided) or (b) a deficiency in their output. Noticing, then, leads to reassessment, which may be an on-the-spot reassessment or involve longer-term, complex thinking about the issue. This latter process may be bolstered by the gathering of additional information through a variety of sources (e.g., input, direct questioning, and looking in grammar books and dictionaries). This, in essence, is the process of learning (see also Swain & Lapkin, 1995).

12.6 THE ROLE OF INPUT AND INTERACTION IN LANGUAGE LEARNING

12.6.1 The Functions of Input and Interaction

What is the function of input and interaction? As a first step to learning, a learner must be aware of a need to learn. Negotiation of the sort that takes place in conversation is a means to focus a learner's attention on just those areas of language that do not match those of the language being learned.

The view of input and interaction that has been presented in this chapter appears to be in opposition to the view of language learning constrained by the principles of Universal Grammar (see Chapter 7). However, the goal of both perspectives is to come to an understanding of how L2 grammars are formulated, in light of the fact that the evidence learners have about the L2 is so limited. In broad terms, as noted in Chapter 7, learners have two kinds of linguistic information at their disposal. The first is known as positive evidence and refers to that limited set of (generally) well-formed utterances to which learners are exposed. The second, negative evidence consists of information provided to a learner that her or his utterance is deviant in some way. Consider the following example:

(12-45) NS: Did you fly to Singapore yesterday?
        NNS: Did I flied here yesterday?
        NS: Pardon?
        NNS: Did I flied here yesterday?
        NS: Yes, did you fly here yesterday?

In 12-45, the first NS utterance provides positive evidence to this NNS about question formation. The second NS utterance provides feedback indicating that there is something incorrect/incomprehensible about the NNS utterance. The third NS utterance also provides indirect feedback to the learner (correct modeling) that the NNS utterance is incorrect. This is what we have been referring to in this chapter as negotiation.

When we look at the literature on child language acquisition, we find that claims have been made that negative evidence is neither frequent nor necessary for acquisition (e.g., Pinker, 1984; Wexler & Cullicover, 1980). As children do not receive much correction, it cannot be a necessary condition for acquisition. In this view, how then does acquisition take place? What has been posited is a set of innate properties that limit the possibilities of grammar formation. The claim is that, if grammar formation is limited, the task of language learning is therefore reduced.

What about L2 learning? With regard to the question of negative evidence, or correction, it is clear that adults (at least those in formal learning situations) do receive more than children. Furthermore, it may be the case that negative evidence is a necessary condition for adult L2 learning (see section 12.5.1).

What function might negative evidence, or error correction, serve? One could argue that, when errors are made and when, as a result, there is feedback, this feedback serves the purpose of providing the learner with information that an utterance is deviant. In an ideal situation, a learner's grammar is then modified. There are obvious limitations to this view. First, corrections cannot occur with all incorrect forms. Second, many so-called errors are errors of interpretation, in which case the learner may not even realize that an error has occurred (as seen in 12-46).

(12-46) NS: When I get to Paris, I'm going to sleep for one whole day. I'm so tired.
NNS: What?
NS: I'm going to sleep for one whole day.
NNS: One hour a day?
NS: Yes.
NNS: Why?
NS: Because I'm so tired.

In 12-46, two women had just boarded a train in Calais after a long trip from London to Dover and a long delay in Dover before crossing the English Channel to Calais. They were both on their way to Paris. They had never met before and were sitting across from each other on the Paris-bound train. In this exchange, it is clear that the NNS had understood the NS to say *one hour a day* rather than *one whole day*. This error of interpretation was never realized. Each thought the other one somewhat peculiar, and both lapsed into silence for the duration of the trip.

A third and perhaps most important limitation is that error acknowledgment, as in the case of expressions of nonunderstanding (e.g., *huh?*), does not provide sufficiently specific information to inform the learner where exactly an error has been made. That is, is the failure in communication the result of incorrect syntax, phonology, morphology, or vocabulary? Error acknowledgment also does not indicate what would have to be done in order to correct the error.

We now turn to another account of how L2 grammars develop. This is an account that takes the linguistic input, coupled with conversational interaction, as the driving force of language development. Thus, understanding the learning environment (including the language information available to learners and the conversational interactions in which L2 learners engage) is central to an understanding of the nature of learning.

It is within this context that Krashen proposed his influential Input Hypothesis, discussed earlier. His main claim is that the *sine qua non* of acquisition is input that is slightly beyond the learner's current level of grammatical knowledge. In his view, given the right kind of input, acquisition will be automatic. As we argued earlier, this account is inadequate. Minimally, one must also consider the role of negotiated interaction, as learning will be promoted in those instances where a conversational partner's assistance in expressing meaning can be relied on. Such assistance comes as a result of negotiation work, including such conversational features as comprehension checks, clarification requests, help with word searches, echoing, and so forth.

376

Wagner-Gough and Hatch (1975) argued that, with regard to SLA, conversational interaction forms the *basis* for the development of syntax, rather than being only a forum for practice of grammatical structures. Syntax, they claimed, develops out of conversation rather than the reverse. The examples in 12-47 and 12-48 illustrate the ways learning can take place within a conversational setting, as the learners in these cases use the conversation to further their lexical development. In 12-47 (Mackey, 1999, pp. 558–559), we see recognition of a new lexical item as a result of negotiation of a new phrase. This example illustrates how the learner may have used the conversation as a resource to learn the new phrase *reading glasses*.

(12-47) NS: There's there's a pair of reading glasses above the plant.
     NNS: A what?
     NS: Glasses reading glasses to see the newspaper?
     NNS: Glassi?
     NS: You wear them to see with, if you can't see. Reading glasses.
→   NNS: Ahh ahh glasses to read you say reading glasses.
     NS: Yeah.

In the penultimate line, the NNS acknowledges the fact that the new phrase *reading glasses* comes from the interaction and, in particular, as a consequence of the negotiation work.

Conversation is, of course, not limited to lexical learning. Example 12-48 is an excerpt from a conversation in which a teacher, an NS of English, is conversing with an NS Punjabi child (from R. Ellis, 1985b, p.79).

(12-48) NS: I want you to tell me what you can see in the picture or what's
          wrong with the picture.
     NNS: A /paik/ (= bike)
     NS: A cycle, yes. But what's wrong?
     NNS: /ret/ (= red)
     NS: It's red yes. What's wrong with it?
     NNS: Black.
     NS: Black. Good. Black what?
     NNS: Black /tæs/ (= tires)

Prior to this point in time, there were no examples of two-constituent utterances in this child's L2 discourse. As can be seen, the conversation itself provides the framework or, as R. Ellis (1985b, p. 79) stated, the breakthrough points for a two-constituent utterance to develop. The teacher broke the task into parts and helped with the crucial vocabulary, which appears to have enabled the child to juxtapose *black* and *tires*, as can be seen in her final utterance. From this time on, there were frequent examples of two-constituent utterances in this child's speech.

interaction helps crack codes

According to R. Ellis (1984, p. 95):

interaction contributes to development because it is the means by which the learner is able to crack the code. This takes place when the learner can infer what is said even though the message contains linguistic items that are not yet part of his competence and when the learner can use the discourse to help him/her modify or supplement the linguistic knowledge already used in production.

Negotiation for meaning: facilitates acquisition because it connects input, internal learner capacities, selective attention and output.

Thus, conversational interaction in an L2 forms the basis for the development of language, rather than being only a forum for practice of specific language features. This idea was expressed by Long (1996) as the Interaction Hypothesis:

negotiation for meaning, and especially negotiation work that triggers inter-actional adjustments by the NS or more competent interlocutor, facilitates acquisition because it connects input, internal learner capacities, particularly selective attention, and output in productive ways.

(pp. 451–452)

It is proposed that environmental contributions to acquisition are mediated by selective attention and the learner's developing L2 processing capacity, and that these resources are brought together most usefully, although not exclusively, during *negotiation for meaning*. Negative feedback obtained during negotiation work or elsewhere may be facilitative of L2 development, at least for vocabulary, morphology, and language-specific syntax, and essential for learning certain specifiable L1–L2 contrasts.

(p. 414)

What this means is that, through focused negotiation work, the learner's attentional resources may be oriented to (a) a particular discrepancy between what he or she knows about the L2 and what is reality vis-à-vis the target language or (b) an area of the L2 about which the learner has little or no information. Learning may take place during the interaction, or negotiation may be an initial step in learning; it may serve as a priming device (Gass, 1997), thereby representing the setting of the stage for learning rather than being a forum for actual learning.

negotiation is an initial step for learning.

We have seen examples where learning appears to take place during the conversation. There is also evidence that conversation stimulates later learning, serving only as a catalyst. Example 12-43, repeated here as 12-49, illustrates delayed learning. Two NNSs are involved in a picture-description task. NNS1 is describing a part of the picture and initiates the description with an incorrectly pronounced word that NNS2 immediately questions. NNS1 most likely ponders the pronunciation problem, never again mispronouncing *cup*. To the contrary, after some time, she correctly pronounces *cup*. In other words, the negotiation itself made her aware of a problem; she was then able to listen for more input until she was able to figure out the correct pronunciation.

(12-49) NNS1: Uh holding the [kʌp].
        NNS2: Holding the cup?

NNS1: Hmm hmmm . . .
        [seventeen turns later]
NNS2: Holding a cup.
NNS1: Yes.
NNS2: Coffee cup?
NNS1: Coffee? Oh yeah, tea, coffee cup, teacup.
NNS2: Hm hm.

But what evidence is there that interaction indeed drives language development? Consider the conversations in 12-50 and 12-51, both of which involve two NNSs (Gass & Varonis, 1989, pp. 79, 81).

(12-50) HIROKO: A man is uh drinking c-coffee or tea uh with the saucer of the uh uh coffee set is uh in his uh knee
     IZUMI: in *him* knee
     HIROKO: uh on *his* knee
     IZUMI: yeah
     HIROKO: on *his* knee.
     IZUMI: so sorry. On *his* knee

(12-51) SHIZUKA: When will you get married?
     AKIHITO: When? I don't know. Maybe . . . uh . . . after thirty.
     SHIZUKA: Thirty?
     AKIHITO: Yeah, after thirty I'll get marriage—I'll get married . . .
          [3 turns]
     AKIHITO: . . . then if I fall in lover with her, I'll get marriage with her .
          [11 turns]
     AKIHITO: And . . . uh . . . when I saw her. I liked to get married with a Chinese girl because she's so beautiful.

In 12-50, Hiroko says *in his knee*, with Izumi responding with an incorrect form, *in him knee*. Hiroko maintains the original form in terms of the pronominal case, although she changes the preposition from the original *in* to the correct *on*. As a result of the negotiation, both participants end up using the same correct form.

Similarly, in 12-51, Akihito hears the correct form *get married* at the beginning of the exchange. It is hypothesized that the form he initially provided (*get marriage*) was his learner-language form, and that the correct modeling by Shizuka resulted in the confusion seen in Akihito's second utterance. It is only 16 turns later when we see the correct form winning out.

In 12-52 is an exchange that involves, not form, but lexical meaning. Three students were in a writing class, negotiating how they were going to write a data commentary based on a graph depicting rental prices in China. In what is excerpted here, the participants are discussing the graph.

(12-52) Data from Loewen and Basturkmen (2005)

Episode 1:

JENNY: <I just write the>
DORIS: the charts
JENNY: th- the-
DORIS: the figure?
(3.0)
JENNY: should I write the charts
DORIS: okay

Episode 2:

JENNY: the chart
DORIS: shows
JENNY: shows or illustrates or
DORIS: indicated (.) <strates>
JONG: actually it's about prime office rebel rental numbers comparison by location

Episode 3:

DORIS: what does prime office mean? Is that like head office for business?
JENNY: I think so.
DORIS: the main office, right?
JONG: uh I'm not quite sure, but mm I think (.) good position, a better place for doing business,
DORIS: mhm
JONG: when good facilities
DORIS: oh okay
JONG: just like offices in Queen street
DORIS: oh okay
JONG: prime
DORIS: okay
JONG: it's actually the—prime means I think the good quality
DORIS: good quality
JONG: yeah good quality
DORIS: prime, prime
JENNY: I should write the chart compares,
DORIS: um
JENNY: prime
DORIS: do we need to write all the cities or we just choose one or two or three the most important ones to discuss

Episode 4:

JONG: it's actually the—prime means I think the (.) good quality
DORIS: good quality
JONG: yeah good quality

In this example, Doris starts off with a question about the meaning of prime office. Through the lengthy discussion, all three finally agree on the meaning of *prime*, as good *quality*.

More direct evidence of the importance of negotiated interaction comes from a number of studies. In one (Pica et al., 1987), the researchers showed that there was better comprehension by a group of L2 learners who were allowed interaction in the completion of a task versus those who were not allowed interaction but who were provided with modified input. A second study (Gass & Varonis, 1994) reported similar results, although, in that study, there was evidence that the effect of interaction was not only on immediate comprehension but was also noted in a follow-up activity that required productive language use. In that study, the learners were given modified input and were either allowed to negotiate or were not allowed to negotiate. In the first part of the task, NSs instructed NNSs as to where to place objects on a board. There were four conditions: (a) modified input, (b) non-modified input, (c) negotiated interaction, and (d) nonnegotiated interaction. In the second part of the task, NNSs described to NSs where to place objects on a different board. In this part, there were two conditions: (a) negotiated interaction and (b) nonnegotiated interaction. The best performance (measured in terms of ability to give accurate instructions on the second part of the task, as reflected in the NSs' ability to appropriately place objects) was obtained in that condition in which learners were allowed to negotiate on the first part of the task. What this suggests is that interaction is indeed beneficial, and not just for the immediate present.

A third study (Loschky, 1989) was similar in that there were several experimental conditions, including modified-input and negotiated-interaction conditions. It differed in that the only effect negotiated interaction had was on online comprehension. There was no positive effect found for syntactic development or vocabulary retention.

A particularly compelling study by Mackey (1999) set out to establish the extent to which a relationship could be found between conversational interaction and L2 development. She looked at the acquisition of question formation, building on the developmental model by Pienemann and Johnston (1987). In that model, originally proposed to account for the acquisition of German word order by L2 speakers, there were discernible and ordered stages of acquisition, each governed by processing mechanisms that constrained the movement from one stage to the next. Although a detailed discussion of the model is not relevant to the present discussion (for details, see Larsen-Freeman & Long, 1991; R. Ellis, 1994), a brief explanation will help in putting Mackey's work in context.

The Pienemann and Johnston (1987) model makes a strong prediction of word-order development, such that a learner will start off (apart from single words and/or chunks) with a canonical order—for example, SVO (*I like Sydney, You are student?*). A second stage involves some movement, but movement that does not interrupt the canonical order (*In Vietnam, I am teacher, Do you have apartment, Why you no eat?*). In the next stage, canonical order is interrupted (*Have you job? I like to eat my friend's house*). In this stage, one can see the beginnings of syntactic development. In the fourth stage, movement entails the recognition that the moved elements are part of

387

grammatical categories (*Why did you go?*—here, the learner needs to know that the auxiliary must be in second position and that tense is marked on the auxiliary). Finally, learners recognize substrings and learn that grammatical operations can operate across the substrings (*He didn't leave, did he?*). Because this model makes a prediction about development, and because conversational interaction within an input–interaction framework is hypothesized to influence development, the Pienemann and Johnston model is a fertile testing ground for the interaction hypothesis.

Mackey (1999) conducted research in which learners of English were engaged in communicative tasks, with questions being the targeted structure and with opportunities for interaction between participants. She noted a positive relationship between interaction and development, in that learners who were involved in structure-focused interaction moved along a developmental path more rapidly than learners who were not. As she noted, interaction was able to step up the pace of development, but was not able to push learners beyond a developmental stage.[6] In other words, developmental stages could not be skipped. In conditions where learners received only premodified input, but where no opportunities were allowed for interaction, little development was noted. It was interesting that evidence for more developmentally advanced structures was noted in delayed posttests rather than taking place immediately. This supports the claim made throughout this book that interaction is a priming device, allowing learners to focus attention on areas that they are working on. In many instances, thinking time is needed before change takes place. It is further noteworthy that, in Mackey's study, the delayed effect is observed more often in more advanced structures, where it is reasonable to assume that more thinking time would be needed before a learner is able to figure out what changes to make and how to make them.

Recall from Chapter 11 that Tarone and Liu (1995) found that different kinds of interactions differentially impacted the rate and route of acquisition. Whereas their findings were similar to those of Mackey with regard to the rate, they diverged from Mackey's with regard to the route. They found that the route could be altered, depending on the context. For example, later-stage interrogatives occurred in interactions with the researcher before the appearance of earlier stages. As suggested by Liu (1991), the explanation for this discrepancy may lie in the context of the interaction itself; in the interaction with the researcher, there were significant amounts of input of later-stage questions. An additional factor may be that the question forms that appeared to be absent from the child's speech were absent because they are ungrammatical in English and there is, presumably, no input (e.g., *Why you do that?*). Thus, it may be that later stages stemming from an input flood of grammatical utterances can be induced when earlier stages are ungrammatical and, hence, devoid of external input.

In this section, we have discussed the relationship between interaction and learning and presented evidence that the former may serve as a forum for, or a facilitator of, language development. We next look at empirical evidence in favor of the effectiveness of feedback, an essential part of interaction.

[handwritten margin note: Interaction doesn't help learners skip developmental stages.]

[handwritten margin note: it is a facilitator though]

12.6.2 Effectiveness of Feedback

Loewen (2012) reviewed the literature on feedback and noted that numerous meta-analyses show an overall positive effect for feedback (see Russell and Spada, 2006; Mackey & Goo, 2007; Li, 2010a, 2010b). Although it is clear that feedback is useful, it is not clear why interaction, generally, is beneficial. We turn to this topic in the following sections: Why is interaction an important source for learning?

12.6.2.1 Attention

Attention "bear[s] on every area of cognitive science" (Allport, 1989, p. 631), and SLA is no exception. In fact, (selective) attention is the mechanism that may be at the heart of the interaction hypothesis, as noted by Long (1996). Negotiation and other types of corrective interaction focus learners' attention on parts of their language that diverge from NS language. In other words, negotiation requires attentiveness and involvement, both of which are necessary for successful communication. As reported, numerous studies suggest that interaction and learning are related. This observation is an important one, but is in need of an explanation in order to advance our understanding of how learning takes place. That is, what happens during a negotiation event that allows learners to utilize the content of the negotiation to advance their own knowledge? Long's (1996) statement, given earlier, suggests an important role for attention, as does Gass's (1997, p. 132) statement that, "attention, accomplished in part through negotiation is one of the crucial mechanisms in this process."

Attention is crucial in the negotiation Process.

In the recent history of SLA research, much emphasis has been placed on the concept of attention and the related notion of noticing (see Doughty, 2003, for an extended and related discussion of actual issues of processing during form-focused instruction). Schmidt (1990, 1993a, 1993b, 1993c, 1994) argued that attention is essential to learning; there can be no learning without attention. Although his strong claim is in dispute (see Gass, 1997; Schachter et al., 1998), it is widely accepted that selective attention plays a major role in learning.

selective attention

It is through interaction (e.g., negotiation, recasts) that a learner's attention is focused on a specific part of the language, particularly on mismatches between TL forms and learner-language forms. There is both anecdotal and empirical evidence that learners are capable of noticing mismatches. Schmidt and Frota (1986) reported on the learning of Portuguese in which the learner documented the noticing and subsequent learning of new forms. This was exemplified earlier with specific examples that mismatches are recognized through interaction (see, for example, 12-47).

Doughty (2003) pointed out that this assumes that these mismatches are indeed noticeable (see Truscott, 1998, for a discussion of attention, awareness, and noticing) and that, if they are noticeable and if a learner is to use these mismatches as a source for grammar restructuring, he or she must have the capacity to hold a representation of the TL utterance in memory, while executing a comparison. Doughty provides three ways in which such a comparison could work (2003, p. 18):

1. Representations of the input and output utterances are held in short-term memory and compared there.
2. Only a deeper (semantic) representation of the already-processed utterance is held in long-term memory, but it leaves useable traces in the short-term memory against which new utterances may be compared.
3. The memory of the utterance passes to the long-term memory but readily can be reactivated if there is any suspicion by the language processor that there is a mismatch between stored knowledge and incoming linguistic evidence.

The role of memory in connection with attention has been noted by others. J. N. Williams (1999) found a strong relationship between individual differences in memory capacity and learning outcomes in an experiment involving a semi-artificial form of Italian. He also recognized the importance of the relationship between long-term memory and vocabulary learning.

12.6.2.2 Contrast Theory

In this chapter, the issue of negative evidence has been raised (see also Chapter 7). We have also pointed out that corrective feedback cannot be relied on in language learning (whether the language is first or second). In this section, we consider a broadened definition of negative evidence, one that relies heavily on conversational interaction. In so doing, we are not making the argument that negative evidence can replace the need for an innate structure; rather, our point is simply that the concept of negative evidence in relation to learners' ability to attend to corrective feedback needs to be broadened. We take the following characterization from Saxton (1997, 2000), whose definition of negative evidence departed somewhat from the more general definition provided by Pinker (1989) and others: "Negative evidence occurs directly contingent on a child error, (syntactic or morphosyntactic), and is characterized by an immediate contrast between the child error and a correct alternative to the error, as supplied by the child's interlocutor" (Saxton, 1997, p. 145). According to this definition of negative evidence, researchers can determine the corrective potential of an utterance vis-à-vis two factors: (a) the linguistic content of the response and (b) the proximity of the response to an error. However, the definition is less clear on the question of whose perspective negative evidence is to be viewed from. It appears that it may be viewed from the point of view of the adult who supplies it. In fact, Saxton (1997, p. 145) stated that, "there is ample evidence that negative evidence, as defined here, is supplied to the child." However, it is more important to view negative evidence from the perspective of the L2 learner (child or adult) and to understand what learners are doing with the information provided.

Saxton (1997, 2000) proposed what he calls the **Direct Contrast Hypothesis**, which he defined within the context of child language acquisition as follows:

> When the child produces an utterance containing an erroneous form, which is responded to immediately with an utterance containing the correct adult

alternative to the erroneous form (i.e. when negative evidence is supplied), the child may perceive the adult form as being in CONTRAST with the equivalent child form. Cognizance of a relevant contrast can then form the basis for perceiving the adult form as a correct alternative to the child form.

(p. 155, emphasis in original)

An example will make this clear:

(12-53) From Saxton, Houston-Price, and Dawson (2005)

> CHILD: I thought they were all womans
> ADULT: They're not all women

Saxton, Houston-Price, and Dawson suggest that this exchange can provide two bits of information that are important as a child learns correct forms: the appropriate grammatical form and the potential ungrammaticality of his/her own form. There have been a number of studies that support this hypothesis (e.g., Saxton et al., 1998; Strapp, 1999; Strapp & Federico, 2000; Otomo, 2001; Chouinard & Clark, 2003; Saxton, Backley, & Gallaway, 2005).

The fact that a correct and an incorrect form are adjacent is important in creating a conflict for the learner. The mere fact of a contrast or a conflict draws a learner's attention to a deviant form, thereby highlighting the contrast through recasts or negotiation work. Saxton specifically tested two competing hypotheses, one based on nativism and one relying on contrast theory. The nativist hypothesis suggests that negative evidence, even when occurring adjacent to a child error, is no more effective than positive evidence in bringing about language change, whereas the contrast theory-based hypothesis suggests that the former is more effective than the latter. Saxton's research with children suggested that contrast theory was a more reliable predictor; that is, children reproduced correct forms more frequently when the correct form was embedded in negative evidence rather than positive evidence.

Saxton and his colleagues (e.g., Saxton, 2005; Saxton, Backley, & Gallaway, 2005; Saxton, Houston-Price, & Dawson, 2005) have conducted a number of experiments in which they investigate corrective input, finding in general that the contrast that occurs in adjacent utterances (contingent models) has a facilitative function, for at least some grammatical functions. Saxton, Houston-Price, and Dawson (2005) specifically considered clarification questions finding support for Saxton's (2000) prompt hypothesis, which assumes that clarification questions can be interpreted as a form of negative feedback, helping the child understand the ungrammaticality of his/her speech:

> This hypothesis is predicated on the assumption that specifically error-contingent CQs [clarification questions] can be interpreted by the child as a form of negative feedback for grammatical errors. The prompt hypothesis predicts that negative feedback can occasionally focus the child's attention on ungrammatical

[handwritten margin note: notice that learner production differs from TL forms. →contrast become apparent through conversations]

aspects of his or her speech, but only in cases where the child has prior knowledge of the correct grammatical form. The idea is that error-contingent CQs can function as a prompt, or reminder, to the child, cuing recall of a previously learned grammatical form. Prior knowledge of the correct form must be assumed, because there is nothing in a clarification request per se that conveys what the correct form is. For this reason, clarification requests are predicted to prompt, rather than teach, the child about preferred grammatical forms.

(pp. 399–400)

[handwritten margin note: correct forms are a result of contrast]

The important point for SLA literature is to ensure that correct forms as a result of contrast not be limited to immediate responses. Long-term effectiveness must be ensured in order to claim that there is validity to this approach.

This is not unlike what has been called in the SLA literature **noticing the gap**—that is, noticing where learner production differs from TL forms. Conversation provides the means for the contrasts to become apparent. The immediate juxtaposition of correct and erroneous forms may lead learners to recognize that their form is, in fact, erroneous. However, as Doughty (2003) pointed out, many questions remain: What is the function of working memory? What happens when learners take the next step, which (at least in the case of syntax or morphosyntax) will undoubtedly involve some sort of analysis? Contrasts occurring within the context of conversation often do not have an immediate outcome. Research has not yet been successful at predicting when a single exposure—for example, through a negotiation sequence or a recast—will or will not suffice to effect immediate learning.

It is likely that there are limitations to what can and cannot be learned through the provision of negative evidence provided through conversation. One possibility is that surface-level phenomena can be learned, but abstractions cannot. This is consistent with Truscott's (1998) claim that competence is not affected by noticing. Negative evidence probably cannot apply to long stretches of speech, given memory limitations (see Philp, 1999), but it may be effective with low-level phenomena such as pronunciation or basic meanings of lexical items. Future research will need to determine the long-term effects of interaction on different parts of language (see Gass et al., 2003). And, one must keep in mind differential effects of perception as noted by Mackey et al. (2000).

[handwritten margin note: language as an object of inquiry (grammar rules/vocab. memorization)]

12.6.2.3 *Metalinguistic Awareness*

[handwritten margin note: As learners think about a language, they learn the language]

Another explanation for the importance of negotiated interaction concerns metalinguistic awareness, an important aspect of language learning. Metalinguistic awareness refers to one's ability to consider language not just as a means of expressing ideas or communicating with others, but also as an object of inquiry. Thus, making puns suggests an ability to think about language, as opposed to only using it for expressive purposes. Similarly, judging whether a given sentence is grammatical in one's NL or translating from one language to another requires thinking about language, as opposed to engaging in pure use of it.

NNSs in a classroom setting often spend more time on metalinguistic activities (e.g., studying rules of grammar or memorizing vocabulary words) than on activities of pure use. The ability to *think* about language is often associated with an increased ability to *learn* a language. In fact, bilingual children have been known to have greater metalinguistic awareness than monolingual children (Bialystok, 1988).

Much classroom activity in earlier language-teaching methodologies engaged learners in just this type of consciousness raising, providing a direct means of making learners aware of the language at the expense of spending classroom time on practice activities. However, there are other ways of increasing metalinguistic awareness in learners in a classroom setting. To specifically relate this to the earlier discussion of negotiation, learners are made aware of errors in their speech (whether in grammar, pronunciation, content, or discourse) through the questioning and clarification that often go on in negotiation. In other words, negotiation is what makes NNSs aware of incongruities between the forms they are using and the forms used by NSs. In order to respond to an inquiry of nonunderstanding, NNSs must modify their output. For this to take place, learners must be aware of a problem and seek to resolve it. Hence, the more learners are made aware of unacceptable speech, the greater the opportunity for them to make appropriate modifications. Although there is limited evidence as to the long-term effects of these modifications, one can presume that, because negotiation leads to heightened awareness, it ultimately leads to increased knowledge of the L2 as well. For example, even though the NNS in the following exchange (from Pica, 1987, p. 6) does not produce the correct form, she is made aware of a pronunciation problem through the NS's indications of nonunderstanding.

Negotiation makes learners aware of differences between NL x TL

(12-54) NNS: And they have the chwach there.
        NS: The what?
        NNS: The chwach—I know someone that—
        NS: What does it mean?
        NNS: Like um like American people they always go there every Sunday
        NS: Yes?
        NNS: You kn—every morning that there pr—that—the American people
             get dressed up to got to um chwach.
        NS: Oh to church—I see.

In sum, there are a number of beneficial aspects to interaction: (1) input is often modified to make it more comprehensible; (2) areas of language difficulty become apparent through interaction, and, thus, learners notice a gap between their knowledge of the L2 and what is actually part of the L2, with noticing being helped through explicit or even indirect correction; and (3) being aware of this difference (i.e., gap), learners are likely to pay greater attention to subsequent input.

> Better in storing, comparing and retrieving.

more things to process = more consolidation

are able to take in more data

high working memory X low working memory

12.6.3 Who Benefits From Interaction?

It is clear that not everyone is able to take advantage of an interactive exchange, and certainly not at all times. The question that needs to be asked is: Why? In this section, we raise the issue of working memory, discussed in Chapter 10, and **inhibitory control** as ways for accounting for an individual's ability to benefit from interaction.

In recent years, there has been interest in the role of working memory as one way of accounting for the differential use of feedback. Philp (2003) was one of the first to acknowledge this relationship, although she did not measure working-memory capacity. Her study of noticing revealed differences among learners in their noticing of differences between what they had said (i.e., their IL) and what was actually said by a NS of the TL. She suggested that working memory and attentional resources may be at the base of this difference. Sagarra (2007), in a computer-based study of feedback, found working-memory capacity to be a variable that predicted whether or not learners benefitted from recasts.

An important study is one by Mackey et al. (2002), who directly investigated the relationship of individual differences in verbal working memory, noticing of interactional feedback, and L2 development, which in their case was measured through the acquisition of English question formation by Japanese L1 speakers. They found different benefits (long term versus short term), depending on the working-memory capacity of the learners. Those with lower working-memory scores had greater benefit immediately from the interaction, but the benefits did not persist when measured two weeks after the treatment. To the contrary, those with higher working-memory scores did have benefits attributable to the interaction that could be seen two weeks later, on a delayed posttest. An explanation that they propose is that those with higher working-memory capacity are better positioned to engage in the types of linguistic comparisons that are known to take place, focusing on both storage and processing. As Mackey et al. note (2002, p. 204), "those with high WM took longer to consolidate and make sense of the feedback given them, reflecting change only after an interval." Those with higher working-memory capacities were able to take in more data. As a consequence, they had more to process and ultimately consolidate; they were better at doing what needs to be done to benefit from interaction: compare, store, and subsequently retrieve. On the other hand, those with lower working-memory capacity, were better at immediate modifications, perhaps because they had fewer data to work with. In sum, the emphasis for high-working-memory individuals is on processing, whereas the emphasis for low-working-memory-capacity individuals is on storage. It is important to note that working-memory scores in this study were a combination of L1 and L2 working-memory scores. Gass et al. (in press) used only L1 working-memory scores (see Gass & Lee, 2011, for arguments against using L2 working-memory scores) and found that working-memory capacity was not a significant variable in determining who does and does not benefit from interaction. Rather, the variable of greater importance was inhibitory control, which we discuss below.

As noted throughout this chapter, another essential part of interaction is output. Mackey et al. (2010) considered the relationship between modified output and working-memory capacity. In their study of 42 college-level, English-speaking learners of Spanish (4th semester), learners participated in interactive, task-based activities and took a verbal working-memory span test, finding a positive relationship between the production of modified output and an individual's working-memory score.

We turn next to **inhibition.** If we think about how much information is present when learning a new language, it is clear that we cannot focus on everything. We have to take in information about syntax, morphology, semantics, phonology, pragmatics, often all at once. At times, it is necessary to block out certain information, so that we can focus on the task at hand. This is what is known as inhibition, namely, the blocking out of some things to focus on others.

[handwritten margin note: inhibition "" = "blocking out system", ←]

There are many ways to determine an individual's ability to do this in real time. One of the most frequently used tests is what is known as the Stroop test, in which participants state the color of the ink/font that a particular word or symbol is written in (Stroop, 1935). Built into the task is a word/color incongruity: the participant is shown a color word (e.g., *red*), written in a color of ink that is incongruent with the word that the participant reads (e.g., the word *red* written in blue ink). Thus, the task for the individual is to *inhibit* the distracting semantic stimulus of the lexical item *red*, in order to correctly state that the color of the ink is blue. The time taken to respond to incongruent items is longer than the time taken to respond to congruent items (e.g., *red* written in red ink) or to neutral items, such as the symbol @ written in red ink).

TIME TO DO ...

Visit www.routledge.com/cw/gass-978415894951. Was it easy to do this in English? Was it easier to do the congruent items (*red* written in red) than the incongruent items (e.g., *red* written in green)? Do you think it would be easy to do this in your L2 (or in your L1, if English is not your L1)?

TIME TO DO ...

Consider the Stroop example located at www.routledge.com/cw/gass-978-415894951/s1/stroop, which is done in Pumlaco, a language you do not know (it is a made-up language). Was it easy to do this? In other words, was there interfering information? Imagine that you know a little bit of Pumlaco: Would that make the task a bit harder? What can you conclude about the relationship between proficiency and the ability to inhibit information?

(handwritten margin note: WORKING MEMORY x inhibition)

Gass et al. (in press) compared interaction results based on working-memory capacity and on inhibition. They looked at actual learning and, from there, considered learner characteristics that might have contributed to that learning. They found that, with two groups of English L1–Italian L2 learners, those who learned from interaction did not differ from those who did not learn from interaction on working-memory scores. They did, however, differ based on their abilities to inhibit information; those who were better able to inhibit information were also better able to learn from interaction. Thus, the ability to inhibit information in the L2 may be one contributing source of a learner's ability to learn from an interactional context.

12.7 LIMITATIONS OF INPUT

(handwritten margin note: 2 types of changes: CONTINUOUS x DISCONTINUOUS)

As with most things, there are limits to what input can do for learners. Sorace (1993a, 1993b, 1995; Bard et al., 1996) argued that there are two kinds of change that occur in learners' grammars: discontinuous and continuous. She considers, in particular, two kinds of verbs in Italian, verbs such as *andare* and *venire*, which mean "to go" and "to come," respectively, and verbs such as *camminare*, which means "to walk." Both *andare* and *venire* are intransitive verbs that require *essere* ("to be") as an auxiliary, whereas *camminare*, also an intransitive verb, requires *avere* ("to have"). She was particularly interested in how learners of Italian learn the appropriate auxiliary to use with these two types of verbs. That is, do they use the auxiliary *essere* or the auxiliary *avere*? Auxiliary choice is dependent on both syntactic and semantic factors; some verbs are sensitive to both lexical–semantic distinctions as well as syntactic configurations.

What Sorace found in looking at data from learners of Italian was a differentiation in terms of input use with regard to auxiliary selection. They were sensitive to the input with regard to lexical–semantic properties of auxiliary selection (regardless of their L1), but they appeared to be impervious to the input with respect to some of the syntactic properties. Also, lexical–semantic properties were acquired incrementally, whereas syntactic properties, if they were acquired at all, developed in a discontinuous fashion (personal communication, January 25, 1993). Thus, in Sorace's work, it is possible for the input, or, in her terms, the evidence available to learners, to have a varying effect depending on the part of the grammar to be affected—more so for lexical semantics and less so for syntax.

12.8 CONCLUSION

In this chapter, we have dealt with the nature and function of input, output, and interaction in SLA. In Chapter 13, we extend these findings and focus attention on L2 learning in a classroom context.

POINTS TO REMEMBER

- Foreigner talk refers to the speech that NSs of a language use with NNSs of that language. It is similar to caretaker talk that is used with young children and is distinguished by slow speech rate, loud speech, long pauses, simple vocabulary, repetitions and elaborations, and paucity of slang.

- Comprehensibility is a characteristic involving NNSs. The NS's ability to understand the NNS's pronunciation, the NNS's ability to contextualize language, and the NNS's ability to understand the NS all affect the comprehensibility of a conversation. Comprehension of an NNS by an NS is facilitated by three factors: (a) familiarity with a particular NNS, (b) familiarity with nonnative speech in general, and (c) familiarity with the discourse topic.

- Backchannel cues are verbal messages, such as *uh huh* or *yeah*, that an NNS can send to an NS in a conversation to indicate understanding (even if there is none).

- Negotiation of meaning refers to episodes when the conversation between an NNS and an NS or two NNSs is interrupted so that one or both parties can understand what the conversation is about. In interactions with NNSs, these episodes are frequent.

- Interaction with NNSs frequently includes confirmation checks (Is this what you mean?), comprehension checks (Do you understand? Do you follow me?), and clarification requests (What? Huh?).

- Comprehensible input is not enough to ensure acquisition. It is also necessary for learners to have the opportunity to produce comprehensible output ("pushed" output). Output serves several functions for learners, including providing information about the success of their utterance, hypothesis testing, automaticity, and a movement from meaning-based to grammar-based processing.

- A recast is a type of feedback where an incorrect utterance is reformulated by the NS (or more proficient speaker of the L2) without losing the meaning of the original utterance.

- Learners can test their hypotheses about how the language works by producing output in their L2.

- An individual L2 learner may benefit more or less than other learners from conversational interaction. Recent studies have considered the role that an individual's working memory and inhibitory control may play in how much they benefit from interaction.

SUGGESTIONS FOR ADDITIONAL READING

Input, interaction and corrective feedback in L2 learning (2012). Alison Mackey. Oxford University Press.

Multiple perspectives on interaction: *Second language research in honor of Susan M. Gass* (2009). Alison Mackey and Charlene Polio (Eds.). Routledge.

Conversational interaction in second language acquisition: A collection of empirical studies (2007). Alison Mackey (Ed.). Oxford University Press.

Learning a second language through interaction (2000). Rod Ellis (Ed.). John Benjamins.

Input, interaction, and the second language learner (1997). Susan Gass. Lawrence Erlbaum Associates.

Input and interaction in language acquisition (1994). Clare Gallaway and Brian J. Richards (Eds.). Cambridge University Press.

The syntax of conversation in interlanguage development (1990). Charlene Sato. Gunter Narr Verlag.

Conversation in second language acquisition: Talking to learn (1986). Richard Day (Ed.). Newbury House.

Input in second language acquisition (1985). Susan Gass and Carolyn Madden (Eds.). Newbury House.

MORE TO DO AND MORE TO THINK ABOUT ...

1. Go to Link #1 in the Link section at the end of the chapter. The exchange took place on February 6, 2011, on CNN's *Reliable Sources*. Candy Crowley was interviewing Ahmed Shafiq, the Egyptian prime minister. This was a telephone interview. She begins by saying: "Mr. Prime Minister, can you hear me?" The rest of the exchange appears on the website:

   Questions:
   (a) In what ways does this conversation seem typical of conversations involving NNSs? In what ways does it not?
   (b) This conversation includes many instances of non-comprehension. Who does not comprehend? How are those instances of non-comprehension made clear to the interlocutor?
   (c) Is there an attempt to resolve the lack of comprehension? In what ways is this done?
   (d) Do you feel that there was truly a lack of comprehension, or was this an example of political side-stepping of the issue? Justify your response.

2. Find an NNS of your language or pretend that you are speaking to an NNS. You need to convey the meanings of the following five sentences. Without letting your partner see the sentences, how would you get your meaning

across (e.g., sentence by sentence)? Make careful note of exactly what you say and what you do.

(a) I don't know the person you're looking at.
(b) She's my cousin, not my friend.
(c) Were you listening to that woman?
(d) Come to my house on Friday. Don't forget!
(e) Yesterday I drove to the zoo and saw some monkeys.

Now reverse roles and do the same with the following five sentences:

(a) She's laughing at that man's accident. She's not nice.
(b) Who is that woman? Is she the president?
(c) He always travels with one suitcase.
(d) Where's the book I gave you yesterday?
(e) He will be leaving tomorrow.

3. Observe an NS and an NNS conversing, taking careful notes on how you think their speech differs from what you would expect in a conversation between NSs. Pay attention to all aspects of the NS's speech, including pronunciation, grammar, vocabulary, rate of speech, and so on. Do the features you note coincide with what is presented in Table 12.1? Are there features you noted that are not included in the table?

4. From Table 12.2, describe the differences in the speech of the kindergarten teacher in each of the instances given. What do you think the effect of the different modifications might be? Do you think that the teacher trained herself to speak like this? What evidence is there that using a modified form of speech is something that we begin doing at a young age? (Hint: Think of speech to NSs as well as to NNSs.)

5. Consider the summary data in Table 12A.1 (p. 394), taken from the teacher's speech referred to in Problem 4 and in Table 12.2.

    Do these data support what you found in looking at the data from Problem 4? What uniform explanation can you give to account for the data in this problem and those from Problem 3?

6. The data that follow come from a telephone conversation in which an NNS was conducting an interview about food and nutrition (Gass & Varonis, 1985). Focus on the language following the NNS's *Pardon me?* How would you describe the difference between that response and the immediately preceding response? What functions do the modifications serve?

> NNS: There has been a lot of talk lately about additives and preservatives in food. In what ways has this changed your eating habits?

(continues on next page)

TABLE 12A.1 Summary Analysis of Data from Table 12.2

Proficiency level	% teacher utterances (n = 269)	Mean length of utterance	Student NL
Beginning	40.5	3.18	Japanese
Low-intermediate	27.9	3.37	Arabic
Intermediate	14.9	4.51	Urdu
Native speaker	16.0	5.27	English

Word usage			
Proficiency level	% total items (n = 933)	Type/token	Student NL
Beginning	37.62	0.33	Japanese
Low-intermediate	24.75	0.41	Arabic
Intermediate	14.50	0.59	Urdu
Native speaker	23.47	0.48	English

NS: Uh, I avoid them, I d—, I don't buy prepackaged foods uh, as much. . . . Uh, I don't buy . . . say . . . potato chips that have a lot of flavoring on them. . . . And uh, I eat better. I think.

NNS: Pardon me?

NS: Ummm, pardon me? I, I eat better, I think. I, I don't buy so much food that's prepackaged.

Example 2:

NNS: How have increasing food costs changed your eating habits?

NS: Well, it doesn't, hasn't really.

NNS: Pardon me?

NS: It hasn't really changed them.

Example 3:

NNS: How have increasing food costs changed your eating habits?

NS: Uh well that would I don't think they've change 'em much right now, but the pressure's on.

NNS: Pardon me?

NS: I don't think they've changed our eating habits much as of now . . .

7. In this chapter, we discussed the role of negotiation. We pointed out that negotiation aids the learner in understanding. What connection can be made between understanding at a particular point in time and actual acquisition (internalization of new linguistic information)? That is, because a learner is

able to understand something in conversation, can we automatically say that he or she will internalize or even understand the same thing at a later point in time?

8. Swain (1985, p. 248) reported the following statement by an L2 learner in Grade 9: "I understand everything anyone says to me, and I can hear in my head how I should sound when I talk, but it never comes out that way." Can you think of examples when this has happened to you in an L2? In your NL? What do you think the reason for this is?

9. Data from NSs engaged in conversations with NNSs follow: (Data from Larsen-Freeman & Long, 1991, pp. 120–124). Describe the ways in which these NSs ask questions of the NNSs. What is the communicative effect of asking questions in these ways? Does it help with language learning? Why or why not?

(12a-1) Did you *like* San Diego?

(12a-2) Do you *like* San Diego? San Diego, did you like it?

(12a-3) Right. When do you take the break? At ten-thirty?

(12a-4) NS: When do you go to the uh Santa Monica? You say you go fishing in Santa Monica, right?
         NNS: Yeah.
         NS: When?

(12a-5) NS: Uh what does uh what does your father do in uh you're from Kyoto, right?
         NNS: Yeah.
         NS: What does your father do in Kyoto?

(12a-6) NS: Are you going to visit San Francisco? Or Las Vegas?
         NNS: Yes I went to Disneyland and to Knottsberry Farm.
         NS: Oh yeah?

(12a-7) NS: Do you like California?
         NNS: Huh?
         NS: Do you like Los Angeles?
         NNS: Uhm.
         NS: Do you like California?
         NNS: Oh! Yeah I like.

10. Find a picture that is relatively easy to describe. Make two recordings of an NS describing the picture to (a) another NS and (b) an NNS. Write down exactly what you hear. In what ways does the structure of the conversation differ? Are there examples of self-corrections, changes in grammar, confirmation checks, comprehension checks, or other interactional

modifications? Is there evidence of cooperation? What are the participants doing to make communication easier?

11. Think about the possibility of success in a study-abroad classroom situation where your fellow students were *not* members of the host community, but speakers of your NL. Thus, the input you receive from your classmates is not the standard language but what Wong-Fillmore (1976) called "junky data." Do you think practice with this type of input data is problematic? If the situation were, instead, a foreign-language classroom, would your answer be the same?

12. In Chapter 11, we discussed CA (section 11.5) and, in the current chapter, we discussed the interaction hypothesis. Both use conversational data as the basis for understanding learning. Consider the following transcript of a conversation from a French language class. Fill in the two columns with a CA interpretation and with an input–interaction interpretation.

	CA interpretation	Input–interaction interpretation
Lines 17–29		
[cette chaîne, *This chain*,		
°chhhh:::::° (.) Lorena une phrase avec ce[tte (trousse) *°chhhh::::::°* *(.) Lorena a* *phrase with* *thi[s pencil* *case*		
[cette trousse est dans ma valise [this pencil case is in my bag		
B [( )]		

P: cette
        trousse   est
        à moi
        this   pencil
        case is mine
24 J: ((cough))		

	CA interpretation	Input–interaction interpretation
25 K: cette trousse est [[(0.3) dans ma:] (0.9) ma sac *this pencil case is [[(0.3) in my: (fem.)] (0.9) my (fem.) bag*		
cette trousse est [[(0.3) dans ma:] (0.9) ma sac *this pencil case is [[(0.3) in my: (fem.)] (0.9) my (fem.) bag*		

°mon:,°
°my:,° (masc.)

mon sac
my bag (28)
sac.
bag.(29)

	Summary:	Summary:

LINK

1. http://transcripts.cnn.com/TRANSCRIPTS/1102/06/rs.01.html

CHAPTER THIRTEEN

Instructed Second Language Learning

[handwritten annotations:]
Instruction: explicit x implicit
duration + intensity of instructional effect
interaction/moderation of effects by variable

Focus on form → meaning
Focus on forms → rule, grammar, structure ...

① learner proficiency
② types of L2 features being taught

13.1 INTRODUCTION

This chapter is devoted to learning that takes place in a classroom context. It is not a chapter intended to be a "how to" manual for teachers; rather, the focus is on learning that is specific to an instructed environment. In the other chapters in this book, we do not differentiate between in- and out-of-classroom contexts of learning. In other words, even though some examples are taken from a classroom context and others from outside the classroom, we do not focus on the contextual difference in the conclusions we draw. This is mainly owing to an assumption that processes involved in learning an L2 can be thought of as independent of the context in which the language is being learned, although they may apply differentially by context. For example, whether or not some mechanism, such as UG, is responsible for the learning of core grammar is not to be thought of as dependent on the context of that learning. Whatever psycholinguistic processing takes place in a naturalistic situation presumably takes place in a classroom situation as well. And whatever theoretical stance one assumes for learning should not depend on where language learning takes place.

[handwritten margin annotations:]
Quality x quantity
environment/social context
classroom

This is not to say that differences do not exist, for clearly they do, the most obvious being differences in the quantity and quality of input. For learners in a foreign-language setting—that is, those learning another language in their home environment—not only is there limited input, but a large part of the input comes from classmates whose knowledge of the foreign language is restricted. Interactional opportunities are also often severely restricted in a foreign-language environment. In this chapter then, our concern is with those opportunities for language learning that are specific to the classroom context. Within this substantial area of SLA, researchers have posed a range of questions related to classroom language/input, the type or types of instruction that are most effective (e.g., explicit vs. implicit), the duration and intensity of instructional effects, and whether those effects might interact with, or be moderated by, other variables, such as learner proficiency or the types of L2 features being taught.

13.2 CLASSROOM LANGUAGE

[handwritten: may be modified depending on students' proficiency level; progression from lesser to greater syntactic complexity]

Spada and Lightbown (2009) provide a review of classroom research, with a focus
on interaction. One of the main differentiating factors between classroom learning and
so-called naturalistic learning is the language available from which learners can come
to understand the workings of the L2 and formulate hypotheses. In language
classrooms, the language addressed to learners may be somewhat modified, as we
saw in Chapter 12.

Gaies (1979) presented data from eight teacher trainees and their speech (a) to
each other and (b) to four groups of ESL students at four proficiency levels. Table
13.1 presents a portion of these data for each of these five groups. As can be seen,
in all cases there is a progression from lesser to greater syntactic complexity as a
function of proficiency level. In fact, the proficiency level is a statistically significant
predictor of the syntactic complexity of these teachers' speech.

In foreign-language instruction, there are generally three sources of input: (a)
teacher, (b) materials, and (c) other learners, with the greatest amount of input coming
from the teacher. We saw earlier that teacher talk can be limited. It is clear that learner
talk to other learners is also limited and often filled with errors. To what extent these
errors are picked up or ignored in the classroom is unclear. Perhaps surprisingly, there
is evidence that learners do not pick up errors from one another to any significant

[handwritten margin: INPUT IN FOREIGN LANGUAGE INSTRUCTION → 1. teacher 2. material 3. other learners]

TABLE 13.1 Complexity of Teacher Speech Directed at Different Proficiency
Levels (*Source*: From "Linguistic input in first and second language
learning" by S. Gaies. In F. Eckman and A. Hastings (Eds.), *Studies in
first and second language acquisition* (p. 190). 1979. Reprinted by
permission.)

Level	Words per T-unit	Ratio of clauses to T-units	Words per clause
Beginner	4.30	1.02	4.20
Upper beginner	5.75	1.14	5.04
Intermediate	6.45	1.24	5.18
Advanced	8.26	1.38	5.98
Baseline	10.97	1.60	6.84

Note: T-Units are defined as "one main clause plus any subordinate clause or nonclausal structure that is
attached to or embedded in it" (Hunt, 1970, p. 4).

degree. For example, Gass and Varonis (1989) reported data from two NNSs of English (different language backgrounds). The learners were performing a classroom task in which they had to go out onto the streets of Ann Arbor, Michigan, with a tape recorder and ask people for directions to the train station. The tape recorder was left on during the entire time they were engaged in the task, including the time between stopping passersby for directions. They alternated stopping strangers to ask for directions. Following is the exhaustive sequence of questions they asked:

(13-1) NNS1: Can you tell me where is the train station?
        NNS2: Can you tell me where the train station is?
        NNS1: Can you tell me where is the train station?
        NNS2: Can you tell me where the train station is?
        NNS1: Can you tell me where is the train station?
        NNS2: Can you tell me where the train station is?
        NNS1: Can you tell me where the train station is?
        NNS2: Can you tell me where the train station is?
        NNS1: Can you tell me where the train station is?

To appreciate the significance of this example, it is important to note that nowhere in the conversation between requests for directions did the students discuss the discrepancy in their versions of indirect questions. Nevertheless, NNS1 made an unprompted change in the form of her utterance, from the incorrect *Can you tell me where is the train station?* to the correct *Can you tell me where the train station is?*, whereas NNS2 made no change. Importantly, the change was in the direction of the TL and not from a correct form to an incorrect form. Hence, it was only input from another NNS that prompted the change from incorrect to correct. Similarly, Bruton and Samuda (1980) listened to 10 hours of taped conversations and found only one example of a change from a correct form to an incorrect one. It may be that learners know when they are right and may also know when they are wrong, or at least have a sense that they are not sure. When learners internalize a new form, they may use the positive evidence they hear/read to strengthen that knowledge. That is, they may receive confirmatory evidence for their correct hypotheses. When a hypothesis is not correct, there is no confirmatory evidence, and the knowledge is loosely structured, resulting in uncertainty.

This is supported by Brooks and Swain (2009), whose four participants were 100 percent accurate on a posttest following a collaborative writing task; they were able to resolve linguistic problems and were able to maintain correct forms on the posttest. Language development, however, required not peer expertise, but NS expertise.

In Chapter 12, we looked at interactions in which negotiation about a form leads to knowledge about the form. Swain (2006) uses the term *languaging, which takes place in collaborative dialogue.* Such dialogue engages learners in both problem-solving as well as knowledge-building. In other words, they are solving linguistic problems and they are building their knowledge about language; that is, they are *languaging*. As Swain et al. (2009) state: "Languaging is a form of verbalization used to mediate the solution(s) to complex problems and tasks. It is defined as 'the process of making meaning and shaping knowledge and experience through language'" (Swain, 2006, p. 89).

We present an example (13-2) of two classroom learners who are jointly writing an essay. They are Grade 8 students who have been in a French immersion program since kindergarten. The vocabulary item *réveille-matin*—"alarm clock"—is in question. On a pretest, Kim knew the word, whereas Rick did not. On a posttest, both students knew the word. What we see in this episode is the use of conversation as a tool for learning. Rick wavers between alternatives for alarm clock and, through questioning of Kim and responses from Kim, he comes to the correct French word *réveille-matin*.

(13-2) Swain and Lapkin (1998, p. 329)

Turn #

2 KIM: On peut pas déterminer qu'est-ce que c'est.
"One can't figure out what it is."

3 RICK: Réveille-matin.
"Alarm clock."

4 KIM: Et il y a un réveille-matin rouge . . . sur une table brune, et le réveille-matin dit six heures, et c'est tout.
"And there is a red alarm clock . . . on the brown table, and the alarm clock says six o'clock, and that's all."

9 RICK: Elle est en train de dormir après que . . . la rêve-matin est encore sonné. Et le rêve-matin dit six heures un.
"She is sleeping after the alarm clock rang again. And the alarm clock says one minute after six o'clock."

55 KIM: Il y a un réveille-matin.
"There is an alarm clock."

56 RICK: Réveille-matin?
"Alarm clock?"

57 KIM: Réveille-matin.
"Alarm clock."

66 RICK: Se réveille à cause . . . du son . . .
"Wakes up because . . . of the sound . . ."

67 KIM: Réveille-matin.
"Alarm clock"

68 RICK: A cause du . . .
"Because of . . ."

69 KIM: Du réveille-matin qui sonne? Does that sound OK?
"Of the alarm clock that rings? Does that sound OK?"

70 RICK: Or what about . . . Jacqueline se lève à cause du . . . du réveille- . . . yeah, qui sonne
"Or what about . . . Jacqueline [the girl in their story] gets up because of the . . . of the alarm- . . . yeah, that rings."

71 KIM: Or you can say, du réveille-matin, or du sonnement du
        réveille-matin.
        "OK. Or you can say, of the alarm clock, or the ring of the
        alarm clock."

72 RICK: No, réveille-matin qui sonne.
        "No, alarm clock that rings."

92 RICK: Sur la rêv- . . . rêve-matin.
        "On the alarm clock."

93 KIM: Sur le réveille-matin pour arrêter le sonnement.
        "On the alarm clock to stop the ring."

94 RICK: Rêve-matin?
        "Alarm clock?"

95 KIM: Réveille-matin
        "Alarm clock." [Stresses component meaning "wake".]

What we see in the example above is an exchange that includes hypothesis generation, hypothesis testing, and the extension of knowledge to new contexts. What is interesting is Rick's initial use of the correct word in Turn 3, followed in Turn 9 by two uses of the incorrect *rêve-matin* (once with the feminine article *la* and once with the masculine article *le*). Clearly, this suggests his uncertainty, which is further seen in his pauses (Turns 9, 70, and 92) and in Turn 94, where he asks his partner if *rêve-matin* is acceptable. So, we see Rick's change to the correct form. The change is not a one-time affair, but shows a back-and-forth wavering between correct and incorrect forms. Rick is seen to generate hypotheses (his questions), and Kim's responses are either confirmatory or disconfirmatory. We note that Rick receives input and uses output as a means of learning the new word. In Turn 56, Rick's attempt to write the word focuses his attention on his own uncertainty, forcing him to make a choice between the alternative hypotheses he has entertained. It is through collaborative dialogues, as evidenced here, that we recall the construct of Zone of Proximal Development discussed in Chapter 11. As noted in that chapter, potential development comes about through problem-solving in collaboration with more capable peers.

However, as mentioned earlier, it is not always the case that learner forms can serve as good input for other learners. In another excerpt (13-3) from these same two learners (Swain & Lapkin, 1998, p. 333), it is clear that, without teacher intervention, these two participants will either walk away uncertain about the correct form or will learn something incorrect in French, that is, they will practice and automatize the IL, perhaps far from TL norms.

(13-3) KIM: [elle voit un] gars.
        "[She sees a] guy."

     RICK: . . . gars, qui s'en va à l'école.
        ". . . guy who is going to school."

     KIM: Qui marche vers l' école . . . marche.
        "Who is walking towards school, walking."

Both *marcher* ("walk") and *s'en aller* ("walk") exist in French, but in this context *marcher* is incorrect. The pair opts for the incorrect form, probably because, as Swain and Lapkin suggested, *marcher* more closely resembles English usage and it is suggested by Kim, the one who in general is seen as having greater expertise in French. Thus, although the classroom is a place where conversational interaction can often provide opportunities for learning, an important caveat is in order—teacher intervention is often essential.

[margin note: Teacher intervention is essential]

Brooks and Swain (2009) show that other sorts of intervention are necessary. In their study, they considered different types of expertise. Four adult ESL learners participated in an initial collaborative writing (in pairs) of a story. The story was then compared with a reformulated version by an NS, and the learners were asked to discuss any differences they noticed between the two versions (this was video-taped). The noticing task was immediately followed by a stimulated recall of the video, in which the researcher stopped the tape to discuss differences or when the students wanted to discuss changes made in the reformulated version. Finally, one week following these activities, there was a posttest in which the participants were given a typed version of their original story and asked to make changes. The researchers found that the relevant sources of expertise depended to some extent on language development. In general, however, most of the important input came from peers, which they conceptualize as the center of input. The next layer of significant input consisted of peers plus the reformulation, and the next was peers plus reformulation plus NS (teacher). As Brooks and Swain (p. 80) note,

[margin note: most important input comes from peers]

> As a pedagogical model this places learners as the first source of expertise rather than the teacher; when learners cannot create a ZPD through interacting with each other or with other forms of mediation such as a reformulation, then the teacher can participate in the activity needed to construct ZPD.

[margin note: teacher intervention x ZPD]

13.3 TEACHABILITY/LEARNABILITY

[margin note: → Language Acquisition takes place in a specific order. ↳ pedagogical intervention does not change their order.]

As early as the morpheme-order studies, there was an emphasis on acquisition orders; that is, the idea that acquisition takes place in some sort of natural order, regardless of input, instruction, or L1 background. In fact, Krashen stated this as part of the entire Monitor Model (see Chapter 5) as the Natural Order Hypothesis, which claims that elements of language (or language rules) are acquired in a predictable order.

The implication of acquisition order is that pedagogical intervention cannot alter (or can alter in only a trivial manner) natural acquisition orders (see Lightbown, 1983). The most explicit statement of this comes from work originally involving German as an L2. Recall from Chapters 10 and 12 the discussion of the acquisition of English questions. Findings based on the natural progression within a classroom context are supported by a number of studies. Pienemann (1984, 1989) argued that stages in this developmental sequence cannot be skipped, even as a result of instruction. He investigated German word-order development among 10 Italian children ranging in

[margin note: stages cannot be skipped with instructions, but they can move faster]

INSTRUCTED SECOND LANGUAGE LEARNING

age from 7 to 9. They all had two weeks of instruction on a particular stage. Some were at the immediately preceding stage, and others were at a much earlier stage. Only the former group learned the instructional target, suggesting that the other children could not learn because they were not developmentally ready.

TIME TO THINK ...

What examples can you think of where learners do not acquire particular forms, regardless of pedagogical intervention? Are there certain structures in your L2 that you have not been able to master, in spite of a great deal of instruction?

As discussed in Chapter 12, Mackey (1995, 1999) set out to determine the extent to which conversational interaction could alter the developmental progression of the acquisition of questions. One couldn't alter the stages of development, although, through interaction, the process could be moved along faster. There are constraints on learning such that even pedagogical intervention is likely to be unsuccessful in altering the order (see discussion on page 253 for an explanation).

In Chapter 9, we dealt with the acquisition of RCs, showing that there is a predictable order of acquisition. Considering the AH from the point of view of learnability, if difficulty is at the base of this universal, we would expect learners to learn to relativize according to the ordering of the AH positions. Yet another prediction comes in the form of learners' capacities to generalize. What would happen if, let's say, through instruction, a learner were to come to learn a more difficult RC position before learning an easier one. Would knowledge of that more difficult RC construction generalize to knowledge of the easier RC positions? This would not be unexpected, because, in some sense, knowledge of a more difficult structure should incorporate knowledge of a related, easier structure. In fact, several studies lend support to this prediction. In Gass (1982), for example, two groups of L2 learners were given specific instruction on RCs. One group was instructed on subject and direct-object relatives; the second group on object-of-preposition relatives only. After the period of instruction, both groups were tested on RC types. The group that had received subject and direct-object instruction only performed well on those two RC types, but not on others, whereas the second group performed well, not only on their instructed RCs (object of preposition), but also on the RCs higher on the Accessibility Hierarchy, that is subject and direct-object RCs, but not those that were lower.

The results from a study by Eckman et al. (1988) were similar. There were four groups of learners: a control group and three experimental groups. Each of the three experimental groups received instruction on one of three RC types: subject, direct object, or object of preposition. Their results are given in Figure 13.1

The figure shows improvement rates for the three types of RCs. As can be seen, the greatest improvement on all three structures occurs in the group that was given

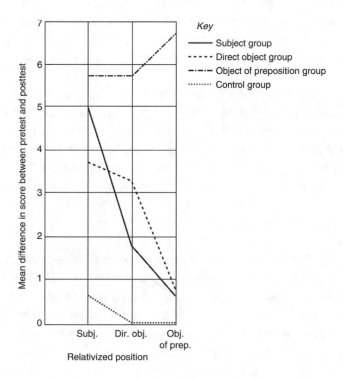

Key
—— Subject group
- - - - Direct object group
—·—·— Object of preposition group
·········· Control group

FIGURE 13.1 Interaction of Group and Relativized Position (*Source*: From "On the generalization of relative clause instruction in the acquisition of English as a second language" by F. Eckman, L. Bell, and D. Nelson, 1988, *Applied Linguistics*, *9*, 1–20. Reprinted by permission.)

instruction on the lowest position (the object of preposition group). The group with the next greatest improvement (i.e., improvement on two structures) was the direct-object group, and then the subject group, although the subject group showed greater improvement than the direct-object group on the RCs on which they had had instruction (subjects). The conclusions of both these studies suggest that learners' maximum generalization occurs from more marked (or difficult, in the terminology used here) structures to the less marked ones (see section 9.2.1). Generalization from less difficult to more difficult does not appear to occur. Hamilton (1994), also using ESL learners, found that learners generalized from the marked to the unmarked. Partial support of generalization of the AH comes from a study by Croteau (1995), who investigated relativization by foreign-language learners of Italian (English as the L1). She found that, when there was instruction on a higher position on the hierarchy, there was not generalization to a lower position. However, when there was instruction on a lower position, generalization did not occur in all instances. Specifically, those instructed on direct-object RCs generalized to subject RCs, but those taught object of preposition RCs generalized to the direct-object position, but not to the subject position. Not surprisingly, those taught genitive RCs did not generalize at all. This is not surprising because the genitive in previous studies did not behave according to the predictions of the hierarchy, possibly because the English genitive may behave as a unit that takes

[handwritten margin notes:]
Generalizations
from more difficult structures (more marked) to less difficult (less marked).
The opposite does not happen.

405

on another position of the hierarchy. For example, the genitive *whose brother* in the sentence *That's the man whose brother I saw* may be interpreted as a direct object of *I saw* and thus takes on the characteristics of the direct-object position rather than a genitive.

More recently, in addition to these and other earlier studies of relativization in ESL (e.g., Pavesi, 1986; Doughty, 1991), a wider of range of languages have been examined, including Chinese (Hu & Liu, 2007) and German (Byrnes & Sinicrope, 2008), among others. In a study of Arabic learners studying English in Tunisia, Ammar and Lightbown (2003) found evidence of generalization to RC types less marked than the RC type on which they received instruction, as is generally predicted, but also found evidence of generalization in the other direction, suggesting bidirectional generalization does occur. This research dealt with learners of languages with post-nominal RCs.

Yabuki-Soh (2007) considered pedagogical effects of RC acquisition by learners of Japanese, a language with pre-nominal RCs. Her study is primarily focused on different treatment types (form-based, meaning-based, and a combination of form-/meaning-based) and the generalization possibilities from the instructed RC (oblique) to easier as well as more difficult RC types. Her instruction was on oblique RCs, which are generally equivalent to object-of-preposition RCs, although, in Japanese, there are postpositions (they occur after the noun) not prepositions. Her results showed that instruction type did affect the ability to generalize RCs. In particular, when there was a detailed analysis of the grammatical structure, comprehension and production were facilitated. With regard to generalization, her study suggests that generalization from more marked to less marked is possible and may indeed be an effective basis of syllabus design.

[margin note: Instruction type affects ability to generalize RC]

A final point to consider is that markedness may not be the only factor that determines the path learners take when acquiring RCs and other features for which developmental sequences have been described (e.g., questions, negation, tense/aspect). A number of other factors, such as saliency, individual cognitive abilities (e.g., working memory, inhibitory control), and frequency may also mediate L2 development (Goldschneider & DeKeyser, 2001; Mackey & Sachs, 2012). From a pedagogical perspective, although little can be done to influence cognitive abilities, there are certainly ways in which teachers can increase the frequency and/or perceptual salience of targeted items (see section 13.4.4 below on input manipulation and input enhancement).

[margin note: L2 DEVELOPMENT VARIABLES ↓ saliency individual cognitive skills frequency]

13.4 FOCUS ON FORM

Spada and Lightbown (2009) provide a rich overview of classroom research, with a focus on interaction. They note the closeness of interaction and classroom-based research in the recent past, with corrective feedback (particularly recasts) being the point of connection. Recall from Krashen's characterization of the input hypothesis,

[margin note: INTERACTION (corrective feedbacks + recasts)]

[Handwritten margin notes at top: "FOCUS ON FORM {need for meaning-focused activity where there is attention to form"; "FOCUS ON FORMS {accumulation of language items (plural, passives)"]

discussed in Chapter 5, that what learners need (at least at the early stages) was input and that other forms of language modification or emphasis (for example, explicit rule presentation, negative feedback) were not necessary. His and the work of others led to numerous studies seeking to test whether instruction as it is traditionally conceived had an effect or not (see Doughty, 1991, and Long, 1983, for early summaries). This line of research showed, relatively quickly, that more than input was needed: for example, interaction and output, discussed in Chapter 12. More explicitly, R. Ellis (2001) and Norris and Ortega (2000), among many others (e.g., Mochizuki & Ortega, 2008), have argued that one needs an explicit focus on language to facilitate acquisition. This has led researchers to consider directly the effects of language focus in instruction. *[Margin note: "Language focus"]*

Throughout this book, we deal with the concept of attention. Implicit in this notion is the concept of **focus on form**.[1] Long (1991) distinguished between focus on *form* and **focus on *formS***. The latter refers to earlier teaching methodologies in which the main organizing principle for language classrooms was the accumulation of individual language items (e.g., plural endings, passives). The former refers to a need for meaning-focused activity into which an attention to form is embedded. As Long (1991, pp. 45–46) stated, focus on form "overtly draws students' attention to linguistic elements as they arise incidentally in lessons whose overriding focus is on meaning or communication." This is similar to what Sharwood Smith (1991, 1993) referred to as enhanced input: that is, input that can be enhanced by an external source (e.g., a teacher) or an internal source (learners relying on their own resources). *[Margin note: "ENHANCED INPUT ↓ input that can be enhanced by external or internal resources."]*

J. Williams (1999) investigated eight classroom learners at different levels of proficiency. She found numerous examples of learner-generated attention to form, as well as considerable variation. The results suggest that learners at low levels of proficiency do not often spontaneously attend to language form. This is not surprising, given the demands necessary just to maintain communication in an L2, particularly when knowledge of the L2 is scant. J. Williams also found that, when there is learner-generated attention to form, the attention is generally given to words rather than to other linguistic features, a result obtained repeatedly in studies investigating focus on form (R. Ellis et al., 2001b; Alcón Soler, 2007; Zhao & Bitchener, 2007; Alcón & Garcia Mayo, 2008; Loewen, 2009).

A study by Gass et al. (1999) supports the notion that freeing up the cognitive burden of focusing on both form and meaning allows greater opportunity to focus on form. In their study, participants performed an online telling of a short video clip. Participants who saw the same video multiple times (i.e., who did not have to focus on meaning during the latter viewings) showed improvement on overall measures of proficiency, morphosyntax, and lexical sophistication. *[Margin note: "Less focus on meaning results in more focus on form."]*

Learner-generated attention to form may not always come naturally and, clearly, may require some pedagogical training. Examples 13-4 and 13-5 come from a classroom context in which a teacher, as part of the curriculum, has assigned what she calls *interaction logs* to students. Interaction logs train students to think about their language use and, particularly, to notice the gap between their L2 language use *[Margin note: "Interaction Logs"]*

[Handwritten margin notes: LEARNERS AS DETECTIVES]

[Handwritten margin note in starburst: Interaction Logs !!!]

[Handwritten margin note: helps students notice how they are using language and how it is differing from native speakers use.]

[Handwritten margin note: LANGUAGE ANALYSIS]

and the language use of native or fluent speakers of the L2. They provide a means for learners to be detectives, in the sense that they are responsible for gathering their own language data, analyzing evidence, and making and testing hypotheses. The logs are language diaries in which students write down what fluent speakers say, how they say it, in what situations and with whom, and how NSs react when a learner says something (Al Cohen, 1999). As the teacher says in her instructions to students, interaction logs are "to help you to notice how you are using language and how it may be different from how native speakers use language." She provides numerous examples of how students can interact, from the very simple task of asking for directions to making small talk with someone at the grocery store. An advantage of interaction logs is that they allow learners to analyze their own language, in a format that goes beyond the ephemeral speech signal. Learners can record their own speech (in writing) and save it until a time when they can appropriately analyze it. Examples 13-4 and 13-5 show how two learners used interaction logs to learn how to analyze their own interaction (data from Al Cohen, 1999):

(13-4) I was talking about the bicycle with a secretary woman in the computer lab. When she said she bought her son Trumpet the day before and being a mother need to spend some money on the children's item, I wanted to "share the responsibility in communication." So I asked whether he liked it or not. She said "yes right now at least, but I'm not sure one month later, then she talked about other instrument she'd already bought for her son. Then I replied "Yes, really. I bought a bicycle for my son a week ago. The bike is expensive than I thought, partly because it has Star Wars decoration on." Then she asked me, "Did you? What kind of bike? The one with tri . . . neee . . . ll?" I couldn't catch her. It's a perfect time to use "manner of asking," because I understood rest of her talk except the last part. At that moment, I could guess it might be one part of bike, "I'm sorry, Deb, Did you say tranee . . . l? What's that?" I just imitated her sound. Then with some gesture she explained, "training . . . eel! The wheels to train the for riding 2 big wheels." Actually I didn't catch her pronunciation at that point, because I have a difficult in listening "W" sound. However, I can understand what's it. "Oh, Training Wheel! O.K . . . I didn't know the name. It's training wheel. I thought it might be 'assisting wheels' or 'supporting wheels'."

(13-5) Last Friday, in the communication class, we talked about the interaction logs, one of the classmates mentioned when she went to the supermarket, the cashier asked her if she wanted to drive out or not. So I learned that phrase from her. Last Sunday, when I went to the supermarket, I was ready to hear that again and I was so excited about it. Because most of time, I was so nervous when the cashier asked me some questions and they all spoke quickly. But not this time, finally, after the cashier packed all my stuff into the plastic bag, he asked "Do you want to drive ____?" "No, thanks . . ." I said. But I noticed he seemed to say some word instead of "out." The last word sounded like "off" or "up" or I was wrong. But I checked it up in the dictionary, "drive out" has a different meaning.

The carryover from metalinguistic sensitization, such as the use of interaction logs into the classroom, can be seen in the following example, observed by one of the authors of this book:

(13-6) T = teacher; S = student

>   S: He finally success.
>   T: What?
>   S: He finally succeed.
>   T: Succeeds.
>   S: Yes.

Even though the student does not appreciate the full force of the teacher's *what?*, he understands that she is making a correction of form (rather than just indicating that she does not understand, which might yield merely a repetition of the early utterance), and he modifies his original utterance accordingly. Whether his *yes* indicates anything more than closure to the exchange is, of course, unclear. This example (as well as the examples from the interaction logs themselves) shows that metalinguistic training in focusing on form can result in sensitivity to grammatical form, rather than just to lexical form, as occurs in most instances.

Ohta (2001) noted that students in a classroom context can assimilate corrective feedback even when it is not directed at them. In 13-7, one student (C) repeats recasts that are intended for a classmate:

(13-7) T = teacher; K and C = students

>   T: Kon shumatsu hima desu ka? Kylie-san.
>   "This weekend are you free? Kylie."
>   K: Um (. . .) iie (.) um (.) uh:: (.) hima- (.) hima: (.) hima nai.
>   "Um, no, um, uh, not, not, not free." [Error: wrong negator]
>   T: Hima ja arimasen?
>   "You're not free?" [T corrects form]
>   K: Oh ja arim[asen
>   C: [hima ja arimasen
>   "Not free." [C repeats correct form]

Student C gives a sotto voce rendition of the correct form, using the classroom as a venue for making a correction.

Mackey (2006) investigated learners' noticing of corrective feedback in a classroom context. Her linguistic focus was question formation and two morphological forms: English plurals and past tense. She found a relationship between noticing and learning for question formation, but not for the two morphological forms (plurals and past tense). One explanation might have to do with salience. Clearly, question formation, with syntactic movement and the addition of an auxiliary, is more salient than the addition of a plural or past-tense marker. Another issue to be sorted out is the type of feedback provided. As Mackey reports, there were more instances of negotiation for questions than for the morphological forms. Morphological errors were more often recast rather than negotiated. Thus, it is not clear what the source of the lack of learning is—the type of feedback or the linguistic entity.

Loewen (2009), in his study of recasts in adult ESL classrooms, points out that recasts are rarely just simple recasts. In fact, 25 percent of those in his large database have multiple responses, with two or three response moves being typical, as in the following example (p. 183):

(13-8) STUDENT (S): and uh you can see some (.) do you know how ca-cheef
        near the sea and there has got a < >chiff or
    TEACHER (T): cliff
    S: uh cluff yeah cluff
    T: cliff
    S: yeah and uh the
    T: cliff
    S: cliff cliff (.) cluff and uh some (.) okay some temple you know

In most instances of multiple responses, miscommunication was the reason, and that miscommunication was generally an issue of pronunciation. There was more uptake in multiple recasts as opposed to simple recasts, but accuracy scores following these episodes did not differ.

Clearly, instructed learning can offer a context for focus on form. This does not mean that all forms are teachable. The English article system, for example, appears to be virtually impermeable to instruction (perhaps because the explanation for its use is, at least, partially semantic, bringing in a number of complex considerations). Furthermore, we have seen in earlier chapters that different kinds of input might be necessary. In particular, we saw that there are limits to what positive evidence can do, and that negative evidence appears to be necessary in some situations. Doughty and J. Williams (1998) outlined four areas to consider in the study of focus on form, two of which are relevant to our current discussion of instructed learning: timing and forms to focus on (see also Spada, 1997). To these we add two others: (1) task design and (2) input enhancement and manipulation.

TIME TO DO ...

Go to Link #1 in the Links section at the end of this chapter and watch the video about content-based language classrooms. What examples of focus on form can you find in these meaning-focused classrooms? Are the focus-on-form episodes learner-generated or teacher-generated? What examples of corrective feedback do you see?

13.4.1 Timing

Harley (1998) investigated early focus-on-form intervention with young learners in order to determine the effect of early instructional focus on form. The learners in her study were Grade 2 students in an early French immersion program. The linguistic focus was acquisition of French gender, which, in Harley's words, is a "quintessentially formal aspect" of French (p. 156). There is little in the way of semantics incorporated into this feature. Gender assignment is a persistent problem for those schooled in an immersion program. Participants were pretested prior to the five-week experimental session and were posttested following the session and again at six months following the treatment. The results indicate that focus-on-form instruction produces better results than no instructional focus, but learners do not extend their knowledge to other words. Harley suggested that, "the experiment was more successful in inducing 'item learning' than 'system learning'" (p. 168). However, in post-experiment stimulated recalls, students tended to demonstrate metalinguistic knowledge of gender and of certain generalizations. This, in fact, may be a part of (or at least a precursor to) learning. In other words, one needs to learn what needs to be learned before being able to sort out the specific facts of what is to be learned.

Lightbown (1998) reviewed a number of studies that deal with timing issues. In particular, she cautioned researchers/teachers not to take too seriously the notion of developmental sequences within a pedagogical context. In other words, although it may be the case that input on stages that may be considerably beyond the learner's current level does not lead to learning, there is no harm done to the learner. What is relevant, however, is the need for teachers to have appropriate expectations of what learners will and will not be able to take from a lesson containing input on stages well beyond their levels. More specifically, whereas in some cases learners may benefit from an explicit focus on a structure that is beyond their current ability (as we saw earlier in the case of RCs), we should not assume that great gains will result from input far beyond the learners' level.

Lightbown's own research (Spada & Lightbown, 1993) was conducted with learners who were essentially at the early stages of the Pienemann model discussed in section 13.4. Following instruction with later-staged questions, the learners were able to produce questions such as *Where is the dog?* and *Where is the shoe?*, as well as even more complex questions such as *How do you say 'tâches' in English?*. However, as Spada and Lightbown pointed out, these may have been little more than

[handwritten margin notes: "Focus on form efficacy → MORE SUCCESS IN ITEM LEARNING THAN IN SYSTEM LEARNING"]

[handwritten margin notes: "Teachers' expectations and awareness of what learners will and what they will not learn."]

substitutions, with little understanding of the syntax underlying them. In other words, these were likely unanalyzed chunks. However, these forms were, nonetheless, present and may then have served as further input for learners' own developing systems. Thus, the fact that they were used in some form, even though not fully acquired, was certainly not detrimental. To the contrary, they served as an aid in future learning. In fact, even following instruction on questions, learners' knowledge increased (Spada & Lightbown, 1993).

ORDERING EFFECTS OF CLASSROOM PRESENTATION

Another way of looking at timing comes from a study by Gass and Alvarez-Torres (2005). They looked at the ordering effects of classroom presentation of input and interaction. Their study consisted of four experimental conditions in which students were (1) only presented with input, (2) only presented with interaction, (3) presented first with input and then interaction, or (4) presented first with interaction and then with input. They considered these different types of information and the ordering of information with regard to vocabulary learning and morphosyntax. The students were English-speaking learners of Spanish, and the morphosyntax structures were gender agreement (Spanish nouns and adjectives agree in number and gender) and the verb *to be*, which in Spanish has two forms and is known to be problematic for English-speaking learners. Examples of gender agreement are given in 13-9 and 13-10, and examples of the use of the two verbs *to be* (*estar* and *ser*) are given in 13-11. Their study only concerned the use of *estar* to express location.

(13-9)   Gender agreement (grammatical and ungrammatical):

Tengo una maleta amarilla.
I have a (f) suitcase (f) yellow (f).
"I have a yellow suitcase."

*Tengo una (f) maleta (f) amarillo (m).
I have a (f) suitcase (f) yellow (m).
"I have a yellow suitcase"

The second example is ungrammatical because the adjective has a masculine ending, but it modifies a feminine noun. Some nouns do not end in a/o, but still have grammatical gender, as in 13-10 below.

(13-10)   Gender agreement with nouns not ending in a/o:

(a)   El bigote pequeño (small mustache)
(b)   La llave rota (broken key)
(c)   El árbol viejo (old tree)
(d)   La luz blanca (white light)

(13-11)   Examples of *ser* (a) and *estar* (b) to express location:

(a)   *La maleta es al lado de la puerta.
The suitcase is to the side of the door.
"The suitcase is next to the door."

(b) La maleta está al lado de la puerta.
   The suitcase is to the side of the door.
   "The suitcase is next to the door."

Their results showed that there were significant gains for all conditions for vocabulary. The gains were not all-encompassing for either gender or *estar* learning. Recall from the discussion in Chapter 12 that attention is the mechanism hypothesized to be at least partially responsible for learning through interaction. Recall also that interaction is what makes learners aware of some problem in their language, although it may not be the source of immediate learning. More input may be needed as a follow-up to the attention-drawing function of interaction. In fact, the only significant gains for gender and *estar* were with the interaction followed by input groups. Another finding of interest was that the groups that had two kinds of input (i.e., input and interaction), regardless of the order, did better than those with only input or only interaction.

[handwritten margin note: Interaction]

[handwritten margin note: Input + Interaction]

13.4.2 Forms to Focus On

It is clear that one cannot use focus-on-form instruction with all grammatical constructions. For example, some structures are so complex (for example, those involving movement of elements in a sentence) that it is not at all clear what could be focused on. J. Williams and Evans (1998) investigated the effect of focus on form on two structures: (a) participial adjectives of emotive verbs (*I am boring* vs. *I am bored*) and (b) passives (*The dog was chased by the cat*). Participial adjectives were used incorrectly by the learners in this study (e.g., *My trip to Niagara Falls was really excited*). Passives were used only rarely. Three groups of learners took part in this study: One group had explicit instruction and feedback, the second group received input only, and the third group served as the control. For the participial adjectives, the group that had explicit instruction and feedback outperformed the other two groups. For the passives, the results were more complex, showing only partial support for the hypothesis that the two experimental groups would outperform the control group, and that there would be a difference between the two experimental groups. The overall results of this study suggest that learners' readiness contributes to their ability to focus on, and take in, new information. A second finding is that not all structures are created equal with regard to input type. For the participial adjectives, the learners had already noticed the form in the input, as is evidenced by their use of the form, albeit incorrectly. Here, explicit instruction was more beneficial than providing input alone. For the passives, there was little difference between the two experimental groups. Any means of highlighting the form (input flood or instruction) serves equally to induce noticing.

[handwritten margin note: Learner Readiness ↓ ability to focus on and take in new info.]

In general, then, one needs to carefully consider what is being targeted to focus on and how best to relate that information to a learner's individual knowledge state and to the means by which a form is focused on.

[Handwritten annotations top: "LONG TERM BENEFITS { Automatization, control, comprehension, Production." — "Task essentialness :{1. is form natural to task? 2. " " " useful to task? 3. " " " essential to task}" — "Involvement Load Hyp. – motivational cognitive model" — "Cognition hypothesis - 1. task complexity 2. task conditions 3. task demands"]

[Handwritten left margin: "focus: vocabulary gain (need, search, evaluation)"; "TASKS WITH HIGH INVOLVEMENT LOADS CONTRIBUTE TO VOCABULARY GAIN"]

13.4.3 Task Design

In addition to determining which forms to focus on, a considerable amount of work in SLA has addressed, at both theoretical and empirical levels, the notion of tasks (see Robinson, 2011, for an overview). More specifically, researchers have sought to describe different types of tasks and to predict which will promote L2 development by focusing learners' attention on form or by other means. At least three models exist for assessing the nature and extent of language demands induced by different tasks: Loschky and Bley-Vroman's (1993) notion of task essentialness, Laufer and Hulstijn's (2001) involvement load hypothesis, and Robinson's (2001, 2003b) **cognition hypothesis**. Each will be introduced in turn.

Loschky and Bley-Vroman's (1993) proposal distinguishes between whether a form is natural in the task, useful to the task, or essential to the task. They used this scheme to predict the effectiveness of different kinds of tasks in terms of automatization, control, and whether a task relates to comprehension or production. Keck et al. (2006) studied the effects of task-based interaction at the meta-analytic level and addressed the relationship between task-essentialness and resulting L2 gains. Their study found only a small advantage for task-essential features on immediate posttests, but a substantial and statistically significant one on delayed posttests, indicating that the benefits of task-essentialness may be more pronounced in the long term. From a methodological standpoint, this finding also highlights the importance of including delayed assessments as a means to understanding the duration of experimental effects (see Plonsky, in press).

Laufer and Hulstijn's involvement load hypothesis is a motivational–cognitive model that attempts to model the vocabulary gains induced by different activities according to both individual and task-related factors. Studies testing their model have sought to determine the extent to which learners' involvement, operationalized as the degree to which *need*, *search*, and *evaluation* are inherent to the task, contributes to gains in vocabulary. In one such study, Hulstijn and Laufer (2001) examined vocabulary development of two groups of EFL learners resulting from tasks with varying degrees of involvement (i.e., reading comprehension, comprehension plus filling in target words, and composition writing with target words). As predicted, the task with the highest involvement load, composition writing, resulted in the greatest vocabulary gains. More recently, the results of Kim (2008) also provide support for the involvement load hypothesis. Similar to Hulstijn and Laufer's (2001) study, Kim found greater gains resulting from tasks of a higher involvement load. Her study also extended beyond that of Hulstijn and Laufer (2001) in two important ways, providing additional support for their hypothesis. Kim's study included a delayed posttest to examine the duration of task effects and found them to hold over a period of two weeks. In Experiment 2, she also tested the effects of two different tasks of the same involvement load and confirmed, as predicted by the hypothesis, that they led to similar gains.

A third and final model for describing tasks and their effects on L2 development is Robinson's (2001, 2003a, b, 2007) Cognition Hypothesis. There are three components to his model: task complexity (i.e., whether the task directs and/or disperses

[Handwritten left margin: "① Task Essentialness / contextualized / target usage of language" ; "② Involvement Load Hypothesis / intention" ; "③ cognition hypothesis"]

414

learner attention), task conditions (e.g., whether the task is carried out uni- or bidirectionally), and task demands. Despite its development as a model and its conceptual appeal, findings of empirical studies seeking to test the Cognition Hypothesis or different components thereof have arrived at mixed results (e.g., Nuevo, 2006; Robinson, 2007; Kim, 2009). We return to this discussion in section 13.5 below.

Although no single model has emerged as dominant, the theoretical work in this area underscores the importance of task design for L2 research and instructed language learning. These models also provide a blueprint for future studies seeking to test task effects across a variety of L2 skills areas (e.g., syntax, vocabulary), additional task characteristics (e.g., contextual support, in Révész, 2009), and theoretical orientations (e.g., interaction).

13.4.4 Input Manipulation and Input Enhancement

A significant function of language instruction is the manipulation of input. That is, teachers can provide varying degrees of explicitness in the input as yet another means to draw learners' attention to targeted forms. A goal of SLA research is to determine the effectiveness of explicitness in terms of learners' developing grammars. The field has changed from a position in the 1970s and 1980s in which, following Krashen, what was needed to create implicit knowledge (more or less equivalent to linguistic competence) was comprehensible input. Explicit input led to explicit knowledge. In later years, the fusion of implicit/explicit input and implicit/explicit knowledge became more apparent. For example, DeKeyser (2003) suggested that explicit learning (e.g., metalinguistic explanation) can result in implicit knowledge through practice.

The concept of practice is important in pedagogical contexts. Practice, as defined by *The American Heritage Dictionary*, is "to exercise or perform repeatedly in order to acquire or polish a skill." It is essential in understanding how explicit information might result in implicit knowledge or how declarative knowledge becomes procedural knowledge; it is also essential in understanding how information might become automatized (see also DeKeyser, 2007; see Chapter 10). In earlier years, practice meant little more than rote repetition and/or substitution drills. In cognitive accounts of language learning, practice takes on a number of forms, but the common ingredient is that the learner interacts with the language in some meaningful (not solely rote) manner. This can include language use (some interactive-based task) or some response to an audio prompt (answering a comprehension question following a listening or reading passage).

The concept of input enhancement highlights ways in which input is made salient to learners (see Sharwood Smith, 1991). As Polio (2007) notes, Sharwood Smith's focus was not on what happened in the learner's mind, but rather on what was done to the input. Input enhancement can take place in a number of ways, through drawing attention to a form (e.g., by coloring or boldfacing in written input).

Underlying the importance of input enhancement is the concept of noticing, discussed in Chapter 12. Given that input enhancement is a means of drawing a

SALIENCE

learner internal device or something externally created.

variables

ellaboration

explicitness

learner's attention to something, an underlying assumption is that noticing is a prerequisite to processing of the input.

Salience, in Sharwood Smith's view, can come about by a learner's own internal devices (his/her own processing mechanisms) or by something that is externally created; this latter is input enhancement. Sharwood Smith refers to two variables involved in externally created salience: elaboration (e.g., repetition) and explicitness (e.g., metalinguistic information).

Input enhancement has not been treated in precisely the same way in all research, and, as a consequence, the results have not always been consistent (cf. Polio, 2007, for an overview). For example, Jourdenais et al. (1995) found that noticing and learning resulted from textual enhancement; Izumi (2002) found noticing, but not learning; and Leow (1997) found neither noticing nor learning. Han et al. (2008), in their review of input-enhancement studies, found numerous methodological differences among studies, making it difficult to state with certainty the extent to which visual input enhancement facilitates learning. Nonetheless, they do note an overall effect for input enhancement .

Taking a more quantitative approach, Lee and Huang (2008) used meta-analytic techniques to assess the evidence to date in this somewhat inconsistent line of research. Synthesizing across 16 studies and 20 treatment groups, the authors found a small but positive advantage for visually enhanced input. Interestingly, they also found evidence for a trade-off of attentional resources: Although learners' performance on targeted grammatical items improved slightly when exposed to visually enhanced input, their reading comprehension was negatively affected by the modified materials. Lastly, the relationship between noticing of, and gains resulting from, enhanced input could not be addressed at the meta-analytic level, owing to the very small number of studies that included measures of noticing in their design.

TIME TO DO ...

Choose a short text in English and decide on a form that you would like to draw learners' attention to in the text.

Design an assignment in which the input is enhanced, that is, an assignment in which learners' attention is drawn to the given form.

13.5 COMPLEXITY, ACCURACY, FLUENCY, AND PLANNING

As we have seen throughout this book, language learning is influenced by numerous factors (see, in particular, the discussion of dynamic systems in Chapter 10). This section looks at what might be thought of as competing factors in terms of a learner's ability to use language: complexity, **accuracy**, **fluency**, and planning.

Think about how you perform in your L2. Can you always use complex language? Does that interfere with your ability to be accurate? Fluent? Which of these do you think is most important and why? Might the context or mode of use (formal, informal, oral, written) be a factor?

Before understanding how these factors may or may not interact, and, importantly, from the perspective of instruction, what the role of planning might be to bring about greater amounts of complexity, accuracy, and/or fluency, we turn to brief definitions. Norris and Ortega (2009) summarize various approaches to measuring complexity (and, hence, defining the locus of concern). These include length of utterances, subordination, coordination, and extent and sophistication of grammatical forms. Thus, a learner who produces primarily simple sentences with frequent vocabulary (e.g., *The girl loves the boy*) would be argued to exhibit less complexity than a learner who produces numerous utterances with RCs. This is known as *linguistic complexity*, and generally refers to the "size, elaborateness, richness, and diversity of the learner's linguistic system" (Housen & Kuiken, 2009, p. 462). Another type of complexity is *cognitive complexity*, which has to do, not with the outcome or production of elements, but with the difficulty that goes into that production (or processing). Complexity in this regard may depend on a number of factors, including one's NL or experience with other languages, working-memory capacity, or even saliency and frequency of input. Accuracy is typically defined as deviations from the norm. On the surface, this seems a straightforward characterization of an error, but there are difficulties even with this relatively simple construct. Are there dialectal differences? Are there things one can say orally, but not in writing? Fluency generally refers to oral fluency and can consist of many subparts, such as speed, paucity of pauses, lack of false starts, and lexical retrieval (see Skehan, 2009).

A major issue in this line of research is the question of the interdependence of these constructs. In other words, is there a trade-off such that, if accuracy increases, complexity decreases, and so forth. Skehan and Foster (2008) offer the following as one way of characterizing the interaction among these factors:

- attentional capacity is limited (Cowan, 2005);
- attending to one of the three performance areas may drain attention from other areas;
- given this limitation, there is, in particular, a form-meaning tension, with meaning normally taking priority and therefore reducing the attention available for form (VanPatten, 1990);
- even when there is attention available for form, there is a still further tension between form directed to the use of more complex, cutting-edge language (form-as-ambition) and attention within form directed to accurate, error-free language (form-as-conservatism);

[Handwritten margin notes:]

COMPLEXITY
size, elaborateness, richness and diversity of linguistic complexity

Difficulty of production

ACCURACY
deviations from the norm.

complexity ↓
accuracy ↓
fluency

417

- a trade-off hypothesis can be formulated that predicts that *under certain conditions*, raised levels in one performance area, when it consumes attention, may take attention away from other areas, with the result that performance in those areas may be lowered.

Central to these propositions is that humans have a limited-attention system and attention to one performance area results in less attention to others. Skehan and Foster (2008) further propose a developmental sequence, as seen in Table 13.2.

TABLE 13.2 A Developmental Sequence for Complexity, Accuracy, and Fluency

Complexity	This represents new, cutting-edge, and possibly risky language and foreshadows growth in the interlanguage system
Accuracy	This represents a striving for control and error avoidance, possibly by the avoidance of cutting-edge language, and by avoiding fluency to enable more time to be used to achieve higher accuracy
Fluency	This represents a focus on meaning, automatization, lexicalization, and a push for real-time processing

In this view, new, complex structures enter the learner's system, and only subsequently do accuracy and then fluency become part of the picture.

Taking a different perspective, Robinson's (2001, 2003a, 2003b, 2007) Cognition Hypothesis assumes not a limited-attentional system, but rather separate attentional pools from which learners can draw, depending in part on communicational needs and demands. The more difficult the task, the more the learner will rise to the occasion by producing language that is more complex and accurate, given that these areas are not in competition. In other words, task complexity is primary in the development of both accuracy and structural complexity, the latter two not being disassociated, as in the trade-off account proposed by Skehan.

Arguments and evidence to support both accounts abound, as can be seen in reports of studies in Skehan (2009) and in reports of empirical studies by Robinson et al. (2009). What has become apparent, however, is that measurements of the constructs are often problematic (see Norris & Ortega, 2009) and operational definitions are not consistent across studies making cross-study comparisons difficult if not impossible.

An issue associated with task performance and issues of complexity is that of planning. When thinking of these issues within a classroom context, it is clear that one can have students perform tasks with or without planning. But, the question is: what is the effect of this on the constructs of complexity, accuracy, and fluency? And what types of planning are beneficial, and how much time should be devoted to planning? R. Ellis (2009) provides a review of the planning literature, distinguishing

[handwritten margin notes: FLUENCY; COGNITION HYPOTHESIS — separate attentional pools that depend on need and demand; PLANNING — pre task planning, during task planning]

418

between pre-task planning and during-task planning. He further subdivides each of these into rehearsal and strategic for pre-task planning, where the first provides an opportunity to practice the task before actually doing the task, and the second allows one to think about what one wants to say in terms of content and linguistic structures before doing the task. Planning that takes place during a task can also be subdivided into pressured (a specific time limit) and unpressured (no time limits). It is difficult to draw conclusions at this point, because there are numerous individual variables that come into play, including proficiency (see Wigglesworth, 1997; Ortega, 1999; Kawauchi, 2005), aptitude (Kormos & Trebits, 2012), and working memory (e.g., Guará-Tavares, 2008 [cited in R. Ellis, 2009]). However, published studies don't always include this information, and, when they do, it is not always clear what proficiency descriptors mean (what does intermediate mean? — Is one researcher's intermediate another researcher's advanced?). R. Ellis (2009, pp. 501–502) provides the following summary points:

1. Rehearsal yields greater fluency and complexity, but these effects do not always transfer to a new task. In other words, the results are not generalizable to a new context.
2. Strategic planning yields greater fluency. The benefits are not clear for complexity and accuracy, where the trade-off model seems to be supported; any given learners will focus on either complexity or accuracy, but not both. Numerous individual variable have an effect (e.g., proficiency).
3. Planning that takes place during a task (within-task planning) yields better complexity and accuracy without negatively impacting fluency.

In sum, planning in the context of instructed language learning is an important construct, although, like most other aspects of language teaching, there are numerous details and variables to be examined as we seek to understand if and how planning promotes learning.

13.6 PROCESSING INSTRUCTION

Processing instruction refers to a type of instruction that takes as its basis how learners process input. In particular, it deals with the conversion of input to intake and specifically focuses on form–meaning relationships (VanPatten & Cadierno, 1993; VanPatten, 1995; VanPatten & Sanz, 1995). Based on a series of experiments, VanPatten and his colleagues presented a model for instructional intervention that relied heavily on the notion of attention to form and its crucial role in a learner's movement from input to intake and, finally, to output. They compared two instructional models, one in which input is provided and learners are prompted to produce the target forms (traditional grammar instruction), and another in which an attempt is made to change the way input is perceived and processed (processing instruction) (see Figures 13.2 and 13.3).

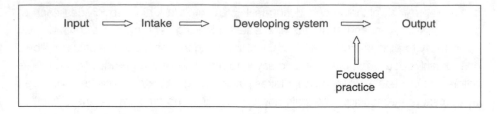

FIGURE 13.2 Traditional Instruction in Foreign-Language Learning (*Source*: From "Explicit instruction and input processing" by B. VanPatten and T. Cadierno, 1993, *Studies in Second Language Acquisition*, *15*, 227. © 1993 by Studies in Second Language Acquisition. Reprinted with the permission of Cambridge University Press.)

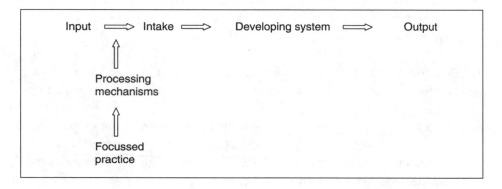

FIGURE 13.3 Processing Instruction in Foreign-Language Teaching (*Source*: From "Explicit instruction and input processing" by B. VanPatten and T. Cadierno, 1993, *Studies in Second Language Acquisition*, *15*, 227. © 1993 by Studies in Second Language Acquisition. Reprinted with the permission of Cambridge University Press.)

Rather than allow an internalized system to (begin to) develop, perhaps erroneously, the goal of this approach is to influence the way that input is processed and, hence, the way the system develops.

VanPatten (2009) presents three premises that form the basis of processing instruction:

1. Learners need input for acquisition.
2. A major problem in acquisition might be the way in which learners process input.
3. If we can understand how learners process input, then we might be able to devise effective input enhancement or focus on form to aid acquisition of formal features of language.

There are a finite number of principles of processing instruction (VanPatten, 2007a, 2007b; see also VanPatten, 2004, 2012). In VanPatten (2012), three main principles are specified.

[handwritten margin note: Basis of processing instruction]

Principles of processing instruction
↓

1. *Primacy of content words*: Learners process content words in the input before anything else.
2. *Lexical-preference principle:* If grammatical forms express a meaning that can also be encoded lexically (e.g., that grammatical marker is redundant), then learners will not initially process those grammatical forms until they have lexical forms to which they can match them.
3. *The first-noun principle:* Learners tend to process the first noun or pronoun they encounter in the sentence as the subject.

    (a) *The lexical-semantics principle*: Learners may rely on lexical semantics, where possible, instead of the *first-noun principle*, to interpret sentences.
    (b) *The event-probabilities principle*: Learners may rely on event probabilities, where possible, instead of the *first-noun principle*, to interpret sentences.

TIME TO THINK ...

Consider the third principle in light of other languages you know, particularly those where the subject of the sentence always appears after the verb or at the end of the sentence. Do you think these same principles apply?

With regard to classroom instruction, VanPatten (2007a) outlines three basic features of processing instruction:

1. Give learners information about a structure or form.
2. Inform learners about a particular processing strategy that may get in the way of selecting the form/structure during comprehension.
3. Structure input so that learners must rely on form/structure to get meaning and not rely on natural processing tendencies.

PROCESSING INSTRUCTION IN THE CLASSROOM.

He presents an example from the French causative, as in 13-12.

(13-12) Jean fait promener le chien à Marie.
John makes to walk the dog to Mary
"John makes Mary walk the dog."

The first step is to have learners answer the question "Who walks the dog?" Most English learners respond that John walks the dog, because that is the first noun. This is part of the first stage in which information is provided to learners about the causative construction in French. This is followed by structured input activities in which other causative constructions might be read aloud, and they have to respond by stating who is doing the action. VanPatten refers to these as referential activities, because there is a right/wrong answer. These are followed by affective structured

Referential activities

activities, which are more open ended and require learners to use information from the real world.

The results of experiments (both sentence-level and discourse-related) suggest that processing instruction may be equally or more effective than traditional, output-based treatments. For example, in experimental studies by VanPatten and colleagues, learners in the processing-instruction group were often better able to understand and produce a target structure than learners in the traditional-instruction group (VanPatten & Cadierno, 1993; VanPatten & Sanz, 1995).

[handwritten margin note: Processing instruction ↓ is equally or more effective than traditional output based treatment.]

This line of research has been conducted in languages other than Spanish, including French (VanPatten & Wong, 2004; Wong, 2004), Italian (Benati, 2004), Russian (Comer & deBenedette, 2010), and German (Henry et al., 2009), which in general find support for this approach (but cf. Fernández, 2008). DeKeyser and Sokalski (1996), DeKeyser et al. (2002), and Salaberry (1997, 1998) have argued against this approach, although VanPatten (2007a) points out that the studies referred to have not dealt with the issue of why there is a processing issue.

In order to determine the overall effects from a number of such studies, Shintani et al. (in press) recently meta-analyzed the effects of processing instruction as part of a larger synthesis of the relative effectiveness of comprehension-based and production-based instruction. Based on the aggregation of results from 35 experiments, the authors found a marked advantage for processing instruction (a subset of the comprehension-based studies) over the traditional production-based instruction on receptive measures. However, there was no significant difference between the two on productive knowledge. This finding puts into question the somewhat counterintuitive position held by many supporters of processing instruction that input-based activities can improve learners' productive abilities as well as receptive ones. These results also underscore the importance of considering the appropriateness of outcome measures when evaluating the results of studies seeking to measure instructional effects.

In sum, this approach to processing instruction attempts to deal, not just with a linguistic difficulty, but with a problematic processing strategy and attempts to interrupt that strategy with overt instruction and practice.

13.7 UNIQUENESS OF INSTRUCTION

Instruction on a particular L2 can have its unique repercussions, that is, effects different from those found among naturalistic learners. In this section, we present two instances where the instruction (or lack thereof) may have produced unique results. Pavesi (1986) specifically compared naturalistic versus instructed learners in terms of their acquisition of RCs. All learners were Italian speakers learning English. There were 48 instructed learners and 38 naturalistic learners. The instructed learners were high-school students (aged 14–18) who had studied English for 4 years on average. They had had virtually no informal exposure to English. Their instruction had been grammar-based, and they had had substantial written input. The second group was made up of 38 Italian workers living in Edinburgh, with menial-type jobs; they ranged in age from 19 to 50 and had lived in the United Kingdom for an average of 6 years (ranging from 3 months to 25 years). Their exposure to English was almost entirely informal, with little, if any, formal instruction. The results from these learners support the findings already discussed elsewhere in this book, that learning proceeds from the unmarked (e.g., subject RC) to the marked structure (e.g., object of comparative RC). The context of learning did not affect this acquisition order. However, a difference was noted in the number of marked RC types used, with the formal group using more. In addition, the informal groups used a greater number of noun copies (*Number five is the boy who the dog is biting the boy*) than the formal group, whereas the formal group used more pronoun copies (*Number five is the boy who the dog is biting him*). Therefore, it appears that the classroom context can provide a richness that an informal environment cannot. However, an important caveat in understanding these results is that the two groups differed in at least two important respects: (a) age differences may have contributed to the more sophisticated use of English by the formal group,[2] and (b) the socioeconomic level of the two groups was sufficiently different to call into question the findings based purely on learning context.

A second example of instructional uniqueness comes from work by Lightbown (1983). She noted that French learners of English tended to make a large number of overuse errors. In Chapter 10, we discussed the concept of U-shaped learning. In that instance, children exposed to *-ing* (progressive) associated that form with the present tense in French and thereby overextended its appropriate use. The overuse continued even when there was little exposure to the form in the input.

Kasper and Rose (2002), with regard to pragmatics, suggest that, without instruction, pragmatic knowledge will be difficult. Specifically, they claim that L2 pragmatics can be taught, and that, in fact, instructional intervention is better than no instruction. In terms of explicitness, they claim that explicit instruction coupled with opportunities for practice provide the best chance for success, a position largely supported among both primary studies and secondary reviews of IL pragmatics intervention research (Jeon & Kaya, 2006; Takahashi, 2010; Taguchi, 2011b; but cf., Li, 2012). Kasper and Rose also report on pragmatic studies in a study-abroad context and find that appropriate pragmatic behavior is not always acquired just by living abroad, a position supported empirically by Taguchi's (2011a) study of Japanese learners of English. This leads them to suggest that instruction coupled with a study-abroad experience provides the optimal condition for pragmatics learning.

Laufer (2005) makes the same point with regard to vocabulary. Input alone is insufficient for vocabulary learning. She takes this a step further and proposes that focus on form instruction is essential and even states that it does not need to be conducted within the context of a communicative task. This notion of decontextualized instruction is somewhat controversial. Nevertheless, evidence in favor of Laufer's claim was found in Won's (2008) meta-analysis of 30 primary studies of vocabulary instruction.

Loewen (2009, p. 192) clearly illustrates the important role of the teacher and supports the Gass and Mackey (2007, p. 184) view of negotiation: "input can be uniquely tailored to individual learners' particular strengths, weaknesses, and communicative needs, providing language that is in line with learners' developmental levels." In 13-13, there is a narrative retelling in which the teacher feels the student should be using the past perfect. Because of this, the teacher's initial response is a clarification request, which does not result in the expected form. The teacher then turns to metalinguistic information. With the correct response still not forthcoming, the teacher provides the correct form (a recast), which the student then repeats. It is this fine-tuning of response types that leads the student to the correct form.

(13-13) S: she told us that was the (.) that she was having the time of her life
        T: she—she told she said that what?
        S: she said she said you are exciting
        T: no no what tense are you [going to use
        S: [< >
        T: past perfect
        S: she said she had the time of her life
        T: she had had
        S: she had had a time of her life he on the Greek island

In general, instructed learning may clearly result in inappropriate conclusions drawn by the learners, precisely because the input is often impoverished and because emphasis on certain forms is selective. With regard to interaction, Bygate and Samuda (2009) note that interaction does not always work. They posit three conditions that provide the greatest likelihood for interaction to be "pedagogically beneficial for learning" (p. 96): field, purpose, and engagement. Field refers to the content of the discourse; purpose refers to the goals of the task and takes tasks out of the realm of a mechanical focus on form; engagement reflects the need for both speaker and listener to be committed to carrying out the task (see also Dörnyei & Tseng, 2009, for a discussion of motivation in interaction). Bygate and Samuda argue that these features of interactive tasks supersede earlier notions of communicative tasks that promote a two-way exchange of information.

13.8 EFFECTIVENESS OF INSTRUCTION

The effectiveness of instruction is often assumed, although not always accepted. For example, in approaches that assume that what is needed is large doses of (comprehensible) input, classroom effectiveness is considered limited. Similarly, in approaches that assume a natural, immutable sequence of natural processes, classroom effectiveness is similarly limited. This was expressed succinctly by Felix (1981, p. 109):

> Foreign language learning under classroom conditions seems to partially follow the same set of natural processes that characterize other types of language acquisition ... there seems to be a universal and common set of principles which are flexible enough and adaptable to the large number of conditions

under which language learning may take place. These observations furthermore suggest that the possibility of manipulating and controlling the students' verbal behavior in the classroom is in fact quite limited.

Despite the uncertainty that has dwelled among certain SLA scholars, the debate over whether or not form-focused instruction is superior to input-only language teaching was largely settled in the early-to-mid 1980s (see discussion above, with citations to Long, 1983b; Doughty, 1991; but cf. Truscott, 2004). Since then, empirical efforts have turned to addressing a wide variety of more nuanced questions related to the effectiveness of different types of instruction, such as focus on forms vs. focus on formS or implicit vs. explicit instruction. Norris and Ortega (2000), in their overview of instructed SLA, found that an explicit focus is more effective than implicit focus, and that a focus on form is more effective than a focus on formS. However, it is important to note, as the authors themselves point out, that these cumulative findings should be treated with caution, given that (1) the measurements of learning outcomes in the studies they included usually favor explicit treatments; (2) implicit treatments may require a longer period of time for learning to take place and, consequently, may necessitate longer post-observation times than explicit treatments; and (3) there was often an inconsistent operationalization of each instructional approach. Finally, the linguistic forms targeted in most of the studies included are (relatively) easy and simple, which potentially favors explicit treatment. In a more recent meta-analysis, Spada and Tomita (2010) took up this issue of the relationship between different types of instruction (implicit vs. explicit) and grammatical features (simple vs. complex). Their results replicate Norris and Ortega's (2000) findings of an advantage for explicit instruction, a difference that is even more pronounced in the case of more complex target features.

We now turn to some of the individual studies reviewed to get a more nuanced view of this area. As with many areas of SLA research, the results are not always clear cut. DeKeyser (1995) found positive effects for explicit rule presentation, as did de Graaff (1997). In this latter study, explicit-rule presentation was beneficial when it was accompanied by two other important ingredients: input and practice. On the other hand, studies such as those by Rosa and O'Neill (1999) and VanPatten and Oikkenon (1996) did not show positive effects. In the case of the former study, the issue of task-demand came into play. Different tasks may elicit different types of output and different types of feedback. For example, in a study by Gass et al. (2005) concerned with a comparison of classroom versus laboratory interaction patterns, the authors used three tasks: a consensus task, a spot-the-difference task, and a one-way map task. Differences were found between task types, but not between different settings.

Explicitness cannot be considered in the abstract. Issues such as rule complexity, language area (e.g., morphosyntax, syntax, lexicon), and proficiency level are equally important variables (see de Graaff, 1997; Robinson, 2002a, 2002b). For example, Gass et al. (2003) found that focused attention (manipulated through an experimental design) was more beneficial for syntactic learning than for morphosyntactic or lexical learning, probably owing to the greater complexity of syntax and the ability of learners to

[handwritten margin note: Focused attention]

self-focus their attention on the lexicon. Additionally, focused attention had a greater role in the early stages of acquisition, most likely owing to the greater linguistic sophistication of more advanced learners, who have sufficient knowledge to focus on complex parts of language. In addition, the question of feedback—when and if, and, if so, how explicit—is relevant to understanding the role of explicitness of input. Here, too, there is not always agreement. Carroll and Swain (1993), in a well-known study of feedback, found that metalinguistic feedback following treatment on dative alternation yielded better performance than other types of feedback (statement of correct/incorrect, recast). On the other hand, Sanz and Morgan-Short (2004), in a study of preverbal direct-object pronouns in Spanish, found no difference between explicit feedback without explanation, feedback with no explanation, and no feedback. The latter study may indicate a difference in the moment of feedback (see feedback discussion in section 12.5.1).

*[handwritten margin note: variables involved in effectiveness in instruction:
1. focus on form
2. explicitness of input
3. Individual differences
   └ learner aptitude
   └ learning style
4. Instructor approach]*

Beyond mere focus on form or explicitness of input, there are numerous other variables that need to be considered when trying to understand the effectiveness of instruction, including, but not limited to, individual differences, such as learner aptitude and matches/mismatches between learning style and instructor approach. For example, two recent studies, Li (2010a) and Goo (2010), tested the interaction of different types of treatment (feedback types and think-aloud protocols, respectively) and working memory (for other recent examples, see Sheen, 2007; Lenet et al., 2011; Mackey & Sachs, 2012). However, very little research has addressed the interactions between types of instruction and individual differences (also referred to as aptitude–treatment interaction (ATI); see Cronbach, 1957), prompting some to call for increased efforts in this area (e.g., DeKeyser, 2009; Plonsky, in press).

[handwritten margin note: INSTRUCTION MAKES THE DIFFERENCE →]

Looking across studies of L2 instruction, we find that there are no easy answers. What is clear is that instruction does make a difference, but how precisely it makes a difference, and what the contributing factors are to its effectiveness continue to be issues that need to be resolved. As it currently stands, empirical and theoretical inquiry into the effectiveness of instruction is not a matter of *yes* or *no*; it is concerned with developing a clearer understanding of what (i.e., particular language features/forms), how (i.e., which instructional techniques, materials, tasks), when (i.e., at which point in terms of learners' developmental readiness), and to what extent these and other variables interact to affect L2 learning.

TIME TO DO ...

Go to Link #2 in the Links section at the end of this chapter and watch the video about a classroom where children are learning Chinese as a foreign language.

How might the input that the learners receive in this classroom be different from the input that they would receive in a naturalistic situation? How does the teacher try to provide the maximum input possible?

13.9 SLA AND CLASSROOM PRACTICES

In this chapter, we have looked at instructed L2 learning, with an eye toward understanding how learning in and out of the classroom may or may not differ. In this final section, we briefly consider how an understanding of SLA might inform classroom practices. Although many treatises exist on this topic (see Gass, 1997), we consider it from the slightly different perspective of Lightbown (1985). In a classic article titled "Great Expectations," Lightbown made the important point that one way L2 research can contribute to successful classroom practice is through the *expectations* that teachers have about what learners can and cannot achieve as a result of instruction. For example, we have discussed the role of interaction (Chapter 12) as a priming device for learning, and even explicit instruction may serve as an introduction to information about a form, rather than being the moment of learning.

[handwritten margin note: some teacher expectations are not achieved through instruction]

Also related to expectations is the uncertainty held by many L2 teachers toward applications of L2 research (see Borg, 2010). Some teachers reading this might identify with this sentiment. Further complicating the issue, many researchers are cautious, or unsure, about how they might apply their findings to classroom contexts. In order to begin to deal with this longstanding disparity of perceptions at the interface of L2 research and practice, Ortega (2012) suggests that researchers and practitioners move toward a different understanding of the potential of their relationship. Specifically, she sees the notion of *relevance*, rather than *application*, as more appropriate and conducive to mitigating unmet expectations. By turning to the more conditional and context-specific notion of relevance, she argues, there is less of an assumption of application, and a greater sense of agency and judgment for teachers. (See also R. Ellis, 2010, for a recent treatment of issues at the research–practice nexus in SLA.)

[handwritten margin note: Relevance x application]

13.10 CONCLUSION

In sum, even though instruction is clearly an aid to learning, it is essential to understand how L2s are acquired in general, if we are to understand how they are acquired in a particular context. In the following chapter, we turn to a consideration of some of the influences on L2 learning that are not dependent on language and that can affect the formation, restructuring, and fossilization of L2 grammars.

POINTS TO REMEMBER

- Although SLA assumes that the processes that take place in naturalistic language learning are the same as those that take place in an instructed language-learning situation, there are differences, for example in the quantity and quality of input.

- There is evidence that learners can change an incorrect form to a more target-like form through interaction with other learners, rather than picking up errors from other learners. There are times, however, that learners can fail to pick up target-like forms if they don't have teacher intervention.

- Although not all forms are teachable, and instruction may not change the order of acquisition, there is evidence that instruction can "step up the pace" of development. For example, leaners who have been instructed on particular RCs on the Accessibility Hierarchy perform well on RCs higher on the hierarchy, even if they did not receive direct instruction on those.

- Focus on formS refers to instruction that is organized around grammatical structures. Focus on form refers to meaning-focused instruction in which attention is drawn to language forms.

- Several issues relevant to focus on form are timing, which forms to focus on, task design, and input manipulation and enhancement.

- Studies have indicated that instruction does make a difference, but it is not completely clear yet how, to what extent, and what contributing factors play a role.

SUGGESTIONS FOR ADDITIONAL READING

Instructed second language acquisition (forthcoming). Shawn Loewen. Routledge.

Language teaching research and language pedagogy (2012). Rod Ellis. Wiley-Blackwell.

Teaching and learning second language listening: Metacognition in action (2012). Larry Vandergrift and Christine Goh. Routledge.

Speaking and instructed foreign language acquisition (2011). Miroslaw Pawlak, Ewa Waniek-Klimczak, and Jan Majer. Multilingual Matters.

Implicit and explicit knowledge in second language learning, testing and teaching (2009). Rod Ellis, Shawn Loewen, Catherine Elder, Rosemary Erlam, Jennifer Philp, and Hayo Reinders (Eds.). Multilingual Matters.

Optimizing a lexical approach to instructed second language acquisition (2009). Frank Boers and Seth Lindstromberg. Palgrave Macmillan.

Second language learning and language teaching (4th ed.). (2008). Vivian Cook. Hodder.

Input for instructed L2 learners: The relevance of relevance (2007). Anna Nizegorodcew. Multilingual Matters.

Learning languages, learning lifeskills: Autobiographical reflexive approach to teaching and learning a foreign language (2007). Riita Jaatinen. Springer Verlag.

Practice in a second language: Perspectives from applied linguistics and cognitive psychology (2007). Robert DeKeyser (Ed.). Cambridge University Press.

Researching second language classrooms (2006). Sandra Lee McKay. Lawrence Erlbaum Associates.

Investigations in instructed second language acquisition (2005). Alex Housen and Michel Pierrard. Mouton de Gruyter.

Input enhancement: From theory and research to the classroom (2005). Wynne Wong. McGraw-Hill.

Planning in task-based performance (2005). Rod Ellis. John Benjamins.

Processing instruction: Theory, research, and commentary (2004). Bill VanPatten (Ed.). Lawrence Erlbaum Associates.

From input to output: A teacher's guide to second language acquisition (2003). Bill VanPatten. McGraw Hill.

Task-based language learning and teaching (2003). Rod Ellis. Oxford Applied Linguistics.

Individual differences and instructed language learning (2002). Peter Robinson (Ed.). John Benjamins.

Cognition in second language instruction (2001). Peter Robinson (Ed.). Cambridge University Press.

Focus on form in classroom second language acquisition (1998). Catherine Doughty and Jessica Williams. Cambridge University Press.

Second language classroom research: Issues and opportunities (1996). Jacquelyn Schachter and Susan Gass. Lawrence Erlbaum Associates.

Second language acquisition and language pedagogy (1992). Rod Ellis. Multilingual Matters.

Instructed second language acquisition (1990). Rod Ellis. Basil Blackwell.

MORE TO DO AND MORE TO THINK ABOUT ...

1. What do you see as the relationship between SLA and L2 pedagogy? How are they different? How might they affect each other, and how might the study of one influence the study or practices of the other? Relate your answers to a specific learning situation. In thinking about the relationship, consider whether or not all aspects of SLA relate (or should be able to relate) to classroom practice.

2. One reason people are interested in the field of SLA is because of their current or future interests in language pedagogy. In Chapter 7, we dealt with the Subset Principle. What are some of the implications of this principle for language teaching? In groups, complete one of the following two sentences.

> If you are a language teacher, you had better know the Subset Principle because _____.
>
> If you are a language teacher, it makes no difference whether or not you know the Subset Principle because _____.

In your answer, you might want to consider the difference between being able to put a name on the phenomenon and understanding the effects of the Subset Principle.

3. In Chapter 5, we described Krashen's view on the function of the Monitor and how it can "get in your way" with its focus on form. Does this mean that, in language classes, there should never be a focus on form, and that, as a result, teachers should only provide well-organized input? When might grammar instruction (i.e., form-focused instruction) be appropriate or necessary?

4. Are all structures equally amenable to focus on form? Why or why not? Can you give examples from your own teaching/learning experience when you could not "figure out" what the correct generalization should be?

5. Consider the concept of negative evidence. When do you think negative evidence might be necessary for learning? (You might want to relate this question to your answer in Problem 4.)

6. To English teachers' dismay, students often omit the third person singular -s, even at fairly advanced proficiency levels. Given what you know about natural orders in L2 acquisition, how do you explain this phenomenon?

7. Do you believe that there is a difference between learning to use the syntax of an L2 correctly and learning to pronounce an L2 correctly? What might the source of those differences be? Do you think that one or the other is easier to teach? Or easier to learn through instruction?

LINKS

1. http://tinyurl.com/c238gx8
2. http://video.pbs.org/video/1533649451

CHAPTER FOURTEEN

Nonlanguage Influences

Individual
Differences
(Dörnyei)

$\left\{ \begin{array}{l} \text{1. APTITUDE} \\ \text{2. MOTIVATION} \\ \text{3. ATTITUDE} \\ \text{4. SOCIOPSYCHOLOGIAL INFLUENYES} \\ \text{5. FOSSILIZATION} \end{array} \right.$

14.1 INTRODUCTION

One of the most widely recognized facts about L2 learning is that some indivduals are more successful in learning an L2 than others. In this chapter, we examine some of the factors that may be responsible for these differences, focusing in particular on nonlanguage factors, such as age, **aptitude**, motivation, **attitude**, and socio-psychological influences. In addition to some learners being more successful language learners, there is also the well-known phenomenon of fossilization, which has been part of the field of SLA since the middle part of the 20th century. The phenomenon of being stuck in the L2 seems to occur to most, if not all, learners, even at the most advanced stages (see Han, 2004).[1] There are many reasons for an apparent lack of success, many of which (but not all) are not related to language or psycholinguistic factors, but relate to the individual him- or herself. These are the subject matter of this chapter.

First of all, a word about the title of the chapter, "Nonlanguage Influences." In much of the SLA literature, the subject matter of this chapter has been described as *individual differences* (see Dörnyei, 2005). The latter term, we maintain, is somewhat misleading. Even though all factors that influence L2 learning can be observed only within an individual, the factors to be discussed in this chapter are not necessarily idiosyncratic. In fact, it may be social backgrounds that are crucial. Even measures of aptitude, which would seem to be the most individualistic, often correlate with societal differences, in that individuals from more privileged backgrounds, as a whole, receive higher scores on aptitude measures. Given space limitations, we have not included all aspects of what can be included in the category of individual differences; other topics have been dealt with in other chapters (e.g., working memory) because they seemed to fit more appropriately there, despite the fact that they are also part of what one might consider an individual difference.

14.2 RESEARCH TRADITIONS

The role of nonlanguage factors in L2 learning has had less of an impact on SLA than has the research based on linguistics, psychology, and psycholinguistics. To understand how the research tradition that investigates such areas as aptitude, attitude, and motivation relates to the entire field of SLA, it is necessary to consider the general goals of those fields that have dominated SLA.

14.2.1 Linguistics

The research tradition in linguistics has tended to downplay a search for aptitude differences in learning an L2. This is not to say that there are explicit statements in theoretical linguistics to the effect that there are no aptitude differences in L2 learning. The influence is more subtle than that.

Competence, as a major concern of modern linguistics, emphasizes what speakers _know_, rather than what they actually _do_ on some particular occasion (performance). The first factor to recognize is that the emphasis on competence has resulted in a minimization of reports of differences in ability in NLs. However, it is not so clear whether the competence that linguists attempt to discover is common to all NSs of a language. Chomsky, in various discussions (e.g., 1995), suggested a common, minimalist sense of competence. That is, the same competence would be shared by all NSs of a language. On the other hand, the methodology is based on the assumption of an ideal speaker–listener (sometimes called a speaker–hearer). The competence of an ideal person may differ from that of most speakers. Early opponents of Chomsky pointed out that many ordinary speakers did not have the same grammaticality judgments reported in the linguistics literature (see Hill, 1961). (Recall from Chapter 3 that judgments about the grammaticality of sentences have been the major source of data about linguistic knowledge/competence.) However, these concerns were not seriously addressed by linguists at that time. Rather than saying that these individuals were less competent in language, the response was that they were less competent in making grammaticality judgments. Hence, the findings of Hill and others were deemed irrelevant for grammatical theory, because these results relate to performance and not to what an individual _knows_ about his or her language. For the purposes of this chapter, it is important to recognize that some individuals are better than others in certain language skills. For example, some are much better storytellers than others. The assumption in mainstream linguistics is that these skills only represent what one can do with language, not what one knows about language. Because it is believed that all children without cognitive deficits learn language in roughly the same way and within the same time frame, and because there is equipotentiality in language (i.e., it is just as easy to learn Chinese as it is to learn Hausa as L1s), discussions of aptitude are not part of mainstream linguistics.

The immediate, negative reaction linguists have toward differences in language abilities in an NL has also affected SLA scholars trained in linguistics. On the one hand, they adhere to the orthodox opinion of linguistics that differences in language ability are not important in NLs. Thus, some resist the tendency to look for such differences in L2 learning. On the other hand, they are faced with the question: If there are differences in ability to learn an L2, how did these differences arise? If they are due to an individual's inherent language ability, then why did they not affect NL learning?

14.2.2 Psychology

[handwritten annotation: motivation, cognition, behaviorism) x]

In Chapter 10, we dealt with some of the major influences on SLA from psychology. It is clear that issues of aptitude/motivation did not fit into that category, as they might have earlier in the study of psychology. As Sorrentino and Higgins (1986, p. 4) noted:

> Early in the history of North American psychology, motivation and cognition were both considered important factors. This can perhaps be traced back to the rise of behaviorism in North American psychology. Until that point, various views relating motivation and/or cognition to behavior were flourishing.

Behaviorism banished both cognition and motivation. Even though cognitive psychology has eventually come to occupy an important place within the field of psychology, it, too, had no role for affect and motivation, at least initially. The implication is that researchers trained in the tradition of cognitive psychology would not have tended to look for a significant role for motivation in the field of SLA.

14.2.3 Psycholinguistics

Psycholinguistics, with roots in both psychology and linguistics, is especially relevant for SLA research. Sorrentino and Higgins, in the introduction to their anthology dealing with the importance of motivation, admit that "motivation had little place in [psycho-linguistics]" (Sorrentino & Higgins, 1986, p. 5). They strongly implied that this is still the case for psycholinguistics.

To summarize to this point, the tradition of linguistics led to a downplaying of aptitude in the explanation of linguistic behavior. The tradition of cognitive psychology led to a downplaying of attitudes and motivation. Thus, it is not surprising that SLA researchers, most influenced by these two research traditions, have tended to look for cognitive factors rather than motivation, for example, in accounting for differential successes in L2 learning. Dörnyei (2005) attributes the process-oriented approach of much SLA research and the conflicting product-oriented approach of most individual-difference research, at least in the areas of attitude and motivation to the lack of full integration of these research areas into the mainstream of SLA research. Another impediment that is both theoretical and methodological exists as well.

Research on motivation, aptitude, and other individual differences has largely been correlational in nature and, therefore, excluded from experimental studies seeking to measure the effect of a particular treatment (i.e., true and quasi-experiments). This trend, however, appears to be changing. A number of researchers have begun to explore ATIs, such as the effectiveness of different feedback types as a function of working memory (see, for example, Li, 2010a, 2010b).

14.3 METHODOLOGICAL CONSIDERATIONS

Before discussing nonlanguage influences studied in SLA, we draw attention to a few methodological issues common to this domain. First, studies of nonlanguage influences usually employ correlational designs. That is, the researchers pose questions such as whether motivation, for example, co-occurs with greater proficiency (and, conversely, lower motivation with lower proficiency). There are four basic outcomes of correlational analyses: positive (as one variable increases, so does the other), negative (as one variable increases, the other decreases), curvilinear (e.g., anxiety; see below), or no correlation or no relationship between the two variables. It is important to remember, when interpreting results from correlational studies, not to view them as causal. For example, it might be tempting to interpret a positive relationship between motivation and proficiency as evidence that having greater motivation affects learners' behaviors and thus leads to greater proficiency. This may very well be the case, but only experimental research—not correlational—allows us to make such claims. Another challenge that also relates to measurement is the fact that most individual differences studied in SLA are not immediately observable. More specifically, whereas some variables can be more or less directly measured (e.g., interactional features such as feedback, accuracy on a particular grammatical feature), variables such as aptitude and learning style must often be measured indirectly, using self-report-type instruments such as questionnaires or surveys. A related challenge is that these types of data-collection instruments introduce a potential threat to validity, because it is hard to be sure that participants will (a) use scales such as strongly disagree to strongly agree in the same way and (b) always respond truthfully, rather than in a way that represents them in a more preferable light (i.e., a prestige bias; see Dörnyei (with Taguchi), 2009, Chapter 3, for more on this and other challenges to using questionnaires). Of course, these issues aren't specific to research on nonlanguage influences; they come into play whenever scaled and/or self-report instruments are used, but they are especially relevant in this area of SLA. The final issue we'd like to mention, one that also relates to instrumentation, is the conceptual or theoretical overlap between constructs. In other words, it is often difficult to isolate the presence, absence, or degree of different non-language influences for comparison with other influences, as in the case of intelligence and aptitude, for example, or willingness to interact and opportunities to interact.

14.4 AGE DIFFERENCES

It is commonly believed that children are better language learners than adults, in the sense that young children typically can gain mastery of an L2, whereas adults cannot. This is reflected in what is known as the **Critical Period Hypothesis (CPH)**. Birdsong (1999a) defines the CPH as follows: "the CPH states that there is a limited developmental period during which it is possible to acquire a language be it L1 or L2, to normal, native-like levels. Once this window of opportunity is passed, however, the ability to learn language declines" (p. 1). Although many researchers use the term

TIME TO THINK ...

Think about individuals you know who learned your L1 as children and about those who learned your L1 as adults. Which ones seem more native-like to you? What characteristics of their language cause you to think they are more native-like? What factors (amount or type of input, time, cognitive differences, etc.) do you think may have caused these differences?

CPH, it is important to note that, in actuality, it is somewhat of a misnomer. Another term used is sensitive period, which is more gradual in its endpoint and allows for greater variation in attainment (Long, 1990).

The original formulation of the CPH came from Lennenberg (1967), who noted that "automatic acquisition from mere exposure to a given language seems to disappear [after puberty], and foreign languages have to be taught and learned through a conscious and labored effort. Foreign accents cannot be overcome easily after puberty" (p. 176). Early observations of this phenomenon come from Penfield and Roberts (1959), who had been concerned with the biological and neurological advantages that humans have for learning language as children rather than as adults. According to this hypothesis, there is an age-related point (generally puberty) beyond which it becomes difficult or impossible to learn an L2 to the same degree as NSs of that language. However, not all researchers agree with this view. The CPH predicts a certain amount of discontinuity—that is, at a certain point, there should be a dramatic drop-off. The Sensitive Period Hypothesis predicts sensitivity, but not absolute drop-offs, such that a learning decline might be gradual. The question of why adult SLA is often difficult and incomplete intrigues researchers and laypeople alike, because, in most cognitive activities, adults have an advantage.

One facet of the dispute is what it means to be a *more successful learner*. An initially attractive measure is speed of learning. In most studies in which measurements have been made of the speed of learning some aspect of an L2 by learners of different ages, no advantages were found for young children. In fact, the advantage typically is in the other direction. College-aged, young adults do quite well on most tests measuring language-learning speed. However, as Larsen-Freeman and Long (1991, pp. 155ff.) pointed out, these studies typically involve the demonstration of mastery of morphological and/or syntactic rules, reflecting speed of learning, not ultimate attainment. The advantages for adults on even these tasks appear short-lived. Snow and Hoefnagle-Höhle (1978), in a study of naturalistic acquisition of Dutch by five groups of English speakers (children [ages 3–5, 6–7, 8–10], adolescents [12–15], and adults), found that adults and adolescents outperformed children on tests given after 3 months of residence in the Netherlands, but, after 10 months, the children had caught up on most measures. This finding leaves many unanswered questions. Is this another example of the tortoise and the hare, with the results due to greater persistence by children, even though they never had an absolute difference in speed? Did children or the older groups somehow change the way in which they went about learning Dutch?

Another set of relevant variables involves types of language-learning tasks. There are some language-learning tasks in which advantages have been shown for children, even with regard to rate. For instance, Tahta et al. (1981) found that American children's ability to replicate intonational patterns in French and Armenian diminished after the age of 8.

In general, results indicate that adults are able to achieve criterion scores on most tests of L2 learning more rapidly than children, at least during the early stages of acquisition. The language skill involved also makes a difference, as the ability of older learners to quickly learn phonology, especially suprasegmental phonology, seems to atrophy rather quickly. This finding has been supported by a number of studies. Moyer (1999) examined highly proficient NNSs of German (English NSs) with an in-country experience as well as classroom instruction in German. They were graduate students in a U.S. university, were highly motivated and had had no significant prepubescent exposure to German. The results showed that, despite all of these positive attributes, their accents were still nonnative-like. Moyer attributes this to motor skills. She argues that, "late learners may face neurological or motor skill constraints, such as entrenched articulatory habits or restricted perceptual targets for phonetic categories, that render the possibility of native-like attainment highly unlikely or impossible" (p. 82).

There is abundant evidence that individuals generally do not achieve a native-like accent in an L2 unless they are exposed to it at an early age. Some researchers have argued that, in large measure, it is not necessarily true that adult learners cannot achieve native-like proficiency in phonology. For example, Neufeld (1979) argued that he was able to teach L2 learners to perform like natives on certain tasks after specialized training. It is quite likely that improved teaching techniques can improve learners' proficiency quite dramatically, but performance on limited tasks is not equivalent to consistent performance in naturalistic situations. After all, it is much easier to mimic someone else's voice over the phone well enough to fool someone in a brief message than to fool them during a long conversation. The shorter and less demanding the task, the easier it is to feign. Neither Neufeld nor anyone else that we are aware of has demonstrated a teaching technique successful enough to guarantee that learners will pass for NSs in everyday encounters. However, the issue is whether or not there is a gradual decline in abilities, as suggested by Flege (1999), or a precipitous drop-off, as would be expected if the CPH were in operation. Flege and others (Patkowski, 1980; Flege et al., 1995; Flege et al., 1999; Yeni-Komshian et al., 2000; Yeni-Komshian et al., 2001) have found that a foreign accent increases as one is exposed later and later to an L2, and that a foreign accent can occur even when exposure begins at age 6 or earlier.

There is a general consensus that most older individuals cannot reasonably hope to ever achieve a native accent in an L2. There is no such consensus about other areas of language. Some studies indicate that L2 learners cannot achieve complete mastery of syntax. Patkowski (1980) used experienced judges to evaluate transcripts of spoken passages by NSs and NNSs of English. The judges rated the transcripts on the basis of syntactic proficiency. He found that learners who acquired English after the age of puberty received lower proficiency scores than did either the NSs or the NNSs who started learning English before puberty. One problem with this method is that it does not show that mastery cannot be achieved, merely that it did not for this group of learners. Another problem is that the method does not directly measure English competence. Perhaps those who learned English later made more errors (even in terms of what they themselves would consider correct), errors they could have caught if allowed to edit their transcripts. Because the transcripts were not provided in the study, we cannot say exactly what the differences were.

In a study carefully designed to assess differences in the acquisition of syntax by learners, Johnson and Newport (1989) investigated learners' proficiency based on different ages of arrival in the country of the L2. Individuals in their study ranged in age of arrival from 3 to 39. Johnson and Newport found that learners' performance on a test intended to measure L2 syntactic knowledge was linearly related to age of arrival only up to puberty. Postpubescent learners generally performed poorly, but there was no correlation with age of arrival. These results can be seen in Figures 14.1 and 14.2.[2] As can be seen in Figure 14.1, there is a linear relationship between the test score and the age of arrival (between the ages of 3 and 15). On the other hand, no such relationship exists for those arriving after the age of 16 (Figure 14.2).

A further study (Slavoff & Johnson, 1995) examined children (NSs of Chinese, Japanese, Korean, and Vietnamese) learning English. The children had arrived in the United States between the ages of 7 and 12 and were tested on specific grammatical structures after various lengths of stay (ranging from 6 months to 3 years). Length of stay, as opposed to age of arrival, was an important variable in predicting knowledge of English syntax (as was gender—females performed better than males). It is important to keep in mind, however, that all of these children were below the age where the CPH is generally thought to take effect (roughly, puberty).

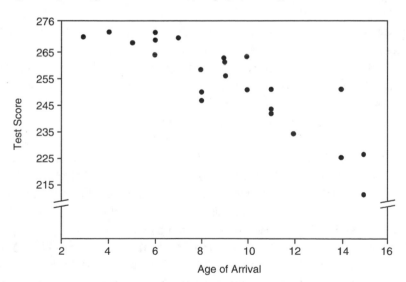

FIGURE 14.1 Learners Arriving, Ages 3–15 (*Source*: From "Critical period effects in second language learning: The influence of maturational state on the acquisition of English as a second language" by J. Johnson and E. Newport, 1989, *Cognitive Psychology*, *21*, 60–99. Reprinted by permission.)

437

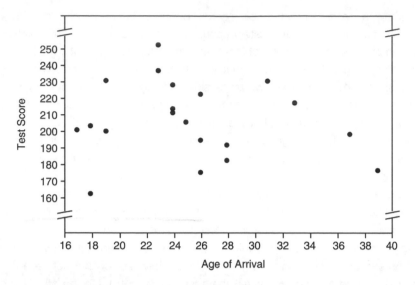

FIGURE 14.2 Learners Arriving, Ages 17–39 (*Source*: From "Critical period effects in second language learning: the influence of maturational state on the acquisition of English as a second language" by J. Johnson and E. Newport, 1989, *Cognitive Psychology*, *21*, 60–99. Reprinted by permission.)

Johnson and Newport (1991) investigated a property of language associated with Universal Grammar (and, hence, supposedly innate) and found that there was a steady decrease in performance according to age of arrival, extending past puberty and with the steepest decline at ages 14–16. These studies and others suggest that there is a critical period for acquisition, and that learners' capabilities for acquiring the syntax of an L2 decline with age.

Bialystok (1987) argued against maturational factors as a determining factor in the success or nonsuccess of L2 learning. In two studies, one looking at the acquisition of French gender marking (which nouns are feminine vs. which are masculine) by English and German NSs, and the other looking at the acquisition of English syntax by Chinese speakers, Bialystok found that age of onset of learning does not have significant effects, and that there is some support for the importance of length of stay in the target culture. She suggested that a factor in the difference between adults and children may be related to processing differences between the two populations. Further, in a reanalysis of Johnson and Newport (1989) data, Bialystok and Hakuta (1994) found age-related effects for some of the structures, but not others. Their recalculations also revealed a deterioration in proficiency starting after age 20—well after the proposed biological changes suggested by the CPH.

Coppieters (1987, p. 544) attempted to investigate the competence question in a more direct manner.[3] He found that NNSs and NSs may have strikingly different intuitions about sentences, although they produce essentially the same structures in actual use. He asked the question: Do native and native-like nonnative (i.e., near-native) speakers develop essentially identical underlying grammars of the same language? Results of extensive interviews indicate that native and near-native adult speakers of

French have strikingly different intuitions on French sentences. In particular, the data indicate that near-native speakers diverge less from NSs in formal features, such as those currently covered by studies in Universal Grammar, than in functional or cognitive aspects of grammar.

Birdsong (1992) also found differences in judgments of many grammatical structures between NSs and very fluent NNSs. However, Universal Grammar provided no basis for predicting on which structures they were like native speakers and on which they were not. And, importantly, unlike in previous studies, individual results indicated that some NNSs performed within the NS range.

It would appear that there are several divergences between the syntax of NSs and the syntax of even near-native speakers, but that these differences are often subtle and difficult to find. This raises a related issue. Does difference imply a lack of mastery? Consider the fact that rules based on Latin grammar had an influence on the views of English grammarians (e.g., do not split infinitives; this is a trivial rule of Latin grammar, because Latin infinitives are single words, not two-word phrases, as in English). In this instance, knowledge of an L2 had an influence on intuitions about an L1. One would not say that these grammarians had failed to master English because they were susceptible to foreign influences.

Patkowski (1980, pp. 462ff.) discusses the Conrad phenomenon, named after Joseph Conrad, the native Pole who learned English at the age of 18 and became one of the greatest English novelists. Patkowski (p. 463) cited the following remarks by Kurt Vonnegut:

> The writing style which is most natural for you is bound to echo the speech you heard when a child. English is the novelist Joseph Conrad's third language, and much that seems piquant in his use of English was no doubt colored by his first language, which was Polish.

Patkowski took this as an indication that Conrad's language was not native-like, but is it necessarily different from the writing style of someone who grew up around many NNSs, as in many neighborhoods of New York? Nabokov's style in *Ada*, in which there are multilingual puns based on French, German, Russian, and English, is different from what one would expect in a typical English speaker, but does this imply lesser or greater mastery? We need to be more precise in describing the acquisition of syntax.

The question of morphosyntax is also at issue. DeKeyser (2000), in a study of Hungarian learners of English with differing ages of arrival in the US, categorized the structures that he investigated as easy or hard, depending on their perceptual saliency, which he claims allows learners to notice an area where there is something to be learned. Examples of easy structures are word order in simple sentences and pronoun gender; examples of difficult structures are articles and subcategorization features. Easy structures did not show age-related effects, whereas difficult structures did. He ties this to explicit and implicit learning, claiming that younger learners have intact the ability for implicit and explicit learning, whereas adults have lost their ability to learn implicitly (see also DeKeyser and Larson-Hall, 2005, and DeKeyser et al., 2010;

cf. Reichle, 2010). In Chapter 12, we discussed research that showed that learners do not interpret morphosyntactic feedback in the way that it is intended, whereas other areas (for example, phonological feedback) are interpreted appropriately. Thus, if we consider interaction to be an important part of learning owing to the feedback received, and if morphosyntactic feedback is not useful, it becomes clear that morphosyntactic learning will be disadvantaged. In explaining the difference between adults and children vis-à-vis rate and ultimate attainment, DeKeyser and Larson-Hall (2005) invoke differences in implicit and explicit learning:

Children necessarily learn implicitly; adults necessarily learn largely explicitly. As a result, adults show an initial advantage because of the shortcuts provided by the explicit structure, but falter in those areas in which explicit learning is ineffective, that is, where rules are too complex or probabilistic in nature to be apprehended fully with explicit rules. Children, on the other hand, cannot use shortcuts to the representation of structure, but eventually reach full native speaker competence through long-term implicit learning from massive input. This long-term effect of age of onset is most obvious to the casual observer in pronunciation, but on closer inspection appears to be no less robust in the domain of grammar.

(2005, p. 103)

In summarizing the results so far, the evidence indicates that young children are more likely to attain native-like proficiency in an L2 than are teenagers or adults. Nevertheless, adults often learn certain parts of a new language more quickly (e.g., some morphological and syntactic features). The evidence is much more solid for an advantage for children in the acquisition of phonology, although there is some support for an advantage in other areas of language as well.

In a detailed review of the literature, Long (1990, p. 251) concluded:

1. Both the initial rate of acquisition and the ultimate level of attainment depend in part on the age at which learning begins.
2. There are sensitive periods governing language development, first or second, during which the acquisition of different linguistic abilities is successful and after which it is irregular and incomplete.
3. The age-related loss in ability is cumulative (not a catastrophic onetime event), affecting first one linguistic domain and then another, and is not limited to phonology.
4. The deterioration in some individuals begins as early as age 6—not at puberty as is often claimed.

The bulk of the evidence comes from the acquisition of English, and, second, the acquisition of other European languages. It is hoped that other languages will be the focus of investigation as the discipline of SLA further develops. Assuming that there is something like a critical period, or at least a sensitive period, the next question is:

Why is this the case? Various explanations have been offered for the well-attested fact that most adults do not (or cannot) become fluent in an L2. Among them are the following:

- Sociopsychological reasons: There are many different versions of this hypothesis. Some suggest that adults do not want to give up the sense of identity their accent provides. Some suggest that adults are unwilling to surrender their ego to the extent required to adopt a new language, which entails a new life-world.
- Cognitive factors: Adults have greater cognitive abilities than children. Ironically, adopting the cognitive abilities in a language-learning task has been hypothesized to result in less successful learning than is found in children, who, according to the hypothesis, rely to a greater extent on a specific language acquisition device.
- Neurological changes: Such changes prevent adults from using their brains in the same way children do on language-learning tasks. This is usually presented as a loss of plasticity, or flexibility, in the brain. As a person ages, there is a progressive lateralization of cerebral functions. The consequence of this and other cerebral changes is that the neural substrate needed for language learning is no longer fully available later in life.
- Exposure to better input: The assumption here is that the type of modifications adults make for children provide better data about language.
- Maladaptive gain of processing capacity: Processing and memory capacities change as a person matures (see Birdsong, 1999b).
- Loss of (access to) the language-learning faculty: Successful language learning cannot take place after puberty because there is a loss of UG and possibly a loss of innate learning strategies (see Chapter 7).
- "Use it, then lose it": This is essentially an evolutionary argument. Once humans have used whatever innate circuitry is available to them at birth, there is no longer any need for it, and the circuitry is dismantled. According to Pinker (1994, pp. 294–295):

> Language-acquisition circuitry is not needed once it has been used; it should be dismantled if keeping it around incurs any costs. And it probably does incur costs. Metabolically, the brain is a pig. It consumes a fifth of the body's oxygen and similarly large portions of its calories and phospholipids. Greedy neural tissue lying around beyond its point of usefulness is a good candidate for the recycling bin.
>
> A version of this is the "use it or lose it" explanation. If one doesn't use the innate faculty, it will atrophy with time. In other words, it is a slow loss rather than an all-at-once dismantling, and adult language learning comes at a greater distance from initial acquisition as a child.

- Learning inhibits learning: In the connectionist models of learning, language learning involves accumulating and strengthening associations (see Chapter 9). Thus, the strength of associations from the NL (or other languages known) might interfere with the possibility of formulating and strengthening new associations.

evolutionary argument

connectionist model

Long (2007) proposes a combination of some of the existing explanations. Exposure to more than one language before the close of the sensitive period, "and probably with no general cognitive correlate, conveys a lasting advantage on early L2 acquirers—an advantage that persists in adulthood" (p. 74). He further proposes that "early richer linguistic exposure leads to the creation of more, and more complex, neural networks before synaptic sheaths harden as part of the myelinization process, making new ones for new languages more difficult to create in older starters" (p. 74).

neural networks → (handwritten margin note)

Long (1990, p. 251) argued that, "affective, input, and current-cognitive explanations for the reduced ability are inadequate." If adults in some cultures do perform as well as children, then explanations based on cognitive or neurological factors are clearly wrong. There is no reason to assume any differences between cultures in these areas. Whereas there are sociopsychological differences between children and adults, children are by no means immune to sociopsychological factors. Input differences do not seem to be the major factor. The primary difference between children and adults is in the mastery of phonology, which can hardly be due to input differences. Moreover, adults are better at negotiating input, which should suggest better acquisition possibilities. Finally, there are indications that children do not receive input divergent from NS speech in certain cultures (i.e., there is no caretaker speech, as it is known in Western cultures).[4] In these cultures, as in others, language learning appears to proceed normally.

Differences between adult and children: (handwritten margin note)
① mastery of phonology (handwritten margin note)
② Adults negotiate better input (handwritten margin note)

If the neurological or cognitive hypotheses were correct, we would expect the process of language learning to be different in children and adults. We would further expect the patterns of acquisition to be different when adult and child learners are compared. Bley-Vroman et al. (1988) investigated this question. In reviewing previous literature, they found that:

> in many crucial domains L2 learners' utterances do, in fact, show structural properties that are at least very similar to those characterizing the speech of first language learners ... Furthermore, the types of interlanguage structures and the order in which certain features of the target language are mastered are close to identical in both L1 and L2 acquisition.
>
> (pp. 1–2)

The major differences noted between L2 and L1 were due to L1 influence, a factor that has nothing to do with age or maturation (with the obvious exception that very young children could not have mastery of a previous language). This indicates that the processes were not very different. Moreover, Bley-Vroman et al. found evidence for UG influence on adult L2 learning, although the patterns are complicated. This suggests that access to UG is not simply lost at some maturational stage.

L1 influence → (handwritten margin note)

In a study of competence, White and Genesee (1996) tested high-proficiency learners (NSs of French, described as "near-natives") on certain English structures known to be influenced by a critical period. The authors found no significant differences between these high-proficiency speakers and NSs of English. Therefore, they concluded that native competence is achievable even by postpubescent learners.

One might argue, though, that studies such as these found no difference simply because their instruments were not sensitive enough to detect one. In a recent study, Abrahamsson and Hyltenstam (2009) examined 195 Spanish–Swedish bilinguals with various ages of exposure who might be considered native-like. After an initial screening, 41 participants were perceived as NSs of their L2, Swedish. However, when a much more stringent battery of 10 tests was administered, none fell within the range of NSs, an empirical finding that echoes and supports their earlier claims, cited below.

Hyltenstam and Abrahamsson (2003) claim that only children reach native-like proficiency. Some do appear to reach native-like proficiency, namely those who have an age of arrival in an L2 environment before puberty, and most likely much earlier (even age 6). As they note, these individuals "reach proficiency levels above *the limit of perceivable non-nativeness*, thus making them *appear* to be nativelike" (p. 571; their emphasis). They go on to say that:

> Nevertheless, given the fact that there are no published accounts of a single adult starter who has reached native-like overall L2 proficiency, and given the frequent observation of non-native features even in very early starters, we would suggest the possibility that absolute native-like command of an L2 may in fact never be possible for any learner. According to such a view, the language learning mechanism would be designed in such a way that it requires immediate triggering from the environment in order for it to develop and work appropriately; that is, the learning mechanism inevitably and quickly deteriorates from birth if not continuously stimulated.
>
> (p. 575)

Future research will need to sort out these various explanations, if indeed there is a critical/sensitive period. It may further be, as with many explanations of L2 learning, that no single explanation can account for age-related differences.

Finally, Marinova-Todd et al. (2000) caution researchers and the lay public alike not to jump to conclusions about early learning. They propose that age differences may reflect more the situation of learning than a capacity for learning. In their words, "the misconception that adults cannot master foreign languages is as widespread as it is erroneous" (p. 27). They argue that the prevailing view that there is a critical period and that the explanation resides in connections to the brain relies on three fallacies:

1. *Misinterpretation*:
   (a) Fallacy: Children are fast and efficient.
   (b) Reality: Children learn languages slowly and effortfully.

2. *Misattribution*:
   (a) Fallacy: Language proficiency is tied to brain functioning.
   (b) Reality: This may in fact turn out to be the case, but data currently in evidence cannot discern this.

3. *Misemphasis*:

   (a) Fallacy: Because there is frequent failure by adults to learn an L2 does not mean that it is impossible to do so.

   (b) Reality: Most adults do end up short of native-like levels of proficiency, but there is often a lack of motivation, a lack of time or energy, and a lack of environmental support.

They suggest that a greater emphasis on those "truly informative cases: successful adults who invest sufficient time and attention in SLA and who benefit from high motivation and from supportive, informative L2 environments" (p. 28) will move the field forward in understanding the role of the critical period and ultimate attainment.

14.5 APTITUDE

[handwritten annotations: → potential for learning new knowledge or new skills/new language ↳ social background plays a role ↳ measuring it is not always clear]

The relationship between aptitude and L2 learning success is an important one, if only because opinions about aptitude can have enormous implications in our everyday lives. If aptitude measures are used to discourage individuals from studying foreign languages, and if the measures are inaccurate, then certain students will be unfairly prevented from receiving whatever advantages may accrue from knowledge of other languages. Given the past history of aptitude measures in school, one could reasonably predict that it is disadvantaged students who are most likely to suffer. Findings relating **language aptitude** to social background do nothing to allay these fears. On the other hand, if (a) an aptitude measure is accurate, and (b) students are placed in an instructional program for which they have little aptitude, and (c) it is possible to either increase their aptitude or place them in another instructional program for which they have greater aptitude, then failure to consider aptitude would penalize students unfairly. Aptitude, therefore, can have real-life consequences.

Aptitude, simply put, refers to one's potential for learning new knowledge or new skills. With regard to language aptitude, it refers to one's ability to learn another language; there is no talk of language aptitude for learning one's L1, at least not for children without cognitive deficits.

Even though aptitude is clearly of crucial importance, it has not always been a focus of investigation, in part for the same reasons illustrated above with regard to the general orientation of L2 studies and, in part, because the construct is somewhat elusive and clearly multicomponential, so that measuring it is not always clear cut. In studies where it has been included, aptitude has been shown to be an important differentiating factor among learners. In fact, Skehan (1989, p. 38) stated that, by definition, if not empirically or theoretically apparent, "aptitude is consistently the best predictor of language learning success." He counters arguments that attempt to diminish the role of aptitude by stressing the centrality of aptitude, which more recently is seen related to working memory, discussed in Chapter 10:

> It has been proposed that motivation . . . or cognitive style . . . or degree of acculturation . . . or personality and attitude . . . are of greater significance than

aptitude. This criticism is really an empirical question, and what is needed is evidence. In fact, such evidence as is available from quantification-based studies generally demonstrates that aptitude is at least as important, and usually more important, than any other variable investigated. Studies have reported multiple correlations between aptitude battery totals and criterion scores as high as 0.70, and values of 0.50 are commonplace. Only motivation indices even approach such high figures. The values one obtains for personality measures and traits such as cognitive style are considerably lower, rarely going much above 0.30.

(1989, p. 38)

J. B. Carroll is the name associated most with early studies of L2 learning aptitude. He is the originator of what Skehan called the "standard 'four component' view of language aptitude" (1989, p. 26):

Standard 4 component view for language aptitude.

1. *Phonemic coding ability.* This is the ability to discriminate among foreign sounds and to encode them in a manner such that they can be recalled later. This would certainly seem to be a skill involved in successful second language learning.
2. *Grammatical sensitivity.* This is the ability to recognize the functions of words in sentences. It does not measure an ability to name or describe the functions, but rather the ability to discern whether or not words in different sentences perform the same function. It appears logical that skill in being able to do this helps in learning another language.
3. *Inductive language learning ability.* This is the ability to infer, induce, or abduct rules or generalizations about language from samples of the language. A learner proficient in this ability is less reliant on well-presented rules or generalizations from a teacher or from materials.
4. *Memory and learning.* Originally this was phrased in terms of associations: the ability to make and recall associations between words and phrases in a native and a second language. It is not clear whether this type of association plays a major role in language learning, but memory for language material is clearly important. Some linguists (e.g., Becker, 1991) suggest that second language learning is much more an accomplishment of memory for text than of the analysis of text. That is, much more is memorized than is broken into parts and subjected to rule formation and/or generalizations.

Skehan (1989) questioned the appropriateness of separating grammatical sensitivity and inductive language-learning ability. He suggested that these be combined into one ability: language analytic ability.

language analytic ability

These abilities seem to be reasonable predictors of L2 learning success, in that a person who is excellent in one or more of these abilities would seem to be at an advantage in learning an L2. There is no a priori reason to believe that individuals will be equally skilled in all abilities. Indeed, Skehan (1989) suggested that all of the abilities (three in his scheme) are independent. If these three abilities are indeed independent, then there should be eight (2^3) learner types, because a person could be good on all three, good on the first but poor on the next two, and so forth. This proposition was tested recently by Sparks et al. (2012), who investigated whether and how many different L2 learner types might exist and what their shared characteristics might be. Using a range of instruments given to 208 learners and designed to measure L1 achievement, intelligence, L2 aptitude, and L2 proficiency, the authors identified three distinct profiles or clusters of learners: one that scored above average on all L1 and L2 measures, another that scored in the average range on all measures, and a third that generally scored below average, except on measures of intelligence. These results suggest a significant role for L1 abilities in defining and measuring L2 aptitude (see also Rysiewicz, 2008).

Role of L1 in learning language ability

In another study, Sparks et al. (2011) used the results from a battery of L1 and L2 tests to propose a somewhat novel model of L2 aptitude. The researchers identified four principal components: (a) language analysis (a combination of features from Carroll's components 2–4 above), (b) phonology/orthography (similar to Carroll's phonemic coding ability), (c) IQ/memory (a combination of features from Carroll's components 3 and 4), and (d) self-perception of language skills (an area related to affect not covered in Carroll's model). All together, the four-component analysis was able to account for 76 percent of the variance in L2 proficiency, thus showing its potential for predictive utility.

It is one thing to agree that these abilities would be useful in learning an L2; it is another thing to say that one has an adequate measure of these abilities. Various attempts have been made to measure them. Perhaps the best known is Carroll and Sapon's (1959) Modern Language Aptitude Test (MLAT). This test consists of five subtests:

- *Part One: Number Learning*: The student is taught, on tape, the Kurdish number system from 1 to 4, plus the "tens" and "hundreds" forms of these numbers, then tested by hearing numbers that are combinations of these elements (e.g., 312, 122, 41). The test aims at measuring associative memory.
- *Part Two: Phonetic Script*: This subtest measures phonemic coding ability. The student learns a system of phonetic notations for some English phonemes. He is then tested on this learning, for example, "Underline the word you hear: Tik; Tiyk; Tis; Tiys."
- *Part Three: Spelling Clues*: This is a high-speed test that measures both NL vocabulary and phonemic coding ability. The student is given clues to the pronunciation of a word (e.g., "ernst" for "earnest") and is then asked to choose a synonym from a list of alternatives.
- *Part Four: Words in Sentences*: This tests grammatical sensitivity. In a typical item, two sentences are presented, with one word in the first sentence underlined. In the second sentence, five words are underlined. The student has to decide which of the underlined words in the second sentence fulfills the same function as the underlined word in the first sentence.

- *Part Five: Paired Associates:* The student studies a written Kurdish–English vocabulary list, practices the stimulus–response pairs seen, and is then tested by means of multiple-choice items. This is a test of associative memory (summary of tests by Skehan, 1989, p. 28).

TIME TO DO ...

Look at these sample questions from a version of the MLAT (see Link #1 in the Links section at the end of the chapter). Did you find the questions difficult? Which section was the easiest? The hardest? Can you make any conclusions about how you might perform on the MLAT were you to take the whole test? Do these questions measure language-learning aptitude in your opinion? Why or why not?

It is important to remember that, although the skills themselves are listed, the only measurements used are those taken from tests, and one must assume that the tests are measuring what they purport to. The *words in sentences* subtest seems to have the best correspondence with the ability it seeks to measure (Skehan, 1989). The *paired associates* test relies on models of memory that are no longer generally accepted. The *spelling clues* test appears to depend heavily on social and regional dialects (because different dialects may have different pronunciations for the same spelling). In other words, what is a good clue for a speaker of one variety may be a poor clue for a speaker of another variety. In general, the abilities themselves are much more persuasive, at first glance, than the subtests used to measure them.

The question arises as to where aptitude comes from. That is, is aptitude innate or does it develop? McLaughlin (1990b) suggested that prior language-learning experience has a positive effect on language learning. This positive effect can manifest itself as better learning (Nation and McLaughlin, 1986) or as better use of language-learning strategies (Nayak et al., 1990). In other words, aptitude develops. However, Harley and Hart (1997) did not find support for aptitude development. Their study compared two groups of students in Grade 11, one that had been in early immersion programs and that had begun L2 (French) study (for the most part) in grade 1, and the other that had begun L2 (French) study in Grade 7. The former group (early immersion experience) did not perform better than the latter group of students (late immersion experience). In other words, language-learning experience did not affect aptitude, and, therefore, the claim cannot be made that aptitude develops as a function of language-learning experience. These arguments have taken place on both theoretical and empirical grounds. One position is that language aptitude is simply due to intelligence in general (see Wesche, 1981). This claim is difficult to maintain. First, it must be made clear that there are many approaches to intelligence (e.g., Gardner, 1983; Sternberg, 2002), and there is not agreement as to the components or hierarchical arrangement of the components of this construct. Many psychologists

447

believe that there are multiple types of intelligence, although it must be recognized that many others claim that there is support for a notion of general intelligence (Carroll, 1992). Second, statistical investigations have demonstrated that language aptitude, generally thought to be one's ability for something, cannot be explained simply on the basis of the most common measurement of intelligence, IQ scores. There are clearly many overlapping traits, but there is not a one-to-one correspondence between measures on a general IQ test and measures of aptitude.

The particular tests devised by Carroll are not the only tests of language aptitude. Other tests have been developed for the U.S. military and for use in other countries. British research (summarized in Skehan, 1989), in particular, has delved into the question of the origins of language aptitude. One discovery is that there are significant differences in the rates of syntactic acquisition in an L1. There is a correlation between the rates (which may be viewed as an indication of NL aptitude, perhaps) and L2 aptitude. Interestingly, the correlation is greater with L2 aptitude than with achievement (what one accomplishes), which supports the idea that capability is being measured, even though various factors may lead children to perform below their capacity.

L2 Aptitude & Social class and parental education

The British studies found that there is an even greater correlation between L2 aptitude and social class and parental education. These two elements have been found to be mixed in with vocabulary development, in a factor termed family background. Not only does family background correlate with L2 aptitude, but it also correlates quite highly with foreign-language achievement.

These relationships should give us pause, because, at least on face value, they seem related to factors that lead to achievement that are not really based on inherent capabilities (i.e., aptitude). Children from more privileged classes and with higher

Achievement x aptitude

parental education are more likely to be rewarded with good grades in schools. Moreover, children with these backgrounds are more likely to be able to use foreign-language skills abroad. Thus, they are good predictors of how likely a student is to get good grades or really use a foreign language, but it is harder to see how they can account for ability in the abstract. In other words, the former is concerned with accomplishments (achievement), and the latter is concerned with ability (aptitude).

More recent measures of aptitude have been devised by Grigorenko et al. (2000) and approach aptitude testing from a perspective of intelligence that takes as its base abilities that are necessary in daily life, as opposed to those needed for successful school learning. Their test, the CANAL-FT (Cognitive Ability for Novelty in Acquisition of Language), as is clear from the name, is grounded in cognitive theory, is dynamic, and is simulation-based. A major underlying idea of this test is that a central ability in foreign-language learning requires the ability to cope with novelty and ambiguity (Ehrman, 1993, 1994, 1996; Ehrman & Oxford, 1995), and this ability is part of Sternberg's theory of human intelligence (1985, 1988, 1997).

There are five knowledge-acquisition processes underlying their test:

- selective encoding—distinguishing between more and less relevant information;
- accidental encoding—understanding the background or secondary information;

- selective comparison—determining the relevance of old information for a current task;
- selective transfer—applying decoded or inferred rules in new contexts and/or tasks;
- selective combination—synthesizing various bits of information gathered through selective and accidental encoding.

The test includes four areas of language (lexical, morphological, semantic, and syntactic) and two modes of input and output (visual and oral). The test is based on the gradual learning of an artificial language. A description of the sections is given below (taken from Dörnyei, 2005, pp. 52–53), followed by sample items taken from Grigorenko et al. (2000, pp. 403–405). There were immediate and delayed recall tests; both immediate and delayed recall items are given here (see Grigorenko et al., 2000, pp. 403–405, for a fuller example of recall items).

The CANAL-FT comprises nine sections: Five involve immediate recall, and the other four are identical to these five sections, except that they are presented later and involve delayed recall (the last section does not have a delayed counterpart). A common element of the sections is that they all focus on the learning of an artificial language, Ursulu. This is presented gradually, so that, initially, participants have no knowledge of the language: by the end of the test, however, they have mastered enough lexical, morphological, semantic, and syntactic knowledge to cope with a small story in Ursulu. The five sections are as follows:

1. Learning meanings of neologisms from context: Participants are presented with 24 brief paragraphs within a 2 × 3 factorial design (type of presentation: oral or visual × density of unknown words: low, medium, or high). Understanding is tested via a multiple-choice format, where students are asked to guess which of five alternatives is most likely to correspond to the meaning of an unknown neologism inserted into the text. Two multiple-choice items are presented immediately after receipt of every passage, and one item relevant to every passage is presented at least 30 minutes after receipt of the passages, in order to measure storage in long-term memory.

   Example item (immediate recall) (partial text): Rising tuition costs and increasingly large loans aren't the only financial issues facing mukulu nafe-de, the latest threat to Yuve-Yuve ya-pama-de pocketbooks comes from mandatory twok-de. One laka will require entering freshmen fru hujuk a mukulu-specified laptop twok at a cost of $3,000.

   Questions: Fru hujuk most likely means: (a) to arrange; (b) having; (c) carrying; (d) to purchase; (e) to rent. Mukulu in line (3) most likely means: (a) schools; (b) student; (c) parent; (d) universities; (e) college.

2. Understanding the meaning of passages: The six test items in this part are identical in form to those in Section 1, but the assessment involves comprehension of whole passages rather than merely of lexical items. Again, half of the items are

presented visually, the other half orally, and the passages differ in terms of the density of unknown words. The test differs from standard reading and oral comprehension tests in the inclusion of unknown words in the passages. Such words render these passages more like those that would be encountered in the process of learning an L2.

> **Example item (immediate recall) (partial text)**: The wealthy hunting femo-de of late glacial Europe might have maintained or even enriched culture, or unta-u erto to stagnate ik decline: Yuve could hardly have advanced erto to a higher form of civilization, for the environment neunta-u erto. But Yuve-Yuve future cutta-u not left in Yuve-Yuve own sima-de.

> **Question (delayed recall)**: The author of the passage about the hunting society apparently believes that levels of civilization are determined by: (a) economic luck; (b) a balance of solar energy; (c) the ambitions of the people; (d) a piece of magic; (e) climatic conditions.

3. Continuous paired-associate learning: In this test, participants are presented with 60 paired associates (word pairs), half of them visually, half of them orally. They are required to learn the successive pairings and, during the process, they are tested at irregular intervals on words learned more recently as well as less recently. The test differs from a straightforward paired-associates memory test in that there are certain rules that can facilitate learning, relating some of the terms to others.

> **Example pairs (immediate recall)**:
> kiss = lutik
> maki smelano = floweret
> to oppose = fru prostoto
> threerish = two
> to luxuriate = fru shikta
> unteriapremu = fairytale
> to learn = fruumbrad
> juk-de = fingers
> yellow = hukoi
> pjze_min-de = workers

> **Questions**: In Ursulu, floweret most likely means (a) maki smelano; (b) ummake; (c) lutik; (d) pjze_min; (e) maki juk. Fru umbrad most likely means: (a) to eat; (b) to go; (c) to learn, (d) to kiss; (e) to dream.

4. **Sentential inference**: Participants receive 20 sets of between three and five sentences in the Ursulu language, with their translations presented either visually or orally. They are then presented with a new sentence, either in English or in Ursulu, and are asked to indicate—based on inferences made from the previously presented sentence pairs—which of five multiple-choice answers best represents the translation.

Example item (immediate recall):

Panlin-u Sumu Twah chuck	means	I handed a stick to him.
Panlin-u Yut Twa dozz	means	He handed an umbrella to me.
Panilcos-u Yut Twa flexta	means	He handed a piece of paper to me.
Panleh-u Sumu Twah chuchu	means	I handed a rope to him.

Question: The sentence Panilcos-u Sumu Twah otikum most likely means:

(a) He handed a rod to me;
(b) I handed a cord to him;
(c) I handed a postcard to him;
(d) I handed a waterhose to him;
(e) I handed a tree-branch to her.

5. **Learning language rules**: Participants are given some vocabulary, some grammar, and some examples of how the Ursulu language works. From this type of information they are expected to learn some of the most evident rules of the language. To measure this learning, they are presented with 12 items (lexical, semantic, morphological, and syntactic) that test their understanding of the Ursulu language.

Example item (immediate recall): In Ursulu, ya-bum baqlo means "the chief's mule," ya being the possessive and ya bum the modifier of the noun baqlo "mule."

Question: Match the corresponding pairs:

(1) ya-fuama pokka   (a) monkey's smile
(2) preumma chicca-de   (b) alligator gloves
(3) ya-xori gazza   (c) sheep wool
(4) prebrutama tepla-de   (d) cat's tail
(5) ya-ayama xrosyo   (e) gigantic tiger
(6) preuntam rutuma   (f) wife's book

Regardless of the type of aptitude measure used, a question arises as to whether there can be any practical applications in terms of tailoring language classrooms to aptitude characteristics of students. Not many studies have investigated this in detail, probably owing to the fact that it is difficult to isolate one factor in a complex learning environment as contributing to success or lack of success. Nonetheless, there are a few relevant studies that would fall under the category of ATI research (see discussion of ATI research in Chapter 13 on instructed SLA).

Wesche (1981) and Skehan (1996) reported that students show greater satisfaction when instruction is matched to learner characteristics, as when more analytic methodologies are used with analytic learners, and more memory-oriented learners did better with methodologies that involved exposure to longer chunks of language.

Similarly, Harley and Hart (1997), in a study of immersion children, found positive relationships between (a) L2 success and analytical measures for immersion beginning in adolescence and (b) L2 success and memory ability for those students beginning immersion in grade 1.

Reves (1983) studied Arabic NSs learning English in school in Israel, and the same group learning Hebrew naturalistically. The aptitude measure was found to be a better predictor of success in the informal, naturalistic setting. Thus, it appears that aptitude is an important indicator of SLA in both classroom and nonclassroom contexts.

Robinson (2001, 2002a, 2002b) has begun to look at aptitude complexes; that is, clusters of traits that lead to efficient learning. Aptitude, in his view, represents the totality of other abilities, which he groups according to cognitive factors that can support learning in different contexts. This is supported by Segalowitz (1997), who places aptitude contextually. It is not a fixed trait, "but rather a complex reflection of the whole learning situation" (p. 108).

Clearly, working memory is part of any discussion of aptitude, and some believe that working memory is aptitude. This is made clear by Miyake and Friedman (1998) when they say that working memory for language may be one (if not the) central component of language aptitude (p. 339), and most models of aptitude have ascribed a role to memory. This idea has led to much research in recent years in the L2 domain. Specifically, the role of working memory as a subconstruct of aptitude has been studied in relation to L2 reading (e.g., Walter, 2006; Leeser, 2007; Jeon & Yamashita, 2011) and writing (e.g., Adams & Guillot, 2008), as well as other individual differences (e.g., Rai et al., 2011) and general proficiency (e.g., van den Noort et al., 2006; Linck & Weiss, 2011), among other variables (see Juffs & Harrington, 2011). Future research will undoubtedly continue to investigate the role of working memory as aptitude.

As Dörnyei (2005) notes, current research views aptitude as a situated phenomenon, for example, in relation to motivation, a discussion of which we turn to next.

> ### TIME TO THINK ...
>
> Are you a good language learner? Which individual differences have helped you in your L2 studies? Are there any individual differences of yours that may have hindered your L2 progress?

14.6 MOTIVATION

A sociopsychological factor frequently used to account for differential success in learning an L2 is motivation. This has an intuitive appeal. It makes sense that individuals who are motivated will learn another language (or anything) faster and to a greater degree. And, quite clearly, some degree of motivation is involved in initial decisions to learn another language and to maintain learning. Furthermore, numerous studies have provided statistical evidence that indicates motivation is a predictor of language-learning success. In recent years, there has been a resurgence of interest in motivation research, with numerous reviews and book-length treatments of the topic, in addition to multiple active lines of empirical inquiry (e.g., Masgoret & Gardner, 2003; Dörnyei & Ushioda, 2009; Ushioda & Dörnyei, 2012).

In general, motivation appears to be the second strongest predictor of success, trailing only aptitude (Skehan, 1989). Nevertheless, an investigation of the role of motivation in L2 learning faces a hurdle just beyond the starting block: the exact nature of motivation is not so clear. Everyone agrees that it has something to do with drive, but, when various definitions are compared, it becomes clear that these definitions differ in significant ways.

Gardner, through his early work with Lambert (1972) and in later work with colleagues at the University of Western Ontario, has become a primary figure in the field of motivation in L2 learning: "Motivation involves four aspects, a goal, effortful behaviour, a desire to attain the goal and favourable attitudes toward the activity in question" (Gardner, 1985, p. 50).

Effort consists of a number of factors, including an inherent need to achieve, good study habits, and the desire to please a teacher or parent. This seems to be a mixed bag of components, as some pertain to what one has done and others to what one would like to do.

Central to this approach is the concept of integration, which refers to an individual's disposition toward the L2 group and the extent to which he or she desires to interact with, and even become similar to, that group. In Figure 14.3 is a representation of Gardner's basic model, showing the roles of both aptitude and motivation in language achievement. Integrativeness is "a complex of attitudes involving more than just the other language community. It is not simply a reason for studying the language" (Gardner, 2001, p. 5).

As can be seen, achievement comes from motivation, of which **integrative motivation** is one component, and aptitude, discussed in the previous section. There are other factors that also contribute to achievement, of which **instrumental motivation**, generally referring to a utilitarian goal such as obtaining a job, is one. But other sources of motivation are also possible, such as an inspiring teacher.

Gardner's basic method in early research was to administer questionnaires that call for self-report answers to questions (often based on a Likert scale), as in this example:

Place a check mark anywhere along the line below to indicate how much you like French compared with all your other courses.

French is my   French is my
least preferred   most preferred
course   course

_____ : _____ : _____ : _____ : _____ : _____ : _____ : _____

453

When you have an assignment to do in French, do you:

_____ (a) do it immediately when you start your homework.

_____ (b) become completely bored.

_____ (c) put it off until all your other homework is finished.

_____ (d) none of these (explain).

(Gardner & Lambert, 1972, p. 153)

Hence, assessments of effort, desire, and attitude are all based on self-reports, without justification for the items of the questionnaire.

In measuring the degree of motivation, scores are added together (except for an anxiety score, which is subtracted). Gardner and his colleagues grouped certain questions into categories, which are further used to account for success in language learning.

As we have seen in Gardner's model, motivation research has viewed motivation in relation to other constructs. However, more than that, motivation research considers

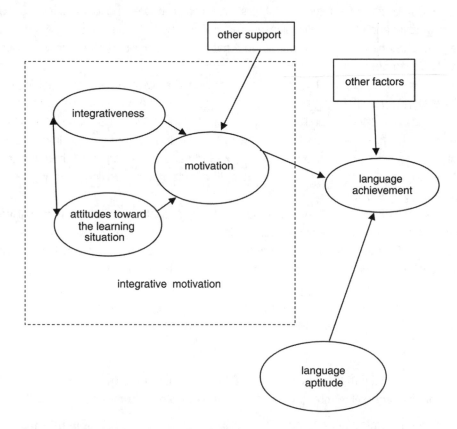

FIGURE 14.3 Basic Model of the Role of Aptitude and Motivation in L2 Learning (*Source*: From "Integrative motivation and second language acquisition" by R. Gardner, 2001. In Z. Dörnyei and R. Schmidt (Eds.), *Motivation and second language acquisition* (pp. 1–19). Honolulu: Second Language Teaching and Curriculum Center. Reprinted by permission.)

motivation as it relates to the context in which learning takes place. For example, Norton (2000) and McKay and Wong (1996) refer to investment—more specifically, investment in the TL. As Potowski (2004) points out, investment "takes into account the factors influencing a learner's decision to speak—or to remain silent—and in which language" (p. 77). If learners are going to engage in a conversation, they need to understand the return on that investment.

[handwritten note: Motivation & context]

What is particularly noteworthy in this approach is considering how motivation affects learning processes and overall disposition (Dörnyei, 2006). In other words, motivation is a dynamic construct.

[handwritten note: Motivation: is a dynamic construct]

14.6.1 Motivation as a Function of Time and Success

Improving proficiency in an L2 is a long-term project. Nevertheless, success in this long-term project depends on success in a series of short activities. A learner who is vigilant about instituting many encounters to gain comprehensible input is more likely to be successful in L2 learning environments. A learner who expends the effort for memorization (even if unconsciously) is more likely to succeed in either foreign- or second-language environments. To obtain good school grades, students must perform many tasks successfully over a term or academic year. Clearly, however, motivation is not static; it changes, depending on the context, and it changes over time.

[handwritten note: Motivation is not static !]

TIME TO THINK ...

Think about your own success (or lack thereof) in learning an L2. Do you believe that motivation or aptitude were more important in determining how successful you were in learning the language? Why?

A question regarding motivation and L2 learning is whether it is better to say that motivation predicts success, in that the more successful one has been in language learning, the more motivated one will be to learn more. This can be broken down into at least two specific questions: (a) Can motivation change over time? and (b) What is the effect of success on performance?

14.6.2 Changes Over Time

Dörnyei and Ottó (1998; and detailed in Dörnyei, 2000, 2001a) proposed a model of motivation that allows for changes over time. Essentially, there are three components to this model, which represent three temporal steps. The model chronicles how initial wishes are transformed into goals, how intentions are operationalized, then how they are enacted, and, finally, how a goal is accomplished and evaluated. The three phases are:

NONLANGUAGE INFLUENCES

generation of motivation →

- *Preactional stage.* This is the stage during which motivation is generated. This leads to the selection of the goal that will be pursued.

executive motivation that sustains the activity →

- *Actional stage:* This is referred to as executive motivation, and it relates to the sustaining of the activity, even with distracting influences.

evaluation →

- *Postactional stage:* The third phase follows the completion of the action. This is referred to as motivational retrospection. This refers to the evaluation of how the activity went and feeds into future activities that might be pursued in the future.

These are schematized in Figure 14.4.

As Dörnyei (2005) points out, the division between stages is not as abrupt as would seem in this diagram on paper. There is most likely overlap: where one stage ends, another begins. The model, however, is intended to show that different motives may be involved at different points in time. Further motives can be reassessed and modified during the process.

change in motivation

There have been some studies that have investigated how motivation changes over time (Lim, 2002; Williams et al., 2002; Gardner et al., 2004; Shedivy, 2004). Shoaib and Dörnyei (2005) found that specific episodes in people's lives had the consequence of restructuring their motivation.

↓

student-teacher relationship can have an impact on students' motivation

Another factor believed to influence learner motivation is what happens in the L2 classroom. Several recent studies have examined the relationship between teacher behavior and both students' motivation and their motivated behaviors. In two related, but independently executed studies, Guilloteaux and Dörnyei (2008) and Papi and Abdollahzadeh (2012) studied EFL classroom behavior in Korea and Iran, respectively, using a coding scheme the former developed for this purpose: the motivation orientation of language teaching (MOLT). The results of Guilloteaux and Dörnyei show strong correlations between all three main variables: teachers' motivating behaviors, learners' motivated behaviors, and learners' motivation. However, the Papi and Abdollahzadeh study only found a significant correlation between teachers' motivational strategies and students' motivated behavior; no relationship was found between student ideal L2 self- and actual motivated behavior. Taken together, these findings underscore that, although teachers can have an impact on their learners' perceptions and behaviors, any discussion or study of motivation and other individual differences must consider the context in question (see also Bernaus & Gardner, 2008).

14.6.3 Influence of Success on Motivation and Demotivation

What is the effect of success on motivation? Does it necessarily increase motivation? The argument earlier suggests that, if learners realize that successful performance in some activity leads toward their goal (whether learning or getting good grades), then expectancies are likely to rise. This would appear to say that success will tend to increase motivation, but matters are not that simple. This argument considers potential motivation and ignores motivational arousal. Motivational arousal, or initiation of motivation, is likely based on a person's assumption of how much effort is needed

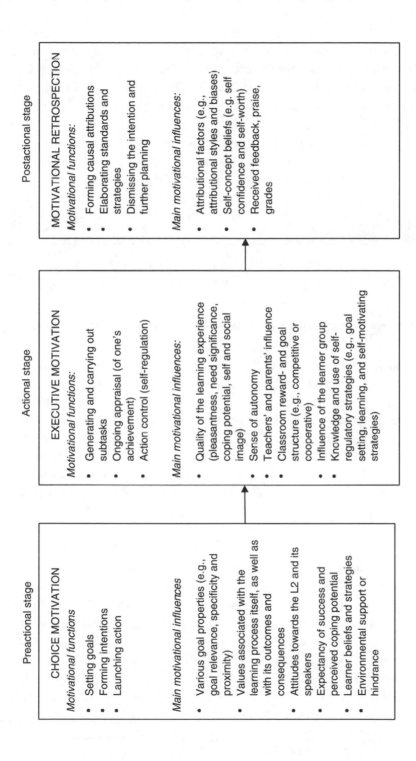

FIGURE 14.4 A Process Model of L2 Motivation (Source: © 2005. From *The psychology of the language learner: Individual differences in second language acquisition* by Z. Dörnyei. Reproduced by permission of Lawrence Erlbaum Associates, a division of Taylor & Francis Group.)

[handwritten margin note:] MOTIVATIONAL AROUSAL : Assumption of how much effort is necessary to complete a task. !!

to perform an activity correctly. Studies indicate that motivational arousal is greatest for tasks that are assumed to be of moderate difficulty (see the discussion in Brehm and Self, 1989). Thus, similar to the relationship between anxiety and performance (see section 14.7.2), we might describe the relationship between motivational arousal and task difficulty as curvilinear, because, when the success rate is considered very high or very low, motivational arousal is weakened. In other words, we try hardest for things we consider challenging but not nearly impossible.

If all of this is still true for language learning, then there is no reason to believe that good grades or good progress in language learning will lead to greater motivation. To the contrary, one may assume that the learners that do the best will find the tasks easy, and, as a result, their motivational intensity should weaken.

TIME TO THINK …

Think about your own L2 learning experience. Have you been motivated to learn? If yes, do you think that helped you succeed. If no, do you think that hindered your learning? Why or why not?

[handwritten margin note:] Success + confidence ↓ more success — success + overconfidence ↓ fall

Does success lead to better performance? There are different results presented in the literature. Moreover, a plausible argument can be made for either direction. Success can breed confidence, which results in greater success. Instead of performance, one might also look at whether a learner persists in their studies as a measure of motivation. Erler and Macaro (2011), for example, found test performance to be a significant predictor of whether or not learners in their sample continued to study French. On the other hand, success can breed overconfidence, which sets one up for a fall. Mizruchi (1991) provided interesting data on this question. Consider the following:

[handwritten margin note:] failure leads to success

The extent to which confidence and motivation affect task performance is a controversial issue among social psychologists. Although most participants believe that prior success breeds present success, many researchers have found no effect of prior performance on current performance. Contrary to the conventional view, I argue that in team competition, prior success breeds failure in current task performance because it decreases the necessity of success. Conversely, I suggest that prior failure breeds current success because it increases the urgency of success. I test this argument with data on playoff games between professional basketball teams from 1947 through 1982. Controlling for the advantage accruing to the home team as well as for the relative strength of the teams, I find that in back-to-back games at the same site, teams that won the previous game are more likely to lose the current game.

(1991, p. 181)

No one would suggest that competition between National Basketball Association teams is exactly analogous to L2 learning situations, but this study provides further reason to doubt the automatic assumption that prior success leads to current or future success.

There is little research on what Dörnyei refers to as demotivation, which is "specific external forces that reduce or diminish the motivational basis of a behavioral intention or an ongoing action" (2001b, p. 143). What he means by this is that the positive motivations that were initially present when a choice was made to undertake some activity were diminished by some negative factor, very often some classroom experience, most notably a teacher. Dörnyei (2005) cites Ushioda (2003, pp. 93–94) to illustrate this point:

> The inevitable problems in classroom motivation arise when there is not a happy fusion between internal and external forces but a negative tension, where the latter dominate at the expense of the former. In other words, individual motivation becomes controlled, suppressed or distorted by external forces . . . this may happen through negative influences in the classroom social dynamic, or through regulating forces in the educational system . . .
>
> Collective motivation can all too easily become collective demotivation, boredom, or at the far end of the spectrum, collective dissatisfaction or rebellion, often in the form of classroom counter-cultures defined by rejection of educational aims and values.

external forces distort individual motivation

As stated earlier, any discussion of attitude, aptitude, or motivation cannot be considered in the abstract; how they relate to an individual depends on that individual's makeup. This is where issues of learning style enter into the picture. Topics such as risk-taking behavior, field dependence/independence, and visual, auditory, or kinesthetic preferences are all related to the general topic of learning styles. These topics have not been prevalent in recent SLA discussions and, thus, will not be dealt with in this book.

feelings + emotions
Language shock → sound comical to NS.
learner realizes he/she may
culture shock → disorientation from exposure to a new culture

14.7 AFFECT

ANXIETY/LANGUAGE + CULTURE SHOCK
SOCIAL DISTANCE

One of the dictionary definitions of *affect* is "a feeling or emotion as distinguished from cognition, thought, or action" (*American Heritage Dictionary*). In other words, it refers to feelings or emotions that individuals have about something. In the case of language learning, it can refer to feelings or emotional reactions about the language, about the people who speak that language, about the culture where that language is spoken, or about the language-learning environment. In the next section, we discuss language shock and culture shock. Language shock refers to the realization that, as a learner, you must seem comical to speakers of the TL, whereas culture shock refers to anxiety relating to disorientation from exposure to a new culture.

14.7.1 Language Shock and Culture Shock

Diary studies suggest that both language shock and culture shock are important for L2 learners, but whether they truly affect acquisition is yet another story. Jones (1977), in her own diary detailing her study of Indonesian in Indonesia, discussed language shock, culture shock, and general stress.

Language shock

June 19

Friday night there was a dinner reception in our honor at the auditorium at school. After we ate dinner, a few of the professors got up and told "funny" stories about their experiences in the U.S. Then they wanted all of us to get up and do the same about our experiences in Indonesia. I politely refused, but Walt and Glenn got up. The guests not only laughed at the stories, but also at the awkward, nonfluent Indonesian used by them. I felt terribly embarrassed. The Indonesians did this because they honestly thought it would be funny and thought we would laugh too. I don't laugh when they try to speak English and I don't think it is funny when I make a mistake. This is one time where I feel I cannot get up and make a fool out of myself for others to laugh at because I wouldn't think it was funny. I find that situations and embarrassment like this inhibits my ability to speak.

July 15

It seems as if all the young people my age laugh at my Indonesian pronunciation and lack of vocabulary. I don't enjoy being laughed at, and I don't think it is funny!! I am unable to reply to even simple sentences after incidents like these.

Culture shock and rejection

July 15

The young married couples sit around with nothing to do and complain about how difficult life is or how tired they are. The young unmarried people don't seem to carry on serious conversations with anyone and spend a lot of time in empty chatter.

July 18

I feel my language has deteriorated while I have been in Yogyakarta because of the way part of the family has behaved towards me. I have felt like an outsider and have rejected them. I am tired of the attitude of some of the family, laughing at me or being impatient with me in my attempt to learn their language.

Stress

June 14

One of the professors is arranging for a play to be given by the participants. I have been cast in a play. I try to get myself out of it but Pak Soesanto (the professor) doesn't seem to understand that I just don't have enough time. I was advised to just not go to the first rehearsal, so I didn't. The next day all the Indonesians connected with the play questioned me. I tried to explain that I had already talked with Pak Soesanto and that I didn't have enough time but I don't think they understand me. I just don't have the vocabulary to adequately express myself and I feel so frustrated and embarrassed in not really being able to make myself completely understood.

June 19

I have gone downtown by myself. The biggest problem is how to ask for "thin" paper for airmail letters. I couldn't make myself understood, so finally I just dropped the whole matter and went home without the paper. This really irritated me as I wanted to write some letters and finally had enough free time to do so.

Anxiety and stress are also prevalent in classroom learning, as well as in individual learning contexts, as shown in the examples above. Bailey (1983) conducted a diary study of her own language-learning experience when studying French at the university. She made frequent journal entries chronicling her own experiences and feelings (see also Mackey and Gass, 2005, and Gass and Mackey, 2007, for additional information regarding diary studies).

Bailey's (1983) entries illustrate such phenomena as the role of self-esteem, competitiveness, and anxiety, as in the following quotations:

I feel very anxious about this class. I know I am (or can be) a good language learner, but I hate being lost in class. I feel like I'm behind the others and slowing down the pace.

(pp. 75–76)

Today I was panicked in the oral exercise where we had to fill in the blanks with either the past definite or the imperfect. Now I know what ESL students go through with the present perfect and the simple past. How frustrating it is to be looking for adverbial clues in the sentence when I don't even know what the words and phrases mean. I realized that the teacher was going around the room taking the sentences in order so I tried to stay one jump ahead of her by working ahead and using her feedback to the class to obtain confirmation or denial of my hypotheses. Today I felt a little scared. I'm so rusty!

(p. 74)

Ard (personal communication) speaks of his own competitiveness as an older person studying Italian in an intensive 4-week program; it was also his first time being a student in nearly 40 years. "I'm somewhat competitive and don't like having a weakness." This, however, played to his advantage in that it made him work harder: "I bought some materials with CDs and have tried practicing at home."

In sum, anxiety, competitiveness, as well as shock in a new, perhaps uncontrollable, situation can make the language-learning situation problematic and stressful, but, as noted above, can also prod some individuals to work even harder.

TIME TO THINK ...

Have you studied abroad? What experiences with culture shock or language shock did you experience? How do you think these experiences might have affected your language learning?

14.7.2 Anxiety

Anxiety seems to represent a trait that falls within the broader scheme of factors affecting learning, but what is not clear is whether it is a matter of personality, an emotional reaction to a situation, or a combination of these (cf. MacIntyre, 2007). The study of anxiety and related issues such as context, of course, are not unique to SLA. However, Horwitz (2001), in a review of the literature, noted that there is something unique about L2 learning anxiety, separate from other types of anxiety (see also MacIntyre, 1999, 2002). Nevertheless, it is somewhat surprising that research in this area has developed largely independent of the larger body of work on academic anxiety (Cassady, 2010).

Anxiety
↑
low levels help
high levels hurt

Anxiety is not always a negative factor in learning. In general, anxiety, like many other factors (see Mizruchi, 1991, for a more general discussion), has a curvilinear effect on performance: low levels help, whereas high levels hurt. As noted earlier, if one doesn't care at all, there is little reason to try to do well. On the other hand, too much concern about failure can get in the way of success.

We provided examples earlier from Bailey's (1983) own diary study. One important point she makes is that anxiety depends on the situation in which learners find themselves. Too often, studies assume some uniform, global relationship between language-learning success and a motivating factor.

Although Bailey and others have catalogued the effects of anxiety on specific situations, there has been very little effort to determine whether general results about anxiety affect L2 learning in what would seem to be the obvious manners. Consider two examples from Geen (1991) and Hoffman (1986). Geen noted that:

SOCIAL
ANXIETY:
↳ *inhibits behavior*
↳ *passive and*
self-defensive
style of verbal
behavior

> Social anxiety essentially inhibits behavior. It may, for example, bring about disengagement—avoidance of social situations, withholding of communication . . . or breaking of eye contact . . . —or replacement of meaningful communication with innocuous sociability . . . Leary et al. (1987) provide evidence that social anxiety is associated with a passive and self-defensive style of verbal behavior in two-person interaction.

(1991, p. 392)

This would seem to have obvious implications for L2 learning, especially for acquisition models or teaching methods that depend on successful interactions. Furthermore, there would appear to exist a kind of tension between learners' anxiety on one hand, which might draw them away from language use and interaction, and motivation or willingness to communicate, more specifically, which might draw them toward these (Liu & Jackson, 2008; MacIntyre, 2007).

More specifically, Hoffman (1986) noted that anxiety can direct attention away from meaning and toward pure form:

> In a [previous] review . . . it was found that intense anxiety directs one's attention to physical features of words (acoustic properties, order of presentation, phonetic similarities) and that occurs to the relative neglect of semantic content. This suggests that affect can determine the extent to which semantic and nonsemantic modes of processing are brought into play.
>
> (p. 261)

This, too, has obvious implications for L2 learning. To the extent that concentration on meaningful use of language is important in learning, anxiety could be a directly negative factor.

Dörnyei (2005) points out that there are two dimensions in the literature that are relevant to understanding anxiety: beneficial/facilitating vs. inhibitory/debilitating anxiety and trait vs. state anxiety. The first dichotomy refers to whether or not anxiety can be a positive or a negative force in learning, and the second refers to whether anxiety is part of an individual's makeup across many situations, or whether it is a reaction in a particular situation (see also Scovel, 2001). Testing is one particular situation where we might expect to find higher levels of anxiety. In order to test this hypothesis and examine other causes and outcomes of anxiety, and to further induce anxiety, MacIntyre and Gardner (1994) introduced a video camera during a vocabulary test. Correlations showed a relationship between anxiety and performance.

As a result of a hypothesized relationship between oral performance and anxiety, we might also expect to see the effects of this individual difference realized in L2 speaking. This area of anxiety research has produced a substantial body of empirical research, most of which has found anxiety to be negatively correlated with oral production. That is, the more anxious the learners, the poorer their performance. Hewitt and Stephenson's (2012) recent replication of Phillips (1992), for example, found a moderate-to-strong relationship between anxiety and speaking. Critically, the study also carried out partial correlations to determine whether poorer performance should be attributed to anxiety or simply to lower proficiency. The authors concluded that both played a role in the participants' production.

In another, perhaps more pedagogically oriented line of research on anxiety, some scholars have tested different techniques for reducing learner anxiety. An early study by D. J. Young (1990), for example, found reduced anxiety for small-group as opposed to whole-class discussions (see also Koch & Terrell, 1991), as well as for classes in which students had positive feelings toward their instructor. For more comprehensive treatments of this topic, see D. J. Young (1999) and Arnold (1999).

[handwritten: a lack of affinity → psychological distance]

14.7.3 Social Distance

[handwritten: reduced input]

[handwritten in left margin: ACCULTURATION MODEL — casual variable in SLA — if learners acculturate, they learn — chain reaction — less contact = less learning]

A related concept to affect is social distance. There are many instances in which an L2 learner does not feel an affinity with the TL community. In such instances, learners create both a psychological distance and a social distance from speakers in the L2 community. An immediate consequence is that this results in a diminished amount of input. The realization of the significance of social (group) distance and psychological (individual) distance formed the basis of Schumann's (1978a, 1978b) **Acculturation Model.** According to the precepts of this model, acculturation (the assimilation of the cultural traits of another group) is the causal variable of SLA. That is, if learners acculturate, they will learn; if learners do not acculturate, they will not learn. Thus, acculturation initiates a chain reaction, including contact in the middle and acquisition as its outcome.

One of the social variables in the model that needs to be considered is the extent to which one group is dominant over another. One can think of situations in which an L2 group is dominant (e.g., colonization), or in which the L1 group is dominant (e.g., immigration). In the former case, learning is less likely to take place.[5] Another social situation to be considered is the extent to which a group integrates. In many immigrant communities, at least in the United States, there has been nearly total assimilation. In such situations, there is a high degree of learning. In others, there is emphasis on preserving one's own lifestyle and language. These situations result in language schooling for one's children in the home language. As a result of less contact, less learning occurs.

What kind of evidence might be adduced to support the Acculturation Model? Schumann based much of his original work on the language development (or lack thereof) of a 33-year-old Costa Rican man named Alberto (see Schumann, 1978b, for greater detail). Alberto graduated from a Costa Rican high school where he had studied English for 6 years. He moved to Cambridge, Massachusetts, at age 33, where he lived with another Costa Rican couple. At his workplace, he was the only Spanish speaker in his department (although other NNSs of English were also employed at the same location). Significantly, he socialized primarily with other Costa Ricans. Alberto's development was followed for a period of 10 months, at the end of which he exhibited little knowledge of English. For example, he continued to place the negative marker before the verb (with no subjects), he did not invert questions, and inflections were minimal. After 10 months of exposure to English in an English-speaking environment, one would expect greater development. However, despite Alberto's claims that he did want to learn English, his actions suggested that he did not. He listened to Spanish music and he socialized and lived with Spanish speakers. Thus, he failed to acculturate in any significant way to the TL community and to speakers of the TL. According to the acculturation hypothesis, it is Alberto's lack of acculturation that resulted in his lack of linguistic development.

However, there is another learner, whose longitudinal development suggests that acculturation cannot be so closely linked to linguistic development. Wes (studied by Schmidt, 1983) is a 33-year-old Japanese artist who moved to Hawai'i. He had every reason to want to be integrated into the Hawaiian community. First and foremost was the need to make a living, but another important dimension of Wes is the fact that one of the reasons for moving to Hawai'i was "a general attraction to the people of Hawai'i." He had an American roommate and, for all intents and purposes, lived in an English-speaking world. However, his grammatical development was limited—although not to the same extent as Alberto's. The following is an example from Wes's speech (Schmidt, 1983, p. 168) (/ = pause breaks):

> I know I'm speaking funny English / because I'm never learning / I'm only just listen / then talk / but people understand / well / some people confuse / before OK / but now is little bit difficult / because many people I'm meeting only just one time / you know demonstrations everybody's first time / sometime so difficult / you know what I mean? / well / I really need English more / I really want speak more polite English / before I'm always I hate school / but I need studying / maybe school / I don't have time / but maybe better / whaddya think? / I need it, right?

Given that Wes realized that his English was "not right," and given that he showed a desire to acculturate and that he appeared to have a desire to speak better English, it is difficult to justify the view that acculturation is the causal variable in SLA. Whereas there may be some personality variables that interact with the variable of acculturation, the data from Wes suggest that one cannot demonstrate a strong causal relationship between social and psychological distance and language learning. It is more accurate to consider distance and other variables discussed in this chapter as providing an impetus for learning, or perhaps even setting the stage for learning, but not as *causing* learning.

Personality interfers in acculturation

there's not a conclusion whether one or another learns better - research shows incongruent results.

14.8 EXTROVERSION AND INTROVERSION

Even though the concepts of **extroversion** and **introversion** are commonly believed to be important in the understanding of L2 learning, a discussion of these concepts has not been central or even common in the literature. The stereotype of an introvert is someone who is much happier with a book than with other people, whereas the stereotype of an extrovert is the opposite: someone happier with people than with a book. These stereotypes have implications for L2 learning success, but the implications are somewhat contradictory. We might expect the introvert to do better in school. This has been borne out in research. For example, Skehan (1989) cited studies of British undergraduates showing a correlation of 0.25 between introversion and academic success. Nonetheless, the gregariousness associated with extroverts would suggest that they would engage in more talking and social activity in an L2 and would thus learn the language better (see Chapter 12). Hence, there are good reasons to think that both extroversion and introversion lead to success in L2 learning, although in different ways.

Research data do not resolve this quandary, but show that extroverts are more fluent in L2 production, especially in stressful situations (Dewaele & Furnham, 1999). Evidence has been given in support of the advantages of extroversion (e.g., Chastain, 1975; Wong & Nunan, 2011) and introversion (Swain & Burnaby, 1976), and both, depending on the context and linguistic focus (van Daele et al., 2006; Zafar & Meenakshi, 2012), as well as with respect to this personality dimension and other individual differences such as strategy use (e.g., Wakamoto, 2009). It is probable that there is no correct global answer. The likely solution is that extroversion is beneficial for certain tasks and certain methods of language teaching, whereas introversion is beneficial for others.

TIME TO THINK ...

Do you consider yourself an introvert? An extrovert? How do you think this affects your ability to learn another language? If you are a language teacher or plan on becoming a language teacher, do you think you do or will consider this distinction in the way you deal with your students? Why or why not?

processes that are consciously selected that enhance language learning

What learners do that underline learning strategies to achieve a goal

14.9 LEARNING STRATEGIES

A common observation is that, not only are some language learners more successful than others, but also that good language learners sometimes do different things than poorer language learners. The term commonly used in the SLA literature to refer to what learners do that underlies these differences is learning strategies. This is a difficult area, because, as with other approaches to SLA, language learning and language use are intricately tied together. Selinker (1972) finds that the endorsement for the separation, in principle, of language-learning strategies and communication or use strategies is laid out, with both being postulated as basic processes leading to the formation of IL, though they are not always easy to disentangle.[6] The centrality of the intersection of structure and strategy use is still robust and can be used as a springboard to integrate the formation of L2 knowledge with strategic use of structural information on the part of learners.

language learning + language use

+ Are intrinsic

We begin with a definition. Cohen (1998, p. 4) defines language-learning (and language-use) strategies as:

LANGUAGE LEARNING STRATEGIES

Those processes which are consciously selected by learners and which may result in action taken to enhance the learning or use of a second or foreign language, through the storage retention, recall, and application of information about that language.

Cohen went on to say that such strategies:

> include strategies for identifying the material that needs to be learned, distinguishing it from other material if need be, grouping it for easier learning (e.g., grouping vocabulary by category into nouns, verbs, adjectives, adverbs, and so forth), having repeated contact with the material (e.g., through classroom tasks or the completion of homework assignments), and formally committing the material to memory when it does not seem to be acquired naturally (whether through rote memory techniques such as repetition, the use of mnemonics, or some other memory technique).
>
> (1998, p. 5)

[handwritten margin note: Language learning strategies:]

In a similar vein, Oxford (1999) refers to learning strategies as:

> Specific actions, behaviors, steps, or techniques that students use to improve their own progress in developing skills in a second or foreign language.
>
> (p. 518)

For example, in order to remember difficult vocabulary, a learner may consciously choose to associate a particular word with the situation in which he or she first seriously noticed that word. This individual would probably continue to do this if it turned out that this strategy of *first serious notice* did, in fact, consistently help you learn vocabulary. Another example comes from the area of IL transfer (Chapter 15). Suppose a NS of English has learned Spanish to a proficient degree and then started to learn Italian. While doing so, he or she substitutes Spanish words for his or her attempted Italian (e.g., *cómo* for the intended *come* "how, what," *por qué/porque* for the intended *perché*, "why, because," and, to take a common phonetic example, [s] for intended [z], [kasa] for intended [kaza]). It turns out to be difficult for him/her to eradicate these substitutions. Let's assume that this individual has a strong visual memory and, during class exercises, refers to a visual chart with the correct forms. The first language learner is using a *learning* strategy, and the second a *language-use* strategy.[7] In this section, we concentrate on learning strategies.

Learning strategies clearly involve internal mental actions, but they may also involve physical actions as well. The claims made in the literature involve potential improvements in language learning related to the selection of information from the input and the organization and integration of it in terms of learner systems. The ways in which information is selected from the input are an important part of the concept.

[handwritten margin note: learning strategies involve internal mental + physical actions → are effortful/goal-directed/intentional]

Some characterizations of learning strategies include such notions as effortful, goal-directed, intentional (see Weinstein et al., 2000; Macaro, 2001). But perhaps the most useful way of thinking of strategic learning is in terms of a larger goal (learning a set of vocabulary items) and the steps that one might take to achieve that goal (tactical steps)—for example, putting them on cards, coloring them, visualizing, and so forth. Thus, strategic learning involves an overall goal (become proficient in an L2),

[Handwritten margin note:]
LEARNING
STRATEGY:
① Goal.
② plan to
   accomplish
   goal.
③ steps needed
   to accomplish
   goal.

a plan to accomplish that goal (learn 10 vocabulary words a day), and the steps needed to achieve the goal (coloring, flashcards).

By now, there are many lists of learning strategies in the literature (O'Malley & Chamot, 1990). The categories include such phenomena as clarification, verification, analyzing, monitoring, memorizing, guessing, deductive versus inductive reasoning, emphasizing one thing over another, and practice and production tricks. O'Malley and Chamot's work attempted to establish a foundation for placing the research on learning strategies in a cognitive context. Since then, several taxonomies and classification schemes have been put forth: (a) learning strategies vs. use strategies; (b) cognitive vs. metacogntive vs. social vs. affective strategies; (c) strategies for reading vs. writing vs. speaking; and so forth. These proposals have expanded our views of strategies and have pushed researchers to examine alternate conceptualizations and relationships. However, competing theoretical models, along with what Tseng et al. (2006) have referred to as "definitional fuzziness" (p. 79), have also contributed to a certain amount of inconsistency among empirical efforts (see Plonsky, 2011).

Recent research in this area has been conducted under the auspices of an organization with the acronym IPOLLS (International Project on Language Learner Strategies). Current issues discussed by researchers in the area relate to:

- defining learning and other related strategies in terms of what actually constitutes a strategy and why it is so hard to define these;
- relating such strategies to not only the short-term goals of learners but their long-term goals as well;
- relating such strategies to individual differences versus what one might find out about group use in various situations (cf. Cohen and Macaro, 2007 for discussion).

In the research agenda of this organization is an attempt to bridge the gap between psychological and sociocultural perspectives on L2 learner strategies and between the role of individual versus group differences. In the words of the editors, the goal is to produce interface work, with "cognitive and metacognitive processes involved in producing meaning within the limitations offered by the learner's interlanguage" (Cohen & Macaro, 2007, Introduction).

One recent proposal relates strategies to working memory, where strategies are conceived of as literally occurring in working memory (Chapter 10) and are related, especially, to a broader framework of cognition, for example, strategic planning. An interesting proposal relates the results from using strategies in a chain or in a cluster to their success at given language tasks. Such strategies would form parts of clusters or combinations, and the whole becomes greater than the sum of the parts through the role of metacognition, which orchestrates the parts and makes the combination effective.

Cohen and Macaro (2007) state that, "there is general agreement that 'strategies' are environment-dependent . . . and/or task dependent . . ." This is a view of strategies that adds empirical support to the discourse domains view of IL (Selinker & Douglas,

[Handwritten margin note:] Learning strategies are environment-dependent and/or task dependent

1985; Douglas, 2000) that claims that important processes of learning function within discourse domains.

Research in this area has considered strategic learning in terms of the pragmatics of speech acts, the practical goal being to provide support for learners who are acquiring pragmatic ability, "by providing them with strategies for enhancing how they learn and use speech acts" (Cohen, 2005, p. 296). In order to "support learners," one first has to understand them and their strategies from a research point of view and then assess whether what they have been taught in terms of learning strategies actually works. Here, L2 pragmatics is viewed from a learner perspective in terms of the learning and performance of pragmatics, focusing on learners approaching the norms of an L2 speech community in terms of a number of relationships concerning strategies and metacognition, aptitude, and motivation.

However, the field is not without its problems, for this is indeed a difficult area to be clear about;[8] in fact, Oxford and Cohen (1992, p. 3) stated, "from the profusion of studies recently devoted to learning strategies . . . one might believe that this research area is fully coherent. However, this coherence is something of an illusion." They then went on to list and discuss "serious conceptual and classificatory problems" that exist in this area. Among them are the problems of the criteria used for classifying language-learning strategies, whether such strategies are conscious or unconscious, the relationship to learning styles, and the difficulty of showing what contributes to language learning. McDonough (1999) has echoed this concern. In listing six ways of conducting research on strategies, he stated that, "none of these methods is without problems, and there is always a danger that method predetermines the kind of results obtained" (p. 3). However, McDonough suggested that the triangulation of various data sources may indeed be a way out and can "provide stabilization of the data and interpretive clarity in particular studies" (p. 3).

Bialystok (1990), in a detailed critique of this area, pointed out that it is difficult, in practice, to distinguish as strategic those learner behaviors that are clearly (a) concerned with problematic tasks, (b) conscious or unconscious, and (c) intentional or unintentional. Cohen (1998) took on such criticisms and claimed that strategies do not have to be directly associated with problematic tasks, in that learners may very well be using their strategy preferences in all or most of their learning. Cohen is more positive about overcoming methodological difficulties, stating that one can devise "various kinds of verbal report tasks to determine the nature of the task for the learner (problematic or not), conscious or unconscious, intentional or unintentional" (Cohen, personal communication) (see Cohen, 1998; Gass & Mackey, 2000, Bowles, 2010, for ways one can go about gathering verbal reports).

In this subdomain, there has traditionally been a conceptual division between so-called good language learners and poor or poorer language learners, the idea being that, if we can discover what the good language learner does, we can teach those strategies to poorer language learners so that they will improve (Rubin, 1975; Naiman et al., 1978) (cf. Cohen, 1998; Chamot et al., 1999; McDonough, 1999; Macaro, 2001; Harris, 2003; Hassan et al., 2005; Taylor et al., 2006; Chamot, 2008; Plonsky, 2011,

[handwritten margin note: Learning strategie variables:
→ learners' style preference
→ personal strategy preference.]

for summaries of strategy training). Such a strict dichotomy is, of course, too simplistic. It is more likely that language learners have personal "style preferences," as well as personal "strategy preferences" (e.g., Cohen, 1998; McDonough, 1999; Lightbown and Spada, 2006). And we must also consider the point made earlier about the appropriateness and effectiveness of strategies being context and task dependent. Thus, we have to ask: Does the teaching of learning strategies[9] that appear to work for better language learners help the poorer ones, given the task in question and the learners' more general approach to, or style of, language learning? Or, if we do not accept this dichotomy, we can pose the question as to whether metacognitive awareness of the processes of strategizing (and self-reports thereof) and the increased use of strategies make a positive difference in language learning. These questions, among others, were at the heart of Plonsky's (2011) meta-analysis of L2 strategy instruction. The study also sought to examine empirically whether the theoretical, methodological, and practical concerns raised about this line of research (see above) were justified. Synthesizing across 61 experimental and quasi-experimental studies, the results showed that strategy instruction is generally and moderately effective. Statistically speaking, treatment groups scored, on average, approximately half of a standard deviation above comparison groups that did not receive strategy instruction. This level of effectiveness, however, was not uniform across the sample of primary studies, and a number of moderators were identified. For example, strategy instruction was found to be substantially more effective when fewer strategies were taught, when interventions lasted longer than 2 weeks, and when the strategies targeted reading, speaking, and vocabulary, rather than writing, listening, and grammar.

[handwritten margin note: strategy instruction is generally and moderately effective]

Yet another critique of the strategies research relates to researchers' sources of information about claimed learning strategies (cf. also Macaro, 2001; Oxford, 2011, Chapter 7). It turns out that the most common sources of information are observations, verbal self-reports, or online protocols (often referred to as think-aloud protocols). Self-reports have weaknesses (see Gass & Mackey, 2000; Bowles, 2010). If learners in a study are asked to give examples of strategies they use, they are likely to mention things that (a) help with difficult tasks, (b) are conscious (at least in retrospect), and (c) seem intentional (again in retrospect), all of which may bias the information given. Also, concerning observation, there are weaknesses, given that it is difficult, though perhaps not impossible, to observe the mental behavior of learners. In the end, a researcher may be forced to only accept reported behavior as strategic if it seems intentional, whereas the most important strategies may in fact not be so. This is all the more reason that reported information must be presented in as accurate and detailed a way as possible.

One clear problem with some of the early examples of **learning-strategy** research is that not all behavior can be accepted as strategic. For instance, Rubin (1975, p. 45) maintained that good language learners are "willing and accurate guesser[s]." This may accurately characterize the learners who were looked at, but it may not be strategic. First of all, a reasonable strategy might be "guess," but "be willing to guess" is problematic as a strategy. More problematic still is the attribution of accuracy. "Guess accurately" cannot be a strategy but a goal, although "willingness to guess" may be part of an individual's learning-style preference and, if so, learners could be taught ways in which to maximize the use of that preference, such as how to guess better using context. Again, however, the learning success of such behavior is open to question, and its relationship to improved IL output must be researched, given individual differences in IL learner outcomes, as emphasized throughout this chapter.

Another problem area is that good or better language learners may self-report actions that all language learners in fact undertake, but only the good learners are somehow aware of. We can only say that these actions are differentiating if it can be shown that poor learners do not use them. Some studies neglect poor learners entirely. Those studies that do not include poor learners cannot then be used to say that poor learners do not do the same things that so-called good language learners do. It is to be noted, however, that sometimes it is difficult to compare good and poorer language learners methodologically. As Skehan (1989) argued, poor learners may be lacking the verbal skills to report what they do as readily as good learners can. If so, then differences in reporting skills may be misinterpreted by analysts as differences in strategies used.

Directionality is also a problem with learning strategies (cf. Skehan, 1989). Good learners may do certain things because they have the prerequisite abilities to do so. Even if poor learners tried to do these things, they may not be able to and might have to improve their L2 skills before they could use these strategies. If so, then one could make the interesting claim that language-learning success causes the use of the strategy, in the sense that successful learning allows for the use of the strategy.

Finally, we return to the point made at the beginning of this section, that some language learners seem better than others at learning languages, and that the better ones sometimes do different things than poorer language learners. It is important to stress, in understanding this area, that, even if we can show that better language learners do X, that this X is strategic, and that X in fact does contribute to their language learning. Logically, it does not follow that, if X is then taught to a poor language learner, it will necessarily lead to language improvement. It is not impossible, of course, that the teaching of that X may in fact lead to language improvement, but the point is that it does not logically follow that it necessarily will, and it must be shown empirically that it does. One way forward is to create procedures that would help individual learners find out (a) if they are better at some language-learning tasks than others and, if so, in what contexts; (b) exactly what they do to help them succeed in these particular tasks; and (c) how such strategies relate to changes (and nonchanges) in their own ILs. This would then help to continue to shift the focus from an absolute emphasis on "good" versus "bad" for particular learners to both good and bad language learners, where the emphasis is on self-discovery to determine in which tasks, in which contexts, and using which strategies the individual learner is successful. In other words, a key is to create self-efficacy and autonomy in learners.

McDonough (1999, p. 17) lists among his conclusions that the teaching of strategies "is not universally successful," although, clearly, success in some contexts has been reported. Although meta-analyses by Plonsky (2011) and Taylor et al. (2006) support the idea that learners benefit from being taught strategies, these results, as the authors make very clear, cannot be generalized to all learners, all contexts, all skills, and so forth. At the least, an understanding of how specific strategies for specific individuals aid in the incorporation of specific TL linguistic features into the L2 system— and not only incorporation of said linguistic features into the short-term system, but, more importantly, incorporation of said linguistic features into one's long-term system. Unfortunately, there appears to be very little longitudinal research of this sort (Graham & Macaro, 2008; Plonsky, 2011). A next, obvious step in the evolution of the research paradigm would be the systematic undertaking of longitudinal studies that attempt to link learning strategies to learners' linguistic abilities, as well as their metacognitive awareness and autonomy (see Cotterall, 2008; Vandergrift & Goh, 2012). This could create a clear link to individual changes and nonchanges in the underlying L2 system over time, becoming a key metric by which to judge the validity of strategy use.

In sum, recent efforts at organizing thought in this area of SLA research appear particularly promising in helping us understand the central question in SLA of how learners strategically use linguistic information to form and restructure their L2 grammars. These various interfaces are in need of longitudinal studies.

TIME TO THINK ...

What language-learning strategies do you use? Which ones are the most successful? Are strategies better for some types of language learning than others (e.g., reading more than writing)?

14.10 CONCLUSION

SLA is complex, being influenced by many factors, both linguistic and nonlinguistic. This chapter has dealt with a number of areas that fall outside of the domain of language-related variables but that impact the acquisition of an L2. In the next chapter, we turn to a discussion of related disciplines.

POINTS TO REMEMBER

- Nonlinguistic influences refer to factors that can affect L2 learning, including motivation, age, attitude, aptitude, and sociopsychological influences.

- Linguistics has traditionally focused on the idea that all NSs of a language have equal competence in their L1; any differences in grammaticality judgments, for example, are due to differences in performance, not in competence. Cognitive psychology has tended to downplay the role of attitude and motivation in SLA.

- Although adults show a faster speed of learning an L2, children seem to have an overall advantage in terms of ultimate attainment, at least for phonology and, possibly, syntax.

- Aptitude, or one's potential for learning new knowledge or new skills, has been measured through various measures, including the Modern Language Aptitude Test and the CANAL-FT. Aptitude, as measured in many tests, may be confounded with other factors, such as general intelligence, working memory, and even socioeconomic factors.

- Motivation is considered, along with aptitude, one of the most important factors determining L2 learning success.

- L2 learning can be complicated by affective variables such as language shock, culture shock, and anxiety.

- Anxiety has a curvilinear relationship with L2 learning: too much anxiety is correlated with a lack of success, as is too little anxiety (i.e., not caring at all).

- The Acculturation Hypothesis predicts that learners who acculturate into the TL community will be more successful in learning the TL.

- The use of language-learning strategies may also explain differences between good and poorer language learners. Finding the strategies that good language learners use and teaching them to poorer language learners does not, however, guarantee that the poorer learners will improve.

SUGGESTIONS FOR ADDITIONAL READING

Individual learner differences in second language acquisition (2011). Janusz Arabski and Adam Wojtaszek. Multilingual Matters.

Strategies in learning and using a second language (2011). Andrew Cohen. Pearson.

Teaching and researching language learning strategies (2011). Rebecca L. Oxford. Pearson.

Questionnaires in second language research: Construction, administration, and processing (2nd ed.) (2009). Zoltán Dörnyei with Tatsuya Taguchi. Routledge.

Lessons from good language learners (2008). Carol Griffiths (Ed.). Cambridge University Press.

Language learner strategies: Thirty years of research and practice (2007). Andrew Cohen and Ernesto Macaro (Eds.). Oxford University Press.

Ultimate attainment in second language acquisition: A case study (2007). Donna Lardiere. Lawrence Erlbaum Associates.

The psychology of the language learner: Individual differences in second language acquisition (2005). Zoltán Dörnyei. Lawrence Erlbaum Associates.

Learning new languages: A guide to second language acquisition (2001). Thomas Scovel. Heinle and Heinle.

Motivation and second language acquisition (2001). Zoltán Dörnyei and Richard Schmidt (Eds.). University of Hawai'i Press.

Second language acquisition and the critical period hypothesis (1999). David Birdsong (Ed.). Lawrence Erlbaum Associates.

Communication strategies: Psycholinguistic and sociolinguistic perspectives (1997). Gabriele Kasper and Eric Kellerman. Longman.

Learning strategies in second language acquisition (1990). J. Michael O'Malley and Anna Chamot. Cambridge University Press.

Communication strategies (1990). Ellen Bialystok. Basil Blackwell.

Individual differences in second-language learning (1989). Peter Skehan. Edward Arnold.

A time to speak: A psycholinguistic inquiry into the critical period for human speech (1988). Tom Scovel. Newbury House.

MORE TO DO AND MORE TO THINK ABOUT ...

1. From your own experience, do you agree that adults learning an L2 have differential success than children learning an L1, or learning an L2? How would you set up an experiment to deal with these questions?

2. Consider the term individual differences. What does this notion mean to you? Ask yourself, in this light, what it means to belong to a particular society or culture. Does everything that you see in an individual belong to that individual, or do some things belong to one culture or another? How would you investigate this issue?

3. Consider age as a factor in language learning and our conclusion that there is no dispute that age may make a significant difference in language learning, but that the dispute, where it exists, is about the reasons. How would this point relate to other variables discussed, such as aptitude, motivation, personality, and strategies?

4. Now consider the notion of ability in language learning. How does ability play a role in accounting for final SLA outcomes?

5. How would your answer differ if aptitude were substituted for ability in problem 4? In considering aptitude, how would we account for the uniform success of children in learning an L1?

6. How can we find valid measures of language aptitude, language ability, motivation, and personality characteristics? If there is always some difficulty and controversy over these measures, will we ever be able to put the entire picture of SLA into one coherent framework? If so, how?

7. In this chapter, we discussed the concept of differential success rates. We can use a measure that is easy to obtain: course grades. What do you think of this measure, especially related to the statement that success in getting good grades in language learning is not necessarily equal to "really learning" an L2? What do you think of the conclusion that success in getting good grades in a foreign-language classroom correlates well with getting good grades in any subject?

8. Is it possible that some people might be better able to learn a closely related L2, whereas others might be better able to learn an unrelated L2? If this is the case, why might this be so?

9. If personality types can affect one's ability to learn an L2, what implications might there be for teaching? That is, would learning be more successful if like learners were put in a classroom with a like teacher and a conducive methodology (e.g., one that requires significant analysis)? Why or why not?

10. Concerning the difficulties of being clear about learning strategies, consider an analogy from basketball. Imagine a National Basketball Association player who always does the following when he goes to the free-throw line: pulls on his shorts, crosses himself, breathes deeply, flexes his knees, looks at the back of the rim, and shoots. Which of these behaviors are strategic, and how would you decide? For example, is tugging at the shorts habitual behavior or strategic? Suppose that all coaches tell their players that breathing deeply, flexing one's knees, and looking at the back of the rim can aid in improving accuracy. Could it then be called strategic? Where does automatic behavior fit in? What about superstition? Does the notion of belief fit in? That is, what if the player believes that crossing himself increases his odds? Does it then become strategic? Now take this analogy and relate it to potential improvement in L2 performance through the use of learning strategies.

11. Consider Dörnyei's characterization of the stages of motivation. Think of an experience that you have had with language learning. Can you identify with the stages that he proposed? Be specific with your examples.

12. The following categories are part of the Learning Style Survey (Cohen et al., 2001). Consider the categories of that survey:

   • how I use my physical senses;
   • how I expose myself to learning situations;

- how I handle possibilities;
- how I deal with ambiguity and with deadlines;
- how I receive information;
- how I further process information;
- how I commit material to memory;
- how I deal with language rules;
- how I deal with multiple inputs;
- how I deal with response time;
- how literally I take reality.

How would you characterize yourself along these dimensions? Now go to Link #2 in the Links section below and take the survey. Do your results coincide with your predictions? Why or why not?

LINKS

1. http://lltf.net/wp-content/uploads/2011/12/MLAT-E-Sample-Items.pd

2. http://goo.gl/mbPSZ

CHAPTER FIFTEEN

Related Disciplines

15.1 INTRODUCTION

As is the case with nearly every discipline, SLA does not operate in a vacuum. There are many research areas that are related to the field of SLA, some of which were mentioned in Chapter 1.

As you have been reading through this book, you have probably thought of how SLA relates to other disciplines that you have studied or other disciplines that interest you. Name some of these related areas and think about specific ways in which the same questions are being asked.

This chapter briefly touches on some of these neighboring disciplines. Although SLA is now an autonomous area of research, it had its roots and initial justification in other areas, for example, language teaching, and it has been strongly influenced by other disciplines, such as linguistics and psychology. It has also had a special relationship with child language acquisition, in that child language acquisition formed the basis of research in SLA, with many of the original L2 research questions stemming from the same questions posed in child language acquisition. Other areas, such as third language acquisition or **heritage language acquisition**, are special instances of SLA and, particularly in the case of heritage-language learning, have developed in recent years. Finally, bilingual acquisition blends issues related to SLA and those related to L1 acquisition.

We begin this chapter with a brief overview of some of the issues addressed in these related fields. We only give cursory coverage, because to do otherwise would take us away from the main focus of this book, SLA. We feel that it is important to give some information on these related areas, however, because they shed light on some of the complexities of SLA. They each have a well-developed history of their own and, in most cases, even have journals devoted to their specific issues. In this chapter, we are able to do little more than summarize the scope of work in these areas.

The relationship of each to SLA is different. Some, namely third language acquisition and heritage language acquisition, have a derivative relationship, developing out of related but more specific concerns. Bilingual research has a parallel development, with concerns that diverge, to some extent, from those of SLA, considering, for example, the onset of learning for both languages. To make divisions of types of acquisition, as we do in this chapter, is somewhat artificial, but necessary for expository purposes. We treat each of these areas below.

15.2 BILINGUAL ACQUISITION

Bilingualism, like heritage language acquisition, to be discussed in section 15.4, is a broad term with many forms and configurations. Often, the term bilingual is used loosely to incorporate multilingualism, as is clear from the introduction to a section of a book by Bhatia and Ritchie (2006). Bhatia (2006) states that, "the investigation of bilingualism is a broad and complex field, including the study of the nature of the individual bilingual's knowledge and use of two (*or more*) languages" (emphasis ours) (p. 5). Cenoz, in her review (2005) of Bhatia and Ritchie's book, states:

> the editors make a remark in the introduction about the use of the word "bilingualism" in the title of the book and say that they do not exclude additional languages and that the chapters in the book include the "full range of multilingualism". However, the use of the term "bilingualism" is problematic because the Latin prefix "bi" means "two."
>
> (p. 638)

The concept of bilingualism is interpreted differently in the field of SLA versus fields such as psychology and education. That is, L2 researchers reserve use of the term for only those that are truly, as shown through some linguistic measure, the equivalent of NSs of two languages. Thus, from the perspective of L2 researchers, bilingual refers to someone whose language is in a steady state and who has learned and now knows two languages. That is, bilingual refers to an endpoint: "someone is bilingual." Within an L2-research context, the endpoint interpretation of the term is generally not a focus of inquiry. Rather, L2 researchers, because of their interest in discovering the SLA process, might focus instead on near-native speakers or advanced language learners. In general, SLA researchers are most interested in individuals who are in the process of learning, not those who have learned two languages earlier.

This use of the term does not appear to be the case in some of the psychological and educational literature on bilingualism.[1] For example, Edwards (2006) starts off his article on the foundations of bilingualism by saying:

Everyone is bilingual. That is, there is no one in the world (no adult, anyway) who does not know at least a few words in languages other than the maternal variety. If, as an English speaker, you can say *c'est la vie* or *gracias* or *guten Tag* or *tovarisch*—or even if you only understand them—you clearly have some command of a foreign tongue . . . The question, of course, is one of degree.

(p. 7)

He goes on to say, "it is easy to find definitions of bilingualism that reflect widely divergent responses to the question of *degree*" (p. 8). Bhatia (2006) states this in an interesting way when he says, "the process of second language acquisition—of becoming a bilingual" (p. 5). In other words, the end result of SLA is a bilingual speaker. Given that bilingualism is seen as the end result, and given that we know that native-like competence in an L2 is rare, there is some difficulty in discussing bilingualism in this way. Thus, Bhatia and Edwards are referring to two different phenomena. Edwards is saying that one is bilingual at any point in the L2 learning process, whereas Bhatia is referring only to the endpoint and does not deal with whether or not that endpoint has to be "native" or not. In other words, the issues seem to be of degree—whether or not one is *bilingual* even if not an NS of the L2—and of endpoint—whether or not one is *bilingual* if still in the process of acquisition. SL researchers are more likely to require native competence and also to reserve use of the term for the end state. The bilingualism literature, it seems, allows more latitude in both of these factors.

Valdés (2001a) also discusses the issue of degree when she says, "the term *bilingual* implies not only the ability to use two languages to some degree in everyday life, but also the skilled superior use of both languages at the level of the educated native speaker" (p. 40). She acknowledges that this is a narrow definition, for it considers the bilingual as someone who can "do everything perfectly in two languages and who can pass undetected among monolingual speakers of each of these two languages" (p. 40). This she refers to as the "mythical bilingual." She argues that there are, in fact, different types of bilinguals, and that it is, therefore, more appropriate to think of bilingualism as a continuum, with different amounts of knowledge of the L1 and L2 being represented. In this view, the term bilingualism can refer to the process of learning as well as the end result, the product of learning.

Some researchers make a distinction between L2 learners and bilinguals, as is clear from the title of an article by Kroll and Sunderman (2003): "Cognitive processes in second language learners and bilinguals: The development of lexical and conceptual representations." In this article, the authors refer to "skilled adult bilinguals," presumably the rough equivalent of *advanced language learners*.

Finally, Deuchar and Quay (2000) define bilingual acquisition as "the acquisition of two languages in childhood" (p. 1), although they point to the difficulties involved in this definition, given the many situations where bilingualism takes place. They point to De Houwer (1995), who talks about *bilingual first language acquisition*, referring to situations when there is regular exposure to two languages within the first month of birth, and *bilingual second language acquisition*, referring to situations where exposure begins later than one month after birth but before age 2. Wei (2000, pp. 6–7) presents a useful table of various definitions/types of bilinguals.

TABLE 15.1 Definitions of Bilingualism (*Source*: From *The bilingual reader* by L. Wei, 2000. Reprinted by permission.)	
Achieved bilingual	Same as *late bilingual*
Additive bilingual	Someone whose two languages combine in a complementary and enriching fashion
Ambilingual	Same as *balanced bilingual*
Ascendant bilingual	Someone whose ability to function in an L2 is developing owing to increased use
Ascribed bilingual	Same as *early bilingual*
Asymmetrical bilingual	See *receptive bilingual*
Balanced bilingual	Someone whose mastery of two languages is roughly equivalent
Compound bilingual	Someone whose two languages are learnt at the same time, often in the same context
Consecutive bilingual	Same as successive bilingual
Co-ordinate bilingual	Someone whose two languages are learnt in distinctively separate contexts
Covert bilingual	Someone who conceals his or her knowledge of a given language due to an attitudinal disposition
Diagonal bilingual	Someone who is bilingual in a nonstandard language or a dialect and an unrelated standard language
Dominant bilingual	Someone who has greater proficiency in one of his or her languages and uses it significantly more than the other language(s)
Dormant bilingual	Someone who has emigrated to a foreign country for a considerable period of time and has little opportunity to keep the first language actively in use
Early bilingual	Someone who has acquired two languages early in childhood
Equilingual	Same as *balanced bilingual*
Functional bilingual	Someone who can operate in two languages, with or without full fluency for the task in hand
Horizontal bilingual	Someone who is bilingual in two distinct languages that have a similar or equal status
Incipient bilingual	Someone at the early stages of bilingualism, where one language is not fully developed
Late bilingual	Someone who has become a bilingual later than childhood
Maximal bilingual	Someone with near native control of two or more languages
Minimal bilingual	Someone with only a few words and phrases in an L2
Natural bilingual	Someone who has not undergone any specific training and who is often not in a position to translate or interpret with facility between two languages
Passive bilingual	Same as *receptive bilingual*
Primary bilingual	Same as *natural bilingual*

TABLE 15.1 *continued*	
Productive bilingual	Someone who not only understands but also speaks and possibly writes in two or more languages
Receptive bilingual	Someone who understands an L2, in either its spoken or written form, or both, but does not necessarily speak or write it
Recessive bilingual	Someone who begins to feel some difficulty in either understanding or expressing him or herself with ease, owing to lack of use
Secondary bilingual	Someone whose L2 has been added to an L1 via instruction
Semibilingual	Same as *receptive bilingual*
Semilingual	Someone with insufficient knowledge of either language
Simultaneous bilingual	Someone whose two languages are present from the onset of speech
Subordinate bilingual	Someone who exhibits interference in his or her language usage by reducing the patterns of the L2 to those of the L1
Subtractive bilingual	Someone whose L2 is acquired at the expense of the aptitudes already acquired in the L1
Successive bilingual	Someone whose L2 is added at some stage after the first has begun to develop
Symmetrical bilingual	Same as *balanced bilingual*
Vertical bilingual	Someone who is bilingual in a standard language and a distinct but related language or dialect

As can be seen from Table 15.1, the terminology used in bilingualism is far-reaching and overlaps to some extent with SLA. For example, successive bilingual describes the scope of SLA research. Importantly, however, it is difficult to pigeon-hole all types of bilingualism, because there are numerous situations in which individuals use two languages, from growing up with two to achieving bilingual status as adults, to having the L2 as virtually their only language (e.g., displaced refugees, immigrants). Further, there are different combinations of ability. For example, there are those who function well in some contexts (talking with one's family), but who are not literate in that language, versus those who function well academically in both languages. Valdés (2001a, p. 41) illustrates what she calls a bilingual continuum in Figure 15.1. The two letters represent two languages; the size and the case of the font reflect different proficiencies.

Despite this range, there have been and continue to be misunderstandings regarding the advantages of being bilingual. One can think of advantages in a number of domains. Baker and Prys Jones (1998) discuss communicative advantages, cultural/economic advantages, and cognitive advantages. With regard to the first of these, some are fairly obvious, including talking to immediate and extended family members. One can imagine a situation in which families emigrate to a country where another language is spoken; the children learn the new language and, for all practical purposes, are NSs of that language; they only barely understand the language of their

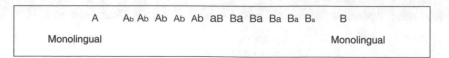

FIGURE 15.1 Bilingual Continuum (*Source*: Adapted from Valdés, G. (2001). "Heritage language students: Profiles and possibilities." In J. Kreeft Peyton, D. A. Ranard, & S. McGinnis (Eds.), *Heritage languages in America: Preserving a national resource*. Washington, DC: Center for Applied Linguistics. Used with permission.)

parents, having become fluent in the language of the new country, whereas the parents do not learn the language of the environment. The communication gap widens between children and parents, with the unfortunate result of virtual noncommunication between the two generations. Beyond these instances of family communication, bilinguals, living in a world of regular language monitoring, often show greater sensitivity to the communicative needs of others. Similarly, having experience in more than one culture provides an understanding of cultural differences among peoples. Further, it is obvious that economic advantages abound in all areas of work.

Finally, there are cognitive advantages, including divergent thinking, creative thinking (e.g., Adi-Japha et al., 2010), and metalinguistic awareness. Metalinguistic awareness is the ability to think about (and manipulate) language. In other words, metalinguistic ability allows one to think about language as an object of inquiry, rather than as something we use to speak and understand language. Bialystok (2001a, 2001b) has found bilingual children to have superior abilities in judging grammatical accuracy compared to monolingual children. Bialystok (1987) also investigated bilingual and monolingual children's abilities to count words, which reflects knowledge of what a word is and knowledge of the relationship between word and sentence meanings. She found that bilinguals were advantaged over monolinguals in both of these domains:

> Bilingual children were most notably advanced when required to separate out individual words from meaningful sentences, focus on only the form of or meaning of a word under highly distracting conditions, and re-assign a familiar name to a different object.
>
> (Bialystok, 1987, p. 138)

In general, bilinguals tend to have better abilities in areas that demand selective attention, because that is what one has to do when there is competing information (e.g., two languages). Thus, bilinguals' awareness of language comes at an early age. Knowing two languages provides them with the skills to separate form from meaning, which in turn facilitates reading readiness. Advantages are found even as early as 7 months. Kovacs and Mehler (2009) found that bilingual children at 7 months of age are significantly faster at adapting to new conditions, as evidenced by looking at a new location when hearing puppets speaking a new language.

Consider the following: Suppose the English-speaking world got together and decided to call the sun "moon" and the moon "sun." What is in the sky when we go to bed at night?

Who will be better at responding to this? Monolinguals or bilinguals. Why?

One of the phenomena of early language development (see discussion in Chapter 5) is babbling. This occurs toward the end of the first year of life. Maneva and Genesee (2002) noted that children exposed to two languages from birth show language-specific patterns in their babbling and, hence, can already differentiate between the two languages before their first birthday. Matching the appropriate language to speakers and/or context is found in children often as young as 2 (e.g., Genesee et al., 1996).

Watch the video (see Link #1 in the Links section at the end of the chapter). Then read the article on the following website (see Link #2 in the Links section at the end of the chapter).

What is the difference between 6-month- and 12-month-old monolingual and bilingual babies in terms of sound discrimination? What cognitive advantages do bilingual babies enjoy over monolingual babies?

A common phenomenon among bilingual speakers is code-switching, which essentially refers to the use of more than one language in the course of a conversation. Sometimes, this might happen because of the lack of a concept in one language and not in the other, sometimes it might be for humor, and sometimes it might happen simply because of the social context. For example, Grosjean (2001, p. 3) presents the following diagram (Figure 15.2) to illustrate the issue of language mode, which is "the state of activation of the bilingual's languages and language processing mechanisms at a given point in time" (p. 2). The NL (here called the base language) is always totally activated; it is the language that controls linguistic activities. The guest language, on the other hand, can be in low-to-high activation, depending on the context. Only in bilingual language mode (the right side of the diagram) is there almost equal activation, and it is in these contexts that code-switching occurs.

Bilingualism, or at least some form of knowledge of more than one language, is so common throughout the world that Cook has proposed that the normal propensity is for humans to know more than one language, rather than taking monolingualism

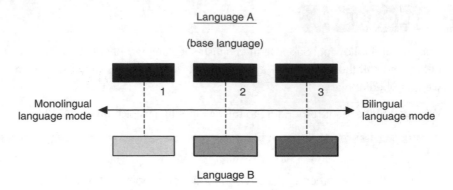

Language A

(base language)

Monolingual language mode ←——1————2————3——→ Bilingual language mode

Language B

FIGURE 15.2 The Language Mode Continuum (*Source*: Grosjean, F. (2001). "The bilingual's language modes." In J. Nicol (Ed.), *One mind, two languages: Bilingual language processing*. Malden, MA: Blackwell.)

TIME TO DO ...

Listen to the recording of a Spanish–English bilingual on the website (see Link #3 in the Links section at the end of the chapter).

What examples of code-switching do you hear? Do you ever code-switch between your L1 and your L2? What words do you tend to code-switch? Do you ever use this as a means of language play?

as the default position. He refers to this as *multicompetence*, which he defines as the "knowledge of two or more languages in one mind" (Cook, 2003, p. 2) (cf. Cook, 1991, 1992). If multicompetence is the norm, then there needs to be a reevaluation of what it means to be an NS of a language. Cook (2005) argued that there are effects of multilingualism on how individuals process their NL, even individuals with a minimal knowledge of an L2. He further argues that the monolingual orientation of SLA belies the reality of the context of language learning in much of the world, where knowledge of more than one language is the norm.

As noted earlier, there are many advantages to being bilingual, in addition to just navigating between two languages. An earlier view of bilingualism maintained that working with two languages might confuse a child, given that there would be interference from one language to the other. In reality, children are quite adept at separating languages, in other words, knowing whom to use which language with (mother versus father; mother versus grandmother). Cognitive flexibility and cognitive development are enhanced with knowledge of more than one language.

15.3 THIRD LANGUAGE ACQUISITION/MULTILINGUALISM

As mentioned in Chapter 1, SLA has become a cover term for acquisition after an L1 has been learned. It often incorporates many different types of acquisition, including third, fourth, and so on, and, in more recent years, has included heritage-language learning (to be discussed in section 15.4). As there are multiple languages involved, the questions addressed are quite interesting and inherently more complex than those involved in true L2 acquisition (see Cenoz, 2003, for a review). In addition, individual histories become important (see Hammarberg, 2009). As noted by Cenoz and Genesee (1998, p. 16):

> Multilingual acquisition and multilingualism are complex phenomena. They implicate all the factors and processes associated with SLA and bilingualism as well as unique and potentially more complex factors and effects associated with the interactions that are possible among the multiple languages being learned and the processes of learning them.

There a number of variables that can impact the extent to which one of the languages involved (the L2 or the L1) will influence the acquisition of the L3. This is often referred to as IL transfer and refers to the influence of one L2 (using the broad sense of this term) over another. Among the factors to be considered are the age at which L3 learning begins, the context of acquisition, individual characteristics, and language distances among the three (or more) languages (cf., Ringbom, 1987, 2001; Möhle, 1989; Cenoz, 2001; Hammarberg, 2001). There are also issues related to the amount of exposure to the L2. For example, Tremblay (2006) reports that the more exposure to the L2, the greater the impact on the L3. Additionally, there is more L2 impact on the L3 during a communicative event. However, there is also a threshold level of proficiency in the L2 that needs to be reached in order for there to be any serious cross-linguistic influence from L2 to L3. Gibbons (2009) concludes, from her study on L3 acquisition of typologically similar and dissimilar languages (French, Spanish, Korean, Japanese, Russian) by native speakers of English, with French or Spanish as their L2, that length of exposure did impact L3 learning. Typological differences had an effect on L3 pronunciation, but not on other areas (grammar, vocabulary, fluency). The recognition of these influences has resulted in some language programs creating special courses for L3 acquisition (for example, Portuguese for Spanish L2 speakers) in U.S. universities.

Examples of language influence can be seen in a number of areas. In 15-1, from Selinker and Baumgartner-Cohen (1995), an English speaker who has just come from France is attempting to speak German.

(15-1) Tu   as   mein   Fax   bekommen?
        you   have   my   Fax   gotten
        French   French   German   German
        "Did you get my fax?"

The sentence is built on German grammar, with split verbs, *as . . . bekommen* ("have . . . gotten"), but with the French subject pronoun (*tu*) and auxiliary *avoir* ("as"). Other examples come from Dewaele (1998), with data from native speakers of Dutch with English as an L2 who produce French as L3 utterances, as in 15-2 and 15-3:

(15-2)   Ils veulent gagner more, euh, plus . . .
         They want to earn more, uh, more. . .

(15-3)   Les gens sont involvés
         The people are involved

In 15-3, the correct word is *impliqués* rather than *involvés*. Another lexical mixture is cited by Herwig (2001). An NS of English who has French as an L2 and German–Swedish as additional languages says *föreslägger* for the Swedish word *föreslär* (the German word is *vorschlagen*—propose).

The difficulty of keeping foreign languages apart was noted by Schmidt and Frota (1986). Their study described an English-speaking learner of Portuguese, with Arabic as a prior L2, who wondered why he couldn't keep the two languages (Portuguese and Arabic) apart. A well-known quote from King Charles V of Spain (1500–1558) suggests that some individuals have no difficulty keeping languages apart and even assign different functions to each: "I speak Spanish to G-d, Italian to women, French to men, and German to my horse."

But most individuals do not have such control and are not so compartmentalized. Why one cannot keep languages and ILs apart, and why the mixing and merging of various languages known and being learned occurs are issues at the heart of research on multilingualism. Many learners have described the experience of influence from even unrelated languages ("talk foreign," as described by Selinker & Baumgartner-Cohen, 1995), as in the case involving Portuguese and Arabic. Another example (personal communication) comes from an NS of English who had been in Turkey for quite some time. He was traveling in Germany, where he had been before, when he reported on his attempt to speak German: "To my horror, out came Turkish."

The concept of third language acquisition from typologically close languages was discussed in Chapter 6 in relation to De Angelis's (2005) study on function words. She found that a determinant of what was and what was not transferred depended in large part on the closeness of source and target language, consistent with early work by Kellerman (1979), discussed in Chapter 6.

In general, however, there are many areas that impact third language acquisition, including sociolinguistic, psycholinguistic, and cross-linguistic influences. With regard to sociolinguistic issues, there are a number of factors to consider, such as the purpose for learning a second or third language. For example, in many parts of the world, or in many industries or professions, English has become the virtual lingua franca, or language used for basic communication, as is the case for Spanish in some areas of the United States. This is quite different from a bilingual home situation. From a psycholinguistic perspective, there are differences for multilingual speakers in how the lexicon is organized. With regard to cross-linguistic influences, we presented examples above that demonstrate how learners of a third language have multiple resources to draw on. Some of the determining variables might be proficiency in the languages known, as well as in the TL, age of user, and linguistic closeness of the languages in question, among others.

An instance of **interlanguage transfer** was provided in 15-1 in the example of a French sentence built on a German syntactic model and produced by an NS of English. Also mentioned earlier was work by Dewaele (1998), who investigated lexical inventions in two versions of oral French IL: one where French was the L2 of NSs of Dutch, with English as a third language, and the other where French was the third language, and English the prior L2. One goal was to see if there was interlanguage transfer in the latter group from its L2 English (with the NL Dutch being blocked). The aim was to establish sources of transfer in French for both groups, which could be either their native Dutch, or their English L2, or English L3. The results showed that the group with French L2 drew heavily on the NL (Dutch) and very little on English L3, whereas the group with French L3 drew on the first foreign language (English L2) in creating French lemmas.

De Angelis (1999) examined the production of Italian by a French–Canadian L1 speaker with three foreign languages: Spanish, English, and Italian. She identified two types of interlanguage transfer: (a) full lexical interlanguage transfer and (b) partial lexical interlanguage transfer. The first type of transfer grouped instances in which an entire nontarget word from an earlier IL was used in the production of the TL (Italian). The second type of transfer grouped instances in which partial morphological information from a nontarget IL word was used in the Italian TL production. De Angelis found occurrences of both types of interlanguage transfer from Spanish into Italian, which, following one of the key principles in this domain, showed strong patterns of phonological similarity between the two languages. The results were discussed in terms of how phonological similarity between or among languages creates the condition for activation to spread to nontarget words in other languages, and how lexical items come to be in competition for selection. A number of suggestions were outlined as to why NL transfer may have been blocked, with the "talk foreign" mode apparently appearing to be important for IL speakers.

In attacking a key question in this research area, Klein (1995, citing a 1994 paper) asked whether knowledge of more than one language might facilitate the acquisition of additional languages within a UG model of acquisition (see Chapter 7). She tested matched groups of monolinguals (English as an L2) and multilinguals learning English as a third or fourth language on the acquisition of (a) lexical learning and (b) syntactic learning. She found that multilinguals outperformed monolinguals in both types of learning and concluded that multilinguals develop qualities that help trigger UG parameters. The qualities were metalinguistic awareness and enhanced lexical learning, as proposed by Thomas (1988), and a less conservative learning procedure, as proposed by Zobl (1992). For the view that multilinguals are better learners than monolinguals, there is both supporting evidence (e.g., Ramsay, 1980) and nonsupporting evidence (Nayak et al., 1990). The interest in the study of third language acquisition from a formal perspective continues, as evidenced by a recent special issue of *Second*

Language Research, (January 2011) devoted to the topic of "the generative study of L3 acquisition."

One recent study (Thompson, 2009) investigated the interface of language aptitude (see Chapter 14) and multilingualism. In her study of learners of English, there were two groups: (1) monolingual speakers of Brazilian Portuguese and (2) NSs of Brazilian Portuguese, with knowledge of another language. In other words, for the second group, English was their L3. She found that previous language experience had an effect on language aptitude, with her second group (multilinguals) outperforming bilinguals on an aptitude test.

Other studies in multiple language acquisition could be interpreted as having an effect on mental structuring and organization of the bilingual lexicon. For example, a study by de Groot and Hoeks (1995) tested the relationship between proficiency and lexico-semantic organization in two sets of "unbalanced" trilinguals (Dutch–English–French). The NL and the weak foreign language were hypothesized to have a "word-association" lexical structure, whereas the NL and the stronger foreign language were hypothesized to have a "concept-mediation" lexical structure. The data suggest that foreign-language proficiency determines lexico-semantic organization in multilingual speakers.

Language similarity and its effects have been discussed by a number of researchers in the area of multiple-language acquisition studies (Vildomec, 1963; Stedje, 1977; Ringbom, 1987; Selinker & Baumgartner-Cohen, 1995; Dewaele, 1998; Williams & Hammarberg, 1998; De Angelis, 1999). Vildomec (1963) made the important and still relevant observation that, in early L3 production, certain functors, such as prepositions, articles, and conjunctions, tend to come from the L2 and not the NL. This may occur even when the two languages are not phonetically similar.

The use of function words from an L2 rather than the NL in third-language production has also been discussed in Stedje (1977), Ringbom (1987), and Williams and Hammerberg (1998). Stedje (1977), who examined Finnish learners of German as a third language with Swedish as the second, found that function words were predominantly transferred from the L2 rather than from the NL. In a study examining the data of essays written in English (L3) by Finnish students with Swedish as an L2, Ringbom (1987) found 187 instances of complete language switches from the Swedish L2 and only 8 from the Finnish L1; in the instances of transfer from Swedish, 67 percent of the lexical items were content words, and 33 percent were functions words. Williams and Hammerberg (1998, p. 296) examined instances of what they called "non-adapted language switches" (i.e., transfer without modification) in a 15-year longitudinal study of a learner of Swedish as a third language, whose NL was English and first L2 was German. An important finding was that, even when no direct similarity could be found, some German L2 lexical or structural features were present in the learner's Swedish L3. The authors proposed that the German L2 was activated in parallel to the third language. To account for this, William and Hammerberg suggested a model of L3 acquisition whereby one non-target language becomes the "default supplier" (p. 295). They argue that there are a number of factors that determine which language assumes that role in L3 acquisition: proficiency, recency, typology, and L2 status.

Cenoz (2001) discussed a number of factors that might influence cross-linguistic influence in general (e.g., age, context of use, proficiency) and provided empirical evidence on the acquisition of English by Spanish/Basque bilinguals, with some dominant in one language and others dominant in the other. She found that linguistic distance is one factor. Basque is unrelated to Spanish or English, and there was greater evidence of transfer from Spanish to English than from Basque to English. This was the case for all learners, regardless of language dominance. Language distance is not the only factor. Age is another, with older learners showing more cross-linguistic influence than younger children. There are language-related factors as well, with more transfer of content words than function words. An interesting finding is that when words in English are *foreignized*, only Spanish words are at the base and not Basque words.

15.4 HERITAGE LANGUAGE ACQUISITION

The heritage-language learner is a relatively recent area of study, having its origins in the education literature.[2] Heritage-language speakers are, broadly speaking, those who have been exposed to a language of personal connection (Fishman, 2001). Valdés (2001a) notes that,

> it is the historical and personal connection to the language that is salient and not the actual proficiency of individual speakers. Armenian, for example, would be considered a heritage language for American students of Armenian ancestry even if the students were English-speaking monolinguals.
>
> (p. 38)

Furthermore, she characterizes a heritage-language learner (living in an English-speaking environment) as someone who is "raised in a home where a non-English language is spoken, who speaks or at least understands the language, and who is to some degree bilingual in that language and in English" (2001a, p. 38).

For research into this type of second- or foreign-language acquisition, an important issue is the exposure to, and use of, the language in childhood. Here, as can be easily imagined, there are numerous problems, because exposure and use vary from individual to individual. Unlike much of the literature on heritage-language learners, which considers the language of the ancestral family, with or without exposure and use, Polinsky (2008) defines heritage language as the language

> which was first for an individual with respect to the order of acquisition but has not been completely acquired because of the switch to another dominant language. An individual may use the heritage language under certain conditions and understand it, but his/her primary language is a different one.
>
> (p. 149)

The recognition of heritage-language learners as a variable in L2 research is recent and has even led to a restructuring of pedagogical programs to include separate learning environments for these individuals (see Kagan & Dillon, 2012, for a review). However, often the concept of heritage-language speaker is (unknowingly) ignored, and these individuals are consequently included in studies. Sorace (1993b) is an exception in that she explicitly controlled for heritage-language speakers in her study on the acquisition of Italian by eliminating them from her database; "none had Italian origins" (p. 35).

Heritage language acquisition is a form of SLA and a form of bilingualism. Heritage-language learners have knowledge of two languages (the home language and the language of the environment/school), and they are usually dominant in the L2. There is a wide range of linguistic knowledge of heritage speakers, including those who were born in the L2 environment and those who came to the L2 environment during their school years. Another consideration is the amount of input in the home, ranging from only the heritage language spoken in the home (with perhaps parents only speaking the heritage language) to those situations in which the heritage language is spoken only sporadically.

Heritage learners often do not become bilingual speakers, because they do not have the opportunity to speak the heritage language as much as they speak the language of the non-home environment. In some cases, they may not have heard or spoken the heritage language since they were very young, because their families switched to the language of the environment. Heritage-language learners form a heterogeneous group, as their experiences of the language are very different. Some learners may have been raised by parents who only spoke the heritage language. However, as soon as they begin to attend school, their L2 generally becomes their dominant language. Other learners may have only received very limited input of the heritage language in the home, while they were young. Nonetheless, it is generally accepted that the nature of language learning for heritage-language learners differs from language learning involving non-heritage-language learners (Valdés, 1995, 2001b; Campbell & Rosenthal, 2000). Heritage speakers often possess a subtly different knowledge base of the heritage language than L2 learners of that language with no prior background. In addition, they often differ from monolingual speakers of their heritage language. Sometimes, these differences may be subtle, and sometimes they may be quite fundamental. Some recent studies have investigated the linguistic differences between heritage language and non-heritage language learners (e.g., Nagasawa, 1995; Polinsky, 1995, 2000, 2008; Ke, 1998; Carreira, 2002; Montrul, 2002, 2004; Gass & Lewis, 2007).

TIME TO THINK ...

There are some obvious experiential differences between heritage-language learners and L2 learners. Think about the time of learning and the amount and place of exposure. How would you characterize those differences? What other differences can you think of?

Heritage speakers rarely have the same competence in their heritage language as do NSs of that language. Some of this is owing to lack of exposure, which over time leads to fossilization; some of this is owing to attrition, because the heritage language often becomes the secondary language and may be subject to influences from the primary language.

When thinking about heritage-language learning, a question arises as to the ways in which L2 learners and heritage-language learners are similar or different. Au et al. (2002) found advantages for aspects of pronunciation for heritage-language learners, but no advantage for morphosyntax. In this latter domain, the two groups patterned alike. To support the advantage of heritage-language learners in the area of pronunciation, Chang et al. (2008) found that heritage-language speakers of Mandarin (particularly advanced learners) are able to keep the two sound systems apart (see also Lukyanchenko & Gor, 2011, for a similar, although not identical, finding, noting that, with regard to speech perception, patterning as NSs is often, but not always, the case). Even though heritage-speaker phonology is more similar to that of NSs of their heritage language than is the case of true L2 learners, it is also the case that there are nonnative elements of pronunciation (see Yeni-Komshian et al., 2000).

Morphosyntax is an area that is not always well controlled by heritage-language learners, particularly when compared with NSs of their heritage language (see Albirini et al., 2011, for Arabic; O'Grady et al., 2011, for Korean; and Polinsky, 2011, for Russian, all of which present recent examples of incomplete grammars). Similar difficulties for syntax are also found among heritage speakers (see Montrul, 2010, for a review) when compared with NSs of the heritage language.

The modality of expression differentiates L2 learners and heritage-language learners. Typically, oral skills are better among heritage-language learners, whereas written skills are better among L2 classroom learners. This is not surprising in that heritage-language learning generally takes place in a home environment and at a young age, prior to access to written materials. On the other hand, L2 learners learn in a formal classroom environment where writing and formal grammar control are emphasized.

TIME TO DO ...

Listen to the podcast about heritage-language learners on the website (see Link #4 in the Links section at the end of the chapter).

What are the differences between heritage-language learners and foreign-language learners? Why does the speaker argue that the two groups of learners should be taught separately?

15.5 SLA BY HEARING IMPAIRED

Research on SLA of sign language (also referred to as **second-modality acquisition,** or M2A) seeks to answer many of the same questions traditionally posed within the field of SLA, such as: What is the initial state of the learner, and what is the role of the L1? In what ways are L1 and L2 acquisition of a sign language similar and different? Which aspects of M2A are language-specific, and which are part of more general cognitive and/or motor abilities? However, unlike SLA and the related field of inquiry into deaf and hearing children who learn a sign language as their L1, M2A research has been sparse, a point explicitly made repeatedly across the M2A literature (Rosen, 2011) and underscored by the rapid increase in sign-language course offerings at secondary and tertiary levels of education (Rosen, 2008).

The principal interest of L2/M2 sign-language research to date has been phonology or "accent." More specifically, researchers have sought to define and describe the features of accentedness among nonnative signers. Kantor's (1978) work with native and nonnative signers found differences between the two groups in rhythm, choice of signs, and especially handshape and facial expression. Others have attempted to explain the sources of difficulty in accurate signing. Rosen (2004), for example, examined handshape, location, movement, palm orientation, and nonmanual phonological segments by novice adult learners of American Sign Language (ASL). This study extends previous descriptions of nonnative signing (e.g., Budding et al., 1995) and attributes learner errors to perceptual difficulties and a lack of dexterity, that is, factors unrelated to language-specific mechanisms (but, see Thompson et al., 2009, and McIntire & Reilly,1988, for evidence in favor of understanding M2A as similar to patterns found in spoken L2 development). Rosen also proposed a **Cognitive Phonology Model** to explain learner errors, dismissing models from the broader SLA literature such as L1 transfer and UG access as lacking applicability to the acquisition of sign languages. In his model, there are two sources of error: inaccurate perception of sign formulation and poor motor dexterity. The errors that are made by L2 signers that result from poor motor dexterity include such error types as substitutions, additions, incompletions within segments, and deletions. On the other hand, errors that are shaped by failures of sign-formulation perception consist of such error types as addition and deletion of features within segments. In contrast, Chen Pichler (2011) has argued for inclusion of language-specific features such as markedness and transfer in models and in future studies of M2A. Her study of novice ASL learners found evidence to support a role for L1/M1 transfer to the M2, as well as for markedness in predicting M2 development. Perhaps equally importantly, her results point to the need for thorough empirical examination of M2 perception and hand-shape development. In one of the few empirical studies of M2 perception, Emmorey et al. (2009) compared eye gazes of deaf native and hearing beginner signers of ASL while watching a fluent signer. Although both groups fixated primarily on the signer's face, learners often looked at the signer's mouth (as opposed to eyes) and hands. The authors attribute these differences, not to difficulty with linguistic complexity or processing, but to the M2 learners' need to attend to mouthing.

In many ways, the current state of research on SLA of sign languages seems to parallel the early work in SLA. Although little empirical work has been done in this area, much can be gained from looking to related disciplines, just as SLA inherited much of its theoretical and methodological foundation from fields such as L1 acquisition, education, and psychology (see Chapter 1). In addition, much like early SLA research that focused largely on English as a second or foreign language, the vast majority of studies of M2A have dealt only with acquisition of American Sign Language (Chen Pichler, 2009).

Chen Pichler (personal communication, 2/29/12) points out that learning across modalities is an underexplored, yet rich, area for research. In particular, instances of hearing speakers of a spoken L1 who learn a signed L2 involve not only a new linguistic system, but also a new modality within which to express that system. As she notes, "there is evidence to suggest that learning in a new modality (L2–M2 or simply M2, in contrast to L2–M1) presents challenges that are not observed when learning an L2 in the same modality as one's L1." Some features are not accessible when looking at L2 learning within the same modality, such as the tendency to proximalize movement. Chen Pichler has argued that new signers take from their inventory of gestures used in their everyday lives and transfer those into their L2 ASL (in her terms, handshape transfer, Chen Pichler, 2011).

Clearly there are numerous questions that remain unaddressed with respect to research on SLA of sign languages, leaving the theoretical and empirical landscapes wide open to researchers interested in this area.

15.6 CONCLUSION

This chapter has focused on different types of acquisition, all of which address issues related to L2 learning, or, in some sense, are part of the same field, namely, one that is concerned with non-monolingual acquisition. In the chapter that follows, we attempt to bring together into one framework the various topics discussed in this book.

POINTS TO REMEMBER

- There are various disciplines related to SLA, including bilingualism, third language acquisition, heritage language acquisition, and SLA by the hearing impaired.

- Definitions of bilingualism vary depending on the field. Bilingualism can refer to individuals who theoretically have native-like knowledge of more than one language, or can refer to individuals who know a couple of words in an L2. Recent definitions of bilingualism have stressed the idea that bilingualism is a continuum.

- The effects of the L2 on the acquisition of a third language may be related to language distance, the age of the learner, the proficiency of the learner, and context of use.

- Heritage-language learners are those learners who have a personal connection to a language that is not dominant in the society.

- M2A refers to second-modality acquisition or to SLA by the hearing impaired, a field that seeks to answer many of the same questions as SLA but is still in its infancy.

SUGGESTIONS FOR ADDITIONAL READING

Processes in third language acquisition (2009). Björn Hammarberg (Ed.). Edinburgh University Press.

The exploration of multilingualism: Development of research on L3, multilingualism and multiple language acquisition (2009). Larissa Aronin and Britta Hufeisen. John Benjamins.

The multiple realities of multilingualism: Personal narratives and researchers' perspectives (2009). Elka Todeva and Jasone Cenoz. Walter de Gruyter.

Heritage language education: A new field emerging (2008). Donna Brinton, Olga Kagan, and Susan Bauckus. Routledge Associates.

Third or additional language acquisition (2007). Gessica De Angelis. Multilingual Matters.

The bilingual edge: Why, when, and how to teach your child a second language (2007). Kendall King and Alison Mackey. Harper Collins.

The bilingualism reader (2006). Li Wei (Ed.). Routledge.

Childhood bilingualism: Research on infancy through school (2006). Peggy D.. McCardle and Erika Hoff (Eds.). Multilingual Matters.

Foundations of bilingual education and bilingualism (4th ed.) (2006). Colin Baker. Multilingual Matters.

Handbook of bilingualism (2006). Tej Bhatia and William Ritchie (Eds.). Blackwell Publishers.

Linguistic awareness in multilinguals: English as a third language (2006). Ulrike Jessner. Edinburgh University Press.

Multiple voices: An introduction to bilingualism (2006). Carol Myers-Scotton. Blackwell.

Handbook of bilingualism: Psycholinguistic approaches (2005). Judith F. Kroll and Annette M. B. De Groot (Eds.). Oxford University Press.

The multilingual lexicon (2003). Jasone Cenoz, Britta Hufeisen, and Ulrike Jessner. Springer Verlag.

A dynamic model of multilingualism: Perspectives of change in psycholinguistics (2002). Philip Heredina and Ulrike Jessner. Multilingual Matters.

Heritage languages in America: Preserving a national resource (2001). Joy Kreeft Peyton, Donald A. Ranard, and Scott McGinnis (Eds.). Delta Publishing Company.

Multilingualism, second language learning, and gender (2001). Aneta Pavlenko. Walter de Gruyter.

Trends in bilingual acquisition (2001). Jasone Cenoz and Fred Genesee (Eds.). John Benjamins.

Cross-linguistic influence in third language acquisition: Psycholinguistic perspectives (2001). Jasone Cenoz, Britta Hufeisen, and Ulrike Jessner (Eds.). Multilingual Matters.

English in Europe: The acquisition of a third language (2000). Jasone Cenoz and Ulrike Jessner (Eds.). Multilingual Matters.

MORE TO DO AND MORE TO THINK ABOUT ...

1. It is a basic premise in SLA that some individuals are more successful at learning L2s than others. Specifically, how might differential language-learning success relate to child language acquisition of various kinds: monolingual, simultaneous bilingual, and consecutive bilingual?

2. If a researcher doesn't obtain sufficient information from her/his participants before carrying out a study, heritage-language learners may be included in the sample without the researcher's knowledge. How could this oversight affect the results of the study? Why would it be important for a researcher to control for this variable?

3. Using Table 15.1, decide which type of bilingual each of the following individuals would be (more than one term may be appropriate).

   (a) A native speaker of Vietnamese who has been living in the United States for 35 years, speaks English with his American family, friends, and colleagues, and has little or no opportunity to use Vietnamese.
   (b) A 4-year-old child who speaks English with his Canadian father and Japanese with his Japanese mother and lives in Canada.
   (c) An Italian university student who speaks Sicilian at home and with friends, but watches television and films in Standard Italian and uses the standard at the university.
   (d) A PhD student who can read Latin texts for her research but doesn't actually speak Latin.
   (e) You.

4. Consider a situation in which an NS of English is in a restaurant in an English-speaking country, speaking to some friends in Italian. At a certain point, the English speaker asks the waitress (a monolingual English speaker), "Could we have another carafe of *vino*?" What has happened here?

5. For the instructor: Prepare a tape of a language that the students do not know and that is related to an L2 that the students may have studied (for example, Portuguese in an English-speaking environment, because many will have studied Spanish). Play the tape once or twice. Ask students how much they understand. Then give them the written version of what they heard. Again, ask what they understood. Then ask what information they used to try to understand this L3—for example, their L1, their L2 (Spanish), real-world knowledge. (We thank Amy Thompson for this suggestion.)

LINKS

1. http://goo.gl/o1FbK

2. http://goo.gl/2HQ04

3. http://goo.gl/6TZWe

4. http://goo.gl/0VRPk

CHAPTER SIXTEEN

An Integrated View of Second Language Acquisition

16.1 AN INTEGRATION OF SUB-AREAS

As has become clear throughout this book, the learning of an L2 is a multifaceted endeavor. In order to fully understand this phenomenon, one must consider what is learned and what is not learned, as well as the contexts in which that learning and nonlearning take place. The latter includes the various influences on the learning process that are the focus of the majority of this book. In Chapters 5 and 6, we explained how the NL plays an important role in learning. In Chapter 7, we presented some of the tenets associated with formal approaches and showed the centrality of UG in an understanding of SLA. We also noted, however, that it accounts for only a portion of the complex phenomenon of SLA. Chapter 8 focused on the importance of the lexicon. In Chapter 9, we discussed the role of typological universals in the acquisition of an L2 and also discussed the acquisition of phonology, as well as the tense–aspect system. In Chapter 10, we discussed psycholinguistic approaches to SLA. In Chapter 11, we considered the role of social and discoursal context in SLA. In Chapter 12, the concepts of input, interaction, and output were presented, and we explained how these ideas are relevant to acquisition itself. Chapter 13 examined how instruction can (or cannot) affect L2 learning. Chapter 14 dealt with nonlinguistic factors involved in SLA, and Chapter 15 dealt with related disciplines.

All of these approaches to acquisition are crucial in dealing with *a part of* what happens in learning an L2. However, none of them alone is able to account for the total picture. In this chapter, a model is presented that will explain where the various pieces discussed throughout this book fit and how each relates to a larger picture of acquisition. The focus of this chapter is a consideration of what a learner must do to convert input to output. There are five stages in this process: (1) apperceived input, (2) comprehended input, (3) intake, (4) integration, and (5) output. We deal with each of these levels and elaborate on the factors that mediate between one level and another.[1]

497

As will be recalled from Chapter 7, a major controversy in language acquisition research (both first and second) is whether or not acquisition can best be characterized by means of innateness. One view holds that a child comes to the learning task with a UG that allows the child to construct a grammar of a language on the basis of limited data. Another view maintains that language acquisition is a form of (and results from) social interaction (Chapters 11 and 12).

Within the first approach, research focuses on the nature of UG (see Chapter 7). Those working within this paradigm take as the scope of investigation linguistic descriptions of grammars. In so doing, an idealized speaker–hearer is assumed, with the claim being made that, in order to understand formal constraints on language, one needs to isolate that linguistic system and investigate it in and of itself, without external (e.g., social) influences. With regard to SLA, the question most often asked is: What is the role of UG in adult SLA? Is UG (which is assumed to be available to children acquiring an L1) available to adults learning an L2?

social interactionist view
↓
language and cognitive development are deeply embedded in context.

In the social interactionist view, it has been argued that language and social interaction cannot be separated without a distorted picture of the development of linguistic and interactive skills resulting (Chapters 11 and 12). From this point of view, language and cognitive development are deeply embedded in context; thus, an understanding of the development of syntax, for example, can only come about as one investigates how syntax interacts with other relevant aspects of the learning situation.

These conflicting positions have resulted in the development of different research traditions as a result of the different questions being asked. This has, at times, created conflicting views about the best way to gather data and/or the correct questions to be asked (see Chapters 2 and 3). When data-gathering methods and research questions are tied to research paradigms, it is far less useful to compare the value of each than it is to question how the various research questions and research findings relate to one another. The model presented in Figure 16.1 and discussed in this chapter is an attempt to do just that.

Input

We begin by referring to the top of the diagram. It is clear that input of some sort is necessary in order for acquisition to take place. What sort of input is necessary is less clear. For example, does it have to be modified (Chapter 12)? If not, are there other ways in which input can be controlled or limited? If so, what are those ways? Can input come from fellow learners, or do learners pay attention only to the input from so-called authority figures, such as teachers or NSs?[2] Once a learner filters out some of the input, what happens next? We consider each of the five stages involved in conversion of input to output: apperceived input, comprehended input, intake, integration, and output.

16.1.1 Apperceived Input

Input ? body of L2 data

The first point to note is that learners are exposed to a body of L2 data. This is known as input, the characteristics of which were discussed in detail in Chapter 12. A well-established fact about SLA is that not everything that learners hear/read is used as they form their L2 grammars. Some language data filter through to learners, and some

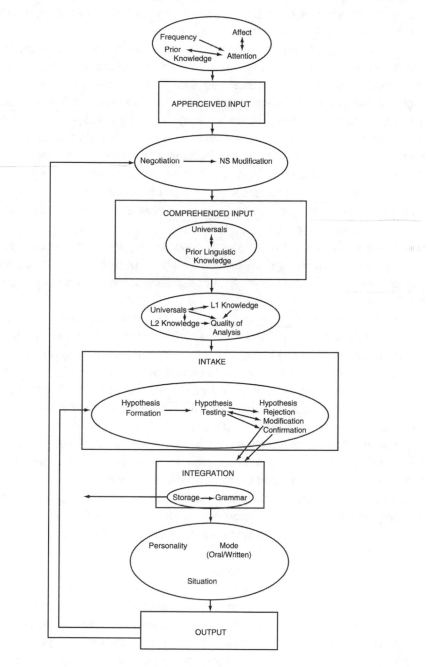

FIGURE 16.1 A Model of Second Language Acquisition (*Source*: From "Integrating research areas: A framework for second language studies" by S. Gass, 1988, *Applied Linguistics*, *9*, 198–217. Reprinted by permission of Oxford University Press.)

do not. A concern in SLA research has been with the limits on what filters through to learners and what determines those limits.

The first stage of input utilization is called apperceived input. Apperception is the process of understanding by which newly observed qualities of an object are related to past experiences. In other words, past experiences relate to the selection of what might be called *noticed* material. Apperception is an internal cognitive act, identifying a linguistic form as being related to some prior knowledge. We can think of apperception as a priming device that tells us which parameters to attend to in analyzing L2 data. That is, it is a priming device that prepares the input for further analysis. What is noticed, or apperceived, then interacts with a parsing mechanism that attempts to segment the stream of speech into meaningful units for the learner. Thus, apperceived input is that bit of language that is noticed in some way by the learner, because of some particular features.

Why are some aspects of language noticed by a learner, whereas others are not? What are the mediating factors at this initial stage? Put differently, what factors serve as input filters? There are a number of possibilities, a few of which are discussed in this chapter.

An obvious factor is *frequency*—possibly at both extremes. Something that is very frequent in the input is likely to be noticed. On the other hand, particularly at more advanced stages of learning, stages at which expectations of language data are well established, something that is unusual because of its *infrequency* may stand out for a learner. For example, given a particular context, one that is familiar to the learner, a new word or phrase may appear. This, then, may be noticed by the learner and is thus available for eventual integration into the learner's system.[3]

A second factor that influences apperception is what has been described as *affect*. Within this category are included such factors as social distance, status, motivation, and attitude. This is exemplified by the work of Krashen, who proposed that individuals have what he called an Affective Filter (see Chapter 5). Another explanation has been put forth by Schumann, who argued that social distance is important in preventing a learner from obtaining input data. If a learner feels psychologically or socially distant from the TL community, the language input will not be available to that learner. This may be the case because a learner physically removes herself or himself from speakers of the TL. These nonlinguistic influences were discussed in detail in Chapter 14.

A third factor that may determine whether language data are apperceived has to do with the broad category of associations and *prior knowledge*. Learning involves integration of new knowledge with prior knowledge. Importantly, one needs some sort of anchor on which to ground new knowledge. Prior knowledge is one of the factors that determine whether the input is meaningful. Prior knowledge is to be interpreted broadly and can include knowledge of the NL, knowledge of other languages, existing knowledge of the L2, world knowledge, language universals, and so forth. All of these play a role in a learner's success or lack of success in interpreting language data, in that they ultimately determine whether a learner understands and what level of understanding takes place. Precisely how these factors ultimately determine acquisition has been a question central to acquisition research over the past decade.

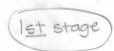

Handwritten margin notes:

1st stage

apperceived input (noticed material)
↓
linguistic form related to some prior knowledge
↓
prepares input for further analysis.
↓
A parsing mechanism tries to segment the speech into meaningful units

FACTORS THAT INFLUENCE PERCEPTION

1. frequency: (frequent input is more likely to be noticed)

2. affect: (social distance, status, motivation, attitude)

3. prior knowledge: (anchor on which to ground new knowledge) determines if input is meaningful

4. Attention (helps learners mismatch between what they know in L2 and how NS actually use the language.)

A final factor to mention is that of *attention*. At a given point in time, does a learner attend to the input? One can think of many reasons why the input is not attended to. Many of these are trivial and don't concern SLA (e.g., falling asleep in class); others are not trivial (e.g., an a priori realization that the input is not manageable, or task demands that make multiple foci of attention difficult or impossible).[4] Why is attention important? It is important because it allows a learner to notice a mismatch between what he or she knows about the L2 and what is produced by speakers of the L2. If one is going to make modifications in one's grammar, one must first recognize that changes need to be made. Thus, readjustment of one's grammar is triggered by the perception of a mismatch.

These categories (i.e., frequency, affect, prior knowledge, and attention) are not intended to be necessarily independent. For example, attention may be related to, or influenced by, affective variables. If a learner has little desire to deal with the TL community, he or she may block out all the input, attending only to that which is necessary to conduct business or to get through the day. Similarly, affective variables may be influenced by prior knowledge. Whether a learner is positively or negatively disposed toward the TL (community) is presumably determined by prior linguistic knowledge (perhaps the learner does or does not like the sound of the language or does or does not find the language difficult to learn) and even by prior experience with speakers of the TL. Thus, a significant role is assigned to prior knowledge and experience as activators of selective attention.

Selective attention activated by prior knowledge and experience

The preceding discussion has dealt with some issues that may determine why or why not some input is noticed by the learner. There are also factors specific to conversational interactions that are relevant to how the input can be shaped so that it can be comprehended. Here are included the concepts of negotiation and foreigner talk, as discussed in Chapter 12. Negotiation and modification differ from the previously mentioned factors in that they involve production and feedback. They are not necessary conditions, but rather serve to increase the possibility of a greater amount of input becoming available for further use.

TIME TO THINK ...

Think about your own acquisition of an L2. Can you recall a particular structure that you apperceived in the input? What factors do you think affected the fact that that structure was apperceived (frequency, prior knowledge, etc.)?

16.1.2 Comprehended Input ≠ comprehensible input

The factors mentioned thus far in this chapter contribute to the potentiality of comprehension of the input. However, there is another point to consider: the concept of comprehended input. There are two differences between the notion of comprehended input and that of comprehensible input, as detailed in Chapter 12. One is that comprehensible input is controlled by the person providing input, generally (but not necessarily) an NS of the L2, whereas comprehended input is learner-controlled: that is, it is the learner who is or who is not doing the "work" to understand. This distinction is crucial in the eventual relationship to intake, because it is the learner who ultimately controls that intake. A second difference is that comprehensible input, in Krashen's sense, is treated as a dichotomous variable; that is, it is either comprehensible or it is not. However, there are different levels of comprehension that can take place. The most typical meaning of comprehension is at the level of semantics.

There is a broader sense of the word, however, one that includes comprehension of structure as well as meaning. Comprehension represents a continuum of possibilities, ranging from semantics to detailed structural analyses. In other words, comprehended input is potentially multistaged. For example, one can comprehend something at the level of meaning; that is, one can have an understanding of the general message, perhaps only understanding isolated words and making sense of the utterances with real-world knowledge to piece those words together. On the other hand, one can imagine a more analytic understanding taking place, with learners performing a mini-linguistic analysis. They might understand what the component parts of an utterance are and thus gain an understanding of the syntactic or phonological pattern represented. This recognition of different levels of analysis is important in relation to the subsequent level of intake.

In dealing with comprehension, one must further remember, from Chapter 1, that there are many aspects of language that L2 learners must learn. These include, not only the more common areas of syntax and phonology (including knowledge about segments, syllable structure, and prosody), but also less commonly thought of areas, such as discourse (Chapter 12), pragmatics (Chapter 11), and vocabulary (Chapter 8).

There are a number of means by which one can reach a particular analysis. For example, the most common way of getting at a syntactic analysis is by first having an understanding of the meaning. However, one can also imagine having an understanding of the syntax, yet not being able to arrive at a meaning. This would be so in the case of idioms, for example, or a proverb.

What is the difference between apperceived and comprehended input? Apperception is conceptualized as a priming device. It prepares the learner for the possibility of subsequent analysis. For example, in learning a language with contrastive vowel length, a learner might apperceive that vowel length is an important feature of the language. In comprehending, however, the task facing the learner is to analyze the input in order to determine what the vowel length is in some particular context and then to relate the particular vowel length to a specific meaning. To take a specific example, Japanese uses vowel length for the purpose of differentiating the meanings of words: /biru/ "building" versus /bi:ru/ "beer." A learner of Japanese has to first recognize that Japanese differentiates between words on this basis (apperception), then recognize the difference between /biru/ and /bi:ru/ (comprehension), and then match /biru/ with the concept of "building" and/or /bi:ru/ with the concept of "beer" (another level of comprehension).

There is another necessary separation of components—that of comprehended input from intake (see Chapter 12). This separation is important because not all input that is comprehended becomes intake. For example, input may be comprehended only for the immediate purpose of a conversational interaction, or it may be used for purposes of learning. Færch and Kasper (1980) proposed something similar when they differentiated between intake as communication and intake as learning, where the first is language intake only for the purpose of immediate meaning in the course of a conversational interaction, and the second is intake incorporated into a learner's grammar. Intake in the approach being discussed in this chapter only includes the second of these possibilities, because intake refers to the *process* of attempted integration of linguistic information. Thus, input that is only used in a conversation and for the sake of that conversation is not regarded as intake.

One factor that determines whether a particular instance of comprehended input will result in intake is the level of analysis of the input a learner achieves. For example, an analysis at the level of meaning is not as useful for intake as an analysis made at the level of syntax. This proposal is supported by Færch and Kasper (1986), who, in the context of foreign-language teaching, argued that one way of improving formal correctness is to provide learners with tasks designed to promote recognition of formal features, rather than overall comprehension of meaning. Support is also found from Call (1985), who argued for the importance of syntax and structural awareness in listening comprehension. A second factor is time. Pressures of conversational interaction may preclude sufficient analysis for the purposes of intake. In this case, the input (even though comprehended) may have no further role in acquisition.

What will determine whether the L2 is comprehended? Prior linguistic knowledge (e.g., knowledge of the NL, of the TL, language universals, knowledge of other languages) is an important aspect (Chapters 6, 7, and 9). These same factors are important in the determination of apperception as well. This is not surprising, because linguistic knowledge is, in some ways, cumulative. One needs a place to attach new information, and one needs some basis for the analysis (i.e., comprehension) of new information. Comprehension cannot take place in a vacuum. Prior knowledge forms the basis for comprehension (in either a narrow or broad sense).

16.1.3 Intake

Intake, the process of assimilating linguistic material, refers to the mental activity that mediates between input and grammars and is different from apperception or comprehension, as the latter two do not necessarily lead to grammar formation. This, of course, suggests that intake is not merely a subset of input. Rather, input and intake refer to two fundamentally different constructs.

What mediates between what has been comprehended and what is eventually important for intake? We have already mentioned that the quality of analysis (i.e., comprehended input) is an important factor. Clearly, knowledge of the L1 and the L2 is also significant. Additionally, whether a particular feature is part of UG (representing

503

something innate) or is part of a universal typological feature will also bear upon eventual intake (Chapters 7 and 9). These factors are not to be understood as being necessarily independent. Features that are part of universal knowledge and/or present in the NL (or other languages known) are most likely to be candidates for a deeper analysis and, hence, candidates for intake.

TIME TO THINK ...

What features of universal knowledge can you think of that may likely become intake in an L2?

[handwritten margin note: psychological processing → incoming info matches up w/ prior knowledge]

How can we describe the intake component? It is that component where psycholinguistic processing takes place (Chapter 10). That is, it is where incoming information is matched up against prior knowledge and where, in general, processing takes place against the backdrop of the existing internalized grammatical rules. It is where generalizations and so-called overgeneralizations are likely to occur; it is where memory traces are formed; and, finally, it is the component from which fossilization stems. Fossilization results when new (correct) input fails to have an impact on the learner's nontarget-like grammar. That is, the correct input is not apperceived or is not comprehended, and thus it is not further processed.

[handwritten margin note: Fossilization: when new input fails to impact learner ↓ new input is not apperceived or not comprehended, thus it is not processed.]

Some of the major processes that take place in the intake component are hypothesis formation, hypothesis testing, hypothesis rejection, hypothesis modification, and hypothesis confirmation.

Hypothesis formation takes place with the addition of new information. A beginning learner (let's assume an NS of Spanish) hears the English sentence *It's pretty* and forms the hypothesis that English sentences can be of the form verb + adjective. The learner arrives at this conclusion by (a) attending to the form, (b) apperceiving it in terms of a Spanish sentence such as *Es bonito*, and (c) understanding the sentence in terms of both its meaning and its syntactic structure. The error in the learner's analysis comes from the fact that *it's* is heard as being similar to *es*, and the learner assumes a similar syntactic structure, that is, she or he analyzes it as one word (*its*). Thus, knowledge of the L1 facilitates that conclusion. Prior knowledge led (a) to apperception, (b) to actual syntactic and semantic comprehension, and (c) to intake, because the analysis matched up with something the learner already knew (*es bonito*).

[handwritten margin note: PROCESSES OF INTAKE: 1. hypothesis formation 2. hypothesis testing 3. hypothesis rejection 4. hypothesis modification 5. hypothesis of confirmation]

The hypothesis of verb + adjective is tested against a reasonable assumption, that of NL–TL similarity. The hypothesis is confirmed. At a later point in time, the learner might see the printed version of *it's* and question the single-word analysis originally given to this form. This would cause the learner to modify this hypothesis and possibly further test it against new data. If the hypothesis is modified in such a way as to eliminate the first hypothesis, that first hypothesis is rejected and is no longer relevant for grammar formation.

development storage
of grammar

16.1.4 Integration

After intake, there are at least two possible outcomes, both of which are a form of _integration:_ (1) the development per se of one's L2 grammar and (2) storage. The distinction made here is between integration and nonintegration of new linguistic information.

Let's consider how this relates to input. There are, essentially, four possibilities for dealing with input. The first two take place in the intake component and result in integration, the third takes place in the integration component, and the fourth represents input that exits the system early on in the process.

1. Hypothesis confirmation/rejection (intake): This first possibility for input is useful as part of the confirmation or rejection of a current hypothesis. This results in integration.

2. Apparent nonuse: Apparent nonuse stems from the fact that the information contained in the input is already incorporated into a learner's grammar. However, the fact that the information is already incorporated into a grammar does not necessarily exclude it from being utilized—but in a different way than what one normally thinks of. When the information contained in the input is already a part of one's knowledge base, the additional input might be used for _rule strengthening_ or _hypothesis reconfirmation._ Part of becoming a fluent speaker of an L2 involves the automatic retrieval of information from one's knowledge base. The knowledge base is developed through practice or repeated exposures to exemplars. Thus, information that may appear to be redundant may in fact be serving an important purpose in terms of the access a learner has to that information.

3. Storage: The third possibility is that input is put into storage, perhaps because some level of understanding has taken place, yet it is not clear how integration into a learner's grammar can or should take place. An example will help to make this clear: A Spanish-speaking ESL student had heard the word _so_ in the following sentence: _So, what did you do yesterday?_ The student could neither figure out what it meant nor how to use it and asked a direct question in an ESL class as to the meaning. From this, one can infer that the learner had stored this information and was waiting for it to be available for integration.

4. Nonuse: In this final possibility, learners make no use of the input at all. This may be because they have not succeeded in comprehending it at a useful level.

What happens after input?

Integration is not necessarily a one-time affair. Rather, there are different levels of analysis and reanalysis from storage into the grammar, and within the grammar itself, as part of integration.

Importantly, the integration component does not function as an independent unit. This is particularly significant in the model we are discussing, because SLA is dynamic and interactive, with knowledge itself being cumulative, interactive, and in flux, as dealt with in Chapter 10 in the discussion of dynamic systems.

processed input that is not storaged becomes the knowledge system (or grammar)

Language information that is processed and deemed appropriate for language development, yet is not put into storage, becomes part of a learner's knowledge system, or grammar. A significant amount of work has been done in this area; indeed, it represents the bulk of the work in SLA over the past few decades. This includes most of the work on linguistic and psycholinguistic aspects of acquisition.

What are some factors that mediate among comprehended input, intake, and integration? Some are similar to those that are also available at the level of apperception. For example, the organizational structure of the NL may shape the way the learner's grammar is structured. Existing knowledge of the L2 will also shape the way integration takes place. Universal principles of language may also play a role in L2 grammar formation (see Chapter 7). Given a particular element in the input, there are universal factors that interact with it, resulting in a generalization of the initial input to other, related domains.

A factor that provides the impetus or motivation for changes in one's knowledge base is the recognition of a mismatch between what is present in the input and the learner's grammar. For learners to modify their speech, they must first recognize that there is something in need of modification—that there is a perceived mismatch between NS speech and their own learner grammars.

Evidence for integrated knowledge can be seen in one of two ways. First, there can be changes in the rule system that surface in the output. This is, in fact, what is typically thought of when one considers developmental changes.

Second, there may be changes in the underlying system, although there is no output change. Changes in underlying systems with no surface manifestation are typically subsumed under the category of reanalysis or restructuring (see Chapter 10).

Re-analysis

Within an L2 context, we can think of reanalysis in two ways. First, a reanalysis of the underlying system may affect the *potential* for output. For example, one can imagine a learner having learned the lexical item *orange juice* as a single lexical item, *orangejuice*, and only at a later point in time reanalyzing it as *orange + juice*. This reanalysis sets the stage for the potential forms *apple juice*, *grapefruit juice*, and so forth.[5] Thus, reanalysis allows for the potential creation of novel forms. Second, on a syntactic level, prefabricated patterns may be analyzed (initially) with little output change. As discussed in Chapter 5, Hakuta (1974b) cited the speech of Uguisu, a 5-year-old child learning English. In the first month of data collection, the following were typical utterances:

(16-1)   Do you know?

(16-2)   Do you want this one?

In later periods, it became obvious that *do you* was a (possibly monomorphemic) question marker. When reanalysis did finally take place and *do you* was analyzed into its component parts, with the result being a productive rule of question formation, there was no output difference. Sentences 16-3 and 16-4 are taken from the fifth month and sixth month, respectively, of data collection:

(16-3)   How do you break it?

(16-4)   Do you put it?

Thus, whereas there was no output difference as a function of reanalysis, the underlying systems were different, as evidenced by other forms in this learner's grammar (see section 10.3.2 on restructuring).

needs a feedback loop to comprehended input
confidence: determining factor for output

16.1.5 Output

The final stage that needs to be examined is that of output. There are two points to emphasize: First, there is the role of comprehensible output in testing hypotheses. Thus, there can be a feedback loop back into the intake component. Second, there is the role output plays in forcing a syntactic, rather than a solely semantic, analysis on language. This conceptualization of output necessitates a feedback loop to comprehended input.

Learners' output is often equated with their grammar. For example, it is frequently inferred that changes in the output represent changes in a learner's grammar. However, as can be seen in Figure 16.1, the two should not be equated. That the output is not identical to one's grammar is suggested by a number of factors. Among these is the recognition that there are individual differences in what learners are willing to say. Personality factors such as confidence in one's ability to produce correct TL sentences may influence whether or not a learner produces TL material. Additionally, learners produce different linguistic forms that have varying amounts of accuracy, depending on the context and the task performed (see Chapter 11). For example, what learners can produce in writing is not what they can produce in speaking; what they can understand from a printed page is not equivalent to what they can understand from an oral stimulus. Finally, different grammatical information may be used in different genres. Undoubtedly, this has to do with the ability to use different channels to express linguistic information. It is also a matter of limitations of access that one has to one's knowledge base.

Not only is confidence in one's ability a determining factor in output, but we can also consider how strongly represented the knowledge is. There may be different degrees of strength of knowledge representation (perhaps related to the automaticity of language processing) that will, in part, determine what output will take place and how it will take place. The following example was provided earlier, but is also relevant here. It comes from Swain (1985, p. 248), who quoted from an eighth-grade immersion student who said: "I can hear in my head how I should sound when I talk, but it never comes out that way." Thus, there appear to be limitations on the translation of knowledge into output.

In sum, the output component represents more than the product of language knowledge; it is an active part of the entire learning process.

OUTPUT: part of the entire learning process.

TIME TO THINK ...

Have you had any experiences where you learned a phrase as a single lexical item in your L2 and later realized that it was made up of more than one part (as in the example of *orangejuice* presented above)?

16.2 CONCLUSION

This chapter has presented a conceptualization of the ways in which the pieces of acquisition fit together, integrating aspects of language acquisition that have been discussed in greater detail in the preceding chapters of this book.

The model in Figure 16.1 is intended to reflect the dynamic and interactive nature of acquisition. It also shows the multiple roles of language transfer and universals. Their roles can only be understood in relation to a specific part of the process. For example, language transfer, as part of prior knowledge, can have a filtering role, as was seen in going from input to apperceived input; a facilitating role when aiding comprehension; and a processing role, as was seen at the level of intake.

Furthermore, such aspects as personality and affect, factors that are under the learner's control to the greatest extent, are important in the initial stages of apperception. Their role is less significant at the levels of intake and integration, areas that are affected by pure linguistic factors (e.g., universals of either a formal or functional type), devoid of cultural and social context and psycholinguistic factors. Finally, personality and affect once again emerge as important factors at the level of output. In other words, those factors that are under the learner's control to the greatest extent have the greatest effect only at the peripheries; that is, at the levels of initial apperceived input and output.

Psycholinguistic processing and linguistic phenomena in the middle are more influenced by mental constraints that are less accessible to direct manipulation. What one would thus expect is (a) a correlation between affective variables and what is apperceived, on the one hand, and what is produced, on the other; and (b) a *lack* of correlation between affective variables and aspects of, for example, Universal Grammar.

In sum, there is a major role for apperceived input, determined to a large extent by selective attention. Without selective attention, grammar development does not take place. In other words, a first step in grammar change is the learner's noticing (at some level) a mismatch between the input and his or her own organization of the TL.

When there is a nonoccurrence of a linguistic phenomenon in the input, change is less likely to come about than in those instances in which forms are overtly present in the TL. It is the areas of the grammar that result from nonoccurrence that are most likely to remain fossilized. Recall the discussion in Chapter 12 (section 12.5.1 on feedback) regarding adverb placement. French speakers learning English frequently produce utterances such as 16-5:

(16-5)   John drinks slowly his coffee.

Because the input does not provide a forum for the learner to readily detect a discrepancy between his or her learner language and the TL, fossilization is likely to occur.

Another area that must be dealt with has to do with variation in learner languages. Variation (both nonrandom and free) (see Chapter 11) in SLA has been well documented. It can be seen diachronically as well as synchronically. Diachronic variation is that variation that represents a change in a learner's knowledge over time; synchronic variation is variation dependent on demands of task type, situation, and language. The important questions are: How do variation and acquisition interact, and what are the constraints on possible variable parts of one's grammar? The concept of automaticity/strength of knowledge discussed in this book is a major factor in the determination of what can and cannot vary. For example, knowledge that is strongly represented is least likely to vary; knowledge that is weakly represented is most likely to vary.

What contributes to the degree of strength of knowledge? If we think of strength of knowledge as being related to memory and prior knowledge, we can understand that the native language and/or language universals are central to this consideration.

Within the present framework, we have pointed to the fact that there is much mileage that needs to be traveled between the input the learner receives and what the learner produces. We cannot assume that, with mere presentation of language information, whether implicitly or explicitly, learners will necessarily convert it to output. It is an arduous task for the learner to (a) extract information from the input, (b) utilize it in forming a grammar, and (c) produce TL forms. Some parts of the process are more accessible to direct learner intervention; others (e.g., psycholinguistic and linguistic phenomena) are less so. It is up to research in future decades to work this process out in all its rich detail.

This book has attempted to integrate components of SLA by presenting a view of acquisition that is dynamic and interactive in nature. It is only by considering SLA in its many and diverse aspects that we can begin to understand the complexities and the interrelationships of this process.

POINTS TO REMEMBER

- There are five stages in the process of converting input to output: (a) apperceived input, (b) comprehended input, (c) intake, (d) integration, and (e) output.

- Apperceived input refers to input that is noticed by the learner because of some particular features such as frequency, infrequency, affect, prior knowledge, and attention.

- Comprehended input differs from intake in that comprehended input may be used only for the immediate purpose of conversational interaction, without becoming intake for learning.

- Intake leads to grammar formation. Hypothesis formation, hypothesis testing, hypothesis rejection, hypothesis modification, and hypothesis confirmation are processes that take place during intake.

- The development of the L2 and the storage of new forms are both forms of integration.

- Apperception and output are both affected by individual differences. Intake and integration are largely affected by language universals and knowledge of the L1 and L2.

MORE TO DO AND MORE TO THINK ABOUT ...

1. If it is the case that there is much mileage to travel from exposure to knowledge, how is it that books and CDs are published that promote fast learning? We frequently encounter advertisements of the sort: "Learn language X in one month." Is this realistic? Why or why not? Other than false advertising, what could be meant?

2. Choose two or three topics dealt with in this book and discuss them in the context of the model of SLA presented in this chapter.

3. In terms of this model, how can one justify the fact that concepts such as transfer and language universals have multiple roles in the acquisition process?

4. Consider standard Spanish, where one has double negatives:

> No   sabe   nada.
> not   know   nothing
> "S/he doesn't know anything."

> No   tiene   nada   de   dinero
> not   have   nothing   of   money
> "S/he doesn't have any money."

And standard English, where one does not:

> He knows nothing.
> She doesn't know anything.

> He has no money.
> She doesn't have any money.

What would you predict would be the forms an NS of Spanish would use in learning English? Consider also the effects of time and environment—that is, the length of time of exposure to English and the location of exposure (classroom vs. naturalistic). What if the Spanish speaker were exposed to a dialect of English in which double negatives were common?

What would you predict would be the forms an NS of English would use in learning Spanish? Would the factors of time and environment have the same effects?

Which of these two groups of learners would have the easier time learning the standard L2 form? Justify your answer.

5. Imagine a particular structure that might be present in the input to a learner. What might and might not happen to that structure as far as the learner is concerned? Trace the path of that structure according to the principles of the model presented in this chapter.

6. The following statements were given in Problem 6 in Chapter 1, where you were asked to determine whether each was true or false. Do so again. Working with a partner, determine whether your answers and your partner's answers are the same or different. Discuss the statements for which your answers differ.

   (a) Any child without cognitive disabilities can learn any language with equal ease.
   (b) Learning an L2 is a matter of learning a new set of habits.
   (c) The only reason that some people cannot learn a second or foreign language is that they are insufficiently motivated.
   (d) All children can learn an L2 accent-free.
   (e) All human beings have an innate capacity to learn language.
   (f) Vocabulary is the most important part of learning an L2.
   (g) Vocabulary is the most difficult part of learning an L2.
   (h) Instruction is a waste of time.
   (i) Learning an L2 takes no more time than learning an L1.

7. The following metaphors were created to represent SLA for a class project. Select one or two and state whether you think these do or do not express the concepts presented in this book.

   (a) Metaphor: Building a house (Margaret Johnson)

   Contrastive Analysis Hypothesis:
   PREMISE: The distances between languages influence SLA.
   METAPHOR: When building a second house, the builder refers to strategies he used in the past and applies them to the construction.

Behaviorism:

PREMISE: Learning by imitation, mimicry, and memorization.

METAPHOR: The builder looks to other houses in the neighborhood and uses them as a model to work off of when constructing his/her own house.

Innatist Perspective:

PREMISE: Proposes that at least some aspects of language are innate and hardwired.

METAPHOR: Before a house is constructed, there is usually a blueprint, or a plan, that guides the builder in creating the house.

Connectionism:

PREMISE: Emphasizes environment influence and exposure to language toward a gradual buildup of language.

METAPHOR: The builder needs the assistance of others to help construct the house; he cannot do it entirely on his own.

Processability Theory:

PREMISE: The sequence of SLA is consistent in order, but not necessarily consistent in rate.

METAPHOR: There is an undeniable order to building a house, beginning with the base, then a lower level, followed by (possibly) more levels, and then a roof. This is true despite the kind of house or where it is built.

(b) Metaphor: Riding a Bicycle (Karen Cheung)

Overview:

When learning to ride a bicycle, many children first start off with training wheels. With training wheels, children don't have to think of balancing the bike; they just have to focus on pedaling and steering the bike. Some children may not even focus on pedaling; they may just put their feet on the pedals and just pedal. When a child has gotten used to the training wheels, the training wheels are taken off so that all is left is two wheels. Someone usually helps the child when the child first rides a two-wheeler. A person may hold the back of the seat to help the child balance on the bicycle. At one point, the person will release their hand to let the child ride by themselves. The child may be able to balance by themselves or fall down, but eventually, the child would get used to riding the two-wheeled bike by themselves. With more and more practice, the child would be more comfortable riding by themselves. Once a person is able to ride the bicycle independently, there may be factors that may affect their ability to ride. The environment can affect the ability for people to ride their bikes. It is easier to ride a bike on a smooth pavement than a rocky pavement or grass. It is easier to ride downhill than uphill. It is easier to ride a bike on a nice sunny/cloudy day than on a raining/snowing/sleeting day. All these factors may make it hard for some to ride their bicycle, but, with motivation and determination, a person can get through anything.

Specifics:

Training Wheels
A two-wheeled bike represents a person learning an L2. Like an adult guiding the child to ride on a two-wheeled bike, there is usually guidance from a teacher when learning an L2. The teacher guides the learner in learning the L2, and, eventually, the learner will be able to communicate in that L2. This concept is similar to the ZPD in that what a child can do with assistance is different than what a child can do independently. The guidance of an adult helping a child during the first day(s) of riding a two-wheeled bike is helpful in that a child may have fewer accidents. The child can feel how the bike is supposed to be balanced, so that they can try to balance on their own. So, in L2 learning, assistance can help a learner so that they will be able to complete their work independently. Once a learner can understand that concept/idea that they are working on, then that concept/idea becomes internalized, just like how a child can then ride their by bike by themselves without assistance.

Similar to learning to ride a bicycle, it may be hard at first when learning an L2, but then it begins to get easier. With more and more practice, a learner can get better at learning an L2. There are factors, however, that may affect the way learners learn an L2 and that is the environment.

Two-Wheeled Bike
Learning to ride a bicycle is just like learning an L2. When a learner first learns a language (first language acquisition), they are like the first stage—training wheels—of riding a bicycle. It starts off pretty easy for the learners because they are born into a language. Everybody around them is speaking the same language. The L1 is innate to the child. When children are on the bike, they just begin to pedal the bike; it is innate for them to pedal the bike. From the innatist perspective, "Chomsky argued that children are biologically programmed for language and that language develops in the child in just the same way that other biological functions develop" (Lightbown & Spada, 2006, p. 15). So it is innate to ride a bicycle, just like it is innate for people to learn languages. Once the child gets used to pedaling the bike, they move on to a two-wheeled bike.

The Environment
When one rides a bicycle, one type of pavement may be easier than another. The weather may make it easier or harder for a person to ride. Hills can make it easier or harder for cyclists. In sociocultural theory, environment plays a vital role in L2 learning. From conversing with others to reading a book, the environment is important in L2 learning.

A learner may learn better if they are in an environment where everyone is speaking that L2, or where they have to speak in that L2. Also, if learners receive positive reinforcement when they do something correct, they are encouraged to continue doing it correctly. Positive reinforcement is part of the behaviorists' perspective, where they believed that, "when children imitated the language produced by those around them, their attempts to reproduce what they heard received 'positive reinforcement.' Thus, encouraged by their environment, children would continue to imitate and practice these sounds and patterns until they formed 'habits' of correct language use" (Lightbown & Spada, 2006, p. 10). So a child may receive positive reinforcement when riding their bicycle when they are doing something correctly. This will help the child to know that they are doing it correctly, and should continue to do it that way.

(c) Metaphor: Mathematics (Jennifer Grima)

The Basics:

The laws
- There are laws in math, but, like the rules of grammar, there are always exceptions.
- When dealing with radicals, there can never be a negative number under the radical, except when dealing with imaginary numbers.
- Only humans are able to comprehend math.
- No other animals can grasp mathematical concepts.

Developmental Sequences
- A person must first learn the basics of math in order to eventually comprehend the other components of math.
- Basic algebra (1 + 2) is the basis of all other levels of math (calculus, trigonometry, geometry).
- Regardless of the country it's learned in, math is learned in the same basic order:
  - Addition and subtraction
  - Multiplication and division
  - Pre-algebra
  - Algebra
  - Pre-calculus
  - Calculus I, II, III
- Acquisition
  - Behaviorist/Interactionist
  - The more you are exposed to math concepts, the more you will learn and the better you will get.
  - Taking a couple of math classes in college will result in better math skills.
  - If a person's math skills aren't used for a while, some aspects will be forgotten, while other aspects will never be forgotten.
  - Once a person learns how to add, he/she will never lose that ability. However, other math skills, such as derivatives, can be easily forgotten.

- – Some people comprehend math faster, while others take longer to acquire the knowledge.
- Critical Period Hypothesis
  - – The older you get, the harder it is to learn math. You have previous experiences and knowledge that may interfere with the laws or rules of math.
  - – Pythagorean Theorem—How did they get this? Older people will analyze it.
  - – Imaginary numbers—There is no such thing.
  - – Previous knowledge of different types of math may interfere with learning another type.
  - – In trigonometry, the sin and cos laws interfere with calculus laws of sin and cos.

(d) Metaphor: Painting a Picture (Amanda Craik)

In order to illustrate SLA, I first need to illustrate L1 acquisition. L1 acquisition is like painting a picture of your immediate surroundings—painting a picture of a place you grew up in and are familiar with. All of your experiences and thoughts are defined by this place you grew up in. This is like L1 acquisition; the L1 is surrounding you all the time, most of your life experiences deal with this L1, and the input of language is always in this L1.

SLA is like painting a picture of a place you have maybe seen in a picture and have heard about from other people. You are given the same paintbrushes and paints to paint this picture as you were given to paint the picture of your immediate surroundings. In some ways, this picture is easy to paint, because you have already used and practiced certain cognitive processes in painting your first picture and understanding the world around you. For example, you already know what a tree is, so when someone tells you to paint a tree you understand what this means. However, this can also hinder you—if someone tells you to paint a tree you may paint a pine tree like in your first painting, because this is what you are familiar with, when in fact you were supposed to paint a palm tree. Even after you learn what a palm tree is, you may continue to accidentally paint pine trees. Also, even if lots of people tell you what this new place is like, or if you get a glimpse of this new place from a postcard, you don't have the same experience of living in that place and having memories of that place. Another factor is that it will be easier to paint the second place if it is similar to the first place, but, the more different it is, the harder it will be to paint. Also, while you are trying to paint this new place, your original familiar surroundings are still all around you, continuing to influence you as you paint. It will be hard to complete the picture; it will probably be an ongoing process that will never look exactly like the place you are trying to paint.

The paintbrushes in this metaphor are like universal grammar. In both first and SLA, we start out with the same basic tools for understanding the grammatical structure of a language. In the L1, though it may be hard to produce (paint) the language perfectly at the beginning, because you are not experienced with the language (or with the place you are painting), eventually the user of the language becomes proficient. There is a constant input of the L1 (the immediate surroundings), and the person catches on. With the L2, there is input from others (pictures and people) in the L2, but there continues to be input in the L1. This makes it more difficult to learn, because the input is not as constant. Another reason it is harder to learn the L2 is because the learner simply does not have background experience with the language. The learner does not have certain connotations or memories that go with certain words. This means, as the sociocultural theory states, the learner will continue to rely on the L1 for internal thinking, because it is comfortable and what he or she is used to. Also, it will be easier to paint the second place if it is more similar to the first place—as the CAH states, it will be easier to acquire a language that is more similar to your L1 than one that is much different.

One main thing my metaphor doesn't address is if a person is immersed into a language (such as if you were to move to another country), or if they acquire an L2 very close to the time they acquire the first (such as when a child is still very young). Rather, it is a metaphor that shows how an L2 is acquired when a person with a lot of experience in their L1 learns from a classroom setting or a setting that is not immersion-based.

(e) Metaphor: Baking a Cake (Megan Sutton)

General Overview

Every culture has food, but not everyone eats sweet masses of dough baked in pans. Similarly, every culture has language, but not everyone speaks the same language. Language and food are universal; specific languages and cake are not.

When learning to make cake after growing up with a diet that does not include it, learners are likely to acquire different taste preferences and baking styles. They may put their own spin on recipes, adding different spices or substituting apple sauce for oil. Parallel to this is the fact that most L2 learners never acquire completely native-like production. They may retain an accent and occasionally use forms that indicate they are using their L2, but, as long as this does not interfere with communication, they are considered proficient. We would not consider a scrumptious cake a failure just because it was slightly different from what we were used to, and we do not consider language acquisition a failure just because it is not completely native-like.

Recipes and Grammar

The rules for combining the ingredients for cake are often written down in recipes. Recipes are helpful, but not sufficient, for learning to make cakes. Handing one to a person who has never made a cake, seen a cake being made, heard of cake, or eaten a cake will not be enough for them to be able to make a cake. Being given written instructions for making cake is no substitute for having background knowledge about cake. On the other hand, observing someone make a cake, if repeated enough times, would probably be enough for a learner to figure out how to make a reasonably tasty dessert. Having a recipe to refer to might be helpful, as it would provide them with a framework of understanding, but watching a demonstration or interacting directly with a baker would be optimal.

In this metaphor, direct instruction in the grammar of a language is the recipe that explains how the ingredients of sounds, words, and phrases are combined. The grammar exists even without the recipe, as is clearly shown by the numerous cooks who can make a cake without referring to instructions. An astute learner could learn these rules by observing a cook, just as motivated learners often pick up an L2 if given enough meaningful input to it. Still, direct instruction may increase the pace of acquisition, because the learner does not have to figure out the rules entirely for themselves.

Theories

Sociocultural Theory

Vygotsky states that learners acquire skills faster if they are supported by a more skilled individual whose goal is to help them reach independence. By this metaphor, a child or adult who wants to learn to make cake will benefit the most from working with a mother, grandmother, or other experienced baker who will take into account their current culinary experience (actual development level) and what they are able to accomplish with help (ZPD).

For example, maybe a learner is familiar with breaking eggs and softening butter. Those two skills are within their actual development level. Perhaps pouring the cake batter into the pan is difficult for them, as they must manage lifting a bowl and holding a spatula simultaneously. The experienced individual might hold the bowl the first time, still requiring the novice to do as much of the work as possible, but allowing them to master one skill before moving on to the next. Similarly with language acquisition, sociocultural theory assumes that learners benefit most from working with more advanced interlocutors who can move them toward self-regulation on an individualized path that takes into account language features they have mastered and others with which they struggle.

Universal Grammar

According to this perspective, all humans possess an innate knowledge of language that allows them to acquire language. This almost instinctive ability is so fundamental it can be compared to the sense of taste by which we analyze food.

The multitude of possible taste sensations we experience stem from a vast array of combinations of just a few flavors: sweet, sour, bitter, and salty.

Similarly, there is a limit to the number of possible phonemes, grammar rules, morphological rules, and other "ingredients" of language. These interact in different ways to create the vast array of human languages.

The taste buds of the tongue are specialized to provide information about the type of food we eat. They tell us if the food we eat contains sugar or salt, bases or acids, and in what proportions they are combined. The language-acquisition device functions in a comparable manner. It analyzes the incoming language data, determining what elements are present in the data and how they are combined. Of course, the comparison is not exactly that simple, as the taste buds themselves can't tell us how to make a cake; we need more overt instruction for that. The language capacity of the human mind is truly remarkable in that it both analyzes incoming data and provides the basis for production.

Input Processing

VanPatten proposes that learners' processing capacity is limited, and therefore when they cannot hold all the information about both form and meaning, they pay attention first to meaning. Therefore, grammar words such as "at" and "that" are overlooked in favor of content words such as "girl" or "house." This process is analogous to learning to make a cake in that a learner would more likely pay more attention to adding the main ingredients than to smaller matters such as what mixer speed to use or sifting the flour.

Imagine someone who has never made a cake. An experienced baker takes them through the entire process. What are they most likely to remember? The order in which everything is placed into the mixing bowl? Or the fact that cake contains eggs, milk, and flour? If they forget the latter ingredients, the cake is likely to be inedible, so, after they've had a bit of experience, they'll probably at least remember the main ingredients. The cake might have a strange consistency without the leavening agent, just as sentences sound strange without proper word order, but the end product would probably be suitable for eating. Eventually, we would expect a novice baker to remember to add all the necessary ingredients in the right amounts and order. Similarly, learners first process the aspects of language that they perceive to be most important and gradually move to a more native-like comprehension of their L2.

Contrastive Analysis Hypothesis

This school of thought surmises that learners pair their L2 with their L1, making it easier for a learner to acquire a language that is more similar to their first, and more difficult to acquire forms that are very different from their NL. Translating this into baking terms, learners should have acquired the ability to bake a cake if they come from a culture that has a similar food, such as brownies. If their cooking background consists of only barbecuing, they may struggle more as they learn about mixers, ovens, and baking ingredients.

The flaw in this theory, in either a language or a baking model, is that learners may have interference if their experience is too similar to what they are learning. For example, the most significant difference between brownies and cake is the presence of leavening. Forgetting to put in baking soda could have considerable consequences for the cake, just as omitting word endings can have disastrous consequences in communication. Additionally, not every mistake learners make can be related to their previous experience; some are equally likely to occur in people with brownie and barbecue backgrounds.

8. As a class project, reflect upon the ideas presented in this book and come up with a metaphor that synthesizes your view of SLA. Create a poster that symbolizes your view of SLA. (Thanks to Ben White (via Jerri Willet) for this idea.)

ODE TO SLA BY ERICH ZIROLL

SLA is like Coin-Star type of machine,
Based on proto-types and frequency,
Separating and connecting different ideas,
Developing a language system oh so fancy.

SLA is like a labyrinth of constraining walls to be navigated,
Figuring out which direction you must go at each turn,
Using principles of language as your guide,
Whilst a second language you begin to learn.

SLA is like a game of throw and catch,
Participating in negotiation of meaning and correction,
Receiving a constant supply of feedback,
Making adjustments for every little detection.

SLA is like a caterpillar "internalized" in a cocoon,
With the intention of becoming a butterfly,
Along with the assistance of others,
To emerge anew, floating toward the sky.

SLA is like a spider in the process of building its web,
Expanding by matching functions to forms and forms to functions,
Following the certain paths to get to the next language stage,
Until the web of language has adequate conjunctions.

SLA is like a switch pad waiting for a code to activate it,
Gaining access to all principles of language through input,
At last the door opens revealing the treasure of language,
With every possible combination given to you afoot.

Glossary

Access to UG Hypothesis   The claim that the innate language facility is operative in SLA and constrains the grammars of second-language learners.

Accessibility Hierarchy (AH)   A continuum of RC types such that the presence of one type implies the presence of other types higher on the hierarchy.

Acculturation Model   A model consisting of social and affective variables. It is based on the notion that learners need to adapt to the target-language culture in order for successful acquisition to take place.

accuracy   Correct use of the target language. (*See also* fluency, complexity.)

Affective Filter   Part of the Monitor Model. The claim is that affect is an important part of the learning process, and that one has a "raised" or "lowered" Affective Filter. The latter leads to better learning.

apperceived input   That part of the language that a learner is exposed to and that is noticed by the learner.

aptitude   An individual-difference characteristic that refers to someone's natural ability to do something; in the case of this book, learn another language. (*See also* language aptitude.)

AS-unit   Analysis-of-speech unit. Used for oral production as a way of dividing oral speech into clauses and phrases.

aspect   A verbal category that marks the way a situation takes place in time (e.g., continuous, repetitive). (*See also* tense.)

Aspect Hypothesis   The claim that first- and second-language learners will initially be influenced by the inherent semantic aspect of verbs or predicates in the acquisition of tense and aspect markers associated with or affixed to these verbs.

attention   The orientation of mental powers; the way we focus on and process elements of our surroundings.

attitude   A tendency to respond in a particular way (positively or negatively) toward something (e.g., a situation, a culture).

automaticity   The degree of routinized control that one has over linguistic knowledge.

Autonomous Induction Theory   A theory that attributes difficulties in learning a second language to parsing problems.

awareness   Conscious orientation; refers to the extent that individuals are conscious of something.

babbling   The sounds infants make that often sound like words to adults.

baby talk   The language addressed to a young child. *(See also* caretaker speech; child-directed speech; motherese.)

backchannel cues   Generally, verbal messages such as *uh huh* and *yeah* that are said during the time another person is talking.

backslide   When a learner seems to make progress (perhaps with the use of a correct form) and then seems to regress.

behaviorism   A school of psychology that bases learning on a stimulus–response paradigm.

Bilingual Syntax Measure (BSM)   A testing instrument that measures the morphological knowledge children have in an second language.

bilingualism   The ability to use more than one language.

Bottleneck Hypothesis   The main challenge to learning a second language is not syntax and semantics, but rather formal features and inflectional morphemes. These cause a bottleneck.

C-unit (Communication unit)   A unit of analysis that can be used with written and oral production. A C-unit is an independent clause and its modifiers. Similar to a T-unit. *(See also* T-unit; AS-unit.)

caretaker speech   The language addressed to a young child. *(See also* baby talk; child-directed speech; motherese.)

chaos theory   An alternative mode of referring to a dynamic system. Chaos theory incorporates order, but not predictability. *(See also* complexity; complex adaptive system; nonlinear system; dynamic system.)

child-directed speech   The language addressed to a young child. *(See also* baby talk; caretaker speech; motherese.)

chunk   A part of language (generally consisting of more than one word) that is considered to be one unit by the learner. *(See also* prefabricated routine/pattern.)

clarification request   A device used in conversation to ask for more information when something has not been understood.

coalescing   A term used in the Hierarchy of Difficulty to refer to the collapsing of two native-language categories into one target-language category. *(See also* Hierarchy of Difficulty.)

Cognition Hypothesis   A claim that pedagogic tasks should be sequenced in order of increasing cognitive complexity.

Cognitive Phonology Model   A model proposed to account for errors made by SLA of sign language.

collocation   Words that belong together, such as *to make a case*.

communication strategies   An approach used by learners when they need to express a concept or an idea in the second language, but do not have or cannot access the linguistic resources to do so.

competence   The mental system that underlies one's ability to use (produce/comprehend) language.

Competition Model   One model of language processing based on how people interpret sentences.

complex adaptive systems   An alternative mode of referring to a dynamic system. (*See also* complexity; chaos; nonlinear system; dynamic system.)

complexity   An alternative mode of referring to a dynamic system; within the planning literature, a term used to determine how difficult it is to produce something (cognitive complexity) or the types of linguistic forms used (linguistic complexity). (*See also* chaos; complex adaptive system; nonlinear system; dynamic system; fluency; accuracy.)

comprehended input   Input that has been understood by the learner; to be contrasted with comprehensible input. (*See also* comprehensible input.)

comprehensible input   Originally formulated as part of the Monitor Model, this concept refers to the understandable input that learners receive. To be useful for learning, comprehensible input needs to be slightly more advanced than the learner's current level of grammatical knowledge. (*See also* comprehended input.)

comprehensible output   The language produced by the learner.

comprehension check   A device used in conversation to ensure that one's interlocutor has understood.

concept-oriented approach   An approach that maps language functions that a learner wants to express to the form that she or he needs to express it.

Conceptualizer   Part of the production process that has to do with the determination of the message that will be communicated. *(See also* formulator.)

confirmation check   A device used in conversation to determine whether one has been understood correctly.

connectionism   An approach that assumes that learning takes place based on the extraction of regularities from the input. (*See also* emergentism.)

contrastive analysis   A way of comparing two languages to determine similarities and dissimilarities.

Contrastive Analysis Hypothesis (CAH)   A prediction that similarities between two languages do not require learning, and that the differences are what need to be learned.

conversation analysis (CH) Uses conversation as a resource for showing how micro-moments of socially distributed cognition are seen in conversation and reflect changes in participants' knowledge.

corpora Bodies of native speaker- or learner-produced text that are analyzed for grammatical or lexical patterns using computers.

corrective feedback An intervention that provides information to a learner that a prior utterance is incorrect. (*See also* feedback.)

correspondence A term used in the Hierarchy of Difficulty to refer to the situation in which there exists a one-to-one relationship between a native-language and target-language form. (*See also* Hierarchy of Difficulty.)

Creative Construction Hypothesis The proposal that child second-language learners construct rules of the second language on the basis of innate mechanisms.

critical period A time after which successful language learning cannot take place. (*See also* sensitive period.)

cross-linguistic influence Any language influence from the first language to the second language, from one interlanguage to another, or from the second language back to the first language. (*See also* language transfer.)

cross-sectional A data-gathering procedure in which data are gathered from groups of learners in order for particular behaviors to be viewed at a single point in time. One often gathers cross-sectional data from learners at different proficiency levels and infers that the differences represent change over time. (*See also* pseudo-longitudinal.)

declarative knowledge Knowledge that one has about something. This information is relatively accessible to conscious awareness. (*See also* procedural knowledge.)

differentiation A term used in the Hierarchy of Difficulty to refer to the situation in which a single form in the native language corresponds to two different forms in the target language. (*See also* Hierarchy of Difficulty.)

Direct Contrast Hypothesis When a child produces an utterance containing an erroneous form, which is responded to immediately with an utterance containing the correct adult alternative to the erroneous form (i.e., when negative evidence is supplied), the child may perceive the adult form as being in contrast with the equivalent child form. Cognizance of a relevant contrast can then form the basis for perceiving the adult form as a correct alternative to the child form.

discourse-completion test A procedure commonly used in gathering data about interlanguage pragmatics and speech acts. Generally, a situation is described, and learners have to write/say what they would typically say in that particular situation.

Discourse Hypothesis A claim that learners distinguished between foregrounded and backgrounded material when telling a narrative.

dynamic systems A class of systems that refers to ways in which complex systems change and develop over time. (*See also* chaos theory; complexity; complex adaptive system; nonlinear system.)

emergentism An approach that assumes that learning takes place based on the extraction of regularities from the input. (*See also* connectionism.)

entrenchment A process of neurodevelopment whereby elements become established in the brain. (*See also* resonance.)

errors The incorrect forms (vis-à-vis the language being learned) that learners produce.

error analysis A procedure for analyzing second-language data that begins with the errors learners make and then attempts to explain them.

explicit knowledge Knowledge about language that involves awareness. (*See also* explicit learning; implicit knowledge; implicit learning; declarative knowledge; procedural knowledge.)

explicit learning Acquisition of language that involves deliberate hypothesis testing as learners search for structure. (*See also* explicit knowledge; implicit knowledge; implicit learning; declarative knowledge; procedural knowledge.)

extroversion Refers to where attention is focused, namely, the world and people outside themselves. (*See also* introversion.)

facilitation The use of the first language (or other languages known) in a second-language context, resulting in a target-like second-language form. (*See also* language transfer; positive transfer.)

Failed Functional Features Hypothesis A claim that, if there are features that are not in the first language, those features cannot be acquired in the second language. Underlying representations remain nontarget-like. (*See also* Representational Deficit Hypothesis.)

feedback An intervention in which information is provided to a learner that a prior utterance is correct or incorrect. (*See also* corrective feedback.)

fluency A measure of how smoothly and quickly one can produce the TL. (*See also* accuracy; complexity.)

focus on form Drawing learners' attention to form within a context of meaning.

focus on formS Instruction that is organized around grammatical structures.

foreign language learning The learning of a second language in a formal classroom situation that takes place in a country where the native language is spoken (e.g., learning French in the United States; learning Hebrew in Japan).

foreigner talk The modified language used when addressing a nonnative speaker.

formulaic language A group of words that often function as a single unit for a learner. (*See also* chunk; collocation.)

Formulator Part of the production process that has to do with putting into words the conceptual notions to be communicated. (*See also* conceptualizer.)

fossilization The cessation of learning. Permanent plateaus that learners reach, resulting from no change in some or all of their interlanguage forms. (*See* also interlanguage; stabilization.)

free variation   An alternation of possible forms, perhaps randomly.

Full Access (without transfer)   A position that maintains that the starting point for acquisition is Universal Grammar, as it is in child language acquisition.

Full Transfer/Full Access   A position that claims that the starting point for SLA is the first language, with full access during the process to Universal Grammar. Learners start with the first language and draw on Universal Grammar when necessary.

functional categories   Categories that carry primarily grammatical meaning, such as morphemes for tense and determiners.

Fundamental Difference Hypothesis (FDH)   The claim that child first language acquisition and adult SLA are different.

general nativism   A position that maintains that there is no specific mechanism designed for language learning. (*See also* special nativism.)

heritage language acquisition   Learning of the language of one's ancestors or home language. (*See also* heritage-language learner.)

heritage-language learner   A learner who is learning the language of his/her ancestors. Often, the learner has had exposure through the home environment to that language. (*See also* heritage language acquisition.)

Hierarchy of Difficulty   A proposed ordering of more-to-less-difficult learning situations.

implicational universals   Common hierarchies across the world's languages in which particular language elements are predicted by the existence of other language elements. (*See also* typological universals.)

implicit knowledge   Knowledge about language that does not involve awareness of that knowledge. (*See also* explicit learning; explicit knowledge; implicit learning; declarative knowledge; procedural knowledge.)

implicit learning   Acquiring knowledge about the underlying structure of a complex stimulus environment without doing so consciously. (*See also* explicit knowledge; explicit learning; implicit knowledge.)

incidental vocabulary   Learning that takes place with an explicit focus on learning: meaning as opposed to having as an explicit goal the learning of new words.

indeterminacy   The incomplete, or lack of, knowledge that a language learner has of the target language.

indirect negative evidence   Evidence based on the lack of occurrence of forms. (*See* also negative evidence; positive evidence.)

inhibition   Blocking out of some things to focus on others. (*See also* inhibitory control.)

inhibitory control   One's ability to control what can be blocked out in order to focus on something else. (*See also* inhibition.)

Initial Hypothesis of Syntax   A position that maintains that the starting point for SLA is Universal Grammar.

initial state   The beginning point of learning.

input   The language that is available to learners; that is, exposure.

input enhancement   A technique that attempts to make parts of the input salient.

input processing   A model of learning that attempts to account for the ways learners connect form and meaning as they comprehend input. Principles and corollaries have been developed that account for the strategies learners adopt. (*See also* processing instruction.)

instrumental motivation   Motivation that comes from the rewards gained from knowing another language. (*See also* integrative motivation.)

intake   That part of the language input that is internalized by the learner.

integrative motivation   Motivation that comes from the desire to acculturate and become part of a target-language community. (*See also* instrumental motivation.)

interaction approach   An approach that considers conversational interaction as a locus of learning.

Interface Hypothesis   Parts of language that involve an interface across components (e.g., pragmatics, syntax, semantics) are more difficult to learn than those that involve only one component (e.g., only syntax, only pragmatics).

interference   The use of the first language (or other languages known) in a second-language context, when the resulting second-language form is incorrect. (*See also* language transfer; negative transfer.)

interlanguage (IL)   The language produced by a nonnative speaker of a language (i.e., a learner's output). Refers to the systematic knowledge underlying learners' production.

interlanguage transfer   The influence of one second language over another in instances where there are multiple languages acquired after the first language.

interlingual   An error type that can be attributed to the native language. (*See also* intralingual.)

interlocutor   The person with whom one is speaking.

internalization   A component of Sociocultural Theory. It is the process that refers to learners gaining greater control over the L2. (*See also* Sociocultural Theory; mediation; regulation; Zone of Proximal Development.)

intralingual   An error type that can be attributed to the language being learned. (*See also* interlingual.)

introversion   Refers to where attention is focused, namely, towards an individual's own inner world. (*See also* extroversion.)

Involvement Load Hypothesis   A hypothesis that claims that vocabulary learning is related to the extent of involvement of the learner in a task.

L1   A person's first language. (*See also* L2.)

L1 = L2 Hypothesis   The claim that a second language is acquired in the same manner as a first language.

L2 A person's second language. To be more specific, one could refer to a person's L3, L4, and so on. However, the general term L2 is frequently used to refer to any language learning or use after the first language has been learned. (*See also* L1.)

Language Acquisition Device (LAD) A language faculty that constrains and guides the acquisition process.

language aptitude A natural ability to learn non-primary languages. (*See also* aptitude.)

language neutral Part of language that learners perceive to be common to (at least) the native and the target languages.

language specific Parts of language that learners perceive to be unique to a specific language.

language transfer The use of the first language (or other languages known) in a second-language context. *(See also* cross-linguistic influence; facilitation; interference; negative transfer; positive transfer.)

learning strategy A strategic plan undertaken by a learner in learning.

learning style The preferred way of taking in, processing new information and/or skills.

longitudinal A data-gathering procedure in which data are gathered from one or more learners over a prolonged period of time in order to gather information about change over time.

markedness A linguistic term that refers to prototypicality and commonality of linguistic features. Unmarked forms are those that are common across languages; marked forms are less common and may be more difficult to learn.

Markedness Differential Hypothesis A proposal based on the markedness values of different forms. Unmarked forms are learned before marked forms.

mean length of utterance (MLU) A measure used in child-language research to determine a child's linguistic development.

mediation Part of Sociocultural Theory whereby the underlying premise is that human activity relates to the world through a symbolic artifact such as language. (*See also* Sociocultural Theory; regulation; internalization; Zone of Proximal Development.)

meta-analysis A systematic and quantitative approach to synthesizing previous research.

metalinguistic knowledge What one knows (or thinks one knows) about the language. It is to be differentiated from what one does in using language.

Minimal Trees Hypothesis A Universal Grammar characterization that claims that both the first language and Universal Grammar are available during the process of learning. Functional categories are not available from the first language, but only from second language input.

Missing Surface Inflectional Hypothesis   A Universal Grammar hypothesis that claims that, rather than having a deficit, learners have intact representations but have difficulty mapping them onto second-language morphology. (*See also* Processing Deficit Approach.)

mistakes   Nonsystematic errors that learners produce. These are "correctable" by the learner.

Monitor Model   A model of SLA based on the concept that learners have two systems (acquisition and learning), and that the learned system monitors the acquired system.

morpheme   The minimal unit of meaning in language. Elements of meaning may be smaller than words (e.g., the word *unclear* contains two units, *un* + *clear*).

morpheme order studies   A series of studies carried out to determine the order in which certain English morphemes are acquired.

morphology   The study of how morphemes form words and function in language.

motherese   The language addressed to a young child. (*See also* baby talk; caretaker speech; child-directed speech.)

motivation   The characteristic that provides the incentive for learning.

native language (NL)   A person's first language.

negative evidence   Information provided to a learner concerning the incorrectness of a form. (*See also* indirect negative evidence; positive evidence.)

negative transfer   The use of the first language (or other languages known) in a second-language context, resulting in a nontarget-like second-language form. (*See also* interference; language transfer; positive transfer.)

negotiation of meaning   The attempt made in conversation to clarify a lack of understanding.

nonlinear systems   An alternative mode of referring to a dynamic system. (*See also* complexity; chaos; complex adaptive system; dynamic system.)

notice the gap   A learner's detection of a difference between his/her interlanguage system and what is said in the target language.

one-to-one principle   A principle that claims that, in early stages of learning, learners learn that each meaning is expressed by one form.

Ontogeny Phylogeny Model   A model that shows the relationship between transfer and developmental processes over time.

Output Hypothesis   A position that holds that output (language production) is a significant factor in second language learning.

overextension   Using a word with a wider referential range than is correct in standard adult language (e.g., when a child uses *doggie* to refer to dogs as well as other animals, such as cows). (*See also* underextension.)

performance   Actual language use.

phoneme   The smallest sound unit that distinguishes meanings.

phonology   The sound patterns of language.

positive evidence   Evidence based on forms that actually occur. (*See also* indirect negative evidence; negative evidence.)

positive transfer   The use of the first language (or other languages known) in a second-language context, when the resulting second-language form is correct. (*See also* cross-linguistic influence; facilitation; interference; language transfer; negative transfer.)

Poverty of the Stimulus   A proposal made within the confines of Universal Grammar that input alone is not sufficiently specific to allow a child to attain the complexities of the adult grammar. (*See also* Universal Grammar.)

pragmatics   The ways in which language is used in context.

prefabricated routine/pattern   Parts of language that are learned as a whole, without knowledge of the component parts. (*See also* chunk.)

private speech   A part of Sociocultural Theory. It refers to language we use when we talk to ourselves. (*See also* Sociocultural Theory.)

procedural knowledge   Knowledge that relates to cognitive skills that involve sequencing information. This information is relatively inaccessible. (*See also* declarative knowledge.)

Processability Theory   A theory that proposes that production and comprehension of second-language forms only takes place to the extent that they can be handled by the linguistic processor. Understanding how the processor functions allows one to understand developmental paths.

Processing Deficit Approach   A Universal Grammar hypothesis that claims that, rather than having a deficit, learners have intact representations but have difficulty mapping them onto second-language morphology. (*See also* Missing Surface Inflectional Hypothesis.)

processing instruction   A type of language instruction that helps to overcome incorrect processing strategies. (*See also* input processing.)

pronominal reflex   A pronoun used (almost) immediately after a noun to refer to that noun (e.g., *The man he went home* or *The man who he went home was ill.*). (*See also* resumptive pronoun.)

Prosodic Transfer Hypothesis   A Universal Grammar hypothesis that claims that second-language morphology is not learned because of first-language transfer of phonological representations.

pseudolongitudinal   The use of cross-sectional data to gather information about change over time. This is frequently done by using groups of learners at different proficiency levels. (*See also* cross-sectional data.)

psychotypology   The organizational structure that learners impose on their native language.

recast   Reformulation of an incorrect utterance that maintain the original's meaning.

regulation   A form of mediation in which learning takes place through less reliance on objects and greater use of the linguistic system, without the support of objects or other individuals. (*See also* Sociocultural Theory; mediation.)

Representational Deficit Hypothesis   A claim that, if there are features that are not in the first language, those features cannot be acquired in the second language. Underlying representations remain nontarget-like. (*See also* Failed Feature Functional Features Hypothesis.)

resonance   A counteracting force to entrenchment, allowing second-language patterns to develop despite entrenchment of first-language patterns. (*See also* entrenchment.)

restructuring   Changes or reorganization of one's grammatical knowledge.

resumptive pronoun   A pronoun used (almost) immediately after a noun to refer to that noun (e.g., *The man he went home* or *The man who he went home was ill*.). (*See also* pronominal reflex.)

second language acquisition (SLA)   The learning of another language after the first language has been learned. The use of this term does not differentiate among learning situations. SLA also refers to the scientific study of this process. (*See also* L2.)

second-modality acquisition   Learning of a language system using a different modality (e.g., learning sign language as a second language).

semantics   The phenomena relating to the meaning of words and sentences.

sensitive period   A time during which most successful learning is likely to take place. (*See also* critical period.)

Shallow Structure Hypothesis   A position that maintains that sentence processing does not involve full/deep syntactic processing. Comprehension takes place with the help of lexical knowledge and real-world knowledge.

Sociocultural Theory   A theory based on work by the Russian psychologist Vygotsky that considers knowledge/learning arising from a social context. Learning, being socially mediated, comes from face-to-face interaction. Knowledge is internalized from learners jointly constructing knowledge in dyadic interactions. (*See also* internalization; mediation; private speech; regulation; Zone of Proximal Development.)

special nativism   A proposal that there exist special principles for language learning. These principles are unique to language (learning) and are not used in other cognitive endeavors. (*See also* general nativism.)

speech act   What one does with language (i.e., the functions for which language is used). Examples include complaining, complimenting, and refusing.

Speech Learning Model   A model of phonological learning that claims that the perceived relationship between first-language and second-language sounds is a determinant of whether or not a new phonetic category is established. The greater the distance, the more likely it is that a new category will be established.

stabilization   The plateaus that learners reach when there is little change in some or all of their interlanguage forms. (*See* also interlanguage; fossilization.)

stimulated recall   A research methodology in which, following completion of a task, individuals are asked to verbalize what they were thinking at the time of the task. A stimulus (such as a video of the individual performing the task) is provided as a prompt. (*See also* verbal reports.)

Structural Conformity Hypothesis   The notion that all universals that are true for primary languages are also true for interlanguages.

suppliance in obligatory context   A method used to determine a second-language learner's knowledge of a given structure by measuring how many times a particular form is used when it is required in the target language.

syntactic priming   Refers to the phenomenon of repetition of a previously uttered structure (known as the prime) when other options are available.

syntax   Generally known as grammar, syntax deals with the order of elements in sentences and sentence structure.

T-unit   One main clause plus any subordinate clause or nonclausal structure that is attached to or embedded in it. (*See also* C-Unit; AS-Unit.)

target language (TL)   The language being learned.

telegraphic   A typical stage of speech in child language acquisition in which only content words are present (e.g., *Mommy go work*).

tense   The time of an event or action, often indicated by an inflectional category. (*See also* aspect.)

think-aloud   A research task used to elicit information on thought processes. Data are collected by having individuals talk through the process of doing a task. (*See also* verbal reports.)

thinking-for-speaking   A perspective on language that claims that the verbalization of events is influenced by the linguistic categories of our language.

Transfer to Somewhere Principle   A principle developed to account for when transfer is likely to occur. It claims that transfer will occur only in those instances when the second-language input allows the learner to see a potential for transfer.

typological universals   Universals derived from an investigation of the commonalities of the world's languages. The goal is to determine similarities in types of language, including implicational universals. (*See also* implicational universals.)

U-shaped patterns   Learning whereby early forms appear to be correct, followed by a period of incorrect forms, with a final stage of correct forms.

UG parameter   A principle of Universal Grammar that is not invariant. It allows for cross-language variation.

UG principle   A constraint that governs all languages.

underextension   Using a word with a narrower referential range than is correct in standard adult language (e.g., a child may not use *tree* to refer to a tree in the dead of winter with no leaves). (*See also* overextension.)

Universal Grammar   A set of innate principles common to all languages.

verbal reports   Based on verbal reporting, it is a type of introspection that consists of gathering information by asking individuals to say what is going through their minds as they are solving a problem or doing a task. (*See also* think-aloud; stimulated recall.)

Voice Contrast Hierarchy   The claim that a voicing contrast in initial position is the least marked, whereas a voicing contrast in final position is the most marked.

working memory   Temporary storage space where processing and storage take place.

Zone of Proximal Development (ZPD)   A concept from Sociocultural Theory that reflects the distance between what learners can do on their own and what they require assistance with. (*See also* Sociocultural Theory.)

Notes

1. Introduction

1. In reality, the picture is more complex, because there are language-learning situations where a variety of the language being learned is spoken widely, although for the most part it is not natively spoken (e.g., English in India).
2. An * is used to indicate a form that does not or cannot exist in a language.
3. Since the early 1970s, a number of terms have been used to describe basically the same concept: *approximative system* (Nemser, 1971), *transitional competence* (Corder, 1967), *idiosyncratic dialect* (Corder, 1971), *learner language* (Færch, Haastrup, & Phillipson, 1984). Each of these terms has a slightly different focus. However, interlanguage is the most commonly used one.

2. Second and Foreign Language Data

1. Many of the examples in this chapter originally appeared in Selinker and Gass (1984). We thank Sandra Deline, Patricia Jensen, and Asma Omari for their assistance in gathering these data.
2. Although not precisely the analogous situation, one can think of the example of Latin categories being imposed on English standards. Some may remember their high-school English teachers telling us not to split infinitives. Yet, we also know that this is common in spoken English (I want to explicitly state . . .). The origin of this rule of English is from Latin, where infinitives are one word (as in Romance languages today) and therefore cannot be split. The rule, as applied to English, is inappropriate in that it results from the imposition of the category of one language onto another.
3. Within the second-language literature, the idea of "spontaneous utterance" is generally opposed to forced elicitation. The latter refers to language samples gathered in an experimental context.
4. This could be a simplification strategy of a common kind: the one-to-many principle, where one form is used for several functions (see Rutherford, 1987).
5. The concept "covert error" was established by Corder (1967) to describe the situation in which the learner has a grammatically correct target-like form, but the form is semantically or pragmatically inappropriate. Corder provided an example in which an NS of German said, "You mustn't take off your hat," when he intended to say, "You don't have to take off your hat."

3. Where do Data Come From?

1.   There is a theoretical distinction to be made between grammaticality judgments and acceptability judgments, despite the fact that the two terms are often used interchangeably. The former, in strict linguistic terms, refers to those sentences that are generated by the grammar, whereas the latter refers to those sentences about which speakers have a feel of well-formedness. As a theoretical construct, grammaticality judgments are not directly accessible, but are inferred through acceptability judgments.

2.   VSO order is somewhat limited in Italian. It can be used for stress (as in the example, 3-25). With a noun rather than a pronoun, there is often a pause after the subject.

3.   The explanation for this phenomenon takes one of two directions. First, one explanation put forth by Freedman and Forster (1985) is that, when a grammatical sentence is seen, a high-level representation of the sentence is immediately created; when a second sentence is seen, a second high-level representation is also immediately created. It is these high-level representations that are matched. In the case of certain ungrammatical sentences, one cannot create a high-level representation, and some less-efficient mechanism must be at work. The second explanation that has been put forth is that by Crain and Fodor (1987), who argue that, in both instances (grammatical and ungrammatical sentences), high-level representations are created, but, in the case of ungrammatical sentences, an individual first creates a so-called corrected version before matching takes place. What slows down the matching process for ungrammatical sentences is the time it takes to make the correction.

4.   More detail is presented in Chapter 9 concerning the acquisition of RCs. Below is preliminary information to make it easier to interpret the tables in this section. Both tables list six types of RCs. These different types refer to the syntactic role of the noun that is being modified in the RC. Below are examples, with the first sentence exemplifying the type of RC. The second sentence in each type has a resumptive pronoun. These latter are indicated with an * because they are not acceptable in standard Englsh (even though they are, at times, used).

Subject RC:
> That's the little boy [*who* ran away] (*who* is the subject of the clause in [ ])
> *That's the little boy who *he* ran away.

Direct-object RC:
> That's the man [*whom* I saw yesterday] (*whom* is the object of the clause in [ ])
> *That's the man whom I saw *him* yesterday.

Indirect-object RC:
> That's the little girl [to *whom* I gave the letter].
> *That's the little girl to whom I gave *her* the letter

Object-of-preposition RC:
> That's the man [*whom* I told you about].
> *That's the man whom I told you about *him*.

Genitive RC:
> That's the dog [*whose* owner I know].
> *That's the man who *his* owner I know.

Object-of-comparative RC:

> That's the woman [*whom* I am taller than].
> *That's the woman whom I am taller than *her.*

4. The Role of the Native Language: An Historical Overview

1. During the 1960s, there were entire books devoted to contrasting the structures of two languages (Agard & Di Pietro, 1965a, 1965b; Stockwell et al., 1965a, 1965b).
2. Those working on linguistic analysis during this period of time (e.g., Bloomfield, Sapir) were primarily involved with languages for which there was no writing system. This may have influenced their views on the primacy of speech over writing. Writing, in this earlier view, was seen as a means of transcribing oral language. "Writing is not language, but merely a way of recording language by means of visible marks" (Bloomfield, 1933, p. 21).
3. There are two distinct traditions of contrastive analysis that emerged. In the North American tradition, the emphasis was on language teaching and, by implication, language learning. Contrastive analyses were conducted with the ultimate goal of improving classroom materials. As Fisiak (1991) noted, this is more appropriately considered "applied contrastive analysis." In the European tradition, the goal of contrastive analysis was not pedagogical. Rather, the goal of language comparison was to gain a greater understanding of language. Within the European tradition, contrastive analysis is a subdiscipline of linguistics, and its goal is to understand the nature of language. In this book, we focus on the North American tradition, as it relates more directly to the field of SLA.
4. Zobl (1980) hypothesized that this discrepancy occurs owing to other factors of the L2. For French speakers learning English, the fact that English always has verb–object order (with both noun and pronominal objects) does not allow the French speaker to find any similarity between the NL and the TL with regard to pronominal placement. Thus, the NS of French is thwarted in his or her efforts to find congruence. However, the NS of English does find congruence between the NL and the TL. Word order of the type verb–object does occur in French (although only with noun objects). Furthermore, the object–verb order seems to be a more complex construction than the verb–object one, with French children showing a bias toward the latter. Hence, one can still employ the concept of NL influence, although clearly not in a simple way, as was predicted by a behaviorist theory.
5. Intralingual errors are also known as developmental errors. The claim here is that they are common to all language learners, thereby being part of language development.

5. The Transition Period

1. There are many interesting issues that surround the acquisition of sign language. We deal with L2 learning by deaf and hard-of-hearing learners in Chapter 15.
2. Foster-Cohen (1999) stated that, although smiling may occur as early as the third week of life, it may not have the precise meaning it has in later life.
3. This assumes that the *I'm* is part of the progressive.
4. These terms are often used without this original technical use of these terms. In this book, the terms *learning* and *acquisition* are used interchangeably.
5. Krashen (1985, p. 2) hypothesized that only two conditions need to be met: focus on form and knowledge of rule. The condition of time was dropped after research by Hulstijn and Hulstijn (1984) showed that, when there was no focus on form, the time condition was no longer valid. In other words, focus on form did make a difference, but, without it, learners did not perform differently as a function of time limits.

6. Alternative Approaches to the Role of Previously Known Languages

1. Some studies (e.g., Felser et al., 2003; Papadopoulo & Clahsen, 2003) have shown different results using a different methodology (eye-tracking in some studies, versus self-paced reading in others). Frenck-Mestre, however, argues that this may be owing to the proficiency level or the mixed results within a group, which could have nullified the transfer effect.

7. Formal Approaches to SLA

1. A notable exception comes from one of the authors of this book who, during a recent trip to New Zealand, had a difficult time resetting her driving parameter from right (United States) to left (New Zealand). She frequently found herself straddling the middle and was thankful for the paucity of cars on many of the roads in New Zealand.

2. In actuality, there is a third type of evidence: *indirect negative evidence*. As Chomsky (1981, p. 9) stated:

   > a not unreasonable acquisition system can be devised with the operative principle that if certain structures or rules fail to be exemplified in relatively simple expressions, where they would be expected to be found, then a (possibly marked) option is selected excluding them in the grammar, so that a kind of "negative evidence" can be available even without corrections, adverse reactions, etc.

   Plough (1994) claimed that the term *indirect negative evidence* is a misnomer, because it is not a form of indirect correction, or any sort of correction. Rather, she claimed the term is an "indirect means of letting the learner know that a feature is not possible because it is never present in the *expected* environment" (p. 30). It may be easier to understand this concept in SLA than in first, because a crucial part of the notion rests on the concept *expected environment*. Essentially, there are two choices for these expectations: (a) from the innately specified principles and parameters of Universal Grammar or (b) from the first language (or other languages known).

   An example can be provided from the animal world. In certain types of primates, babies must learn the difference between predatory birds and nonpredatory birds. In the case of the former, the entire community screeches loudly when these birds approach. However, in the case of nonpredatory birds, the absence of screeches (in the context that screeches are to be expected) provides information to the babies that allows them to distinguish between predatory and nonpredatory birds.

3. This is, of course, a performance-level phenomenon and does not directly relate to learners' underlying knowledge of a language system. It only relates to the ways in which that knowledge system is put to use.

4. Even though this new lexical item has permeated the English lexicon, the spelling is not yet codified; *Time* uses *dotcoms*; *Newsweek* uses *dot-com*.

5. This practice, which is less common today than it once was, is akin to the practice of a woman taking her husband's name.

6. In fact, U.S. policy in Iraq has been framed in terms of preposition substitution; as President Bush and acolytes, during his term in office, said numerous times: We will stand DOWN when the Iraquis stand UP.

7. The interested reader might also want to refer to the Interpretability Hypothesis (Hawkins & Hattori, 2006; Tsimpli & Dimitrakopoulou, 2007) for a related approach.

8. A comparable distinction between approaches to L2 morphological difficulties has been described in the processing literature. For example, Jiang (2004) delineates a Competence Deficit Approach from a Performance Deficit Approach. The former holds that learners' difficulties with L2 morphology are due to representational or competence deficits arising from incomplete acquisition, whereas the Performance Deficit Approach claims that such problems are based at the level of processing or control, in that learners are not able to readily access the morphological knowledge that they have internalized.

9. For those familiar with the theory on which this is based, this violation occurs because elements cannot jump over more than one bounding node. In English, IP and NP are bounding nodes. The underlying structure of the sentence is as follows:

$$[_{CP}Who_i \ do \ [_{IP} \ you \ agree \ with \ [_{NP} \ the \ idea \ [_{CP} \ that \ [_{IP} \ David \ loves \ t_i]]]]]$$

Hence, the movement of the question word to the front of the sentence involves jumping over three nodes and, therefore, is a violation of subjacency.

10. See White (1989) for a theoretical discussion of alternative explanations for Schachter's data.

11. White (2003) presents data from Kellerman et al. (1999) that purport to refute the claims of Kanno, arguing that Kellerman et al.'s data do not truly reflect the conclusions that they came to.

12. Arabic is similar to Spanish in that it allows optional pronouns in subject position. Japanese allows zero topics that can be either subjects or objects. As far as word order is concerned, Arabic has verb–subject word order as basic; Japanese is rigidly verb-final and, hence, does not allow verb–subject order. Japanese does not allow *that*-trace; Arabic is more complex in that extraction of a subject is dependent on the main verb.

13. The analogy is, of course, limited as, in a kaleidoscope, the elements in the system are fixed. No new elements can enter or leave. This is not the same with SLA, where new elements/patterns are added, as is the case when a new grammatical structure is learned.

14. Voicing contrasts (i.e., the difference between voiced and voiceless sounds) have to do with whether or not the vocal cords are vibrating during speech. They distinguish between a number of sounds that are made with the same tongue and lip position. Examples are sounds such as [b] and [p] and [s] and [z].

8. The Lexicon

1. Receptive vocabulary is often referred to as passive vocabulary. This term is inappropriate in that receptive knowledge of vocabulary is not passive at all. Learners are actively involved in the use of receptive knowledge.

2. Chunking is a concept associated with working-memory capacity. In general 7 (+/-2) is the average amount of information that we can hold in active memory, as determined by looking at responses to a digit span task (see Chapter 10). To understand this concept, consider the following sequence of numbers: 5821647856231548. If you were to hear the numbers, you would be hard-pressed to remember them in order. If, on the other hand, you were to hear the following sequence of numbers, 1111222233334444, you could probably remember them more easily, even though the number of numbers is the same. That is because we can chunk the numbers into units (presumably 1111, 2222, 3333, 4444), thereby reducing the memory burden.

3. Interestingly, although Levelt did not note this fact, English used to have a three-way distinction, with the additional term *yon*, with the word *yonder* and *hither and yon* being relics of that distinction.

4. See also Hatch and Hawkins (1985), Kempen (1977, 1978), and Kempen and Hoenkamp (1981, 1987).

9. Typological and Functional Approaches

1. See note 4 in Chapter 3 for an explanation of these RC types.

2. The interested reader is referred to Keenan and Comrie (1977) and Comrie and Keenan (1979) for further elaboration on their claim and on possible exceptions.

3. See Fox (1987) and Keenan (1975) for further elaboration.

4. For an explanation of the unpredicted findings of the genitive, refer to Gass (1979a, 1979b).

5. As with the results of the Gass study, the genitive results in Hyltenstam's study were out of hierarchical order.

6. There are exceptions to this generalization in these data that are accounted for by assuming that these learners have an optional rule of devoicing rather than an obligatory one. They are represented by /p/, /t/, /k/, /f/, /s/, /θ/ (*th* as in *forth*), /ʃ/ (as in *shin*), /tʃ/ (as in *church*), /b/, /d/, /g/, /v/, /z/ /ð/ (as in *then*), /dž/ (as in *judge*).

7. NP refers to noun phrase. T-Units are defined as "one main clause plus any subordinate clause or nonclausal structure that is attached to or embedded in it" (Hunt, 1970, p. 4).

8. See Gass and Ard (1980) for an explanation based on prototypicality and core meanings.

10. Looking at Interlanguage Processing

1. Thanks go to Caroline Latham for bringing this example to our attention.

2. U-shaped learning is documented in the child language literature, as well as in other areas of cognition (see Carlucci et al., 2005).

3. Numerous commentaries can be found in *Applied Psycholinguistics* (2006), volume *27*, issue 1.

4. Some successful network simulations of L2 learner data were reviewed by Broeder and Plunkett (1994).

5. As might be predicted, the picture is more complex. L1/L2 cue similarities/differences, cue type (grammatical vs. semantic), and L2 proficiency all interact to produce the observed patterns. For example, Japanese ESL learners actually continue to use case-marking cues as their dominant strategy in the L2, but they do rely on animacy more heavily than in their NL (see Sasaki, 1994). In Heilenman and McDonald (1993) and McDonald and Heilenman (1992), English learners of French quickly lost their L1 word-order strategy, yet did not show stronger animacy-cue use. Dutch learners of English and English learners of Dutch, similarly, transferred inappropriate L1 grammatical strategies, but showed no animacy effect (McDonald, 1987).

6. Van Valin (1991) has shown that, in languages where aspect is expressed through morphology, it is acquired before or at the same time as tense, but never after.

7. This is similar to the case in French immersion brought up earlier (Harley & Swain, 1984), where the learner equates one word in the IL (e.g., *j'ai*, with two words in the target, producing forms like *j'ai as*.

11. Interlanguage in Context

1. There were two acceptable TL variants in this study, given that these speakers were living in New York City, where there is great variation as to the acceptable form.
2. Major (1987) argued against Beebe's interpretation of the source of the variants. He pointed out that, in Thai, the trilled /r/ characterizes formal speech, but, in running speech (reading of sentences in Thai), a variant similar to an American /r/ occurs. Major claimed that, in the English of these speakers, the prevalence of the trilled /r/ in formal speech and that of the American /r/ in casual conversation are both due to transfer.
3. We thank LeAnne Spino for this suggestion and for providing the table.
4. Clearly, these are not the only areas of L2 study. Rather, they are taken as examples of what legitimately is part of SLA and what needs to be argued to be a part of SLA.
5. Interestingly, the term *learning strategy* seems to be rooted in a neighboring field (psychology); the term *communication strategy* seems indigenous to early SLA. Selinker (1972) attributes the term to Coulter (1968). The data from his study are described in Selinker (1992, Chapter 5).

12. Input, Interaction, and Output

1. In a matched-guise format, the same speaker is used for two different sets of tape-recorded utterances or passages. Listeners are then asked to characterize the speakers according to a variety of possible attributes, which vary depending on the purpose of the study in question.
2. Within the field of conversation analysis, these are often seen as continuers, whose function it is to keep the conversation going. As Varonis and Gass (1985b) pointed out in their discussion of "conversational continuants," these utterances are often ambiguous; it is not always possible to determine whether their function is to keep the conversation going or to indicate understanding.
3. As with other kinds of learning, one must put one's knowledge to use. One cannot imagine learning how to play tennis by watching, observing, and understanding the motions involved. Parts of the game of tennis can be learned that way (e.g., knowledge of the rules of the game, strategies), but actual implementation cannot.
4. In actuality, only the past-tense part of the study could be analyzed owing to the paucity of examples of plural markers that could be corrected in the experimental group.
5. We are not including here so-called "reading knowledge" of a language, necessary for many graduate degree programs. In those instances, it may indeed be possible to know little of the syntax (perhaps other than basic word-order phenomena) and to rely on lexical knowledge and knowledge of the subject matter as the sole decoding cues. It is often the case that individuals who have "reading knowledge" are incapable of encoding that language or of decoding the language in anything but a written format.
6. This is in some sense reminiscent of early work by Zobl (1982), who, in discussions of the role of the NL, noted that NL background affects the speed at which certain developmental stages are transversed.

13. Instructed Second Language Learning

1. In this discussion of focus on form, we do not intend to imply that language is the only aspect focused on. McNeill et al. (1994) suggested that we also pay attention to communication through gesture and integrate gestural information with verbal information. We are grateful to Elizabeth Hauge for pointing this reference out to us.

2. Keenan (1975) reported that, in a comparison between a sophisticated writer (in this case, a philosopher) and tabloid newspaper writers, there was a greater amount of lower-position use of RCs among the former.

14. Nonlanguage Influences

1. The phenomenon of fossilization seemed to force early SLA researchers, working within a contrastive-analysis framework (e.g., Nemser, 1961; Brière, 1966, 1968; Selinker, 1966), into independently positing intermediate linguistic systems that, in some sense, did not always exhibit perceptible change. These systems were thought to be "intermediate" between, and different from, the NL and the TL, an "approximative" system in Nemser's terms. Fossilization is a much discussed, yet little understood, SLA concept.

2. Note that these figures do not have the same scale.

3. Coppieters' data are based on elicitations of grammaticality judgments. This elicitation methodology focuses on a determination of a learner's knowledge. It is important to note that, whereas grammaticality judgment tasks are frequently used as an indirect *reflection* of competence, they in no way *directly* reflect competence.

4. In cultures where modified input, as is known in Western cultures, does not exist, speech to children nonetheless differs from that addressed to adults. Schieffelin (1986) reported on the acquisition of Kaluli, pointing out that, when small children are addressed, it is often a "language instruction" format. Speech will be preceded by *a:la:ma*, which translates as "Say like that." This serves the function of "framing" the speech and may serve a similar function to the modifications used in Western cultures.

5. This situation often sees the rise of pidgin varieties of language.

6. Cohen and Macaro (2007) acknowledge this difficulty and suggest the cover term *language-learner strategies*.

7. Strategizing is not confined to language learning and appears to be basic to human cognition. An example of nonlanguage-learning strategizing would be in the area of the learning of hatha yoga. To learn to get "deeply" into some postures, it is usually thought necessary to "warm up" with simpler yoga postures. Suppose you are a runner and, instead of doing your yoga stretching first, you realize that you can learn to get deeper into difficult yoga practice *after* you do your running, then you will probably tend to continue with this strategy. The interested reader may wish to turn to Riding and Rayner (1998) or Riding (2002, 2003), where many of the general problems of strategy learning and identification are discussed in more general cognitive terms.

8. Dörnyei (2005, 2006) introduces the conundrum of what exactly a learning strategy is. He provides the following example:

    > If someone memorises vocabulary by simply looking at a bilingual vocabulary list, most people would say that this is an example of learning. But if the person applies some colour marking code to highlight the words in the list which he or she still does not know, suddenly we can start talking about strategic learning. But what is the difference? The colour code?

    > (2006, p. 57)

    See Grenfell and Macaro (2007) for a counter-argument.

9. McDonough (1999, p. 2), in a useful review of the literature, pointed out that "strategies have been isolated and described" in a wide area (e.g., learning an L2, learning to learn, learning to use the L2, learning to communicate, learning to compensate for communication breakdowns, and in macro-skill areas, such as reading, writing, and

so forth). Given this range, he pointed to a change in some parts of the literature away from the term *learning strategies* to use of the term *learner strategies*, where the emphasis shifts to the learner as "a problem-solver and reflective organizer" (p. 2) of the knowledge and skills necessary for "effective language use" (p. 2).

15. Related Disciplines

1. This may be an oversimplification, because there is also variation from individual to individual within each of these disciplines.
2. Valdés (2001a) points out that, up until 1996, heritage speakers of Spanish had been primarily referred to as NSs of Spanish.

16. An Integrated View of Second Language Acquisition

1. Much of this chapter is based on an article entitled, "Integrating research areas: A framework for second language studies," originally published as Gass (1988a).
2. See Beebe (1985) for an extensive discussion of the role of different types and sources of input.
3. This issue is related to the general notion of salience and to what is noticed. For example, phonological salience owing to syllable stress may result in a form being noticed to a greater extent than unstressed syllables.
4. In many cases, learners will find themselves engaged in a conversation with an NS and know beforehand that they will understand very little. The learners may do nothing more than provide minimal feedback to the NS so as not to appear rude, while at the same time tune out completely to the conversation. This is likely the case of the NNS in Chapter 12, who called about the price of TV sets.
5. One could also imagine the reanalysis coming from the other direction. A learner might encounter *apple juice*. Once the learner realizes *apple juice* is made up of two words, that knowledge could serve as a trigger for reanalysis of the original *orangejuice*.

References

Abrahamsson, N., & Hyltenstam, K. (2009). Age of onset and nativelikeness in a second language: Listener perception versus linguistic scrutiny. *Language Learning*, *59*, 249–306.

Adams, A.-M., & Guillot, K. (2008). Working memory and writing in bilingual students. *International Journal of Applied Linguistics*, *156*, 13–28.

Adamson, H. D. (1988). *Variation theory and second language acquisition*. Washington, DC: Georgetown University Press.

Adi-Japha, E. J., Banbrich-Artzi, J., & Libnawi, A. (2010). Cognitive flexibility in drawings of bilingual children. *Child Development*, *81*, 1356–1366.

Adjemian, C. (1976). On the nature of interlanguage systems. *Language Learning*, *26*, 297–320.

Adjemian, C. (1983). The transferability of lexical properties. In S. Gass & L. Selinker (Eds.), *Language transfer in language learning* (pp. 250–268). Rowley, MA: Newbury House.

Agard, F., & Di Pietro, R. (1965a). *The sounds of English and Italian*. Chicago: University of Chicago Press.

Agard, F., & Di Pietro, R. (1965b). *The grammatical structures of English and Italian*. Chicago: University of Chicago Press.

Akhmatova, O. (1974). *Word–combination: Theory and method*. Moscow: Izdatel'stvo Moskovskogo Universiteta.

Akmajian, A., Demers, R., Farmer, A., & Harnish, R. (1995). *Linguistics: An introduction to language and communication*. Cambridge, MA: MIT Press.

Albirini, A., Benmamoun, E., & Saadah, E. (2011). Grammatical features of Egyptian and Palestinian Arabic heritage speakers' oral production. *Studies in Second Language Acquisition*, *33*, 273–303.

Alcón Soler, E. (2007). Incidental focus on form, noticing and vocabulary learning in the EFL classroom. *International Journal of English Studies*, *7*, 41–60.

Alcón Soler, E., & García Mayo, M. P. (2008). Incidental focus on form and learning outcomes with young foreign language classroom learners. In J. Philp, R. Oliver, & A. Mackey (Eds.), *Second language acquisition and the younger learner* (pp. 173–192). Philadelphia: John Benjamins.

Alexander, R. (1982). Vocabulary acquisition and the "advanced learner of English": A brief survey of the issues. *Arbeiten aus Anglistik und Amerikanistik*, *7*, 59–75.

Aljaafreh, A., & Lantolf, J. (1994). Negative feedback as regulation and second language learning in the zone of proximal development. *The Modern Language Journal*, *78*, 465–483.

Allport, A. (1989). Visual attention. In M. Posner (Ed.), *Foundations of cognitive science* (pp. 631–682). MIT Press, Cambridge, MA.

Altman, G. (1990). Cognitive models of speech processing: An introduction. In G. Altman (Ed.), *Cognitive models of speech processing: Psycholinguistic and computational perspectives* (pp. 1–23). Cambridge, MA: MIT Press.

The American Heritage Book of English Usage (1996). Boston, New York: Houghton Mifflin Harcourt.

American Psychological Association (2010). *Publication manual of the American Psychological Association* (6th ed.). Washington, DC: American Psychological Association.

Ammar, A., & Lightbown, P. M. (2003). Teaching marked linguistic structures—more about the acquisition of relative clauses by Arab learners of English. In A. Housen & M. Pierrard (Eds.), *Investigations in instructed second language learning* (pp. 167–198). Berlin, Germany: Mouton de Gruyter.

Ammar, A., & Spada, N. (2006). One size fits all? Recasts, prompts and L2 learning. *Studies in Second Language Acquisition*, *28*, 543–574.

Andersen, R. (1976, March). *A functor acquisition study in Puerto Rico*. Paper presented at the 10th annual meeting of the Teachers of English to Speakers of Other Languages, New York.

Andersen, R. (1977). The impoverished state of cross–sectional morpheme acquisition accuracy methodology. In C. Henning (Ed.), *Proceedings of the Second Language Research Forum* (pp. 308–319). Los Angeles: University of California, Department of Applied Linguistics.

Andersen, R. (1983). Transfer to somewhere. In S. Gass & L. Selinker (Eds.), *Language transfer in language learning* (pp. 177–201). Rowley, MA: Newbury House.

Andersen, R. (1984). The one-to-one principle of interlanguage construction. *Language Learning*, *34*, 77–95.

Andersen, R. (1986). El desarrollo de la morfologia verbal en el español como segundo idioma [The development of verbal morphology in Spanish as a second language]. In J. Meisel (Ed.), *Adquisición de lenguaje/Aquisição da linguagem* [Acquisition of language] (pp. 115–138). Frankfurt, Germany: Vervuert.

Andersen, R. (1990). Models, processes, principles and strategies: Second language acquisition inside and outside the classroom. In B. VanPatten & J. F. Lee (Eds.), *Second language acquisition–foreign language learning* (pp. 45–78). Clevedon, UK: Multilingual Matters.

Andersen, R. (1991). Developmental sequences: The emergence of aspect marking in second language acquisition. In T. Huebner & C. Ferguson (Eds.), *Crosscurrents in second language acquisition and linguistic theories* (pp. 305–324). Amsterdam: John Benjamins.

Andersen, R., & Shirai, Y. (1994). Discourse motivations for some cognitive acquisition principles. *Studies in Second Language Acquisition*, *16*, 133–156.

Andersen, R., & Shirai, Y. (1996). The primacy of aspect in first and second language acquisition: The pidgin–creole connection. In W. Ritchie & T. Bhatia (Eds.), *Handbook of second language acquisition* (pp. 527–570). San Diego, CA: Academic Press.

Anderson, J. (1987). The markedness differential hypothesis and syllable structure difficulty. In G. Ioup & S. Weinberger (Eds.), *Interlanguage phonology* (pp. 279–291). Rowley, MA: Newbury House.

Antinucci, F., & Miller, R. (1976). How children talk about what happened. *Journal of Child Language*, *3*, 167–189.

Aoyama, K., Flege, J., Guion, S., Yamada, T., & Akahane-Yamada, R. (2004). Perceived phonetic dissimilarity and L2 speech learning: The case of Japanese /r/ and English /l/ and /r/. *Journal of Phonetics*, *23*, 233–250.

Ard, J. (1989). A constructivist perspective on non–native phonology. In S. Gass & J. Schachter (Eds.), *Linguistic perspectives on second language acquisition* (pp. 243–259). Cambridge, UK: Cambridge University Press.

Ard, J., & Gass, S. (1987). Lexical constraints on syntactic acquisition. *Studies in Second Language Acquisition*, *9*, 235–255.

Ard, J., & Homburg, T. (1983). Verification of language transfer. In S. Gass & L. Selinker (Eds.), *Language transfer in language learning* (pp. 157–176). Rowley, MA: Newbury House.

Ard, J., & Homburg, T. (1992). Verification of language transfer. In S. Gass & L. Selinker (Eds.), *Language transfer in language learning* (2nd ed., pp. 47–70). Amsterdam: John Benjamins.

Ardila, A. (2003). Language representation and working memory with bilinguals. *Journal of Communication Disorders*, *36*, 233–240.

Ardila, A., Rosselli, M., Ostrosky-Sois, F., Marcos, J., Granda, G., & Soto, M. (2000). Syntactic comprehension, verbal memory, and calculation abilities in Spanish–English bilinguals. *Applied Neuropsychology*, *7*, 3–16.

Arnold, J. (Ed.) (1999). *Affect in language learning*. Cambridge, UK: Cambridge University Press.

Aston, G. (1986). Trouble-shooting in interaction with learners: The more the merrier? *Applied Linguistics*, *7*, 128–143.

Au, T. K., Knightly, L., Jun, S.-Ah., & Oh, J. (2002). Overhearing a language during childhood. *Psychological Science*, *13*(3), 238–243.

Ayoun, D., & Salaberry, R. (2008). The expression of temporality in English as a foreign language by French native speakers. *Language Learning*, *58*, 555–595.

Baddeley, A. D. (2000). The episodic buffer: A new component of working memory? *Trends in Cognitive Sciences*, *4*, 417–423.

Baddeley, A. D. (2003a). Working memory and language: An overview. *Journal of Communication Disorders*, *36*, 189–208.

Baddeley, A. D. (2003b). Working memory: Looking back and looking forward. *Neuroscience*, *4*, 829–839.

Baddeley, A. D., & Hitch, G. (1974). Working memory. In G. H. Bower (Ed.), *The psychology of learning and motivation* (pp. 47–90). New York: Academic Press.

Bader, M., & Häussler, J. (2010). Toward a model of grammaticality judgments. *Journal of Linguistics*, *46*, 273–330.

Bailey, K. M. (1983). Competitiveness and anxiety in adult second language learning: Looking at and through the diary studies. In H. W. Seliger & M. H. Long (Eds.), *Classroom oriented research in second language acquisition* (pp. 67–103). Rowley, MA: Newbury House.

Bailey, N., Madden, C., & Krashen, S. (1974). Is there a "natural sequence" in adult second language learning? *Language Learning*, *24*, 235–243.

Baker, C. L. (1979). Syntactic theory and the projection problem. *Linguistic Inquiry, 10*, 533–581.

Baker, C., & Prys Jones, S. (Eds.) (1998). *Encyclopedia of bilingualism and bilingual education*. Clevedon, UK: Multilingual Matters.

Bard, E., Robertson, D., & Sorace, A. (1996). Magnitude estimation of linguistic acceptability. *Language, 72*, 32–68.

Bardovi-Harlig, K. (1987). Markedness and salience in second–language acquisition. *Language Learning, 37*, 385–407.

Bardovi-Harlig, K. (1992a). The relationship of form and meaning: A cross–sectional study of tense and aspect in the interlanguage of learners of English as a second language. *Applied Psycholinguistics, 13*, 253–278.

Bardovi-Harlig, K. (1992b). The use of adverbials and natural order in the development of temporal expression. *International Review of Applied Linguistics, 30*, 299–320.

Bardovi-Harlig, K. (1994). Anecdote or evidence? Evaluating support for hypotheses concerning the development of tense and aspect. In E. Tarone, A. Cohen, & S. Gass (Eds.), *Research methodology in second language acquisition* (pp. 41–60). Hillsdale, NJ: Lawrence Erlbaum Associates.

Bardovi-Harlig, K. (1998). Narrative structure and lexical aspect: Conspiring factors in second language acquisition of tense–aspect morphology. *Studies in Second Language Acquisition, 20*, 471–508.

Bardovi-Harlig, K. (1999a). From morpheme studies to temporal semantics: Tense–aspect research in SLA. *Studies in Second Language Acquisition, 21*, 341–382.

Bardovi-Harlig, K. (1999b). Exploring the interlanguage of interlanguage pragmatics: A research agenda for acquisitional pragmatics. *Language Learning, 49*, 677–713.

Bardovi-Harlig, K. (2000). *Tense and aspect in second language acquisition: Form, meaning, and use*. Malden, MA: Blackwell.

Bardovi-Harlig, K. (2004a). The emergence of grammaticalized future expression in longitudinal production data. In B. VanPatten, J. Williams, S. Rott, & M. Overstreet (Eds.), *Form-meaning connections in second language acquisition* (pp. 115–137). Mahwah, NJ: Erlbaum.

Bardovi-Harlig, K. (2004b). Monopolizing the future OR How the *go*-future breaks into *will*'s territory and what it tells us about SLA. In S. Foster Cohen (Ed.), *EuroSLA yearbook* (pp. 177–201). Amsterdam: Benjamins.

Bardovi-Harlig, K. (2004c). *Pragmatic competence of the advanced learner*. Unpublished manuscript, Indiana University.

Bardovi-Harlig, K. (2005). The future of desire: Lexical futures and modality in L2 English future expression. In L. Dekydtspotter, R. A. Sprouse, & A. Liljestrand (Eds.), *Proceedings of the 7th Generative Approaches to Second Language Acquisition Conference (GASLA 2004)* (pp. 1–12). Somerville, MA: Cascadilla Press.

Bardovi-Harlig, K. (2006). Interlanguage development: Main routes and individual paths. In K. Bardovi-Harlig & Z. Dörnyei (Eds.), *Themes in SLA Research, AILA Review, 19* (pp. 69–82). Amsterdam: John Benjamins.

Bardovi-Harlig, K. (2007). One functional approach to second language acquisition: The concept-oriented approach. In B. VanPatten & J. Williams (Eds.), *Theories in second language acquisition: An introduction* (pp. 57–75). Mahwah, NJ: Lawrence Erlbaum Associates.

Bardovi-Harlig, K. (2012). Pragmatics in second language acquisition. In S. Gass & A. Mackey (Eds.), *The Routledge handbook of second language acquisition* (pp. 147–162). New York: Routledge.

Bardovi-Harlig, K., & Bergström, A. (1996). The acquisition of tense and aspect in SLA and FLL: A study of learner narratives in English (SL) and French (FL). *Canadian Modern Language Review, 52*, 308–330.

Bardovi-Harlig, K., & Dörnyei, Z. (1998). Do language learners recognize pragmatic violations? Pragmatic versus grammatical awareness in instructed L2 learning. *TESOL Quarterly, 32*, 233–262.

Bardovi-Harlig, K., & Reynolds, D. W. (1995). The role of lexical aspect in the acquisition of tense and aspect. *TESOL Quarterly, 29*, 107–131.

Bates, E., & MacWhinney, B. (1981). Second language acquisition from a functionalist perspective: Pragmatics, semantics and perceptual strategies. In H. Winitz (Ed.), *Annals of the New York Academy of Sciences Conference on Native Language and Foreign Language Acquisition* (pp. 190–214). New York: New York Academy of Sciences.

Bates, E., & MacWhinney, B. (1982). Functionalist approach to grammar. In E. Wanner & L. Gleitman (Eds.), *Language acquisition: The state of the art* (pp. 173–218). New York: Cambridge University Press.

Bayley, R., & Preston, D. (Eds.) (1996). *Second language acquisition and linguistic variation*. Amsterdam: John Benjamins.

Bayley, R., & Tarone, E. (2012). Variationist perspectives. In S. Gass & A. Mackey (Eds.), *The Routledge handbook of second language acquisition* (pp. 41–56). New York: Routledge.

Becker, A. L. (1991). Language and languaging. *Language & Communication, 11*, 33–35.

Beebe, L. (1980). Sociolinguistic variation and style shifting in second language acquisition. *Language Learning, 30*, 433–447.

Beebe, L. (1985). Input: Choosing the right stuff. In S. Gass & C. Madden (Eds.), *Input in second language acquisition* (pp. 404–430). Rowley, MA: Newbury House.

Beebe, L., & Takahashi, T. (1989). Do you have a bag?: Social status and patterned variation in second language acquisition. In S. Gass, C. Madden, D. Preston, & L. Selinker (Eds.), *Variation in second language acquisition: Discourse and pragmatics* (pp. 103–125). Clevedon, UK: Multilingual Matters.

Beebe, L., Takahashi, T., & Uliss-Weltz, R. (1990). Pragmatic transfer in ESL refusals. In R. C. Scarcella, E. S. Andersen, & S. D. Krashen (Eds.), *Developing communicative competence in a second language* (pp. 55–73). New York: Newbury House.

Beebe, L., & Zuengler, J. (1983). Accommodation theory: An explanation for style shifting in second language dialects. In N. Wolfson & E. Judd (Eds.), *Sociolinguistics and second language acquisition* (pp. 195–213). Rowley, MA: Newbury House.

Behney, J. (2008, October). *L2 syntactic priming of Italian relative clauses*. Presented at the Second Language Research Forum (SLRF) Conference, University of Hawai'i Manoa, Honolulu, HI.

Behney, J. & Gass, S. (in press). Interaction and the Noun Phrase Accessibility Hierarchy: A study using syntactic priming. In J. Schwieter (Ed.), *Innovative research and practices in second language acquisition and bilingualism*. Amsterdam: John Benjamins.

Benati, A. (2004). The effects of structured input activities and explicit information on the acquisition of the Italian future tense. In B. VanPatten (Ed.), *Processing instruction: Theory, research, and commentary* (pp. 207–225). Mahwah, NJ: Lawrence Erlbaum Associates.

Berko, J. (1958). The child's learning of English morphology. *Word, 14*, 150–177.

Berman, I. M., Buchbinder, V. A., & Beznedeznych, M. L. (1968). Formirovanie potentialnogo slovarnogo pri obu(enii russkomu jazyku kak inostannomu [Forming a potential vocabulary in teaching Russian as a foreign language]. *Russkij jazyk za rubez(om, 4*, 57–60.

Bernaus, M., & Gardner, R. C. (2008). Teacher motivation strategies, student perceptions, student motivation, and English achievement. *The Modern Language Journal, 92*, 387–401.

Bhatia, T. (2006). Introduction to part I. In T. Bhatia & W. Ritchie (Eds.), *The handbook of bilingualism* (pp. 5–6). Malden, MA: Blackwell.

Bhatia, T. & Ritchie, W. (Eds.) (2006). *The handbook of bilingualism*. Malden, MA: Blackwell.

Bialystok, E. (1978). A theoretical model of second language learning. *Language Learning, 28*, 69–84.

Bialystok, E. (1987). Words as things: Development of word concept by bilingual children. *Studies in Second Language Acquisition, 9*, 133–140.

Bialystok, E. (1988). Levels of bilingualism and levels of linguistic awareness. *Developmental Psychology, 24*, 560–567.

Bialystok, E. (1990). *Communication strategies*. Oxford, UK: Basil Blackwell.

Bialystok, E. (2001a). *Bilingualism in development: Language, literacy and cognition*. Cambridge, UK: Cambridge University Press.

Bialystok, E. (2001b). Metalinguistic aspects of bilingual processing. *Annual Review of Applied Linguistics, 21*, 169–181.

Bialystok, E., & Hakuta, K. (1994). *In other words: The science and psychology of second-language acquisition*. New York: Basic Books.

Bialystok, E., & Sharwood Smith, M. (1985). Interlanguage is not a state of mind: An evaluation of the construct for second-language acquisition. *Applied Linguistics, 6*, 101–117.

Binon, J., & Cornu, A. M. (1985). A semantic approach to collocations: A means to reduce the random character of the co-occurrence of lexical items. *ABLA Papers, 9*, 37–61.

Birdsong, D. (1989). *Metalinguistic performance and interlinguistic competence*. New York: Springer Verlag.

Birdsong, D. (1992). Ultimate attainment in second language acquisition. *Language, 68*, 706–755.

Birdsong, D. (1999a). Introduction: Whys and why nots of the Critical Period Hypothesis for second language acquisition. In D. Birdsong (Ed.), *Second language acquisition and the critical period hypothesis* (pp. 1–22). Mahwah, NJ: Lawrence Erlbaum Associates.

Birdsong, D. (Ed.) (1999b). *Second language acquisition and the critical period hypothesis*. Mahwah, NJ. Lawrence Erlbaum Associates.

Blaas, L. (1982). *Fossilization in the advanced learner's lexicon*. Unpublished manuscript, University of Utrecht, Department of English, The Netherlands.

Bley-Vroman, R. (1983). The comparative fallacy in interlanguage studies: The case of systematicity. *Language Learning, 33*, 1–17.

Bley-Vroman, R. (1989). What is the logical problem of foreign language learning? In S. Gass & J. Schachter (Eds.), *Linguistic perspectives on second language acquisition* (pp. 41–68). Cambridge, UK: Cambridge University Press.

Bley-Vroman, R. (2009). The evolving context of the fundamental difference hypothesis. *Studies in Second Language Acquisition, 31*, 175–198.

Bley-Vroman, R., Felix, S., & Ioup, G. (1988). The accessibility of Universal Grammar in adult language learning. *Second Language Research, 4*, 1–32.

Bloomfield, L. (1933). *Language*. New York: Holt, Rinehart & Winston.

Blum-Kulka, S., & Levenston, E. (1987). Lexical–grammatical pragmatic indicators. *Studies in Second Language Acquisition, 9*, 155–170.

Bock, J. K. (1986). Syntactic persistence in language production. *Cognitive Psychology, 18*, 355–387.

Bock, J. K. (1989). Closed-class immanence in sentence production. *Cognition, 31*, 163–186.

Bock, J. K., & Griffin, Z. (2000). The persistence of structural priming: Transient activation or implicit learning? *Journal of Experimental Psychology: General, 129*, 177–192.

Bock, J. K., & Loebell, H. (1990). Framing sentences. *Cognition, 35*, 1–39.

Bogaards, P. (2001). Lexical units and the learning of foreign language vocabulary. *Studies in Second Language Acquisition, 23*, 321–343.

Bogaards, P., & Laufer, B. (Eds.) (2004). *Vocabulary in a second language: Selection, acquisition and testing*. Amsterdam: John Benjamins.

Borg, S. (2010). Language teacher research engagement. *Language Teaching, 43*, 391–429.

Bowles, M. (2010). *The think-aloud controversy in second language research*. New York: Routledge

Boyland, J. T., & Anderson, J. R. (1998). Evidence that syntactic priming is long-lasting. In *Proceedings of the 20th Annual Conference of the Cognitive Science Society* (p. 1205). Hillsdale, NJ: Erlbaum.

Brehm, J., & Self, E. A. (1989). The intensity of motivation. *Annual Review of Psychology, 40*, 109–131.

Brière, E. (1966). An investigation of phonological interference. *Language, 42*, 768–796.

Brière, E. (1968). *A psycholinguistic study of phonological interference*. The Hague, The Netherlands: Mouton.

Broeder, P., & Plunkett, K. (1994). Connectionism and second language acquisition. In N. Ellis (Ed.), *Implicit and explicit learning of languages* (pp. 421–453). San Diego, CA: Academic Press.

Brooks, L., & Swain, M. (2009). Languaging in collaborative writing: Creation of and response to expertise. In A. Mackey & C. Polio (Eds.), *Multiple perspectives on interaction: Second language research in honor of Susan M. Gass* (pp. 58–89). New York: Routledge.

Broselow, E. (1987). An investigation of transfer in second language phonology. In G. Ioup & S. Weinberger (Eds.), *Interlanguage phonology* (pp. 261–278). Cambridge, MA: Newbury House.

Broselow, E., & Finer, D. (1991). Parameter setting in second language phonology and syntax. *Second Language Research, 7*, 35–59.

Broselow, E., Chen, S.-I., & Wang, C. (1998). The emergence of the unmarked in second language phonology. *Studies in Second Language Acquisition, 20*, 261–280.

Brown, D. F. (1974). Advanced vocabulary teaching: The problems of collocation. *RELC Journal, 5*, 1–11.

Brown, J. D. (2011). Quantitative research in second language studies. In E. Hinkel (Ed.), *Handbook of research on second language teaching and learning* (Vol. 2) (pp. 190–206). New York: Routledge.

Brown, R. (1973). *A first language*. Cambridge, MA: Harvard University Press.

Brown, R., & Hanlon, C. (1970). Derivational complexity and the order of acquisition in child speech. In J. Hayes (Ed.), *Cognition and the development of language* (pp. 155–207). New York: Wiley.

Brown, R., Waring, R., & Donkaewbua, S. (2008). Incidental vocabulary acquisition from reading, reading-while-listening, and listening to stories. *Reading in a Foreign Language*, *20*, 136–163.

Bruton, A., & Samuda, V. (1980). Learner and teacher roles in the treatment of error in group work. *RELC Journal*, *11*, 49–63.

Buchanan, T., Johnson, J. & Goldberg, L. (2005). Implementing a five-factor personality inventory for use on the internet. *European Journal of Psychological Assessment*, *21*, 115–127.

Budding, C., Hoopes, R., Mueller, M., & Scarcello, K. (1995). Identification of foreign sign language accents by the Deaf. In L. Byers et al. (Eds.), *Gallaudet University Communication Forum*, Vol. 4.

Butler, Y. G., & Lee, J. (2006). On-task versus off-task self-assessments among Korean elementary school students studying English. *The Modern Language Journal*, *90*(4), 506–518.

Butler, Y. G., & Lee, J. (2010). The effects of self-assessment among young learners of English. *Language Testing*, *27*(1), 5–31.

Bygate, M., & Samuda, V. (2009). Creating pressure in task pedagogy: The joint roles of field, purpose, and engagement within the interaction approach. In A. Mackey & C. Polio (Eds.), *Multiple perspectives on interaction: Second language research in honor of Susan M. Gass* (pp. 90–116). New York: Routledge.

Byrnes, H., & Sinicrope, C. (2008). Advancedness and the development of relativization in L2 German: A curriculum-based longitudinal study. In L. Ortega & H. Byrnes (Eds.), *The longitudinal study of advanced L2 capacities* (pp. 109–138). New York: Routledge.

Call, M. (1985). Auditory short-term memory, listening comprehension, and the input hypothesis. *TESOL Quarterly*, *19*, 765–781.

Campbell, R. N., & Rosenthal, J. W. (2000). Heritage languages. In J. W. Rosenthal (Ed.), *Handbook of undergraduate second language education* (pp. 165–84). Mahwah, NJ: Lawrence Erlbaum Associates.

Carlisle, R. (1998). The acquisition of onsets in a markedness relationship: A longitudinal study. *Studies in Second Language Acquisition*, *20*, 245–260.

Carlucci, L., Jain, S., Kimber, E., & Stephan, F. (2005). Variations on U-shaped learning. In P. Auer & R. Meir (Eds.), *Learning Theory, Proceedings of the 18th Annual Conference on Learning Theory, COLT 2005. Lecture Notes in Computer Science* (No. 3559, pp. 382–397). New York: Springer Verlag.

Carreira, M. (2002). A Connectionist approach to enhancing the phonological competence of heritage language speakers of Spanish. In J. Sullivan (Ed.), *Literacy and the second language learner* (pp. 239–259). Greenwich, CT: Information Age Publishing.

Carroll, J. B. (1992). Cognitive abilities: The state of the art. *Psychological Science*, *3*, 266–270.

Carroll, J. B., & Sapon, S. (1959). *Modern language aptitude test—Form A*. New York: The Psychological Corporation.

Carroll, S. (2001). *Input and evidence: The raw material of second language acquisition*. Amsterdam: John Benjamins.

Carroll, S. (2006). Salience, awareness and SLA. In M. G. O'Brien, C. Shea, & J. Archibald (Eds.), *Proceedings of the 8th Generative Approaches to Second Language Acquisition Conference* (pp. 17–24). Somerville, MA: Cascadilla Proceedings Project.

Carroll, S. (2007). Autonomous induction theory. In B. VanPatten & J. Williams (Eds.), *Theories in second language acquisition: An Introduction* (pp. 155–74). Mahwah, NJ: Lawrence Erlbaum.

Carroll, S., Roberge, Y., & Swain, M. (1992). The role of feedback in adult second language acquisition, error correction, and morphological generalizations. *Applied Psycholinguistics, 13*, 173–198.

Carroll, S., & Swain, M. (1993). Explicit and implicit negative feedback: An empirical study of the learning of linguistic generalizations. *Studies in Second Language Acquisition, 15*, 357–386.

Cassady, J. C. (2010). Introduction. In J. C. Cassady (Ed.), *Anxiety in the schools: The causes, consequences, and solutions for academic anxieties* (pp. 1–3). New York: Peter Lang.

Cazden, C. (1972). *Child language and education*. New York: Holt, Rinehart & Winston.

Cazden, C. (1976). Play with language and metalinguistic awareness: One dimension of language experience. In J. S. Bruner, A. Jolly, & K. Silva (Eds.), *Play: Its role in development and evolution* (pp. 603–618). New York: Basic.

Cenoz, J. (2001). The effect of linguistic distance, L2 status and age on cross-linguistic influence in third language acquisition. In J. Cenoz, B. Hufeisen, & U. Jessner (Eds.), *Cross-linguistic influence in third language acquisition: Psycholinguistic perspectives* (pp. 8–20). Clevedon, UK: Multilingual Matters.

Cenoz, J. (2003). The additive effect of bilingualism on third language acquisition: A review. *The International Journal of Bilingualism, 7*, 71–87.

Cenoz, J. (2005). Review of the book *Handbook of bilingualism*, T. Bhatia & W. Ritchie (Eds.). *Studies in Second Language Acquisition, 27*, 638–639.

Cenoz, J., & Genesee, F. (1998). Psycholinguistic perspectives on multilingualism and multilingual education. In J. Cenoz & F. Genesee (Eds.), *Beyond bilingualism: Multilingualism and multilingual education* (pp. 16–32). Clevedon, UK: Multilingual Matters.

Chamot, A. U. (2008). Strategy instruction and good language learners. In C. Griffiths (Ed.), *Lessons from good language learners* (pp. 266–281). New York: Cambridge University Press.

Chamot, A., Barnhardt, S., El-Dinary, P. B., & Robbins, J. (1999). *The learning strategies handbook*. New York: Longman.

Chang, C., Haynes, E., Rhodes, R., & Yao, Y. (2008). A tale of two fricatives: Consonantal contrast in heritage speakers of Mandarin. Paper presented at the 32nd Penn Linguistics Colloquium.

Chao, W. (1981). Pro-drop languages and nonobligatory control. *Occasional Papers in Linguistics, 7*, 46–74. Amherst: University of Massachusetts.

Chastain, K. (1975). Affective and ability factors in second-language acquisition. *Language Learning, 25*, 153–161.

Chaudron, C. (1983). Research in metalinguistic judgments: A review of theory, methods and results. *Language Learning, 33*, 343–377.

Chaudron, C., & Russell, G. (1990). *The validity of elicited imitation as a measure of second language competence*. Unpublished manuscript.

Chen Pichler, D. (2009). The development of sign language. In K. de Bot et al. (Eds.), *Language development over the life-span* (pp. 217–241). Mahwah, NJ: Lawrence Erlbaum Associates.

Chen Pichler, D. (2011). Sources of handshape error in first-time signers of ASL. In D. Napoli & G. Mathur (Eds.), *Deaf around the world* (pp. 96–121). Oxford, UK: Oxford University Press.

Cho, S. (1999). *The acquisition of relative clauses: Experimental studies on Korean*. Unpublished doctoral dissertation, University of Hawai'i at Manoa.

Choi, S., & Lantolf, J. (2008). Representation and embodiment of meaning in L2 communication: Motion events in the speech and gesture of advanced L2 Korean and L2 English speakers. *Studies in Second Language Acquisition*, *30*, 191–224.

Chomsky, N. (1959). Review of B. F. Skinner, *Verbal behavior*. *Language*, *35*, 26–58.

Chomsky, N. (1968). *Language and mind*. New York: Harcourt Brace Jovanovich.

Chomsky, N. (1975). *Reflections on language*. New York: Pantheon.

Chomsky, N. (1981). *Lectures on government and binding*. Dordrecht, The Netherlands: Foris.

Chomsky, N. (1986). *Barriers*. Cambridge, MA: MIT Press.

Chomsky, N. (1989). Some notes on economy of derivation and representation. *MIT Working Papers in Linguistics*, *10*, 43–74.

Chomsky, N. (1995). *The minimalist program*. Cambridge, MA: MIT Press.

Chomsky, N. (2000). *New horizons in the study of language and mind*. Cambridge, UK: Cambridge University Press.

Chomsky, N. (2002). *On nature and language*. Cambridge, UK: Cambridge University Press.

Chouinard, M. M., & Clark, E. V. (2003). Adult reformulations of child errors as negative evidence. *Journal of Child Language*, *30*, 637–669.

Churchill, E., & DuFon, M. (2006). Evolving threads in SA research. In M. DuFon & E. Churchill (Eds.), *Language learners in SA contexts* (pp. 1–27). Clevedon, UK: Multilingual Matters.

Clahsen, H. (1984). The acquisition of German word order: A test case for cognitive approaches to L2 development. In R. Andersen (Ed.), *Second languages: A cross-linguistic perspective* (pp. 219–242). Rowley, MA: Newbury House.

Clahsen, H., & Felser, C. (2006a). Grammatical processing in language learners. *Applied Psycholinguistics*, *27*(1), 3–42.

Clahsen, H., & Felser, C. (2006b). Continuity and shallow structures in language processing: A reply to our commentators. *Applied Psycholinguistics*, *27*(1), 107–126.

Clahsen, H., and Felser, C. (2006c). How native-like is non-native language proceessing? *Trends in Cognitive Science*, *10*(12), 564–570.

Clark, H., & Clark, E. (1977). *Psychology and language: An introduction to psycholinguistics*. New York: Harcourt Brace.

Coady, J., Magoto, J., Hubbard, P., Graney, J., & Mokhtari, K. (1993). High frequency vocabulary and reading proficiency in ESL readers. In T. Huckin, M. Haynes, & J. Coady (Eds.), *Second language reading and vocabulary learning* (pp. 217–228). Norwood, NJ: Ablex.

Cohen, A. D. (1998). *Strategies in learning and using a second language*. London: Longman.

Cohen, A. D. (2005). Strategies for learning and performing L2 speech acts. *Intercultural Pragmatics*, *2*, 275–301.

Cohen, A. D., & Macaro, E. (2007). *Language learner strategies: 30 years of research and practice*. Oxford, UK: Oxford University Press.

Cohen, A. D., & Olshtain, E. (1993). The production of speech acts by EFL learners. *TESOL Quarterly*, *27*, 33–56.

Cohen, A. D., Oxford, R., & Chi, J. C. (2001). *Learning styles survey for young learners*. Retrieved March 9, 2007, from www.carla.umn.edu/about/profiles/CohenPapers/LearningStylesSurvey.pdf

Cohen, A. D., & Upton, T. A. (2007). *Language Testing*, *24*(2), 209–250.

Cohen, Al. (1999, October). *Helping students to help themselves*. Paper presented at MITESOL Conference, Ann Arbor, MI.

Collentine, J., & Asención-Delaney, Y. (2010). A corpus-based analysis of the discourse functions of ser/estar + adjective in three levels of Spanish as FL learners. *Language Learning, 60*, 409–445.

Collentine, J., & Freed, B. (Eds.) (2004). *Studies in Second Language Acquisition* [Special Issue], *26* (2).

Comer, W. J., & deBenedette, L. (2010). Processing instruction and Russian: Issues, materials, and preliminary experimental results. *Slavic and East European Journal, 54*, 118–146.

Comrie, B. (1981). *Language universals and language typology*. Chicago: University of Chicago Press.

Comrie, B. (2003). Typology and language acquisition: The case of relative clauses. In A. Ramat (Ed.), *Typology and second language acquisition* (pp. 19–37). Berlin: de Grutyer.

Comrie, B., & Keenan, E. (1979). Noun phrase accessibility revisited. *Language, 55*, 649–664.

Conklin, K., & Schmitt, N. (2008). Formulaic sequences: Are they processed more quickly than nonformulaic language by native and nonnative speakers? *Applied Linguistics, 29*, 72–89.

Conway, A., Kane, M., Bunting, M., Hambrick, D. Z., Wilhelm, O., & Engle, R. W. (2005). Working memory span tasks: A methodological review and user's guide. *Psychonomic Bulletin & Review, 12*, 769–786.

Cook, V. (1991). The poverty of stimulus argument and multi-competence. *Second Language Research, 7*, 103–117.

Cook, V. (1992). Evidence for multi-competence. *Language Learning, 42*, 557–591.

Cook, V. (1997). *Inside language*. London: Edward Arnold.

Cook, V. (Ed.) (2003). *Effects of the second language on the first*. Clevedon, UK: Multilingual Matters.

Cook, V. (2005, October). *Multi-competence: Black-hole or worm-hole?* Paper presented at the Second Language Research Forum, Teachers College, Columbia University, New York.

Coppieters, R. (1987). Competence differences between native and non-native speakers. *Language, 63*, 544–573.

Corder, S. P. (1967). The significance of learners' errors. *International Review of Applied Linguistics, 5*, 161–170.

Corder, S. P. (1971). Idiosyncratic dialects and error analysis. *International Review of Applied Linguistics, 9*, 147–159.

Corder, S. P. (1973). The elicitation of interlanguage. In J. Svartvik (Ed.), *Errata: Papers in error analysis* (pp. 36–48). Lund, Sweden: CWK Gleerup.

Corder, S. P. (1981). *Error analysis in interlanguage*. Oxford, UK: Oxford University Press.

Corder, S. P. (1983). A role for the mother tongue. In S. Gass & L. Selinker (Eds.), *Language transfer in language learning* (pp. 85–97). Rowley, MA: Newbury House.

Corder, S. P. (1992). A role for the mother tongue. In S. Gass & L. Selinker (Eds.), *Language transfer in language learning* (2nd ed., pp. 18–31). Amsterdam: John Benjamins.

Cornelius, E. T. (1981). *Interviews*. New York: Longman.

Costa, A., Caramazza, A., & Sebastian-Galles, N. (2000). The cognate facilitation effect: Implications for models of lexical access. *Journal of Experimental Psychology: Learning, Memory, and Cognition, 26*, 1283–1296.

Cotterall, S. (2008). Autonomy and good language learners. In C. Griffiths (Ed.), *Lessons from good language learners* (pp. 110–120). New York: Cambridge University Press.

Coulter, K. (1968) *Linguistic error analysis of the spoken English of two native Russians*. Unpublished thesis, University of Washington.

Cowan N. (2005) *Working memory capacity*. New York: Psychology Press.

Cowan, R., & Hatasa, Y. (1994). Investigating the validity and reliability of native speaker and second-language learner judgments about sentences. In E. Tarone, S. Gass, & A. Cohen (Eds.), *Research methodology in second-language acquisition* (pp. 287–302). Hillsdale, NJ: Lawrence Erlbaum Associates.

Cowie, A. P. (1978). Vocabulary exercises within an individualized study programme. *ELT Documents*, *103*, 37–44.

Craik, F. I. M., & Lockhart, R. S. (1972). Levels of processing: A framework for memory research. *Journal of Verbal Learning and Verbal Behavior*, *11*, 671–684.

Craik, F. I. M., & Tulving, E. (1975). Depth of processing and the retention of words in episodic memory. *Journal of Experimental Psychology: General*, *104*, 268–294.

Crain, S., & Fodor, J. (1987). Sentence matching and overgeneration. *Cognition*, *26*, 123–169.

Cronbach, L. J. (1957). The two disciplines of scientific psychology. *American Psychologist*, *12*, 671–684.

Crookes, G. (1989). Planning and interlanguage variation. *Studies in Second Language Acquisition*, *11*, 367–383.

Crookes, G. (1991). Second language speech production research: A methodologically oriented review. *Studies in Second Language Acquisition*, *13*, 113–132.

Croteau, K. (1995). Second language acquisition of relative clause structures by learners of Italian. In F. Eckman, D. Highland, P. Lee, J. Mileham, & R. Rutkowski Weber, (Eds.), *Second Language Acquisition Theory and Pedagogy* (pp. 115–128). Mahwah, NJ: Lawrence Erlbaum Associates.

Cutler, A. (1990). Exploiting prosodic probabilities in speech segmentation. In G. Altman (Ed.), *Cognitive models of speech processing: Psycholinguistics and computational perspectives* (pp. 105–121). Cambridge, MA: MIT Press.

Dagut, M., & Laufer, B. (1985). Avoidance of phrasal verbs—A case for contrastive analysis. *Studies in Second Language Acquisition*, *7*, 73–79.

Dahl, Ö. (1985). *Tense and aspect systems*. Oxford, UK: Blackwell.

Dahl, Ö. (2000). *Tense and aspect in the languages of Europe*. Berlin, Germany: de Gruyter.

Daneman, M., & Capenter, P. A. (1980). Individual differences in working memory and reading. *Journal of Verbal Learning and Verbal Behavior*, *19*, 450–466.

De Angelis, G. (1999, March). *Interlanguage transfer and multiple language acquisition: A case study*. Paper presented at the annual TESOL conference, New York.

De Angelis, G. (2005). Interlanguage transfer of function words. *Language Learning*, *55*(3), 379–414.

de Bot, K. (2008). Introduction: Second language development as a dynamic process. *The Modern Language Journal*, *92*, 166–178.

de Bot, K., Paribakht, S., & Wesche, M. (1997). Toward a lexical processing model for the study of second language vocabulary acquisition: Evidence from ESL reading. *Studies in Second Language Acquisition*, *19*, 309–329.

de Graaff, R. (1997). The eXperanto experiment: Effects of explicit instruction on second language acquisition. *Studies in Second Language Acquisition*, *19*, 249–276.

de Groot, A. M. B., & Hoeks, J. (1995). The development of bilingual memory: Evidence from word translation by trilinguals. *Language Learning*, *45*, 683–724.

De Houwer, A. (1995). Bilingual language acquisition. In P. Fletcher & B. MacWhinney (Eds.), *The handbook of child language* (pp. 219–250). Oxford, UK: Blackwell.

de Jong, N. (2005). Can second language grammar be learned through listening? An experimental study. *Studies in Second Language Acquisition*, *27*, 205–234.

de la Fuente, M. J. (2006). Classroom L2 vocabulary acquisition: Investigating the role of pedagogical tasks and form-focused instruction. *Language Teaching Research*, *10*, 263–295.

De Saint Leger, D. (2009). Self-assessment of speaking skills and participation in a foreign language class. *Foreign Language Annals*, *42*(1), 158–178.

de Villiers, J., & de Villiers, P. (1973). A cross-sectional study of the acquisition of grammatical morphemes in child speech. *Journal of Psycholinguistic Research*, *2*, 267–278.

DeKeyser, R. (1995). Learning second language grammar rules: An experiment with a miniature linguistic system. *Studies in Second Language Acquisition*, *17*, 379–410.

DeKeyser, R. (1997). Beyond explicit rule learning: Automatizing second language morphosyntax. *Studies in Second Language Acquisition*, *19*, 195–221.

DeKeyser, R. (2000). The robustness of critical period effects in second language acquisition. *Studies in Second Language Acquisition*, *22*, 499–533.

DeKeyser, R. (2001). Automaticity and automatization. In N. P. Robinson (Ed.), *Cognition and second language instruction* (pp. 125–151). Cambridge, UK: Cambridge University Press.

DeKeyser, R. (2003). Implicit and explicit learning. In C. Doughty & M. H. Long (Eds.), *The handbook of second language acquisition* (pp. 313–347). Oxford, UK: Blackwell.

DeKeyser, R. (2007). Skill acquisition theory. In B. VanPatten & J. Williams (Eds), *Theories in second language acquisition* (pp. 97–113). Mahwah, NJ: Lawrence Erlbaum Associates.

DeKeyser, R. (2009, October). *Variable interaction in SLA: Much more than a nuisance*. Plenary address given at the Second Language Research Forum, East Lansing, MI.

DeKeyser, R., Alfi-Shabtay, I., & Ravid, D. (2010). Cross-linguistic evidence for the nature of age effects in second language acquisition. *Applied Psycholinguistics*, *31*, 413–438.

DeKeyser, R., & Larson-Hall, J. (2005). What does the critical period really mean? In J. F. Kroll & A. M. B. De Groot (Eds.), *Handbook of bilingualism: Psycholinguistic approaches* (pp. 88–108). Oxford, UK: Oxford University Press.

DeKeyser, R., Salaberry, R., Robinson, P., & Harrington, M. (2002). What gets processed in processing instruction? A commentary on Bill VanPatten's "Processing Instruction: An Update." *Language Learning*, *52*, 805–823.

DeKeyser, R., & Sokalski, K. (1996). The differential role of comprehension and production practice. *Language Learning*, *35*, 613–642.

Deuchar, M., & Quay, S. (2000). *Bilingual acquisition: Theoretical implications of a case study*. Oxford, UK: Oxford University Press.

Dewaele, J.-M. (1998). Lexical inventions: French interlanguage as L2 versus L3. *Applied Linguistics*, *19*, 471–490.

Dewaele, J.-M., & Furnham, A. (1999). Extraversion: The unsolved variable in applied linguistic research. *Language Learning*, *49*, 509–544.

Dickerson, L. (1975). The learner's interlanguage as a system of variable rules. *TESOL Quarterly*, *9*, 401–407.

Dickerson, L., & Dickerson, W. (1977). Interlanguage phonology: Current research and future directions. In S. P. Corder & E. Roulet (Eds.), *The notions of simplification, interlanguages and pidgins and their relation to second language learning* (Actes du 5ème Colloque de Linguistique Appliquée de Neuchâtel, pp. 18–29). Paris: AIMAV/ Didier.

Dietrich, R., Klein, W., & Noyau, C. (1995). *The acquisition of temporality in a second language*. Amsterdam: John Benjamins.

Dijkstra, T., Grainger, J., & Van Heuven, W. J. B. (1999). Recognition of cognates and interlingual homographs: The neglected role of phonology. *Journal of Memory and Language, 41*, 496–518.

Dijkstra, T., Miwa, K., Brummelhuis, B., Sappelli, M., & Baayen, H. (2010). How cross-language similarity and task demands affect cognate recognition. *Journal of Memory and Language, 62*, 284–301.

Dinnsen, D., & Eckman, F. (1975). A functional explanation of some phonological typologies. In R. E. Grossman, L. J. San, & T. J. Vance (Eds.), *Functionalism* (pp. 126–134). Chicago: Chicago Linguistic Society.

Domínguez, L., Tracy-Ventura, N., Arche, M. J., Mitchell, R., & Myles, F. (2012). The role of dynamic contrasts in the L2 acquisition of Spanish past tense morphology. *Bilingualism: Language and Cognition, 15*, 1–20.

Dörnyei, Z. (2000). Motivation in action: Towards a process-oriented conceptualization of student motivation. *British Journal of Educational Psychology, 70*, 519–538.

Dörnyei, Z. (2001a). *Motivational strategies in the language classroom*. Cambridge, UK: Cambridge University Press.

Dörnyei, Z. (2001b). *Teaching and researching motivation*. Harlow, UK: Longman.

Dörnyei, Z. (2005). *The psychology of the language learner: Individual differences in second language acquisition*. Mahwah, NJ: Lawrence Erlbaum Associates.

Dörnyei, Z. (2006). Individual differences in second language acquisition. In K. Bardovi-Harlig & Z. Dörnyei (Eds.), *Themes in SLA Research. AILA Review, 19* (pp. 42–68). Amsterdam: John Benjamins.

Dörnyei, Z., & Ottó, I. (1998). Motivation in action: A process model of L2 motivation. *Working Papers in Applied Linguistics* (London: Thames Valley University), *4*, 43–69.

Dörnyei, Z., & Scott, M. (1997). Communication strategies in a second language: Definitions and taxonomies. *Language Learning, 47*, 173–210.

Dörnyei, Z. with Taguchi, T. (2009). *Questionnaires in second language research: Construction, administration, and processing* (2nd ed.). New York: Routledge.

Dörnyei, Z., & Tseng, W.-T. (2009). Motivational processing in interactional tasks. In A. Mackey & C. Polio (Eds.), *Multiple perspectives on interaction: Second language research in honor of Susan M. Gass* (pp. 117–134). New York: Routledge.

Dörnyei, Z., & Ushioda, E. (2009). *Motivation, language identity and the L2 self*. Clevedon, UK: Multilingual Matters.

Doughty, C. (1991). Second language instruction does make a difference: Evidence from an empirical study of SL relativization. *Studies in Second Language Acquisition, 13*, 431–469.

Doughty, C. (2003). Instructed SLA: Constraints, compensation, and enhancement. In C. Doughty & M. H. Long (Eds.), *The handbook of second language acquisition* (pp. 256–310). Oxford, UK: Blackwell.

Doughty, C., & Williams, J. (1998). *Focus on form in classroom second language acquisition*. Cambridge, UK: Cambridge University Press.

Douglas, D. (2000). *Assessing languages for specific purposes*. Cambridge, UK: Cambridge University Press.

Duchowski, A. T. (2002). A breadth-first survey of eyetracking applications. *Behavior, Methods, Research, Instruments, and Computers, 1*, 1–15.

Dulay, H., & Burt, M. (1973). Should we teach children syntax? *Language Learning, 23*, 245–258.

Dulay, H., & Burt, M. (1974a). Natural sequences in child second language acquisition. *Language Learning, 24*, 37–53.

Dulay, H., & Burt, M. (1974b). You can't learn without goofing. In J. Richards (Ed.), *Error analysis: Perspectives on second language acquisition* (pp. 95–123). London: Longman.

Dulay, H., & Burt, M. (1975). Creative construction in second language learning and teaching. In M. Burt & H. Dulay (Eds.), *On TESOL '75: New directions in second language learning, teaching and bilingual education* (pp. 21–32). Washington, DC: Teachers of English to Speakers of Other Languages.

Dulay, H., Burt, M., & Krashen, S. (1982). *Language two*. New York: Oxford University Press.

Durrant, P., & Schmitt, N. (2009). To what extent do native and non-native writers make use of collocations? *IRAL, 47*, 157–177.

Dušková, L. (1983). On sources of errors in foreign language learning. In B. Robinett & J. Schachter (Eds.), *Second language learning: Contrastive analysis, error analysis, and related aspects* (pp. 215–233). Ann Arbor: University of Michigan Press.

Dušková, L. (1984). Similarity—An aid or hindrance in foreign language learning? *Folia Linguistica, 18*, 103–115.

Dussias, P. E. (2010). Uses of eye-tracking data on second language sentence processing research. *Annual Review of Applied Linguistics, 30*, 149–166.

Dussias, P., & Sagarra, N. (2007). The effect of exposure on syntactic parsing in Spanish–English. *Bilingualism: Language and Cognition, 10*, 101–116.

Eckman, F. (1977). Markedness and the Contrastive Analysis Hypothesis. *Language Learning, 27*, 315–330.

Eckman, F. (1981a). On predicting phonological difficulty in second language acquisition. *Studies in Second Language Acquisition, 4*, 18–30.

Eckman, F. (1981b). On the naturalness of interlanguage phonological rules. *Language Learning, 31*, 195–216.

Eckman, F. (1992, April). *Secondary languages or second-language acquisition? A linguistic approach*. Plenary address at the Second Language Research Forum, East Lansing, MI.

Eckman, F. (1994a). Local and long distance anaphora in second-language acquisition. In E. Tarone, S. Gass, & A. Cohen (Eds.), *Research methodology in second-language acquisition* (pp. 207–225). Hillsdale, NJ: Lawrence Erlbaum Associates.

Eckman, F. (1994b). The competence–performance issue in second-language acquisition theory: A debate. In E. Tarone, S. Gass, & A. Cohen (Eds.), *Research methodology in second-language acquisition* (pp. 3–15). Hillsdale, NJ: Lawrence Erlbaum Associates.

Eckman, F. (1996). On evaluating arguments for special nativism in second language acquisition theory. *Second Language Research, 12*, 398–419.

Eckman, F. (2007). Hypotheses and methods in second language acquisition: Testing the noun phrase accessibility hierarchy on relative clauses. *Studies in Second Language Acquisition, 29*, 321–327.

Eckman, F., Bell, L., & Nelson, D. (1988). On the generalization of relative clause instruction in the acquisition of English as a second language. *Applied Linguistics, 9*, 1–20.

Eckman, F., Elreyes, A., & Iverson, G. (2003). Some principles of second language phonology. *Second Language Research, 19*, 169–208.

Eckman, F., Moravcsik, E., & Wirth, J. (1989). Implicational universals and interrogative structures in the interlanguage of ESL learners. *Language Learning, 39*, 173–205.

Edwards, J. (1994). *Multilingualism*. London: Routledge.

Edwards, J. (2006). Foundations of bilingualism. In T. Bhatia & W. Ritchie (Eds.), *The handbook of bilingualism* (pp. 5–29). Oxford, UK: Blackwell.

Ehrman, M. (1993). Ego boundaries revisited: Toward a model of personality and learning. In J. A. Alatis (Ed.), *Georgetown University Roundtable on Languages and Linguistics* (pp. 330–362). Washington, DC: Georgetown University Press.

Ehrman, M. E. (1994). The type differentiation indictor and adult foreign language learning success. *Journal of Psychological Type, 30*, 10–29.

Ehrman, M. E. (1996). *Understanding second language learning difficulties*. Thousand Oaks, CA: Sage Publications.

Ehrman, M. E., & Oxford, R. (1995). Cognition plus: Correlates of language learning success. *Modern Language Journal, 79*, 67–89.

Eisenstein, M., & Starbuck, R. (1989). The effect of emotional investment on L2 production. In S. Gass, C. Madden, D. Preston, & L. Selinker (Eds.), *Variation in second language acquisition: Psycholinguistic issues* (pp. 125–137). Clevedon, UK: Multilingual Matters.

Elgort, I. (2011). Deliberate learning and vocabulary acquisition in a second language. *Language Learning, 61*, 367–413.

Ellis, N. (1994). Implicit and explicit language learning—An overview. In N. Ellis (Ed.), *Implicit and explicit learning of languages* (pp. 1–31). London: Academic Press.

Ellis, N. (2001). Memory for language. In P. Robinson (Ed.), *Cognition and second language instruction*. Cambridge, UK: Cambridge University Press.

Ellis, N. (2002). Frequency effects in language processing: A review with implications for theories of implicit and explicit language acquisition. *Studies in Second Language Acquisition, 24*, 143–188.

Ellis, N. (2005). At the interface: Dynamic interactions of explicit and implicit language knowledge. *Studies in Second Language Acquisition, 27*, 305–352.

Ellis, N. (2007). The associate-cognitive CREED. In B. VanPatten & J. Williams (Eds.), *Theories in second language acquisition: An introduction*. Mahwah, NJ: Lawrence Erlbaum Associates.

Ellis, N. (2009). The psycholinguistics of the interaction approach. In A. Mackey & C. Polio (Eds.), *Multiple perspectives on interaction: Second language research in honor of Susan M. Gass* (pp. 11–40). New York: Routledge.

Ellis, N. (2012) Frequency-based accounts of second language acquisition. In S. Gass & A. Mackey (Eds.), *The Routledge handbook of second language acquisition* (pp. 193–210). New York: Routledge.

Ellis, N. C., & Larsen-Freeman, D. (Eds.) (2006). Language emergence: Implications for applied linguistics [Special issue]. *Applied Linguistics, 27*(4), 558–559.

Ellis, N., & Schmidt, R. (1997). Morphology and longer distance dependencies: Laboratory research illuminating the A in SLA. *Studies in Second Language Acquisition, 19*, 145–171.

Ellis, R. (1984). *Classroom second language development: A study of classroom interaction and language acquisition*. Oxford, UK: Pergamon.

Ellis, R. (1985a). *Understanding second language acquisition*. Oxford, UK: Oxford University Press.

Ellis, R. (1985b). Teacher–pupil interaction in second language development. In S. Gass & C. Madden (Eds.), *Input in second language acquisition* (pp. 69–86). Rowley, MA: Newbury House.

Ellis, R. (1987a). Interlanguage variability in narrative discourse: Style shifting in the use of the past tense. *Studies in Second Language Acquisition, 9*, 1–20.

Ellis, R. (Ed.) (1987b). *Second language acquisition in context*. London: Prentice–Hall.

Ellis, R. (1990a). Grammaticality judgments and learner variability. In H. Burmeiser & P. Rounds (Eds.), *Variability in second language acquisition: Proceedings of the Tenth Meeting of the Second Language Research Forum* (pp. 25–60). Eugene: University of Oregon, Department of Linguistics.

Ellis, R. (1990b). A response to Gregg. *Applied Linguistics*, *11*, 118–131.

Ellis, R. (1991). Grammaticality judgments and second language acquisition. *Studies in Second Language Acquisition*, *13*, 161–186.

Ellis, R. (1994). *The study of second language acquisition*. Oxford, UK: Oxford University Press.

Ellis, R. (2001). Methodological options in grammar teaching materials. In E. Hinkel & S. Fotos (Eds.), *New perspectives on grammar teaching in second language classrooms*. Mahwah, NJ: Lawrence Erlbaum.

Ellis, R. (2005). Measuring implicit and explicit knowledge of a second language: A psychometric study. *Studies in Second Language Acquisition*, *27*, 141–172.

Ellis, R. (2007). The differential effect of corrective feedback on two grammatical structures. In A. Mackey (Ed.), *Conversational interaction and second language acquisition: A series of empirical studies* (pp. 339–360). Oxford, UK: Oxford University Press.

Ellis, R. (2008). *The study of second language acquisition* (2nd ed.). Oxford, UK: Oxford University Press.

Ellis, R. (2009). The differential effects of three types of task planning on the fluency, complexity, and accuracy in L2 oral production. *Applied Linguistics*, *19*, 474–509.

Ellis, R. (2010). Second language acquisition, teacher education and language pedagogy. *Language Teaching*, *43*, 182–201.

Ellis, R., Basturkmen, H., & Loewen, S. (2001a). Learner uptake in communicative ESL lessons. *Language Learning*, *51*, 281–318.

Ellis, R., Basturkmen, H., & Loewen, S. (2001b). Pre-emptive focus on form in the ESL classroom. *TESOL Quarterly*, *35*, 407–432.

Ellis, R., & He, X. (1999). The roles of modified input and output in the incidental acquisition of word meanings. *Studies in Second Language Acquisition*, *21*, 285–301.

Ellis, R. & Loewen, S. (2007). Confirming the operational definitions of explicit and implicit knowledge in Ellis (2005): Responding to Isemonger. *Studies in Second Language Acquisition*, *29*, 119–126.

Ellis, R., Loewen, S., & Erlam, R. (2006). Implicit and explicit corrective feedback and the acquisition of L2 grammar. *Studies in Second Language Acquisition*, *28*, 339–368.

Ellis, R., & Sheen, Y. (2006). Re-examining the role of recasts in L2 acquisition. *Studies in Second Language Acquisition*, *28*, 575–600.

Emmorey, K., Thompson, R., & Colvin, R. (2009). Eye gaze during comprehension of American Sign Language by native and beginning signers. *Journal of Deaf Studies & Deaf Education*, *14*, 237–243.

Epstein, S., Flynn, S., & Martohardjono, G. (1996). Second language acquisition: Theoretical and experimental issues in contemporary research. *Brain and Behavioral Sciences*, *19*, 677–714.

Epstein, S., Flynn, S., & Martohardjono, G. (1998). The strong continuity hypothesis in adult L2 acquisition of functional categories. In S. Flynn, G. Martohardjono, & W. O'Neil (Eds.), *The generative study of second language acquisition* (pp. 61–77). Mahwah, NJ: Lawrence Erlbaum Associates.

Erler, L., & Macaro, E. (2011). Decoding ability in French as a Foreign Language and language learning motivation. *The Modern Language Journal*, *95*, 496–518.

Ervin-Tripp, S. (1974). Is second language learning like the first? *TESOL Quarterly*, *8*, 111–127.

Færch, C., Haastrup, K., & Phillipson, R. (1984). *Learner language and language learning*. Clevedon, UK: Multilingual Matters.

Færch, C., & Kasper, G. (1980). Processes in foreign language learning and communication. *Interlanguage Studies Bulletin*, *5*, 47–118.

Færch, C., & Kasper, G. (1986). The role of comprehension in second language learning. *Applied Linguistics*, *7*, 257–274.

Færch, C., & Kasper, G. (1987). From product to process—introspective methods in second language research. In C. Færch & G. Kasper (Eds.), *Introspection in second language research* (pp. 5–23). Clevedon, UK: Multilingual Matters.

Felix, S. (1981). The effect of formal instruction on second language acquisition. *Language Learning*, *31*, 87–112.

Felser, C., Roberts, L., Gross, R., & Marinis, T. (2003). The processing of ambiguous sentences by first and second language learners of English. *Applied Psycholinguistics*, *24*, 453–489.

Ferguson, C. (1971). Absence of copula and the notion of simplicity: A study of normal speech, baby talk, foreigner talk and pidgins. In D. Hymes (Ed.), *Pidginization and creolization of languages* (pp. 141–150). Cambridge, UK: Cambridge University Press.

Fernández, C. (2008). Reexamining the role of explicit information in processing instruction. *Studies in Second Language Acquisition*, *30*, 277–305.

Ferreira, V., & Bock, J. K. (2006). The functions of structural priming. *Language and Cognitive Processes*, *21*, 1011–1029.

Firth, A., & Wagner, J. (1997). On discourse, communication and (some) fundamental concepts in SLA research. *The Modern Language Journal*, *81*, 285–300.

Firth, A., & Wagner, J. (1998). SLA property: No trespassing! *The Modern Language Journal*, *82*, 91–94.

Fishman, J. (2001). 300-plus years of heritage language education in the United States. In J. Kreeft Peyton, D. A. Ranard, & S. McGinnis (Eds.), *Heritage languages in America: Preserving a national resource* (pp. 81–97). McHenry, IL: The Center for Applied Linguistics/Delta Systems.

Fisiak, J. (1991, April). *Contrastive linguistics and language acquisition*. Paper presented at the Regional English Language Center (RELC) Conference, Singapore.

Flashner, V. E. (1989). Transfer of aspect in the English oral narratives of native Russian speakers. In H. Dechert & M. Raupach (Eds.), *Transfer in language production* (pp. 71–97). Norwood, NJ: Ablex.

Flege, J. E. (1987a). The production of "new" and "similar" phones in a foreign language: Evidence for the effect of equivalence classification. *Journal of Phonetics*, *15*, 47–65.

Flege, J. E. (1987b). Effects of equivalence classification on the production of foreign language speech sounds. In A. James & J. Leather (Eds.), *Sound patterns in second language acquisition* (pp. 9–39). Dordrecht, The Netherlands: Foris.

Flege, J. E. (1990). English vowel production by Dutch talkers: More evidence for the "similar" vs. "new" distinction. In J. Leather & A. James (Eds.), *New Sounds 90: Proceedings of the Amsterdam Symposium on the Acquisition of Second-Language Speech* (pp. 255–293). Amsterdam: The University of Amsterdam.

Flege, J. E. (1992). The intelligibility of English vowels spoken by British and Dutch talkers. In R. D. Kent (Ed.), *Intelligibility in speech disorders: Theory, measurement, and management* (Vol. 1, pp. 157–232). Philadelphia: Amsterdam.

Flege, J. E. (1993). Production and perception of a novel, second language phonetic contrast. *Journal of the Acoustical Society of America*, *93*, 1589–1608.

Flege, J. E. (1995). Second language speech learning: Theory, findings, and problems. In W. Strange (Ed.), *Speech perception and linguistic experience: Issues in cross-linguistic research* (pp. 233–277). Timonium, MD: York Press.

Flege, J. E. (1999). Age of learning and second language speech. In D. Birdsong (Ed.), *Second language acquisition and the critical period hypothesis* (pp. 101–131). Mahwah, NJ: Lawrence Erlbaum Associates.

Flege, J. E. (2007). Language contact in bilingualism: Phonetic system interactions. In J. Cole & J. I. Hualde (Eds.), *Laboratory phonology 9*. Berlin: Mouton de Gruyter.

Flege, J. E., Birdsong, D., Bialystok, E., Mack, M., Sung, H., & Tsukada, K. (2006). Degree of foreign accent in English sentences produced by Korean children and adults. *Journal of Phonetics*, *34*, 153–175.

Flege, J. E., Munro, M., & Mackay, I. (1995). Factors affecting degree of perceived foreign accent in a second language. *Journal of the Acoustical Society of America*, *97*, 3125–3134.

Flege, J. E., Yeni-Komshian, G. E., & Liu, S. (1999). Age constraints on second language acquisition. *Journal of Memory and Language*, *41*, 78–104.

Flexner, S. B., and Hauck, L. C. (Eds.) (1988). *Random House dictionary of the English language* (2nd ed.). New York: Random House.

Flynn, S. (1987). *A parameter-setting model of L2 acquisition*. Dordrecht, The Netherlands: Reidel.

Flynn, S. (1996). A parameter-setting approach to second language acquisition. In W. Ritchie & T. Bhatia (Eds.), *Handbook of second language acquisition* (pp. 121–158). San Diego, CA: Academic Press.

Flynn, S., & Martohardjono, G. (1994). Mapping from the initial state to the final state: The separation of universal principles and language-specific principles. In B. Lust, M. Suner, & J. Whiteman (Eds.), *Syntactic theory and first language acquisition: Cross-linguistic perspectives. Vol. 1. Heads, projections and learnability* (pp. 319–335). Hillsdale, NJ: Lawrence Erlbaum Associates.

Foss, D., & Hakes, D. (1978). *Psycholinguistics*. Englewood Cliffs, NJ: Prentice-Hall.

Foster, P., Tonkyn, A., & Wigglesworth, G. (2000). Measuring spoken language: A unit for all reasons. *Applied Linguistics*, *21*, 354–375.

Foster-Cohen, S. (1999). *An introduction to child language development*. London: Longman.

Fox, B. (1987). The noun phrase accessibility hierarchy revisited. *Language*, *63*, 856–870.

Fraser, C. (1999). Lexical processing strategy use and vocabulary through reading. *Studies in Second Language Acquisition*, *21*, 225–241.

Frawley, W., & Lantolf, J. P. (1985). L2 discourse: A Vygotskian perspective. *Applied Linguistics*, *6*, 19–44.

Freed, B. (1990). Language learning in a SA context: The effects of interactive and non-interactive out of class contact on grammatical achievement and oral proficiency. In J. Alatis (Ed.), *Linguistics, language teaching and language acquisition: The interdependence of theory, practice and research* (pp. 459–477). Georgetown University Round Table on Languages and Linguistics. Washington, DC: Georgetown University Press.

Freedman, S., & Forster, K. (1985). The psychological status of overgenerated sentences. *Cognition*, *24*, 171–186.

Frenck-Mestre, C. (2005). Eye-movement recording as a tool for studying syntactic processing in a second language. A review of methodologies and experimental findings. *Second Language Research*, *21*, 175–198.

Fries, C. (1945). *Teaching and learning English as a foreign language*. Ann Arbor: University of Michigan Press.

Fries, C. (1957). Foreword. In R. Lado, *Linguistics across cultures*. Ann Arbor: University of Michigan Press.

Gabriele, A. (2009). Transfer and transition in the SLA of aspect: A bidirectional study of learners of English and Japanese. *Studies in Second Language Acquisition, 31*, 371–402.

Gaies, S. (1979). Linguistic input in first and second language learning. In F. Eckman & A. Hastings (Eds.), *Studies in first and second language acquisition* (pp. 185–193). Rowley, MA: Newbury House.

Gairns, R., & Redman, S. (1986). *Working with words: A guide to teaching and learning vocabulary*. New York: Cambridge University Press.

Gardner, R. C. (1983). *Frames of mind: The theory of multiple intelligences*. New York: Basic Books.

Gardner, R. C. (1985). *Social psychology and second language learning: The role of attitudes and motivation*. London: Edward Arnold.

Gardner, R. C. (2001). Integrative motivation and second language acquisition. In Z. Dörnyei & R. Schmidt (Eds.), *Motivation and second language acquisition* (pp. 1–19). Honolulu: The University of Hawai'i, Second Language Teaching and Curriculum Center.

Gardner, R. C., & Lambert, W. (1972). *Attitudes and motivation in second language learning*. Rowley, MA: Newbury House.

Gardner, R. C., Masgoret, A.-M., Tennant, J., & Mihic, L. (2004). Integrative motivation: Changes during a year-long intermediate-level language course. *Language Learning, 54*, 1–34.

Gass, S. (1979a). *An investigation of syntactic transfer in adult second language acquisition*. Unpublished doctoral dissertation, Indiana University, Bloomington.

Gass, S. (1979b). Language transfer and universal grammatical relations. *Language Learning, 29*, 327–344.

Gass, S. (1980). An investigation of syntactic transfer in adult L2 learners. In R. Scarcella & S. Krashen (Eds.), *Research in second language acquisition* (pp. 132–141). Rowley, MA: Newbury House.

Gass, S. (1982). From theory to practice. In M. Hines & W. Rutherford (Eds.), *On TESOL '81* (pp. 129–139). Washington, DC: Teachers of English to Speakers of Other Languages.

Gass, S. (1984). A review of interlanguage syntax: Language transfer and language universals. *Language Learning, 34*, 115–132.

Gass, S. (1986). An interactionist approach to L2 sentence interpretation. *Studies in Second Language Acquisition, 8*, 19–37.

Gass, S. (1987). The resolution of conflicts among competing systems: A bidirectional perspective. *Applied Psycholinguistics, 8*, 329–350.

Gass, S. (1988a). Integrating research areas: A framework for second language studies. *Applied Linguistics, 9*, 198–217.

Gass, S. (1988b). Second language vocabulary acquisition. *Annual Review of Applied Linguistics, 9*, 92–106.

Gass, S. (1989). Language universals and second language learning. *Language Learning, 39*, 497–534.

Gass, S. (1994). The reliability of second-language grammaticality judgments. In E. Tarone, S. Gass, & A. Cohen (Eds.), *Research methodology in second-language acquisition* (pp. 303–322). Hillsdale, NJ: Lawrence Erlbaum Associates.

Gass, S. (1997). *Input, interaction and the second language learner*. Mahwah, NJ: Lawrence Erlbaum Associates.

Gass, S. (1998). Apples and oranges: Or, why apples are not orange and don't need to be. *The Modern Language Journal, 82*, 83–90.

Gass, S. (1999). Discussion: Incidental vocabulary learning. *Studies in Second Language Acquisition, 21*, 319–333.

Gass, S. (2001). Sentence matching: A reexamination, *Second Language Research, 17*, 421–444.

Gass, S. (2003). Input and interaction. In C. Doughty & M. H. Long (Eds.), *The handbook of second language acquisition* (pp. 224–255). Oxford, UK: Basil Blackwell.

Gass, S. (2004). Conversation and input-interaction. *The Modern Language Journal, 88*, 597–616.

Gass, S., & Alvarez-Torres, M. (2005). Attention when? An investigation of the ordering effect of input and interaction. *Studies in Second Language Acquisition, 27*, 1–31.

Gass, S. & Ard, J. (1980). L2 data: Their relevance for language universals. *TESOL Quarterly, 14*, 443–452.

Gass, S., & Ard, J. (1984). L2 acquisition and the ontology of language universals. In W. Rutherford (Ed.), *Second language acquisition and language universals* (pp. 33–68). Amsterdam: John Benjamins.

Gass, S., Behney, J., & Uzum, B. (in press). Inhibitory control, working memory, and L2 interaction gains. In K. Droździał-Szelest & M. Pawlak, *Psycholinguistic and sociolinguistic perspectives on second language learning and teaching: Studies in honor of Waldemar Marton*. Berlin: Springer Verlag.

Gass, S., & Houck, N. (1999). *Interlanguage refusals: A cross-cultural study of Japanese–English*. Berlin, Germany: Mouton de Gruyter.

Gass, S. & Lee, J. (2011). Working memory capacity, inhibitory control, and proficiency in a second language. In M. Schmid & W. Lowie (Eds.), *Modeling bilingualism: From structure to chaos* (pp. 59–84). Amsterdam: John Benjamins.

Gass, S., Lee, J., & Roots, R. (2007). Firth and Wagner (2007): New ideas or a new articulation? *The Modern Language Journal, 91*, 788–799.

Gass, S., & Lewis, K. (2007). Perceptions of interactional feedback: Differences between heritage language learners and non-heritage language learners. In A. Mackey (Ed.), *Conversational interaction in second language acquisition: A series of empirical studies* (pp. 173–196). Oxford, UK: Oxford University Press.

Gass, S., & Mackey, A. (2000). *Stimulated recall methodology in second language research*. Mahwah, NJ: Lawrence Erlbaum Associates.

Gass, S., & Mackey, A. (2006). Input, interaction and output: An overview. In K. Bardovi-Harlig & Z. Dörnyei (Eds.), *AILA Review* (pp. 3–17). Amsterdam: John Benjamins.

Gass, S., & Mackey, A. (2007). *Data elicitation for second and foreign language research*. Mahwah, NJ: Lawrence Erlbaum Associates.

Gass, S., Mackey, A., Alvarez-Torres, M., & Fernández-García, M. (1999). The effects of task repetition on linguistic output. *Language Learning, 49*, 549–581.

Gass, S., Mackey, A., & Ross-Feldman, L. (2005). Task-based interactions in classroom and laboratory settings. *Language Learning, 55*, 575–611.

Gass, S., & Madden, C. (Eds.) (1985). *Input in second language acquisition*. Rowley, MA: Newbury House.

Gass, S., & Schachter, J. (Eds.) (1989). *Linguistic perspectives on second language acquisition*. Cambridge, UK: Cambridge University Press.

Gass, S., Svetics, I., & Lemelin, S. (2003). Differential effects of attention. *Language Learning, 53*, 497–545.

Gass, S., & Varonis, E. (1984). The effect of familiarity on the comprehension of nonnative speech. *Language Learning*, *34*, 65–89.

Gass, S., & Varonis, E. (1985). Variation in native speaker speech modification to non-native speakers. *Studies in Second Language Acquisition*, *7*, 37–57.

Gass, S., & Varonis, E. (1989). Incorporated repairs in NNS discourse. In M. Eisenstein (Ed.), *Variation and second language acquisition* (pp. 71–86). New York: Plenum.

Gass, S., & Varonis, E. (1994). Input, interaction and second language production. *Studies in Second Language Acquisition*, *16*, 283–302.

Gatbonton, E. (1978). Patterned phonetic variability in second language speech: A gradual diffusion model. *Canadian Modern Language Review*, *34*, 335–347.

Geen, R. G. (1991). Social motivation. *Annual Review of Psychology*, *42*, 377–399.

Genesee, F., Boivin, I., & Nicoladis, E. (1996). Talking with strangers: A study of bilingual children's communicative competence. *Applied Psycholinguistics*, *17*, 427–442.

George, H. (1972). *Common errors in language learning*. Rowley, MA: Newbury House.

Giacalone Ramat, A., & Banfi, E. (1990). The acquisition of temporality: A second language perspective. *Folia Linguistica*, *XXIV*(3–4), 405–428.

Gibbons, E. (2009). *The effects of second language experience on typologically similar and dissimilar third languages*. Unpublished PhD dissertation. Brigham Young University, Salt Lake City, UT.

Giles, H., & Smith, P. M. (1979). Accommodation theory: Optional levels of convergence. In H. Giles & R. N. St. Clair (Eds.), *Language and social psychology* (pp. 45–65). Oxford, UK: Basil Blackwell.

Giles, H., & St. Clair, R. N. (Eds.) (1979). *Language and social psychology*. Oxford, UK: Basil Blackwell.

Glew, M. (1998).*The acquisition of reflexive pronouns among adult learners of English*. Unpublished doctoral dissertation, Michigan State University, East Lansing, MI.

Goad, H., White, L., & Steele, J. (2003). Missing surface inflection in L2 acquisition: A prosodic account. In B. Beachley, A. Brown, & F. Conlin (Eds.), *BUCLD 27 Proceedings* (pp. 264–275). Sommerville, MA: Cascadilla Press.

Godfroid, A., Boers, F., & Housen, A. (in press). An eye for words: Gauging the role of attention in L2 vocabulary acquisition by means of eye-tracking. *Studies in Second Language Acquisition, 35*(3).

Goldschmidt, M. (1996). From the addressee's perspective: Imposition in favor-asking. In S. Gass & J. Neu (Eds.), *Speech acts across cultures* (pp. 241–256). Berlin, Germany: Mouton de Gruyter.

Goldschneider, J., & DeKeyser, R. (2001). Explaining the "Natural order of L2 morpheme acquisition" in English: A meta-analysis of multiple determinants. *Language Learning*, *51*(1), 1–50.

Goldschneider, J., & DeKeyser, R. (2005). Explaining the "Natural order of L2 morpheme acquisition" in English: A meta-analysis of multiple determinants. *Language Learning*, *55*(Suppl. 1), 27–77.

Goo, J. (2010). Working memory and reactivity. *Language Learning*, *60*, 712–752.

Goo, J., & Mackey, A. (2013). The case against the case against recasts. *Studies in Second Language Acquisition*, *35*.

Gosling, S. D., Srivastava, S., Pand, O., & John, O. P. (2004). Should we trust web-based studies? A comparative analysis of six preconceptions about internet questionnaires. *American Psychologist*, *59*, 93–104.

Goss, N., Ying-Hua, Z., & Lantolf, J. (1994). Two heads may be better than one: Mental activity in second-language grammaticality judgments. In E. Tarone, S. Gass, &

A. Cohen (Eds.), *Research methodology in second-language acquisition* (pp. 263–286). Hillsdale, NJ: Lawrence Erlbaum Associates.

Graham, S., & Macaro, E. (2008). Strategy instruction in listening for lower-intermediate learners of French. *Language Learning*, *58*, 747–783.

Granger, S. (2012). How to use foreign and second language learner corpora? In A. Mackey & S. Gass (Eds.), *Research methodologies in second language acquisition* (pp. 7–29). London: Blackwell.

Greenberg, J. H. (1963). Some universals of grammar with particular reference to the order of meaningful elements. In J. H. Greenberg (Ed.), *Universals of language* (pp. 73–113). Cambridge, MA: MIT Press.

Gregg, K. (1984). Krashen's monitor and Occam's razor. *Applied Linguistics*, *5*, 79–100.

Gregg, K. (1990). The variable competence model of second language acquisition and why it isn't. *Applied Linguistics*, *11*, 364–383.

Grenfell, M., & Macaro, E. (2007). Language learner strategies: Claims and critiques. In A. D. Cohen & E. Macaro (Eds.), *Language learner strategies: 30 years of research and practice* (pp. 9–28). Oxford, UK: Oxford University Press.

Grigorenko, E., Sternberg, R., & Ehrman, M. E. (2000). A theory based approach to the measurement of foreign language learning ability: The CANAL-F theory and test. *The Modern Language Journal*, *84*, 390–405.

Grosjean, F. (2001). The bilingual's language modes. In J. Nicol (Ed.), *One mind, two languages: Bilingual language processing*. Malden, MA: Blackwell.

Gu, Y., & Johnson, R. (1996). Vocabulary learning strategies and language learning outcomes. *Language Learning*, *46*, 643–679.

Guará-Tavares, M. G. (2008). *Pre-task planning, working memory capacity and L2 speech performance*. Unpublished doctoral thesis, Universidade Federal de Santa Catarina, Brazil.

Guilloteaux, M. J., & Dörnyei, Z. (2008). Motivating language learners: A classroom-oriented investigation of the effects of motivational strategies on student motivation. *TESOL Quarterly*, *42*, 55–77.

Gullberg, M. (1998). *Gesture as a communication strategy in second language discourse: A study of learners of French and Swedish*. Lund, Sweden: Lund University Press.

Gullberg, M., & McCafferty, S. (2008). Introduction to gesture and SLA: Toward an integrated approach. *Studies in Second Language Acquisition*, *30*, 133–146.

Gumperz, J., & Tannen, D. (1979). Individual and social differences in language use. In C. Fillmore, D. Kempler, & W. S.-Y. Wang (Eds.), *Individual differences in language ability and language behavior* (pp. 305–325). New York: Academic.

Hakuta, K. (1974a). Prefabricated patterns and the emergence of structure in second language learning. *Language Learning*, *24*, 287–297.

Hakuta, K. (1974b). A preliminary report on the development of grammatical morphemes in a Japanese girl learning English as a second language. *Working Papers in Bilingualism*, *3*, 18–43.

Hakuta, K. (1976a). A report on the development of grammatical morphemes in a Japanese girl learning English as a second language. In E. Hatch (Ed.), *Second language acquisition: A book of readings* (pp. 132–147). Rowley, MA: Newbury House.

Hakuta, K. (1976b). Becoming bilingual: A case study of a Japanese child learning English. *Language Learning*, *26*, 321–351.

Hama, M., & Leow, R. P. (2010). Learning without awareness revisited: Extending Williams (2005). *Studies in Second Language Acquisition*, *32*, 465–491.

Hamilton, R. (1994). Is implicational generalization unidirectional and maximal? Evidence from relativization instruction in a second language. *Language Learning*, *44*, 123–157.

Hamilton, R. (1996). Against underdetermined reflexive binding. *Second Language Research, 12,* 420–446.

Hammarberg, B. (2001). Roles of L1 and l2 in L3 production and acquisition. In J. Cenoz, B. Hufeisen, & U. Jessner (Eds.), *Cross-linguistic influence in third language acquisition: Psycholinguistic perspectives* (pp. 21–41). Clevedon, UK: Multilingual Matters.

Hammarberg, B. (Ed.) (2009). *Processes in third language acquisition.* Edinburgh, UK: Edinburgh University Press.

Han, Z.-H. (2000). Persistence of the implicit influence of L1: The case of the pseudo-passive. *Applied Linguistics, 21,* 78–105.

Han, Z.-H. (2002). A study of the impact of recasts on tense consistency in L2 output. *TESOL Quarterly, 36,* 543–72.

Han, Z.-H. (2004). *Fossilization in adult second language acquisition.* Clevedon, UK: Multilingual Matters.

Han, Z-H., Park, E., & Combs, C. (2008). Textual enhancement of input: issues and possibilities. *Applied Linguistics, 29,* 597–618.

Hanania, E. (1974). *Acquisition of English structures: A case study of an adult native speaker of Arabic in an English-speaking environment.* Unpublished doctoral dissertation, Indiana University, Bloomington.

Hancin-Bhatt, B. (2000). Optimality in second language phonology: Codas in Thai ESL. *Second Language Research, 16,* 201–232.

Hancin-Bhatt, B., & Bhatt, R. (1997). Optimal L2 syllables: Interactions of transfer and developmental effects. *Studies in Second Language Acquisition, 19,* 379–400.

Hankamer, J. (1989). Morphological parsing in the lexicon. In W. Marslen-Wilson (Ed.), *Lexical representation and process* (pp. 392–408). Cambridge, MA: MIT Press.

Harley, B. (1998). The role of focus-on-form tasks in promoting child L2 acquisition. In C. Doughty & J. Williams (Eds.), *Focus on form in classroom second language acquisition* (pp. 156–174). Cambridge, UK: Cambridge University Press.

Harley, B., & Hart, D. (1997). Language aptitude and second language proficiency in classroom learners of different starting ages. *Studies in Second Language Acquisition, 19,* 379–400.

Harley, B., & Swain, M. (1984). The interlanguage of immersion students and its implications for second language teaching. In A. Davies, C. Criper, & A. Howatt (Eds.), *Interlanguage* (pp. 291–311). Edinburgh, UK: Edinburgh University Press.

Harrington, M. (1987). Processing transfer: Language-specific strategies as a source of interlanguage variation. *Applied Psycholinguistics, 8,* 351–378.

Harrington, M., & Sawyer, M. (1992). L2 working memory capacity and L2 reading skill. *Studies in Second Language Acquisition, 14,* 25–38.

Harris, V. (2003). Adapting classroom-based strategy instruction to a distance learning context. *TESL-EJ, 7,* 1–19.

Hartsuiker, R. J., & Kolk, H. H. J. (1998). Syntactic persistence in Dutch. *Language and Speech, 41,* 143–184.

Hartsuiker, R. J., Kolk, H. H. J., & Huiskamp, P. (1999). Priming word order in sentence production. *Quarterly Journal of Experimental Psychology, 52A,* 129–147.

Hartsuiker, R. J., & Westenberg, C. (2000). Word order priming in written and spoken sentence production. *Cognition, 75*(2), B27–B39.

Hasbún, L. (1995). *The role of lexical aspect in the acquisition of tense and grammatical aspect in Spanish as a foreign language.* Unpublished doctoral dissertation, Indiana University, Bloomington.

Hassan, X., Macaro, E., Mason, D., Nye, G., Smith, P., & Vanderplank, R. (2005). *Strategy training in language learning: A systematic review of available research.* Retrieved

October 1, 2007, from University of London, EPPI–Centre Social Science Research Unit, Institute of Education website: http://eppi.ioe.ac.uk/EPPIWeb/home.aspx?page=/reel/ review_groups/mfl/review_one.htm

Hatch, E. (1978). Discourse and second language acquisition. In E. Hatch (Ed.), *Second language acquisition: A book of readings* (pp. 401–435). Rowley, MA: Newbury House.

Hatch, E. (1983). *Psycholinguistics: A second language perspective*. Rowley, MA: Newbury House.

Hatch, E., & Hawkins, B. (1985). Second-language acquisition: An experiential approach. In S. Rosenberg (Ed.), *Advances in applied psycholinguistics, Vol. 2* (pp. 241–283). New York: Cambridge University Press.

Hawkins, B. (1985). Is an "appropriate response" always so appropriate? In S. Gass & C. Madden (Eds.), *Input in second language acquisition* (pp. 162–178). Rowley, MA: Newbury House.

Hawkins, R. (2003). *"Representational deficit" theories of (adult) SLA: Evidence, counterevidence and implications*. Paper presented at European Second Language Association, Edinburgh.

Hawkins, R., & Chan, C. Y.-H. (1997). The partial availability of universal grammar in second language acquisition: The "failed functional features hypothesis." *Second Language Research, 13*, 187–226.

Hawkins, R., & Hattori, H. (2006). Interpretation of English multiple wh-questions by Japanese speakers: A missing uninterpretable feature account. *Second Language Research, 22*, 269–301.

Haynes, M., & Baker, I. (1993). American and Chinese readers learning from lexical familiarizations in English text. In T. Huckin, M. Haynes, & J. Coady (Eds.), *Second language reading and vocabulary learning* (pp. 130–150). Norwood, NJ: Ablex.

Heilenman, K., & McDonald, J. (1993). Processing strategies in L2 learners of French: The role of transfer. *Language Learning, 43*, 507–557.

Henkes, T. (1974). *Early stages in the non-native acquisition of English syntax: A study of three children from Zaire, Venezuela, and Saudi Arabia*. Unpublished doctoral dissertation, Indiana University, Bloomington.

Henriksen, B. (1999). Three dimensions of vocabulary development. *Studies in Second Language Acquisition, 21*, 303–317.

Henry, N., Culman, H., & VanPatten, B. (2009). More on the effects of explicit information in processing instruction: A partial replication and response to Fernández (2008). *Studies in Second Language Acquisition, 31*, 359–375.

Herwig, A. (2001). Plurilingual lexical organization: Evidence from lexical processing in L1–L2–L3–L4 translation. In J. Cenoz, B. Hufeisen, & U. Jessner (Eds.), *Cross-linguistic influences in third language acquisition: Psycholinguistic perspectives* (pp. 115–137). Clevedon, UK: Multilingual Matters.

Hewitt, E., & Stephenson, J. (2012). Foreign language anxiety and oral exam performance: A replication of Phillips's MLJ study. *The Modern Language Journal, 96*(2), 170–189.

Hill, A. (1961). Grammaticality. *Word, 17*, 1–10.

Hilles, S. (1986). Interlanguage in the pro-drop parameter. *Second Language Research, 2*, 33–52.

Hoek, D., Ingram, D., & Gibson, D. (1986). Some possible causes of children's early word extensions. *Journal of Child Language, 13*, 477–494.

Hoffman, M. L. (1986). Affect, cognition and motivation. In R. M. Sorrentino & E. T. Higgins (Eds.), *Handbook of motivation and cognition* (pp. 244–280). New York: Guilford.

Horst, M. (2010). How well does teacher talk support incidental vocabulary acquisition? *Reading in a Foreign Language, 22*, 161–180.

Horwitz, E. K. (2001). Language anxiety and achievement. *Annual Review of Applied Linguistics*, *21*, 112–126.

Houck, N., & Gass, S. (1996). Non-native refusals: A methodological perspective. In S. Gass & J. Neu (Eds.), *Speech acts across cultures* (pp. 45–64). Berlin: Mouton de Gruyter.

Housen, A. (1995). *It's about time*. Unpublished doctoral dissertation, Vrije Universiteit, Brussels, Belgium.

Housen, A., & Kuiken, F. (2009). Complexity, accuracy, and fluency in second language acquisition. *Applied Linguistics*, *30*, 461–473.

Hu, X., & Liu, C. (2007). Restrictive relative clauses in English and Korean learners' second language Chinese. *Second Language Research*, *23*, 263–287.

Huebner, T. (1979). Order-of-acquisition vs. dynamic paradigm: A comparison of method in interlanguage research. *TESOL Quarterly*, *13*, 21–28.

Huebner, T. (1983). *A longitudinal analysis of the acquisition of English*. Ann Arbor, MI: Karoma.

Hulstijn, J. (2005). Theoretical and empirical issues in the study of implicit and explicit second-language learning: Introduction. *Studies in Second Language Acquisition*, *27*, 129–140.

Hulstijn, J., Hollander, M., & Greidanus, T. (1996). Incidental vocabulary learning by advanced foreign language students: The influence of marginal glosses, dictionary use, and reoccurrence of unknown words. *The Modern Language Journal*, *80*, 327–339.

Hulstijn, J., & Hulstijn, W. (1984). Grammatical errors as a function of processing constraints and explicit knowledge. *Language Learning*, *34*, 23–43.

Hulstijn, J., & Laufer, B. (2001). Some empirical evidence for the involvement load hypothesis in vocabulary acquisition. *Language Learning*, *51*, 539–558.

Hulstijn, J., & Marchena, E. (1989). Avoidance: Grammatical or semantic causes? *Studies in Second Language Acquisition*, *11*, 241–255.

Hunt, K. W. (1965). *Grammatical structures written at three grade levels* (NCTE Research Report No. 3). Champaign, IL: National Council of Teachers of English.

Hunt, K. W. (1970). Syntactic maturity in school-children and adults. *Monographs for the Society for Research in Child Development*, *35*(1, Serial No. 134).

Hyams, N. (1983). *The acquisition of parameterized grammars*. Unpublished doctoral dissertation, City University of New York.

Hyltenstam, K. (1977). Implicational patterns in interlanguage syntax variation. *Language Learning*, *27*, 383–411.

Hyltenstam, K. (1984). The use of typological markedness conditions as predictors in second language acquisition: The case of pronominal copies in relative clauses. In R. Andersen (Ed.), *Second languages: A crosslinguistic perspective* (pp. 39–58). Rowley, MA: Newbury House.

Hyltenstam, K., & Abrahamsson, N. (2003). Maturational constraints in SLA. In C. Doughty & M. H. Long (Eds.), *The handbook of second language acquisition* (pp. 539–588). Oxford, UK: Blackwell.

In'nami, Y., & Koizumi, R. (2010). Database selection guidelines for meta-analysis in applied linguistics. *TESOL Quarterly*, *44*, 169–184.

Ioup, G. (1984). Is there a structural foreign accent? A comparison of syntactic and phonological errors in second language acquisition. *Language Learning*, *34*, 1–17.

Isemonger, I. (2007). Operational definitions of explicit and implicit knowledge: A response to R. Ellis (2005) and some recommendations for future research in this area. *Studies in Second Language Acquisition*, *29*, 101–118.

Ishida, M. (2004). Effects of recasts on the acquisition of the aspectual form *te i(ru)* by learners of Japanese as a foreign language. *Language Learning*, *54*, 311–394.

Iwashita, N. (2003). Negative feedback and positive evidence in task-based interaction: Differential effects on L2 development. *Studies in Second Language Acquisition*, *25*, 1–36.

Izquierdo, J., & Collins, L. (2008). The facilitative role of L1 influence in tense–aspect marking: A comparison of Hispanophone and Anglophone learners of French. *The Modern Language Journal*, *92*, 350–368.

Izumi, S. (2002). Output, input enhancement and the noticing hypothesis: An experimental study on ESL relativization. *Studies in Second Language Acquisition*, *24*, 541–577.

Izumi, S., & Bigelow, M. (2000). Does output promote noticing in second language acquisition? *TESOL Quarterly*, *34*, 239–278.

Izumi, S., Bigelow, M., Fujiwara, M., & Fearnow, S. (1999). Testing the output hypothesis: Effects of output on noticing and second language acquisition. *Studies in Second Language Acquisition*, *21*, 421–452.

Izumi, Y., & Izumi, S. (2004). Investigating the effects of oral output on the learning of relative clauses in English: Issues in the psycholinguistic requirements for effective output tasks. *The Canadian Modern Language Review*, *60*, 587–609.

Jannedy, S., Poletto, R., & Weldon, T. (Eds.) (1994). *Language files* (6th ed.). Columbus, OH: Ohio State University Press.

Jared, D., & Kroll, J. F. (2001). Do bilinguals activate phonological representations in one or both of their languages when naming words? *Journal of Memory and Language*, *44*, 2–31.

Jarvis, S. (2002). Topic continuity in L2 English article use. *Studies in Second Language Acquisition*, *24*, 387–418.

Jeon, E. H., & Kaya, T. (2006). Effects of L2 instruction on interlanguage pragmatic development: A meta-analysis. In J. M. Norris & L. Ortega (Eds.), *Synthesizing research on language learning and teaching* (pp. 165–211). Philadelphia: John Benjamins.

Jeon, E. H., & Yamashita, J. (2011, October). *The relationship of second language reading comprehension to its components: A meta-analysis of correlation coefficients*. Paper presented at the Second Language Research Forum, Ames, Iowa.

Jeon, K. S. (2007). Interaction-driven L2 learning: Characterizing linguistic development. In A. Mackey (Ed.), *Conversational interaction in second language acquisition: A collection of empirical studies* (pp. 379–403). Oxford, UK: Oxford University Press.

Jeon, K. S., & Kim, H.-Y. (2007). Development of relativization in Korean as a foreign language: Noun Phrase Accessibility Hierarchy in head-internal and head-external relative clauses. *Studies in Second Language Acquisition*, *29*, 253–276.

Jiang, N. (2000). Lexical representation and development in a second language. *Applied Linguistics*, *21*, 47–77.

Jiang, N. (2002). Form–meaning mapping in vocabulary acquisition in a second language. *Studies in Second Language Acquisition*, *24*, 617–637.

Jiang, N. (2004). Semantic transfer and its implications for vocabulary teaching in a second language. *The Modern Language Journal*, *88*, 416–432.

Jiang, N. (2012). *Conducting reaction time research in second language studies*. New York: Routledge.

Johansson, S. (1978). *Studies in error gravity: Native reactions to errors produced by Swedish learners of English*. Göteberg, Sweden: Acta Universitatis Gothoburgensis.

Johnson, J., & Newport, E. (1989). Critical period effects in second language learning: The influence of maturational state on the acquisition of ESL. *Cognitive Psychology*, *21*, 60–99.

Johnson, J., & Newport, E. (1991). Critical period effects on universal properties of language: The status of subjacency in the acquisition of a second language. *Cognition*, *39*, 215–258.

Johnson, K. E. (2009). *Second language teacher education: A sociocultural perspective*. New York: Routledge.

Jones, R. (1977). Social and psychological factors in second language acquisition: A study of an individual. In C. Henning (Ed.), *Proceedings of the Second Language Research Forum* (pp. 331–341). Los Angeles: University of California, Department of Applied Linguistics.

Jordan, G. (2005). *Theory construction in second language acquisition*. Amsterdam: John Benjamins.

Jourdenais, R., Ota, M., Stauffer, S., Boyson, B., & Doughty, C. (1995). Does textual enhancement promote noticing: A think-aloud protocol analysis. In R. Schmidt (Ed.), *Attention and awareness in foreign language learning* (pp. 183–216). Honolulu: University of Hawai'i Press.

Juffs, A., & Harrington, M. (2011). Working memory in L2 learning. *Language Teaching*, *44*, 137–166.

Kagan, O., & Dillon, K. (2012). Heritage languages and L2 learning. In S. Gass & A. Mackey (Eds.), *The handbook of second language acquisition* (pp. 491–505). New York: Routledge.

Kanno, K. (1996). The status of a nonparameterized principle in the L2 initial state. *Language Acquisition*, *5*, 317–332.

Kanno, K. (2007). The role of an innate acquisition device in second language acquisition. In M. Nakayama, R. Mazuka, & Y. Shirai (Eds.), *Handbook of Japanese psycholinguistics* (pp. 144–150). Cambridge, UK: Cambridge University Press.

Kantor, R. (1978). Identifying native and second language signers. *Communication and Cognition*, *11*, 39–55.

Kaplan, M. A. (1987). Developmental patterns of past tense acquisition among foreign language learners of French. In B. VanPatten, T. R. Dvorak, & J. F. Lee (Eds.), *Foreign language learning: A research perspective* (pp. 52–60). Rowley, MA: Newbury House.

Kasper, G. (1997). "A" stands for acquisition. *The Modern Language Journal*, *81*, 307–312.

Kasper, G. (2004). Participant orientations in German conversation-for-learning. *The Modern Language Journal*, *88*, 551–567.

Kasper, G., & Rose, K. R. (2002). *Pragmatic development in a second language*. Oxford, UK: Blackwell.

Kasper, G., & Schmidt, R. (1996). Developmental issues in interlanguage pragmatics. *Studies in Second Language Acquisition*, *18*, 149–169.

Kawaguchi, S. (2005). Argument structure and syntactic development in Japanese as a second language. In M. Pienemann (Ed.), *Cross-linguistic aspects of Processability Theory* (pp. 253–298). Amsterdam: John Benjamins.

Kawauchi, C. (2005). The effects of strategic planning on the oral narratives of learners with low and high intermediate proficiency. In R. Ellis (Ed.), *Planning and task-performance in a second language* (pp. 143–164). Amsterdam: John Benjamins.

Ke, C. (1998). Effects of language background on the learning of Chinese characters among foreign language students. *Foreign Language Annals*, *31*, 91–100.

Keck, C., Iberri-Shea, G., Tracy-Ventura, N., & Wa-Mbalaka, S. (2006). Investigating the empirical link between interaction and acquisition: A quantitative metananlysis. In J. M. Norris & L. Ortega (Eds.), *Synthesizing research on language learning and teaching* (pp. 91–131). Amsterdam: John Benjamins.

Keenan, E. (1975). Variation in Universal Grammar. In R. Fasold & R. Shuy (Eds.), *Analyzing variation in language* (pp. 136–148). Washington, DC: Georgetown University Press.

Keenan, E., & Comrie, B. (1977). Noun phrase accessibility and Universal Grammar. *Linguistic Inquiry, 8*, 63–99.

Kellerman, E. (1979). Transfer and non-transfer: Where we are now. *Studies in Second Language Acquisition, 2*, 37–57.

Kellerman, E. (1987). *Aspects of transferability in second language acquisition*. Unpublished doctoral dissertation, Katholieke Universiteit te Nijmegen.

Kellerman, E., & Sharwood Smith, M. (Eds.) (1986). *Cross-linguistic influence in second language acquisition*. Oxford, UK: Pergamon Press.

Kellerman, E., van Ijzendoorn, J., & Takashima, H. (1999). Retesting a universal: The Empty Category Principle & learners of (pseudo) Japanese as a second language. In K. Kanno (Ed.), *Studies on the acquisition of Japanese as a second language* (pp. 71–87). Amsterdam: John Benjamins.

Kempen, G. (1977). Conceptualizing and formulating in sentence production. In S. Rosenberg (Ed.), *Sentence production: Developments in research and theory* (pp. 259–274). Hillsdale, NJ: Lawrence Erlbaum Associates.

Kempen, G. (1978). Sentence construction by a psychologically plausible formulator. In R. N. Campbell & P. T. Smith (Eds.), *Recent advances in the psychology of language: Formal and experimental approaches* (pp. 103–123). New York: Plenum.

Kempen, G., & Hoenkamp, E. (1981). *A procedural grammar for sentence production* (Internal Report No. 81). Nijmegen, The Netherlands: Katholieke Universiteit, Vakgroep psychologische functieleer, Psychologisch taboratorium.

Kempen, G., & Hoenkamp, E. (1987). An incremental procedural grammar for sentence formulation. *Cognitive Science, 11*, 201–258.

Kilborn, K., & Ito, T. (1989). Sentence processing strategies in adult bilinguals. In B. MacWhinney & E. Bates (Eds.), *The crosslinguistic study of sentence processing* (pp. 257–291). Cambridge, UK: Cambridge University Press.

Kim, Y. (2008). The role of task-induced involvement and learner proficiency in L2 vocabulary acquisition. *Language Learning, 58*, 285–325.

Kim, Y. (2009). The effects of task complexity on learner–learner interaction. *System, 37*, 254–268.

Kim, Y., & McDonough, K. (2008). Learners' production of passives during syntactic priming activities. *Applied Linguistics, 29*, 149–154.

Kinginger, C. (2004). Alice doesn't live here anymore: Foreign language learning and identity reconstruction. In A. Pavlenko & A. Blackledge (Eds.), *Negotiation of identities in multilingual contexts* (pp. 219–242). Clevedon, UK: Multilingual Matters.

Kleifgen, J. A. (1985). Skilled variation in a kindergarten teacher's use of foreigner talk. In S. Gass & C. Madden (Eds.), *Input in second language acquisition* (pp. 59–85). Cambridge, MA: Newbury House.

Klein, E. (1994). *Second versus third language acquisition: Does prior linguistic knowledge make a difference?* Unpublished manuscript.

Klein, E. (1995). Evidence for a "wild" L2 grammar: When PP's rear their empty heads. *Applied Linguistics, 16*, 87–117.

Klein, W., & Perdue, C. (1989). The learner's problem of arranging words. In B. MacWhinney & E. Bates (Eds.), *The crosslinguistic study of sentence processing* (pp. 292–327). Cambridge, UK: Cambridge University Press.

Kleinmann, H. (1977). Avoidance behavior in adult second language acquisition. *Language Learning, 27*, 93–107.

Klima, E., & Bellugi, U. (1966). Syntactic regularities in the speech of children. In J. Lyons & R. J. Wales (Eds.), *Psycholinguistics Papers* (pp. 183–219). Edinburgh, UK: Edinburgh University Press.

Koch, A. S., & Terrell, T. D. (1991). Affective reactions of foreign language students to natural approach activities and teaching techniques. In E. K. Horwitz & D. J. Young (Eds.), *Language anxiety: From theory and research to classroom implications* (pp. 109–126). Englewood Cliffs, NJ: Prentice Hall.

Koda, K. (1989). The effects of transferred vocabulary knowledge on the development of L2 reading proficiency. *Foreign Language Annals, 22*, 529–540.

Kormos, J. (1999). The timing of self-repairs in second language speech production. *Studies in Second Language Acquisition, 22*, 145–167.

Kormos, J., & Sáfár, A. (2008). Phonological short-term memory and foreign language performance in intensive language learning. *Bilingualism: Language and Cognition, 11*, 261–271.

Kormos, J., & Trebits, A. (2012). The role of task complexity, modality, and aptitude in narrative task performance. *Language Learning, 62*, 439–472.

Kovacs, A., & Mehler, J. (2009). Flexible learning of multiple speech structures in bilingual infants. *Science, 325*, 611–612.

Krashen, S. (1977). Some issues relating to the monitor model. In H. Brown, C. Yorio, & R. Crymes (Eds.), *On TESOL '77: Teaching and learning English as a second language: Trends in research and practice* (pp. 144–158). Washington, DC: Teachers of English to Speakers of Other Languages.

Krashen, S. (1982). *Principles and practice in second language acquisition*. London: Pergamon.

Krashen, S. (1985). *The Input Hypothesis: Issues and implications*. New York: Longman.

Krashen, S., Butler, J., Birnbaum, R., & Robertson, J. (1978). Two studies in language acquisition and language learning. *ITL: Review of Applied Linguistics, 39–40*, 73–92.

Krashen, S., Houck, N., Giunchi, P., Bode, S., Birnbaum, R., & Strei, G. (1977). Difficulty order for grammatical morphemes for adult second language performers using free speech. *TESOL Quarterly, 11*, 338–341.

Kreeft Peyton, J., Ranard, D., & McGinnis, S. (Eds.) (2001). *Heritage languages in America: Preserving a national resource*. McHenry, IL: The Center for Applied Linguistics/Delta Systems.

Kroll, J. F., & Stewart, E. (1994). Category interference in translation and picture naming: Evidence for asymmetric connections between bilingual memory representations. *Journal of Memory and Language, 33*, 149–174.

Kroll, J. F., & Sunderman, G. (2003). Cognitive processes in second language learners and bilinguals: The development of lexical and conceptual representations. In C. Doughty & M. H. Long (Eds.), *The handbook of second language acquisition* (pp. 104–129). Cambridge, MA: Blackwell.

Kumpf, L. (1984). Temporal systems and universality in interlanguage: A case study. In F. Eckman, L. Bell, & D. Nelson (Eds.), *Universals of second language acquisition* (pp. 132–143). Rowley, MA: Newbury House.

Labov, W. (1969). Contraction, deletion, and inherent variability of the English copula. *Language, 45*, 715–762.

Labov, W. (1970). The study of language in its social context. *Studium Generale, 23*, 30–87.

Labov, W., & Fanshel, D. (1977). *Therapeutic discourse*. New York: Academic.

Lado, R. (1957). *Linguistics across cultures*. Ann Arbor: University of Michigan Press.

Lafford, B. (2006). The effects of study abroad vs. classroom contexts on Spanish SLA: Old assumptions, new insights and future research directions. In C. Klee & T. Face (Eds.), *Selected proceedings of the 7th conference on the acquisition of Spanish and Portuguese as first and second languages* (pp. 1–25). Somerville, MA: Cascadilla Proceedings Project.

Lakshmanan, U. (1986). The role of parametric variation in adult second language acquisition: A study of the "pro-drop" parameter. *Papers in Applied Linguistics–Michigan, 2*, 97–118.

Lakshmanan, U. (1995). Child second language acquisition of syntax. *Studies in Second Language Acquisition, 17*, 301–329.

Lakshmanan, U., & Teranishi, K. (1994). Preferences versus grammaticality judgments: Some methodological issues concerning the governing category parameter in second language acquisition. In E. Tarone, S. Gass, & A. Cohen (Eds.), *Research methodology in second language acquisition* (pp. 185–206). Hillsdale, NJ: Lawrence Erlbaum Associates.

Lantolf, J. (2012). Sociocultural theory: A dialectical approach to L2 research. In S. Gass & A. Mackey (Eds.), *The Routledge handbook of second language acquisition* (pp. 57–72). New York: Routledge.

Lantolf, J. P., & Thorne, S. (2006). *Sociocultural theory and the genesis of second language development*. Oxford, UK: Oxford University Press.

Lantolf, J. P., & Thorne, S. (2007). Sociocultural theory and second language learning. In B. VanPatten & J. Williams (Eds.), *Theories in second language acquisition: An introduction* (pp. 201–224). Mahwah, NJ: Lawrence Erlbaum Associates.

Lantolf, J. P., & Yáñez, M. C. (2003). Talking yourself into Spanish: The role of private speech in second language learning. *Hispania, 86*, 98–110.

Lardiere, D. (2007). *Ultimate attainment in second language acquisition: A case study*. Mahwah, NJ: Lawrence Erlbaum Associates.

Lardiere, D. (2009). Some thoughts on the contrastive analysis of features in second language acquisition. *Second Language Research, 25*, 173–227.

Lardiere, D. (2012). Linguistic approaches to second language morphosyntax. In S. Gass & A. Mackey (Eds.), *The Routledge handbook of second language acquisition* (pp. 106–126). New York: Routledge.

Larsen-Freeman, D. (1975a). *The acquisition of grammatical morphemes by adult learners of English as a second language*. Unpublished doctoral dissertation, University of Michigan, Ann Arbor.

Larsen-Freeman, D. (1975b). The acquisition of grammatical morphemes by adult ESL students. *TESOL Quarterly, 9*, 409–430.

Larsen-Freeman, D. (1976). An explanation for the morpheme acquisition order of second language learners. *Language Learning, 26*, 125–134.

Larsen-Freeman, D. (1978). An explanation for the morpheme accuracy order of learners of English as a second language. In E. Hatch (Ed.), *Second language acquisition: A book of readings* (pp. 371–379). Rowley, MA: Newbury House.

Larsen-Freeman, D. (1997). Chaos/complexity science and second language acquisition. *Applied Linguistics, 18*, 141–165.

Larsen-Freeman, D. (2006). The emergence of complexity, fluency, and accuracy production of five Chinese learners of English. *Applied Linguistics, 27*, 590–619.

Larsen-Freeman, D. (2012). Complexity theory. In S. Gass & A. Mackey, *The Routledge handbook of second language acquisition* (pp. 73–87). New York: Routledge.

Larsen-Freeman, D., & Long, M. (1991). *An introduction to second language acquisition research*. London: Longman.

Larsen-Freeman, D., Schmid, M., & Lowie, W. (2011). From structure to chaos: Twenty years of modeling bilingualism. In M. Schmid & W. Lowie (Eds.), *Modeling bilingualism: From structure to chaos* (pp. 1–11). Amsterdam: John Benjamins.

Laufer, B. (1997a). What's in a word that makes it hard or easy: Some intralexical factors that affect the learning of words. In N. Schmitt & M. McCarthy (Eds.), *Vocabulary: Description, acquisition and pedagogy* (pp. 140–180). Cambridge, UK: Cambridge University Press.

Laufer, B. (1997b). The lexical plight in second language reading: Words you don't know, words you think you know, and words you can't guess. In J. Coady & T. Huckin (Eds.), *Second language vocabulary acquisition: A rationale for pedagogy* (pp. 20–33). Cambridge, UK: Cambridge University Press.

Laufer, B. (1998). The development of passive and active vocabulary in a second language: Same or different? *Applied Linguistics*, *19*, 255–271.

Laufer, B. (2005). Focus on form in second language vocabulary learning. In S. Foster-Cohen, M. del Pilar García Mayo, & J. Cenoz (Eds.), *EuroSLA Yearbook* (pp. 223–150). Amsterdam: John Benjamins.

Laufer, B., & Eliasson, S. (1993). What causes avoidance in L2 learning: L1–L2 difference, L1–L2 similarity, or L2 complexity? *Studies in Second Language Acquisition*, *15*, 33–48.

Laufer, B., & Hulstijn, J. (2001). Incidental vocabulary acquisition in a second language: The construct of task-induced involvement. *Applied Linguistics*, *23*, 1–26.

Laufer, B., & Nation, I. S. P. (2012). Vocabulary. In S. M. Gass & A. Mackey (Eds.), *The Routledge handbook of second language acquisition* (pp. 163–176). New York: Routledge.

Laufer, B., & Paribakht, S. (1998). The relationship between passive and active vocabularies: Effects of language learning context. *Language Learning*, *48*, 365–391.

Laufer, B., & Rozovski-Roitblat, B. (2011). Incidental vocabulary acquisition: The effects of task type, word occurrence and their combination. *Language Teaching Research*, *15*, 391–411.

Leary, M. R., Knight, P. D., & Johnson, K. A. (1987). Social anxiety and dyadic conversation: A verbal response analysis. *Journal of Social and Clinical Psychology*, *5*, 34–50.

LeBlanc, R., & Painchaud, G. (1985). Self-assessment as a second language placement instrument. *TESOL Quarterly*, *19*(4), 673–687.

Lee, J. (2007). *The inside of the L2 lexicon and semantic overgeneralization*. Unpublished manuscript, Michigan State University.

Lee, S.-K., & Huang, H.-T. (2008). Visual input enhancement and grammar learning: A meta-analytic review. *Studies in Second Language Acquisition*, *30*, 307–331.

Leeman, J. (2003). Recasts and second language development: Beyond negative evidence. *Studies in Second Language Acquisition*, *25*, 37–63.

Leeser, M. J. (2007). Learner-based factors in L2 reading comprehension and processing grammatical form: Topic familiarity and working memory. *Language Learning*, *57*, 229–270.

Lemhöfer, K., & Dijkstra, T. (2004). Recognizing cognates and interlingual homographs: Effects of code similarity in language-specific and generalized lexical decision. *Memory and Cognition*, *32*, 533–550.

Lenet, A., Sanz, C., Lado, B., Howard, J. H., & Howard, D. V. (2011). Aging pedagogical conditions, and differential success in SLA: An empirical study. In C. Sanz (Ed.), *Implicit and explicit language learning: Conditions, processes, and knowledge in SLA and bilingualism* (pp. 73–84). Washington, DC: Georgetown University Press.

Lennenberg, E. (1967). *Biological foundations of language.* New York: John Wiley.

Leow, R. (1997). Attention, awareness, and foreign language behavior. *Language Learning, 47,* 467–505.

Leow, R. (2000). A study of the role of awareness in foreign language behavior: Aware versus unaware learners. *Studies in Second Language Acquisition, 22,* 557–584.

Leow, R. (2001). Attention, awareness, and foreign language behavior. *Language Learning, 51*(Suppl. 1), 113–155.

Leung, J., & Williams, J. (2012). Constraints on implicit learning of grammatical form-meaning connections. *Language Learning, 62,* 634–662.

Levelt, C., Schiller, N., & Levelt, W. J. M. (1999). A developmental grammar for syllable structure in the production of child language. *Brain and Language, 68,* 291–299.

Levelt, W. J. M. (1989). *Speaking: From intention to articulation.* Cambridge, MA: MIT Press.

Levenston, E. (1979). Second language acquisition: Issues and problems. *Interlanguage Studies Bulletin, 4,* 147–160.

Li, S. (2010a). *Corrective feedback in perspective: The interface between feedback type, proficiency, the choice of target structure, and learners' individual differences in working memory and language analytic ability.* Unpublished doctoral dissertation, Michigan State University, East Lansing, MI.

Li, S. (2010b). The effectiveness of corrective feedback in SLA: A meta-analysis. *Language Learning, 60,* 309–365.

Li, S. (2012). The effect of input-based practice on pragmatic development in L2 Chinese. *Language Learning, 62,* 403–438.

Lightbown, P. (1983). Exploring relationships between developmental and instructional sequences in L2 acquisition. In H. Seliger & M. H. Long (Eds.), *Classroom oriented research in second language acquisition* (pp. 217–243). Rowley, MA: Newbury House.

Lightbown, P. (1985). Great expectations: Second language acquisition research and classroom teaching. *Applied Linguistics, 6,* 173–189.

Lightbown, P. (1992). Can they do it themselves? A comprehension-based ESL course for young children. In R. Courchêne, J. Glidden, J. St. John, & C. Thérien (Eds.), *Comprehension-based second language teaching* (pp. 353–370). Ottawa, Canada: University of Ottawa Press.

Lightbown, P. (1998). The importance of timing in focus on form. In C. Doughty & J. Williams (Eds.), *Focus on form in classroom second language acquisition* (pp. 177–196). Cambridge, UK: Cambridge University Press.

Lightbown, P., & Spada, N. (2006). *How languages are learned.* Oxford, UK: Oxford University Press.

Lim, H. Y. (2002). The interaction of motivation, perception, and environment: One EFL learner's experience. *Hong Kong Journal of Applied Linguistics, 7,* 91–106.

Lin, Y.-H., & Hedgcock, J. (1996). Negative feedback incorporation among high-proficiency and low-proficiency Chinese-speaking learners of Spanish. *Language Learning, 46,* 567–611.

Linck, J. A., & Weiss, D. J. (2011). Working memory predicts the acquisition of explicit L2 knowledge. In C. Sanz (Ed.), *Implicit and explicit language learning: Conditions, processes, and knowledge in SLA and bilingualism* (pp. 101–113). Washington, DC: Georgetown University Press.

Linell, P. (1982). The concept of phonological form and the activities of speech production and speech perception. *Journal of Phonetics, 10,* 37–72.

Linell, P. (1985). Problems and perspective in the study of spoken interaction. In L. S. Evensen (Ed.), *Nordic research in text linguistics and discourse analysis* (pp. 103–136). Trondheim, Norway: TAPIR.

Liu, D., & Jiang, P. (2009). Using a corpus-based lexicogrammatical approach to grammar instruction in EFL and ESL contexts. *The Modern Language Journal*, *93*, 61–78.

Liu, G. (1991). *Interaction and second language acquisition: A case study of a Chinese child's acquisition of English as a second language*. Unpublished doctoral dissertation, La Trobe University, Australia.

Liu, M., & Jackson, J. (2008). An exploration of Chinese EFL learners' unwillingness to communicate and foreign language anxiety. *The Modern Language Journal*, *92*, 71–86.

Loewen, S. (2003). *Grammaticality judgment tests: What do they really measure?* Paper presented at the Second Language Research Forum, Tucson, AZ.

Loewen, S. (2009). Recasts in multiple response focus on form episodes. In A. Mackey & C. Polio (Eds.), *Multiple perspectives on interaction: Second language research in honor of Susan M. Gass* (pp. 176–196). New York: Routledge.

Loewen, S. (2012). The role of feedback. In S. Gass & A. Mackey (Eds.), *The Routledge handbook of second language acquisition* (pp. 24–40). New York: Routledge.

Loewen, S., & Basturkmen, H. (2005). Interaction in group writing tasks in genre-based instruction in an EAP classroom. *Journal of Asian Pacific Communication*, *15*, 171–189.

Loewen, S., & Reinders, H. (2011). *Key concepts in second language acquisition*. New York: Palgrave Macmillan.

Lombardi, L. (2003). Second language data and constraints on Manner: Explaining substitutions for the English interdentals. *Second Language Research*, *19*, 225–250.

Long, M. H. (1980). *Input, interaction and second language acquisition*. Unpublished doctoral dissertation, University of California, Los Angeles.

Long, M. H. (1983). Does second language instruction make a difference? *TESOL Quarterly*, *17*, 359–382.

Long, M. H. (1990). Maturational constraints on language development. *Studies in Second Language Acquisition*, *12*, 251–285.

Long, M. H. (1991). Focus on form: A design feature in language teaching methodology. In K. de Bot, R. Ginsberg, & C. Kramsch (Eds.), *Foreign language research in cross-cultural perspective* (pp. 39–52). Amsterdam: John Benjamins.

Long, M. H. (1996). The role of the linguistic environment in second language acquisition. In W. Ritchie & T. Bhatia (Eds.), *Handbook of second language acquisition* (pp. 413–468). San Diego, CA: Academic Press.

Long, M. H. (1997). Construct validity in SLA research. *The Modern Language Journal*, *81*, 318–323.

Long, M. H. (2007). *Problems in SLA*. Mahwah, NJ: Lawrence Erlbaum Associates.

Long, M. H., Inagaki, S., & Ortega, L. (1998). The role of implicit negative feedback in SLA: Models and recasts in Japanese and Spanish. *The Modern Language Journal*, *82*, 357–371.

Long, M. H., & Sato, C. (1983). Classroom foreigner talk discourse: Forms and functions of teachers' questions. In H. Seliger & M. H. Long (Eds.), *Classroom oriented research in second language acquisition* (pp. 268–285). Rowley, MA: Newbury House.

Loschky, L. C. (1989). *The effects of negotiated interaction and premodified input on second language comprehension and retention* (Occasional Papers No. 16). University of Hawai'i at Manoa.

Loschky, L. C., & Bley-Vroman, R. (1993). Grammar and task-based methodology. In G. Crookes & S. Gass (Eds.), *Tasks and language learning: Integrating theory and practice* (pp. 122–167).Clevedon, UK: Multilingual Matters.

Luk, Z., & Shirai, Y. (2009). Is the acquisition order of grammatical morphemes impervious to L1 knowledge? Evidence from the acquisition of plural -s, articles, and possessive 's. *Language Learning*, *59*, 721–754.

Lukyanchenko, A., & Gor, K. (2011). Perceptual correlates of phonological representations in heritage speakers and L2 learners. In N. Danis, K. Mesh, & H. Sung (Eds.), *Proceedings of the 35th Annual Boston University Conference on Language Development* (pp. 414–426). Somerville, MA: Cascadilla Press.

Lyster, R. (1998). Recasts, repetition, and ambiguity in L2 classroom discourse. *Studies in Second Language Acquisition*, *20*, 51–81.

Lyster, R. (2004). Differential effects of prompts and recasts in form-focused instruction. *Studies in Second Language Acquisition*, *26*, 399–432.

Lyster, R., & Ranta, L. (1997). Corrective feedback and learner uptake: Negotiation of form in communicative classrooms. *Studies in Second Language Acquisition*, *20*, 37–66.

Macaro, E. (2001). *Learning strategies in foreign and second language classrooms*. London: Continuum Press.

MacIntyre, P. D. (1999). Language anxiety: A review of the research for language teachers. In D. J. Young (Ed.), *Affect in foreign language and second language learning* (pp. 24–45). Boston, MA: McGraw-Hill.

MacIntyre, P. D. (2002). Motivation, anxiety and emotion in second language acquisition. In P. Robinson (Ed.), *Individual differences and instructed language learning* (pp. 45–68). Amsterdam: John Benjamins.

MacIntyre, P. D. (2007). Willingness to communicate in the second language: Understanding the decision to speak as a volitional process. *The Modern Language Journal*, *91*, 564–576.

MacIntyre, P. D., & Gardner, R. C. (1994). The subtle effects of language anxiety on cognitive processing in the second language. *Language Learning*, *44*, 283–305.

Mackey, A. (1995). *Stepping up the pace—Input, interaction and interlanguage development: An empirical study of questions in ESL*. Unpublished doctoral dissertation, University of Sydney, Australia.

Mackey, A. (1999). Input, interaction and second language development. *Studies in Second Language Acquisition*, *21*, 557–587.

Mackey, A. (2002). Beyond production: Learners' perceptions about interactional processes. *International Journal of Educational Research*, *37*, 379–394.

Mackey, A. (2006). Feedback, noticing and instructed second language learning. *Applied Linguistics*, *27*, 405–430.

Mackey, A., Abbuhl, R., & Gass, S. (2012). Interactionist approach. In S. Gass & A. Mackey (Eds.), *The Routledge handbook of second language acquisition* (pp. 7–23). New York: Routledge.

Mackey, A., Adams, R., Stafford, C., & Winke, P. (2010). Exploring the relationship between modified output and working memory capacity. *Language Learning*, *60*, 501–533.

Mackey, A., & Gass, S. (2005). *Second language research: Methodology and design*. Mahwah, NJ: Lawrence Erlbaum Associates.

Mackey, A., Gass, S., & McDonough, K. (2000). Learners' perceptions about feedback. *Studies in Second Language Acquisition*, *22*, 471–497.

Mackey, A., & Goo, J. (2007). Interaction research in SLA: A meta-analysis and research synthesis. In A. Mackey (Ed.), *Conversational interaction in second language acquisition: A series of empirical studies* (pp. 407–452). Oxford, UK: Oxford University Press.

Mackey, A., & Oliver, R. (2002). Interactional feedback and children's L2 development. *System*, *30*, 459–477.

Mackey, A., & Philp, J. (1998). Conversational interaction and second language development: Recasts, responses, and red herrings. *The Modern Language Journal*, *82*, 338–356.

Mackey, A., & Sachs, R. (2012). Older learners in SLA research: A first look at working memory, feedback, and L2 development. *Language Learning*, *62*, 704–740.

Mackey, A., Philp, J., Egi, T., Fujii, A., & Tatsumi, T. (2002). Individual differences in working memory, noticing of interactional feedback, and L2 development. In P. Robinson (Ed.), *Individual differences and instructed language learning* (pp. 181–209). Philadelphia: John Benjamins.

MacWhinney, B. (2002). The Competition Model: The input, the context, and the brain. In P. Robinson, *Cognition and second language instruction* (pp. 69–90). New York: Cambridge University Press.

MacWhinney, B. (2005). A unified model of language acquisition. In J. F. Kroll & A. M. B. de Groot (Eds.), *Handbook of bilingualism: Psycholinguistic approaches* (pp. 49–67). Oxford, UK: Oxford University Press.

MacWhinney, B. (2008). A unified model. In P. Robinson & N. Ellis (Eds.), *Handbook of cognitive linguistics and second language acquisition*. Mahwah, NJ: Lawrence Erlbaum Associates.

MacWhinney, B. (2012). The logic of the unified model. In S. Gass & A. Mackey (Eds.), *The Routledge handbook of second language acquisition* (pp. 211–227). New York: Routledge.

MacWhinney, B., Bates, E., & Kliegl, R. (1984). Cue validity and sentence interpretation in English, German, and Italian. *Journal of Verbal Learning and Behavior*, *23*, 127–150.

Magnan, S., & Lafford, B. (2012). Learning through immersion during study abroad. In S. Gass & A. Mackey (Eds.), *The Routledge handbook of second language acquisition* (pp. 525–540). New York: Routledge.

Maier, P. (1992). Politeness strategies in business letters by native and non-native English speakers. *ESP Journal*, *11*, 189–205.

Major, R. (1987). Foreign accent: Recent research and theory. *International Review of Applied Linguistics*, *25*, 185–202.

Major, R. (2001). *Foreign accent*. Mahwah, NJ: Lawrence Erlbaum Associates.

Major, R., & Kim, E. (1999). The similarity differential rate hypothesis. *Language Learning*, *49*, 151–183.

Makino, T. (1979). Acquisition order of English morphemes by Japanese secondary school students. *Journal of Hokkaido University of Education*, *30*, 101–148.

Malabonga, V. A., Kenyon, D. M., & Carpenter, H. (2005). Self-assessment preparation and response time on a computerized oral proficiency test. *Language Testing*, *22*(1), 59–92.

Mandell, P. (1999). On the reliability of grammaticality judgment tests in second language acquisition research. *Second Language Research*, *15*, 73–99.

Maneva, B., & Genesee, F. (2002). Bilingual babbling: Evidence for language differentiation in dual language acquisition. In B. Skarabela et al. (Eds.), *The Proceedings of the 26th Boston University Conference on Language Development* (pp. 383–392). Somerville, MA: Cascadilla Press.

Marian V., & Spivey, M. (2003). Bilingual and monolingual processing of competing lexical items. *Applied Psycholinguistics*, *24*, 173–193.

Marinova-Todd, S., Marshall, D. B., & Snow, C. E. (2000). Three misconceptions about age and second-language learning. *TESOL Quarterly*, *34*, 9–34.

Masgoret, A.-M., & Gardner, R. C. (2003). Attitudes, motivation, and second language learning: A meta-analysis of studies conducted by Gardner and associates. *Language Learning*, *53*, 123–163.

McCafferty, S. (1994). Adult second language learners' use of private speech: A review of studies. *The Modern Language Journal*, *78*, 421–436.

McCafferty, S. (2004a). Introduction. *International Journal of Applied Linguistics*, 14, 1–6.

McCafferty, S. (2004b). Space for cognition: Gesture and second language learning. *International Journal of Applied Linguistics*, 14, 148-165.

McDonald, J. (1987). Sentence interpretation in bilingual speakers of English and Dutch. *Applied Psycholinguistics*, *8*, 379–413.

McDonald, J., & Heilenman, K. (1992). Changes in sentence processing as second language proficiency increases. In R. J. Harris (Ed.), *Cognitive processing in bilinguals* (pp. 375–396). Amsterdam: North-Holland.

McDonough, K. (2005). Identifying the impact of negative feedback and learners' responses on ESL question development. *Studies in Second Language Acquisition*, *27*, 79–103.

McDonough, K. (2006). Interaction and syntactic priming. *Studies in Second Language Acquisition*, *28*, 179–207.

McDonough, K. (2007). Interactional feedback and the emergence of simple past activity verbs in L2 English. In A. Mackey (Ed.), *Conversational interaction and second language acquisition: A series of empirical studies* (pp. 323–338). Oxford, UK: Oxford University Press.

McDonough, K., & Mackey, A. (2006). Responses to recasts: Repetitions, primed production, and linguistic development. *Language Learning*, *56*, 693–720.

McDonough, K., & Mackey, A. (2008). Syntactic priming and ESL question development. *Studies in Second Language Acquisition*, *30*, 31–47.

McDonough, K., & Trofimovich, P. (2009). *Using priming methods in second language research*. New York: Routledge.

McDonough, S. H. (1999). Learner strategies: State of the art article. *Language Teaching*, *32*, 1–18.

McIntire, M., & Reilly, J. (1988). Nonmanual behaviors in L1 & L2 learners of American Sign Language. *Sign Language Studies*, *61*, 351–375.

McKay, S. L., & Wong, S. C. (1996). Multiple discourses, multiple identities: Investment and agency in second-language learning among Chinese adolescent immigrant students. *Harvard Educational Review*, *66*, 577–608.

McLaughlin, B. (1978). *Second-language acquisition in childhood*. Hillsdale, NJ: Lawrence Erlbaum Associates.

McLaughlin, B. (1987). *Theories of second language learning*. London: Edward Arnold.

McLaughlin, B. (1990a). Restructuring. *Applied Linguistics*, *11*, 113–128.

McLaughlin, B. (1990b). The relationship between first and second languages: Language proficiency and language aptitude. In B. Harley, P. Allen, J. Cummins, & M. Swain (Eds.), *The development of second language proficiency* (pp. 158–178). Cambridge, UK: Cambridge University Press.

McLaughlin, B., & Heredia, R. (1996). Information-processing approaches to research on second language acquisition and use. In W. Ritchie & T. Bhatia (Eds.), *Handbook of second language acquisition* (pp. 213–228). San Diego: Academic Press.

McLaughlin, B., Rossman, T., & McLeod, B. (1983). Second language learning: An information processing perspective. *Language Learning*, *33*, 135–158.

McNeill, D. (1966). Developmental psycholinguistics. In F. Smith & G. Miller (Eds.), *The genesis of language* (pp. 15–84). Cambridge, MA: MIT Press.

McNeill, D. (2000a). Introduction. In D. McNeill (Ed.), *Language and gesture* (pp. 1–10). New York: Cambridge University Press.

McNeill, D. (Ed.) (2000b). *Language and gesture.* New York: Cambridge University Press.

McNeill, D. (2005). *Gesture and thought.* Chicago: Chicago University Press.

McNeill, D., Cassell, J., & McCullough, K.-E. (1994). Communicative effects of speech mismatched gesture. *Research on Language and Social Interaction, 27,* 223–237.

Meara, P. (1978). Learners' word associations in French. *Interlanguage Studies Bulletin, 43,* 192–211.

Meara, P. (Ed.) (1983). *Vocabulary in second language* (Vol. 1). London: Centre for Language Teaching and Research.

Meara, P. (1984). The study of lexis in interlanguage. In A. Davies, C. Criper, & A. Howatt (Eds.), *Interlanguage* (pp. 225–235). Edinburgh, UK: University of Edinburgh Press.

Meara, P. (Ed.). (1987). *Vocabulary in second language* (Vol. 2). London: Centre for Language Teaching and Research.

Meara, P. (1996). The dimensions of lexical competence. In G. Brown, K. Malmkjaer, & J. Williams (Eds.), *Performance and competence in second language acquisition* (pp. 35–53). Cambridge, UK: Cambridge University Press.

Meara, P., & Fitzpatrick, T. (2000). Lex-30: An improved method of assessing productive vocabulary in an L2. *System, 28,* 19–30.

Milon, J. (1974). The development of negation in English by a second language learner. *TESOL Quarterly, 8,* 137–143.

Mitchell, R., & Myles, F. (2004). *Second language theories* (2nd ed.). London: Hodder Arnold.

Miyake, A., & Friedman, N. (1998). Individual differences in second language proficiency: Working memory as language aptitude. In A. F. Healy & L. E. Bourne, Jr. (Eds.), *Foreign language learning: Psycholinguistic studies on training and retention* (pp. 339–364). Mahwah, NJ: Lawrence Erlbaum Associates.

Miyake, A., & Shah, P. (Eds.) (1999). *Models of working memory: Mechanisms of active maintenance and executive control.* Cambridge, UK: Cambridge University Press.

Mizruchi, M. S. (1991). Urgency, motivation, and group performance: The effect of prior success on current success among professional basketball teams. *Social Psychology Quarterly, 52,* 181–189.

Mochizuki, N., & Ortega, L. (2008). Balancing communication and grammar in beginning-level foreign language classrooms: A study of guided planning and relativization. *Language Teaching Research, 12,* 13–37.

Mode, B. (1995). *Fully Committed.* New York: Dramatists Play Service.

Möhle, D. (1989). Multilingual interaction in foreign language production. In H. W. Dechert & M. Raupach (Eds.), *Interlingual processes* (pp. 179–194). Tübingen, Germany: Gunter Narr Verlag.

Montrul, S. (2002). Incomplete acquisition and attrition of Spanish tense/aspect distinctions in adult bilinguals. *Bilingualism: Language and Cognition, 5,* 39–68.

Montrul, S. (2004). Subject and object expression in Spanish heritage speakers: A case of morphosyntactic convergence. *Bilingualism: Language and Cognition, 7,* 125–142.

Montrul, S. (2010). Current issues in heritage language. *Annual Review of Applied Linguistics, 30,* 3–23.

Mori, J. (2004). Negotiating sequential boundaries and learning opportunities: A case from a Japanese language classroom. *The Modern Language Journal, 88,* 536–550.

Mourelatos, A. (1981). Events, processes, states. In P. Tedeschi & A. Zaenen (Eds.), *Tense and aspect* (Syntax and Semantics 14) (pp. 191–212). New York: Academic Press.

Moyer, A. (1999). Ultimate attainment in L2 phonology: The critical factors of age, motivation, and instruction. *Studies in Second Language Acquisition*, *21*, 81–108.

Nabei, T., & Swain, M. (2002). Learner awareness of recasts in classroom interaction: A case study of an adult EFL student's second language learning. *Language Awareness*, *11*, 43–63.

Nagasawa, F. (1995). L1, L2, bairingaru no nihongo bunpoo nooryoku [Comparative grammatical competence among L1, L2, and bilingual speakers of Japanese]. *Nohongo kyooiku*, *86*, 173–89.

Naiman, N., Fröhlich, M., Stern, H. H., & Todesco, A. (1978). *The good language learner*. Research in Education Series 7. Toronto, Ontario: Ontario Institute for Studies in Education.

Nassaji, H. (2004). The relationship between depth of vocabulary knowledge and L2 learners' lexical inferencing strategy use and success. *The Canadian Modern Language Review*, *61*, 107–134.

Nassaji, H. (2012). Significance tests and generalizability of research results: A case for replication. In G. Porte (Ed.), *Replication research in applied linguistics* (pp. 92–115). Cambridge, UK: Cambridge University Press.

Nation, I. S. P. (2001). *Learning vocabulary in another language*. Cambridge, UK: Cambridge University Press.

Nation, R., & McLaughlin, B. (1986). Experts and novices: An information-processing approach to the "good language learner" problem. *Applied Psycholinguistics*, *7*, 41–56.

Nayak, N., Hansen, N., Krueger, N., & McLaughlin, B. (1990). Language learning strategies in monolingual and multilingual adults. *Language Learning*, *40*, 221–240.

Negueruela, E., Lantolf, J. Jordan, S., & Gelabert, J. (2004). The "private function" of gesture in second language speaking activity: A study of motion verbs and gesturing in English and Spanish. *International Journal of Applied Linguistics*, *14*, 113–147.

Nemser, W. (1961). *The interpretation of English stops and interdental fricatives by native speakers of Hungarian*. Unpublished doctoral dissertation, Columbia University.

Nemser, W. (1971). Approximative systems of foreign learners. *International Review of Applied Linguistics*, *9*, 115–124.

Neufeld, G. (1979). Towards a theory of language learning ability. *Language Learning*, *29*, 227–241.

Newton, J. (1995). Task-based interaction and incidental vocabulary learning: A case study. *Second Language Research*, *11*, 159–177.

Nicholas, H., Lightbown, P. M., & Spada, N. (2001). Recasts as feedback to language learners. *Language Learning*, *51*(4), 719–758.

Nobuyoshi, J., & Ellis, R. (1993). Focused communication tasks and second language acquisition. *English Language Teaching*, *47*, 203–210.

Norris, J., & Ortega, L. (2000). Effectiveness of L2 instruction: A research synthesis and quantitative meta-analysis. *Language Learning*, *50*, 417–528.

Norris, J., & Ortega, L. (2009). Towards an organic approach to investigating CAF in instructed SLA: The case of complexity. *Applied Linguistics*, *30*, 555–578.

Norris, J. M., & Ortega, L. (2010). Timeline: Research synthesis. *Language Teaching*, *43*, 61–79.

Norris, J., & Ortega, L. (2012). Assessing learner knowledge. In S. Gass & A. Mackey (Eds.), *The Routledge handbook of second language acquisition* (pp. 573–589). New York: Routledge.

Norton, B. (2000). *Identity and language learning: Gender, ethnicity and educational change*. Essex, UK: Pearson Education Limited.

Nuevo, A. (2006). *Task complexity and interaction: L2 learning opportunities and development*. Unpublished doctoral dissertation, Georgetown University, Washington, DC.

O'Brien, I., Segalowitz, N., Freed, B., & Collentine, J. (2007). Phonological memory predicts second language oral fluency gains in adults. *Studies in Second Language Acquisition*, *29*, 557–582.

O'Grady, O., Kwak, H.-Y., Lee, O.-S., & Lee, M. (2011). An emergentist perspective on heritage language acquisition. *Studies in Second Language Acquisition*, *33*, 223–245.

O'Grady, W. (1996). Language acquisition without Universal Grammar: A general nativist proposal for L2 learning. *Second Language Research*, *12*, 374–397.

O'Grady, W. (2003). The radical middle: Nativism without universal grammar. In C. Doughty & M. H. Long (Eds.), *The handbook of second language acquisition* (pp. 43–62). Malden, MA: Blackwell.

O'Grady, W. (2005). *Syntactic carpentry: An emergentist approach to syntax*. Mahwah, NJ: Lawrence Erlbaum Associates.

O'Grady, W. (2006, July). *The problem of verbal inflection in second language acquisition*. Paper presented at the 11th PAAL Conference, Chuncheon, Korea.

O'Grady, W., Lee, M., & Choo, M. (2003). A subject–object asymmetry in the acquisition of relative clauses in Korean as a second language. *Studies in Second Language Acquisition*, *25*, 433–448.

O'Malley, J. M., & Chamot, A. (1990). *Learning strategies in second language acquisition*. Cambridge, UK: Cambridge University Press.

Odlin, T. (1989). *Language transfer*. Cambridge, UK: Cambridge University Press.

Odlin, T. (2005). Cross-linguistic influence and conceptual transfer: What are the concepts? *Annual Review of Applied Linguistics*, *25*, 3–25.

Odlin, T. (2008). Conceptual transfer and meaning extensions. In P. Robinson & N. Ellis (Eds.), *Handbook of cognitive linguistics and second language acquisition* (pp. 306–340). London: Routledge.

Odlin, T., & Alonso-Vázquez, C. (2006). Meanings in search of the perfect form: A look at interlanguage verb phrases. *Rivista di psicolinguistica applicata*, *6*, 53–63.

Ohta, A. (2001). *Second language acquisition processes in the classroom: Learning Japanese*. Mahwah, NJ: Lawrence Erlbaum Associates.

Oliver, R. (1995). Negative feedback in child NS–NNS conversation. *Studies in Second Language Acquisition*, *17*, 459–481.

Oliver, R. (1998). Negotiation of meaning in child interactions. *The Modern Language Journal*, *82*, 372–386.

Oliver, R. (2002). The patterns of negotiation of meaning in child interactions. *The Modern Language Journal*, *86*, 97–111.

Oliver, R., & Mackey, A. (2003). Interactional context and feedback in child ESL classrooms. *The Modern Language Journal*, *87*, 519–533.

Oller, J., & Ziahosseiny, S. (1970). The Contrastive Analysis Hypothesis and spelling errors. *Language Learning*, *20*, 183–189.

Olshtain, E. (1987). The acquisition of new word formation processes in second language acquisition. *Studies in Second Language Acquisition*, *9*, 223–234.

Ortega, L. (1999). Planning and focus on form in L2 oral performance. *Studies in Second Language Acquisition*, *21*, 109–148.

Ortega, L. (2012). Language acquisition research for language teaching: Choosing between application and relevance. In B. Hinger, D. Newby, & E. M. Unterrainer (Eds.), *Sprachen lernen: Kompetenzen entwickeln? Performanzen (über)prüfen* (pp. 24–38). Wien: Präsens Verlag.

Osaka, M., & Osaka, N. (1992). Language-independent working memory as measured by Japanese and English reading span tests. *Bulletin of the Psychonomic Society, 30*, 287–289.

Oswald, F. L., & Plonsky, L. (2010). Meta-analysis in second language research: Choices and challenges. *Annual Review of Applied Linguistics, 30*, 85–110.

Otomo, K. (2001). Maternal responses to word approximations in Japanese children's transition to language. *Journal of Child Language, 28*, 29–57.

Otsu, Y., & Naoi, K. (1986, September). *Structure dependence in L2 acquisition*. Paper presented at the meeting of the Japan Association of College English Teachers (JACET), Keio University, Tokyo.

Oxford, R. (1999). Learning strategies. In B. Spolsky (Ed.), *Concise encyclopedia of educational linguistics* (pp. 518–522). Oxford, UK: Elsevier.

Oxford, R. L. (2011). *Teaching and researching language learning strategies*. White Plains, NY: Pearson.

Oxford, R., & Cohen, A. (1992). Language learning strategies: Crucial issues of concept and classification. *Applied Language Learning, 3*, 1–35.

Ozeki, H., & Shirai, Y. (2007). Does the Noun Phrase Accessibility Hierarchy predict the difficulty order in the acquisition of Japanese relative clauses? *Studies in Second Language Acquisition, 29*, 169–196.

Palmberg, R. (1987). Patterns of vocabulary development in foreign-language learners. *Studies in Second Language Acquisition, 9*, 203–222.

Papadopoulou, D., & Clahsen, H. (2003). Parsing strategies in L1 and L2 sentence processing: A study of relative clause attachment in Greek. *Studies in Second Language Acquisition, 25*, 501–528.

Papagno, C., & Vallar, G. (1992). Phonological short-term memory and the learning of novel words: The effect of phonological similarity and item length. *Quarterly Journal of Experimental Psychology, 44A*, 47–67.

Papi, M., & Abdollahzadeh, E. (2012). Teacher motivational practice, student motivation, and possible L2 selves: An examination in the Iranian EFL context. *Language Learning, 62*, 571–594.

Paribakht, T., & Wesche, M. (1993). Reading comprehension and second language development in a comprehension-based ESL program. *TESL Canada Journal, 11*, 9–29.

Paribakht, T., & Wesche, M. (1997). Vocabulary enhancement activities and reading for meaning in second language vocabulary development. In J. Coady & T. Huckin (Eds.), *Second language vocabulary acquisition: A rationale for pedagogy* (pp. 174–200). New York: Cambridge University Press.

Paribakht, T., & Wesche, M. (1999). Reading and "incidental" L2 vocabulary acquisition: An introspective study of lexical inferencing. *Studies in Second Language Acquisition, 21*, 195–223.

Park, H. (2004). A minimalist approach to null subjects and objects in second language acquisition. *Second Language Research, 20*, 1–32.

Parker, K., & Chaudron, C. (1987). The effects of linguistic simplifications and elaborative modifications on L2 comprehension. *University of Hawai'i Working Papers in English as a Second Language, 6*, 107–133.

Patkowski, M. (1980). The sensitive period for the acquisition of syntax in a second language. *Language Learning, 30*, 449–472.

Pavesi, M. (1986). Markedness, discoursal modes, and relative clause formation in a formal and informal context. *Studies in Second Language Acquisition, 8*, 38–55.

Pavlenko, A., Blackledge, A., Piller, I., & Teutsch-Dwyer, M. (Eds.) (2001). *Multilingualism, second language learning, and gender*. Berlin, Germany: Walter de Gruyter.

Penfield, W., & Roberts, L. (1959). *Speech and brain mechanisms*. New York: Athenaeum.

Phillips, E. M. (1992). The effects of language anxiety on students' oral test performance and attitudes. *The Modern Language Journal, 76*, 14–26.

Philp, J. (1999). *Interaction, noticing and second language acquisition: An examination of learners' noticing of recasts in task-based interaction*. Unpublished doctoral dissertation, University of Tasmania, Australia.

Philp, J. (2003). Constraints on noticing the gap: Nonnative speakers' noticing of recasts in NS-NNS interaction. *Studies in Second Language Acquisition, 25*, 99–126.

Philp, J. (2009). Epilogue. In A. Mackey & C. Polio (Eds.), *Multiple perspectives on interaction: Second language research in honor of Susan M. Gass* (pp. 254–273). New York: Routledge.

Philp, J., & Duchesne, S. (2008). When the gate opens: The interaction between social and linguistics goals in child second language development. In J. Philp, R. Oliver, & A. Mackey (Eds.), *Child's play? Second language acquisition and the younger learner*. Amsterdam: John Benjamins.

Pica, T. (1984). Methods of morpheme quantification: Their effect on the interpretation of second language data. *Studies in Second Language Acquisition, 6*, 69–78.

Pica, T. (1987). Second-language acquisition, social interaction, and the classroom. *Applied Linguistics, 8*, 3–21.

Pica, T. (1988). Interlanguage adjustments as an outcome of NS–NNS negotiated interaction. *Language Learning, 38*, 45–73.

Pica, T. (1992). The textual outcomes of native speaker-nonnative speaker negotiation: What do they reveal about second language learning? In C. Kramsch & S. McConnell-Ginet (Eds.), *Text and context: Cross-disciplinary perspectives on language study* (pp. 198–237). Lexington, MA: D. C. Heath and Co.

Pica, T. (1994). Research on negotiation: What does it reveal about second-language learning conditions, processes, and outcomes? *Language Learning, 44*, 493–527.

Pica, T., Holliday, L., Lewis, N., & Morgenthaler, L. (1989). Comprehensible output as an outcome of linguistic demands on the learner. *Studies in Second Language Acquisition, 11*, 63–90.

Pica, T., Young, R., & Doughty, C. (1987). The impact of interaction on comprehension. *TESOL Quarterly, 21*, 737–758.

Pickering, M., & Branigan, H. (1998). The representation of verbs: Evidence from syntactic priming in language production. *Journal of Memory & Language, 39*, 633–651.

Pienemann, M. (1984). Psychological constraints on the teachability of languages. *Studies in Second Language Acquisition, 6*, 186–214.

Pienemann, M. (1989). Is language teachable? *Applied Linguistics, 10*, 52–79.

Pienemann, M. (1999). *Language processing and second language development: Processability Theory*. Amsterdam: John Benjamins.

Pienemann, M. (2007). Processability theory. In B. VanPatten & J. Williams (Eds.), *Theories in second language acquisition: An introduction* (pp. 137–154). Mahwah, NJ: Lawrence Erlbaum Associates.

Pienemann, M., & Johnston, M. (1987). Factors influencing the development of language proficiency. In D. Nunan (Ed.), *Applying second language acquisition research* (pp. 45–141). Adelaide, Australia: National Curriculum Resource Centre, AMEP.

Pienemann, M., & Keßler, J.-U. (2012). Processability theory. In S. Gass & A. Mackey (Eds.), *The Routledge handbook of second language acquisition* (pp. 228–246). New York: Routledge.

Pimsleur, P. (1967). A memory schedule. *The Modern Language Journal*, *51*, 73–75.

Pinker, S. (1984). *Language learnability and language development*. Cambridge, MA: Harvard University Press.

Pinker, S. (1987). The bootstrapping problem in language acquisition. In B. MacWhinney (Ed.), *Mechanisms of language acquisition* (pp. 399–441). Hillsdale, NJ: Lawrence Erlbaum Associates.

Pinker, S. (1989). *Learnability and cognition*. Cambridge, MA: MIT Press.

Pinker, S. (1994). *The language instinct: How the mind creates language*. New York: Morrow.

Pintzuk, S. (1988). *VARBRUL programs*. Philadelphia: University of Pennsylvania, Department of Lingistics.

Platzack, C. (1996). The initial hypothesis of syntax. In H. Clahsen (Ed.), *Generative perspectives on language acquisition* (pp. 369–414), Amsterdam: John Benjamins.

Plonsky, L. (2009, October). *"Nix the null": Why statistical significance is overrated*. Paper presented at the Second Language Research Forum (SLRF), East Lansing, MI.

Plonsky, L. (2011). The effectiveness of second language strategy instruction: A meta-analysis. *Language Learning*, *61*, 993–1038.

Plonsky, L. (2012a). Effect sizes. In P. Robinson (Ed.), *The Routledge encyclopedia of Second Language Acquisition* (pp. 200–202). New York: Routledge.

Plonsky, L. (2012b). Replication, meta-analysis, and generalizability. In G. Porte (Ed.), *Replication research in applied linguistics* (pp. 116–132). New York: Cambridge University Press.

Plonsky, L. (in press). Study Quality in SLA: An assessment of designs, analyses, and reporting practices in quantitative L2 research. *Studies in Second Language Acquisition*.

Plonsky, L., & Gass, S. (2011). Quantitative research methods, study quality, and outcomes: The case of interaction research. *Language Learning*, *61*, 325–366.

Plonsky, L., & Loewen, S. (in press). Focus on form and vocabulary acquisition in the Spanish L2 classroom. *Language, Interaction and Acquisition*.

Plonsky, L., & Oswald, F. L. (2012). How to do a meta-analysis. In A. Mackey & S. Gass (Eds.), *A guide to research methods in second language acquisition* (pp. 275–295). London: Basil Blackwell.

Plough, I. (1994). *A role for indirect negative evidence in second language acquisition*. Unpublished doctoral dissertation, Michigan State University, East Lansing.

Polinsky, M. (1995). Cross-linguistic parallels in language loss. *Southwestern Journal of Linguistics*, *14*, 87–125.

Polinsky, M. (2000). A composite linguistic profile of a speaker of Russian in the USA. In O. Kagan & B. Rifkin (Eds.), *The learning and teaching of Slavic languages and cultures* (pp. 437–466). Bloomington, IN: Slavica.

Polinsky, M. (2008). Heritage language narratives. In D. Brinton, O. Kagan, & S. Bauckus (Eds.), *Heritage languages: A new field emerging* (pp. 149–164). Hillsdale, NJ: Lawrence Erlbaum Associates.

Polinsky, M. (2011). Reanalysis in adult heritage language: New evidence in support of attrition. *Studies in Second Language Acquisition*, *33*, 305–328.

Polio, C. (2007). A history of input enhancement: Defining an evolving concept. In C. Gascoigne (Ed.), *Assessing the impact of input enhancement in second language education*. Stillwater, OK: New Forums Press.

Polio, C., & Gass S. (1997). Replication and reporting: A commentary. *Studies in Second Language Acquisition*, *19*, 499–508.

Polio, C., & Mackey, A. (Eds.) (2009). *Multiple perspectives on interaction: Second language research in honor of Susan M. Gass*. New York: Routledge.

Politzer, R. (1978). Errors of English speakers of German as perceived and evaluated by German natives. *The Modern Language Journal*, 62, 253–261.

Porte, G. (Ed.) (2012). *Replication research in Applied Linguistics*. Cambridge, UK: Cambridge University Press.

Porter, J. (1977). A cross-sectional study of morpheme acquisition in first language learners. *Language Learning*, 27, 47–62.

Porter, P. (1983). *Variations in the conversations of adult learners of English as a function of the proficiency level of the participants*. Unpublished doctoral dissertation, Stanford University, California.

Postman, L. (1971). Transfer, interference and forgetting. In J. W. Kling & L. A. Riggs (Eds.), *Woodworth and Schlosberg's experimental psychology* (pp. 1019–1132). New York: Holt, Rinehart & Winston.

Potowski, K. (2004). Student Spanish use and investment in a dual immersion classroom: Implications for second language acquisition and heritage language maintenance. *The Modern Language Journal*, 88, 75–101.

Poulisse, N. (1997). Some words in defense of the psycholinguistic approach. *The Modern Language Journal*, 81, 324–328.

Preston, D. (1989). *Sociolinguistics and second language acquisition*. Oxford, UK: Basil Blackwell.

Preston, D. (2000). Three kinds of sociolinguistics and SLA: A psycholinguistic perspective. In B. Swierzbin, F. Morris, M. E. Anderson, C. A. Klee, & E. Tarone (Eds.), *Social and cognitive factors in second language acquisition: Selected proceedings of the 1999 Second Language Research Forum* (pp. 3–30). Sommerville, MA: Cascadilla Press.

Preston, D. (2002). A variationist perspective on second language acquisition: Psycholinguistic concerns. In R. Kaplan (Ed.), *The Oxford handbook of applied linguistics* (pp. 141–159). Oxford, UK: Oxford University Press.

Prévost, P., & White, L. (2000). Missing surface inflection or impairment in second language acquisition? Evidence from tense and agreement. *Second Language Research*, 16, 103–133.

Prince, A., & Smolensky, P. (1997). Optimality: From neural networks to Universal Grammar. *Science*, 275, 1604–1610.

Pulido, D. (2003). Modeling the role of second language proficiency and topic familiarity in second language incidental vocabulary acquisition through reading. *Language Learning*, 53, 233–284.

Qasem, M., & Foote, R. (2010). Crosslanguage lexical activation: A test of the Revised Hierarchical and morphological decomposition models in Arabic–English bilinguals. *Studies in Second Language Acquisition*, 32, 111–140.

Qian, D. (1999). Assessing the roles of depth and breadth of vocabulary knowledge in reading comprehension. *The Canadian Modern Language Review*, 56, 282–308.

Rai, M. K., Loschky, L. C., Harris, R. J., Peck, N. R., & Cook, L. G. (2011). Effects of stress and working memory capacity on foreign language readers' inferential processing during comprehension. *Language Learning*, 61, 187–218.

Ramsay, R. (1980). Language-learning approach styles of adult multilinguals and successful language learners. *Annals of the New York Academy of Sciences*, 75, 73–96.

Rand, D., & Sankoff, D. (1990). GoldVarb: A variable rule application for the Macintosh (version 2.0) [Computer software]. Montreal: Centre de Recherche Mathématiques, Université de Montréal.

Ravem, R. (1968). Language acquisition in a second language environment. *International Review of Applied Linguistics*, *6*, 175–186.

Ravem, R. (1974). The development of *Wh-* questions in first and second language learners. In J. Richards (Ed.), *Error analysis: Perspectives on second language acquisition* (pp. 134–155). London: Longman.

Read, J. (1993). The development of a new measure of L2 vocabulary knowledge. *Language Testing*, *10*, 355–371.

Read, J. (2000). *Assessing vocabulary*. Cambridge, UK: Cambridge University Press.

Read, J. (2004). Plumbing the depths: How should the construct of vocabulary knowledge be defined? In P. Bogaards & B. Laufer (Eds.), *Vocabulary in a second language* (pp. 209–227). Amsterdam: John Benjamins.

Reichle, R. V. (2010). Judgments of information structure in L2 French: Nativelike performance and the Critical Period Hypothesis. *International Review of Applied Linguistics in Language Teaching*, *48*, 53–85.

Reves, T. (1983). *What makes a good language learner?* Unpublished doctoral dissertation, Hebrew University of Jerusalem.

Révész, A. (2009). Task complexity, focus on form, and second language development. *Studies in Second Language Acquisition*, *31*, 437–470.

Richards, J. C., & Sampson, G. (1974). The study of learner English. In J. C. Richards (Ed.), *Error analysis: Perspectives on second language acquisition* (pp. 3–18). London: Longman.

Riding, R. (2002). *School learning and cognitive style*. London: David Fulton.

Riding, R. (2003). On the assessment of cognitive style: A commentary on Peterson, Deary, and Austin. *Personality and Individual Differences*, *34*, 893–897.

Riding, R., & Rayner, S. (1998). *Cognitive styles and learning strategies: Understanding style differences in learning and behaviour*. London: David Fulton Publishers.

Ringbom, H. (1987). *The role of the first language in foreign language learning*. Clevedon, UK: Multilingual Matters.

Ringbom, H. (2001). Lexical transfer in L3 production. In J. Cenoz, B. Hufeisen, & U. Jessner (Eds.), *Cross-linguistic influence in third language acquisition: Psycholinguistic perspectives* (pp. 59–68). Clevedon, UK: Multilingual Matters.

Robinson, P. (1995). Attention, memory, and the "Noticing" Hypothesis. *Language Learning*, *45*, 283–331.

Robinson, P. (1996). *Consciousness, rules, and instructed second language acquisition*. New York: Peter Lang.

Robinson, P. (2001). Individual differences, cognitive abilities, aptitude complexes and learning conditions in second language acquisition. *Second Language Research*, *17*, 368–392.

Robinson, P. (2002a). Individual differences, cognitive abilities, aptitude complexes and learning conditions in second language acquisition. *Second Language Research*, *17*, 368–92.

Robinson, P. (2002b). Learning conditions, aptitude complexes and SLA: A framework for research and pedagogy. In P. Robinson (Ed.), *Individual differences and instructed language learning* (pp. 113–133). Amsterdam: John Benjamins.

Robinson, P. (2003a). Attention and memory during SLA. In C. J. Doughty & M. H. Long (Eds.), *Handbook of second language acquisition* (pp. 633–678). Malden, MA: Wiley-Blackwell.

Robinson, P. (2003b). The cognition hypothesis, task design, and adult task-based language learning. *Second Language Studies*, *21*, 45–105.

Robinson, P. (2007). Task complexity, theory of mind, and intentional reasoning: Effects on L2 speech production, interaction, uptake and perceptions of task difficulty. *International Review of Applied Linguistics*, *45*, 193–213.

Robinson, P. (2011). Task-based language learning: A review of issues. *Language Learning*, *61*(Suppl. 1), 1–36.

Robinson, P., Cadierno, T., & Shirai, Y. (2009). Time and motion: Measuring the effects of the conceptual demands of tasks on second language speech production. *Applied Linguistics*, *30*, 533–554.

Robinson, P., Mackey, A., Gass, S., & Schmidt, R. (2012). Attention and awareness in second language acquisition. In S. Gass & A. Mackey, *The Routledge handbook of second language acquisition* (pp. 247–267). New York: Routledge.

Robison, R. (1990). The primacy of aspect: Aspectual marking in English interlanguage. *Studies in Second Language Acquisition*, *12*, 315–330.

Robison, R. (1995). The Aspect Hypothesis revisited: A cross-sectional study of tense and aspect marking in interlanguage. *Applied Linguistics*, *16*, 344–370.

Rocca, S. (2002). Lexical aspect in child second language acquisition of temporality: A bidirectional study. In R. Salaberry & Y. Shirai (Eds.), *Tense–aspect morphology in L2 acquisition*. Amsterdam: John Benjamins.

Rocca, S. (2007). *Child second language acquisition: A bi-directional study of English and Italian tense–aspect morphology*. Amsterdam: John Benjamins.

Rohde, A. (1996). The Aspect Hypothesis and emergence of tense distinction in naturalistic L2 acquisition. *Linguistics*, *34*, 1115–1138.

Rohde, A. (2002). The Aspect Hypothesis in naturalistic L2 acquisition—What uninflected verb forms in early interlanguage tell us. In R. Salaberry & Y. Shirai (Eds.), *Tense and aspect morphology in L2 acquisition*. Amsterdam: John Benjamins.

Rosa, E., & O'Neill, M. D. (1999). Explicitness, intake, and the issue of awareness. *Studies in Second Language Acquisition*, *21*, 511–556.

Rosa, E., & Leow, R. (2004). Awareness, different learning conditions, and L2 development. *Applied Psycholinguistics*, *25*, 269–292.

Rosansky, E. (1976). Method and morphemes in second language acquisition research. *Language Learning*, *26*, 405–425.

Rosen, R. (2004). Beginning L2 production errors in ASL lexical phonology: A cognitive phonology model. *Sign Language & Linguistics*, *7*, 31–61.

Rosen, R. (2008). American Sign Language as a foreign language in US high schools: State of the art. *The Modern Language Journal*, *92*(1), 10–38.

Rosen, R. (2011). Modality and language in second language acquisition of ASL. In: D. J. Napoli & G. Mathur (Eds.), *Deaf around the World: The impact of language* (pp. 123–126). Oxford, UK: Oxford University Press.

Ross, S. (1998). Self assessment in second language testing: A meta-analysis and analysis of experiential factors. *Language Testing*, *15*(1), 1–20.

Rott, S. (1999). The effect of exposure frequency on intermediate language learners' incidental vocabulary acquisition and retention through reading. *Studies in Second Language Acquisition*, *21*, 589–619.

Rounds, P., & Kanagy, R. (1998). Acquiring linguistic cues to identify AGENT: Evidence from children learning Japanese as a second language. *Studies in Second Language Acquisition*, *20*, 509–542.

Rubin, J. (1975). What the good language learner can teach us. *TESOL Quarterly*, *9*, 41–51.

Russell, J., & Spada, N. (2006). The effectiveness of corrective feedback for the acquisition of L2 grammar: A meta-analysis of the research. In J. Norris & L. Ortega (Eds.),

Synthesizing research on language learning and teaching (pp. 133–164). Amsterdam: John Benjamins.

Rutherford, W. (1987). *Second language grammar: Learning and teaching*. New York: Longman.

Rysiewicz, J. (2008). Cognitive profiles of (un)successful FL learners: A cluster analytical study. *The Modern Language Journal*, *92*, 87–99.

Sachs, R., & Polio, C. (2007). Learners' uses of two types of written feedback on a L2 revision task. *Studies in Second Language Acquisition*, *29*, 67–100.

Safir, K. (1982). *Syntactic chains and the definiteness effect*. Unpublished doctoral dissertation, MIT, Cambridge, MA.

Safire, W. (1999, May 9). On language; McCawley, *New York Times Magazine*.

Sagarra, N. (2007). Working memory and L2 processing of redundant grammatical forms. In Z. Han (Ed.), *Understanding second language process* (pp. 133–147). Clevedon, UK: Multilingual Matters.

Salaberry, R. (1997). The role of input and output practice in second language acquisition. *The Canadian Modern Language Review*, *53*, 422–451.

Salaberry, R. (1998). On input processing, true language competence, and pedagogical bandwagons: A reply to Sanz and VanPatten. *The Canadian Modern Language Review*, *54*, 274–285.

Sanz, C., & Morgan-Short, K. (2004). Positive evidence versus explicit rule presentation and explicit negative feedback: A computer-assisted study. *Language Learning*, *54*(l), 35–78.

Sasaki, Y. (1991). English and Japanese comprehension strategies: An analysis based on the competition model. *Applied Psycholinguistics*, *12*, 47–73.

Sasaki, Y. (1994). Paths of processing strategy transfers in learning Japanese and English as foreign languages: A competition model approach. *Studies in Second Language Acquisition*, *16*, 43–72.

Sasaki, Y. (1997a). Individual variation in a Japanese sentence comprehension task: Form, functions, and strategies. *Applied Linguistics*, *18*, 508–537.

Sasaki, Y. (1997b). Material and presentation condition effects on sentence interpretation task performance: Methodological examinations of the competition experiment. *Second Language Research*, *13*, 66–91.

Sato, C. (1984). Phonological processes in second language acquisition: Another look at interlanguage syllable structure. *Language Learning*, *34*, 43–57.

Sato, C. (1985). Task variation in interlanguage phonology. In S. Gass & C. Madden (Eds.), *Input in second language acquisition* (pp. 181–196). Rowley, MA: Newbury House.

Saxton, M. (1997). The contrast theory of negative input. *Journal of Child Language*, *24*, 139–161.

Saxton, M. (2000). Negative evidence and negative feedback: Immediate effects on the grammaticality of child speech. *First Language*, *20*, 221–252.

Saxton, M. (2005). 'Recast' in a new light: Insights for practice from typical language studies. *Child Language Teaching and Therapy*, *21*, 23–38.

Saxton, M., Backley, P., & Gallaway, C. (2005). Negative input for grammatical errors: Effects after a lag of 12 weeks. *Journal of Child Language*, *32*, 643–672.

Saxton, M., Houston-Price, C., & Dawson, N. (2005). The prompt hypothesis: Clarification requests as corrective input for grammatical errors. *Applied Psycholinguistics*, *26*, 393–413.

Saxton, M., Kulcsar, B., Marshall, G., & Rupra, M. (1998). The longer term effects of corrective input: An experimental approach. *Journal of Child Language*, *25*, 701–721.

Scarcella, R. (1979). On speaking politely in a second language. In C. A. Yorio, K. Perkins, & J. Schachter (Eds.), *On TESOL '79* (pp. 275–287). Washington, DC: TESOL.

Schachter, J. (1974). An error in error analysis. *Language Learning, 24*, 205–214.

Schachter, J. (1983). A new account of language transfer. In S. Gass & L. Selinker (Eds.), *Language transfer in language learning* (pp. 98–111). Rowley, MA: Newbury House.

Schachter, J. (1988). Second language acquisition and its relationship to Universal Grammar. *Applied Linguistics, 9*, 219–235.

Schachter, J. (1989). Testing a proposed universal. In S. Gass & J. Schachter (Eds.), *Linguistic perspectives on second language acquisition* (pp. 73–88). New York: Cambridge University Press.

Schachter, J. (1990). On the issue of completeness in second language acquisition. *Second Language Research, 6*, 93–124.

Schachter, J. (1992). A new account of language transfer. In S. Gass & L. Selinker (Eds.), *Language transfer in language learning* (pp. 32–46). Amsterdam: John Benjamins.

Schachter, J. (1998). Recent research in language learning studies: Promises and problems. *Language Learning, 48*, 557–83.

Schachter, J., & Celce-Murcia, M. (1971). Some reservations concerning error analysis. *TESOL Quarterly, 11*, 441–451.

Schachter, J., Rounds, P. L., Wright, S., & Smith, T. (1998). *Comparing conditions for learning syntactic patterns: Attention and awareness*. Unpublished manuscript.

Schachter, J., & Rutherford, W. (1979). Discourse function and language transfer. *Working Papers in Bilingualism, 19*, 3–12.

Schachter, J., Tyson, A., & Diffley, F. (1976). Learner intuitions of grammaticality. *Language Learning, 26*, 67–76.

Scheepers, C. (2003). Syntactic priming of relative clause attachments: Persistence of structural configuration in sentence production. *Cognition, 89*(3), 179–205.

Schieffelin, B. (1986). Teasing and shaming in Kaluli children's interactions. In B. Schieffelin & E. Ochs (Eds.), *Language socialization across cultures* (pp. 165–181). Cambridge, UK: Cambridge University Press.

Schmidt, R. (1977). Sociolinguistic variation and language transfer in phonology. *Working Papers on Bilingualism, 12*, 79–95.

Schmidt, R. (1983). Interaction, acculturation, and the acquisition of communicative competence: A case study of an adult. In N. Wolfson & E. Judd (Eds.), *Sociolinguistics and language acquisition* (pp. 137–174). Rowley, MA: Newbury House.

Schmidt, R. (1990). The role of consciousness in second language learning. *Applied Linguistics, 11*, 129–158.

Schmidt, R. (1993a). Awareness and second language acquisition. *Annual Review of Applied Linguistics, 13*, 206–226.

Schmidt, R. (1993b). Consciousness, learning and interlanguage pragmatics. In G. Kasper & S. Blum-Kulka (Eds.), *Interlanguage pragmatics* (pp. 21–42). New York: Oxford University Press.

Schmidt, R. (1993c). *Consciousness in second language learning: Introduction*. Paper presented at the meeting of AILA Tenth World Congress of Applied Linguistics, Amsterdam.

Schmidt, R. (1994). Implicit learning and the cognitive unconscious: Of artificial grammars and SLA. In N. Ellis (Ed.), *Implicit and explicit learning of languages* (pp. 165–209). London: Academic Press.

Schmidt, R. (1995). Consciousness and foreign language learning: A tutorial on the role of attention and awareness in learning. In R. Schmidt (Ed.), *Attention and awareness in foreign language learning* (Tech. Rep. No. 9, pp. 1–64). Honolulu: University of Hawai'i at Manoa, Second Language Teaching and Curriculum Center.

Schmidt, R. (2001). Attention. In P. Robinson (Ed.), *Cognition and second language instruction* (pp. 3–32). Cambridge, UK: Cambridge University Press.

Schmidt, R., & Frota, S. (1986). Developing basic conversational ability in a second language: A case study of an adult learner of Portuguese. In R. Day (Ed.), *Talking to learn: Conversation in second language acquisition* (pp. 237–326). Rowley, MA: Newbury House.

Schmitt, N. (1998a). Quantifying word association responses: What is native-like? *System, 26*, 389–401.

Schmitt, N. (1998b). Tracking the incremental acquisition of second language vocabulary: A longitudinal study. *Language Learning, 48*, 281–317.

Schmitt, N. (2008). Instructed second language vocabulary learning. *Language Teaching Research, 12*, 329–363.

Schmitt, N., & Meara, P. (1997). Researching vocabulary through a word knowledge framework: Word associations and verbal suffixes. *Studies in Second Language Acquisition, 19*, 17–36.

Schmitt, N., & Schmitt, D. (in press). A reassessment of frequency and vocabulary size in L2 vocabulary teaching. *Language Teaching*.

Schmitt, N., Jiang, X., & Grabe, W. (2011). The percentage of words known in a text and reading comprehension. *The Modern Language Journal, 95*, 26–42.

Schumann, J. (1978a). The acculturation model for second language acquisition. In R. Gingras (Ed.), *Second language acquisition and foreign language teaching* (pp. 27–50). Arlington, VA: Center for Applied Linguistics.

Schumann, J. (1978b). *The pidginization process: A model for second language acquisition.* Rowley, MA: Newbury House.

Schumann, J. (1979). The acquisition of English negation by speakers of Spanish: A review of the literature. In R. Andersen (Ed.), *The acquisition and use of Spanish and English as first and second languages* (pp. 3–32). Washington, DC: Teachers of English to Speakers of Other Languages.

Schwartz, A. I., Kroll, J. F., & Diaz, M. (2007). Reading words in Spanish and English: Mapping orthography to phonology in two languages. *Language and Cognitive Processes, 22*, 106–129.

Schwartz, B. (1998). On two hypotheses of "transfer" in L2A: Minimal trees and absolute influence. In S. Flynn, G. Martohardjono, & W. O'Neil (Eds.), *The generative study of second language acquisition* (pp. 35–59). Mahwah, NJ: Lawrence Erlbaum Associates.

Schwartz, B., & Sprouse, R. (1994). Word order and nominative case in nonnative language acquisition: A longitudinal study of (L1 Turkish) German interlanguage. In T. Hoekstra & B. Schwartz (Eds.), *Language acquisition studies in generative grammar: Papers in honor of Kenneth Wexler from the 1991 GLOW Workshops* (pp. 317–368). Amsterdam: John Benjamins.

Schwartz, B., & Sprouse, R. (1996). L2 cognitive states and the full transfer/full access model. *Second Language Research, 12*, 40–72.

Schwartz, B., & Sprouse, R. (2000). When syntactic theories evolve: Consequences for L2 acquisition research. In J. Archibald (Ed.), *Second language acquisition and linguistic theory* (pp. 156–186). Oxford, UK: Basil Blackwell.

Scovel, T. (2001). *Learning new languages: A guide to second language acquisition.* Boston: Heinle & Heinle.

Segalowitz, N. (1997). Individual differences in second language acquisition. In A. M. B. de Groot, & J. F. Kroll (Eds.), *Tutorials in bilingualism: Psycholinguistic perspectives* (pp. 85–112). Mahwah, NJ: Lawrence Erlbaum Associates.

Segalowitz, N. (2003). Automaticity and second languages. In C. Doughty & M. H. Long (Eds.), *The handbook of second language acquisition* (pp. 382–408). Malden, MA: Blackwell.

Segalowitz, N., & Hulstijn, J. (2005). Automaticity in bilingualism and second language learning. In J. F. Kroll & A. M. B. de Groot (Eds.), *Handbook of bilingualism: Psycholinguistic approaches* (pp. 371–388). Oxford, UK: Oxford University Press.

Seliger, H. (1983). The language learner as linguist: Of metaphors and realities. *Applied Linguistics, 4,* 179–191.

Selinker, L. (1966). *A psycholinguistic study of language transfer.* Unpublished doctoral dissertation, Georgetown University.

Selinker, L. (1972). Interlanguage. *International Review of Applied Linguistics, 10,* 209–231.

Selinker, L. (1992). *Rediscovering interlanguage.* London: Longman.

Selinker, L., & Baumgartner-Cohen, B. (1995). Multiple language acquisition: "Damn it, why can't I keep these two languages apart?" In M. Ben-Soussan & I. Berman (Eds.), *Language Culture and Curriculum* [special issue], *8,* 1–7.

Selinker, L., & Douglas, D. (1985). Wrestling with "context" in interlanguage theory. *Applied Linguistics, 6,* 190–204.

Selinker, L., & Gass, S. (1984). *Workbook in second language acquisition.* Rowley, MA: Newbury House.

Selinker, L., & Lakshmanan, U. (1992). *Language transfer and fossilization: The "multiple effects principle."* In S. Gass & L. Selinker (Eds.), *Language transfer in language learning* (2nd ed., pp. 47–70). Amsterdam: John Benjamins.

Selinker, L., Swain, M., & Dumas, E. (1975). The interlanguage hypothesis extended to children. *Language Learning, 25,* 139–152.

Service, E., & Craik, F. (1993). Differences between young and older adults in learning a foreign vocabulary. *Journal of Memory and Language, 32,* 608–623.

Service, E., & Kohonen, V. (1995). Is the relation between phonological memory and foreign language learning accounted for by vocabulary acquisition? *Applied Psycholinguistics, 16,* 155–172.

Service, E., Simola, M., Metsaenheimo, O., & Maury, S. (2002). Bilingual working memory span is affected by language skill. *European Journal of Cognitive Psychology, 13,* 383–407.

Sharwood Smith, M. (1978). *Strategies, language transfer and the simulation of the second language learner's mental operations.* Unpublished manuscript.

Sharwood Smith, M. (1988). L2 acquisition: Logical problems and empirical solutions. In J. Pankhurst, M. Sharwood Smith, & P. Van Buren (Eds.), *Learnability and second languages. A book of readings* (pp. 9–35). Dordrecht, The Netherlands: Foris.

Sharwood Smith, M. (1991). Speaking to many minds: On the relevance of different types of language information for the L2 learner. *Second Language Research, 7,* 118–132.

Sharwood Smith, M. (1993). Input enhancement in instructed SLA: Theoretical bases. *Studies in Second Language Acquisition, 15,* 165–179.

Shea, M. (2011). *Cohesion in second language writing.* Unpublished doctoral dissertation, Michigan State University. East Lansing, MI.

Shedivy, S. L. (2004). Factors that lead some students to continue the study of foreign language past the usual 2 years in high school. *System, 32,* 103–119.

Sheen, Y. (2007). The effects of corrective feedback, language aptitude, and learner attributes on the acquisition of English articles. In A. Mackey (Ed.), *Conversational interaction in second language acquisition: A collection of empirical studies* (pp. 301–322). Oxford, UK: Oxford University Press.

Shintani, N., Li, S., & Ellis, R. (in press). Comprehension-based versus production-based grammar instruction: A meta-analysis of comparative studies. *Language Learning, 63*.

Shirai, Y. (1995). Tense–aspect marking by L2 learners of Japanese. In D. MacLaughlin & S. McEwen (Eds.), *Proceedings of the Nineteenth Annual Boston University Conference on Language Development* (Vol. 2, pp. 575–586). Somerville, MA: Cascadilla Press.

Shirai, Y., & Kurono, A. (1998). The acquisition of tense–aspect marking in Japanese as a second language. *Language Learning, 48*, 245–279.

Shoaib, A., & Dörnyei, Z. (2005). Affect in life-long learning: Exploring L2 motivation as a dynamic process. In P. Benson & D. Nun (Eds.), *Learners' stories: Difference and diversity in language learning* (pp. 22–41). Cambridge, UK: Cambridge University Press.

Singleton, D. (1999a). *Exploring the second language mental lexicon*. Cambridge, UK: Cambridge University Press.

Singleton, D. (1999b). *Vocabulary learning in another language*. Cambridge, UK: Cambridge University Press.

Siyanova, A., & Schmitt, N. (2008). L2 learner production and processing of collocation: A multi-study perspective. *The Canadian Modern Language Review, 64*, 429–458.

Siyanova-Chanturia, A., Conklin, K., & Schmitt, N. (2011). Adding more fuel to the fire: An eye-tracking study of idiom processing by native and non-native speakers. *Second Language Research, 27*, 1–22.

Sjoholm, K. (1976). A comparison of the test results in grammar and vocabulary between Finnish and Swedish-speaking applicants for English, 1974. In H. Ringbom & R. Palmberg (Eds.), *Errors made by Finns and Swedish-speaking Finns in the learning of English* (AFRIL, Vol. 5, pp. 54–137). Åbo, Finland: Åbo Åkademi, Publications of the Department of English.

Skehan, P. (1989). *Individual differences in second-language learning*. London: Edward Arnold.

Skehan, P. (1996). A framework for implementation of task-based instruction. *Applied Linguistics, 17*, 38–62.

Skehan, P. (2009). Modelling second language performance: Integrating complexity, accuracy, fluency, and lexis. *Applied Linguistics, 30*, 510–532.

Skehan, P., & Foster, P. (2008). Complexity, accuracy, fluency and lexis in task-based performance: A meta-analysis of the Ealing research. In S. Van Daele, A. Housen, F. Kuiken, M. Pierrard & I. Vedder (Eds.), *Complexity, accuracy, and fluency in second language use, learning, and teaching*. Brussels: University of Brussels Press.

Slabakova, R. (2006). Is there a critical period for the acquisition of semantics? *Second Language Research, 22*(3), 302–338.

Slabakova, R. (2008). *Meaning in the second language*. Berlin, Germany: Mouton de Gruyter.

Slabakova, R. (2012). L2 semantics. In S. Gass & A. Mackey (Eds.), *The handbook of second language acquisition* (pp. 127–146). New York: Routledge.

Slavoff, G., & Johnson, J. (1995). The effects of age on the rate of learning a second language. *Studies in Second Language Acquisition, 17*, 1–16.

Sleight, W. G. (1911). Memory and formal training. *British Journal of Psychology, 4*, 386–457.

Slobin, D. (1996). From "thought and language" to "thinking for speaking." In S. Gumperz & S. Levinson (Eds.), *Rethinking linguistic relativity* (pp. 70–96). New York: Cambridge University Press.

Slobin, D. (2003). Language and thought online: Cognitive consequences of linguistic relativity. In D. Gentner & S. Goldin-Meadow (Eds.), *Language in mind: Advances in the study of language and thought* (pp. 157–192). Cambridge, MA: MIT Press.

Smith, M., & Wheeldon, L. (2001). Syntactic priming in spoken sentence production: An online study. *Cognition*, *78*(2), 123–164.

Smith, N. (1973). *The acquisition of phonology: A case study*. Cambridge, UK: Cambridge University Press.

Snow, C., & Hoefnagle-Höhle, M. (1978). The critical age for second language acquisition: Evidence from second language learning. *Child Development*, *49*, 1114–1128.

Söderman, T. (1993). Word associations of foreign language learners and native speakers: The phenomenon of a shift in response type and its relevance for lexical development. In H. Ringbom (Ed.), *Near-native proficiency in English* (pp. 91–182). Åbo: ÅboAkademi, English Department Publications.

Sokolik, M. (1990). Learning without rules: PDP and a resolution of the adult language learning paradox. *TESOL Quarterly*, *24*, 685–696.

Sokolik, M., & Smith, M. (1992). Assignment of gender to French nouns in primary and secondary language: A connectionist model. *Second Language Research*, *8*, 39–58.

Sorace, A. (1993a). Unaccusativity and auxiliary choice in non-native grammars of Italian and French: Asymmetries and predictable indeterminancy. *Journal of French Language Studies*, *3*, 71–93.

Sorace, A. (1993b). Incomplete vs. divergent representations of unaccusativity in non-native grammars of Italian. *Second Language Research*, *9*, 22–47.

Sorace, A. (1995). Acquiring linking rules and argument structures in a second language: The unaccusative/unergative distinction. In L. Eubank, L. Selinker, & M. Sharwood Smith (Eds.), *The current state of interlanguage: Studies in honor of William E. Rutherford* (pp. 153–175). Amsterdam: John Benjamins.

Sorace, A. (2000). Syntactic optionality in non-native grammars. *Second Language Research*, *16*, 93–102.

Sorace, A. (2003). Near-nativeness. In C. Doughty & M. Long (Eds.), *The handbook of second language acquisition* (pp. 130–153). Oxford, UK: Blackwell Publishers.

Sorace, A. (2005). Syntactic optionality at interfaces. In L. Cornips & K. Corrigan (Eds.), *Syntax and variation: Reconciling the biological and the social* (pp. 46–111). Amsterdam: John Benjamins.

Sorace, A. (2011). Pinning down the concept of "interface" in bilingualism. *Linguistic Approaches to Bilingualism*, *1*, 1–33.

Sorrentino, R. M., & Higgins, E. T. (1986). Motivation and cognition: Warming up to synergism. In R. M. Sorrentino & E. T. Higgins (Eds.), *Handbook of motivation and cognition* (pp. 3–19). New York: Guilford.

Spada, N. (1997). Form-focussed instruction and second language acquisition: A review of classroom and laboratory research [State of the Art Article]. *Language Teaching*, *30*(2), 73–87.

Spada, N., & Lightbown, P. (1993). Instruction and the development of questions in the L2 classroom. *Studies in Second Language Acquisition*, *15*, 205–221.

Spada, N., & Lightbown, P. (2009). Interaction research in second/foreign language classrooms. In A. Mackey & C. Polio (Eds.), *Multiple perspectives on interaction: Second language research in honor of Susan M. Gass* (pp. 157–175). New York: Routledge.

Spada, N., & Tomita, Y. (2010). Interactions between type of instruction and type of language feature: A meta-analysis. *Language Learning*, *60*, 263–308.

Sparks, R. L., Patton, J., & Ganschow, L. (2012). Profiles of more and less successful L2 learners: A cluster analysis study. *Learning and Individual Differences*, *22*, 463–472.

Sparks, R. L., Patton, J., Ganschow, L., & Humbach, N. (2011). Subcomponents of second-language aptitude and second-language proficiency. *The Modern Language Journal*, *95*, 153–173.

Spinner, P., Gass, S., & Behney, J. (in press). Coming eye-to-eye with attention. In J. Bergsleithner & S. Frota, *Noticing in SLA*.

Spinner, P., & Juffs, A. (2008). L2 grammatical gender errors: Seeking the source of the problem. *International Review of Applied Linguistics*, *46*, 315–348.

Stæhr, L. S. (2009). Vocabulary knowledge and advanced listening comprehension in English as a foreign language. *Studies in Second Language Acquisition*, *31*, 577–607.

Stedje, A. (1977). Tredjerspråksinterferens i fritt tal—en jämförande studie. In R. Palmberg & H. Ringbom (Eds.), *Papers from the conference on contrastive linguistics and error analysis*. Åbo, Finland: Åbo Åkademi.

Sternberg, R. J. (1985). *Beyond IQ: A triarchic theory of human intelligence*. New York: Cambridge University Press.

Sternberg, R. J. (1988). *The triarchic mind: A new theory of human intelligence*. New York: Viking.

Sternberg, R. J. (1997). *Thinking styles*. New York: Cambridge University Press.

Sternberg, R. J. (2002). The theory of successful intelligence and its implications for language-aptitude testing. In P. Robinson (Ed.), *Individual differences and instructed language learning* (pp. 13–43). Amsterdam: John Benjamins.

Stewart, J., Batty, A. O., & Bovee, N. (2012). Comparing multidimensional and continuum models of vocabulary acquisition: An empirical examination of the Vocabulary Knowledge Scale. *TESOL Quarterly*, *46*, 695–721.

Stockwell, R., & Bowen, J. ((1965). *The sounds of English and Spanish*. Chicago, IL: University of Chicago Press.

Stockwell, R., Bowen, J., & Martin, J. (1965a). *The grammatical structures of English and Italian*. Chicago: University of Chicago Press.

Stockwell, R., Bowen, J., & Martin, J. (1965b). *The grammatical structures of English and Spanish*. Chicago: University of Chicago Press.

Strapp, C. M. (1999). Mothers', fathers', and siblings' responses to children's language errors: Comparing sources of negative evidence. *Journal of Child Language*, *26*, 373–391.

Strapp, C. M., & Federico, A. (2000). Imitations and repetitions: What do children say following recasts? *First Language*, *20*, 273–290.

Strapp, C. M., Helmick, A. L., Tonkovich, H. M., & Bleakney, D. M. (2011). Effects of negative and positive evidence on adult word learning. *Language Learning*, *61*, 506–532.

Stroop, J. R. (1935). Studies of interference in serial verbal reactions. *Journal of Experimental Psychology*, *12*, 643–662.

Sumara, D. (2000). Critical issues: Researching complexity. *Journal of Literacy Research*, *32*, 267–281.

Sunderman, G., & Kroll, J. F. (2006). First language activation during second language lexical processing: An investigation of lexical form, meaning and grammatical class. *Studies in Second Language Acquisition*, *28*, 387–422.

Swain, M. (1985). Communicative competence: Some roles of comprehensible input and comprehensible output in its development. In S. Gass & C. Madden (Eds.), *Input in second language acquisition* (pp. 235–253). Rowley, MA: Newbury House.

Swain, M. (1995). Three functions of output in second language learning. In G. Cook & B. Seidlhofer (Eds.), *Principle and practice in applied linguistics* (pp. 125–144). Oxford, UK: Oxford University Press.

Swain, M. (2005). The output hypothesis: Theory and research. In E. Hinkel (Ed.), *Handbook of research in second language teaching and learning* (pp. 471–483). Mahwah, NJ: Lawrence Erlbaum Associates.

Swain, M. (2006). Language, agency, and collaboration in advanced language proficiency. In H. Byrnes (Ed.), *Advanced language learning: The contribution of Halliday and Vygotsky* (pp. 95–108). London: Continuum.

Swain, M., & Burnaby, B. (1976). Personality characteristics and second language learning and younger children: A pilot study. *Working Papers on Bilingualism*, *11*, 115–128.

Swain, M., & Lapkin, S. (1995). Problems in output and the cognitive processes they generate: A step towards second language learning. *Applied Linguistics*, *16*, 371–391.

Swain, M., & Lapkin, S. (1998). Interaction and second language learning: Two adolescent French immersion students working together. *The Modern Language Journal*, *82*, 320–337.

Swain, M., Lapkin, S., Knouzi, I., Suzuki, W., & Brooks, L. (2009). Languaging: University students learn the grammatical concept of voice in French. *The Modern Language Journal*, *93*, 5–24.

Taguchi, N. (2011a). Do proficiency and study-abroad experience affect speech act production? Analysis of appropriateness, accuracy, and fluency. *International Review of Applied Linguistics*, *49*, 265–293.

Taguchi, N. (2011b).Teaching pragmatics: Trends and issues. *Annual Review of Applied Linguistics*, *31*, 289–310.

Tahta, S., Wood, M., & Lowenthal, K. (1981). Foreign accents: Factors relating to transfer of accent from the first language to the second language. *Language and Speech*, *24*, 265–272.

Takahashi, S. (2010). Assessing learnability in second language pragmatics. In A. Trosborg (Ed.), *Handbook of pragmatics* (Vol. VII) (pp. 391–421). Berlin, Germany: Mouton de Gruyter.

Takashima, H. (1995). *A study of focused feedback, or output enhancement, in promoting accuracy in communicative activities*. Unpublished doctoral dissertation, Temple University, Japan.

Talmy, L. (2000). *Toward a cognitive semantics. Vol. II: Typology and process in concept structuring*. Cambridge, MA: MIT Press.

Tarone, E. (1977). Conscious communication strategies in interlanguage. In H. D. Brown, C. A. Yorio, & R. C. Crymes (Eds.), *On TESOL '77: Teaching and learning English as a second language: Trends in research and practice* (pp. 194–203). Washington, DC: Teachers of English to Speakers of Other Languages.

Tarone, E. (1979). Interlanguage as chameleon. *Language Learning*, *29*, 181–191.

Tarone, E. (1980). Some influences on the syllable structure on interlanguage phonology. *International Review of Applied Linguistics*, *18*, 139–152.

Tarone, E. (1983). On the variability of interlanguage systems. *Applied Linguistics*, *4*, 142–163.

Tarone, E. (1985). Variability in interlanguage use: A study of style-shifting in morphology and syntax. *Language Learning*, *35*, 373–404.

Tarone, E. (1988). *Variation in interlanguage*. London: Edward Arnold.

Tarone, E. (1990). On variation in interlanguage: A response to Gregg. *Applied Linguistics*, *11*, 392–399.

Tarone, E. (2000). Still wrestling with "context" in interlanguage theory. In W. Grabe (Ed.), *Annual review of applied linguistics: Applied linguistics as an emerging discipline* (pp. 182–198). New York: Cambridge University Press.

Tarone, E. (2009). A variationist perspective on the interaction approach. In A. Mackey and C. Polio (Eds.), *Multiple perspectives on interaction: Second language research in honor of Susan M. Gass* (pp. 41–57). New York: Routledge.

Tarone, E., Frauenfelder, U., & Selinker, L. (1976). Systematicity/variability and stability/instability in interlanguage systems. *Language Learning* [Special Issue], *4*, 93–134.

Tarone, E., & Liu, G. (1995). Situational context, variation, and second language acquisition theory. In G. Cook & B. Seidlhofer (Eds.), *Principle and practice in applied linguistics: Studies in honour of H. G. Widdowson* (pp. 107–124). Oxford, UK: Oxford University Press.

Taylor, A., Stevens, J. R., & Asher, J. W. (2006). The effects of explicit reading strategy training on L2 reading comprehension. In J. M. Norris & L. Ortega (Eds.), *Synthesizing research on language learning and teaching* (pp. 213–244). Philadelphia: John Benjamins.

Teichroew, F. M. (1982). A study of receptive versus productive vocabulary. *Interlanguage Studies Bulletin, 6*, 3–33.

Tesar, B., & Smolensky, P. (1996). *Learnability in optimality theory* (Tech. Rep. JHU-CogSci-96-3). Baltimore, MD: John Hopkins University.

Tesar, B., & Smolensky, P. (1998). Learnability in optimality theory. *Linguistic Inquiry, 29*, 229–268.

Thakerar, J. N., Giles, H., & Cheshire, J. (1982). Psychological and linguistic parameters of speech accommodation theory. In C. Fraser & K. R. Scherer (Eds.), *Advances in the social psychology of language* (pp. 205–255). New York: Cambridge University Press.

Thomas, J. (1988). The role played by metalinguistic awareness in second and third language learning. *Journal of Multilingual and Multicultural Development, 9*, 235–246.

Thomas, M. (1989). The interpretation of English reflexive pronouns by non-native speakers. *Studies in Second Language Acquisition, 11*, 281–303.

Thomas, M. (1991). Universal Grammar and the interpretation of reflexives in a second language. *Language, 67*, 211–239.

Thomas, M. (1993). *Knowledge of reflexives in a second language*. Amsterdam/Philadelphia: John Benjamins.

Thomas, M. (1994). Assessment of L2 proficiency in second language acquisition research. *Language Learning, 44*, 307–336.

Thomas, M. (1995). Acquisition of the Japanese reflexive zibun and movement of anaphors in logical form. *Second Language Research, 11*, 206–234.

Thompson, A. (2009). *The multilingual/bilingual dichotomy: An exploration of individual differences*. Unpublished doctoral dissertation, Michigan State University, East Lansing, MI.

Thompson, A., Li, S., White, B., Loewen, S., & Gass, S. (2012). Preparing the future professoriate. In G. Gorsuch (Ed.), *Working theories for TA and ITA development*. Stillwater, OK: New Forums Press.

Thompson, R. L., Emmorey, K., & Kluender, R. (2009). Learning to look: The acquisition of eye gaze agreement during the production of ASL verbs. *Bilingualism: Language and Cognition, 12*, 393–409.

Titone, D., Libben, M., Mercier, J. Whitford, V., & Pivneva, I. (2011). Bilingual lexical access during L1 sentence reading: The effects of L2 knowledge, semantic constraint, and L1-L2 intermixing. *Journal of Experimental Psychology: Learning, Memory, and Cognition, 37,* 1412–1431.

Tomasello, M. (2003). *Constructing a language. A usage based theory of language acquisition.* Cambridge, MA: Harvard University Press.

Tomlin, R. S., & Villa, V. (1994). Attention in cognitive science and second language acquisition. *Studies in Second Language Acquisition, 16,* 183–203.

Trahey, M. (1996). Positive evidence in second language acquisition: Some long-term effects. *Second Language Research, 12,* 111–139.

Trahey, M., & White, L. (1993). Positive evidence and preemption in the second language classroom. *Studies in Second Language Acquisition, 15,* 181–204.

Tremblay, M.-C., (2006). Cross-linguistic influence in third language acquisition: The role of L2 proficiency and L2 exposure. *Cahiers Linguistiques d'Ottawa, 34,* 109–119.

Truscott, J. (1998). Noticing in second language acquisition: A critical review. *Second Language Research, 14,* 103–135.

Truscott, J. (2004). The effectiveness of grammar instruction: Analysis of a meta-analysis. *English Teaching & Learning, 28,* 17–29.

Truscott, J., & Sharwood Smith, M. (2011). Input, intake, and consciousness: The quest for a theoretical foundation. *Studies in Second Language Acquisition, 33,* 497–528.

Tseng, W.-T., Dörnyei, Z., & Schmitt, N. (2006). A new approach to assessing strategic learning: The case of self-regulation in vocabulary acquisition. *Applied Linguistics, 27,* 78–102.

Tsimpli, I.-M., & Dimitrakopoulou, M. (2007). The interpretability hypothesis: Evidence from *wh*-interrogatives in second language acquisition. *Second Language Research, 23,* 215–242.

Tyler, L. (1989). The role of lexical representations in language comprehension. In W. Marslen-Wilson (Ed.), *Lexical representation and process* (pp. 439–462). Cambridge, MA: MIT Press.

Uggen, M. (2012). Reinvestigating the noticing function of output. *Language Learning, 62,* 506–540.

Ushioda, E. (2003). Engaging with the curriculum through the European Language Portfolio. *Neusprachliche Mitteilungen, 3,* 147–153.

Ushioda, E., & Dörnyei, Z. (2012). Motivation. In S. M. Gass & A. Mackey (Eds.), *The Routledge handbook of second language acquisition* (pp. 396–409). New York: Routledge.

Vainikka, M., & Young-Scholten, M. (1994). Direct access to X'-theory: Evidence from Korean and Turkish adults learning German. In T. Hoekstra & B. Schwartz (Eds.), *Language acquisition studies in generative grammar* (pp. 265–316). Amsterdam: John Benjamins.

Vainikka, M., & Young-Scholten, M. (1996a). The early stages of adult L2 syntax: Additional evidence from Romance speakers. *Second Language Research, 12,* 140–176.

Vainikka, M., & Young-Scholten, M. (1996b). Gradual development of L2 phrase structure. *Second Language Research, 12,* 7–39.

Valdés, G. (1995). The teaching of minority languages as "foreign" languages: Pedagogical and theoretical challenges. *Modern Language Journal, 79,* 299–328.

Valdés, G. (2001a). Heritage language students: Profiles and possibilities. In J. Peyton, D. Ranard, & S. McGinnis (Eds.), *Heritage languages in America: Preserving a national resource.* Washington, DC: Center for Applied Linguistics.

Valdés, G. (2001b). *Learning and not learning English: Latino students in American schools.* New York: Teachers College Press.

Van Assche, E., Duyck, W., & Brysbaert, M. (in press). Verb processing by bilinguals in sentence contexts: The effect of cognate status and verb tense. *Studies in Second Language Acquisition*.

van Daele, S., Housen, A., Pierrard, M., & Debruyn, L. (2006). The effect of extraversion on oral L2 proficiency. *EuroSLA Yearbook, 6*, 213–236.

van den Noort, M., Bosch, P., & Hugdahl, K. (2006). Foreign language proficiency and working memory capacity. *European Psychologist, 11*, 289–296.

van Someren, M., Barnard, Y., & Sandberg, J. (1994). *The think aloud method: A practical guide to modelling cognitive processes.* London: Academic Press.

Van Valin, R. (1991). Functionalist linguistic theory and language acquisition. *First Language, 11*, 7–40.

Vandergrift, L., & Goh, C. C. M. (2012). *Teaching and learning second language listening: Metacognition in action.* New York: Routledge.

VanPatten, B. (1990). Attending to content and form in the input: An experiment in consciousness. *Studies in Second Language Acquisition, 12*, 287–301.

VanPatten, B. (1995). Input processing and second language acquisition: On the relationship between form and meaning. In P. Hashemipour, R. Maldonado, & M. van Naerssen (Eds.), *Festschrift in honor of Tracy D. Terrell* (pp. 170–183). New York: McGraw-Hill.

VanPatten, B. (2004). Input processing in SLA. In B. VanPatten (Ed.), *Processing instruction: Theory, research, and commentary* (pp. 5–31). Mahwah, NJ: Lawrence Erlbaum Associates.

VanPatten, B. (2007a). Processing instruction. In C. Sanz (Ed.), *Mind and context in adult second language acquisition* (pp. 267–281). Washington, DC: Georgetown University Press.

VanPatten, B. (2007b) Input processing in adult second language acquisition. In B. VanPatten & J. Williams (Eds.), *Theories in second language acquisition: An introduction* (pp. 115–135). Mahwah, NJ: Lawrence Erlbaum Associates.

VanPatten, B. (2009). Processing matters in input enhancement. In T. Piske & M. Scholten-Young (Eds.), *Input Matters* (pp. 47–61). Clevedon, UK: Multilingual Matters.

VanPatten, B. (2012). Input processing. In S. Gass & A. Mackey (Eds.), *The Routledge handbook of second language acquisition* (pp. 268–281). New York: Routledge.

VanPatten, B., & Benati, A. (2010). *Key terms in second language acquisition.* London: Continuum.

VanPatten, B., & Cadierno, T. (1993). Explicit instruction and input processing. *Studies in Second Language Acquisition, 15*, 225–243.

VanPatten, B., & Keating, G. (2007, April). *Getting tense.* Paper delivered at the annual meeting of the American Association for Applied Linguistics, Costa Mesa, CA.

VanPatten, B., & Oikkenon, S. (1996). The causative variables in processing instruction: Explicit information versus structured input activities. *Studies in Second Language Acquisition, 18*, 495–510.

VanPatten, B., & Sanz, C. (1995). From input to output: Processing instruction and communicative tasks. In F. Eckman, D. Highland, P. Lee, J. Mileham, & R. Weber (Eds.), *Second language acquisition theory and pedagogy* (pp. 169–186). Hillsdale, NJ: Lawrence Erlbaum Associates.

VanPatten, B., & Wong, W. (2004). Processing instruction and the French causative: Another replication. In B. VanPatten (Ed.), *Processing instruction: Theory, research, and commentary* (pp. 97–118). Mahwah, NJ: Lawrence Erlbaum Associates.

Varonis, E., & Gass, S. (1982). The comprehensibility of non-native speech. *Studies in Second Language Acquisition, 4*, 114–136.

Varonis, E., & Gass, S. (1985a). Miscommunication in native/non-native conversation. *Language in Society, 14*, 327–343.

Varonis, E., & Gass, S. (1985b). Non-native/non-native conversations: A model for negotiation of meaning. *Applied Linguistics, 6*, 71–90.

Vidal, K. (2011). A comparison of the effects of reading and listening on incidental vocabulary acquisition. *Language Learning, 61*, 219–258.

Vihman, M. (1996). *Phonological development: The origins of language in the child*. Oxford, UK: Basil Blackwell.

Vildomec, V. (1963). *Multilingualism*. Leyden, The Netherlands: A. W. Sythoff.

Vygotsky, L. S. (1978). *Mind in society: The development of higher psychological processes*. Cambridge, MA: Harvard University Press.

Vygotsky, L. S. (1987). *The collected works of L. S. Vygotsky. Vol. 1. Problems of general psychology. Including the volume Thinking and Speech*. New York: Plenum Press.

Wagner-Gough, K., & Hatch, E. (1975). The importance of input in second language acquisition studies. *Language Learning, 25*, 297–308.

Wakabayashi, S. (1996). The nature of interlanguage: SLA of reflexives. *Second Language Research, 12*, 266–303.

Wakamoto, N. (2009). *Extroversion/introversion in foreign language learning: Interactions with learner strategy use*. New York: Peter Lang.

Waldrop, M. (1992). *Complexity: The emerging science at the edge of order and chaos*. New York: Simon & Schuster.

Walter, C. (2006). Transfer of reading comprehension skills to L2 is linked to mental representations of text and to L2 working memory. *Applied Linguistics, 25*, 315–339.

Wei, L. (2000). *The bilingual reader*. London: Routledge.

Weinstein, C. E., Husman, J., & Dierking, D. R. (2000). Self-regulation interventions with a focus on learning strategies. In M. Boekaerts, P. R., Pintrich & M. Zeldner (Eds.), *Handbook of self-regulation* (pp. 727–747). San Diego, CA: Academic Press.

Weir, R. (1962). *Language in the crib*. The Hague, The Netherlands: Mouton.

Weist, R., Wysocka, H., Witkowska-Stadnik, K., Buczowska, E., & Konieczna, E. (1984). The defective tense hypothesis: On the emergence of tense and aspect in child Polish. *Journal of Child Language, 11*, 347–374.

Wesche, M. (1981). Language aptitude measures in streaming, matching students with methods, and diagnosis of learning problems. In K. C. Diller (Ed.), *Individual differences and universals in language learning aptitude*. Rowley, MA: Newbury House.

Wesche, M., & Paribakht, S. (1999a). Introduction. *Studies in Second Language Acquisition, 21*, 175–180.

Wesche, M., & Paribakht, S. (Eds.) (1999b). Incidental L2 vocabulary acquisition: Theory, current research, and instructional implications. *Studies in Second Language Acquisition, 21*.

Wexler, K., & Cullicover, P. (1980). *Formal principles of language acquisition*. Cambridge, MA: MIT Press.

White, L. (1985). The "pro-drop" parameter in adult second language acquisition. *Language Learning, 35*, 47–62.

White, L. (1989). *Universal Grammar and second language acquisition*. Amsterdam: John Benjamins.

White, L. (1991). Adverb placement in second language acquisition: Some effects of positive and negative evidence in the classroom. *Second Language Research, 7*, 133–161.

White, L. (1992). Universal Grammar: Is it just a new name for old problems? In S. Gass & L. Selinker (Eds.), *Language transfer in language learning* (pp. 219–234). Amsterdam: John Benjamins.

White, L. (2003). *Second language acquisition and Universal Grammar*. Cambridge, UK: Cambridge University Press.

White, L., Bruhn-Garavito, J., Kawasaki, T., Pater, J., & Prévost, P. (1997). The researcher gave the subject a test about himself: Problems of ambiguity and preference in the investigation of reflexive binding. *Language Learning*, *47*, 145–172.

White, L., & Genesee, F. (1996). How native is near-native? The issue of ultimate attainment in adult second language acquisition. *Second Language Research*, *12*, 233–265.

White, L., Valenzuela, E., Kozlowska-Macgregor, M., & Leung, I. (2004). Gender agreement in non-native Spanish. *Applied Psycholinguistics*, *25*, 105–133.

Whitman, R., & Jackson, K. (1972). The unpredictability of contrastive analysis. *Language Learning*, *22*, 29–41.

Whong-Barr, M. (2005). Transfer of argument structure and morphology. In L. Dekydtspotter, R. Sprouse, & A. Liljestrand (Eds.), *Proceedings of the 7th Generative Approaches to Second Language Conference (GASLA 2004)* (pp. 269–282). Somerville, MA: Cascadilla Press.

Wigglesworth, G. (1997). An investigation of planning time and proficiency level on oral test discourse. *Language Testing*, *14*, 21–44.

Williams, J. (1990, March). *Discourse marking and elaboration and the comprehensibility of second language speakers*. Paper presented at the Second Language Research Forum, Eugene, OR.

Williams, J. N. (1999). Learner-generated attention to form. *Language Learning*, *49*, 583–625.

Williams, J. N. (1999). Memory, attention, and inductive learning. *Studies in Second Language Acquisition*, *21*, 1–48.

Williams, J. N. (2004). Implicit learning of form-meaning connections. In B. VanPatten, J. Williams, S. Rott, & M. Overstreet (Eds.), *Form meaning connections in second language acquistion* (pp. 203–218). Mahwah, NJ: Lawrence Erlbaum Associates.

Williams, J. N. (2005). Learning without awareness. *Studies in Second Language Acquisition*, *27*, 269–304.

Williams, J. N. (2012). Working memory and SLA. In S. Gass & A. Mackey (Eds.), *The Routledge handbook of second language acquisition* (pp. 427–441). New York: Routledge.

Williams, J. N., & Evans, J. (1998). What kind of focus and on which forms? In C. Doughty & J. Williams (Eds.), *Focus on form in classroom second language acquisition* (pp. 139–155). Cambridge, UK: Cambridge University Press.

Williams, J. N., & Lovatt, P. (2003). Phonological memory and rule learning. *Language Learning*, *53*, 67–121.

Williams, M., Burden, R., & Lanvers, U. (2002). "French is the language of love and stuff": Student perceptions of issues related to motivation in learning a foreign language. *British Educational Research Journal*, *28*, 503–528.

Williams, S., & Hammarberg, B. (1998). Language switches in L3 production: Implications for a polyglot speaking model. *Applied Linguistics*, *19*, 295–333.

Wilson, R., & Dewaele, J.-M. (2010). The use of web questionnaires in second language acquisition and bilingualism research. *Second Language Research*, *26*, 103–123.

Winke, P., Gass, S., & Sydorenko, T. (2010). The effects of captioning videos used for foreign language listening activities. *Language Learning & Technology*, *14*, 65–86.

Witzel, J. D., Witzel, N. O., & Nicol, J. (2009). *Deeper than shallow: Evidence for structurally-based parsing biases in L2 sentence processing*. Poster presented at the 22nd Annual Meeting of the CUNY Conference on Human Sentence Processing, University of California, Davis, CA.

Wode, H. (1976). Developmental principles in naturalistic L1 acquisition. *Arbeitspapiere zum Spracherwerb* (No. 16). Kiel, Germany: Kiel University, Department of English.

Wode, H. (1977). On the systematicity of L1 transfer in L2 acquisition. *Proceedings from 1977 Second Language Research Forum (SLRF)* (pp. 160–169). Los Angeles: University of California, Department of Applied Linguistics.

Woken, M., & Swales, J. (1989). Expertise and authority in native–non-native conversations: The need for a variable account. In S. Gass, C. Madden, D. Preston, & L. Selinker (Eds.), *Variation in second language acquisition: Discourse and pragmatics* (pp. 211–227). Clevedon, UK: Multilingual Matters.

Wolfe-Quintero, K. (1996). Nativism does not equal Universal Grammar. *Second Language Research*, *12*, 335–373.

Won, M. (2008). *The effects of vocabulary instruction on English language learners: A meta-analysis*. Unpublished doctoral dissertation, Texas Tech University, Lubbock, TX.

Wong-Fillmore, L. (1976). *The second time around: Cognitive and social strategies in second language acquisition*. Unpublished doctoral dissertation, Stanford University, Palo Alto, CA.

Wong, L. L. C., & Nunan, D. (2011). The learning styles and strategies of effective language learners. *System*, *29*, 144–163.

Wong, W. (2004). Processing instruction in French: The roles of explicit information and structured input. In B. VanPatten (Ed.), *Processing instruction: Theory, research, and commentary* (pp. 187–205). Mahwah, NJ: Lawrence Erlbaum Associates.

Wray, A. (2002). *Formulaic language and the lexicon*. Cambridge, UK: Cambridge University Press.

Wulff, S., Ellis, N., Römer, U., Bardovi-Harlig, K., & Leblanc, C. (2009). The acquisition of tense-aspect: Converging evidence from corpora and telicity ratings. *The Modern Language Journal*, *93*, 354–369.

Yabuki-Soh, N. (2007). Teaching relative clauses in Japanese: Exploring the explicitness of instruction and the projection effect. *Studies in Second Language Acquisition*, *29*, 219–252.

Yeni-Komshian, G. H., Flege, J. E., & Liu, S. (2000). Pronunciation proficiency in the first and second languages of Korean–English bilinguals. *Bilingualism, Language and Cognition*, *3*, 131–149.

Yeni-Komshian, G. H., Robbins, M., & Flege, J. E. (2001). Effects of word class differences on L2 pronunciation accuracy. *Applied Psycholinguistics*, *22*, 283–299.

Young, D. J. (1990). An investigation of students' perspectives on anxiety and speaking. *Foreign Language Annals*, *23*, 539–553.

Young, D. J. (Ed.) (1999). *Affect in foreign language and second language learning: A practical guide to creating a low-anxiety classroom atmosphere*. Boston, MA: McGraw-Hill College.

Young, R. (1986). The acquisition of a verbal repertoire in a second language. *Penn Working Papers in Educational Linguistics*, *2*, 85–119.

Young, R. (1991). *Variation in interlanguage morphology*. New York: Peter Lang.

Young, R. (1999). Sociolinguistic approaches to SLA. In W. Grabe (Ed.), *Annual review of applied linguistics, 19. Survey of applied linguistics* (pp. 105–132). New York: Cambridge University Press.

Young-Scholten, M. (1995). The negative effects of "positive" evidence in phonology. In L. Eubank, L. Selinker, & M. Sharwood Smith (Eds.), *The current state of interlanguage* (pp. 107–121). Amsterdam: John Benjamins.

Young-Scholten, M. (1997). Second language syllable simplification: Deviant development or deviant input? In J. Leather & A. James (Eds.), *New sounds 97*. Klagenfurt, Austria: University of Klagenfurt.

Young-Scholten, M., & Archibald, J. (2000). Second language syllable structure. In J. Archibald (Ed.), *Second language acquisition and linguistic theory* (pp. 64–101). Oxford, UK: Basil Blackwell.

Young-Scholten, M., Akita, M., & Cross, N. (1999). Focus on form in phonology: Orthographic exposure as a promoter of epenthesis. In P. Robinson & J. O. Jungheim (Eds.), *Pragmatics and pedagogy. Proceedings of the Third PacSLRF* (Vol. 2). Tokyo: Aoyama Gakuin University.

Zafar, S., & Meenakshi, K. (2012). A study on the relationship between extroversion–introversion and risk-taking in the context of second language acquisition. *International Journal of Research Studies in Language Learning*, *1*, 33–40.

Zhao, S. Y., & Bitchener, J. (2007). Incidental focus on form in teacher–learner and learner–learner interactions. *System*, *35*, 431–447.

Zobl, H. (1980). The formal and developmental selectivity of L1 influence on L2 acquisition. *Language Learning*, *30*, 43–57.

Zobl, H. (1982). A direction for contrastive analysis: The comparative study of developmental sequences. *TESOL Quarterly*, *16*, 169–183.

Zobl, H. (1992). Prior linguistic knowledge and the conservatism of the learning procedure: Grammaticality judgments of unilingual and multilingual learners. In S. Gass & L. Selinker (Eds.), *Language transfer in language learning* (pp. 176–196). Amsterdam: John Benjamins.

Zuengler, J. (1989). Performance variation in NS–NNS interactions: Ethnolinguistic difference, or discourse domain? In S. Gass, C. Madden, D. Preston, & L. Selinker (Eds.), *Variation in second language acquisition: Discourse and pragmatics* (pp. 228–244). Clevedon, UK: Multilingual Matters.

Zyzik, E. (2006). Transitivity alternations and sequence learning insights from L2 Spanish production data. *Studies in Second Language Acquisition*, *28*, 449–485.

Zyzik, E., & Polio, C. (2008). Incidental focus on form in university Spanish literature courses. *The Modern Language Journal*, *92*, 53–70.

Author Index

Subject Index

Note: References in **bold** are to the Glossary.

SECOND LANGUAGE ACQUISITION